Lecture Notes in Artificial Intelligence 11311

Subseries of Lecture Notes in Computer Science

LNAI Series Editors

Randy Goebel
  University of Alberta, Edmonton, Canada
Yuzuru Tanaka
  Hokkaido University, Sapporo, Japan
Wolfgang Wahlster
  DFKI and Saarland University, Saarbrücken, Germany

LNAI Founding Series Editor

Joerg Siekmann
  DFKI and Saarland University, Saarbrücken, Germany

More information about this series at http://www.springer.com/series/1244

Max Bramer · Miltos Petridis (Eds.)

Artificial Intelligence XXXV

38th SGAI International Conference
on Artificial Intelligence, AI 2018
Cambridge, UK, December 11–13, 2018
Proceedings

Editors
Max Bramer
University of Portsmouth
Portsmouth, UK

Miltos Petridis
Middlesex University
London, UK

ISSN 0302-9743   ISSN 1611-3349   (electronic)
Lecture Notes in Artificial Intelligence
ISBN 978-3-030-04190-8   ISBN 978-3-030-04191-5   (eBook)
https://doi.org/10.1007/978-3-030-04191-5

Library of Congress Control Number: 2018961017

LNCS Sublibrary: SL7 – Artificial Intelligence

This Springer imprint is published by the registered company Springer Nature Switzerland AG
The registered company address is: Gewerbestrasse 11, 6330 Cham, Switzerland

Preface

This volume, entitled *Artificial Intelligence XXXV*, comprises the refereed papers presented at AI-2018, the thirty-eighth SGAI International Conference on Innovative Techniques and Applications of Artificial Intelligence, held in Cambridge in December 2018, in both the technical and the application streams. The conference was organized by SGAI, the British Computer Society Specialist Group on Artificial Intelligence.

The technical papers included here present new and innovative developments in the field, divided into sections on "Neural Networks," "Planning and Scheduling," and "Machine Learning." This year's Donald Michie Memorial Award for the best refereed technical paper was won by a paper entitled "Secure Third-Party Data Clustering Using Φ Data: Multi-User Order-Preserving Encryption and Super Secure Chain Distance Matrices" by Nawal Almutairi (University of Liverpool, UK, and King Saud University, Saudi Arabia), Frans Coenen, and Keith Dures (University of Liverpool, UK).

The application papers included present innovative applications of AI techniques in a number of subject domains. This year, the papers are divided into sections on "Industrial Applications of Artificial Intelligence," "Planning and Scheduling in Action," "Machine Learning in Action," "Applications of Machine Learning," and "Applications of Agent Systems and Genetic Algorithms."

This year's Rob Milne Memorial Award for the best refereed application paper was won by a paper entitled "Beat the Bookmaker – Winning Football Bets with Machine Learning" by Johannes Stübinger (Friedrich-Alexander-Universität Erlangen-Nürnberg, Germany) and Julian Knoll (Technische Hochschule Nürnberg, Germany)

The volume also includes the text of short papers in both streams presented as posters at the conference.

On behalf of the conference Organizing Committee, we would like to thank all those who contributed to the organization of this year's programme, in particular the Programme Committee members, the Executive Programme Committees, and our administrators Mandy Bauer and Bryony Bramer.

October 2018

Max Bramer
Miltos Petridis

Organization

AI-2018 Conference Committee

Conference Chair

Max Bramer   University of Portsmouth, UK

Technical Programme Chair

Max Bramer   University of Portsmouth, UK

Application Programme Chair

Miltos Petridis   Middlesex University, UK

Deputy Application Programme Chair

Jixin Ma   University of Greenwich, UK

Workshop Organizer

Adrian Hopgood   University of Portsmouth, UK

Treasurer

Rosemary Gilligan

AI Open Mic and Panel Session Organizer

Andrew Lea   Amplify Life, UK

Publicity Organizer

Frederic Stahl   University of Reading, UK

FAIRS 2018

Giovanna Martinez   University of Nottingham, UK

UK CBR Organizer

Miltos Petridis   Middlesex University, UK

Cambridge Walking Tour Organizer

Nadia Abouayoub

Conference Administrator

Mandy Bauer   BCS

Paper Administrator

Bryony Bramer

Technical Executive Programme Committee

Max Bramer (Chair)	University of Portsmouth, UK
Adrian Hopgood	University of Portsmouth, UK
John Kingston	University of Brighton, UK
Dan Neagu	University of Bradford, UK
Gilbert Owusu	BT, UK

Application Executive Programme Committee

Miltos Petridis (Chair)	Middlesex University, UK
Richard Ellis	RKE Consulting, UK
Rosemary Gilligan	.
Stelios Kapetanakis	University of Brighton, UK
Andrew Lea	Amplify Life, UK
Jixin Ma	University of Greenwich, UK

Technical Programme Committee

Andreas Albrecht	Middlesex University, UK
Per-Arne Andersen	University of Agder, Norway
Raed Sabri Hameed Batbooti	Southern Technical University/Basra Engineering Technical College, Iraq
Lluís Belanche	Universitat Politecnica de Catalunya, Spain
Yaxin Bi	Ulster University, UK
Mirko Boettcher	University of Magdeburg, Germany
Soufiane Boulehouache	University of 20 Août 1955-Skikda, Algeria
Max Bramer	University of Portsmouth, UK
Krysia Broda	Imperial College, University of London, UK
Ken Brown	University College Cork, Ireland
Marcos Bueno	Radboud University Nijmegen, The Netherlands
Nikolay Burlutskiy	ContextVision AB, Sweden
Philippe Chassy	University of Liverpool, UK
Daren Chitty	University of Bristol, UK

Frans Coenen	University of Liverpool, UK
Ireneusz Czarnowski	Gdynia Maritime University, Poland
Nicolas Durand	Aix-Marseille University, France
Frank Eichinger	DATEV eG, Nuremberg, Germany
Mohamed Gaber	Robert Gordon University Aberdeen, UK
Adriana Giret	Universidad Politecnica de Valencia, Spain
Peter Hampton	Ulster University, UK
Chris Headleand	University of Lincoln, UK
Xia Hong	University of Reading, UK
Adrian Hopgood	University of Portsmouth, UK
Zina Ibrahim	Kings College, London, UK
Said Jabbour	CRIL CNRS - University of Artois, France
Navneet Kesher	Facebook, Seattle WA, USA
John Kingston	University of Brighton, UK
Ivan Koychev	University of Sofia, Bulgaria
Nicole Lee	University of Hong Kong, SAR China
Anne Liret	British Telecom, France
Fernando Lopes	LNEG-National Research Institute, Portugal
Jixin Ma	University of Greenwich, UK
Fady Medhat	University of York, UK
Silja Meyer-Nieberg	Universität der Bundeswehr München, Germany
Roberto Micalizio	Università di Torino, Italy
Daniel Neagu	University of Bradford, UK
Joanna Isabelle Olszewska	University of Gloucestershire, UK
Dan O'Leary	University of Southern California, USA
Fernando Saenz-Perez	Universidad Complutense de Madrid, Spain
Miguel A. Salido	Universidad Politecnica de Valencia, Spain
Isabel Sargent	Ordnance Survey, UK
Rainer Schmidt	University Medicine of Rostock, Germany
Frederic Stahl	University of Reading, UK
Simon Thompson	BT Innovate, UK
Jon Timmis	University of York, UK
M. R. C. van Dongen	University College Cork, Ireland
Martin Wheatman	Yagadi Ltd., UK
Honghan Wu	King's College London, UK

Application Programme Committee

Hatem Ahriz	Robert Gordon University, UK
Tony Allen	Nottingham Trent University, UK
Ines Arana	Robert Gordon University, UK
Mercedes Arguello Casteleiro	University of Manchester, UK
Vasileios Argyriou	Kingston University, UK
Juan Carlos Augusto	Middlesex University, UK

Contents

Short Technical Papers

Application Papers

Industrial Applications of Artificial Intelligence

Planning and Scheduling in Action

Machine Learning in Action

Applications of Machine Learning

Technical Papers

Papers Included in the Technical Stream
of AI-2018

The following four sections comprise refereed papers accepted for the technical stream of AI-2018, divided into the following categories:

- Neural Networks
- Planning and Scheduling
- Machine Learning
- Short Technical Papers

The Donald Michie Memorial Award for the best refereed technical paper in the conference was won by a paper entitled "Secure Third Party Data Clustering Using Φ Data: Multi-User Order Preserving Encryption and Super Secure Chain Distance Matrices" by Nawal Almutairi (University of Liverpool, UK, and King Saud University, Saudi Arabia), Frans Coenen and Keith Dures (University of Liverpool, UK).

The final section comprises the text of short technical papers which were presented as posters at the conference.

Secure Third Party Data Clustering Using Φ Data: Multi-User Order Preserving Encryption and Super Secure Chain Distance Matrices (Best Technical Paper)

Nawal Almutairi[1,2]([⊠]), Frans Coenen[1]([⊠]), and Keith Dures[1]([⊠])

[1] Department of Computer Science, University of Liverpool, Liverpool, UK
{n.m.almutairi,coenen,dures}@liverpool.ac.uk
[2] Information Technology Department, College of Computer and Information Sciences, King Saud University, Riyadh, Saudi Arabia
nawalmutairi@ksu.edu.sa

Abstract. The paper introduces the concept of Φ-data, data that is a proxy for some underlying data that offers advantages of data privacy and security while at the same time allowing particular data mining operations without requiring data owner participation once the proxy has been generated. The nature of the proxy representation is dependent on the nature of the desired data mining to be undertaken. Secure collaborative clustering is considered where the Φ-data is in the form of a Super Secure Chain Distance Matrices (SSCDM) encrypted using a proposed Multi-User Order Preserving Encryption (MUOPE) scheme. SSCDMs can be produced with respect to horizontal and vertical data partitioning. The DBSCAN clustering algorithm is adopted for illustrative and evaluation purposes. The results indicate that the proposed solution is efficient and produces comparable clustering configurations to those produced using an unencrypted, "standard", algorithm; while maintaining data privacy and security.

Keywords: Privacy Preserving Data Mining
Order preserving and homomorphic encryption · Φ-data
Super Secure Chain Distance Matrices

1 Introduction

The resources facilitated through cloud computing have allowed for the delivery of a great variety of services to businesses that would not otherwise be available. One example, and that of interest with respect to this paper, is Data Mining as a Services (DMaaS). The emergence of the potential for third party data analysis using DMaaS has changed the way that data mining is traditionally conducted. However, an issue of significant concern is data privacy and security, a legitimate concern that has served to limit the uptake of DMaaS and which has instigated the research domain of Privacy Preserving Data Mining (PPDM) [2].

© Springer Nature Switzerland AG 2018
M. Bramer and M. Petridis (Eds.): SGAI-AI 2018, LNAI 11311, pp. 3–17, 2018.
https://doi.org/10.1007/978-3-030-04191-5_1

Early work on PPDM adopted the idea of Secure Multi-Party Computation (SMPC) which resolved data privacy concerns by precluding any form of data sharing [8,9,12]. The idea was for the individual data owners to locally process their data to produce local statistical characteristics describing their data which could then be used as an input to computation protocols that securely computed global characteristics. Although, to a certain extent, SMPC addressed the problem of data confidentiality, the requirement for data owner participation, as the data mining progressed, resulted in a significant computation and communication overhead and a consequent drain on local resources. These, in turn, effected scalability; thus rendering the approach infeasible for any form of large scale collaborative data mining.

A more desirable PPDM solution, that does not feature the limitations of SMPC, is to entirely outsource the data mining to a third party while maintaining data privacy and security. The idea here is to modify that data either by transforming it or encrypting it, in such a way that data mining activities can still be applied effectively. However, many transformation methods have been shown to adversely affect accuracy. Further, in the collaborative data mining context [3,4,6], data owners are all required to transfer their data in the same manner, which makes the solution vulnerable to breaches of privacy. A further criticism is that it has been shown that the data distribution may be reconstructed from the modified data [1]. Cryptography, in turn, provides a substantial guarantee for data privacy. A potential solution is the use of Homomorphic Encryption (HE) schemes that permit limited calculation over cyphertexts without compromising security. Although HE schemes support primitive operations that go some way to supporting data mining, they do not provide an entire solution. For example they do not support record comparison. One mechanism whereby this can be addressed is with recourse to bespoke SMPC protocols, such as "Yao's Millionaires Problem" protocol as used in [12], or by recourse to data owners as in the case of [15]; in either case undesired communication and/or computational overheads are introduced.

This paper presents a solution to the above in the context of distributed/collaborative data clustering using a third party data miner. More specifically the paper proposes the idea of using a proxy for the real data, an idea referred to as the "Φ-data" concept, where Φ data is a secure transform of the actual data (not a modification of the data), that supports some specific form of secure data mining that does not entail data owner participation once the proxy has been constructed. The concept of Φ data can be implemented in a variety of ways. In this paper it is illustrated using Super Secure Chain Distance Matrices (SSCDMs), a data proxy designed for secure collaborative data clustering using the DBSCAN algorithm. The exemplar scenario is that of a number of data owners who wish to produce collaboratively a cluster configuration without sharing their data. A CDM is a 2D matrix M where one dimension represents the set of records in a dataset (-1) and the other the set of attributes. Each cell $M_{i,j}$ holds the distance between the jth attribute value in $i$the record and the value of the same attribute in $i+1$th record. A SCDM is then an encrypted

CDM. This paper also proposes an order preserving encryption scheme, Multi-User Order Preserving Encryption (MUOPE), suited to encrypting CDMs. A SSCDM is then the union set of two or more SCDMs. The SSCDM construction process is facilitated by a Semi-honest Third Party (STP). Once complete it can be passed to a third party data miner who can produce a cluster configuration without requiring further data owner participation and without ever having had access to the original datasets held by individual data owners.

2 Related Works

This section presents a review of previous work directed at collaborative secure data clustering. The focus is on DBSCAN clustering; the clustering mechanism used to illustrate the solution proposed in this paper. Generally, the main challenge in collaborative data clustering is that of maintaining data confidentiality during processing without adversely affecting the calculation accuracy; thus in the case of DBSCAN when calculating distances between records and when comparing such distances against a threshold ϵ. As noted in the introduction, the proposed solutions can be categorised as being founded on either: (i) SMPC or (ii) secure outsourcing to a third party who has the permissions to carry out the required calculations. Both approaches are considered in further detail below.

The fundamental idea of SMPC is for the collaborating parties to jointly compute functions concerning their data while maintaining the privacy of their data. The nature of these functions, and the protocols used to calculate them, depend on the nature of the application. There are a number of examples where multiparty DBSCAN has been implemented using SMPC [8,9,12] where: (i) distance between data records is calculated using either a "secure multi-party scalar product" protocol or the homomorphic properties of a HE scheme, and (ii) secure comparison was achieved using either "Yao's Millionaires' Problem" protocol (YMPP) [18] or Cachin's scheme [5]. However, the solutions presented in [8,9,12] all entailed a significant computational overhead and consequently they were only suited to two party collaborative data clustering. In terms of security, involving data owners in the calculation of distances, and the comparison of distances, gives rise to the potential for "overlapping attacks" where a non-honest participant uses knowledge of their local data, and the computation results, to identify intersections with the data held by other parties and then uses this information to estimate records held by other parties. In the specific context of SMPC-based DBSCAN clustering a further security risk is that the total number of points within the ϵ-radius is revealed to all participants. Theses limitations render SMPC-based solution inadequate for many instances of DMaaS.

The alternative solution is to outsource the data and data analysis to a third party data miner. In this case privacy is preserved by modifying the data in some way. Two well documented modification techniques are data perturbation and encryption. The basic idea of data perturbation is to distort individual values by adding additive or multiplicative noise, or by applying some form of randomisation, so that the statistical characteristics of the data are retained.

From the literature a variety of perturbation methods have been proposed, both two party [2] and multiparty [3,4,6]. However, it has been demonstrated that the higher the level of security provided by the perturbation the worse the final data mining result, this is especially the case where each party applies a local perturbation method. This is why in [3] it was proposed that all parties use the same perturbation method so that an acceptable accuracy is achieved. Whatever the case, perturbation has two major disadvantages. The first is that the final results are adversely affected. The second is that the original data distribution can be reconstructed from the perturbed data [1]. Homomorphic Encryption provides an effective alternative that does not feature these disadvantages. In [15] a HE scheme was used to encrypt multiple source data before outsourcing to a third party data miner who then utilised the HE properties to calculate the required distances. However, the generated cyphers do not preserve the data ordering, thus data owner participation was still required to determine whether the distances were below or above the DBSCAN threshold ϵ value.

In [17] a mechanism is presented for applying DBSCAN in a secure distributed manner that combines the SMPC idea with the usage of a third party data miner. The basic idea is for each party to first apply DBSCAN to their local data and then to share the resulting boundary points and cluster labels using a third party data miner. The data miner's role is then to determine global boundary points which are then used by the individual data owner to update their local clusters. However, the local boundary points are sent to the data miner in plaintext form, which presents a security threat.

3 Paillier Homomorphic Encryption

Before considering the proposed secure DBSCAN clustering algorithm, and the SSCDM concept, in detail, Paillier Homomorphic Encryption, utilised in the context of the proposed MUOPE scheme, is briefly described in this section. The Paillier encryption scheme [14] is an additive, probabilistic and asymmetric HE scheme that encodes a plaintext value m to a cyphertext value c using the equation $c = g^m r^N \pmod{N^2}$ where N is the Rivest-Shamir-Adleman (RSA) modulus, g is a non-zero integer of order divisible by N; and r is a random number, $r \in \mathbb{Z}_N$, used to ensure the probabilistic feature of the scheme. The scheme has an additive homomorphic feature that maps plaintext addition ($+$) to cypher multiplication ($\otimes$) as given in Eq. 1, where $a, b \in \mathbb{Z}_N$.

$$E(a + b) = E(a) \otimes E(b) \pmod{N^2} \tag{1}$$

The decryption function decodes c to the original plaintext value m using Algorithm 1 where: LCM is a *Least Common Multiple* function, L is a function defined as $L(x) = \frac{x-1}{N}$, (N, g) is the public key and (λ, μ) is the secret key.

Algorithm 1. Paillier decrypt function

1: **procedure** DECRYPT(c)
2:      $\lambda = LCM(p-1, q-1)$ ▷ p and q are two prime numbers
3:      $\mu = (L(g^\lambda \pmod{N^2})))^{-1} \pmod{N}$
4:      $m = L(c^\lambda \pmod{N^2}))\mu \pmod{N}$
5:      **Exit** with m

---

4   The Multi-User Order Preserving Encryption (MUOPE) Scheme

The CDM, generated by individual data owners and described further in Sect. 5 below, is essentially a set of linear equations that might support the undesirable re-engineering of the original data distribution. Therefore, to prevent such re-engineering, while still permitting comparison of distances, in this paper it is proposed that CDMs are encrypted to give Secure CDMs (SCDMs) using a bespoke encryption scheme, the MUOPE scheme.

The idea of the proposed MUOPE scheme is founded on the scheme presented in [13] which was directed at encrypting data in such a way that the order of data items was preserved; however the scheme was not applicable to data from multiple sources. The main objective of the proposed MUOPE scheme is to encrypt two or more SCDMs, that are to be combined into a single SSCDM, in such a way that any data distribution that might exist in the generated cyphertexts is entirely obscured. To this end, the concepts of *message space splitting* and *non-linear cypher space expansion* were adopted so that the third party data miner could have access to the ordering of distances between records and not the original CDM distance values themselves.

In the proposed MUOPE scheme a Semi-honest Third Party (STP) is used to act as a mediator between u participating parties (data owners), $P = \{p_1, \ldots, p_u\}$. The STPs role is to: (i) derive MUOPE encryption parameters and (ii) manage the SSCDM generation process. The STP starts by determining the required "interval" of message space $M = [l, h]$ and the associated expanded "interval" of cypher space $C = [l', h']$ where h is the maximum interval boundary and l is the minimum boundary in such a way that $|C| \gg |M|$. The STP then randomly splits the message space into t consecutive intervals, where t is a random number, to give $M = \{m_1, \ldots, m_t\}$, where $m_i = [l_i, h_i]$; as demonstrated in Fig. 1. The message space interval boundaries are then sent to the data owners.

To generate the cypher space intervals, the STP needs to know how many distances fall into each interval. The STP does this by creating a list V comprised of t items $\{v_1, \ldots, v_t\}$ where each item in a list will eventually hold a count of the number of distances that fall in each interval. The STP populates V with a random set of values and encrypts it using the Paillier encryption from Sect. 3. Thus the STP is also responsible for generating Paillier public-private key pairs. The Paillier encrypted list V' is then sent, together with the Paillier public key, to the first data owner p_1 who then updates V' with their data density, for

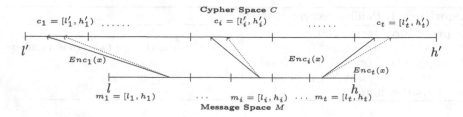

Fig. 1. Message and expanded cypher space splitting

each interval, using the additive feature of the Paillier scheme. The updated list V' is then sent in turn to the remaining data owners. The last party p_u will return V' to the STP who decrypts it and subtracts the original values used to populate V. The results (the data density for each interval) is then used to dimension the cypher space C to give $C = \{c_1, \ldots, c_t\}$, in such a way that the length of each interval c_i is determined according to the density of the data in the corresponding message space interval m_i. The aim is to ensure that message space intervals with a high "density" correspond to larger (expanded) cypher space intervals, and vice versa. The cypher space boundaries are then sent to the data owners. The intervals boundaries represent MUOPE encryption keys.

On receiving the MUOPE encryption keys, from the STP, the data owners encrypt their individual CDMs to give SCDMs, the process for this is discussed in Sect. 5 below. The encryption is conducted as indicated by Eq. 2, where: i represents the ID number of an "interval" within which a distance $dist$ is contained; l_i and h_i are the boundaries for the ith message space interval; and l'_i and h'_i are the boundaries for the ith cypher space interval. The variable δ_i is a random number sampled from the range 0 to $Sens \times Scale$ where $Sens$ is defined, as in [11], as the data sensitivity value that represents the minimum distance between plaintext values.

$$Scale = \frac{(l'_i - h'_i)}{(l_i - h_i)}, \quad Enc(dist) = l'_i + (Scale \times (dist - l_i)) + \delta_i \qquad (2)$$

The STP then commences the SSCDM generation process. How this is done depends on whether we have horizontally or vertically partitioned data and is described in Sect. 5. Once the SSCDM has been calculated, the STP passes this on to the third party data miner. The STPs role is now complete.

5   The Super Secure Chain Distance Matrix (SSCDM)

A SCDM is a mechanism for realising the envisioned Φ-data concept in the context of collaborative data clustering, specifically DBSCAN clustering. A SCDM allows for secure data comparison in the absence of the original data. A Super SCDM (SSCDM) is then a combination of a number of SCDMs generated by individual data owners. In the following subsections the SSCDM generation process is given in further detail. The generation of SCDM is presented in Subsect. 5.1. This is followed, Subsects. 5.2 and 5.3, with discussion of the "binding" process to give SSCDM given either horizontally or vertically partitioned data.

5.1 The Secure Chain Distance Matrix (SCDM)

A CDM is a 2D matrix that holds the distances (differences) between each attribute value within a record i and the corresponding attribute value in the following record $i + 1$ according to whatever ordering is featured in the dataset D. The matrix thus measures $(|R| - 1) \times |A|$, where $|R|$ is the number of records in D and $|A|$ is the size of the attribute set A. A SCDM is then an encrypted CDM. The SCDM is generated in two steps: (i) CDM calculation and (ii) CDM encryption to arrive at a SCDM. Algorithm 2 gives the CDM calculation process. The algorithm commences by dimensioning the desired CDM (line 2) which is then populated (lines 3 to 5) by calculating the distances between the values for attributes in the ith and $i + 1$th data records (line 5).

Algorithm 2. Chain Distance Matrix Calculation

1: **procedure** CDMCALCULATION(D)
2:     **CDM** $= \emptyset$ array of $|R| - 1$ rows and $|A|$ column
3:     **for** $i = 1$ to $i = |R| - 1$ **do**
4:         **for** $j = 1$ to $j = |A|$ **do**
5:             **CDM**$_{[i,j]} = D_{[i,j]} - D_{[i+1,j]}$
6:     **Exit** with **CDM**

The next step is to encrypt the calculated CDM to give a SCDM. To this end the MUOPE scheme presented in Sect. 4 was used. The key feature of the resulting SCDM is that a third party has access to the distance value ordering, but not the actual distance values. In addition, the chain feature of SCDMs allows a number of SCDMs to be "bound" to form a SSCDM that then permits similarity calculations between data records, possibly owned by different parties, without involving the data owners. The similarity between a record r_x and a record r_y (where $x < y$), is calculated according to Eq. 3. In the case of $x = y$ the distance will clearly be 0.

$$Sim(SCDM, r_x, r_y) = \sum_{j=1}^{j=|A|} \sum_{i=x}^{i=(y-1)} |SCDM_{[i,j]}| \qquad (3)$$

5.2 SSCDM for Horizontal Data Partitioning

Horizontally distributed data is where each partition conforms to the same set of attributes A, but features different records; in other words the global dataset D has been partitioned by dividing it up "horizontally". To "bind" two SCDMs,

$SCDM_i$ and $SCDM_{i+1}$, representing horizontally partitioned data, belonging to two data owners p_i and p_{i+1} respectively, an additional "pivot" record, with $|A|$ attributes, needs to be inserted between the two SCDMs, recording the differences between attribute values in the last record in D_i owned by P_i, and the first record in D_{i+1} owned by P_{i+1}. The process is as shown in Algorithm 3. The inputs to the process are the two SCDMs ($SCDM_i$ and $SCDM_{i+1}$) and the global SSCDM accumulated so far. The algorithm commences with the STP randomly generating a record, $R = \{r_1, r_2, \ldots, r_{|A|}\}$ and encrypting this using the MUOPE scheme (line 2); this is then sent to p_i and p_{i+1}. Data owner p_i calculates the distances between the MUOPE cypher of the last record in its dataset and the content of R to give a record C_1 (line 3); whilst data owner p_{i+1} calculates the distances between the content of R and the MUOPE cypher of the first record in its dataset to give a record C_2 (line 4). Both C_1 and C_2 are returned to the STP who calculates the pivot record, $pivot = C_1 + C_2$. The pivot record is then used to bind $SCDM_i$ and $SCDM_{i+1}$ (line 6) and append this to the SSCDM so far. The process repeats with $SCDM_{i+1}$ and $SCDM_{i+2}$ and continues until the entire SSCDM has been generated.

Algorithm 3. Horizontal binding process

1: **procedure** HORIZONTALBINDING($SCDM_i, SCDM_{i+1}, SSCDM$)
2:     $R = \{r_1, \ldots, r_{|A|}\}$ ▷ Encrypted using MUOPE
3:     $C1 =$ Distances between last record in D_i and R
4:     $C2 =$ Distances between R and first record in D_{i+1}
5:     $Pivot = C_1 + C_2$
6:     $SSCDM = concatenate(SSCDM, SCDM_i, Pivot, SCDM_{i+1})$
7:     **Exit** with **SSCDM**

5.3   SSCDM for Vertical Data Partitioning

Vertically distributed data is where each partition features the same set of records but a specific sub-set of attributes from a global set of attributes A; the global dataset has been partitioned by being divided up "vertically". The binding process for vertically partitioned data is as shown in Algorithm 4. The inputs are: a SCDM, $SCDM_i$ belonging to data owner p_i, and the SSCDM so far. On start up the SSCDM so far will simply be $SCDM_1$, belonging to data owner p_1. The algorithm operates by simply appending records to one another, (line 2), there is no need for a pivot record. As before, the process will continue until the entire SSCDM has been generated.

Algorithm 4. Vertical binding process

1: **procedure** VERTICALBINDING($SCDM_i, SSCDM$)
2:     $SSCDM = concatenate(SSCDM, SCDM_i)$
3:     **Exit** with **SSCDM**

---

6   Secure DBSCAN (SDBSCAN)

The SDBSCAN clustering is conducted by the third party data miner following a processes very similar to the standard DBSCAN [7]. The pseudo code is given in Algorithm 5. The inputs are the SSCDM received from the STP and the desired density parameters, $MinPts$ and ϵ', that are agreed by the participating parties. The ϵ value is encrypted using the proposed MUOPE scheme to give ϵ' so that the third party data miner does not have the real radius value. The algorithm uses a "virtual" dataset VR where the indexes refer to the data held by data owners, thus $VR = \{vr_1, vr_2, \ldots, vr_{|SSCDM|+1}\}$. The order of the data indexes matches the order used to bind the SCDMs. For example, indexes 0 to $|SCDM_1 + 1|$ represent the p_1 virtual dataset. The algorithm commences by creating the ordered set VR, creating an empty set of clusters C and setting the number of clusters so far to 1 (line 2). The set VR is then processed. For each "virtual" record $vr_i \in VR$ that has not been previously assigned to a cluster, is "unclustered", the set S is determined. The set S is the ϵ-neighbourhood of vr_i and comprises the set of record IDs in VR whose distance from vr_i is less than or equals to ϵ'. The set is determined by calling the $RegionQuery$ procedure (line 5) where the SSCDM is used to determine the overall distances between records (see Eq. 3). If the number of records in S is greater than $MinPts$ the density requirement is satisfied thus vr_i is marked as "clustered" and considered to represent a new cluster C_k (lines 6 to 8). This cluster is then expanded by considering the points in S using the $ExpandCluster$ procedure called in line 9. The inputs to the $ExpandCluster$ procedure are: the cluster C_k so far, the set S, SSCDM and the density parameters $MinPts$ and ϵ'. The $ExpandCluster$ procedure is a recursive procedure. For each record in S which has not been previously clustered we add the record to C_k and then determine the ϵ-neighbourhood S_2 for the record. If the size of S_2 is greater than $MinPts$ we call the $ExpandCluster$ procedure again and so on until all the "virtual" records in VR are processed at which point the algorithm will exit with the cluster configuration C. For the purpose of data privacy each participating party will receive their own data clustering results.

7   Experimental Evaluation

This section reports on the evaluation of the Φ-data concept in the context of MUOPE and SSCDM as implemented with respect to SDBSCAN. The objectives of the evaluation were to consider the proposed approach in terms: (i) data

---

Algorithm 5. Secure DBSCAN clustering algorithm

1: **procedure** SDBSCAN($SSCDM$, $MinPts$, ϵ')
2:     $C = \emptyset$, VR =list of record IDs, $k = 1$
3:     **for** $\forall\, vr_i \in VR$ **do**
4:         **if** vr_i *is Unclustered* **then**
5:             $S = $ RegionQuery($vr_i, \epsilon', SSCDM$)
6:             **if** $|S| > MinPts$ **then**
7:                 mark vr_i as *clustered*
8:                 $C_k = vr_i$ (new cluster)
9:                 $C_k = $ ExpandCluster(C_k,S, $SSCDM$,ϵ',$MinPts$)
10:                $C = C \cup C_k$
11:                $k = k + 1$
12:    **Exit** with **C**
13: **procedure** EXPANDCLUSTER(C,S, $SSCDM$,ϵ',$MinPts$)
14:    **for** $\forall\, vr_i \in S$ **do**
15:        **if** vr_i *is Unclustered* **then**
16:            mark vr_i as *clustered*
17:            $C = C \cup vr_i$
18:            $S_2 = $ RegionQuery($vr_i, \epsilon', SSCDM$)
19:            **if** $|S_2| > MinPts$ **then**
20:                $C = $ ExpandCluster(C,S_2, $SSCDM$,ϵ',$MinPts$)
21:    **Exit** with **C**
22: **procedure** REGIONQUERY($Index$, ϵ', $SSCDM$)
23:    $N_\epsilon = \emptyset$
24:    **for** $\forall\, vr_j \in VR$ **do**
25:        $distance = Sim(SSCDM, Index, j)$ ▷ (Eq. 3)
26:        **if** $distance \leq \epsilon'$ **then**
27:            $N_\epsilon.add(j)$
28:    **Exit** with N_ϵ

---

owners participation, (ii) clustering efficiency, (iii) clustering accuracy, (iv) security and (v) scalability. Two different types of data were used, synthetic data and data from the UCI machine learning repository [10].

7.1 Data Owner Participation

Individual data owner participation was measured in terms of the runtimes (ms) required to: (i) generate CDMs (CDM Gen.), (ii) encrypt CDMs (CDM Enc) and (iii) calculate the data density required to dimension the MUOPE cypher space (Dens Cal). Experiments were conducted using a sequence of ten synthetic datasets increasing in size from 1000 to 10,000 records, in steps of 1,000; the number of attributes ($|A|$) was kept constant at 125. The results are presented in Fig. 2. Inspection of the figure indicates that, as was expected, time complexity increases in a linear manner as the number of records ($|R|$) increases. For example, in the case of the $|R| = 1$K dataset, the recorded runtimes for *CDM Gen* and *Dens Cal* are both 163 ms, while for the 10K dataset the recorded run times were 445 ms and 493 ms respectively. The time complexity for *CDM Gen* is $O(|R| - 1 \times |A|)$. The *CDM Enc* is slightly higher; the 1K required 0.5 s which increased to 2.4 s for 10K. What is noteworthy is that, regardless of the number of records considered, the run times are not significantly high; hence the amount of data owner participation can be argued to be minimal. Recall that once the SSCDM has been generated no further data owner participation is required other than instructing the third party data miner to undertake specific clustering exercises.

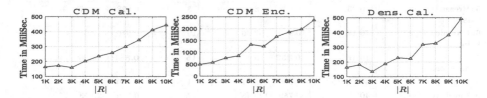

Fig. 2. Time required (ms) for data owner participation in term of number of records in a data owner's local dataset

7.2   Clustering Efficiency

A comparison of the runtimes required to cluster data using standard (unencrypted) DBSCAN and the proposed SDBSCAN is given in columns 6 and 9 of Table 1 which gives clustering outcomes using fifteen UCI datasets [10]. Note that runtimes for standard DBSCAN are reported in milliseconds (ms), while runtimes for SDBSCAN are reported in seconds (s). The *MinPts* and ϵ values reported in the table are randomly selected; in practice these are prescribed by the data owners. From the table, it can be seen that reported runtimes were larger for SDBSCAN than in the case of the standard approach. The difference is due to the utilisation of SSCDMs. Note that the bigger the dataset the larger the SSCDM, hence the greater the time required to process the SSCDM to determine record similarity. However, inspection of the recorded results indicates that usage of SSCDMs did not introduce an unreasonable overhead.

7.3   Clustering Accuracy

Clustering accuracy was measured by comparing the clustering configurations obtained using SDBSCAN with those obtained using standard DBSCAN. The intuition was that the secure algorithm should produce comparable configurations to those produced using the standard algorithm; if so the secure algorithm could be said to be operating correctly. The measure used was the established Silhouette Coefficient (Sil. Coef.) [16]; a value between −1 and 1, the closer the values is to 1 the better the clustering. The Sil. Coef. values obtained are presented in columns 5 and 8 of Table 1, and the number of generated clusters in Columns 4 and 7. From the table, it can be seen that the cluster configurations produced using the proposed SDBSCAN were the same in 12 out of 15 cases,

Table 1. Cluster configuration for standard and secure DBSCAN (differing results highlighted in bold font)

DataSet	$MinPts$	ϵ	Standard DBSCAN			Secure DBSCAN		
			Num. clus.	Sil. coef.	Exec. time (ms)	Num. clus.	Sil. coef.	Exec. time (s)
1. Arrhythmia	2	600	6	0.472	187.16	6	0.472	367.24
2. Banknote Auth	2	3	7	0.922	686.37	7	0.922	254.25
3. Blood Trans	2	10	**27**	**0.971**	54.20	**33**	**0.976**	4.73
4. Breast Cancer	2	5	**4**	**0.678**	61.64	**1**	**0.485**	9.60
5. Breast Tissue	2	100	3	0.628	3.93	3	0.628	0.27
6. Chronic kidney	2	70	19	0.970	57.36	19	0.970	12.64
7. Dermatology	2	10	**16**	**0.853**	19.46	**15**	**0.881**	5.86
8. Ecoli	2	60	1	−1.000	45.81	1	−1.000	4.58
9. Ind. Liver Patient	3	40	7	0.789	120.48	7	0.789	25.53
10. Iris	5	2	2	0.722	11.89	2	0.722	0.33
11. Libras Move	5	5	11	0.715	61.75	11	0.715	120.62
12. Lung Cancer	2	20	1	0.053	0.32	1	0.053	0.01
13. Parkinsons	3	10	5	0.829	14.84	5	0.829	4.06
14. Pima Disease	5	20	4	0.691	221.87	4	0.691	30.15
15. Seeds	5	1	7	0.852	16.90	7	0.852	1.43

and slightly different in three cases (Blood Trans., Breast Cancer and Dermatology). It is interesting to note that in two of these three cases (Blood Trans. and Dermatology) SDBSCAN produced better Sil. Coef. values. The reason for the differences was because the proposed MUOPE scheme produced different cyphertexts for the same plaintext value, which meant that "equality" was not supported; thus if a dataset had many identical values these would result in different cyphertexts which in turn would effect the nature of the clustering (sometimes in a positive manner). This feature of the MUOPE scheme was introduced to hide data value frequency so as to prevent statistical attacks that can be instigated when attackers have knowledge of the data distribution (frequency).

7.4   Security Analysis

Security was evaluated by identifying the potential attacks that may threaten the proposed secure data clustering. In the proposed solution, data preservation relies on the Φ data concept and the security of the MUOPE scheme used to encrypt the SSCDMs. The concept of Φ data, prevents the data from being confided (in any form) to a third party data miner or shared with any other participants. Therefore, the Φ data concept precludes any form of attack directed at the actual data, including the overlapping attack possible with respect to other solutions (see Sect. 2). The only data proxy received by the third party data miner is the SSCDM; there is no further data owner involvement. Hence, the only potential form of attack is Cyphertexts Only Attacks (COAs) that may occur if an adversary somehow has access to a SSCDM. As a countermeasure to COAs the proposed MUOPE was designed to reduce information leakage in cyphertexts by avoiding the deterministic feature that is usually used in COAs. More specifically the MUOPE scheme uses an encryption function that generates different cyphertexts for the same plaintext values on each occasion that the encryption function is applied; this feature makes inferences using COAs harder. COAs are more likely to succeed when attackers have a background knowledge of the data distribution, or frequency, of the original data values. Knowledge associated with the ordering features of some order preserving encryption schemes might allow an adversary to infer the ranges containing dense data. Alternatively, frequency analysis could allow attackers to highlight cyphertexts with the same frequency as plaintexts (if such plaintexts were available) and then identify cyphertexts that have the same frequency. However, this will not be possible in the case of the MUOPE scheme, which incorporates *message space splitting*, *non-linear cypher space expansion* and a *one-to-many encryption function*, that serves to obscure the statistical features of the generated cyphertexts.

7.5   Scalability

The scalability of the proposed SDBSCAN approach, founded on the concept of Φ data realised using SSCDMs, encrypted using the proposed MUOPE scheme, was evaluated by considering the effect on time complexity as the number of data owners (participants) increased. In the proposed approach data owner collaboration occurs when generating: (i) MUOPE encryption keys (Key Gen.) and (ii) SSCDMs (Super SCDM Gen.). For the evaluation a sequence of experiments was conducted where the number of participants was increased from 10 to 100 in steps of 5 (for completeness experiments using two and four participants were also conducted). A synthetic dataset, comprised of 7000 records and 125 attributes, was equally distributed across the parties in each case. The recorded total runtime results are presented in Fig. 3. From the figure it can be seen that the overall time required to generate the encryption keys was negligible; even in the 100 participants case the recorded runtime was 1, 213 ms. The scalability, as demonstrated by the reported results, indicates that the MUOPE scheme has potential benefits for many other forms of DMaaS and collaborative PPDM.

With respect to the overall time required to generate a SSCDM the results reported in Fig. 3(b) show that, as expected, the time required will increase linearly with the number of participants. Recall that the usage of SSCDMs allows collaborative data clustering to be implemented without requiring extensive communication between participants when calculating distances between data points as in the case of [8,9,12]. From the figure it can also be seen that vertical partitioning produced the best performance because we are simply "bolting" one SCDM to another.

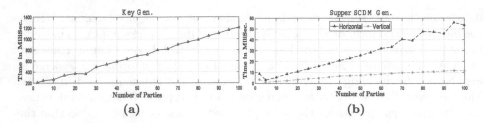

Fig. 3. Runtime to generate OPE keys and construct SSCDMs as the number of participants (data owners) increases

8   Conclusion and Future Work

This paper has proposed a novel solution for third party privacy preserving collaborative data clustering using the concept of Φ-data and SSCDMs encrypted using MUOPE. The Φ-data concept obviates the need for any form of data sharing between data owners and/or a third party data miner. The proposed approach offers three main advantages. Firstly, the SSCDM proxy representation allows multiple data sources to be compared without data owner involvement or any communication overhead. Secondly, the MUOPE scheme encrypts SSCDMs, in such a way that protection against Cyphertexts Only Attacks (COAs) is provided (other forms of attack are precluded). Thirdly, the secure data clustering is entirely delegated to a third party data miner (over encrypted data), no data owner participation is required. The accuracy of the clustering produced using the SDBSCAN approach was shown to be compatible with those produced using standard DBSCAN, whilst the time complexity was not significantly greater. It was also shown that the proposed approach was readily scalable. For future work, the authors intend to investigate the utility of SSCDMs with respect to alternative clustering algorithms and other data mining techniques.

References

1. Aggarwal, C.C., Yu, P.S.: A general survey of privacy-preserving data mining models and algorithms. In: Aggarwal, C.C., Yu, P.S. (eds.) Privacy-Preserving Data Mining. Advances in Database Systems, vol. 34, pp. 11–52. Springer, Boston (2008). https://doi.org/10.1007/978-0-387-70992-5_2
2. Agrawal, R., Srikant, R.: Privacy-preserving data mining. SIGMOD Rec. **29**(2), 439–450 (2000)
3. Anikin, I.V., Gazimov, R.M.: Privacy preserving DBSCAN clustering algorithm for vertically partitioned data in distributed systems. In: IEEE International Siberian Conference on Control and Communications, pp. 1–4. IEEE (2017)
4. Bhaduri, K., Stefanski, M.D., Srivastava, A.N.: Privacy-preserving outlier detection through random nonlinear data distortion. IEEE Trans. Syst. Man Cybern. Part B (Cybern.) **41**(1), 260–272 (2011)
5. Cachin, C.: Efficient private bidding and auctions with an oblivious third party. In: Proceedings of the 6th ACM Conference on Computer and Communications Security, pp. 120–127. ACM (1999)

6. Chen, K., Liu, L.: Privacy-preserving multiparty collaborative mining with geometric data perturbation. IEEE Trans. Parallel Distrib. Syst. **20**(12), 1764–1776 (2009)
7. Ester, M., Kriegel, H.P., Sander, J., Xu, X., et al.: A density-based algorithm for discovering clusters in large spatial databases with noise. In: KDD 1996, pp. 226–231 (1996)
8. Jiang, D., Xue, A., Ju, S., Chen, W., Ma, H.: Privacy-preserving DBSCAN on horizontally partitioned data. In: IEEE International Symposium on Medicine and Education, pp. 1067–1072. IEEE (2008)
9. Kumar, K.A., Rangan, C.P.: Privacy preserving DBSCAN algorithm for clustering. In: Alhajj, R., Gao, H., Li, J., Li, X., Zaïane, O.R. (eds.) ADMA 2007. LNCS (LNAI), vol. 4632, pp. 57–68. Springer, Heidelberg (2007). https://doi.org/10.1007/978-3-540-73871-8_7
10. Lichman, M.: UCI machine learning repository (2013). http://archive.ics.uci.edu/ml
11. Liu, D., Wang, S.: Nonlinear order preserving index for encrypted database query in service cloud environments. Concurr. Comput. Pract. Exp. **25**(13), 1967–1984 (2013)
12. Liu, J., Xiong, L., Luo, J., Huang, J.Z.: Privacy preserving distributed DBSCAN clustering. Trans. Data Priv. **6**(1), 69–85 (2013)
13. Liu, Z., Chen, X., Yang, J., Jia, C., You, I.: New order preserving encryption model for outsourced databases in cloud environments. J. Netw. Comput. Appl. **59**, 198–207 (2016)
14. Paillier, P.: Public-key cryptosystems based on composite degree residuosity classes. In: Stern, J. (ed.) EUROCRYPT 1999. LNCS, vol. 1592, pp. 223–238. Springer, Heidelberg (1999). https://doi.org/10.1007/3-540-48910-X_16
15. Rahman, M.S., Basu, A., Kiyomoto, S.: Towards outsourced privacy-preserving multiparty DBSCAN. In: 22nd IEEE Pacific Rim International Symposium on Dependable Computing, pp. 225–226. IEEE (2017)
16. Rousseeuw, P.J.: Silhouettes: a graphical aid to the interpretation and validation of cluster analysis. J. Comput. Appl. Math. **20**, 53–65 (1987)
17. Tong, Q., Li, X., Yuan, B.: Efficient distributed clustering using boundary information. Neurocomputing **275**, 2355–2366 (2018)
18. Yao, A.C.: Protocols for secure computations. In: 23rd Annual Symposium on Foundations of Computer Science, pp. 160–164. IEEE (1982)

Neural Networks

Implementing Rules with Artificial Neurons

Christian Huyck[✉] and Dainius Kreivenas

Middlesex University, London NW4 4BT, UK
c.huyck@mdx.ac.uk

Abstract. Rule based systems are an important class of computer languages. The brain, and more recently neuromorphic systems, is based on neurons. This paper describes a mechanism that converts a rule based system, specified by a user, to spiking neurons. The system can then be run in simulated neurons, producing the same output. The conversion is done making use of binary cell assemblies, and finite state automata. The binary cell assemblies, eventually implemented in neurons, implement the states. The rules are converted to a dictionary of facts, and simple finite state automata. This is then cached out to neurons. The neurons can be simulated on standard simulators, like NEST, or on neuromorphic hardware. Parallelism is a benefit of neural system, and rule based systems can take advantage of this parallelism. It is hoped that this work will support further exploration of parallel neural and rule based systems, and support further work in cognitive modelling and cognitive architecture.

Keywords: Rule based system · Simulated neurons
Cognitive architecture · Compilation to neurons

1 Introduction

Simulated and emulated neural systems can be used for practical applications, have massive parallelism, and can be used for exploring human and other animal neural processing. Rule based systems are a standard programming paradigm that has been widely used for expert systems and for cognitive modelling. Consequently, the ability to easily translate a rule based system into a neural system that can execute the same system has many potential uses in modern AI and cognitive science. This paper describes such a translation mechanism, and the neural execution of two particular rule bases (Monkeys and Bananas Sect. 4.1, and the Tower of Hanoi Sect. 4.2).

The idea is based around finite state automata (FSAs) as each rule is a simple FSA moving from one set of facts to another. Facts are implemented neurally as binary cell assemblies (CAs) (see Sect. 2.2).

This translation ability expands the potential easy use of large neural systems, as large rule based systems can be directly translated to them. This supports the exploration of large, parallel rule based systems, and the exploration of neural cognitive architectures.

© Springer Nature Switzerland AG 2018
M. Bramer and M. Petridis (Eds.): SGAI-AI 2018, LNAI 11311, pp. 21–33, 2018.
https://doi.org/10.1007/978-3-030-04191-5_2

2   Literature Review

Rule based systems are powerful, have a long history, and are widely used in modern cognitive science (see Sect. 2.1). FSAs are an important standard computational theoretical construct that can be readily implemented in neurons using binary CAs; CAs more broadly are important standard neuropsychological constructs that form the neural basis of concepts (see Sect. 2.2). Biological neurons can be accurately simulated and emulated in modern computers; moreover, standard mechanisms are available to increase the reusability of neural systems (see Sects. 2.3 and 3.2).

2.1   Rule Based Systems

Rule based systems have been in use since at least the 1940s [17], and are Turing complete. They were important in early AI systems (e.g. [16]). Many expert systems in the 1970s and since have been implemented in rule based systems, in part because experts can explain their reasoning in rules, and thus it is relatively simple for a programmer to translate this expertise into a rule based program. Rules are also the most common mechanism for procedural knowledge in cognitive architectures, including ACT-R [2], Soar [13], and EPIC [12].

As the name suggests, rule based systems are built around if then rules. For example **if** *Banana at A, and Monkey at A* **then** *Monkey has Banana.* Facts, like *Banana at A* are boolean. Rule based systems are readily implemented on standard computers. While developing the system described in this paper, CLIPS [18] was used to develop particular systems, and as a test that the same results were produced. Rule based systems are often easier for people to learn to program than standard programming languages like Java.

In most rule based systems, one rule is applied in each time step. However, it is also possible to apply all supported rules in parallel. For example, the rule based component of EPIC [12] applies many rules in each cycle. This parallel application may be useful in cognitive modelling, but it is also useful as parallel processing. It is possible to have a parallel rule based system that fires thousands or even millions of rules in parallel, allowing a rapid processing speed increase.

While rules are simple, an FSA is perhaps simpler.

2.2   Finite State Automata and Cell Assemblies

Finite state automata are standard computational theoretical models based around states [14]. They can be used to recognise that an input is valid, so starting from a state, they will move to another state depending on the next input. They are powerful and widely used mechanisms, in for example compilers. They are, however, not Turing complete.

A long standing theory of neuropsychology is that concepts are represented by reverberating circuits of neurons called cell assemblies (CAs) [10]. These neurons have a large number of synapses to each other, and the weights of these synapses are large. So, if enough of the neurons start to fire, the neurons will continue to fire causing a reverberating circuit. Once the CA starts to fire, it is said to be ignited. An ignited CA is a psychological short-term memory. When the neurons in the CA stop firing at an elevated rate, the CA is no longer in short-term memory.

While the topology of biological CAs is complex and poorly understood, it is relatively simple to develop binary CAs in simulated neurons. These binary CAs are either firing, or not. They persist indefinitely, unless inhibited by neurons outside the CA, which can switch the CA off.

These binary CAs can act as states in a finite state automata. Once a state is active (firing persistently), it will persist indefinitely. A second state can be activated by a combination of the current state, and input. The second state can inhibit the first, and the neural implementation of the automata has transitioned to the second state. Any FSA can be implemented in this fashion [6].

The attentive reader will note that while rule based systems are Turing complete, FSAs are not. How then can FSAs be used to implement rule based systems. The answer is in the neural facts. An FSA can be combined with an infinite tape to make a Turing machine, which is, as the name suggests, Turing complete. In this case, an infinite number of neurons to implement facts replaces the tape. Do note that any finite calculation can be done with a finite sized tape, and similarly with a finite number of neurons. This should not be particularly surprising as it has been shown that a system based on neurons is Turing complete [4].

2.3   Artificial Neurons

There a many artificial neural models with complexities varying from simple integrate-and-fire neurons [15], to compartmental models [11] and beyond. There is a trade-off between biological accuracy and computational efficiency. This work makes use of leaky-integrate-and-fire (LIF) models [3]. These point models are widely used in biological neural modelling, and are available on neuromorphic hardware [8]. Unlike standard Von Neumann architectures, neuromorphic hardware is not general purpose, but instead emulates neurons; this hardware supports a large degree of parallelism.

A simple description of LIF models is that they collect activation from other neurons. If a neuron collects enough activation to surpass its threshold, it fires, and sends activation to the neurons it is connected to. These can be modelled continuously, but the systems typical run in discrete time steps. If a neuron does not fire in a time step, some if its activation leaks away. The time step used in the simulations described below is 1 ms.

The connections between neurons are weighted uni-directional synapses. These weights may be positive (excitatory) or negative (inhibitory).

3   System

The system described in this paper translates rules to a neural implementation of those same rules. These rules are run in simulated neurons, but could easily be run on neuromorphic hardware. In the simulations below, execution of the neural rule based system is done by externally stimulating the neural implementation of the initial facts, causing them to become persistently active (putting them into memory). The firing neurons in the fact spreads activation to the rules they support, causing the rules to be applied, putting new facts into memory, and removing old facts.

3.1   Translating Rules to Neurons

The translation system takes as input the rules defined as python structures, and the initial facts. It stores the rules internally as a dictionary of definitions, which determine what facts activate or deactivate other facts. It then takes each rule and translates it to one or more FSAs.

The translation engine uses the rules to create new facts by scanning the existing facts. In essence, these are the facts that may become true during execution. As new facts and rules are added to the system a recursive mapping process ensures that all new facts that are needed are created.

Through the system's recursive translation engine, the facts are mapped to rules. Every time a new fact or rule is added to the system, new facts may be added. For example, Eq. 1 is a simple rule approximating CLIPS syntax.

$$(MonkeyCanReach\ ?x) \Rightarrow (MonkeyGrab\ ?x)$$
$$(remove\ (MonkeyCanReach\ ?x)) \tag{1}$$

In the rule 1, the $?x$ is a variable. When it is defined, the system has no facts. If a fact $(MonkeyCanReach\ Banana)$ is defined, the system will put the fact into the dictionary. It will also add the $(MonkeyGrab\ Banana)$ fact to the dictionary because of rule 1. If the rule had a constant fact (e.g. $(MonkeyCanReach\ Banana)$) as the antecedent, it would have added that fact to the dictionary while reading the rule. The consequent of sets up an FSA that both adds new facts and removes the old ones.

With this rule and the associated two facts, the system will create an FSA that links the two facts so that if the $(MonkeyCanReach\ Banana)$ fact becomes active, it will turn on the $(MonkeyGrab\ Banana)$ fact, and in turn be turned off.

If a new fact is added, say $MonkeyCanReach\ Apple$, the corresponding $MonkeyGrab\ Apple$ fact will be created and another linking FSA for the rule will be created.

Note that in this context the fact is true if its associated state is on, and is made false by turning that state off. Of course, there is no turning on or off at this stage. The structure is just set up in an internal python dictionary. This structure relates to a Rete net [7] typically used in rule based engines.

Once all of the rules and initial facts are read, the system caches out the fact and rule structures to neurons and synapses. This involves translating each state into a CA, implemented in neurons and synapses. These CAs are linked so that they implement the FSAs underlying the rules; this is done by adding synapses to turn fact states on and turn them off. There are extra assertion neurons, for turning the fact CAs on, and retraction neurons for turning them off (see Fig. 1).

If the rule has more than two if clauses, the system makes use of intermediate states. So, the if portion $A\&B\&C$, would be represented by an FSA with A and B turning on the intermediate state AB. The if clause is true if AB and C are both on.

The translation engine needs to make sure that every possibility is exhausted. One way the engine is made more efficient is to find the matching facts for a rule using fact groups. Each fact group is a named item that is stored in a key valued dictionary. Each dictionary value is a list of facts that belong to this group. This concept separates the facts into groups allowing rule conditions to be found and attributes matched faster.

Finally, the translation engine needs to set up external activation for the initial facts. This is done with PyNN spike source generators.

Monkey Grab (banana) Rule Architecture

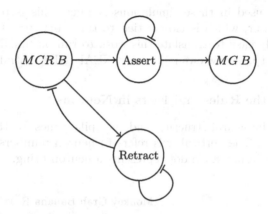

Fig. 1. Neural architecture for the rule *MonkeyGrab* when a fact *MonkeyCanReach Banana* is added. Where each state is a CA. Arrows represent excitatory connections, and blocks represent inhibitory connections; so the MCRB CA turns on the retract CA, which in turn extinguishes MCRB and itself.

Figure 1 illustrates the neural CA structure of the rule from Eq. 1 along with the fact (*MonkeyCanReach Banana*). This shows that, when ignited, the CA for (*MonkeyCanReach Banana*) starts a spread of neural activation that leaves the (*MonkeyGrab Banana*) CA ignited, while the reach is extinguished.

This system is a simple rule based system translation engine. It converts rules and initial facts to simple FSAs. It then converts these to neurons, synapses, and spike sources. The neural system can then be run in a simulator or emulator (see Sect. 4.1).

3.2   Simulating Neurons

The simulations described in this paper make use of the NEST [9] neuron simulator, and uses PyNN [5] as middleware. That is PyNN, python classes for managing neural net simulations, is used to specify the neural topology, and manages starting the simulation, initial inputs to the neurons, and recording the resulting firing. Once PyNN specifies the topology and initial inputs, it calls NEST to simulate the neurons.

The neurons that are used are adaptive exponential integrate and fire neurons [3]. These are leaky integrate and fire neurons, and the default parameters are used with three exceptions. The refractory period is increased from 1 ms to 2 ms; the firing threshold is decreased from −50.0 to −53.0 mV; and the reset after firing is decreased from −65.0 to −70.0 mV. These neurons are a standard set used in the authors' neural FSA work to assure consistent firing behaviour.

Each state consists of 10 neurons, with the first eight being excitatory, and the last two inhibitory. The excitatory neurons connect to the other neurons in the state with the same weight, and the inhibitory neurons connect to the other neurons with the same weight. The supports regular firing speeds (every 5 ms), once the state is ignited.

The time step used in these simulations is 1 ms. This is to conform with SpiNNaker behaviour, which is closely tied to this 1 ms step. Consequently it should be relatively easy to translate this work to run on SpiNNaker. All code can be found at http://www.cwa.mdx.ac.uk/NEAL/NEAL.html.

3.3   Executing the Rules and Facts in Neurons

Figure 2 displays the neural structure and the spike times for the *monkey grab banana* rule (Eq. 1). The vertical axis refers to neuron numbers, and the horizontal axis to time in ms. Each dot represents a neuron firing.

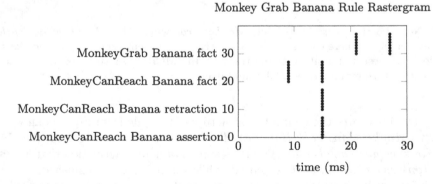

Fig. 2. Spike times for rule *MonkeyGrabBanana*. Neuron numbers represent: 0–9 - *MonkeyGrabBanana* assertion neurons; 10–19 - *MonkeyCanReachBanana* retraction neurons; 20–29 - *MonkeyCanReach Banana* fact; 30–39 - *MonkeyGrab Banana* fact

Figure 2 shows that the initial fact $MonkeyCanReach\,Banana$ fires at 9 ms. With no rule, it would repeatedly fire indefinitely. However, the rule is applied, and the assertion CA fires at 15 ms and that ignites the $MonkeyGrab\,Banana$ fact CA at 21 ms. The fact $MonkeyCanReach\,Banana$ is also retracted at 15 ms by being inhibited by the retraction neurons. The whole simulation took only 28 ms to progress from initial state to the end state. It will persist in this state indefinitely, unless other rules are available.

4 Examples

Two examples of complete systems are provided. The first is a simple monkeys and Bananas problem. The second shows the more complex Tower of Hanoi problem.

4.1 Monkeys and Bananas

The monkey and banana problems is a good old fashioned artificial intelligence problem. The problem involves a monkey and bananas suspended from the ceiling. There is also a chair in the room and the only way to reach the fruit is to move the chair, and stand on it to reach the bananas.

The following scenario describes rules and facts in a format approximating CLIPS syntax. There are three initial facts: $(ChairAt\ 2)$, $(Fruit\ banana\ 0)$, $(Fruit\,apple\,1)$. The $ChairAt$ fact represents the position of the chair. The $Fruit$ facts represent the type of fruits and their position. As long as the chair position is the same of that of a fruit, it is considered that the fruit can be reached. The scenario also consists of four rules: $MonkeyGrab$ Eq. 1 defined earlier, $EatFruit$ Eq. 2, $MonkeyHasFruit$ Eq. 3 and $PushChair$ Eq. 4.

$$(MonkeyHas\ ?type) \Rightarrow$$
$$(assert\ (MonkeyAte\ ?type)) \tag{2}$$
$$(remove\ (MonkeyHas\ ?type))$$

$$(ChairAt\ ?position)\&(Fruit\ ?type\ ?position) \Rightarrow$$
$$(assert\ (MonkeyHas\ ?type)) \tag{3}$$
$$(remove\ (Fruit\ ?type\ ?position))$$

$$(Fruit\ ?type\ ?position)\&(not\ ChairAt\ ?position) \Rightarrow$$
$$(assert\ (ChairAt\ ?position)) \tag{4}$$
$$(remove\ (not\ ChairAt\ ?position))$$

Note that the $PushChair$ rule has the not operator, meaning the $ChairAt$ fact is not in the same position as the $Fruit$ fact. This is done by a dictionary process that links facts where the variable $?position$ differs between the two antecedent clauses.

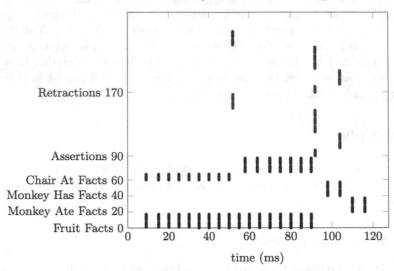

Fig. 3. Spikes of the neurons that implement the Monkeys and Bananas Problem.

The system converts the rules and facts to neurons. When it is run, it completes the task. The spike times are shown in Fig. 3.

The bottom 20 neurons represent the initial *Fruit* facts. As Fig. 3 shows, the fruit is grabbed at 90 ms. Neurons 21–40 represent *MonkeyAte* facts and 41–60 represent *MonkeyHas* facts. Neurons 61–90 are the *ChairAt* facts. At 58 ms, the rule is applied changing the facts. Neurons 230–249 fire and retract the (*ChairAt* 2) fact. Neurons 150–169 fire and assert the (*ChairAt* 0) and (*ChairAt* 2) facts.

The parallel nature of the execution of the rules leads to an unanticipated, and probably unwanted, effect. The system does not understand that the *ChairAt* fact is a single object Therefore, the 61–70 neurons of (*ChairAt* 2) fact, after 58 ms are replaced by two facts (*ChairAt* 1) and (*ChairAt* 0) represented by 71–90 neurons to match both the initial *Fruit* facts. This triggers the *MonkeyHasFruit* rule for both apple and banana. From this point on the conflict carries through to the end of the simulation, which takes around 110 ms to rest at the end state.

The rest of the spikes belong to retractions and assertions. The 91–170 neurons are the assertions and 171–250 are the retractions, which get activated to transition the simulation through different states. The final state, which will persist indefinitely, is (*MonkeyAte apple*) and (*MonkeyAte banana*).

4.2 Tower of Hanoi

The Tower of Hanoi is a widely known problem and widely used problem involving three towers and a number of discs of increasing size. Each disc can fit on the base of a tower, or on a larger disc already on a tower, but not on a smaller disc. Only the top disc of a tower can be moved to another tower. Figure 4 shows an example starting state of the problem with four discs.

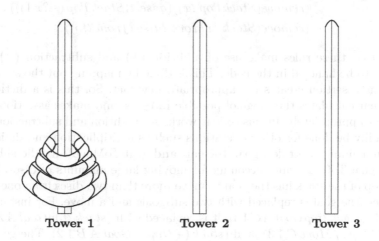

Tower 1   **Tower 2**   **Tower 3**

Fig. 4. The tower of Hanoi four disc start state.

To solve the Tower of Hanoi, a goal stack is used. The system uses a series of facts to represent the stack. This paper presents facts as tuples in parenthesis, like CLIPS. So, the fact (*StackTop* 3) says that the stack has three elements in it. The stack contains two types of items: goals, and moves. A move fact is of the form (*Stack ?stackLevel Move ?disc ?from ?to*). Again, as in rules, variables are prefixed with a question mark. So, the stack at the *stackLevel*, moves, the disc *disc* from tower *from* to tower *to*. So if the fact were instantiated as (*Stack* 3 *Move C* 1 3), the disc *C* would move from tower 1 to tower 3 when the third stack item was popped.

The stack can also contain goals. They are of the form (*Stack ?stackLevel Goal ?topDisc?bottomDisc?from?to*). So there is goal to move the discs between *topDisc* and *bottomDisc* from tower *from* to tower *to*. The first goal that is added to the stack for one three disc problem is (*Stack* 1 *Goal A C* 1 3), which states move the discs A to C from tower 1 to tower 3.

The system consists of five rules: addDisc, addFinalDisc, makeMove, goals ToGoals, and goalsToMoves. The first two rules are used to initialize the facts with the initial positions of the discs. Typically this has discs A to N on tower 1. The initial fact that says how large N is must be specified.

The makeMove rule accounts for the primitive disc moves, and is described by Eq. 5. It is relatively complex, but even very complex rules can be cached out to neurons. The rule only works on the item that is on top of the stack. If this item is a *Move*, it removes it by popping the stack (the bottom two lines), and moves the disc (the first two clauses after the arrow).

$(StackTop\,?x)\&(Stack\,?xMove\,?disc\,?from\,?to)\&$

$\qquad (Disc?disc\,?from) \Rightarrow (assert(Disc?disc\,?to))$

$\qquad (remove(Disc\,?disc\,?from)) \qquad\qquad\qquad\qquad\qquad (5)$

$\qquad (remove(StackTop\,?x))(assert(StackTop\,(-?x\,1)))$

$\qquad (remove(Stack\,?xMove\,?disc\,?from\,?to))$

Note that these rules make use of addition (+) and subtraction (−), and they have to be handled in the code. This is done by mapping out the structure so that the assertion creates the appropriate new fact. So, this is a dictionary process that calculates the range of possible integers, and makes assertions and retractions appropriately. In this code it works for addition and subtraction, but could readily be done for other operations such as multiplication and division.

The remaining two rules, goalsToGoals and goalsToMoves, handle subgoaling. The goalsToGoals rules accounts for moving large amounts of discs. If the current top of the stack has the goal to move more than two discs from one place to another, the goal is replaced with two subgoals and a move. For instance, if the goal is $(stack\,?topGoal\,A\,C\,1\,3)$, it is replaced with $(stack\,?topGoal\,A\,B\,2\,3)$, $(stack\,(+?top\,1)\,Move\,C\,1\,3)$, and $(stack\,(+?top\,2)\,Goal\,A\,B\,1\,2)$. The goalsToMoves rule accounts for moving two discs. It replaces a goal with two discs with three moves. For instance, if the goal is $(stack\,?top\,Goal\,A\,B\,1\,3)$, it is replaced with $(stack\,?top\,Move\,A\,2\,3)$, $(stack\,(+?top\,1)\,Move\,B\,1\,3)$, and $(stack\,(+?top\,2)\,Move\,A\,1\,2)$. These five rules can solve any problems with any number of discs by using the minimum amount of moves required.

Tower of Hanoi 3 Disc Rastergram

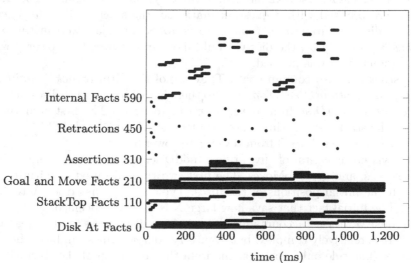

Fig. 5. Tower of Hanoi 3 disc problem neuron spikes. Neuron number on the horizontal axis with many labels omitted.

Figure 5 displays the rastergram of the neuron spike times of the Tower of Hanoi problem with three discs implemented using the rules described above converted to neurons. As the neurons are binary CAs, and all the neurons in the CA behave the same, only one neuron per CA is shown in the rastergram. The neurons represented in the figure shows the full system of neurons.

The bottom 80 neurons represent the *discAt* facts, so the movement of the largest disc from tower 1 to tower 3 can be seen at 600 ms. The neurons from 590–909 are the internal neurons used for combining multiple if clauses. Neurons 450–589 are retraction neurons. Neurons 310–449 are assertion neurons; 210–309 are the goal and move facts; and 180–209 are the towers, which stay on throughout the simulation. Neurons 120–179 are the *stackTop* neurons; 110–119 are the neurons for the initial fact saying there are three discs; and neurons 80–109 are the neurons for adding the discs at the start of the simulation.

Figure 6 shows the simulated times between moves on the five disc Tower of Hanoi problem. This closely echoes the human times and cognitive model times reported by Altmann and Trafton [1]. The difference is that times of the neural system are about 20 times faster.

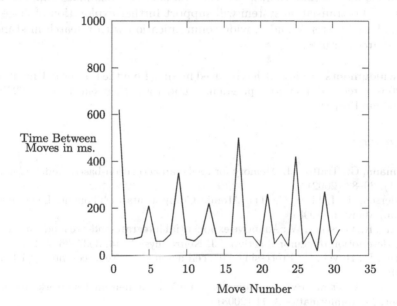

Fig. 6. Latencies for moves in the 5 disc tower of Hanoi problem

5   Conclusion

This paper has briefly discussed the importance of rule based systems. It has shown how they can be automatically translated into neural systems.

Though this paper shows that rule based systems can be readily implemented in neurons, and indeed can be directly translated, a number of improvements can be made to the system. There are relatively straight forward issues about usability, and more complex issues. Relatively straight forward improvements include a parser for the rule based system, a closer link to, for instance, CLIPS, and tools for recognition of issues like the forking of multiple facts as shown in Sect. 4.1.

More complex issues include parallelism, number of neurons, expansion to other types of memory, and cognitive improvements. For instance a large number of neurons might be needed for certain systems; if a rule based system were to use real numbers, it would need an uncountably infinite number of CAs to cope with this. The actual number could be determined at translation time, but it is possible that number could be very large. The translation system might also note when this number is large, and warn the user. The translation process assumes that possible values are known before hand. Dynamically interacting with a virtual environment via neural facts and neural outputs can lead to the introduction of new facts. In this case, the system would have to specify a range of possible values.

One of the benefits of neural systems is that time emerges naturally. Biological neurons have a time course, and the artificial versions make explicit use of this time. This translation system will support further exploration of large parallel rule based systems, and provide communication with research in standard cognitive architectures.

Acknowledgments. This work has received funding from the European Union's Horizon 2020 research and innovation programme under grant agreement No. 720270 (the Human Brain Project).

References

1. Altmann, G., Trafton, J.: Memory for goals: an activation-based model. Cogn. Sci. **25**(1), 39–83 (2002)
2. Anderson, J., Lebiere, C.: The Atomic Components of Thought. Lawrence Erlbaum, Mahwah (1998)
3. Brette, R., Gerstner, W.: Adaptive exponential integrate-and-fire model as an effective description of neuronal activity. J. Neurophysiol. **94**, 3637–3642 (2005)
4. Byrne, E., Huyck, C.: Processing with cell assemblies. Neurocomputing **74**, 76–83 (2010)
5. Davison, A., et al.: PyNN: a common interface for neuronal network simulators. Front. Neuroinformatics **2**, 11 (2008)
6. Fan, Y., Huyck, C.: Implementation of finite state automata using flif neurons. In: IEEE Systems, Man and Cybernetics Society, pp. 74–78 (2008)
7. Forgy, C.: Rete: a fast algorithm for the many pattern/many object pattern match problem. In: Readings in Artificial Intelligence and Databases, pp. 547–559 (1988)
8. Furber, S., et al.: Overview of the spinnaker system architecture. IEEE Trans. Comput. **62**(12), 2454–2467 (2013)
9. Gewaltig, M., Diesmann, M.: NEST (neural simulation tool). Scholarpedia **2**(4), 1430 (2007)
10. Hebb, D.O.: The Organization of Behavior: A Neuropsychological Theory. Wiley, New York (1949)

11. Hodgkin, A., Huxley, A.: A quantitative description of membrane current and its application to conduction and excitation in nerve. J. Physiol. **117**, 500–544 (1952)
12. Kieras, D., Wood, S., Meyer, D.: Predictive engineering models based on the epic architecture for a multimodal high-performance human-computer interaction task. ACM Trans. Comput. Hum. Interact. **4**(3), 230–275 (1997)
13. Laird, J., Newell, A., Rosenbloom, P.: Soar: an architecture for general cognition. Artif. Intell. **33**(1), 1–64 (1987)
14. Lewis, H., Papadimitriou, C.: Elements of the Theory of Computation. Prentice-Hall, Inc., Englewood Cliffs (1981)
15. McCulloch, W., Pitts, W.: A logical calculus of ideas immanent in nervous activity. Bull. Math. Biophys. **5**, 115–133 (1943)
16. Newell, A., Simon, H.: The logic theory machine-a complex information processing system. IRE Trans. Inf. Theory **2**(3), 61–79 (1956)
17. Post, E.: Formal reductions of the general combinatorial decision problem. Am. J. Math. **65**(2), 197–215 (1943)
18. Riley, G., Culbert, C., Lopez, F.: C language integrated production system. Technical report, NASA (1989)

Informed Pair Selection for Self-paced Metric Learning in Siamese Neural Networks

Kyle Martin$^{(\boxtimes)}$, Nirmalie Wiratunga , Stewart Massie ,
and Jérémie Clos

Robert Gordon University, Aberdeen, Scotland
{k.martin,n.wiratunga,s.massie,j.clos}@rgu.ac.uk

Abstract. Siamese Neural Networks (SNNs) are deep metric learners that use paired instance comparisons to learn similarity. The neural feature maps learnt in this way provide useful representations for classification tasks. Learning in SNNs is not reliant on explicit class knowledge; instead they require knowledge about the relationship between pairs. Though often ignored, we have found that appropriate pair selection is crucial to maximising training efficiency, particularly in scenarios where examples are limited. In this paper, we study the role of informed pair selection and propose a 2-phased strategy of exploration and exploitation. Random sampling provides the needed coverage for exploration, while areas of uncertainty modeled by neighbourhood properties of the pairs drive exploitation. We adopt curriculum learning to organise the ordering of pairs at training time using similarity knowledge as a heuristic for pair sorting. The results of our experimental evaluation show that these strategies are key to optimising training.

Keywords: Deep learning · Siamese Neural Networks
Active learning · Case-based reasoning · Machine learning
Metric learning

1 Introduction

The Siamese Neural Network (SNN) is a deep learning architecture which trains upon pairs of input data to learn a metric space in which training instances can be placed. The expectation of paired learning is that the learned space can better represent salient relationships between pairs which can then be better captured in Euclidean space. Originally used in binary classification tasks such as signature verification [2] and face recognition [3], SNNs have recently been generalised to multi-class classification [6].

Central to SNN learning is the use of similarity knowledge to gauge closeness of data points such that it provides a meaningful matching criterion. The expected outcome of SNN training is to have instances deemed similar to be

© Springer Nature Switzerland AG 2018
M. Bramer and M. Petridis (Eds.): SGAI-AI 2018, LNAI 11311, pp. 34–49, 2018.
https://doi.org/10.1007/978-3-030-04191-5_3

mapped closer together. As SNNs are metric learners that develop a new representation of the original data, in a classification setting they require a non-parametric learner (such as k-NN) to perform the explicit classification. However, a benefit of SNNs is that they do not require full class knowledge during training, as they are learning on the basis of whether pairs meet the matching criteria, not whether they belong to a specific label. For this reason, recent work has demonstrated these networks can perform effectively even when working with extremely limited training data, such as in a one-shot learning environment [6].

Surprisingly, pair selection and ordering have been given little attention in SNNs, despite showing promising results in the closely-related Triplet Networks (TNs) [17,20]. Pair selection and ordering directly informs the data relationships that the network will learn and be trained upon, thereby directly influencing the metric developed by the network. It is our view that these strategies play an important role in both improving training time and ensuring high overall performance of SNNs. Pair selection and presentation order are likely to be particularly relevant in data-budgeted scenarios where there are only a small number of annotated examples.

In this paper we discuss the importance of pair selection strategies and their effect on training. We are of the opinion that only by understanding the impact of sample selection in multiple-input networks can we build upon these ideas for application towards recent advancements in deep metric learners. For this reason we start with SNNs. Although we limit our scope to SNNs, the contribution from this paper is applicable to other neural network architectures that learn from multiple examples - particularly triplet [5] and matching networks [19].

The contributions of this paper are four fold: (1) we demonstrate the importance of having a pair selection strategy in SNNs; and (2) we introduce several pair selection strategies, including methods for informed pair selection that optimise pair creation using explorative and exploitative strategies. Taking inspiration from self-paced learning; (3) we demonstrate that pair ordering can improve SNN network performance; and (4) we introduce a pair complexity heuristic for ordering that draws on knowledge about the neighbourhood properties of pairs[1].

This paper is organised as follows: in Sect. 2 we explore work related to pair selection and curriculum learning; in Sect. 3 we formalise pair creation and its role in SNN learning before we introduce the concepts of pair ordering and informed pair selection employed in our work; a comparative study of proposed methods appear in Sect. 4 with results on the MNIST, Large Movie Review Dataset (LMRD) and SelfBACK[2] datasets appearing in Sect. 5; and finally conclusions in Sect. 6.

---

[1] The code associated with this paper is publicly accessible from https://github.com/RGU-AI/Informed-Pair-Selection.

[2] The SelfBACK project is funded by European Union's H2020 research and innovation programme under grant agreement No. 689043. More details available: http://www.selfback.eu. The SelfBACK dataset associated with this paper is publicly accessible from https://github.com/selfback/activity-recognition.

2 Related Work

Employing informed selection for training data is increasingly gaining attention for deep learning architectures. Both optimising for batch size and the order in which training examples are processed have shown to be effective for achieving performance improvements [1,10]. Typically network loss is exploited to create ranking heuristics with significant speed-up gains observed when processing harder examples first. Training on an increasing ratio of 'hard' samples can be seen as adopting an 'exploitation' strategy where focus is maintained on known 'hard' problems. It is interesting to note that meta-learning strategies, such as boosting, do precisely this with weak learners; whereby model learning is focused on examples that were incorrectly solved previously [18]. However such a strategy alone in the context of informed sample selection can be detrimental, if 'exploration' of the space of possible problems is ignored [10]. We study how both exploration and exploitation strategies can be utilised for informed pair selection. Specifically we consider budgeted learning scenarios associated with learning an embedding function [9], where it has been shown that picking more suitable examples will return greater results in circumstances where labeled data is limited [4].

Paired examples in relation to triplet networks (TNs) [5] help learn useful feature embeddings (representations) by distance comparisons [17,20]. Like SNNs, the goal of training is to develop an embedding function which minimises distance between the positive examples and the query examples, while maximising the distance between the negative example and the query. Unlike with SNNs, TNs form a triplet instance from a negative and positive pair given a query. Heuristics that are static (neither exploratory or exploitative) based on initial similarity (relevance) alone were found to perform poorly [20]. Using heuristics that continually update to reflect the triplets the network is likely to find difficult in the next iteration, such as exploiting according to the loss value, was found to give superior performance [17]. However, loss information is not available from the start of training so the network must complete an initial 'dry run' to retrieve this information. In our work we consider how heuristics that utilise similarity knowledge calculated from the most recent network embedding can contribute towards formulating a more dynamic ranking heuristic for training examples.

Curriculum Learning (CL) is the concept of introducing examples to a network in a meaningful order, most often by difficulty from 'easy' to 'hard'. The idea is that by ranking so that the network is initially exposed to simpler examples and then gradually introduced to more complex examples, the network will converge faster [1]. Though a simple concept, CL has demonstrated excellent generalisability, showing success in areas such as motif finding, noun phrase conference [7] and multi-task learning [14]. Research has also shown that self-paced CL where the ordering of examples is based on feedback from the network itself (dynamic), rather than a (static) curriculum set by a teacher [7], results in model improvements. In this way, the order in which examples are presented to the network is continuously updated, such that the curriculum presented at the start and that presented at the end of training may be vastly different. In our work we apply self-paced learning to sequence the presentation of training examples to SNNs.

3   Training and Testing with Pairs in a SNN

The SNN architecture consists of two neural networks that share identical weights and are joined at one or more layers [2]. SNNs receive pairs of examples as input to during both training and testing to develop similarity knowledge at an object-to-object level.

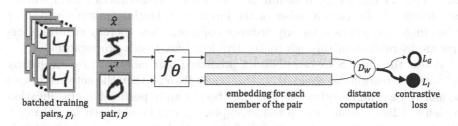

batched training pairs, p_i pair, p embedding for each member of the pair   distance computation   contrastive loss

Fig. 1. The SNN learning process

We first introduce the notation used in this paper to assist presentation of the different pair creation strategies. Let $\mathcal{X}$ be a set of labeled examples, such that example, $x \in \mathcal{X}$ and $y(x)$ is a function that returns the class label, y, of x. $\mathcal{P}$ is a set of pairs $(p_1, ...p_n)$ that form the paired training batches for input to the SNN (see Fig. 1). Each training pair, $p \in \mathcal{P}$, consists of a pair of examples, $p = (\hat{x}, x')$, where $\hat{x}$ is a pivot example whose relationship to passive example x' dictates whether the pair is of class genuine, or impostor. Here the pair's relationship class is easily established by comparing class labels $y(\hat{x})$ with $y(x')$. For this we use function, $Y(p)$ or $Y(\langle \hat{x}, x' \rangle)$, which returns, p's relationship class label, such that $Y(p) = 0$ when $y(\hat{x}) = y(x')$, and $Y(p) = 1$ when $y(\hat{x}) \neq y(x')$. Typically $\hat{x}, x'$ are randomly selected, to form the genuine and impostor relationship pairs for training.

During training the network develops a multi-dimensional embedding based upon the input training pairs, $\mathcal{P}$. This is facilitated by having the shared layers; essentially these layers enable the SNN to generate an embedding for each member of a pair (see Fig. 1). Thereafter members can be compared using a distance metric, D_W, which influences the computation of the two loss components: loss due to pairs being further apart when they should not be, L_G; and loss due to pairs being too close when they should be further apart, L_I. Contrastive loss, L (as in Eq. 3), is commonly used to guide the sub-network weight update for model learning by combining these two losses - genuine L_G and impostor L_I [3]. It essentially formulates the pair prediction error on the basis of genuine and impostor error predictions. The use of both genuine and impostor error means that the similarity metric can be directly learned by the network through the comparison of the actual pair label Y_A (equal to 0 for genuine and 1 for impostor pairs) and the distance, Euclidean or otherwise, between pair members, D_W.

This means that distance between constituents of genuine pairs are minimised over the course of training, whilst ensuring that impostor pairs maintain at least a set margin of M distance apart.

$$L_G = (1 - Y_A) \cdot D_W{}^2 \tag{1}$$

$$L_I = Y_A \cdot (max(0, \; M - D_W))^2 \tag{2}$$

$$L = L_G + L_I \tag{3}$$

The output of the identical neural networks (or 'sub-networks') form feature embeddings, f_θ, for each member of the input pair. During training it is these embeddings that are used for any distance computations, thereby ensuring iterative model refinement through contrastive loss based back propagation.

At test time, the SNN can obtain a predicted pair label, Y_P, by comparing D_W with the margin threshold M. If D_W is less than M then the network judges the pair to be genuine, otherwise it is classified as an impostor. For classification problems, a label for an unseen test example, x_q, can be obtained by pairing it with a representative training example from each class, $(\bar{x}_i, ..., \bar{x_m})$, where m is the number of classes, and $\bar{x}_i$ is a prototypical example for class i. The trained SNN is then used to provide a pair label prediction for each such pair. We then use a distance weighted voting algorithm to determine the classification of a query example from its nearest class prototype neighbour ($\bar{x}_i$). Note that only genuine pairings with $\bar{x}_i$ contribute to the classification vote:

$$vote(c_i) = \sum_{j=1}^{m} w_j * [EQ(c_i, y(\bar{x}_j)) \, (1 - Y(\bar{x}_j, x_q))] \tag{4}$$

$$w_j = \frac{1}{\sqrt{(\sum_i |f_\theta^i(x_q) - f_\theta^i(\bar{x}_j)|^2)}} \tag{5}$$

Here EQ compares two parameters and returns 1 when they match or 0 otherwise; in this case checks for matching class labels. The classification with the highest vote is deemed to be the classification of x_q. The weighting is based on Euclidean distance between examples using their feature embeddings from the network.

In the following sections we introduce pair creation strategies for SNN training, with strategies that are informed by knowledge about areas of difficulty (exploitation) and strategies that balance this with the need for problem space coverage (exploration).

3.1   Explorative Pair Selection

It is important to note that $\mathcal{P}$ only represents a small subset of all possible pairs which can be obtained by exhaustively pairing all examples in the training set (the total size of which would be $|\mathcal{X}|^2$). The result is that $\mathcal{P}$ gives a narrow view of instance relationships. We can improve this by initiating multiple pair selection sessions throughout training. Doing so allows us to explore the relationships between examples more thoroughly. Specifically instead of a static $\mathcal{P}$, as in Sect. 3, we can create a $\mathcal{P}$ for each cycle of training, where a cycle will consist of a set number of training epochs.

Algorithm 1. Algorithm to create the Explore Set

---

1   **Explore:** $\mathcal{P}_{RND}(n)$
2   $P_I,\, P_G := \emptyset$
3   **for** $i = 1 \ldots n/2$ **do**
4      $\hat{x} := \text{rnd\_selection}(\mathcal{X})$
5      $x_1' := \text{rnd\_selection}(\mathcal{X}) \wedge y(\hat{x}) \neq y(x_1')$
6      $x_2' := \text{rnd\_selection}(\mathcal{X}) \wedge y(\hat{x}) = y(x_2')$
7      $P_I := P_I \cup p(\hat{x}, x_1')$
8      $P_G := P_G \cup p(\hat{x}, x_2')$
9   **end**
10   $Explore := P_I \cup P_G$
11   **return** $Explore$

Algorithm 1 lists the steps involved with random creation of a *Explore* pair set, where given n, a call to $\mathcal{P}_{RND}(n)$ assigns n pairs to $\mathcal{P}:= \mathcal{P}_{RND}(n)$. Here $\hat{x}$ and its paired members x_1' and x_2' are randomly selected from $\mathcal{X}$ with the only condition that the two pairs formed must provide the necessary genuine and impostor representatives; such that $Y(P_I)$ is 0 and $Y(P_G)$ is 1.

3.2   Exploitative Pair Selection

Inspired by uncertainty sampling and boosting we can utilise information that we gain during the previous training cycle to inform pair selection for the next training cycle. Here instead of only exploring the problem space randomly, we integrate an exploitation phase such that pair selection will be guided by sampling in areas found to be 'hard' for the learner. Specifically for each $p_i \in \mathcal{P}$ we use the network's predictions, $Y(p_i)$ and associated loss to rank elements in $\mathcal{P}$. We extract the 'hardest' ranked pairs (i.e. pairs with the highest loss), from which we generate new pairs to form the exploitation set. We represent the ratio of exploit to explore as α. The main idea is to use this ratio to guide pair creation in areas of uncertainty (see Algorithm 2).

For each selected pair, we find the nearest neighbour of each member within each pair using function, NN_i. By taking the neighbours of the original difficult pair, we generalise network attention to the complex area of the space without overfitting on specific examples. These neighbours form the basis for a new pair for our training set. It is worth noting here that it is possible to develop the entire training set by using the exploit algorithm and setting α equal to 1. We found this to be detrimental to training, as the network tended to overfit to specific

---

Algorithm 2. Algorithm to create the Exploit Set

---

1 **Exploit:** $\mathcal{P}_{NN}(\mathcal{P}')$
2 $P_I, P_G := \emptyset$
3 **for** $p_i \in \mathcal{P}'$ where $\mathcal{P}' \subset \mathcal{P}$ and $|\mathcal{P}'| = \alpha$ **do**
4 $\quad$ $p'_i = (NN_1(\hat{x}), NN_1(x'))$
5 $\quad$ **if** $Y(p'_i) = 0$ **then**
6 $\quad\quad$ $P_G := P_G \cup p'_i$
7 $\quad$ **end**
8 $\quad$ **if** $Y(p'_i) = 1$ **then**
9 $\quad\quad$ $P_I := P_I \cup p'_i$
10 $\quad$ **end**
11 **end**
12 $Exploit := P_I \cup P_G$
13 **return** $Exploit$

---

difficult areas, become trapped and develop a distorted feature embedding as a result. Hence we suggest using an Explore-Exploit ratio to prevent this.

3.3 Explorative and Exploitative Pair Selection

A mixed approach that allows the learner to both explore and exploit requires pair selection that can utilise pairs formed using both strategies from previous Sects. 3.1 and 3.2. We accomplish this by randomly creating pairs to perform early exploration of the feature space through a 'dry run' of training the network for a small number of epochs (typically ten or less) which helps to initialise network weights. Thereafter we use the ratio α to generate a new set of exploit pairs (as in Algorithm 2); and the rest will consist of a new set of explore pairs (as in Algorithm 1).

Algorithm 3. Algorithm to combine Explore and Exploit Sets

---

1 **Explore&Exploit:** $\mathcal{P}_{HYBRID}(\mathcal{P})$
2 $b := \alpha \cdot |\mathcal{P}|$
3 **for** $p_i \in \mathcal{P}$ **do**
4 $\quad$ $\mathcal{L} := \mathcal{L}.\textbf{append}(L(\theta, p_i))$
5 **end**
6 $\mathcal{P} := \mathcal{P}.\textbf{sort}(\mathcal{P}, \mathcal{L}, <)$
7 **for** $i = 1 \ldots b$ **do**
8 $\quad$ $\mathcal{P}' := \mathcal{P}'.\textbf{add}(p_i)$
9 **end**
10 $Exploit := P_{NN}(\mathcal{P}')$
11 $Explore := P_{RND}(\mathcal{P} \setminus \mathcal{P}')$
12 **return** $Explore \cup Exploit$

The loss, L, for each p_i is maintained in $\mathcal{L}$, which is based on current network parameters θ. Pairs are sorted in decreasing order of loss and the top α pairs are used for exploit pair generation and the rest generated through the explore strategy. This process is repeated multiple times during training, as the areas of the feature space that the network will find complex will very likely change as the network 'learns' by refining θ. Note that NN_i's similarity computations are influenced by feature embeddings on the basis of the latest θ - i.e. they are based on activations of the last network layer at the current point in training.

It is also important to note that the suggested algorithms do not sample from a larger training set than the baseline method. It is merely the way in which instances are paired that changes. For example, in a data-budgeted scenario where only 1% of a dataset is available (such as in one of our evaluations later in this paper), these algorithms will operate within that budget and will not sample additional data from the training set.

3.4 Heuristic Ordering for Self-paced Learning

To develop a structured ordering method for our pairs, we take inspiration from complexity measures used in neighbourhood analysis for case-based reasoning systems [12]. The basic idea is that an area is considered complex when neighbourhoods of examples are found to be non-homogeneous in terms of their class labels. We adopt this for complexity analysis C for a given pair p (instead of a single example) as in Eq. 6.

$$C(p) = \frac{\sum_i \sum_j EQ(Y(p), Y(\langle NN_i(\hat{x}), NN_j(x')\rangle))}{\sum_i \sum_j (1 - EQ(Y(p), Y(\langle NN_i(\hat{x}), NN_j(x')\rangle))} \qquad (6)$$

The numerator in the complexity ratio counts the number of pairs formed in the neighbourhood that differ from the class of the original pair and denominator counts those that are of the same pair label (i.e. is it an impostor or genuine pair). Here $NN_i(.)$ denotes the ith nearest neighbour of a given example. We create all possible pairs between $\hat{x}$'s and x''s neighbourhoods. For any given pair, function Y returns the pair's class label (0 for genuine and 1 impostor). With self-paced learning we can use any of the pair selection strategies and sort pairs by the complexity metric for model training.

4   Evaluation

The aim of our experiments is two fold. Firstly, we aim to investigate the effect of incorporating a pair creation method by analysing three variations of pairing strategies: no strategy, a dynamic strategy (exploration) and an informed dynamic strategy (exploration/exploitation). Secondly, we aim to investigate the effect of complexity-based ordering, giving us an unordered and an ordered variation of each strategy and a total of six candidate approaches:

1. **Base:** Pairs are unordered, and are not updated throughout training. As such this is a static, standard paired-training used for SNNs - the baseline (Sect. 3).

2. **Base***: As BASE but now with pairs ordered (Sect. 3.4).
3. **DynE**: Pairs are unordered, but pair are updated (hence dynamic) using the exploration algorithm throughout training (Sect. 3.1).
4. **DynE***: As DYNE but now with pairs ordered (Sect. 3.4).
5. **DynEE**: Pairs are unordered, and are updated (hence dynamic) using the explore and exploit algorithm according to some α ratio (Sect. 3.3).
6. **DynEE***: As DYNEE but now with pairs ordered (Sect. 3.4).

We use the '*' postfix to indicate complexity-based ordering over those that have no ordering. We evaluate these algorithms using two different criteria. First, we perform a one-tail t-test to establish statistical significance at a confidence level of 95% on classification accuracy from network output on image classification, sentiment analysis and HAR tasks. Secondly, we examine each algorithm's capacity to learn over time by analysing averaged accuracy on each test set for increasing number of training epochs.

4.1   Datasets

Four datasets were used in our evaluation: MNIST, LMRD, SelfBACK-Thigh and SelfBACK-Wrist. MNIST has been used extensively for image classification [6,7,10] and the Large Movie Review Dataset is an extension of the popular movie review dataset [11], whilst SelfBACK is a recent dataset used for Human Activity Recognition (HAR) focused on muscular skeletal disorders [15].

Image Dataset. The MNIST dataset is comprised of 70,000 images of handwritten single-digit numbers which are 28×28 pixels and have one of ten classes (the numbers zero to nine). We split this into 60,000 training and 10,000 test images. We allocated a budget of 1% of the full training set (600 images) and tested on the full test set.

Sentiment Analysis Dataset. The Large Movie Review Dataset (LMRD) is comprised of 50,000 labeled film reviews scraped from the Internet Movie Database (IMDB) and evenly split between training and test sets [11]. These reviews are labeled as either 'positive' or 'negative' to create a binary classification task. Though the dataset contains a significant number of unlabeled reviews, we did not use these in our experiments.

We adopted a budget of 10% of the training set (2,500 reviews) and tested against the full test set (25,000). Reviews were preprocessed before submission to the network using Word2Vec [13] and averaging the word vectors to form a document vector [8]. This resulted in a single movie review being represented as a vector of 300 features.

HAR Datasets. The SelfBACK dataset features time series data collected from 34 users performing different activities over a short period of time. Data was collected by mounting a tri-axial accelerometer on the thigh and right-hand wrist of participants at a sampling rate of 100 Hz [15]. For our experiments, we remove any users that have less than 60 s of recorded data per activity, leaving 24 users. Data was split into 3 s windows, with 900 features per example.

Our goal in the SelfBACK dataset is to classify user activity based on minimal information pertaining to them. This is important for personalised HAR model generation to minimise demand on the user for labels [16]. Data is split into training and test sets within each user so that our training set consists of 4 windows (12 s) of data for each activity and the test set is the remaining data.

4.2 Experimental Setup

In MNIST and LMRD we performed our evaluation using a 10-fold cross-validation design, while in SelfBACK we divide each user into their own train and test set and average the results from all users. Each algorithm is therefore compared based upon the same initial sample as taken from the dataset, though the way in which this is exploited to form training pairs differ between algorithms.

4.3 Network Architecture

For the MNIST and LMRD datasets we used a 3-layer perceptron with a batch size of 16 for each of our sub-networks. We then trained these architectures for 100 epochs. For the SelfBACK dataset, we used a 5-layer convolutional network (as in [15]) with a batch size of 8 for each sub-network. This architecture was trained for 50 epochs to prevent overfitting on the smaller dataset. All architectures used ReLU activations and computations for test classification adopt Euclidean distance on feature embeddings at the similarity layer. Table 1 provides information on network hyperparameters.

We found that increasing regularization by decreasing batch size improves convergence speed on all methods, likely due to the limited number of examples. Decreasing the batch size gives DYNEE and DYNEE* flexibility to extract a relevant exploitation set, and offers more opportunity to update network weights appropriately.

Table 1. Summary of relevant network hyperparameters

	Sub-network (layers)	Total epochs	Exploitation ratio α
MNIST	MLP (3 Dense)	100	$^{|P|}/_6$
LMRD	MLP (3 Dense)	100	$^{|P|}/_{10}$
SelfBACK	Convolutional (3 Conv., 2 Dense)	50	$^{|P|}/_4$

4.4   Ratio of Exploration to Exploitation

We experimented to understand the impact of the ratio of exploration to exploitation, α, for each dataset. As identified above, over-exploiting a given dataset can cause overfitting and have negative effects on accuracy. We therefore sampled various α to determine the optimum for each dataset. We observed that high levels of exploitation are beneficial at the start of training, but cause overfitting towards the end. Intuitively, this suggests that exploitation would function optimally as a decay parameter - something we will explore in future work.

We established optimal α for each dataset: $|P|/6$ for MNIST, $|P|/10$ for LMRD and $|P|/4$ for both SelfBACK datasets. This means that for DYNEE and DYNEE*, at every training cycle, this proportion of the pairs were generated based upon exploiting knowledge from the previous training iterations and the rest of the pairs were sampled according to the explore strategy. We repeat the pair selection process every five epochs for DYNE, DYNE*, DYNEE and DYNEE*.

5   Results

Our results demonstrate that using a pairing strategy will improve network performance on all of the investigated datasets (see Table 2 and Fig. 2). On every dataset using either DYNE or DYNEE boasts faster convergence and greater accuracy than the BASE method. In one instance (MNIST), DYNEE achieves a statistically significant higher optima than any other method. Though complexity-based ordering offers mixed results, we observe that an ordered method (DYNE*) ultimately achieves the greatest accuracy on three of the four compared datasets. The results for each dataset appear in Table 2 with bold font used to indicate maximum accuracy for a dataset and asterisks indicating statistical significance with 0.95 confidence.

5.1   Dynamic Informed Pair Selection

On MNIST, we can distinguish that both DYNEE and DYNE begin to outperform BASE from as little as 15 and 20 epochs respectively. The difference between DYNEE and BASE is statistically significant from epoch 40 onward. In LMRD we observe that DYNE and DYNEE reach superior performance to that of BASE with only 60% and 70% of the training epochs required. Similarly, DYNE and DYNEE demonstrate faster convergence to optima on the SelfBACK-Wrist dataset, though not on SelfBACK-Thigh. On both SelfBACK datasets, the proposed methods ultimately converge to a higher optima than BASE can achieve.

These results suggest that the informed explorative and exploitative pair selection strategies present greater insight into the space than can be achieved through the static pairing method of the baseline. They support our hypothesis that a suitable training strategy can improve the performance of SNNs.

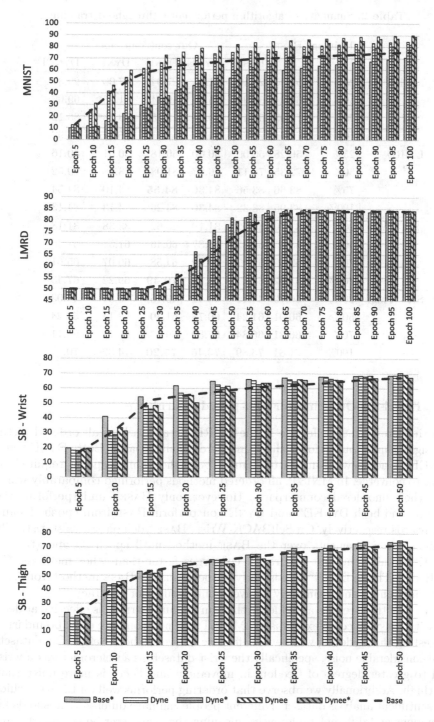

Fig. 2. Results on the MNIST, LMRD and SelfBACK datasets

Table 2. Summary of algorithm performance throughout training

	Training	BASE	Our contributions				
			BASE*	DYNE	DYNE*	DYNEE	DYNEE*
MNIST	25%	57.50	29.19	61.05	27.04	67.00	29.37
	50%	68.24	52.96	75.16	59.24	81.93*	69.09
	75%	72.03	63.47	80.76	72.78	86.78*	83.12
	100%	75.51	70.74	84.53	82.21	**90.05***	88.92
LMRD	25%	50.28	50.00	50.00	50.18	50.01	50.16
	50%	72.35	78.11	76.87	81.08*	73.08	79.52
	75%	83.66	83.56	84.36	**84.55**	84.10	84.54
	100%	83.95	83.32	84.30	84.26	84.13	84.13
SB - Wrist	20%	31.70	40.92*	31.19	28.62	33.38	31.18
	50%	58.25	64.82*	62.37	60.46	61.54	57.46
	70%	62.39	67.07	66.02	64.58	66.07	65.61
	100%	67.32	68.71	68.72	**70.49**	69.22	67.43
SB - Thigh	20%	40.79	44.46	43.12	43.76	45.31	46.03
	50%	60.91	61.24	60.78	61.30	58.11	58.24
	70%	66.31	66.84	67.59	69.37	65.71	63.71
	100%	71.81	73.89	73.46	**75.20**	74.39	70.63

5.2 Heuristic Ordering for Self-paced Learning

Ordering proves most effective in the LMRD dataset, where all ordered methods significantly outperform their unordered counterparts. Both DYNE* and DYNEE* reach new optima at 65% and 70% of the training epochs required for BASE to converge. In MNIST, all ordered methods performed comparably worse than their unordered counterparts. However, only BASE* underperforms the baseline and both DYNEE* and DYNE* outperform BASE from epochs 55 and 80 onwards respectively. On SelfBACK-Wrist, BASE* demonstrates statistically significant improvements over the BASE method until epoch 30 and (though DYNE* obtains the best accuracy), converges faster than other methods. On SelfBACK-Thigh, DYNE* consistently outperforms the BASE method from very early in training and ultimately achives a much superior accuracy.

We take these results as evidence that curriculum learning is effective at dealing with noisy or complex datasets. MNIST has non-complex class boundaries, suggesting that ordering will be less effective. However, both SelfBACK datasets have considerable noise, specifically the wrist dataset, as accelerometers on wrist lead to greater degrees of freedom in movement and hence is more noisy than the thigh. Additionally we observe that ordering performs well on LMRD, which is a sentiment analysis dataset. Different people can have different thresholds for enjoyment and different preferences, meaning they can describe the exact same event with different sentiments. This means there can be considerable complexity at the boundary between positive and negative classes.

In summary, the results demonstrate that a pair selection strategy will improve the performance of an SNN. In every tested dataset, the use of a non-ordered pairing strategy offers faster convergence and enables greater accuracy to be achieved, though selecting the most effective strategy depends on the task. In one domain DYNEE even allows the SNN architecture to significantly out-perform the baseline in terms of classification accuracy. Furthermore, although ordering is not effective in every scenario, incorporating a sample ordering based upon neighbourhood-complexity analysis can speed up convergence on noisy or complex datasets. Specifically, DYNE* operates very effectively in these situations. This is likely because it is performing an ordered exploration of the feature space, which allows it to gradually improve its knowledge to better deal with complex areas.

6   Conclusions and Future Work

In conclusion, we have demonstrated the need for a reasoned training strategy for SNNs. We have presented four contributions towards addressing this need, highlighting the importance of a pair selection strategy and noting both an explo-rative algorithm, explore-exploit algorithm and an ordering method for pairs and have shown on four different datasets that each is suitable in different scenarios. Namely, informed pair selection offers a greater view on the problem space when needed and ordering allows a network to develop a structured training regime which is robust to dataset complexity. Thus we conclude that use of an appro-priate pairing strategy will improve network performance, though selecting an optimal strategy is task dependant.

In future work, we aim to further optimise elements of training. We also plan to pursue a method to extend the benefits of curriculum learning further throughout training.

References

1. Bengio, Y., Louradour, J., Collobert, R., Weston, J.: Curriculum learning. In: Pro-ceedings of the 26th Annual International Conference on Machine Learning, ICML 2009, pp. 41–48. ACM, New York, June 2009
2. Bromley, J., Guyon, I., LeCun, Y.: Signature verification using a 'siamese' time delay neural network. Int. J. Pattern Recognit. Artif. Intell. **7**(4), 669–688 (1993)
3. Chopra, S., Hadsell, R., LeCun, Y.: Learning a similarity metric discriminatively, with application to face verification. In: Proceedings of the 2005 IEEE Computer Society Conference on Computer Vision and Pattern Recognition, CVPR 2005, pp. 539–546. IEEE Computer Society, Washington, DC, June 2005
4. Deng, K., Zheng, Y., Bourke, C., Scott, S., Masciale, J.: New algorithms for bud-geted learning. Mach. Learn. **90**(1), 59–90 (2013)
5. Hoffer, E., Ailon, N.: Deep metric learning using triplet network. In: Feragen, A., Pelillo, M., Loog, M. (eds.) SIMBAD 2015. LNCS, vol. 9370, pp. 84–92. Springer, Cham (2015). https://doi.org/10.1007/978-3-319-24261-3_7

6. Koch, G., Zemel, R., Salakhutdinov, R.: Siamese neural networks for one-shot image recognition. In: Deep Learning Workshop, ICML 2015, July 2015
7. Kumar, M.P., Packer, B., Koller, D.: Self-paced learning for latent variable models. In: Advances in Neural Information Processing Systems, NIPS 2010, vol. 23, pp. 1189–1197. Curran Associates Inc., Red Hook, December 2010
8. Le, Q., Mikolov, T.: Distributed representations of sentences and documents. In: Proceedings of the 31st International Conference on International Conference on Machine Learning, ICML 2014, vol. 32. pp. II-1188–II-1196. JMLR.org (2014)
9. Lizotte, D.J., Madani, O., Greiner, R.: Budgeted learning of naive-bayes classifiers. In: Proceedings of the Nineteenth Conf. on Uncertainty in Artificial Intelligence, UAI 2003, pp. 378–385. Morgan Kaufmann Publishers Inc., San Francisco, August 2003
10. Loshchilov, I., Hutter, F.: Online batch selection for faster training of neural networks. In: ICLR Workshops, ICLR 2016, May 2016
11. Maas, A.L., Daly, R.E., Pham, P.T., Huang, D., Ng, A.Y., Potts, C.: Learning word vectors for sentiment analysis. In: Proceedings of the 49th Annual Meeting of the Association for Computational Linguistics: Human Language Technologies, HLT 2011, vol. 1. pp. 142–150. Association for Computational Linguistics, Stroudsburg (2011)
12. Massie, S., Craw, S., Wiratunga, N.: Complexity-guided case discovery for case-based reasoning. In: Proceedings of the 20th AAAI Conference on AI, pp. 216–221. AAAI Press (2005)
13. Mikolov, T., Chen, K., Corrado, G., Dean, J.: Efficient estimation of word representations in vector space. CoRR abs/1301.3781 (2013)
14. Pentina, A., Sharmanska, V., Lampert, C.H.: Curriculum learning of multiple tasks. In: Proceedings of the 2015 IEEE Computer Society Conference on Computer Vision and Patter Recognition, CVPR 2015, pp. 5492–5500. IEEE Computer Society, Washington, DC, June 2015
15. Sani, S., Wiratunga, N., Massie, S., Cooper, K.: SELFBACK—activity recognition for self-management of low back pain. In: Bramer, M., Petridis, M. (eds.) Research and Development in Intelligent Systems XXXIII, pp. 281–294. Springer, Cham (2016). https://doi.org/10.1007/978-3-319-47175-4_21
16. Sani, S., Wiratunga, N., Massie, S., Cooper, K.: kNN sampling for personalised human activity recognition. In: Aha, D.W., Lieber, J. (eds.) ICCBR 2017. LNCS (LNAI), vol. 10339, pp. 330–344. Springer, Cham (2017). https://doi.org/10.1007/978-3-319-61030-6_23
17. Schroff, F., Kalenichenko, D., Philbin, J.: Facenet: a unified embedding for face recognition and clustering. In: Proceedings of the IEEE Conference on Computer Vision and Pattern Recognition, CVPR 2015, pp. 815–823. IEEE Computer Society, Washington, DC, June 2015
18. Shapire, R.E.: The boosting approach to machine learning: An overview. In: Denison, D.D., Hansen, M.H., Holmes, C.C., Mallick, B., Yu, B. (eds.) Nonlinear Estimation and Classification. LNS, vol. 171, pp. 149–172. Springer, New York (2003). https://doi.org/10.1007/978-0-387-21579-2_9

19. Vinyals, O., Blundell, C., Lillicrap, T., kavukcuoglu, k., Wierstra, D.: Matching networks for one shot learning. In: Lee, D.D., Sugiyama, M., Luxburg, U.V., Guyon, I., Garnett, R. (eds.) Advances in Neural Information Processing Systems, vol. 29, pp. 3630–3638. Curran Associates, Inc. (2016)
20. Wang, J., et al.: Learning fine-grained image similarity with deep ranking. In: Proceedings of the 2014 IEEE Conference on Computer Vision and Pattern Recognition, CVPR 2014, Washington, DC, USA, pp. 1386–1393. IEEE Computer Society, June 2014. https://doi.org/10.1109/cvpr.2014.180

A Brain-Inspired Cognitive System that Mimics the Dynamics of Human Thought

Yuehu Ji[✉], David Gamez, and Christian Huyck

Middlesex University, London, UK
yj097@live.mdx.ac.uk

Abstract. In recent years, some impressive AI systems have been built that can play games and answer questions about large quantities of data. However, we are still a very long way from AI systems that can think and learn in a human-like way. We have a great deal of information about how the brain works and can simulate networks of hundreds of millions of neurons. So it seems likely that we could use our neuroscientific knowledge to build brain-inspired artificial intelligence that acts like humans on similar timescales. This paper describes an AI system that we have built using a brain-inspired network of artificial spiking neurons. On a word recognition and colour naming task our system behaves like human subjects on a similar timescale. In the longer term, this type of AI technology could lead to more flexible general purpose artificial intelligence and to more natural human-computer interaction.

Keywords: Spiking neural network · Small-world topology
Cell assembly · Stroop effect

1 Introduction

In recent years there has been an explosion of interest in AI. This has partly been the result of developments in deep neural networks, which have achieved success in a wide range of areas, such as face recognition [40] and games [31,37]. AI systems are also capable of doing impressive feats of natural language processing - for example, IBM's recent successes with Watson [8] and Project Debater [22]. These systems have generated a lot of excitement as well as doom-laden predictions about widespread job losses and apocalyptic takeovers by malevolent machine intelligence.

The recent successes in AI have occurred in situations where a large amount of data is available or there is a highly constrained environment. These AI systems are poor at finding new solutions to problems and they do not think in a human-like way. This creates problems when humans have to interact with the AI. Humans typically use their own minds to model the minds of other people, but this breaks down when humans try to understand an AI system, whose behaviour might be controlled by the processing of vast quantities of text. The mind of an artificial intelligence is opaque to the human mind, which makes it difficult for

ⓒ Springer Nature Switzerland AG 2018
M. Bramer and M. Petridis (Eds.): SGAI-AI 2018, LNAI 11311, pp. 50–62, 2018.
https://doi.org/10.1007/978-3-030-04191-5_4

humans to collaborate with AI systems and teach them new things. It also leads to major issues with transparency, accountability and trust.

Neuroscience has made big advances in recent years. We have a great deal of information about how the brain works and can simulate hundreds of millions of neurons in real time [9]. Models have been built of the fruit fly brain [1], worms [41] and there are ongoing attempts to simulate the human brain with increasing accuracy [29]. These networks not only aim to build an 'in silico' duplicate of a static brain, but also to simulate the learning and developmental processes: capturing how groups of neurons evolve to perform highly complex cognitive functions.

The human brain is the best example of a general-purpose intelligence that we have. So one way of addressing AI's current limitations could be to build brain-inspired systems that 'think' in a similar way to the human brain. A system that works in a similar way to humans could be more easily understood by humans, which would help to address the issues of trust, accountability and transparency.

In our research we are investigating how cognitive systems can be built using brain-inspired spiking neural networks. The basic unit for these models is a cell assembly [21]: a group of neurons that displays persistent activation. Groups of cell assemblies can be wired together, potentially using learning, into brain-inspired cognitive systems. One of our aims is to produce systems that think in a human-like way. A good way of evaluating this is to measure the system using tests that have been developed by experimental psychology. For example, in this paper we describe a system that shows a similar Stroop effect to human subjects. The construction of brain-inspired systems can also help us to understand the human brain. This can lead to a positive feedback loop in which the results from neuroscience and experimental psychology help us to build AI systems and these AI systems lead to better explanations in neuroscience and experimental psychology.

This paper describes an AI system that performs a word recognition and colour naming task in a human-like way on a similar time scale to humans. It is based on a brain-inspired architecture and implemented using spiking neurons. To evaluate the extent to which our system thinks in a human-like way we measured the timing of its word recognition and colour naming when the colour of the word was congruent with its meaning (for example, 'red' written in red ink) and when the colour of the word was incongruent with its meaning (for example, the word 'red' written in blue ink). When humans perform this task there is a well known interference effect, known as the Stroop effect [38], such that human reaction times vary between the congruent and incongruent tasks. We were hoping to reproduce this Stroop effect in our system.

The first part of the paper gives some background on the word recognition and colour naming tasks and the Stroop effect that is observed when humans perform them. The background section also covers previous computer simulations of the Stroop effect and some of the earlier cognitive systems that have been built with cell assemblies. Section 3 describes how we constructed our system and Sect. 4 gives the results of our experiments and compares the behaviour of our system with that of human subjects. The paper concludes with a discussion and our plans for creating AI systems that use learning to develop complex cognitive functions.

2   Background

2.1   Word Recognition and Colour Naming Stroop Effect

In word recognition and colour naming tasks the subjects are presented with a colour word, such as 'red' or 'blue', which is written in coloured ink. In the congruent situation, the colour of the ink matches the meaning of the word (for example, 'red' written in red ink). In the incongruent situation the colour of the word is different from the colour of the ink (for example, the word 'red' written in blue ink). The subjects have to recognize and repeat the word (WR) or name the colour of the ink (CN). When humans perform these tasks they have a faster reaction time in WR tasks compared with CN tasks. Subjects also have slower reaction times on CN tasks in the incongruent situation where the word and ink colour disagree, but the difference in reaction time is not significant in incongruent WR tasks (see Table 1). This shows that word-reading interferes with colour-naming but colour-naming does not significantly interfere with word-reading. This difference in response times is known as the Stroop effect [38].

The Stroop effect is one of the most studied phenomena of cognitive interference and many variations on Stroop's original experiments have been carried out. For example, Glaser and Glaser [13] introduced stimulus onset asynchrony (SOA) when presenting colour and word stimuli at different temporal positions; the compensated processing time for colour-naming did not result in interference on reading words. Dunbar and Macleod [6] modified the words in different rotations so that participants took longer to read the word. In this situation the hindered word reading still interfered with colour naming. Macleod, Colin and Dunbar [27] introduced shape naming and associated different shapes to different colours. After intensive practicing, slower shape naming interfered with faster colour-naming tasks when participants were asked to name the colour of a shape.

A number of theories have been proposed to explain the Stroop effect [26]. Stroop [39] assumed that people can read words much faster than name colours and attributed the interference on colour-naming to incomplete inhibition on the faster processed word-reading. This model was challenged when slow word reading was shown to strongly interfere with fast colour naming. A different theory was put forward by Cohen, Dunbar and McClelland [4], who suggested that there are parallel distributed processes of word-reading and colour-naming. The strength of the word-reading pathway is stronger than the colour-naming pathway, as there are more experiences of reading words. The pathway strength affects the processing speed and priority in the interference scenario. Melara and Algom [30] suggested that there could be perceptual biases towards word reading compared with colour naming. The attention selection is biased by the dimensional imbalance and uncertainty in linking the stimulus to word or colour perceptions. As words are more salient than colours, word-naming would interfere with colour naming. Roelofs [35] argues that there are architectural difference in the processing of colours and words. In this proposal, colour-naming requires more steps than word reading, so colour-naming requires more attention and is less automatic than word reading.

2.2 Computer Simulations of the Stroop Effect

One of the most influential computer simulations of the Stroop effect was built by Cohen et al. [4]. A multilayer perceptron (MLP) network was trained on control conditions when only colour or word inputs were present. The input layer had input nodes for ink colour, word text and task and it was connected to the output layers via a hidden layer. The activation of sensory inputs and commands were fed through the network to produce output vectors. Training in word or colour conditions increased the strength of the pathways. As reading is highly practiced, there were ten times as many word training items than colour training items. The trained MLP was run repeatedly to generate the output time, which was determined when the accumulated output of one of the output vectors exceeded a response threshold. The system was able to reproduce the basic Stroop effect and predicted a reverse-Stroop effect that has been recently observed [45].

Based on the architecture of the Cohen model, Laeng et al. [25] replaced the single unit colour inputs with three input nodes that worked in combination to represent a much wider range of colours. Kaplan et al. [23] introduced a number of models of neuroanatomic components: a habitual response module, an attentional module, an inhibition module and an error detection module. The authors claimed that the multi-perception network was a duplicate of prefrontal circuits. Benbassat and Henik [2] applied an evolutionary algorithm to the Cohen model to generate the outputs. Different parameters of the networks were imported as part of the genome segments and the system evolved based on its performance in control conditions when only colour or word input was present. This network was able to produce the basic Stroop effect. Kello [24] implemented a simplified articulation process with an inhibition model (gain) to control the information flow through the system. By varying response latencies, a different stimulus onset asynchrony effect was simulated. Phaf [34] built representations of experimental conditions as different feature attributes. By manipulating connection weights, the multi-layer perceptron system was able to perform winner-take-all filtering on input patterns. The recurrent connection between different modules forced the system to converge to a stable state for any given input. This system was able to demonstrate the cooperative and competitive interferences that are detected in some of the Stroop tests.

Roelofs [35] simulated the Stroop effect in a interactive activation model [36] of word production. Based on similar architecture, Van Maanen et al. [43] focused on semantic interference during retrieval. Although colour-naming and word-reading had similar input structure and the symbolic processing unit was biased towards words during retrieval, the system was able to duplicate results for semantic gradient effects [14] and the SOA effects. Fennell [7] further parameterized the decision process by introducing both boundary and diffusion models [15]. Yusoff, Gruning and Browne [46] simulated the Stroop tests in an auto-associative Hopfield network. This network was initiated with partially enabled (turned on) bits forming colour or word memory as task requirements, and the system took different numbers of cycles to converge on a stable state under different conditions.

2.3 Cognitive Models with Cell Assemblies

The Cell Assembly hypothesis is that CAs are the neural basis of internal resentations of concepts, ideas and mental states [16]. A CA is a group of neurons that has relatively high synaptic connectivity, and relatively highly weighted synaptic connectivity. Thus, once some neurons with in a given CA start to fire, there is a cascade of firing that causes the larger portion of the CA population to fire. This firing is the neural basis of a psychological short-term memory. The synaptic change required to make this connectivity is a long-term memory. When a concept (for example, a word red) is presented to a participant, a group activation pattern of neurons will emerge and persist when a 'red' word is recognized by the participant.

One of the core principles of Hebbian theory [16] is that CAs emerge from Hebbian plasticity; if a group of neurons often fire together, their connecting weights will increase and the particular co-firing neurons will form a CA that acts as a basic unit for neuronal computation. There is considerable theoretical support for CAs (e.g. [3]) and there is a large community of researchers that, in essence, assumes that the CA hypothesis is correct (see [21] for a review). Although imaging data is consistent with the idea of CAs, it cannot provide conclusive evidence because it is not currently possible to record the spiking behaviour of all neurons [11].

In previous work, CAs have been used to build a number of cognitive systems. Researchers have been developing CA based systems for quite some time [33]. In particular, the authors have done work on, for example, associative memory [18], natural language parsing [19], and category learning [20]. Others have developed, for example, systems for robot control [42], and the semantics of words [10]. Simualted spiking neurons are powerful computational devices. It is relatively simple to build systems based on spiking neurons that are incompatible with the CA hypothesis. These systems are suspect as models of human psychological behaviour.

3   Methodology

Our cognitive system was constructed using the spiking neuron simulation platform NEST [12][1].

---

[1] The code can be found on http://www.cwa.mdx.ac.uk/NEAL/NEAL.html.

Integrate and fire neurons were programmatically connected together into eight Cell Assemblies (CAs) (see Fig. 3). There is no learning in the neural network described in this paper. All of the CAs contained one thousand neurons except for the two word reading CAs, which contained two thousand neurons. A CA group was inter-connected with excitatory synapses that has static and identical weights.

The internal connections in a CA follow a small-world-topology [44]. A small world topology is a sparse topology, where nodes can reach most other nodes in a small number of, in this case, synapses. In this paper, we adopted a small world topology that was consistent with neural biology, in which neurons that have more connections are more likely to be connected, which has been reported with 'hub' neurons that are highly connected to other neurons in brain networks [17]. A demonstration of small world topology is shown in Fig. 1 that shows a network of 12 neurons with a small world topology (left) and a random topology (right). Notice how some neurons in the small world topology are receiving more synaptic connections while the synaptic connections in the random topology are more evenly distributed.

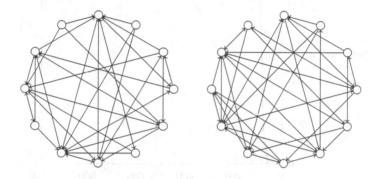

Fig. 1. Small-world topology.

The small world topology in our project are implemented as follows: initially, each neuron in the CA is connected to its adjacent neuron in a ring. Each connection is then rewired according to Eq. 1, which shows how likely each of the other neurons is to be selected as the post-synaptic neuron. In this terminology, the connections are one directional synaptic connections. This is a 'rich get richer' policy: post-synaptic neurons that already have may incoming connections have a higher chance of getting a new connection.

$$p_i = \frac{c_i + 1}{\sum_{j=1}^{n \neq m} (c_j + 1)} \tag{1}$$

n is the total number of neurons and $n \times s$ is the total number of uni-directional synaptic connections, with s being the number of synapses leaving each neuron. p_i is the probability of the ith neuron being selected by a presynaptic neuron whose connection is being rewired. c_i is the number of presynaptic neurons that are currently connecting to the ith neuron. If a connection is to be rewired from neuron m, it will always reconnect to another postsynaptic neuron. Note that we are not implying that small world topologies develop in the brain using this rewiring mechanism, just that they are common topologies in the brain.

One of the properties of a CA is the ability to 'ignite' when some of the neurons in the CA are stimulated. In our experiment, 10 neurons (20 for word CAs) were stimulated repeatedly. The CA will gradually have more neurons starting to fire. A demonstration of CA ignition is shown in Fig. 2. There are 30 connections leaving each neuron to connect to post-synaptic neurons. It is the same with the random connection condition. Note how the random line never really has any extra firing, while the small world line slowly builds up firing. The random 100 line does increase its firing and rapidly goes to saturation.

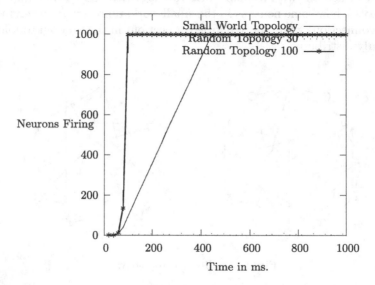

Fig. 2. Firing behaviour of groups of neurons with clamped input, and differing topologies.

The small-world topology was also applied between CAs following the same 'rich get richer' policy under Eq. 1, however only the count of synapses between these populations was used in the equation. Each neuron in a CA was connected to 1.1% of other neurons in the CA. A gross network structure is shown in Fig. 3. All CAs had excitatory internal connections, neurons in colour and word CAs had both excitatory and inhibitory external connections. Neurons in task-selection and output CAs only had inhibitory external connections. Excitatory connections are shown as solid arrows and inhibitory connections are shown as dotted lines.

At the start of a simulation run the task, word and ink CAs were externally activated by injecting a current of 378 mA into a percentage of their neurons.

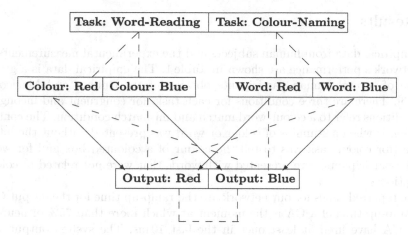

Fig. 3. Network Structure. There are eight Cell Assemblies consisting of neurons with excitatory connections between them. There are also inhibitory connections between CAs, represented by dashed lines, and excitatory connections between CAs, represented by solid lines. All inhibitory connections are from top to bottom except the output CAs are mutually inhibitory.

For instance, if it was a word naming (WN) task and the word red was presented in blue ink, then neurons in the word naming task CA, the red word CA and the blue ink CA were activated with the 378 mA injection current, which was continued throughout the simulation of 1000 milliseconds (ms). Activated neurons continued firing throughout the simulation. The percentage of neurons that were externally stimulated for each CA is 0.13% for the ink colour and word CAs, and 0.26% for the task CAs.

The ink colour and word CAs had excitatory connections to the output CAs. Each of these were connected to 0.5% of the appropriate output neurons. They also had inhibitory connections to 0.6% of the appropriate output neurons. The task neurons had connections to 1.2% of the appropriate neurons. (Appropriate here refers to the arcs in Fig. 3).

The synaptic weights were static and did not change with training or repeated exposure to the task. The synaptic weights were initially set at the minimum weight to evoke spikes in post-synaptic neurons. Then the connecting weights and nodes inside and across different CAs were manually tuned to produce the firing delays in output neurons that matched the empirical data from human subjects.

Six conditions were simulated, which are shown in Table 1. In the two control conditions either a single word or ink colour CA is stimulated. In the other four conditions, one task, one word and one ink colour CA was stimulated. These four conditions were the congruent or incongruent, colour naming or word reading conditions. So, when one incongruent word reading task was run, the word reading CA, the red ink CA, and the blue word CA were turned on. In this case the correct answer was blue.

4   Results

The empirical data from human subjects and the experimental measurements of our network's performance are shown in Table 1. The empirical data is a group average of several human participants obtained from Dunbar and Macleod's work [6]. There are three conditions for each task, for congruent and incongruent conditions refer to a colour-word match and mismatch condition. The control condition is when a stimulus of colour or word was presented without the interference (for colour task was to tell the colour of a coloured box and for word task the participants were presented with words that were not related to colour descriptions).

The reported times for our network are the ramp-up time for the output CA. The ramp-up time of a CA is the moment at which more than 75% of neurons in the CA have fired at least once in the last 10 ms. The system output was recorded when a target CA had ramped-up. If both CAs were ramping-up, the CA that first reached 75% was reported. In isolation, the ramp-up time for the task CAs is 90 ms, for colour-naming it is 188 ms, and for word-reading it is 146 ms, that is faster than colour-naming

Human participants take roughly 300 ms to process visual input and produce a behaviour response. As our system only performs the cognitive task, the time for perception and movement can be discounted. Consequently, Table 1 shows the reported results in brackets, with the results minus 300 ms first. The incongruent times match exactly and the others are within 13 ms.

Table 1. Empirical and simulation results

Human subjects	Congruent (ms)	Incongruent (ms)	Control (ms)
Colour naming	310(610)	490(790)	330(630)
Word reading	210(510)	220(520)	215(515)
Simulation	Congruent (ms)	Incongruent (ms)	Control (ms)
Colour naming	297	490	370
Word reading	203	220	216

5   Discussion and Future Work

The results in the previous section show that our system successfully executes the word and colour naming tasks with similar timings to human subjects. While the tasks that our system performs are not particularly intelligent, we believe that this type of system could eventually lead to the development of AIs that think in a human-like way and can be more easily understood and trusted by human subjects.

There is no one size fits all recipe for producing an AI system. When large amounts of data are available, deep neural networks are often the best solution.

However, deep learning has limitations [28] and other situations have different requirements, such as one shot learning, transparency, symbol manipulation, etc. This paper has demonstrated how a symbol manipulating AI system can be implemented in spiking neurons in a way that is constrained by the brain architecture and measurements of human performance in experimental psychology. In some situations this approach to AI could be a better choice. In the longer term this type of brain-inspired system could prove to be better at flexible general purpose AI than the current state of the art systems.

Although our neural network is a very approximate model of the brain structures that are responsible for naming colours and words, it does have features that might point towards novel explanations of the Stroop effect in the human brain. For example, the small world topology provides important functionality in our CA based system (see Sect. 3) and our network's Stroop effect is partly driven by the fact that the number of neurons in the word CAs is twice that of those in the ink CAs.

Humans learn new concepts by modifying synaptic connectivity in the brain. Synaptic connectivity modifications inlude as long-term potentiation and long-term depression of synapses caused by the spiking patterns of pre and post synaptic neurons [32]. Some of the co-activation patterns are found to follow Hebbian plasticity: if a neuron repeatedly causes another neuron to fire, their connecting weight will tend to be strengthened [16]. In the future, we are planning to add learning rules to our network so that it could develop its topology dynamically by interacting with its environment. Part of this research will be to develop a collection of learning rules that enables the training of simulated neurons to yield desired functional behaviours.

The hope is that a set of learning rules [47] will lead to a stable usable memory system. One cognitive task is a question answering task around semantic nets [5]. This work will be based around encoding known symbolic associative memories into neurons, a form of symbolic boot-strapping. Large scale neural associative memories, run in large neuromorphic systems, can be used in, for example, text mining. Stroop effects should emerge naturally from the behaviour of large associative memories learned in this fashion as a benchmark test of the system.

Beyond this, symbol grounding will be explored, with long term memory units being learned from an environment by a behaving agent; while learning these units, associations will also be learned. These systems will understand their environment in ways similar to humans, and that understanding will grow as they continue to operate in that environment.

6   Conclusion

This paper has described a system that performs word recognition and colour naming tasks. It was implemented using spiking neurons and it operated in a human-like way on a human-like time scale - displaying a similar Stroop effect to human subjects. In the longer term this type of system could potentially address some of the limitations of the current generation of AI systems. It can also serve as a cognitive model that can help us to understand the brain.

The next step on the authors' plan is to build spiking neural network that can produce CAs automatically instead of hand-wiring. Another potential direction is to build associative memories that would eventually scaffold the capability to conduct word and colour recognitions and then we could re-test the system on the Stroop task.

Acknowledgment. This work has received funding from the European Union's Horizon 2020 research and innovation programme under grant agreement No. 720270 (the Human Brain Project).

References

1. Arena, P., Patané, L., Termini, P.S.: An insect brain computational model inspired by drosophila melanogaster: simulation results. In: The 2010 International Joint Conference on Neural Networks (IJCNN), pp. 1–8. IEEE (2010)
2. Benbassat, A., Henik, A.: Examining the stroop effect using a develomental spatial neuroevolution system. In: Proceedings of the Companion Publication of the 2015 Annual Conference on Genetic and Evolutionary Computation, pp. 747–748. ACM (2015)
3. Buzsáki, G.: Neural syntax: cell assemblies, synapsembles, and readers. Neuron **68**(3), 362–385 (2010)
4. Cohen, J.D., Dunbar, K., McClelland, J.L.: On the control of automatic processes: a parallel distributed processing account of the stroop effect. Psychol. Rev. **97**(3), 332 (1990)
5. Collins, A., Quillian, M.: Retrieval time from semantic memory. J. Verbal Learn. Verbal Behav. **8**(2), 240–247 (1969)
6. Dunbar, K., MacLeod, C.M.: A horse race of a different color: stroop interference patterns with transformed words. J. Exp. Psychol. Hum. Percept. Perform. **10**(5), 622 (1984)
7. Fennell, A.: Does response modality influence conflict? Modelling vocal and manual response stroop interference. Ph.d. thesis, The Ohio State University (2017)
8. Ferrucci, D., et al.: Building watson: an overview of the deepQA project. AI Mag. **31**(3), 59–79 (2010)
9. Furber, S.B., Galluppi, F., Temple, S., Plana, L.A.: The spinnaker project. Proc. IEEE **102**(5), 652–665 (2014). https://doi.org/10.1109/JPROC.2014.2304638
10. Garagnani, M., Wennekers, T., Pulvermüller, F.: Recruitment and consolidation of cell assemblies for words by way of hebbian learning and competition in a multi-layer neural network. Cogn. Comput. **1**(2), 160–176 (2009)
11. Gerstein, G.L., Kirkland, K.L.: Neural assemblies: technical issues, analysis, and modeling. Neural Netw. **14**(6–7), 589–598 (2001)
12. Gewaltig, M., Diesmann, M.: NEST (NEural Simulation Tool). Scholarpedia **2**(4), 1430 (2007)
13. Glaser, M.O., Glaser, W.R.: Time course analysis of the stroop phenomenon. J. Exp. Psychol. Hum. Percept. Perform. **8**(6), 875 (1982)
14. Glaser, W.R., Düngelhoff, F.J.: The time course of picture-word interference. J. Exp. Psychol. Hum. Percept. Perform. **10**(5), 640 (1984)

15. Gold, J.I., Shadlen, M.N.: The neural basis of decision making. Annu. Rev. Neurosci. **30**, 535–574 (2007)
16. Hebb, D.O., et al.: The Organization of Behavior: A Neuropsychological Theory. Wiley, New York (1949)
17. van den Heuvel, M.P., Sporns, O.: Network hubs in the human brain. Trends Cogn. Sci. **17**(12), 683–696 (2013)
18. Huyck, C.: Creating hierarchical categories using cell assemblies. Connect. Sci. **19**(1), 1–24 (2007)
19. Huyck, C.: A psycholinguistic model of natural language parsing implemented in simulated neurons. Cogn. Neurodynamics **3**(4), 316–330 (2009)
20. Huyck, C., Mitchell, I.: Post and pre-compensatory Hebbian learning for categorisation. Comput. Neurodynamics **8**(4), 299–311 (2014)
21. Huyck, C.R., Passmore, P.J.: A review of cell assemblies. Biol. Cybern. **107**(3), 263–288 (2013)
22. IBM: Project debater. https://www.research.ibm.com/artificial-intelligence/project-debater/
23. Kaplan, G.B., Şengör, N., Gürvit, H., Güzeliş, C.: Modelling the stroop effect: a connectionist approach. Neurocomputing **70**(7–9), 1414–1423 (2007)
24. Kello, C.T., Plaut, D.C., MacWhinney, B.: The task dependence of staged versus cascaded processing: an empirical and computational study of stroop interference in speech perception. J. Exp. Psychol. Gen. **129**(3), 340 (2000)
25. Laeng, B., Låg, T., Brennen, T.: Reduced stroop interference for opponent colors may be due to input factors: evidence from individual differences and a neural network simulation. J. Exp. Psychol. Hum. Percept. Perform. **31**(3), 438 (2005)
26. MacLeod, C.M.: The stroop effect. In: Luo, R. (ed.) Encyclopedia of Color Science and Technology, pp. 1–6. Springer, Heidelberg (2014). https://doi.org/10.1007/978-3-642-27851-8_67-1
27. MacLeod, C.M., Dunbar, K.: Training and stroop-like interference: evidence for a continuum of automaticity. J. Exp. Psychol. Learn., Mem., Cogn. **14**(1), 126 (1988)
28. Marcus, G.: Deep learning: a critical appraisal. CoRR abs/1801.00631 (2018). http://arxiv.org/abs/1801.00631
29. Markram, H.: The human brain project. Sci. Am. **306**(6), 50–55 (2012)
30. Melara, R.D., Algom, D.: Driven by information: a tectonic theory of stroop effects. Psychol. Rev. **110**(3), 422 (2003)
31. Mnih, V., et al.: Human-level control through deep reinforcement learning. Nature **518**, 529–33 (2015)
32. Nabavi, S., Fox, R., Proulx, C.D., Lin, J.Y., Tsien, R.Y., Malinow, R.: Engineering a memory with LTD and LTP. Nature **511**(7509), 348 (2014)
33. Palm, G.: Neural Assemblies. An Alternative Approach to Artificial Intelligence. Springer, Heidelberg (1982). https://doi.org/10.1007/978-3-642-81792-2
34. Phaf, R.H., Van der Heijden, A., Hudson, P.T.: Slam: a connectionist model for attention in visual selection tasks. Cogn. Psychol. **22**(3), 273–341 (1990)
35. Roelofs, A.: Goal-referenced selection of verbal action: modeling attentional control in the stroop task. Psychol. Rev. **110**(1), 88 (2003)
36. Rumelhart, D.E., McClelland, J.L.: An interactive activation model of context effects in letter perception: II. The contextual enhancement effect and some tests and extensions of the model. Psychol. Rev. **89**(1), 60 (1982)
37. Silver, D., et al.: Mastering the game of go without human knowledge. Nature **550**, 354–59 (2017)

38. Stroop, J.R.: Studies of interference in serial verbal reactions. J. Exp. Psychol. **18**(6), 643 (1935)
39. Stroop, J.R.: Factors affecting speed in serial verbal reactions. Psychol. Monogr. **50**(5), 38 (1938)
40. Sun, Y., Liang, D., Wang, X., Tang, X.: Deepid3: face recognition with very deep neural networks. CoRR abs/1502.00873 (2015). http://arxiv.org/abs/1502.00873
41. Szigeti, B., et al.: Openworm: an open-science approach to modeling caenorhabditis elegans. Front. Comput. Neurosci. **8**, 137 (2014)
42. Tetzlaff, C., Dasgupta, S., Kulvicius, T., Wörgötter, F.: The use of hebbian cell assemblies for nonlinear computation. Sci. Rep. **5**, 12866 (2015)
43. Van Maanen, L., Van Rijn, H.: An accumulator model account of semantic interference in memory retrieval. In: Proceedings of the Seventh International Conference on Cognitive Modeling, pp. 322–327 (2006)
44. Watts, D.J., Strogatz, S.H.: Collective dynamics of 'small-world' networks. Nature **393**(6684), 440 (1998)
45. Yamamoto, N., Incera, S., McLennan, C.T.: A reverse stroop task with mouse tracking. Front. Psychol. **7**, 670 (2016)
46. Yusoff, N., Grüning, A., Browne, A.: Modelling the stroop effect: dynamics in inhibition of automatic stimuli processing. In: Wang, R., Gu, F. (eds.) Advances in Cognitive Neurodynamics (II), pp. 641–645. Springer, Dordrecht (2011). https://doi.org/10.1007/978-90-481-9695-1_95
47. Zenke, F., Agnes, E.J., Gerstner, W.: Diverse synaptic plasticity mechanisms orchestrated to form and retrieve memories in spiking neural networks. Nat. Commun. **6**, 6922 (2015)

Enhancing Human Decision Making for Workforce Optimisation Using a Stacked Auto Encoder Based Hybrid Genetic Algorithm

R. Chimatapu[1]($\boxtimes$), H. Hagras[1], A. J. Starkey[2], and G. Owusu[2]

[1] University of Essex, Colchester, UK
{rcl6956,hani}@essex.ac.uk
[2] British Telecom, Ipswich IP5 3RE, UK
{andrew.starkey,gilbert.owusu}@bt.com

Abstract. In organisations with a large mobile workforce there is a need to improve the operational efficiency of the engineers who form the mobile workforce. This improvement can lead to significant savings in operational costs and a corresponding increase in revenue. The operational efficiency of the engineers can be improved by optimising the geographic areas within which the engineers operate. This process is known as Work Area Optimization and it is a subdomain of Workforce Optimization. In this paper, we will present a Hybrid Genetic Algorithm where we will use Deep Neural Networks to generate prior knowledge about the Work Area Optimization problem and use this knowledge to generate improved initial estimates which in turn improves the performance of an existing Genetic Algorithm that does Work Area Optimization. We will also compare our approach with prior knowledge generated with the help of human experts with years of experience in the field. We show that our new approach is as good as or better in generating the prior knowledge when compared to human experts.

Keywords: Deep Neural Network · Hybrid Genetic Algorithm Workforce Optimization

1 Introduction

In industries which employ a large mobile workforce, there is a need to improve operational efficiency of the mobile workforce (engineers). This is because improvement in operational efficiency will lead to significant saving in cost, improved revenues and improvement in customer satisfaction.

One way in which operational efficiency of engineers is improved is by optimising the geographic areas in which the engineers operate. These areas, known as work areas (WAs) [1], are the boundaries within which a team of engineers work. These work areas then generate the demand or tasks that the engineers perform, such as installing new connections, repairing faults, general maintenance etc.

© Springer Nature Switzerland AG 2018
M. Bramer and M. Petridis (Eds.): SGAI-AI 2018, LNAI 11311, pp. 63–75, 2018.
https://doi.org/10.1007/978-3-030-04191-5_5

These WAs are created by grouping of Service Delivery Points (SDPs) together. The SDPs are locations from which services such as electricity, water, telecom etc. are delivered to individual homes or businesses. Work area optimisation is the process of combining SDPs into WAs while optimising a set of constraints such as

- Coverage: Maximise the number of tasks that are expected to be completed
- Utilisation: Maximise the amount of time the engineers work
- Travel: Minimise the amount of travel for the engineers
- Balance: WAs should be evenly balanced with the amount of work that they contain
- Team Balance: WAs should have a similar number of team members.

These types of problem are called combinatorial optimisation problems. Previous work such as [1, 2], have used Multi-Objective Genetic Algorithms (MOGAs) to solve the problem. Where the problem is solved by trying to find a set of SDPs around which the rest of the SDPs can be clustered to form the WAs, one SDP for each of the WA that has to be generated. The initial population of these solutions is created by randomly selecting the SDPs. Selecting random solutions is an intuitive way of generating unbiased solutions when the algorithm has no prior information on the search space.

A number of researchers have found that if prior knowledge exists or can be generated at a low computational cost, seeding Genetic Algorithms (GAs) with good initial estimates may generate better solutions with faster convergence [3].

In this paper, we propose a hybrid GA approach where we will create a Stacked Autoencoder to generate prior knowledge about the SDPs. We also took the help of human experts to generate prior knowledge about the SDPs. We will show that the new approach provides similar or better performance when compared to manually generating prior knowledge. There by reducing the cost and time required to generate the prior knowledge.

The rest of this paper is organised as follows. In Sect. 2 we will provide a brief overview of Deep Neural Networks and Stacked Auto Encoders. Section 3 will present an overview of Genetic Algorithms. Section 4 will present the description of the DNN based seeding. Section 5 will be experiments and results and Sect. 6 will provide the conclusion.

2   A Brief Overview of Deep Neural Networks

A Deep Neural Network (DNN) is an Artificial Neural Network (ANN) with multiple hidden layers between the input and the output layers [4, 5]. The extra hidden layers allow composition of features from lower layers, potentially modelling complex data with fewer units [4].

There are many variants of DNNs including Recurrent Neural Network (RNN) [6], Convolutional Neural Networks (CNN) [7], Deep Belief Networks (DBN) [8] and Stacked Auto-Encoders (SAE) [9]. We will be using SAEs in this paper as they can be effectively used for unsupervised feature learning on complex data sets and they can be easily adapted to new data sets with minimal redesign [10]. Details of how to build a Stacked Auto Encoder are explained in the following subsections.

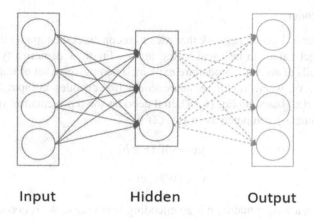

Input   **Hidden**   **Output**

Fig. 1. Autoencoder

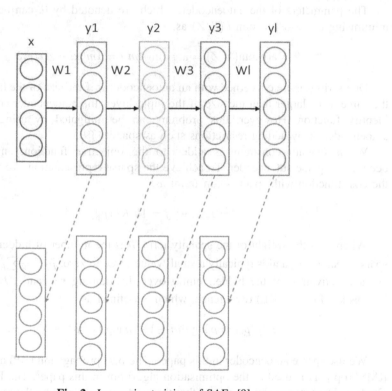

Fig. 2. Layerwise training of SAEs [9]

2.1   Autoencoder

An Autoencoder is a neural network that tries to reconstruct the input at the output i.e., setting the target values to be equal to the inputs. Figure 1 depicts a typical autoencoder. The details of an Autoencoder are explained here: given a set of training samples $[x_1, x_2, x_3, x_4, \ldots x_i]$, where $x_i \in R$, an autoencoder first encodes an input x_i to a hidden representation $y(x_i)$ based on Eq. (1). Then it decodes the representation $y(x_i)$ back into a reconstruction $z(x_i)$ computed as in Eq. (2) [9]:

$$yx = (W1x + b) \tag{1}$$

$$zx = (W2y(x) + c) \tag{2}$$

Where W_1 is a weight matrix, b is an encoding bias vector, W_2 is decoding matrix, c is a decoding bias vector. We use the logistic sigmoid function $1/(1 + \exp(-x))$ for $f(x)$ and $g(x)$ in this paper.

The parameters of the autoencoder, which are denoted by θ, can be obtained by minimising the cost function $L(X, Z)$ as:

$$\theta = \arg\min(X, Z) = \arg\min 1m \ i = 1m \|xi - z(xi)\|2 \tag{3}$$

One serious issue concerned with an autoencoder is if the size of the hidden layer is the same as or larger than the size of the input layer, the autoencoder could learn the identity function. However, this problem can be mitigated by using a nonlinear autoencoder or by adding restrictions such as sparsity [9].

When sparsity constraint is added to the objective function, an autoencoder becomes a sparse autoencoder. To achieve the sparse representation, we will minimise the cost function with sparsity constraint as:

$$\theta = LX, + \gamma j = 1h \ KL(\rho \| \rho j) \tag{4}$$

Where γ is the weight of the sparsity term, h is the number of hidden units, ρ is a sparsity parameter and is typically a small value close to zero, $\hat{\rho}_j = \frac{1}{N}\sum_{i=1}^{N} y_i(x_i)$ is the average activation of the hidden unit j over the training set, and $KL(\rho\|\hat{\rho}_j)$ is the Kullback – Leibler (KL) divergence, which is defined as

$$K(\rho|\rho j) = \rho \log \rho\rho j + 1 - \rho \log 1 - \rho 1 - \rho j \tag{5}$$

We use sparse autoencoder in this paper. The backpropagation (BP) algorithm with RMSProp [11] is used as the optimisation algorithm in this paper. The RMSProp and Gradient Descent are similar except that the gradient is divided by the moving average of the squared gradient for each weight i.e., the square root of the output of Eq. (6).

$$M(w, t) = 0.9 \, MS(w, t - 1) + 0.1(\partial E\partial w(t))2 \tag{6}$$

2.2 Stacked Autoencoders

An SAE model (depicted in Fig. 2), is created by stacking autoencoders to form a deep network by taking the output of the autoencoder found on the layer below as the input of the current layer [12]. More clearly, consider an SAE of l layers, the first layer is trained as an autoencoder, with the training set as the input. After obtaining the parameters of the first hidden layer, the output of the first hidden layer is used as the input for the 2nd hidden layer. Similarly, after training the kth hidden layer the output of that layer is used as input for the $(k+1)^{th}$ hidden layer. In this way, multiple autoencoders can be stacked hierarchically.

3 A Brief Overview of Genetic Algorithm

Genetic Algorithms (GAs) are based on the theory of evolution where over time a population or species will adapt to the environment. This is based on the idea of the survival of the fittest. This means that the individuals that are best suitable for the environment survive to reproduce the next generation [2].

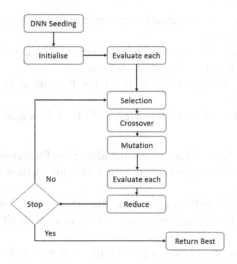

Fig. 3. Genetic algorithm with DNN seeding

The algorithm for a standard GA is explained below.

Initialize the population: This is normally done by creating N solutions and randomly initialising the genes for each solution.

Evaluate: The solutions created in the previous step are evaluated using a fitness function. Each solution is then given a score to represent the solution fitness.

Selection: There are a number of selection operators such as tournament or roulette [13]. In tournament selection, a subset of solutions from the population is chosen. Then the solution with the highest fitness will be chosen as the first parent. The process is repeated to find the second parent.

Crossover: The parents chosen in the previous step will crossover their genes using a crossover operator (1-point, 2-point or uniform) [14]. The crossover operation will generate 2 child solutions that will be added to the new population set.

Mutation: Some of the genes in the child solutions are changed randomly.

Evaluate: The child solutions in the previous steps are evaluated using a fitness function.

The above steps are repeated again until the stopping criteria are reached.

4   Hybrid GA Based on DNN Seeding

The flow of a Hybrid GA is shown in Fig. 3 where the initial population is generated using initial estimates produced by the Stacked Auto Encoder. The Stacked Auto Encoder is trained using a greedy layer-wise unsupervised learning algorithm [8].

The Training method for the DNN Model is as follows:

- Train the first layer as an autoencoder by minimising the objective function with the training sets as the input
- Train the second layer as an autoencoder taking the first layer's output as the input
- Repeat Step 2 for the desired number of layers
- Use the output of the last layer as input for the output layer and initialise its parameters randomly
- Fine Tune the parameters of all the layers with Back Propagation (BP) method in a supervised way.

We used Adam [15] algorithm as the BP algorithm for training.

Once the DNN model is trained we use the following method to generate the initial Population of the GA.

First, the details of the SDPs are passed to the DNN model, which provides a rating for each of the SDP. These ratings are values from 1 to 10 with 10 for the best and 1 for the worst SDPs.

These ratings are used to create a p-value for each SDP using the Eq. (7).

$$p_i = \frac{r_i}{\sum_{j=1}^{n} r_j} \tag{7}$$

Where n is the number of exchanges and r_i is the rating of the SDPs. This is similar to a roulette wheel algorithm [13].

The p values provide the probability of being selected. The higher the rating of an SDP the higher the probability of it being part of the initial population.

5 Experiments and Results

In our experiments, we used SDP data collected from BT in the UK. The data contained unsupervised information about more than 5500 SDPs and with supervised ratings available for 883 SDPs. We randomly divided both the unsupervised and supervised data sets into three parts: 70% for training, 15% for validation and 15% for testing.

The input data contained the following information for each SDP.

- Number of SDPs that are directly accessible from the current SDP
- Number of Resources in the SDP
- Total Number of Tasks in the SDP on average
- Total Task time of all the tasks in the SDP
- Distance from the Northern most SDP in the sub-region being optimized.
- Distance from the Southernmost SDP in the sub-region being optimized
- Distance from the Eastern most SDP in the sub-region being optimized.
- Distance from the Western most SDP in the sub-region being optimised
- Mean distance to all the other SDPs in the sub-region being optimised
- Mean distance to all the resources in the sub-region being optimised.
- Mean distance from all the SDPs that are directly accessible from the current SDP

A Stacked Autoencoder with three layers (100, 60, 30 neurons respectively in each layer) trained using greedy layer-wise training was found to have the best performance on the available dataset.

The following GA parameters were used for all the experiments.

- Crossover Rate: 0.1
- Mutation Rate: 0.05
- Population Size: 100
- Number of Generations: 100

The four different GA configurations were used to optimise the WAs for 15 different sub-regions. The four GA configurations are as follows.

- Original: Conventional GA
- DNN Based Seeding: The proposed Stacked Auto Encoder based Hybrid GA
- Expert Seeding: The SDP ratings were provided by human experts who are familiar with these SDPs
- Previous run Ratings: The SDP ratings were built using the fitness values obtained from the optimisation runs of the Conventional GA.

The optimisation of the fifteen sub-regions was done for three of the GA configurations and we obtained human expert ratings for six of the sub-regions (due to the difficulty and the time-consuming nature of generating these ratings) and repeated seven times and the average of these seven runs are shown in Tables 1, 2, 3, 4, 5, 6, 7, 8, 9, 10, 11, 12, 13, 14 and 15. The optimisation was done using five objectives which are Max Coverage, Max Utilisation, Min Travel, Min Balance and Min Team Balance.

The DNN Based Seeding and Previous run Ratings were compared against the Original GA for all fifteen sub-regions and the average of the changes is shown in Table 16. From Table 16 it can be seen that the DNN based seeding produces a 13% overall improvement in fitness and 38% improvement in Team Balance.

Analysing the results shown in Tables 1, 2, 3, 4, 5 and 6, where we can compare all the four approaches, we can see that the original GA does better in only one of the sub-regions in all other sub-regions the other approaches do better. The Human Expert Seeding beats the DNN based seeding in only sub-region 2 and they are about equal in sub-region 4. In all other sub-regions the DNN based seeding beats the Human Expert Seeding.

Table 1. Sub-region 1

Objective	Original	DNN based seeding	Expert seeding	Previous run ratings
Coverage	57	57	57	57
Travel	35	35	34	34
Utilization	22	22	22	22
Balance	50	38	40	40
Team bal.	1	2	2	2
Overall fitness	0.00591	0.00644	0.00666	0.00732

Table 2. Sub-region 2

Objective	Original	DNN based seeding	Expert seeding	Previous run ratings
Coverage	53	52	52	52
Travel	7	7	7	7
Utilization	14	14	14	14
Balance	39	37	35	33
Team bal.	6	6	5	5
Overall fitness	0.00478	0.00565	0.00603	0.00653

Table 3. Sub-region 3

Objective	Original	DNN based seeding	Expert seeding	Previous run ratings
Coverage	56	56	57	56
Travel	20	20	21	20
Utilization	20	20	20	20
Balance	49	47	46	47
Team bal.	1	1	1	1
Overall fitness	0.01259	0.0133	0.01249	0.01334

Table 4. Sub-region 4

Objective	Original	DNN based seeding	Expert seeding	Previous run ratings
Coverage	56	56	56	56
Travel	40	40	39	40
Utilization	23	23	23	23
Balance	26	37	26	39
Team bal.	4	4	7	4
Overall fitness	0.00356	0.00269	0.00248	0.00282

Table 5. Sub-region 5

Objective	Original	DNN based seeding	Expert seeding	Previous run ratings
Coverage	51	51	51	51
Travel	2	2	2	2
Utilization	16	16	16	16
Balance	38	42	48	50
Team bal.	2	1	1	2
Overall fitness	0.08944	0.10242	0.07535	0.06437

Table 6. Sub-region 6

Objective	Original	DNN based seeding	Expert seeding	Previous run ratings
Coverage	47	48	48	48
Travel	38	38	39	39
Utilization	20	20	20	20
Balance	44	42	42	39
Team bal.	2	2	2	2
Overall fitness	0.00324	0.00394	0.00385	0.00378

Analysing the results shown in Tables 7, 8, 9, 10, 11, 12, 13, 14 and 15 we can see that the DNN based seeding is beaten by the Original GA in only one of the sub-regions, region 8. In four of the regions DNN Seeding beats the Original by a good margin and in all other regions its performance is comparable to that of the original GA algorithm.

Table 7. Sub-region 7

Objective	Original	DNN based seeding	Previous run ratings
Coverage	60	60	60
Travel	44	45	44
Utilization	21	21	21
Balance	24	18	17
Team bal.	1	1	1
Overall fitness	0.0125	0.01975	0.02221

Table 8. Sub-region 8

Objective	Original	DNN based seeding	Previous run ratings
Coverage	49	50	49
Travel	5	5	5
Utilization	10	10	10
Balance	28	34	28
Team bal.	4	4	4
Overall fitness	0.00972	0.00753	0.00981

Table 9. Sub-region 9

Objective	Original	DNN based seeding	Previous run ratings
Coverage	55	54	55
Travel	36	35	36
Utilization	19	19	19
Balance	21	20	21
Team bal.	4	4	5
Overall fitness	0.0045	0.00418	0.00376

Table 10. Sub-region 10

Objective	Original	DNN based seeding	Previous run ratings
Coverage	48	47	48
Travel	11	11	11
Utilization	13	13	13
Balance	51	45	39
Team bal.	11	11	9
Overall fitness	0.00159	0.00179	0.00205

Table 11. Sub-region 11

Objective	Original	DNN based seeding	Previous run ratings
Coverage	55	55	55
Travel	20	19	20
Utilization	15	15	15
Balance	43	64	64
Team bal.	9	4	3
Overall fitness	0.00184	0.0023	0.00294

Table 12. Sub-region 12

Objective	Original	DNN based seeding	Previous run ratings
Coverage	50	51	51
Travel	16	16	16
Utilization	15	15	15
Balance	34	28	38
Team bal.	2	1	1
Overall fitness	0.01091	0.01842	0.01424

Table 13. Sub-region 13

Objective	Original	DNN based seeding	Previous run ratings
Coverage	51	51	51
Travel	49	49	50
Utilization	26	26	26
Balance	23	24	29
Team bal.	1	1	1
Overall fitness	0.01405	0.01262	0.01164

Table 14. Sub-region 14

Objective	Original	DNN based seeding	Previous run ratings
Coverage	51	51	51
Travel	31	30	30
Utilization	21	21	21
Balance	55	71	69
Team bal.	4	1	1
Overall fitness	0.0046	0.00476	0.00448

Table 15. Sub-region 15

Objective	Original	DNN based seeding	Previous run ratings
Coverage	49	49	49
Travel	4	4	4
Utilization	10	10	10
Balance	40	35	35
Team bal.	2	2	2
Overall fitness	0.0153	0.01934	0.01835

Table 16. Overall improvement

Type	ML improvement	Human rating improvement	Previous run ratings
Overall fitness	**13%**	2%	14%
Coverage	0%	0%	0%
Travel	1%	0%	0%
Utilization	0%	0%	0%
Balance	1%	**4%**	0%
Team balance	**38%**	5%	38%

6 Conclusions and Future Work

This paper presented a new approach where a Deep Neural Network was used to generate prior knowledge about SDPs, this knowledge was then used to initialise a Genetic Algorithm for solving the Work Area Optimization Problem.

We compared the proposed model against a Conventional Genetic Algorithm. Moreover, against similar ratings provided by Human Experts, the results show that the proposed model showed improvement in most of the Sub Regions on which it was tested. It also showed an overall improvement of 13% and it also showed a 38% improvement in team balance. This contrasts with the Human Expert Ratings which showed only 2% overall improvement and only 5% improvement in the team balance. However, the Human Expert Ratings beat our proposed model in the Balance objective by 3%.

In conclusion, our proposed model beats the Human Expert Ratings in 2 of the 5 objectives and the Human Expert Ratings beat our proposed model in 1 of the 5 objectives. This shows that our model can generate better prior knowledge about the SDPs when compared to human experts. It is also cheaper and quicker to produce prior knowledge using our proposed model.

For future work, we aim to compare our approach against other types of Genetic Algorithms also we would like to use other types of DNN models such as Convolutional Neural Network, Recurrent Neural Networks etc., for generating the SDP ratings.

References

1. Starkey, A., Hagras, H., Shakya, S., Owusu, G.: A genetic type-2 fuzzy logic based approach for the optimal allocation of mobile field engineers to their working areas. Presented at the IEEE International Conference on Fuzzy Systems (FUZZ-IEEE), Istanbul, 2–5 August 2015
2. Starkey, A., Hagras, H., Shakya, S., Owusu, G.: A Multi-objective Genetic Type-2 Fuzzy Logic Based System for Mobile Field Workforce Area Optimization (2016)
3. Keedwell, E., Khu, S.-T.: A hybrid genetic algorithm for the design of water distribution networks. Eng. Appl. Artif. Intell. **18**(4), 461–472 (2005)
4. Bengio, Y.: Learning deep architectures for AI. Found. Trends® Mach. Learn. **2**(1), 1–127 (2009)
5. Schmidhuber, J.: Deep learning in neural networks: an overview. Neural Netw. **61**, 85–117 (2015)
6. Mikolov, T., Karafiát, M., Burget, L., Cernocký, J., Khudanpur, S.: Recurrent neural network based language model. In: Interspeech, vol. 2, p. 3 (2010)
7. LeCun, Y., Bengio, Y.: Convolutional networks for images, speech, and time series. Handb. Brain Theory Neural Netw. **3361**(10), 1995 (1995)
8. Hinton, G., Osindero, S., Teh, Y.-W.: A fast learning algorithm for deep belief nets. Neural Comput. **18**(7), 1527–1554 (2006)
9. Lv, Y., Duan, Y., Kang, W., Li, Z., Wang, F.-Y.: Traffic flow prediction with big data: a deep learning approach. IEEE Trans. Intell. Transp. Syst. **16**(2), 865–873 (2015)
10. Shin, H., Orton, M., Collins, D., Doran, S., Leach, M.: Stacked autoencoders for unsupervised feature learning and multiple organ detection in a pilot study using 4D patient data. IEEE Trans. Pattern Anal. Mach. Intell. **35**(8), 1930–1943 (2013)
11. Tieleman, T., Hinton, G.: Lecture 6.5-RMSProp: divide the gradient by a running average of its recent magnitude. COURSERA Neural Netw. Mach. Learn. **4**(2), 26–31 (2012)
12. Bengio, Y., Lamblin, P., Popovici, D., Larochelle, H.: Greedy layer-wise training of deep networks. In: Advances in Neural Information Processing Systems, pp. 153–160 (2007)
13. Jebari, K., Madiafi, M.: Selection methods for genetic algorithms. Int. J. Emerg. Sci. **3**(4), 333–344 (2013)
14. Murata, T., Ishibuchi, H.: Positive and negative combination effects of crossover and mutation operators in sequencing problems, pp. 170–175. IEEE (1996)
15. Kingma, D.P., Ba, J.: Adam: a method for stochastic optimization. arXiv preprint arXiv: 1412.6980 (2014)

Planning and Scheduling

A Versatile Executive Based on T-REX for Any Robotic Domain

Fernando Ropero[✉][iD], Pablo Muñoz[iD], and María D. R-Moreno[iD]

Computer Engineering Department, University of Alcalá,
28871 Alcalá de Henares, Spain
{fernando.ropero,malola.rmoreno,pablo.munoz}@uah.es

Abstract. Autonomous controllers are highly expertise entities that integrate the *sensing-planning-act* cycle to operate robotic platforms in unaffordable environments. Its complexity usually makes them to be focused on a single robotic platform which is ostensibly inefficient. The Teleo-Reactive EXecutive (T-REX) is an autonomous controller envisaged as a multi-agent architecture where sensing, planning and execution are interleaved on a single agent. In this paper, we present a T-REX executive module to manage the execution cycle of actions during the planning phase. Our executive module, called GER, aims to state generic execution policies which make a T-REX controller turns into a heterogeneous entity able to operate over any robotic domain. The experimental section demonstrates that GER allows current T-REX architectures, such as GOAC, to manage different robotic domains as Unmanned Aerial Vehicles (UAV) or Unmanned Ground Vehicles (UGV).

Keywords: Intelligent agents · Planning and scheduling
Distributed AI algorithms

1 Introduction

Autonomous controllers represent a key technology in the development of fully autonomous robotic platforms. During the last decades, there have appeared a lot of autonomous control architectures aiming to operate advanced autonomous vehicles such as Unmanned Aerial Vehicles (UAV) or Autonomous Underwater Vehicles (AUV). However, autonomous controllers are built on several heterogeneous technologies which hinder their adaptability to those robotic platforms. Then, flexibility and scalability are significant aspects highly demanded in autonomous controllers. Ingrand et al. [10] present a global overview of the state of the art in autonomous controllers where there are outlined a vast variety of technologies. There, we find a discreteness classification about autonomous controllers depending on its robotic domains. We appreciate that autonomous controllers are focused on a specific robotic domain such as autonomous exploration robots, AUVs, rescue robots or military robots. In order to encourage the development of heterogeneous (capability to adapt to any robotic domain)

M. Bramer and M. Petridis (Eds.): SGAI-AI 2018, LNAI 11311, pp. 79–91, 2018.
https://doi.org/10.1007/978-3-030-04191-5_6

autonomous controllers, we develop an execution module based on the Teleo-Reactive EXecutive (T-REX) architecture [19]. T-REX was built for a specific underwater robotic application, but it can be applied in many robotic platforms with a proper interpretation of its guidelines. We focus on these guidelines to help T-REX achieve its high potential.

The T-REX architecture is a goal-oriented system which follows the Teleo-Reactive paradigm [17]. It is based on a multi-agent architecture where planning and execution are intertwined in every agent. A T-REX agent is a singular framework for formally managing the interactions among a set of reactors, and so, the robotic platform. A reactor is a control-loop that encapsulates all the world knowledge (of the robotic platform) to accomplish its goals. There exist several T-REX instances which are oriented to operate a particular robotic platform such as AUVs [12] or exploration robots [3].

The purpose of this work is to contribute to this framework by providing an executive reactor which is flexible enough to manage the execution of any robotic domain. This feature abstracts the execution level to the T-REX controllers which can be focused on high-level planning tasks and so, develop complex architectures. Indeed, we demonstrate that a single T-REX instance is able to fully operate an exploration rover and an exploration UAV.

The rest of the paper is organized as follows. Next section briefly explains the literature around autonomous controllers. Sect. 3 defines the key concepts and definitions related to T-REX. Sect. 4 describes the executive reactor. Experimental results are discussed in Sect. 5. Finally, conclusions are outlined.

2   Related Work

Autonomous control architectures are being under a deep study since the past two decades. There are different approaches to model a control architecture, but all of them require an executive operator to manage the task monitoring and execution.

Layered architectures are highly used schemas to build autonomous controllers. Specifically, the Three Tiers (3T) architectures [9] made up by a deliberative layer (top-tier), an executive layer (middle-tier) and a functional layer (bottom-tier). A pioneer of 3T architectures is the Three-Layer Architecture for Navigating Through Intricate Situations (ATLANTIS) [8] which combines a reactive control mechanism with a traditional planning system. ATLANTIS was originally designed for exploration UGVs and consists of three components: the *controller*, the *sequencer* and the *deliberator*. The *sequencer* is the executive operator which controls the initiation and termination of primitive activities previously planned by the *deliberative* in a determined time-window. The Remote Agent (RA) [2] is an autonomous controller based on a closed-loop system fully demonstrated by running on-board the Deep Space 1, so it was developed for spacecraft commanding. RA uses EXEC [18] as a reactive executive operator to translate high-level actions into low-level commands to the *System Software* (bottom-tier). The Laboratory of Analysis and Architecture of Systems (LAAS)

[1,11] implements as an executive operator, the Open Procedural Reasoning Systems (OpenPRS). OpenPRS is a open source version of the Procedural Reasoning Systems (PRS) [16]. It provides a high-level language to represent goals, parallel processing of activities and a bounded reaction time to new events as main attributes. PRS has been used for a wide variety of applications, from mobile robot execution control to space shuttle operational procedure execution. The Wallenberg Information Technology and Autonomous Systems (WITAS) [6,7] is a framework focused on temporal-logic planning and monitoring execution. The *plan executor* is the executive operator which translates the high-level plans provided by its *TALplanner* (deliberative layer) into command sequences to the *command executor*. The WITAS architecture has been specifically designed for the autonomous control of UAVs. Also, the Model-Based Architecture (MoBAr) [14] is a 3 T architecture in which the executive operator is the *Universal Executive* using its own Plan Execution Interchange Language (PLEXIL) [21] to model and control the robot behaviours and monitor the plan execution.

Multi-agent architectures are another schema in autonomous controller designing. These divide the problem into interconnected sub-problems in which each sub-problem is processed by a single agent. The architecture is described in a high level, defining the agents which will form part of the system, their roles, interactions among them and resources that will need. The Intelligent Distributed Execution Architecture (IDEA) [15] represents an unifying framework of the RA architecture, where every IDEA agent has the same layered structure that the RA agent. Here, each IDEA agent has the *Plan Runner*, which is the executive operator for executing and monitoring the actions sended by its *Reactive Planner* or the *Central Plan Database*. The goal of IDEA is to extend RA to domains of higher complexity than spacecraft commanding. The Autonomous Robot Multi-agent Architecture with Distributed Coordination (ARMADICo) can be described in its main elements: an interface agent, mission-task-path planning agents, a battery charger agent, a localization agent, behavioural agents, sensor agents and back agents. The executive operator in ARMADICo is formed by the behavioural agents, which process the goals: go to a point, avoid obstacles and go through narrow spaces. The Goal Oriented Autonomous Controller (GOAC) [3] is an instance of the T-REX architecture designed for exploration rovers. Particularly, GOAC is a T-REX agent where the executive operator is the *Command Dispatcher Reactor*. This executive translates the goals received from other T-REX reactors (deliberative layer) into requests to the functional layer, and it translates replies from the functional layer into observations to the deliberative reactors.

Usually, the executive operators of the layered architectures are highly focused on a specific (robotic or not) domain, which implies an added complexity to adjust these executives to other domains. Furthermore, as we mentioned about T-REX, the multiple combinations and synchronizations of agents in multi-agent architectures entail difficulties in the execution process in different robotic domains. Thus, both architectures approaches present resilience problems for different robotic platforms. Hence, we propose a generic executive for T-REX-based architectures which can be shaped to any robotic platform, such as rovers, UAVs or AUVs.

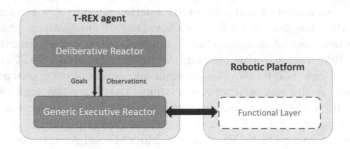

Fig. 1. An instance of the T-REX architecture with the Generic Executive Reactor (GER) as the manager of the execution predicates of the system.

3 Key Concepts and Definitions

The purpose of this section is to introduce to the reader the concepts and definitions of the T-REX architecture [12,19] required to understand the contribution of this paper, so it is out of the scope of this paper a detailed explanation of T-REX. Thus, T-REX is a goal-oriented system which represents the world of the robotic platform in state variables describing its evolution from a time perspective. A state variable (called timelines) is a collection of states (called predicates) which defines its temporal progress. These state variables are distributed into smaller modules called reactors, which in turn build a specific T-REX agent. Then, a T-REX agent is composed by a set of deliberative and executive reactors deployed to change the world through actions on their state variables in order to accomplish mission goals. The role of the T-REX agent is to ensure that all reactors interact concurrently so that they are informed of any state evolution that may impact them, being able to deliberate and dispatch appropriated plans. The T-REX architecture can be briefly summarized in the following statements:

- The current predicate of the state variables is pronounced through observations into the T-REX agent.
- The future predicate of the state variables is declared through goals.
- The communication among reactors is carried out via observations and goals of the state variables.
- Internal state variables are those which are controlled by the owner reactor. The owner reactor has sole responsibility to update them via observations and also to plan ahead on any goal state.
- External state variables describe world information to a reactor which does not control them but it needs the information to define its own internal state. It may be able to request changes via goals of these state variables to the owner reactor.

Additionally, our executive module, which it is known as an executive reactor in the T-REX architecture, identifies two kind of predicates:

- The execution predicate is required to be performed by the robotic platform to alter the status of its state variable, e.g., the *RobotBase*, which is the navigation module of the robotic platform, has the *GoingTo* predicate to indicate a moving action from one location to another. In this case, *GoingTo* needs to be executed on the robotic platform to perform the movement action.
- The static predicate does not need to be performed by the robotic platform. It represents the consequence after achieving the execution predicate. Our executive reactor uses them to monitor the robotic platform response, e.g., *RobotBase* uses the *GoingTo* execution predicate to move to a particular location, and it uses the *At* static predicate to represent the consequence, that is, being in a particular location.

4   The Generic Executive Reactor

The contribution of this paper is the *Generic Executive Reactor* (GER), a module designed for autonomous controllers based on the T-REX architecture. It is *Generic* because it can adapt itself to any robotic platform by stating global execution policies which can manage any execution routine. It is *Executive* because its role is to dispatch and monitor the execution predicates of its internal state variables to the functional layer of the robotic platform. Therefore, it provides an interface between the deliberative reactor and the functional layer without creating knowledge dependencies between them (see Fig. 1).

Despite of the previous aspects, GER is considered as a reactive reactor too, where the latency $\lambda = 0$ and the look-ahead $\pi = 1$ within the timing model of the T-REX application, i.e., it does not deliberate beyond the execution frontier. Then, attending to the T-REX notation [19], the GER dispatching window H_D can be defined as follows:

$$H_D(GER) = [\tau + \lambda, \tau + \lambda + \pi]$$
$$= [\tau, \tau + \pi] \rightarrow \lambda = 0, \pi = 1 \tag{1}$$

where τ is the execution frontier expressing the boundary between the past and the future.

4.1   Goal Dispatching

It is related to manage a goal over an internal execution cycle. GER follows a synchronous execution where it dispatches one-by-one the goals received by other reactors. This execution is managed by an internal clock of the T-REX agent. The general policy of GER is: to execute every goal individually without overlapping in the Robotic Platform (RP). The unit of time is a tick, defined in external units depending on the application design. Figure 2 represents a state diagram to describe the execution cycle for execution predicates (remember that static predicates do not need to be executed). It is explained in the following steps:

(1) The GER receives a new goal encapsulating an execution predicate from another reactor, and it is queued into an execution waiting list.
(2) GER waits until the last dispatched goal has been properly performed by the RP, i.e., the RP notified that the goal was achieved.
(3) The new goal has been sent to execution and GER remains in a waiting mode for an asynchronous reply from the RP.
(4) GER runs a monitoring routine to check the RP reply.
(5) GER updates the RP world on the T-REX agent. Finally, it notifies to the T-REX agent that the goal was executed, enabling the execution of the next goal.

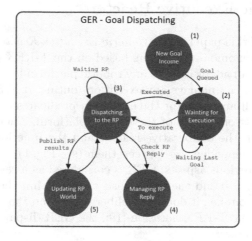

Fig. 2. A state diagram to describe the internal behaviour of GER when receives a goal with an execution predicate and GER dispatches their execution to the Robotic Platform (RP). The arrows represent the transitions among the different states represented as circles.

4.2   GER's Coordination into a T-REX Agent

The behaviour of GER inside a T-REX agent is described through a sequence diagram representing the interactions among reactors. Figure 3 shows a basic T-REX agent instance formed by a Deliberative Reactor and the GER. The interactions are described tick-by-tick as follows:

- (t): the Deliberative Reactor posts a new planned goal with an encapsulated execution predicate.

- *(t+1)*: the Deliberative Reactor posts a new planned goal with an static predicate representing the consequence of performing the action described by the previous execution predicate.
- *(t+n)*: the GER dispatches the goal (with the execution predicate) to the robotic platform. n represents any time so that, $t+n$ is between the minimum and maximum start time of the goal planned by the Deliberative Reactor.
- *(t+n+1)*: the GER notifies the T-REX agent that the goal is already in execution by posting its observation (updating the world) just a tick later.
- *(t+m)*: the robotic platform sends the consequence of performing the execution predicate as a reply. The GER checks that it is the reply expected and notifies to the T-REX agent of this fact. If not, just store the reply to be dispatched when it is needed. m is any time so that, $t + m$ is between the minimum and maximum end time of the goal planned by the Deliberative Reactor.

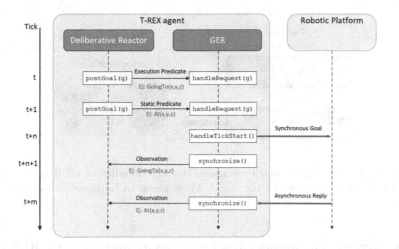

Fig. 3. A sequence diagram of a possible instance of T-REX formed by a Deliberative Reactor and GER. The arrows represent the interactions between the reactors managed by the T-REX agent. The two arrows on the right represent the interaction of the T-REX agent with a robotic platform. On the left, there is a temporal axis representing the tick in which each interaction happens.

The last two steps allows the GER to manage the start and end times of every planned goal.

5 Experimental Evaluation

The goal of the experimental evaluation of the GER is to demonstrate that T-REX instances embedding GER, such as GOAC, are able to adapt to any robotic platform. In this experiment, GER has been tested over a UAV and a UGV, but the same principles can be applied to any robotic platform.

For the experiments, we have set up a T-REX Agent formed by a deliberative reactor and an executive reactor (see Fig. 4) as a fully autonomous controller to control a simulated UAV (first experiment) and a real UGV (second experiment). The deliberative reactor is based on ESA APSI technology [4], deployed in the context of the GOAC project. The APSI reactor is responsible for the plan generation. The associated planner to the APSI reactor uses the Domain Definition Language (DDL.3) [4] to encode the components and physical constraints that describe the temporal behaviour of the robotic platform and the Problem Definition Language (PDL) [5] to specify planning and scheduling problems. The executive reactor is the GER, which is responsible of managing the coordination with the deliberative reactor and the functional layer of the robotic platforms as explained in Sect. 4. GER uses a XML configuration file to describe the robotic layout, which allows it to adjust to both robotic platforms.

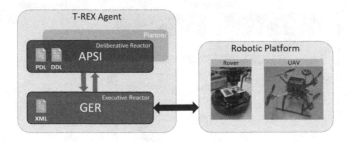

Fig. 4. The T-REX Agent used to evaluate the functionality of GER in a UAV and a real UGV. The behaviour of the real UAV is going to be simulated due to safety reasons.

The experimental evaluation consists of two instances of the T-REX Agent shown in Fig. 4. Each instance sets up the APSI reactor with the DDL and PDL, and the GER reactor with the configuration file of the specific robotic platform. The two experiments are briefly defined as follows:

- The UAV Simulation Experiment. The T-REX Agent is set up with two mission goals: to take a picture in a location and to perform a landing in another location. We simulate the real behaviour of the UAV shown in Fig. 4, because of the difficulties in regard of ensuring a proper safety level.
- The UGV Real Experiment. The T-REX Agent is set up with two mission goals: to take a picture in a location A and to take a picture in a location B. The robotic platform deployed (Fig. 4) has been the modified TurtleBot II[1] version presented in Ropero et al. [20].

---

[1] www.turtlebot.com.

The On-Ground Autonomy Test Environment (OGATE) [13] framework has been used to evaluate the GER performance. It is able to assess the behaviour of an autonomous control architecture managing a robotic platform, gathering relevant data of the operations involved and generating user-friendly reports.

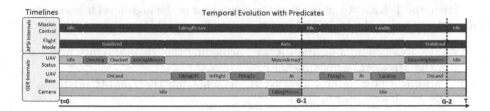

Fig. 5. The T-REX Agent solution to the UAV mission described in the first experiment. The timelines are deployed at the left square, and its predicates evolve to the right. The predicates of APSI are painted in black colour. The execution predicates of the GER are painted in dark gray and the static predicates in light gray. The execution frontier is represented by τ.

5.1   UAV Simulation Experiment

The first experiment deploys the T-REX Agent shown in Fig. 4 to control a simulated UAV in a specific mission.

Leaving aside the APSI reactor configuration, the GER setting is achieved through a XML configuration file in which there are defined every GER internal state variable (called timeline) (see Sect. 3) related to the UAV and their possible temporal states (called predicates). The internal UAV timelines of the GER are:

- *UAVStatus*: to manage the hardware status through the predicates:
    - *Idle*. Initial state.
    - *Checking*. Execution predicate to check the critical hardware components.
    - *Checked*. Static predicate.
    - *ArmingMotors*. Execution predicate to arm the motors.
    - *MotorsArmed*. Static predicate.
    - *DisarmingMotors*. Execution predicate to disarm the motors.
- *UAVBase*: to control the UAV navigation with the predicates:
    - *OnLand(x,y,z)*. Initial predicate.
    - *TakingOff(x,y,z)*. Execution predicate to take off on a specific location.
    - *InFlight(x,y,z)*. Static predicate.
    - *FlyingTo(x,y,z)*. Execution predicate to go to a specific location.
    - *At(x,y,z)*. Static predicate.
    - *Landing(x,y,z)*. Execution predicate to land on a specific location.
- *Camera*: to control the camera with the predicates:
    - *Idle*. Initial predicate.
    - *TakingPicture(pic,x,y,z)*. Execution predicate to take a picture on a specific location.

Additionally, the *MissionControl* timeline is used by the APSI reactor as internal timeline to plan the high-level mission goals and send low-level goals to the GER internal timelines. Also, the *FlightMode* is an APSI internal timeline to show the UAV flight mode at any time. The GER internal timelines are externals for APSI.

Then, the T-REX Agent requires the statement of the high-level mission goals (named as G-id). The high-level mission goals for the UAV are the following:

G-1. Take a picture in a location A, i.e., achieving the *TakingPicture* predicate in the *MissionControl* timeline.

G-2. Perform a landing in a location B, or achieving the *LandAt* predicate in the *MissionControl* timeline.

The solution obtained by the T-REX Agent for the high-level mission goals is presented as shows Fig. 5. The issue to address in this experiment is the synchronous execution policy of the GER reactor. We can observe that every GER internal timeline has executed its predicates following the state diagram shown in Fig. 2 (any goal is executed until the last goal was successfully performed). The parallel execution of various execution predicates is forbidden in the GER. When an execution predicate has been performed by the robotic platform, the GER publishes the related static predicate into the T-REX agent, to notify to the APSI reactor that the predicate has been achieved as shows the sequence diagram in Fig. 3.

5.2   UGV Real Experiment

The second experiment sets up the T-REX Agent (Fig. 4) to control a real UGV in a controlled environment.

Following the same guidelines as in the previous experiment, the GER requires a XML configuration file in which it is defined every GER internal timeline of the UGV and their temporal states. The internal UGV timelines of GER are:

- *Communication*: to manage the communication with the ground control station through the predicates:
    - *Idle*. Initial state.
    - *Communicating(pic)*. Execution predicate to communicate a picture.
- *PanTilt*: to control the angle of the camera with the predicates:
    - *PointintAt(pan_angle,tilt_angle)*. Initial predicate.
    - *MovingTo(pan_angle,tilt_angle)*. Execution predicate to position the camera.
- *RobotBase*: to control the UGV navigation with the predicates:
    - *At(x,y)*. Initial predicate.
    - *GoingTo(x,y)*. Execution predicate to go to a specific location.
- *Camera*: to control the camera with the predicates:
    - *Idle*. Initial predicate.

– *TakingPicture(pic,x,y,pan_angle,tilt_angle)*. Execution predicate to take a picture on a specific location.

Additionally, as in the first experiment, *MissionControl* is the APSI internal timeline to plan the high-level mission goals and send low-level goals to the GER internal timelines. The GER internal timelines are externals for APSI.

Then, the high-level goals of the UGV mission for this experiment are the following:

G-1. Take a picture in a location A, or achieving the *TakingPicture* predicate in *MissionControl*.
G-2. Take a picture in a location B, or achieving another *TakingPicture* predicate (its attributes, such as the location B, denote a different predicate) in *MissionControl*.

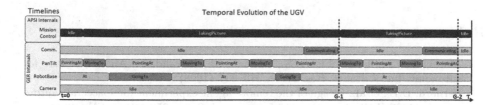

Fig. 6. The T-REX Agent solution to the UGV mission described in the second experiment. The timelines are deployed at the left square, and its predicates evolve to the right. The predicates of APSI are painted in black colour. The execution predicates of GER are painted in dark gray and the static predicates in light gray. The execution frontier is represented by τ.

The solution to the UGV mission is presented in Fig. 6. We can appreciate that, as we demonstrated in the UAV experiment, GER reactor keeps following the synchronous execution policy. This experiment allow us to highlight the clear difference between the two GER configurations. The UGV navigation module (*RobotBase*) requires only two predicates to describe every possible state of its temporal evolution in the navigation process (*GoingTo* and *At*). However, the UAV navigation module requires six predicates (*FlyingTo*, *At*, *TakingOff*, *InFlight*, *OnLand*, *Landing*). Despite the difference, the GER is able to adapt to the UGV and UAV with only the configuration file. This GER capability allows the T-REX architecture to abstract the execution layer and to design complex T-REX agents focused on deliberative issues.

6   Conclusions

In this paper we have presented the GER, a generic executive operator based on T-REX which gives to a T-REX instance the ability to adapt to any robotic domain. Therefore, it provides an abstraction layer for future T-REX architectures which are focused on other high-level tasks such as deliberative or coordination issues. The GER module has the capability of managing a synchronous execution for any robotic platform. The results show that the executive can handle the execution of UGV and UAV goals. In spite of this results, there are relevant issues which need to be addressed, such as the implementation of a fail safe mode able to manage in real-time any contingency. Maybe, some deliberative capabilities aiming to deterministically react to opportunistic events.

Acknowledgements. The authors want to thank Dr. David F. Barrero for the fruitful discussions. The work is supported by the UAH project 2016/00351/001.

References

1. Alami, R., Chatila, R., Fleury, S., Ghallab, M., Ingrand, F.: An architecture for autonomy. Int. J. Robot. Res. **17**(4), 315–337 (1998)
2. Bernard, D.E., et al.: Design of the remote agent experiment for spacecraft autonomy. In: 1998 IEEE Aerospace Conference, vol. 2, pp. 259–281. IEEE (1998)
3. Ceballos, A., et al.: A goal-oriented autonomous controller for space exploration. In: ASTRA, p. 11 (2011)
4. Cesta, A., Cortellessa, G., Fratini, S., Oddi, A.: Developing an end-to-end planning application from a timeline representation framework. In: IAAI (2009)
5. Cesta, A., Oddi, A.: Ddl. 1: a formal description of a constraint representation language for physical domains. New directions in AI planning, pp. 341–352 (1996)
6. Doherty, P.: Advanced research with autonomous unmanned aerial vehicles. In: KR, pp. 731–732 (2004)
7. Doherty, P., Kvarnström, J., Heintz, F.: A temporal logic-based planning and execution monitoring framework for unmanned aircraft systems. Auton. Agent. Multi-Agent Syst. **19**(3), 332–377 (2009)
8. Gat, E.: Integrating planning and reacting in a heterogeneous asynchronous architecture for controlling real-world mobile robots. In: AAAI, pp. 809–815 (1992)
9. Gat, E., Bonnasso, R.P.: On three-layer architectures. Artif. Intell. Mobile Robot. **195**, 210 (1998)
10. Ingrand, F., Ghallab, M.: Deliberation for autonomous robots: a survey. Artif. Intell. **247**, 10–44 (2017)
11. Ingrand, F., Lacroix, S., Lemai-Chenevier, S., Py, F.: Decisional autonomy of planetary rovers. J. Field Robotic. **24**(7), 559–580 (2007)
12. McGann, C., Py, F., Rajan, K., Thomas, H., Henthorn, R., McEwen, R.: A deliberative architecture for AUV control. In: IEEE International Conference on Robotics and Automation ICRA 2008, pp. 1049–1054. IEEE (2008)
13. Muñoz, P., Cesta, A., Orlandini, A., R-Moreno, M.D.: First steps on an on-ground autonomy test environment. In: 2014 IEEE International Conference on Space Mission Challenges for Information Technology (SMC-IT), pp. 30–37. IEEE (2014)

14. Munoz, P., R-Moreno, M.D.: Model-based architecture on the ESA 3DROV simulator. In: Policella, N., Onder, N. (ed.), p. 6 (2013)
15. Muscettola, N., Dorais, G.A., Fry, C., Levinson, R., Plaunt, C.: IDEA: planning at the core of autonomous reactive agents (2002)
16. Myers, K.L.: A procedural knowledge approach to task-level control. In: AIPS, pp. 158–165 (1996)
17. Nilsson, N.: Teleo-reactive programs for agent control. Journal of artificial intelligence research (1994)
18. Pell, B., et al.: A hybrid procedural/deductive executive for autonomous spacecraft. In: Proceedings of the Second International Conference on Autonomous Agents, pp. 369–376. ACM (1998)
19. Rajan, K., Py, F.: T-REX: partitioned inference for AUV mission control. Further advances in unmanned marine vehicles. The Institution of Engineering and Technology (IET), pp. 171–199 (2012)
20. Ropero, F., Vaquerizo, D., Muñoz, P., R-Moreno, M.D.: An advanced teleassistance system to improve life quality in the elderly. In: Benferhat, S., Tabia, K., Ali, M. (eds.) IEA/AIE 2017. LNCS (LNAI), vol. 10350, pp. 533–542. Springer, Cham (2017). https://doi.org/10.1007/978-3-319-60042-0_59
21. Verma, V., Jónsson, A., Pasareanu, C., Iatauro, M.: Universal-executive and plexil: engine and language for robust spacecraft control and operations. In: Space 2006, p. 7449 (2006)

Tuning the Discount Factor in Order to Reach Average Optimality on Deterministic MDPs

Filipo Studzinski Perotto[✉] and Laurent Vercouter

Normandy University / INSA / LITIS, Rouen, France
{filipo.perotto,laurent.vercouter}@litislab.fr

Abstract. Considering Markovian Decision Processes (MDPs), the meaning of an optimal policy depends on the optimality criterion chosen. The most common approach is to define the optimal policy as the one that maximizes the sum of discounted rewards. The intuitive alternative is to maximize the average reward per step. The former has strong convergence guarantees but suffers from the dependency on a discount factor. The latter has the additional inconvenience of being insensitive to different policies with equivalent average. This paper analyzes the impact of such different criteria on a series of experiments, and then provides a threshold for the discount factor in order to ensure average optimality for discounted-optimal policies in the deterministic case.

Keywords: Average dynamic programming
Sensitive dynamic programming · Reinforcement learning
Markovian decision process

1 Introduction

Dynamic Programming (DP) refers to a set of algorithms that can efficiently compute optimal policies for *Markovian Decision Processes* (MDPs), providing essential foundations for *Reinforcement Learning* (RL) methods [22,26]. DP and RL algorithms are fundamentally based on *discounted-optimality*. In this setting, an optimal policy maximizes the sum of discounted rewards over time using a discount factor γ.

When considering infinite time-horizon, the use of discounted rewards constitutes an important key on guarantying polynomial time convergence for such methods [2]. However, in many domains, the use of a discount factor does not present any relation to the optimization problem itself. Typically, when facing recurrent MDPs (where terminal states do not exist), discounting future rewards in favor of immediate rewards can introduce a kind of "distortion" on the real utility of a policy of actions [17,21,27].

The *crawling robot* problem [29] offers an illustrative example of such issue. The robot is endowed with a single articulated arm, and some of its movements cause the displacement of the robot. The objective is finding the optimal cyclical sequence of actions in order to make the robot walk forward as fast as possible. Rewards correspond to immediate progressions. However, depending on the discount factor, a discounted-optimal policy can be unable to reach the maximum velocity. In other words, an intuitively optimal behavior can be seen as sub-optimal under the discounted framework. In fact, the robot reaches its maximum speed when it enters in the recurrent cycle of states that offers the highest average displacement per step. Other examples of this issue are given in [17]. For such scenarios, maximizing the average reward per step is, in some sense, more appropriate, but a key limitation of such approach is that *average-optimality* cannot distinguish among policies which have the same recurrent average reward per step, but which are not necessarily equivalent in terms of transient rewards [19].

The discussion about optimality is not new [4,8,14], and is summarized in Sect. 2. In practice, the discounted framework had been largely preferred. Such algorithms are easier to implement, and the polynomial convergence bounds are guaranteed for the general case [23,34].

In fact, if the discount factor γ is sufficiently high, *discounted-optimal* policies become also *average-optimal*. How high γ needs to be depends on each particular setting (topology and rewards), and cannot be calculated beforehand. For that reason, it is a hard-to-tune parameter. Without any other information, such average optimality is only guaranteed in the limit when $\gamma \to 1$ [3,4,12]. However, the higher the discount factor, the slower the convergence of iterative methods. When γ approaches 1, the necessary time for convergence approaches ∞ [34].

How often are discounted-optimal policies not average-optimal? The first contribution of this paper is an analysis on the difference between discounted-optimality and average-optimality in terms of total reward loss on the long run depending on how γ is tuned. Using a set of experiments with random MDPs we show that the impact of the use of too low γ values is not negligible.

How can the discount factor be optimally tuned in practice? The second contribution of this paper is a method for calculating a threshold for γ in order to ensure average-optimality to discounted-optimal policies. In this paper, as it consists on a first approach to the problem, only deterministic MDPs will be considered.

The rest of the paper is organized as follows. Section 2 reviews related concepts and methods on computational sequential decision-making. Section 3 presents our contributions: an analysis about the impact in terms of reward loss on choosing either discounted or average optimality, and the deduction of a formula for identifying average-optimal discount factors. Section 4 concludes the paper.

2 Background: Markovian Decision Processes

Markovian Decision Processes (MDPs) are in the center of a widely-used framework for approaching *automated control, sequential decision-making, planning,* and *computational reinforcement learning* problems [21,22,25,26,30,32].

An MDP works like a discrete stochastic finite state machine: at each time step the machine is in some state s, the agent observes that state and interacts with the process by choosing some action a to perform, then the machine changes into a new state s' and gives the agent a corresponding reward r.

An MDP can be defined as a set $\mathcal{M} = \{S, A, T, R\}$ in the form:

$$\mathcal{M} = \begin{cases} S = \{s_1, s_2, ..., s_n\} & \text{is the finite set of states} \\ A = \{a_1, a_2, ..., a_m\} & \text{is the finite set of actions} \\ T = \Pr(s'|s, a) & \text{is the transition function} \\ R = \Pr(r|s, a, s') & \text{is the reward function} \end{cases}$$

where $n = |S|$ is the number of states, and $m = |A|$ is the number of actions.

The transition function T defines the system dynamics by determining the next state s' given the current state s and the executed action a. The reward function R defines the immediate reward $r \in \mathbb{R}$ after moving from state s to s' with action a. *Deterministic MDPs* (D-MDPs) constitute the particular set of MDPs where the transitions are deterministic, in the form $T : S \times A \rightarrow S$.

Solving an MDP means finding a policy of actions that maximizes the rewards received by the agent, according to a given optimality criterion and a given time-horizon. The optimality criterion is defined by an utility function U. An optimal policy π^* is a policy that cannot be improved:

$$U(s, \pi^*) \geq U(s, \pi), \forall s \in S, \forall \pi \in \Pi \tag{1}$$

where $U(s, \pi)$ is the utility of following the policy π from the state s.

A deterministic stationary policy π is a mapping between states and actions in the form $\pi : S \rightarrow A$. The number of such policies contained in Π, the set of possible policies, is exponential, and corresponds to $|\Pi| = m^n$.

2.1 Discounted Optimality

When the stopping time h is finite and known, a simple solution consists in evaluating policies by estimating their *total rewards*. The utility function U is then equivalent to Z, the (undiscounted) sum of expected rewards:

$$Z_h(s, \pi) = \sum_{t=1}^{h} R_t(s, \pi) \tag{2}$$

where $R_t(s, \pi)$ corresponds to the expected reward in time t starting from state s and following policy π. In that case an exact optimal policy can be found through *backward recursion* [2] in polynomial time, $\mathcal{O}(nmh)$. However, such solution cannot be applied when the time-horizon is infinite, unbounded or unknown.

The standard approach to the infinite horizon setting consists in applying a *discount factor* $\{\gamma \in \mathbb{R} \mid 0 < \gamma < 1\}$ that reduces the weight of future rewards compared to immediate rewards in the sum. Such sum is always finite, which guarantees the convergence of iterative methods to an optimal solution [22, 32].

The sum of discounted rewards $V_\gamma(s, \pi)$, starting in a given state s, following a given policy π, and for a given discount factor γ, is:

$$V_\gamma(s, \pi) = \lim_{h \to \infty} \sum_{t=1}^{h} \gamma^{t-1} R_t(s, \pi) \tag{3}$$

Tuning the discount factor implies a trade-off: the higher γ is (closer to 1), the better the chances of ensuring average optimality for discounted-optimal policies, but the bigger the computational costs for calculating the solution. The convergence time bound to compute discounted-optimal policies using iterative methods increases with rate $\mathcal{O}(\frac{1}{1-\gamma} \log \frac{1}{1-\gamma})$ [24,34]

Typical values of γ in the literature are 0.9 and 0.99. The inconvenience of using such generic suggestions is that, in certain circumstances, when γ is too low, discounted-optimality can lead the agent to a sub-optimal behavior in terms of average reward. We would like to call such phenomenon a "discount trap".

2.2 Average (or Gain) Optimality

In many domains, there is no grounded interpretation for the discount factor γ. In addition, the value corresponding to the sum of discounted rewards is less human readable (i.e. harder to interpret) than the average reward per step. Moreover, in recurrent domains (where later rewards are as important as earlier rewards) the use of low values of γ can "distort" the utility of some sequence of actions. For such reasons, maximizing the average reward received per time step can be preferable [9,28]. The *average reward* over an infinite time-horizon, called *gain*, of a policy π starting on state s, is:

$$G(s, \pi) = \lim_{h \to \infty} \frac{1}{h} \sum_{t=1}^{h} R_t(s, \pi) \tag{4}$$

The convenience of *average-optimality* compared to *discounted-optimality* can be observed regarding the MDPs shown in Fig. 1. On both problems, depending on the discount factor, the discounted-best policy can correspond to a clearly worse solution on the long run.

Considering unichain MDPs running over an infinite time-horizon, the average reward (or gain) of a given policy π converges to a single value g independently of the starting state [22], i.e. $G(s, \pi) = g, \forall s \in S$. Considering multichain MDPs, there is a convergent gain for each communicant subset of states (i.e. for each recurrent class within the process). The major drawback of average-optimal methods is that they have weaker convergence guarantees compared to discounted methods, even with the strong constraint of unichainess [11]. Worse yet, they are insensitive for distinguishing different policies with same average reward per step [15].

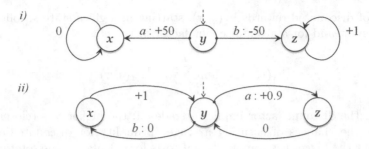

Fig. 1. In (i), there is a unique decision to be taken, on the middle state y. The gain of choosing the action a is $G(y, a) = 0$. It corresponds to the reward on the loop of the recurrent left state x. The gain of choosing the action b is $G(y, b) = +1$. It corresponds to the reward on the loop of the recurrent right state z. Because $G(y, b) > G(y, a)$, the action b constitutes the *average-optimal* policy. The action a earns a unique and immediate positive reward of 50 in time $t = 1$. At the same time, the action b loses 50, but then earns an additional reward of $+1$ per each subsequent time-step. In time $t = 101$, the policy b "reaches" the policy a, both having accumulated the same total rewards $Z_{101}(y, a) = Z_{101}(y, b) = +50$. Then, after 101 execution steps, b becomes better than a up to the infinity. So, considering an unbounded time-horizon (where the stopping time h of the process is likely to be greater than 100), the policy b would be preferred. However, given that $V_{0.99}(y, a) = +50$ and $V_{0.99}(y, b) = +49$, the discounted-optimal policy for any discount factor $\gamma \leq 0.99$ is a. In (ii), the average of the policy starting on the middle state y and choosing the action a is $G(y, a) = +0.45$ (the average per step on the cycle $\{y, z\}$, on the right). The action b presents $G(y, b) = +0.5$ (the average per step on the cycle $\{y, x\}$, on the left) and is *gain-optimal*. However, given that $V_{0.9}(y, a) = V_{0.9}(y, b) \approx 4.737$, the discounted-optimal policy for any discount factor $\gamma < 0.9$ is a. In fact b becomes definitely better (i.e. get better total rewards) than a after 20 execution steps and up to the infinity.

2.3   Sensitive (or Blackwell) Optimality

For a same MDP there may be several *average-optimal* policies which are not necessarily equivalent. That is the case regarding the examples in Fig. 2. On both cases, two possible policies converge to a common average reward as time approaches infinity. They are, for that reason, indistinguishable from an average reward point of view.

The problem is that rewards obtained in the transient path toward the recurrent states disappear on the infinite averaging. In the same way, the position of each reward inside a sequence of cyclical rewards also disappears. However, such differences are important when considering an unbounded (but finite) time-horizon. Even though the gain of a policy π is mathematically independent of the starting state s on the infinite, the total expected reward in a given time h is not, i.e. $G(s, \pi) \neq \frac{1}{h} Z_h(s, \pi)$. Such differences are generally called *bias* [15,17,19,28].

In fact, for a given MDP, there is a discount factor γ^* from which the optimal policies do not change [3]. Such common "unanimous" optimal policies correspond to a *sensitive-optimality* [18,31].

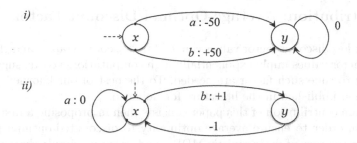

Fig. 2. In (*i*), the gain of both possible policies is equivalent, $G(x,a) = G(x,b) = G(y) = 0$, but their initial steps (in $t = 1$) are not equivalently rewarded, $R_1(x,a) = -50$ and $R_1(x,b) = +50$. In this case, both policies a and b are *average-optimal*, but b offers a better transient reward and would be preferred over a. In fact, the total rewards accumulated by the policy b are greater than the rewards accumulated by a after the first step, i.e. $Z_h(x,b) > Z_h(x,a), \forall h \in \mathbb{Z} \mid h \geq 1$. In (*ii*), the gain of both possible policies is equivalent, $G(x,a) = G(x,b) = 0$, but the policy b presents a bigger total reward compared to a every time when t is odd. Then $Z_h(x,b) \geq Z_h(x,a), \forall h \in \mathbb{Z}^+$, and for such reason, b would be the preferred policy.

2.4 Dynamic Programming

Dynamic Programming (DP) refers to iterative optimization methods which can be used to efficiently compute optimal policies of Markovian Decision Processes (MDPs) when a model is given [2,22]. *Value-Iteration* (VI) [1] and *Policy-Iteration* (PI) [13] are the two fundamental and widely used DP algorithms for infinite time-horizon MDPs. It had been demonstrated that PI converges at least as quickly as VI [21], and, in practice, PI has been shown to be most effective [16].

There is a significant research effort for understanding the complexity of PI. The demonstration of its tight upper and lower bounds is still an open problem. Considering stochastic MDPs under discounted optimality, with a fixed discount rate $0 \leq \gamma < 1$, PI is proved to be *strongly polynomial* [10,23,34], i.e. the number of operations required to compute an optimal policy has an upper bound that is polynomial in the number of state-action pairs. Unfortunately, the convergence time increases with rate $\mathcal{O}(\frac{1}{1-\gamma} \log \frac{1}{1-\gamma})$ [24,34]. It constitutes a major impediment for using high discount factors ($\gamma \to 1$) in practice.

Typically, average optimization is a more difficult problem than discounted optimization [7]. PI can need an exponential number of iterations under average-optimality for stochastic MDPs in the general case [6]. In contrast, a deterministic MDP under average-optimality can be solved in strongly polynomial-time, $\mathcal{O}(n^2m)$ [11,20] as the well-known *Minimum-Mean-Cost-Cycle* problem. Experimental studies suggest that PI works very efficiently in this context [5]. Recent advances in average optimisation have been proposed in [33].

3   Contribution: Average-Optimal Discount Factor

Given that low discount factor values can lead to "discount traps", and that high discount factor values imply exponentially high computational costs, suggestions about how to tune such factor are needed. To the best of our knowledge, there is no method published in the literature for doing so.

The main contribution of this paper consists then in proposing a first threshold for γ in order to ensure average optimality to discounted-optimal policies, considering the case of deterministic MDPs, and based on simple characteristics of the target process. It means deducing a value for γ ensuring that discounted-optimal policies will correspond to average-optimal policies for any D-MDP which fits the given characteristics.

3.1   Tuning the Discount Factor

Let a *discount trap* be characterized by the situation where, for a given MDP $\mathcal{M}$, and for a given discount factor γ, there is a state s from where the gain of discounted-optimal policies is smaller than the gain of average-optimal policies. Formally, a *discount trap* exists if:

$$\exists \pi \in \Pi, \exists s \in S \begin{cases} V_\gamma(s, \pi^*) \geq V_\gamma(s, \pi) \\ G(s, \pi^*) < G(s, \pi) \end{cases} \tag{5}$$

Let a *family* $\mathcal{F}$ of deterministic MDPs be the set of all possible D-MDPs presenting the following identical characteristics:

$$\mathcal{F} = \begin{cases} n = |S| & \text{number of states} \\ m = |A| & \text{number of actions} \\ r_{\min} \in \mathbb{R} & \text{worst immediate reward value} \\ r_{\max} \in \mathbb{R} & \text{best immediate reward value} \\ \delta \in \mathbb{R}^+ & \text{the smallest non-zero immediate reward difference} \\ \Delta = r_{\max} - r_{\min} & \text{the range of the reward support} \end{cases}$$

In order to avoid discount traps, the discount factor must be tuned over a certain threshold. It is known that there exists an optimal discount factor γ^* from where the optimal policies do not change [3,12]. Such value can be called the *sensitive-optimal* discount factor. γ is guaranteed to be over such threshold on the limit when it approaches 1, i.e. $\lim \gamma \to 1 \implies \gamma > \gamma^*$. Another threshold, generally smaller than γ^*, ensures that discounted-optimal policies are also average-optimal. We would like to call it the *average-optimal* discount factor, and denote it $\gamma^{\bowtie}$.

When looking for the average-optimal discount factor $\gamma^{\bowtie}$ for a given family of D-MDPs $\mathcal{F}$, we must look for the worst case within the family, i.e. the process $\mathcal{M} \in \mathcal{F}$ which requires the highest value of γ to ensure average-optimality for discounted-optimal policies.

3.2   Deterministic Worst Case

Let an *optimal loop* L within a given D-MDP $\mathcal{M}$ be a cycle over a single state s, with some action a, presenting the maximum possible reward $r_{\max}$. Let an *almost optimal cycle* C be a cycle containing a subset of states, having a period $|C|$ that can vary from 1 (a single state) to $n - 1$, and presenting a sequence of $|C| - 1$ maximum rewards $r_{\max}$ followed by an almost maximum reward $r_{\max} - \delta$. Let a *maximally penalizing path* W be a path having a length $|W|$ that can vary from 1 (a single step) to $n - 1$, and presenting the worst possible reward $r_{\min}$ on every step. When such 3 structures appear connected within a D-MDP, we discover a graph topology similar to the cases presented in Fig. 3.

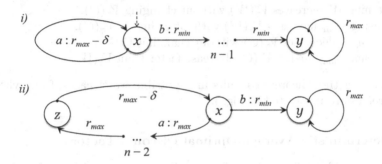

Fig. 3. In (i), the recurrent optimal loop on the state y can be reached by choosing the action b on state x. It offers a better gain than the almost optimal cycle reached with the action a in x, i.e. $G(x, b) = G(y) = R(y) = r_{\max} > G(x, a) = R(x, a) = r_{\max} - \delta$. However, a long and hardly penalizing transient path must be traversed in order to get from x to y. Such path counts the maximum possible distance between x and y, and is rewarded with the worst possible reward $r_{\min}$ at each step. The period of the almost optimal cycle is 1 (a loop), and the size of the maximally penalizing path is $n - 1$. **In (ii),** the almost optimal cycle constitutes the biggest possible cycle disjoint from the optimal loop in the MDP. Its period is $n - 1$, which reduces the length of the path to 1. However, the gain difference is also smaller, $G(x, b) = r_{\max} > G(x, a) = r_{\max} - \frac{\delta}{n-1}$. Such are the two intuitively possible worst situations within a given MDP family for defining an average-optimal discount factor.

The infinite discounted sum of rewards on the almost optimal cycle C, denoted $V_\gamma(C)$, can be calculated by the difference between the infinite discounted sum of $r_{\max}$ and the infinite discounted sum of δ discounted by its position in the cycle:

$$V_\gamma(C) = \frac{r_{\max}}{1 - \gamma} - \frac{\gamma^{|C|-1}\delta}{1 - \gamma^{|C|}} \tag{6}$$

The infinite discounted sum of rewards on the path W followed by the loop L, denoted $V_\gamma(W)$, corresponds to the finite discounted sum of r_{min} on the maximally penalizing path plus the infinite discounted sum of r_{max} on the optimal loop discounted by the size of the path:

$$V_\gamma(W) = \frac{r_{min}(1 - \gamma^{|W|})}{1 - \gamma} + \frac{r_{max}\gamma^{|W|}}{1 - \gamma} \qquad (7)$$

When the discount factor is average-optimal, there is no discount trap.

Theorem 1. *Let $\mathcal{F}$ be a family of D-MDPs, corresponding to the set of processes presenting identical characteristics $n, m, r_{min}, r_{max}, \delta, \Delta$. The set of D-MDPs within such family which requires the highest average-optimal discount factor is characterized by: (i) an almost optimal cycle C disjoint from (ii) an optimal loop L, both separated by a unique (iii) maximally penalizing path W.*

The Theorem 1 necessarily holds because:

1. Shortening W increases $V_\gamma(W)$ without changing $V_\gamma(C)$.
2. Increasing r_{min} increases $V_\gamma(W)$ without changing $V_\gamma(C)$.
3. Increasing δ decreases $V_\gamma(C)$ without changing $V_\gamma(W)$.
4. Decreasing r_{max} makes $V_\gamma(C)$ decrease faster than $V_\gamma(W)$.

Developing the Theorem 1 results in n possible worst cases, from where the two extremes are illustrated in Fig. 3.

3.3   Deterministic Average-Optimal Discount Factor

In order to avoid a "discount trap", the utility of staying in an *almost optimal cycle* must be worse than the utility of traveling across all the states of the *maximally penalizing path* to the *optimal loop*. In the precedent section, two candidate worst cases have been presented. In this section the formula for an optimal discount factor is deduced for both examples. Such procedure allows to confirm what is effectively the worst case. An optimal discount factor for such worst case must necessarily be an optimal discount factor for any other case within the same MDP family. Such formulas can be deduced by simply developing the statement:

$$\gamma > \gamma^\bowtie \implies V_\gamma(W) > V_\gamma(C) \qquad (8)$$

Firstly, we consider the case presented in Fig. 3 (i), which contains a long penalizing path. The value of the average-optimal discount factor $\gamma^\bowtie$ from which the discounted-optimal policies are also average-optimal for such D-MDP is:

$$V_\gamma(x, b) > V_\gamma(x, a)$$

$$\implies \quad \sum_{i=0}^{n-2} \gamma^i r_{\min} + \sum_{i=n-1}^{\infty} \gamma^i r_{\max} > \sum_{i=0}^{\infty} \gamma^i (r_{\max} - \delta)$$

$$\implies \quad \frac{(1 - \gamma^{n-1}) r_{\min}}{1 - \gamma} + \frac{\gamma^{n-1} r_{\max}}{1 - \gamma} > \frac{r_{\max} - \delta}{1 - \gamma}$$

$$\implies \quad r_{\min} - \gamma^{n-1} r_{\min} + \gamma^{n-1} r_{\max} > r_{\max} - \delta$$

$$\implies \quad \gamma^{n-1} r_{\max} - \gamma^{n-1} r_{\min} > r_{\max} - r_{\min} - \delta$$

$$\implies \quad \gamma^{n-1} \Delta > \Delta - \delta$$

$$\implies \quad \gamma > \sqrt[n-1]{1 - \frac{\delta}{\Delta}}$$

Then we consider the case presented in Fig. 3 (*ii*), which contains a short penalizing path. The value of the average-optimal discount factor $\gamma^{\bowtie}$ from which the discounted-optimal policies are also average-optimal for such D-MDP is:

$$V_\gamma(x, b) > V_\gamma(x, a)$$

$$\implies \quad r_{\min} + \gamma V_\gamma(y) > V_\gamma(y) - \frac{\gamma^{n-2} \delta}{1 - \gamma^{n-1}}$$

$$\implies \quad V_\gamma(y) - r_{\max} + r_{\min} > V_\gamma(y) - \frac{\gamma^{n-2} \delta}{1 - \gamma^{n-1}}$$

$$\implies \quad -r_{\max} + r_{\min} > -\frac{\gamma^{n-2} \delta}{1 - \gamma^{n-1}}$$

$$\implies \quad \frac{\gamma^{n-2} \delta}{1 - \gamma^{n-1}} > \Delta$$

$$\implies \quad \gamma^{n-2} \delta > \Delta (1 - \gamma^{n-1})$$

$$\implies \quad \gamma^{n-2} > \frac{-\delta \pm \sqrt{\delta^2 + 4\Delta^2}}{2\Delta}$$

$$\implies \quad \gamma > \sqrt[n-2]{\frac{-\delta + \sqrt{\delta^2 + 4\Delta^2}}{2\Delta}}$$

Effectively, the second case is the worst case, which can be algebraically confirmed:

$$\sqrt[n-2]{\frac{-\delta + \sqrt{\delta^2 + 4\Delta^2}}{2\Delta}} > \sqrt[n-1]{1 - \frac{\delta}{\Delta}}$$

$$\implies \left(\frac{-\delta + \sqrt{\delta^2 + 4\Delta^2}}{2\Delta}\right)^2 > 1 - \frac{\delta}{\Delta}$$

$$\implies \frac{2\delta^2 - 2\delta\sqrt{\delta^2 + 4\Delta^2} + 4\Delta^2}{4\Delta^2} > 1 - \frac{\delta}{\Delta}$$

$$\implies \frac{2\delta^2 - 2\delta\sqrt{\delta^2 + 4\Delta^2}}{4\Delta^2} > -\frac{\delta}{\Delta}$$

$$\implies 2\delta^2 - 2\delta\sqrt{\delta^2 + 4\Delta^2} > -4\Delta\delta$$

$$\implies \delta - \sqrt{\delta^2 + 4\Delta^2} > -2\Delta$$

$$\implies \delta - \sqrt{\delta^2 + 4k^2\delta^2} > -2k\delta$$

$$\implies k > 0$$

$$\implies \frac{\Delta}{\delta} > 0$$

Hence, the formula for calculating the optimal discount factor is:

$$\gamma^{\bowtie} = \sqrt[n-2]{\frac{-\delta + \sqrt{\delta^2 + 4\Delta^2}}{2\Delta}} \tag{9}$$

Figure 4 plots the function $\gamma^{\bowtie}$ for two different settings. Parameter i indicates the number of states, $n = i$, and the two different series represent reward granularity $\delta = 1/i$ and $\delta = 1$ (binary rewards).

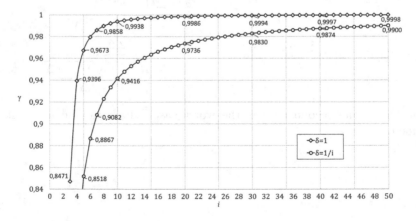

Fig. 4. The average-optimal discount factor for $n = i$ and reward support in $[0, 1]$. The two different series represent reward granularity $\delta = 1/i$ and $\delta = 1$ (Bernoulli).

3.4   Discount Trap Frequency

The choice of the optimality criterion has an impact on the calculated optimal policies. When using the discounted framework, if the discount factor γ is not sufficiently high, discounted-optimal policies could not correspond to gain-optimal policies, and it means a worst performance in terms of total rewards in the long run. In order to be able to measure the impact of such choice, we made a series of experiments, verifying how often a "discount trap" is detected.

Each experiment consists in generating 10000 random D-MDPs for a given setting (or family) i, varying the number of states $n = i$ and the reward granularity $\delta = 1/i$. It means that the MDP size and the reward granularity are both gradually incremented. The number of actions is fixed to $m = 2$, as well as the minimum reward $r_{min} = 0$ and the maximum reward $r_{max} = 1$. We make the parameter i vary from 2 to 50. The results presented in Fig. 5 confirm that, for standard "naive" values of γ, like 0.9 and 0.99, the frequency of "discount traps" is not negligible, even for such small MDPs.

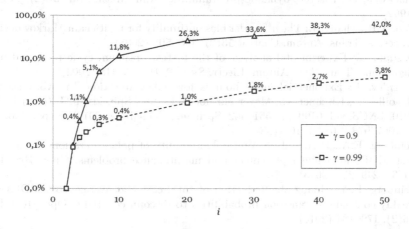

Fig. 5. The frequency of discount traps, when the discounted-optimal policy is not gain-optimal, considering $\gamma = 0.9$ and $\gamma = 0.99$. The parameter i indicates the number of states $n = i$ and the reward granularity $\delta = 1/i$.

4   Conclusion

Using a set of experiences with randomly generated MDPs, we demonstrated that the occurrence of *discount traps*, inherent to all mechanisms that calculate utility functions using a discount factor, can cause sub-optimal behaviors on several recurrent MDPs in terms of total (undiscounted) rewards, and can be observed more often than usually suspected. In our experiments, we show that the use of "naive" but classical values for γ can result in discounted-optimal policies which are not average-optimal in 40% of the simulations when $\gamma = 0.9$, and almost 4% when $\gamma = 0.99$, which is far from being negligible.

In this paper, a formula for calculating an average-optimal discount factor is deduced, given the target family of deterministic MDPs characterized by n (the number of states), $r_{\max}$ and $r_{\min}$ (the reward bounds), and δ (the "reward granularity", equivalent to the smallest difference between any two rewards into the reward function). It represents an upper bound that could be improved by taking other characteristics into account. This paper was limited to deterministic MDPs. The next step of the work is understanding how such γ threshold can be defined on the stochastic case.

References

1. Bellman, R.: Dynamic Programming. Princeton University Press, Princeton (1957)
2. Bertsekas, D.P.: Dynamic Programming and Optimal Control, 3rd edn. Athena Scientific, Belmont (2005)
3. Blackwell, D.: Discrete dynamic programming. Ann. Math. Stat. **33**(2), 719–726 (1962)
4. Cao, X.R., Zhang, J.: The nth-order bias optimality for multichain Markov decision processes. Trans. Autom. Control **53**(2), 496–508 (2008)
5. Dasdan, A.: Experimental analysis of the fastest optimum cycle ratio and mean algorithms. Trans. Des. Autom. Electr. Syst. **9**(4), 385–418 (2004)
6. Fearnley, J.: Exponential lower bounds for policy iteration. In: Abramsky, S., Gavoille, C., Kirchner, C., Meyer auf der Heide, F., Spirakis, P.G. (eds.) ICALP 2010. LNCS, vol. 6199, pp. 551–562. Springer, Heidelberg (2010). https://doi.org/10.1007/978-3-642-14162-1_46
7. Feinberg, E.A., Huang, J.: Strong polynomiality of policy iterations for average-cost MDPs modeling replacement and maintenance problems. Oper. Res. Lett. **41**(3), 249–251 (2013)
8. Feinberg, E.A., Huang, J.: Reduction of total-cost and average-cost MDPs with weakly continuous transition probabilities to discounted MDPs. Oper. Res. Lett. **46**(2), 179–184 (2018)
9. Gosavi, A.: A reinforcement learning algorithm based on policy iteration for average reward: empirical results with yield management and convergence analysis. Mach. Learn. **55**(1), 5–29 (2004)
10. Hansen, T.D., Miltersen, P.B., Zwick, U.: Strategy iteration is strongly polynomial for 2-player turn-based stochastic games with a constant discount factor. J. ACM **60**(1), 1–16 (2013)
11. Hansen, T.D., Zwick, U.: Lower bounds for Howard's algorithm for finding minimum mean-cost cycles. In: Cheong, O., Chwa, K.-Y., Park, K. (eds.) ISAAC 2010. LNCS, vol. 6506, pp. 415–426. Springer, Heidelberg (2010). https://doi.org/10.1007/978-3-642-17517-6_37
12. Hordijk, A., Yushkevich, A.: Blackwell optimality. In: Feinberg, E.A., Shwartz, A. (eds.) The Handbook of Markov Decision Processes: Methods and Applications, chap. 8, pp. 231–268. Kluwer (2002)
13. Howard, R.: Dynamic Programming and Markov Processes. MIT Press, Cambridge (1960)

14. Kallenberg, L.: Finite state and action MDPS. In: Feinberg, E.A., Shwartz, A. (eds.) Handbook of Markov Decision Processes. International Series in Operations Research and Management Science, vol. 40, pp. 21–87. Springer, Boston (2003). https://doi.org/10.1007/978-1-4615-0805-2_2
15. Lewis, M.E., Puterman, M.L.: Bias optimality. In: Feinberg, E.A., Shwartz, A. (eds.) The Handbook of Markov Decision Processes: Methods and Applications, chap. 3, pp. 89–111. Kluwer (2002)
16. Littman, M.L., Dean, T.L., Kaelbling, L.P.: On the complexity of solving Markov decision problems. In: Proceedings of the 11th UAI, p. 394402 (1994)
17. Mahadevan, S.: Average reward reinforcement learning: foundations, algorithms, and empirical results. Mach. Learn. 22(1–3), 159–195 (1996)
18. Mahadevan, S.: Sensitive discount optimality: unifying discounted and average reward reinforcement learning. In: Saitta, L. (ed.) Proceedings of the 13th ICML, pp. 328–336. Morgan Kaufmann (1996)
19. Mahadevan, S.: Learning representation and control in Markov decision processes: new frontiers. Found. Trends Mach. Learn. 1(4), 403–565 (2009)
20. Papadimitriou, C., Tsitsiklis, J.N.: The complexity of Markov decision processes. Math. Oper. Res. 12(3), 441–450 (1987)
21. Puterman, M.: Markov Decision Processes: Discrete Stochastic Dynamic Programming. Wiley, New York (1994)
22. Puterman, M., Patrick, J.: Dynamic programming. In: Sammut, C., Webb, G. (eds.) Encyclopedia of Machine Learning, pp. 298–308. Springer (2010)
23. Kalyanakrishnan, S., Mall, U., Goyal, R.: Batch-switching policy iteration. In: Proceedings of the 25th IJCAI. AAAI Press (2016)
24. Scherrer, B.: Improved and generalized upper bounds on the complexity of policy iteration. Math. Oper. Res. 41(3), 758–774 (2016)
25. Sigaud, O., Buffet, O. (eds.): Markov Decision Processes in Artificial Intelligence. iSTE - Wiley (2010)
26. Sutton, R., Barto, A.: Introduction to Reinforcement Learning. MIT Press, Cambridge (1998)
27. Tadepalli, P.: Average-reward reinforcement learning. In: Sammut, C., Webb, G. (eds.) Encyclopedia of Machine Learning, pp. 64–68. Springer (2010)
28. Tadepalli, P., Ok, D.: Model-based average reward reinforcement learning. Artif. Int. 100(1–2), 177–224 (1998)
29. Tokic, M., Fessler, J., Ertel, W.: The crawler, a class room demonstrator for reinforcement learning. In: Lane, C., Guesgen, H. (eds.) Proceedings of the 22th FLAIRS, pp. 160–165. AAAI Press, Menlo Park (2009)
30. Uther, W.: Markov decision processes. In: Sammut, C., Webb, G. (eds.) Encyclopedia of Machine Learning, pp. 642–646. Springer (2010)
31. Veinott, A.: Discrete dynamic programming with sensitive discount optimality criteria. Ann. Math. Stat. 40(5), 1635–1660 (1969)
32. van Otterlo, M., Wiering, M.: Reinforcement learning and Markov decision processes. In: Wiering, M., van Otterlo, M. (eds.) Reinforcement Learning. Adaptation, Learning, and Optimization, vol. 12, pp. 3–42. Springer, Heidelberg (2012). https://doi.org/10.1007/978-3-642-27645-3_1
33. Yang, S., Gao, Y., An, B., Wang, H., Chen, X.: Efficient average reward reinforcement learning using constant shifting values. In: Proceedings of the 30th AAAI. AAAI Press/The MIT Press (2016)
34. Ye, Y.: The simplex and policy-iteration methods are strongly polynomial for the Markov decision problem with a fixed discount rate. Math. Oper. Res. 36(4), 593603 (2011)

A Strategical Path Planner
for UGV-UAV Cooperation
in Mars Terrains

Fernando Ropero$^{(\boxtimes)}$ ⓘ, Pablo Muñoz ⓘ, and María D. R-Moreno ⓘ

Computer Engineering Department, University of Alcalá,
28871 Alcalá de Henares, Spain
{fernando.ropero,malola.rmoreno,pablo.munoz}@uah.es

Abstract. Mars exploration is an ongoing researching topic mainly due to the technological breakthroughs in robotic platforms. Space agencies as NASA, are considering future Mars explorations where multi-robot teams cooperate to maximize the scientific return. In this regard, we present a cooperative team formed by a Unmanned Aerial Vehicle (UAV) and a Unmanned Ground Vehicle (UGV) to autonomously perform a Mars exploration. We develop a strategical path planner to compute a route plan for the UGV-UAV team to reach all the target points of the exploration. The key problems that we have considered in Mars explorations for the UGV-UAV team are: the UAV energy constraints and the UGV functionality constraints. Our strategical path planner models the UGV as a moving charging station which will carry the UAV through secure locations close to the target points locations, and the UAV will visit the target points using the UGV as a recharging station. Our solution has been tested in several scenarios and the results demonstrate that our approach is able to carry out a coordinated plan in a local optimal mission time on a real Mars terrain.

Keywords: Planning and scheduling · Intelligent agents
Distributed AI algorithms · Systems and applications

1 Introduction

Over the last decades the technological growth in robotics has been enhancing the development of advanced autonomous vehicles, such as the Unmanned Aerial Vehicle (UAV) or the Autonomous Underwater Vehicle (AUV), which provide additional capabilities (e.g., aerial images or underwater autonomous exploration) to the classical ones provided by Unmanned Ground Vehicles (UGVs). This is a driving factor for many research institutions to develop novel solutions based on these robotic systems, e.g., using UAVs for aerial exploration [3], reconnaissance [22] or persistent surveillance [12], or using AUVs for oceanic exploration [4]. Furthermore, a large amount of these solutions build multi-robot platforms to overcome the performance of single-robot platforms in scenarios

© Springer Nature Switzerland AG 2018
M. Bramer and M. Petridis (Eds.): SGAI-AI 2018, LNAI 11311, pp. 106–118, 2018.
https://doi.org/10.1007/978-3-030-04191-5_8

such as the exploration [1] or the persistence coverage [15]. This is naturally revealing a deep scientific study on robotics cooperation ever since.

1.1 Motivation

This article is motivated by the Mars explorations with a cooperative UGV-UAV team where the key issues to face are the UAV energy constraints and UGV functionality constraints. This exploration is related to autonomously perform a routing which includes unreachable goals for a UGV single-robot system (functionality constraint) and it takes too much time to be reached by a UAV single-robot system (energy constraint). For instance, a UGV cannot take pictures of a cliff and the UAV cannot visit that cliff on its own because it is too far away from its initial position, so it does not have enough energy to reach it. Our solution proposes the UGV to carry the UAV to the cliff edge, and then, the UAV can take pictures around the cliff and it can recharge its energy on the UGV. This problem can be extrapolated to a real setting such as the planned for the Mars 2020 mission, in which NASA plans to launch the Mars Helicopter Scout (MHS) along with the Mars Rover. The MHS and the Mars Rover will cooperate to study and plan the best driving route as a multi-robot team.

In our solution, the multi-robot team is formed by a single UGV with functionality constraints and a single UAV with energy constraints. We define the UGV as a moving charging station which carries the UAV through Secure Locations (SLs) close to the Target Points (TPs). Then, the UAV will visit the subset of connected TPs from every SL. A SL is a particular map coordinate which meets the terrain features requirements, such as the terrain slope, to be crossed by a UGV. A sub-set of target points is delimited by the circle representing the UAV farthest distance (see Fig. 1) centered on a SL. The fully UAV charged battery determines the farthest distance the UAV can travel.

Therefore, we have implemented a strategical path planner which follows an ordered set of stages to give a cooperative routing for the UGV-UAV multi-robot system in order to accomplish the Mars exploration problem considered.

1.2 Related Work

The heterogeneous multi-robot cooperation has been extensively studied in the existing literature. Over the last decade, there have emerged several cooperation paradigms which perform different UGV-UAV multi-robot cooperation approaches depending on the problem to address. Hence, we can highlight the following three widely studied problems: guidance, persistent surveillance and exploration. Our path planner has been designed under the idea of being applied on each problem.

The guidance problem is related to use a robotic system to provide help in the navigation process to others systems. Usually, the UAV is the robotic system chosen to collect aerial information to guide the UGV on the ground. Sofman et al. [19] describe methods to extract relevant information from the environment using a UAV to enhance the navigation of the UGV. Mueggler et al. [16] present

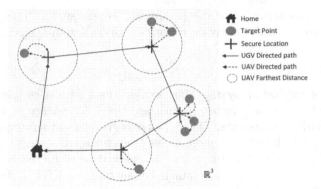

Fig. 1. A possible scenario for the UGV-UAV multi-robot system. Both systems start at the Home location. The black lines represent the path of the UGV. The dashed black lines are the paths of the UAV. The dashed black circles represent the boundaries of the UAV farther distance.

a path planner in which the UAV scans the area and search for the fastest route for the UGV in order to deliver a first-aid kit. Gurin et al. [7] propose a guidance scheme in which a UAV provides target points to a UGV which carries objects in unsafe industrial areas. The main difference of these path planners from ours is that there is no information about the environment before running the planner, otherwise the UAV has to previously collect aerial data of the terrain to provide the suitable route for the UGV.

The surveillance problem is another well-studied problem whose goal is to guarantee a proper safety level to a specific target. Grocholsky et al. [6] propose different algorithms based on a network of UGVs and UAVs which are constantly searching for and localizing targets in a specified area. Hsieh et al. [10] consider the UAVs to generate a navigation map and the UGVs to build a radio-signal strength map in order to monitor and control a village. Tokekar et al. [23] present a collaborative UGV-UAV system in which each robot performs soil and aerial measurements respectively, in order to achieve a precision agriculture in an optimal time. Indeed, our work is motivated by the same cooperation paradigm in which the UGV carries the UAV through the computed target points. But, the UGV does not have the capability of a recharging station so the UAV cannot recharge its energy, and the stated problem is slighly different.

The exploration problem in long-term autonomy missions focuses on reaching a set of target points on a specific area, and it is referred to find a path for the multi-robot system optimizing the overall mission time. The problem of finding an optimal solution among a set of target points is the Travelling Salesman Problem (TSP) [2], which is a well-known NP-Hard optimization combinatorial problem [8]. Nowadays, there are a lot of works which deploy a UGV-UAV multi-robot system to solve the exploration problem. Maini et al. [13] formulate the Fuel Constrained UAV Refueling Problem with Mobile Refueling Station (FCURP-MRS) in which the UAV has to reach the target points and it uses the

UGV as a moving charging station to place charging stops around the UGV's path. The FCURP-MRS uses an equivalent cooperation paradigm as Tokekar et al. [23]. In fact, both strategies model the path planning problem as TSPs, and also, both solve the Hitting Set Problem (HSP) [18] to select the optimal number of UGV locations. Nonetheless, none of them compute Voronoi Tessellations to find SLs as an initial stage. Manyam et al. [14] define the cooperative air-ground vehicle routing problem (CAGVRP) in which a multiple UGV-UAV system is involved. The aim of the CAGVRP is to visit a set of target points either by the UAV or the UGV, keeping alive the communication link between both vehicles. The cooperation paradigm used in CAGVRP is also equivalent to our approach. However, in our problem, the UAV has to visit every target point and we do not consider communication problems. Also, the CAGVRP does not introduce the SLs variable into the problem equation.

The rest of the paper is organized as follows. Next section defines the UGV-UAV cooperation paradigm assessed. Section 3 describes the strategical path planner. Experimental results are presented in Sect. 4. Finally, conclusions are outlined.

2   Cooperation Paradigm

The cooperation paradigm designed is aimed to solve the Mars exploration problem considered. This problem is raised by the energy and functionality constraint related to the UAV and UGV respectively. Thus, it is required to state the problem and the synergies for the UGV-UAV cooperation.

2.1   Mars Exploration Problem

The **problem** considered in this work remains stated as follows (see Fig. 2a):

 (i) A Mars terrain modelled as an Euclidean space $\mathbb{R}^3$.
 (ii) A set of target points distributed around the Mars terrain.
 (iii) A UGV-UAV multi-robot system.
 (iv) A UAV energy constraint. It is modelled as the farther distance the UAV can travel with a fully charged battery.
 (v) A UGV functionality constraint. The UGV cannot reach the target points and it cannot travel around the whole area because of the terrain features.
 (vi) A home location where both systems start and end the mission.

The **goal** related to this problem is:

To find a cooperative routing for the UGV-UAV multi-robot system in order to allow the UAV to visit every target point while trying to minimize the overall mission time.

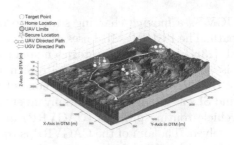

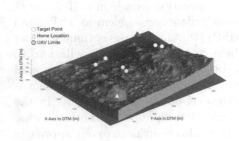

(a) The stated Mars exploration problem.

(b) Solving the problem with the strategical path planner proposed. The normal line is the UGV's directed path. The dashed line is the UAV's directed path.

Fig. 2. A real Mars Digital Terrain Model (DTM) solving the Mars exploration problem considered in Sect. 2.1. The UGV-UAV multi-robot system starts at the Home Location, which initially shows the UAV energy constraint in a sphere.

The distance travelled by both robotic systems is directly proportional to the time spent and the energy consumed in a trip. Therefore, the shorter the distance travelled, the shorter the time spent and the lower the energy consumed, and viceversa. Taking this into consideration, the goal can be summarized into finding the shortest path for the UGV and the UAV in order to minimize the mission time.

The Mars terrain is computed as a real Digital Terrain Model (DTM) captured by the High Resolution Imaging Science Experiment on board the Mars Reconnaissance Orbiter. For instance, Fig. 2 shows the central uplift of a 30-Km diameter crater in Noachis Terra. Its identification in the HiRISE database is: DTEED_030808_1535_031230_1535_A01.

2.2 UGV-UAV Cooperation Synergy

The cooperation synergy laid out aims to solve the long-term autonomy exploration problem through the useful mixing of the UGV-UAV multi-robot system capabilities. The cooperation synergy represents the interaction ways between both systems. Therefore, taking into account the stated constraints (iv and v), this interactions are defined as follows:

- The UGV is a moving charging station which carries the UAV through secure locations from where the UAV will visit the target points. A secure location is a particular map coordinate which meets the terrain features requirements (terrain slope, rocks, etc) to be crossed by the UGV. This terrain features are explained by Muñoz et al. [17].
- Each secure location is linked to a sub-set of target points (see Fig. 1), so on each sub-set, the UAV plans a route taking into account the possibility to fly back to the UGV to recharge its battery to avoid run out of energy in the next sub-set of target points.

Algorithm 1. Strategical Path Planner Stages

Require: A 3-D Area, a set of TPs and a Home Location
Ensure: A UGV-UAV route

    A. **Finding Secure Locations:** Voronoi Tessellations [24] are computed to find a suitable set of SLs aiming to reduce its number and thus, minimize the UGV's path.
    B. **Secure Locations Optimization:** the HSP is computed to select an optimal number of SLs aiming to minimize UGV's path.
    C. **TSP Computation:** a genetic algorithm is applied to solve the TSP for the UGV. It gives as output a sorted set of SLs.
    D. **UGV Path Planning:** the 3Dana Algorithm [17] is computed to obtain the UGV three-dimensional route from the sorted set of SLs obtained in C.
    E. **UAV Path Planning:** a search algorithm is computed to obtain the UAV three-dimensional route for every sub-set of TP linked to a SL.

- The UAV can recharge its battery on the onboard UGV charging station while the UGV is at a secure location. The autonomous charging method used is out of the scope of this article, but for instance, we can mention two processes using battery swapping systems [20,21].
- Once the UAV has achieved a sub-set of target points, it flies back to the UGV. Then, the UGV carries the UAV to the next planned secure location to visit the associated sub-set of target points.
- Finally, the UGV returns with the UAV to the Home Location and it concludes the mission.

3 Path Planner

The main contribution of this paper is the strategical path planner which follows a coordinated set of five stages to allow the UGV-UAV multi-robot system to autonomously accomplish a Mars exploration. It is based on the divide-and-conquer approach in which each stage deals with a single issue in order to solve the real problem (see Algorithm 1).

3.1 Finding Secure Locations

The first stage of the strategical path planner look for a set of SLs which guarantee the full covering of the stated TPs. The selected computational method is based on Voronoi Tessellations [24].

It computes N iterations of Voronoi Tessellations to ensure that every TP is inside the boundaries of a SL, which means it can be visited by the UAV. On each iteration, it applies a Voronoi Tessellation taking as inputs: the set of remaining uncovered TPs plus the set of Voronoi vertices (those points delimited by the intersections shaping the Voronoi regions) computed in the last iteration. The objective is to find a Voronoi vertex which covers the remaining TPs. The set of Voronoi vertices computed on each iteration help us to cut down the area around the TPs in order to increase the probabilities of finding near suitable SLs in future iterations. Nevertheless, all the Voronoi vertices do not provide a feasible location due to it can be located out of the map boundaries, or represent a risky location for the UGV, such a rock or crater edge. Therefore, the Voronoi vertices computed in the $n - 1$ iteration are classified on three types of vertices in order to used them properly in the n iteration:

- Legitimate vertices: those which represent a feasible option for a SL.
- Illegitimate vertices: represent terrain features locations where the UGV cannot cross around.
- Artificial vertices: always ensure a feasible option for a SL. Usually, these vertices are computed when the algorithm does not find legitimate vertices due to hard terrain features.

Our computational method selects the nearest legitimate vertice to each target point ensuring that every target point is covered. Then, the output is formed by a set of legitimate vertices which we have formally called as SLs.

3.2   Secure Locations Optimization

The second stage aims to find the minimum set of SLs which guarantee the full covering of the set of TPs in order to minimize the distance travelled by the UGV. In computer science this is known as the HSP. The problem is modelled as a bipartite graph where the SLs are represented on the left side, the universe represented by TPs on the right side, and the edges representing the SLs covering the TPs.

We have tailored the implementation developed by Gori et al. [5], taking as input the SLs computed in the A stage and the TPs stating the initial problem. The output is an optimized set of SLs (see Fig. 2b).

3.3   TSP Computation

The third stage is referred to solve the TSP for the set of SLs given in the B stage. The result will be an ordered set of SLs which will guide the UGV's path. It is important to mention that the TSP is computed with the Euclidean distances in two dimensions. The three dimensional path planning will be computed in the next stage.

We adapted the genetic algorithm of Kirk et al. [11] to compute the TSP. Each chromosome represents an ordered combination of a possible route. On each iteration, the algorithm computes the travel cost in every chromosome and it selects the four chromosomes with minimum travel costs. Then, it applies flipping, swapping and sliding as mutation techniques to those four chromosomes and it adds them to the new population. Note that we do not apply mutation techniques in the first and last gen because the mission starts and finishes at the home location (*vi* statement in Sect. 2.1).

3.4 UGV Path Planning

The fourth stage considers the ordered set of SLs of the previous stage to compute the complete three dimensional path among these SLs. We have used 3Dana [17] to compute the three dimensional UGV's path taking into account different terrain features such as the terrain slope or different obstacles. The output is the UGV's path which solves the long-term autonomy exploration problem (see Fig. 2b).

3.5 UAV Path Planning

The fifth stage implements a classical planning technique to compute the path planning for each sub-set of TPs. We have developed a search algorithm based on the A* algorithm [9] aiming to minimize the UAV distance travelled. This algorithm has particularly been designed to minimize the number of intermediate charging stops for the UAV to accomplish the sub-set of TPs. To do that, as well as A*, we use the evaluation function $f = g + h$. The cost function (g) is the accumulated distance to reach a TP. As well, the heuristic function (h) represents the remaining TPs to visit. However, we integrate the UAV energy constraint in the searching process as the farther distance the UAV can travel, so the computational cost of the heuristic search is minimized. This algorithm has been designed taking into account that the UAV will fly on straight line. The output is the UAV's path which solves the long-term autonomy exploration problem (see dashed line on Fig. 2b).

4   Experimental Evaluation

The described path planner has been developed and tested in a real Mars DTM over different TPs distributions. The TPs distributions have been generated using a random scenario generator specifically designed for this evaluation. To the best of our knowledge there are not previous works applying such UGV-UAV cooperation synergies in this kind of Mars exploration problems. Thus, the experimental assessment consist of two experiments:

- The Clustering Optimization Experiment: assessment of the path planner capability to find the minimal number of SLs required to cover the set of TPS.
- The Performance Vs Safety Experiment: testing the overall performance of the path planner under different safety levels.

The algorithm has been implemented in MATLAB and all the experiments are carried out on a 2.6 GHz Intel Core i7 with 16 GB of RAM under Windows 10.

4.1 3-D Random Scenario Generator

The random scenario generator uses key parameters to create well-defined TPs distributions where we can properly assess the path planner performance. These key parameters are defined as follows:

- A: the area size of the Real Mars DTM.
- N: number of TPs.
- R: farther distance the UAV can travel.
- δ: optimal number of SLs to cover the set of TPs, i.e., the TPs cannot be clustered with less SLs than δ.

The random map generator creates every scenario ensuring that N target points are distributed in δ secure locations, inside a specific radius R and allocated around a real Mars DTM with a specific area size A. Here, the δ parameter allows us to define the optimal number of SLs to cluster every TP on each scenario. This means that the path planner could compute, at the very least, δ secure locations.

4.2 Clustering Optimization Experiment

The first experiment evaluates the A and B path planner stages (Sects. 3.1 and 3.2). As we mentioned, the goal of these stages is to minimize the number of SLs, denoted as N_{SL}, required to cover the whole set of TPs. But, we cannot ensure that N_{SL} is optimal on every distribution. Then, we use the random scenario generator to define the optimal number of SLs, known as δ, on every distribution. Therefore, we are able to compare N_{SL} and δ to detect when the path planner has computed an optimized scenario. We have defined as an optimized scenario when $N_{SL} = \delta$.

Also, we wanted to assess the optimized scenarios according to the UGV-UAV multi-robot safety along the exploration. Then, let R denote the UAV energy constraint as the farthest distance the UAV can travel in meters. Let P denote the UGV functionality constraint as the terrain slope of every DTM coordinate in degrees. We have defined four different safety levels based on R and P (L1 = low safety, L4 = high safety) to evaluate the optimized scenarios percentage on each level. These safety levels allows us to describe several risky environments settings through the next two parameters:

- Terrain slope (P): 3Dana uses the terrain slope as a threshold to compute a UGV path where every point has less slope than this threshold. A high safety level will be determined by a lower slope because the UGV path will avoid dangerous terrain features.
- Security range (β): represents the distance percentage that is going to be subtracted from a theoretical farther distance (R_{th}) the UAV can travel without running out of energy, e.g., with $R_{th} = 300$ m and $\beta = 0.1$ (10%) then, $R = R_{th} - (R_{th} * \beta) = 270$ m. The objective of β is to avoid the UAV runs out of energy due to unpredictable environmental conditions.

This experiment consists of the execution of 10000 random scenarios over the Mars DTM shown in Fig. 2 with the safety levels displayed in Table 1. P is ranged from 20° (a normal inclination) to 1° (plain terrain). β goes from 10% (low security range) to 90% (high security range). Then, the goal of this experiment is to determine the optimized scenarios percentage in the L1-L4 safety levels. The results in Table 1 show that as long as the safety level increases from L1 to L4, the percentage of optimized scenarios (when $S = \delta$) decreases. L1 shows the highest percentage of optimized scenarios, because a high P and a low β represents more possibilities to find SLs around the TPs, and then, to achieve $S = \delta$. L4 shows the lowest percentage of optimized scenarios, because of the highest β and the lowest P, so there are hardly any SLs around the TPs. Also, we can appreciate that the computational time increases as long as it does the safety level, because the path planner finds less legitimate vertices to ensure SLs for the UGV close to the TPs. So, if a SL cannot be reached by the UGV, its means that the TP cannot be visited by the UAV and then, the scenario does not have solution. As shows the L4 results, the path planner estimates that there are not solution in 2759 scenarios.

Table 1. Clustering optimization of the first two path planner stages in different safety levels over the Mars DTM shown in Fig. 2. It has been computed a total of 10000 random scenarios for each safety level.

Level	β (%)	P (°)	Scenarios with solution	Scenarios without solution	Failed scenarios	Optimized scenarios (%)	Average time (ms)
L1	10	20	10000	0	0	71,03	6,47
L2	30	10	10000	0	0	62,35	12,2
L3	60	5	10000	0	0	63,13	16,7
L4	90	1	7241	2759	0	39,22	26,1

4.3 Performance vs Safety Experiment

The second experiment evaluates the performance of the path planner (A-E stages) against different safety levels. The performance has been assessed in terms of the computational time to solve every scenario and the distance travelled by the UGV-UAV multi-robot system.

This experiment consist of the evaluation of the same 100 scenarios over the Mars DTM shown in Fig. 2 with the safety levels displayed in Table 2. P is ranged from 20° (a normal inclination) to 5° (almost a plain terrain). Note that $P = 1°$ has no been computed because even with $P = 5°$, the path planner does not find any solution. β goes from 10% (low security range) to 90% (high security range). The results in Table 2 shows that as long as the safety level increases from L1 to L4, the distance travelled clearly increases, the number of scenarios with solution decreases and the computational time increases exponentially. The distance travelled by both robotic systems is minimum in the lowest safety level

Table 2. Performance of the five stages of the path planner in different safety levels over DTEED_030808_1535_031230_1535_A01 shown in Fig. 2. Every level has been tested over the same 100 random scenarios.

Level	β (%)	$P(°)$	UGV avg. dist. (m)	UAV avg. dist. (m)	Scenarios with solution	Scenarios without solution	Avg. comp. time (s)
L1	10	20	$1,0679.10^4$	$1,0955.10^3$	93	7	226,6
L2	30	15	$1,0727.10^4$	$1,0957.10^3$	65	35	485,6
L3	60	10	$1,1807.10^4$	$1,1097.10^3$	4	96	3562
L4	90	5	0	0	0	100	0

L1 due to the UGV has more ability to avoid obstacles (high P) and the UAV can fly a farther distance (low β). Then, it is easier to reach a SL close to a TP, which in turn minimize the distance travelled by the UGV-UAV multi-robot system. Also, the computed scenarios with solution decreases in a higher safety level due to the UGV has less ability to avoid obstacles (low P) and the UAV can fly a shorter distance (high β). Then, it is more difficult to reach a legitimate vertice complaining the SL requirements. Consequently, the computational time increases because of the UGV path planning in the D stage, i.e., the 3Dana algorithm needs to expand more nodes around the scenario to find a way to reach a SL.

5   Conclusions

In this paper, we have formulated a cooperation paradigm defining a UGV-UAV cooperation synergy to address the Mars exploration problem with UAV energy and UGV functionality constraints. Then, we have proposed a path planner based on a coordinated set of stages to solve different isolated issues of the problem. Our technique has been evaluated over different simulated scenarios in a real Mars DTM. The results show a great optimization capability of the path planner and reveal a multi-objective optimization between the distance travelled by both robotic systems.

Despite of these encouraging results, there is still a lot of work ahead. An interesting research direction could be adding a group of UAVs to the problem, in which these UAVs have different functionalities and can achieve specific target points. Other interesting research line is to establish different priority levels to the target points, in order to be visited in certain conditions.

Acknowledgements. The authors want to thank Dr. David F. Barrero for the fruitful discussions and his help to carry out the experiments. The work is supported by the UAH project 2016/00351/001.

References

1. Burgard, W., Moors, M., Stachniss, C., Schneider, F.E.: Coordinated multi-robot exploration. IEEE Trans. Robot. **21**(3), 376–386 (2005)
2. Dantzig, G., Fulkerson, R., Johnson, S.: Solution of a large-scale traveling-salesman problem. J. Oper. Res. Soc. Am. **2**(4), 393–410 (1954)
3. Ergezer, H., Leblebiciolu, K.: 3D path planning for multiple UAVs for maximum information collection. J. Intell. Robot. Syst. **73**(1–4), 737 (2014)
4. Eriksen, C.C., et al.: Seaglider: a long-range autonomous underwater vehicle for oceanographic research. IEEE J. Oceanic Eng. **26**(4), 424–436 (2001)
5. Gori, F., Folino, G., Jetten, M.S., Marchiori, E.: MTR: taxonomic annotation of short metagenomic reads using clustering at multiple taxonomic ranks. Bioinformatics **27**(2), 196–203 (2011)
6. Grocholsky, B., Keller, J., Kumar, V., Pappas, G.: Cooperative air and ground surveillance. IEEE Robot. Autom. Mag. **13**(3), 16–25 (2006)
7. Guérin, F., Guinand, F., Brethé, J.F., Pelvillain, H., et al.: UAV-UGV cooperation for objects transportation in an industrial area. In: 2015 IEEE International Conference on Industrial Technology (ICIT), pp. 547–552. IEEE (2015)
8. Gutin, G., Punnen, A.P.: The Traveling Salesman Problem and Its Variations, vol. 12. Springer, Heidelberg (2006)
9. Hart, P.E., Nilsson, N.J., Raphael, B.: A formal basis for the heuristic determination of minimum cost paths. IEEE Trans. Syst. Sci. Cybern. **4**(2), 100–107 (1968)
10. Hsieh, M.A., et al.: Adaptive teams of autonomous aerial and ground robots for situational awareness. J. Field Robot. **24**(11–12), 991–1014 (2007)
11. Kirk, J.: Traveling salesman problem-genetic algorithm. Retrieved from the MATLAB File Exchange website: www.mathworks.com/matlabcentral/fileexchange/13680-travelingsalesman-problem-genetic-algorithm (2007)
12. Leahy, K., Zhou, D., Vasile, C.I., Oikonomopoulos, K., Schwager, M., Belta, C.: Persistent surveillance for unmanned aerial vehicles subject to charging and temporal logic constraints. Autonom. Robots **40**(8), 1363–1378 (2016)
13. Maini, P., Sujit, P.: On cooperation between a fuel constrained UAV and a refueling UGV for large scale mapping applications. In: 2015 International Conference on Unmanned Aircraft Systems (ICUAS), pp. 1370–1377. IEEE (2015)
14. Manyam, S.G., Casbeer, D.W., Sundar, K.: Path planning for cooperative routing of air-ground vehicles. In: 2016 American Control Conference (ACC), pp. 4630–4635. IEEE (2016)
15. Mitchell, D., Corah, M., Chakraborty, N., Sycara, K., Michael, N.: Multi-robot long-term persistent coverage with fuel constrained robots. In: 2015 IEEE International Conference on Robotics and Automation (ICRA), pp. 1093–1099. IEEE (2015)
16. Mueggler, E., Faessler, M., Fontana, F., Scaramuzza, D.: Aerial-guided navigation of a ground robot among movable obstacles. In: 2014 IEEE International Symposium on Safety, Security, and Rescue Robotics (SSRR), pp. 1–8. IEEE (2014)
17. Muñoz, P., R-Moreno, M.D., Castaño, B.: 3Dana: a path planning algorithm for surface robotics. Eng. Appl. Artif. Intell. **60**, 175–192 (2017)
18. Mustafa, N.H., Ray, S.: Improved results on geometric hitting set problems. Discrete Comput. Geom. **44**(4), 883–895 (2010)
19. Sofman, B., Bagnell, J.A., Stentz, A., Vandapel, N.: Terrain classification from aerial data to support ground vehicle navigation (2006)

20. Suzuki, K.A., Kemper Filho, P., Morrison, J.R.: Automatic battery replacement system for UAVs: analysis and design. J. Intell. Robot. Syst. **65**(1), 563–586 (2012)
21. Swieringa, K.A., et al.: Autonomous battery swapping system for small-scale helicopters. In: 2010 IEEE International Conference on Robotics and Automation (ICRA), pp. 3335–3340. IEEE (2010)
22. Tian, J., Shen, L., Zheng, Y.: Genetic algorithm based approach for Multi-UAV cooperative reconnaissance mission planning problem. In: Esposito, F., Raś, Z.W., Malerba, D., Semeraro, G. (eds.) ISMIS 2006. LNCS (LNAI), vol. 4203, pp. 101–110. Springer, Heidelberg (2006). https://doi.org/10.1007/11875604_13
23. Tokekar, P., Vander Hook, J., Mulla, D., Isler, V.: Sensor planning for a symbiotic UAV and UGV system for precision agriculture. IEEE Trans. Robot. **32**(6), 1498–1511 (2016)
24. Watson, D.F.: Computing the n-dimensional Delaunay tessellation with application to Voronoi polytopes. Comput. J. **24**(2), 167–172 (1981)

Machine Learning

GEP-Based Ensemble Classifier
with Drift-Detection

Joanna Jędrzejowicz[1]([✉]) [ID] and Piotr Jędrzejowicz[2] [ID]

[1] Institute of Informatics, Faculty of Mathematics, Physics and Informatics,
University of Gdańsk, 80-308 Gdańsk, Poland
jj@inf.ug.edu.pl
[2] Department of Information Systems, Gdynia Maritime University,
Morska 83, 81-225 Gdynia, Poland
pj@am.gdynia.pl

Abstract. The paper proposes a new ensemble classifier using Gene Expression Programming as the induction engine. The approach aims at predicting unknown class labels for datasets with concept drift. For constructing the proposed ensemble we use the two-level scheme where at the lower level base classifiers are induced and at the upper level, the meta-classifier is produced. The classification process is controlled by the well-known early drift detection mechanism. To validate the approach computational experiment has been carried out. Its results confirmed that the proposed classifier performs well.

Keywords: Gene Expression Programming · Classifier ensemble
Datasets with concept drift

1 Introduction

Gene Expression Programming (GEP) was introduced by Ferreira [11]. In GEP programs are represented as linear character strings of fixed length called chromosomes which, in the subsequent fitness evaluation, evolve into expression trees without any user intervention. This property makes GEP induced expression trees a useful tool for constructing classifiers, as noticed by Ferreira [12]. Expression Trees induced by Gene Expression Programming can be used as base classifiers in the ensemble of classifiers. The idea was proposed by Jedrzejowicz and Jedrzejowicz [17] and further developed in [18–20]. In these papers, several approaches to combining expression trees including majority-voting, boosting and clustering were suggested. The current paper investigates the possibility of using GEP as the induction engine for classifiers working in non-stationary data environments.

Classification is one of the most important machine learning problems. To solve a classification task it is required to induce from training data a classifier, that is a function or a model able to predict the class of unlabelled instances. In case of the stationary data environment, the problem domain has a stationary

© Springer Nature Switzerland AG 2018
M. Bramer and M. Petridis (Eds.): SGAI-AI 2018, LNAI 11311, pp. 121–131, 2018.
https://doi.org/10.1007/978-3-030-04191-5_9

distribution and a classifier does not have to be changed over time. If however, distribution of future instances differs substantially from the original one, the problem domain might be characterized by the presence of, so called, concept drift, typical for a non-stationary distribution.

There have been numerous attempts to construct classifiers able to deal, in general with data stream mining and, in particular with non-stationary data environments. Basically, there are two main research directions trying to respond to challenges of such environments. The first one assumes that the learner is periodically re-induced from the most recent chunk of data. The approach is often referred to as the incremental learning, online learning or sliding window-based pattern mining.

Incremental learners allow an existing model to be updated using only newly arriving data instances, without having to re-process all of the past instances. Incremental learners date back to eighties with the paper of Schlimmer et al. [27]. Later on Utgoff et al. [29] proposed an efficient method for incrementally inducing decision trees. A fast incremental decision tree learner was suggested by Hulten et al. [15]. Effective incremental learners have been constructed using the info-fuzzy approach by Cohen et al. [8]. Well-performing learner based on a sliding window concept was proposed by Tanbeer et al. [28]. Recently, several Extreme Learning Machine (ELM) approaches to incremental learning have been discussed by Liu et al. [25], and Xu and Wang [30].

Incremental learners can also profit from advantages of using ensembles of classifiers. Combining base classifiers for incremental learning was proposed by Fern and Givan [10]. Another useful approach to ensemble incremental learning was suggested by Kotsiantis [23] where several different base classifiers form input to the voting scheme. Further examples, where ensembles consisting of base learners have been proposed to deal with concept drift, include the dynamic weighted majority scheme of Kolter and Maloof [22], adaptable diversity-based online boosting by de Carvalho Santos et al. [7] and fast adaptive stacking of ensembles by Frias-Blanco et al. [13].

The second approach to learning from a non-stationary data uses concept-drift detectors which signal concept changes. A drift detector is a light-weight program invoking base models replacement or modification upon detecting a concept drift. According to Barros and Santos [4] among the most well-known drift-detectors are drift detection method of Gama et al. [14], early drift detection method of Baena-Garcia et al. [3], adaptive windowing of Bifet and Gavalda [6] and statistical test of equal proportions of Nishida and Yamauchi [26]. Among recent ones one should mention drift detection methods based on Hoeffding's bounds by Frias-Blanco et al. [13] and Fisher test drift detector by de Lima Cabral et al. [24].

The goal of this paper is to propose GEP-based ensemble classifier with drift detection denoted as GEP-DD. As the detector we use the early drift detection method of Baena-Garca et al. [3]. To evaluate its performance we recall the GEP-based incremental classifier (GEP-INCR) proposed by the authors in [16] and compare both approaches in the computational experiment. The remainder of this paper is organized as follows. Section 2 describes the idea of gene expression programming when used as a classification method. Section 3 presents the proposed GEP-DD, gives a short overview of the GEP-INCR and finally, gives an account on computational complexity of both algorithms. Section 4 includes computational experiment settings and results. Final Sect. 5 contains conclusions and suggestions for future research.

2   GEP as Base Classifier

The idea of gene expression programming (GEP) is based on evolving the population of genes which is subject to genetic variation according to fitness calculation. Each gene is divided into two parts as in the original head-tail method, see Ferreira [11]. The tail part of a gene always contains terminals and head can have both, terminals and functions. The size of the head (h) is determined by the user and for classification task, the suggested size is not less than the number of attributes in the dataset. The size of the tail (t) is computed as $t = h(m-1)+1$ where m is the largest arity found in the function set. In the computational experiments, the functions are: logical AND, OR, XOR, NOR and NOT. Thus $m = 2$ and the size of the gene is $h + t = 2h + 1$.

The terminal set contains triples ($op, attrib, const$) where op is one of relational operators $<, \leq, >, \geq, =, \neq$, $attrib$ is the attribute number, and finally, $const$ is a value belonging to the domain of the attribute $attrib$. Thus for a fixed gene g and fixed row from the data set r the value $g(r)$ is boolean and for binary classification, each gene naturally differentiates between two classes. Attaching an expression tree to a gene is done in exactly the same manner as in all GEP systems.

Consider the gene g with head = 6, defined below.

0	1	2	3	4	5	6	7	8	9
OR	AND	AND	$(=,1,8)$	$(=,2,0)$	$(>,1,0)$	$(>,4,10)$	$(>,1,0)$	$(<,1,10)$	$\cdots$

The start position (position 0) in the chromosome corresponds to the root of the expression tree (OR, in the example). Then, below each function branches are attached and there are as many of them as the arity of the function - 2 in that case. The following symbols in the chromosome are attached to the branches on a given level. The process is complete when each branch is completed with a terminal. The number of symbols from the chromosome to form the expression tree is denoted as the termination point. For the discussed example, the termination point is 6. For the attribute vector $rw = (8.0, 1.0, 0.0, 20.0, 1.0, \cdots)$ the value of the above gene g is $true$.

To introduce variation in the population the following genetic operators are used:

- mutation,
- transposition of insertion sequence elements (IS transposition),

– root transposition (RIS transposition),
– one-point recombination,
– two-point recombination.

For a fixed training set D and fixed gene g the fitness function counts the proportion of vectors from D classified correctly

$$fit_D(g) = \frac{\sum_{rw \in D,\ g(rw)\ is\ true} sg(\text{rw is from class 1})}{|D|} \tag{1}$$

where

$$sg(\varphi) = \begin{cases} 1 & \text{if } \varphi \text{ is true} \\ 0 & \text{otherwise} \end{cases}$$

Metagenes are representing ensemble classifiers. Similarly, as above, the set of functions contains logical ones and terminals are identifiers of genes from the trained population. For example, the metagene mg makes use of two genes g and h defined below:

$$mg: \quad \begin{array}{c|c|c|c|c} 0 & 1 & 2 & 3 & 4 \\ \hline \text{AND} & \text{NOT} & g & h & \cdots \end{array} \qquad h: \quad \begin{array}{c|c|c} 0 & 1 & 2 \\ \hline \text{NOT} & (=, 2, 7) & \cdots \end{array}$$

For a fixed attribute vector rw each terminal (i. e gene) has a boolean value and thus the value of metagene can be computed. For the above metagene mg and rw as before we have

$$g(rw) = true, \ h(rw) = true, \ mg(rw) = false$$

Similarly as in (1), for a fixed training set D and fixed metagene mg the fitness function counts the proportion of vectors classified correctly:

$$FIT_D(mg) = \frac{\sum_{rw \in D,\ mg(rw)\ is\ true} sg(\text{rw is from class 1})}{|D|} \tag{2}$$

The procedure described above works for the binary classification. For the multi-class classification two approaches, OVA or OVO, can be applied. In the first case OVA (one-versus-all) the number of training steps is proportional to $|C|$ - the number of classes, as training takes place separately for each class. For OVO (one-versus-one) approach the training is computationally demanding, as for each pair of classes $c1, c2 \in C$ the population of genes which separates best instances from $c1$ and $c2$ is evolved. In this case, the cost of training is proportional to $|C|^2$. In the experiments OVA approach was applied and the gene classifier was a vector of length $|C|$ containing genes specialized for distinguishing instances for each separate class. For the testing stage the value of $g = (g_1, \ldots, g_{|C|})$ for a given instance r is a majority vote of $|C|$ counters.

To generate the population of genes, values of the following parameters have to be set: number of iterations (nG), population size ($popS$) and elite size ($eliteS$). Procedure for selecting the best fitted metagene requires setting values of the metagene population size ($popG$), and the number of iterations (nG).

More details on GEP operators and GEP classification can be found in [17–19].

3   Ensemble Classifiers

3.1   Classification with Drift Detection

Following Gama et al. [14] we consider the online learning framework. Let $(\mathbf{x_i}, y_i)$ stand for a sequence of data rows $\mathbf{x_i}$ with label y_i arriving online. For each arriving example, a decision is taken which predicts the label $\hat{y}_i$ that can be either True $(\hat{y}_i = y_i)$ or False $(\hat{y}_i \neq y_i)$. It is assumed that the error p_i is a random variable and represents the number of wrong decisions in a sample of i data. Standard deviation is equal $s_i = \sqrt{p_i(1 - p_i)/i}$. It is further assumed that the error rate decreases when the number of examples i increases but a significant error increase suggests a change in the class distribution (called drift). To manage drift detection two parameters are examined and updated during classification, that is p_{min} and s_{min}. Once $p_i + s_i \geq p_{min} + 2s_{min}$ is satisfied, so called warning level is reached, and further reaching $p_i + s_i \geq p_{min} + 3s_{min}$ means finding the drift level which indicates the need of new classifier generation.

Algorithm 1. Classification with drift detection GEP-DD.

Input: data D, number of gene classifiers K, $initW$ - size of initial window
Output: accuracy of classification

1 initialize $noCorrect$, $noWrong$ to 0;
2 use $initW$ rows of dataset to induce K genes;
3 use next $initW$ rows and generated genes to induce best metagene mg;
4 $indF \leftarrow 2 \cdot initW$;
5 **while** *not all rows in D considered* **do**
6   use **Algorithm** 2 to detect maximal window with no drift and perform classification;
7   update $noCorrect$, $noWrong$;
8      $windowSize \leftarrow$ distance between drift level and warning level;
       // **new classifier training**
9   use $windowSize$ rows from D to generate K genes and metagene classifier mg;
10   update $initF$ to the first row not considered yet;
11 accuracy$\leftarrow noCorrect/(noWrong + noCorrect)$;
12 **return** *accuracy of classification*

The general idea of drift detection is shown in Algorithm 1. The initial classifier is generated with $initW$ rows of the dataset, where $initW$ is a parameter of the process. Then the following procedure is iterated. With a fixed classifier the coming data rows are classified and the error is calculated. Once the warning level is reached the next data rows are moved to the context window as long as no drift level is reached. Data from the context window are then used to generate a new classifier. The procedure of finding the maximal window with no drift is shown as Algorithm 2. Base classifiers are generated as described in Sect. 2 and applied in Algorithm 1 (line 2, 9).

Algorithm 2. Detection of a maximal window with no drift.

Input: classifier mg, data D, index of first row $indF$, parameter $initT$
Output: boundaries of the maximal window with no drift: k_w index of
warning row, k_d - index of drift row

1   $warning, drift \leftarrow$ false;
2   trainSet$\leftarrow initT$ rows from D starting from $indF$;
3   classify trainSet with classifier mg;
4   $noCorrect \leftarrow$ number of correct classification results;
5   $noWrong \leftarrow$ number of wrong classification results;
6   $p_{min} \leftarrow noWrong/(noWrong + noCorrect)$;
7   $s_{min} \leftarrow \sqrt{p_{min}(1 - p_{min})/(noWrong + noCorrect)}$;
8   $rowNo \leftarrow indF + 2 \cdot initT$;
9   **while** not all rows in D considered yet $\wedge$ not $drift$ **do**
10   classify row $rowNo$ with classifier mg;
11   modify $noCorrrect, noWrong$;
12     $p \leftarrow noWrong/(noWrong + noCorrect)$;
13     $s \leftarrow \sqrt{p(1 - p)/(noWrong + noCorrect)}$;
14   modify p_{min}, s_{min};
15   warning$\leftarrow (p + s \geq p_{min} + 2s_{min})$;
16   **if** $warning$ **then**
17       $k_w = rowNo$;
18   drift$\leftarrow (p + s \geq p_{min} + 3s_{min})$;
19   **if** $warning\wedge drift$ **then**
20       $k_d = rowNo$;
21     $rowNo + +$;
22 **return** $k_d, k_w, noWrong, noCorrect$

3.2   GEP-Based Incremental Classifier

A detailed description of the GEP-based incremental classifier (GEP-INCR) can
be found in [16]. The process of generating base classifiers and creating metagens
is identical as in case of the classification with drift detection. The incremental
classification algorithm is shown as Algorithm 3.

To run the incremental classifier two main parameters have to be set by the
user. The first is the chunk size (ch) and the second - the number of genes (K).

3.3   Computational Complexity of GEP-DD and GEP-INCR

For the case of binary GEP classification, the computational complexity of generating the population of genes and choosing one best metagene as a classi-
fier is $O(nG \cdot posS \cdot \log(posS) \cdot |D|)$, where nG is the maximum of number
of iterations for gene and meta-gene learning, $popS$ is the size of the popula-
tion and $|D|$ is the size of the dataset. For the multi-class OVA approach it is
$O(nG \cdot posS \cdot \log(posS) \cdot |D| \cdot |C|)$, with $|C|$ number of classes. In what follows
let $ComplBase$ stand for the complexity of generating base classifiers.

Algorithm 3. Incremental algorithm GEP-INCR.

Input: data D, chunk size ch, K-number of genes in population

Output: qc - quality of the incremental classification

1   initialize $correctClsf \leftarrow 0$

2   $dataTrain \leftarrow$ first ch vectors from D

3   **for** $i = 1$ *to* K **do**

4   apply GEP learning to generate gene g

5      $dataTest \leftarrow$ next ch vectors from D

6      $corr \leftarrow$ number of vectors from $dataTest$ correctly classified by g

7      $correctClsf \leftarrow correctClsf + corr$

8   add g to population of genes pop

9      $dataTrain \leftarrow dataTest$

10   $dataTrainMeta \leftarrow$ next ch vectors from D

11   **while** *vectors in D not considered yet* **do**

12   apply GEP learning to $dataTrain$ to generate gene g

13   add g to population of genes pop

14   delete from pop the gene with the lowest fitness

15   apply GEP learning to $dataTrainMeta$ and pop to generate metagene mg

16      $dataTest \leftarrow$ next ch vectors from D

17      $corr \leftarrow$ number of vectors from $dataTest$ correctly classified by mg

18      $correctClsf \leftarrow correctClsf + corr$

19      $dataTrain \leftarrow dataTrainM$

20      $dataTrainM \leftarrow dataTest$

21   $qc \leftarrow \frac{correctClfs}{|D| - 2 \cdot ch}$

22   **return** qc

For drift detection algorithm, the number of iterations it (lines $5 - 10$ in Algorithm 1) depends on the dataset and is equal to the number of detected drift changes. Thus the complexity of GEP-DD is $O(it \cdot K) \cdot ComplBase$ where K is a parameter denoting the number of classifiers. For incremental learning GEP-INCR the formula for complexity is the same, here the number of iterations $it = |D|/ch$ depends on the parameter ch-chunk size.

4   Computational Experiment Settings and Results

The computational experiment aimed to evaluate the performance of the proposed GEP based ensemble classifier with drift detection versus the performance of the GEP-based incremental ensemble classifier. In the experiment publicly available real-life datasets listed in Table 1 have been used.

In the experiment, each classifier has been run 50 times for each of the considered datasets. Classifier performance has been measured in terms of the average accuracy (Acc) and standard deviation ($\pm$). In case of both GEP-DD and GEP-INCR following settings have been used: number of base classifiers $K = 50$, number of iterations in the procedure producing genes - 100, number of

Table 1. Benchmark datasets used in the experiment.

Dataset	Instances	Attributes	Classes	Source
Airlines	539383	8	2	[1]
Covertype	581012	55	7	[9]
Electricity	44976	6	2	[2]
KDD99-10%	1025010	11	9	[9]
Poker Hand	141179	11	10	[9]

Table 2. Settings and experiment results for GEP-DD.

Dataset	Accuracy	±	$initW$	$initT$
Airlines	**0,6484**	0,0061	20	3
Covertype	0,8801	0,0064	20	4
Electricity	**0,9356**	0,0416	100	4
KDD99-10%	**0,9769**	0,0059	100	4
Poker Hand	0,5816	0,0096	100	4

Table 3. Settings and experiment results for GEP-INCR.

Dataset	Accuracy	±	ch
Airlines	0,6413	0,0186	200
Covertype	**0,8808**	0,0214	200
Electricity	0,8814	0,0365	50
KDD99-10%	0,9586	0,0093	100
Poker Hand	**0,5943**	0,0109	1000

iterations in the procedure producing metagenes - 50. Further settings are shown in Tables 2 and 3 together with performance results of the respective classifier.

Comparing the discussed classifiers it can be observed that GEP-DD seem to perform slightly better than GEP-INCR in terms of both - higher accuracy and lower standard deviations.

To better compare both discussed approaches we have analysed two series of 250 accuracies each, produced in the experiment by GEP-DD and GEP-INCR. Analysis using the paired Two Sample t-Test for equality of means shows that the null hypotheses stating that the respective means are statistically equal, holds (Test t two-tailed = 2,032, t stat = 3,306, $P(T \leq t)two-tailed = 0,00224$, confidence level = 0,05).

To confront results obtained by both discussed classifiers (GEP with drift detector and incremental GEP) with some literature reported ones, we show in Table 4 some recently published results for state-of-the-art classifiers with drift detectors and for some incremental classifiers. The proposed GEP-DD algorithm performs, for some real-life datasets, better in terms of the classification accuracy than the recently proposed ones. On the other hand, there are datasets where GEP-based approaches are outperformed by other classifiers. The above finding supports what intuitively is generally accepted. So far no single kind of classifier with a concept drift detection or no other single incremental/online classifier can be considered as superior to all other of such classifiers.

Table 4. Literature reported results.

Dataset	Accuracy	Base classifier	D.D. algorithm	Source
Airlines	0,6691	Naïve Bayes	FSDD	[24] 2018
Airlines	0,6544	Hoeffding Tree	SEED	[24] 2018
Covertype	0,6838	Naïve Bayes	FTDD	[24] 2018
Covertype	0,7564	Hoeffding Tree	DDM	[24] 2018
Electricity	0,9070	KFCM	Incremental	[21] 2016
KDD99-10%	0,9749	KAOGINC	Incremental	[5] 2013
Poker Hand	0,5011	Naïve Bayes	DDM	[24] 2018
Poker Hand	0,5185	Hoeffding Tree	DDM	[24] 2018

5   Conclusion

The paper contributes through proposing Gene Expression Programming ensemble classifier with drift detection. Main features of the approach include using the two levels classification scheme where at the base level expression trees serving as base classifiers are induced and at the meta level metagenes used for predicting class labels are evolved. The approach incorporates one of the well-known concept drift detectors. The computational experiment confirmed that the proposed classifier performs well and for some real-life datasets produces competitive class predictions. Basing on the above it can be concluded that the proposed GEP-DD classifier extends the family of classifiers suitable for dealing with non-stationary data streams environments.

Future research will concentrate on integrating GEP-based classifiers with some other drift detection mechanisms with a view to further improve its predictive power when dealing with datasets characterized by a concept drift. Another direction of research will concentrate on finding measures to decrease computational complexity of the approach, thus making it more practical when dealing with huge datasets.

References

1. Airlines dataset (2017). http://www.kaggle.com/datasets
2. Analysis, M.O.: UCI machine learning repository (2013). http://moa.cms.waikato.ac.nz/datasets/

3. Baena-Garća, M., del Campo-Ávila, J., Fidalgo, R., Bifet, A., Gavaldà, R., Morales-Bueno, R.: Early drift detection method. In: International Workshop on Knowledge Discovery from Data Streams, pp. 77–86 (2006)
4. Barros, R.S.M., Santos, S.G.T.C.: A large-scale comparison of concept drift detectors. Inf. Sci. **451–452**, 348–370 (2018). https://doi.org/10.1016/j.ins.2018.04.014
5. Bertini, J.R.J., Zhao, L., Lopes, A.A.: An incremental learning algorithm based on the k-associated graph for non-stationary data classification. Inf. Sci. **246**, 52–68 (2013)
6. Bifet, A., Gavaldà, R.: Learning from time-changing data with adaptive windowing. In: Proceedings of the Seventh SIAM International Conference on Data Mining, 26–28 April 2007, Minneapolis, Minnesota, USA, pp. 443–448. SIAM (2007). https://doi.org/10.1137/1.9781611972771.42
7. de Carvalho Santos, S.G.T., de Barros, R.S.M., Júnior, P.M.G.: Optimizing the parameters of drift detection methods using a genetic algorithm. In: 27th IEEE International Conference on Tools with Artificial Intelligence, ICTAI 2015, Vietri sul Mare, Italy, 9–11 November 2015, pp. 1077–1084. IEEE Computer Society (2015). https://doi.org/10.1109/ICTAI.2015.153
8. Cohen, L., Avrahami, G., Last, M., Kandel, A.: Info-fuzzy algorithms for mining dynamic data streams. Appl. Soft Comput. **8**(4), 1283–1294 (2008). https://doi.org/10.1016/j.asoc.2007.11.003
9. Dheeru, D., Karra Taniskidou, E.: UCI machine learning repository (2017). http://archive.ics.uci.edu/ml
10. Fern, A., Givan, R.: Online ensemble learning: an empirical study. Mach. Learn. **53**(1–2), 71–109 (2003). https://doi.org/10.1023/A:1025619426553
11. Ferreira, C.: Gene expression programming: a new adaptive algorithm for solving problems. CoRR cs.AI/0102027 (2001)
12. Ferreira, C.: Gene Expression Programming: Mathematical Modeling by an Artificial Intelligence. Studies in Computational Intelligence, vol. 21. Springer, Heidelberg (2006). https://doi.org/10.1007/3-540-32849-1
13. Frías-Blanco, I., Verdecia-Cabrera, A., Ortiz-Díaz, A., Carvalho, A.: Fast adaptive stacking of ensembles. In: Proceedings of the 31st Annual ACM Symposium on Applied Computing, SAC 2016, pp. 929–934. ACM, New York (2016). https://doi.org/10.1145/2851613.2851655
14. Gama, J., Medas, P., Castillo, G., Rodrigues, P.: Learning with drift detection. In: Bazzan, A.L.C., Labidi, S. (eds.) SBIA 2004. LNCS (LNAI), vol. 3171, pp. 286–295. Springer, Heidelberg (2004). https://doi.org/10.1007/978-3-540-28645-5_29
15. Hulten, G., Spencer, L., Domingos, P.M.: Mining time-changing data streams. In: Lee, D., Schkolnick, M., Provost, F.J., Srikant, R. (eds.) Proceedings of the Seventh ACM SIGKDD International Conference on Knowledge Discovery and Data Mining, San Francisco, CA, USA, August 26–29, 2001, pp. 97–106. ACM (2001). http://portal.acm.org/citation.cfm?id=502512.502529
16. Jedrzejowicz, J., Jedrzejowicz, P.: Incremetal GEP-based ensemble classifier. In: Czarnowski, I., Howlett, R.J., Jain, L.C. (eds.) IDT 2017. SIST, vol. 72, pp. 61–70. Springer, Cham (2018). https://doi.org/10.1007/978-3-319-59421-7_6
17. Jędrzejowicz, J., Jędrzejowicz, P.: GEP-Induced Expression Trees as Weak Classifiers. In: Perner, P. (ed.) ICDM 2008. LNCS (LNAI), vol. 5077, pp. 129–141. Springer, Heidelberg (2008). https://doi.org/10.1007/978-3-540-70720-2_10
18. Jędrzejowicz, J., Jędrzejowicz, P.: A Family of GEP-Induced Ensemble Classifiers. In: Nguyen, N.T., Kowalczyk, R., Chen, S.-M. (eds.) ICCCI 2009. LNCS (LNAI), vol. 5796, pp. 641–652. Springer, Heidelberg (2009). https://doi.org/10.1007/978-3-642-04441-0_56

19. Jędrzejowicz, J., Jędrzejowicz, P.: Experimental evaluation of two new gep-based ensemble classifiers. Expert Syst. Appl. **38**(9), 10932–10939 (2011). https://doi. org/10.1016/j.eswa.2011.02.135
20. Jędrzejowicz, J., Jędrzejowicz, P.: Combining expression trees. In: 2013 IEEE International Conference on Cybernetics, CYBCONF 2013, Lausanne, Switzerland, 13– 15 June 2013, pp. 80–85. IEEE (2013). https://doi.org/10.1109/CYBConf.2013. 6617448. http://ieeexplore.ieee.org/xpl/mostRecentIssue.jsp?punumber=6599033
21. Jędrzejowicz, J., Jędrzejowicz, P.: Distance-based online classifiers. Expert Syst. Appl. **60**, 249–257 (2016). https://doi.org/10.1016/j.eswa.2016.05.015
22. Kolter, J.Z., Maloof, M.A.: Dynamic weighted majority: an ensemble method for drifting concepts. J. Mach. Learn. Res. **8**, 2755–2790 (2007)
23. Kotsiantis, S.B.: An incremental ensemble of classifiers. Artif. Intell. Rev. **36**(4), 249–266 (2011). https://doi.org/10.1007/s10462-011-9211-4
24. de Lima Cabral, D.R., de Barros, R.S.M.: Concept drift detection based on Fisher's Exact test. Inf. Sci. **442–443**, 220–234 (2018). https://doi.org/10.1016/j.ins.2018. 02.054
25. Liu, S., Liu, Z., Sun, J., Liu, L.: Application of synergetic neural network in online writeprint identification. Int. J. Digit. Content Technol. Appl. **5**(3), 126–135 (2011)
26. Nishida, K., Yamauchi, K.: Detecting concept drift using statistical testing. In: Corruble, V., Takeda, M., Suzuki, E. (eds.) DS 2007. LNCS (LNAI), vol. 4755, pp. 264–269. Springer, Heidelberg (2007). https://doi.org/10.1007/978-3-540-75488-6_27
27. Schlimmer, J.C., Granger, R.H.: Incremental learning from noisy data. Mach. Learn. **1**(3), 317–354 (1986). https://doi.org/10.1023/A:1022810614389
28. Tanbeer, S.K., Ahmed, C.F., Jeong, B., Lee, Y.: Sliding window-based frequent pattern mining over data streams. Inf. Sci. **179**(22), 3843–3865 (2009). https:// doi.org/10.1016/j.ins.2009.07.012
29. Utgoff, P.E., Berkman, N.C., Clouse, J.A.: Decision tree induction based on efficient tree restructuring. Mach. Learn. **29**(1), 5–44 (1997). https://doi.org/10.1023/A: 1007413323501
30. Xu, S., Wang, J.: A fast incremental extreme learning machine algorithm for data streams classification. Expert Syst. Appl. **65**(C), 332–344 (2016). https://doi.org/ 10.1016/j.eswa.2016.08.052

Dynamic Process Workflow Routing Using Deep Learning

Kareem Amin[1,3], Stelios Kapetanakis[4(✉)], Klaus-Dieter Althoff[1,2],
Andreas Dengel[1,3], and Miltos Petridis[5]

[1] German Research Center for Artificial Intelligence, Smart Data
and Knowledge Services, Kaiserslautern, Germany
{kareem.amin, klaus-dieter.althoff,
andreas.dengel}@dfki.uni-kl.de
[2] Institute of Computer Science, Intelligent Information Systems Lab,
University of Hildesheim, Hildesheim, Germany
[3] Kaiserslautern University, Kaiserslautern, Germany
[4] School of Computing Engineering and Mathematics,
University of Brighton, Brighton, UK
s.kapetanakis@brighton.ac.uk
[5] Department of Computing, Middlesex University, London, UK
m.petridis@mdx.ac.uk

Abstract. Dynamic business processes are challenged by constant changes due to unstable environments, unexpected incidents and difficult to predict behaviours. In industry areas like customer support, complex incidents can be regarded as instances of a dynamic process since there can be no static planning against their unique nature. Support engineers will work with any means at their disposal to solve any emerging case and define a custom prioritization strategy, to achieve the best possible result. To assist with this, in this paper we describe a novel workflow application to address the tasks of high solution accuracy and shorter prediction resolution time. We describe how workflows can be generated to assist experts and how our solution can scale over time to produce domain-specific reusable cases for similar problems. Our work is evaluated using data from 5000 workflows from the automotive industry.

Keywords: Business processes · Case-based reasoning · Deep learning
Natural Language Processing

1 Introduction

Customer support is the most important service of a business. Speaking from a customer's experience there are only a few times where customer service was great, without the feeling of treating her/him as just another ticket. Effective customer support poses several challenges for a company since any solitary case can involve a variety of complex factors as well as substantial obscurity and uncertainty in its description. For a trained engineer to complete a series of workflow cases with all cases must be prioritized and executed on a daily schedule. Routing must be determined based on each case problem definition, complexity, priority in accordance with any historical

M. Bramer and M. Petridis (Eds.): SGAI-AI 2018, LNAI 11311, pp. 132–142, 2018.
https://doi.org/10.1007/978-3-030-04191-5_10

evidence (past workflow cases) that may lead to a solution. This work proposes a hybrid solution using deep learning and case-based reasoning (CBR) on business process workflows to increase solution accuracy and minimize the cost of a solution retrieval.

The growth of intensive data-driven decision-making has caused broad recognition [1], and the promise that Artificial Intelligence (AI) technologies can augment it even further. Within the Case-based Reasoning community there have been several examples of applying data-driven methods to fast changing work environments with several benefits from it. Recently, the customer experience industry has adopted a data-centric vision in an equivalent way, as companies embrace the power of data to optimize their business workflows and the quality of their services [1].

This work focuses on large-scale customer support, helping help-desk managers to optimize their prioritization strategies and achieve increased performance. A key concept in that is timely case resolution, measured in resolved cases per minute, which usually leads to high resolution vs. lower accuracy. Research on successful customer support ticket resolutions has identified several features that influence resolutions results. For example, the work of Maddern et al. [14] looks at the effect of grammatically incorrect sentences, abbreviations, mixes among different languages and semantic challenges. Besides the knowledge containers domain vocabulary: how similarity measures are formulated and can identify the adaptation knowledge [7].

Customer support cases usually resemble an application workflow which follows a certain business process. Business processes can be represented sets of activities with temporal relationships and constraints. Business processes are highly standardized to be monitored automatically [30–32]. Several standards are now available to that can be integrated with bespoke large scale portals. The Business Process Modelling Notation (BPMN) developed by the Business Process Management Initiative (BPMI) and Object Management Group (OMG) provides a standard for the graphical representation of workflow-based business processes [27]. Standards produced for business process representation aim to cover the definition, orchestration and choreography of a business process. Over the last few years, several standards have emerged and are widely accepted and supported by mainly Service Oriented Architecture (SOA) enterprise technologies. An example is the OASIS Business Process Execution Language (BPEL), short for Web Services BPEL (WS-BPEL) [28] and the XML Process Definition Language (XPDL) which is standardized to interchange Business Process definitions between different workflow products and systems [29].

Deep Learning algorithms are effective when dealing with learning from substantial amounts of both structured and unstructured data. Within the CBR paradigm, Deep Learning models can benefit from any available data, any integration of the two faces substantial challenges [3]. While Deep Learning can be applied to learn from large volumes of labeled data, it can also be attractive for learning from substantial amounts of unlabeled/unsupervised data [4–6], making it attractive for extracting meaningful representations and patterns from large volumes of Workflow Data.

This paper proposes a hybrid approach using CBR and Deep Learning to mitigate the challenges that come from complex workflow domains. This approach is being evaluated with Help-Desk support engineers while prioritizing and solving new, raw-content workflows. We present DeepTMS, a hybrid Textual Case-based reasoning (hTCBR) approach using Deep Neural Networks while (a) not relying on manually constructed similarity measures as with traditional CBR and (b) it does not require domain expertise to decode any domain knowledge.

This paper is structured as follows: First we describe the related work to our approach. Section 3 explains our approach, our domain challenges and the followed solution architecture. Section 4 presents the carried-out evaluation with domain experts to ensure the efficiency of our proposed approach. Finally Sect. 5 concludes this work and presents our future directions.

2 Related Work

A business process is tightly dependent on its workflow representation. When monitoring information about a business process, the current workflow state must be analysed and compared using domain/model knowledge and knowledge gained from experience. As problems usually recur, if similar cases are found this can provide the context for reasoning about the workflow or, if no such precedent can be found, new knowledge can be derived in the form of a new case that can be stored in the system for later use. This approach matches the behaviour and process of Case-Based Reasoning (CBR) systems which follows the Retrieve, Reuse, Revise, Retain model [2]. CBR seems an effective way of monitoring business processes [30, 31] when represented as graphs and spatio-temporal [33] or structural similarity measures are applied [26].

Related work to this research also relates to text processing with mixed languages, customer support and CBR systems and automation of text relation extraction. Textual CBR supports cases represented as text. Text representation states several challenges since text is unstructured and can have grammatically incorrect sentences. This research can be compared to the work presented in [18–20], where hybrid CBR approaches (CBR with Natural Language Processing – NLP-) frameworks were used to process the knowledge written in free text. In this work, NLP frameworks were not able to process text spanned across different languages since there were several issues related to accurate sentence parsing. Therefore, we suggest a different approach using Deep Neural Networks to ease the task of finding similarities between workflows and automate the knowledge from textual workflows.

HOMER [21, 22] is a help desk support system designer for the same purpose of DeepTMS. HOMER used an object-oriented approach to represent cases and used a question-answering approach to retrieve cases. HOMER showed very good results when it first presented in 1998 and after its further improvement in 2004. However, any existing fast-pace work environments demand solutions that can deal with big amounts of data in real time with minimum human interference. Comparing to DeepTMS, we focused more on how to automate the extraction of similarities and deal with unstructured or mixed-languages text, but this approach also can't be automated to be integrated in business environments.

Finding the relation between text and extract features are key criteria in the success of any textual CBR system. These tasks require a lot of effort and normally can take a long time to be done accurately. Different approaches have been presented to build text similarities and find higher order relationships [23]. The work of automating knowledge extraction using Neural Networks can be compared to the work presented in [24] where authors represented the text using dubbed Text Reasoning Relevant work has been seen in Graph (TRG), a graph- based representation with expressive power to represent the chain of reasoning underlying the analysis as well as facilitate the adaptation of a past analysis to a new problem. The authors have used manually constructed lexico-syntactic patterns developed by Khoo [25] to extract the relations between texts.

3 Hybrid Textual CBR Approach on Workflows

Text is used to express knowledge. Text is a collection of words in any well- known language that can convey a meaning (i.e., ideas) when interpreted in aggregation [8]. To build a textual CBR system we follow the system process and how normally the workflow experts prioritize and route cases. From this process key attributes are identified as key ones to decide. In a support ticket management system these can be:

1. Subject
2. Content
3. Sender Group (The company was organized internally in diverse groups and each group had its own applications and systems)
4. Case priority assigned as assigned by the team who reported it.

Upon the above attributes, an expert can decide how to proceed with this workflow and the CBR case can be defined as:

1. Case Generation: Since attributes are few, workflow cases can have flat attribute-value representation features
2. Case Retrieval: Since NLP has substantial complexity case similarities require a rich, context-aware similarity measure. As such a trained neural network for identifying and recommending solutions from the historical case base can be selected.
3. Case Adaptation: Adaptation rules can be generated based on agent behavioral patterns and be recorded in the case management workflow "memory" of the CBR system

NLP challenges in Business process workflows include tedious and time-consuming building cases task for domain experts since they are not able to cope with the cases numbers. Any existing knowledge base as well as new tickets can be received in a multi-lingual format (e.g. English, German, French, etc.). Multi-languages add substantial complexity in the text analysis and pre-processing both in building and retrieving similar cases. Cases can be written by non-native speakers and can contain several grammar mistakes or vague domain abbreviations. Due to the last two challenges it is not possible to resort to any traditional NLP frameworks for text understanding like TwitterNLP and Stanford NLP, since their application does not return sufficient results.

Our approach is based on Deep Neural Networks and Word Embeddings to improve the text pre-processing and similarity measures. Therefore, we propose a solution architecture which connects end to end: data, the CBR process and workflow experts.

DeepTMS solution architecture consists of three main modules (See Fig. 1):

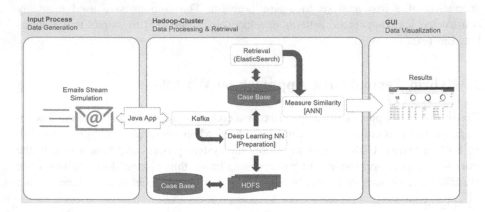

Fig. 1. DeepTMS Solution Architecture

1. Input Process (Data Generation) Module: This module is responsible for generating and simulating the emails (tickets) stream.
2. Map/Reduce -Hadoop- Cluster (Data Processing & Retrieval): This module is responsible for receiving the tickets and doing the ticket content pre-processing/processing, then retrieve the similar tickets from the Case Base (Case Generation, Retrieval & Retain).
3. Graphical User Interface (Data Visualization): This module is responsible for visualizing the results to the system end-users.

Our proposed architecture combines a Deep Neural Network with CBR to capture and decode domain knowledge in the context of NLP. It is applied throughout the task of prioritizing cases based on their content and it measures text similarity based on their semantics. We present several Neural Network types to represent a sequence of sentences as a convenient input for our different models.

The proposed methodology supports several NLP modules to handle workflow cases. These can include Support Vector Machines (SVM) and/or Vectorization to prioritize cases. Large volumes of case can be used to test the methodology as well as several states of the art neural network models like: Convolutional Neural Networks (CNNs), Recurrent Neural Network (RNNs), and Long Short- Term Memory (LSTMs) [16] to test and compare results.

3.1   Vocabulary

Vocabulary is one of the knowledge containers that represents information collected from the domain to express knowledge [7]. By filling in this container we identify terms that are useful for the main system tasks. The acquisition of the domain vocabulary can have direct effects on any system performance, and that's why it is usually done with intensive help from domain experts. To improve any domain acquired vocabulary, we can follow the typical three methods described in [7]. Out of domain words and extracted key features that represent certain text can be identified by using the Word2Vec models [12]. In the next section we describe how exactly Word2Vec worked to build neural word embeddings.

3.2 Word Embedding

Most of the Deep Learning models can't process strings or plain text. They require vectorized representation as inputs to perform any sort of job, classification, regression, etc. Several NLP systems and techniques treat words as atomic units, therefore, in order to apply a Deep Learning model on NLP, words are vectorized using word embeddings is the process of converting text into a numerical representation for further processing. The distinct types of word embeddings can fall into two main categories:

1. Frequency-based embedding (FBE):

FBE algorithms focus mainly on the number of occurrences for each word, which requires a lot of time to process and exhaustive memory allocation to store the co-occurrence matrix. A severe disadvantage of this approach is that quite important words may be skipped since they may not appear frequently in the text corpus.

2. Prediction-based embedding (PBE):

PBE algorithms are based on Neural Networks. These methods are prediction based in the sense that they assign probabilities to seen words. PBE algorithms seem the present state of the art for tasks like word analogies and word similarities.

PBE methodologies were known to be limited in their word representations until Mitolov et al. introduced Word2Vec to the NLP community [12]. Word2vec consists of two neural network language models: A Continuous Bag of Words (CBOW) and Skip-gram. In both models, a window of predefined length is moved along the corpus, and in each step the network is trained with the words inside the window. Whereas the CBOW model is trained to predict the word in the center of the window based on the surrounding words, the Skip-gram model is trained to predict the context based on the central word. Once the neural network has been trained, the learned linear transformation in the hidden layer is regarded as the word representation. In this work we have used Skip-gram model since it demonstrates better performance in semantic task identification [13].

3.3 Text Pre-processing

In the text Pre-Processing stage, raw text corpus preparation tasks are taking place in anticipation of text mining or NLP. Models like Word2Vec can be trained over case corpuses to build cases used in similarity measures. As any text pre-processing tasks, two main components can be identified, these of Tokenization and Normalization. Tokenization is a step which splits longer strings of text into smaller pieces, or tokens. Normalization generally refers to a series of related tasks meant to put all text on a level playing field: converting all text to the same case (upper or lower), removing punctuation, converting numbers to their word equivalents, and so on. Normalization puts all words on equal footing and allows processing to proceed uniformly. Normalizing text can mean performing several tasks, but for our approach, we will apply normalization in four steps: 1. Stemming, 2. Lemmatization 3. Eliminating any stopping words (German or English) 4. Noise Removal (e.g. greetings & signatures). The Word2Vec model or any other model that could be built as a substitution to the traditional taxonomies.

3.4 Similarity Measures

Similarity measures are highly domain dependent and used to describe how cases are related to each other. In CBR, comparison of cases can be performed along multiple important dimensions [9, 11]. Cases that only match partially, can be adapted to a problem situation, using domain knowledge contained in the system [10]. Thus methods Information Retrieval (IR) that are based only on statistical inferences over word vectors, are not appropriate or sufficient. Instead, mechanisms for mapping textual cases onto a structured representation are required. A basic assumption for applying the principle for similarity measures is that both arguments of the measure follow the same construction process. This allows comparing the corresponding sub-objects in a systematic way. For our system we defined the two types of similarity measures: Local Similarity Measures and Global Similarity Measures. Local Similarity Measures describe the similarity between two attributes and the Global Similarity Measures describe the similarity between two complete cases.

Local Similarity Measures (LSM): LSM are heavily dependent on local domain expertise. We have mainly four attributes which are distinctive except for the email subject and content. For the Priority (integer) and Sending Groups (distinctive strings) we used distance functions. For the email subject and content, we counted upon the Word2Vec model to give us the similarity degrees between different texts, after applying all the prepossessing tasks.

Global Similarity Measures (GSM): GSM defines the relations between attributes and gives an overall weight to the retrieved case. The weight of each attribute demonstrates its importance within the case. Methods like the weighted Euclidean distance for the calculation of the global similarity can be applied, as also shown in [15].

4   Experimental Evaluation

Our proposed methodology is being evaluated on a real helpdesk environment which offers customer support service. This work has been a joint application between the German Research Center for Artificial Intelligence (DFKI) and a Multinational Automotive Company (the company) with multiple offices throughout the world. Inside the company, most of the helpdesk cases come through emails to a dedicated team. Once received experts prioritize the cases and assign them to specialist engineers both inside and outside the team to work on it. The company has several historical datasets describing a plethora of issues they have happened along with given solutions.

A historical workflow case could be represented in the form of Problem Description, Solution and Keywords. When new tickets arrive, an expert should search within the company's knowledge base to confirm whether any solution(s) exists or not.

The system evaluation is considering the workflow priority (as provided by the neural network) and any retrieved neighbor cases and the suggested solutions to the visited case.

During our system testing and evaluation phase, we decided to use different Neural Network models to explore, validate and compare accuracy results for each model. We applied three Neural Network models: CNNs, RNNs, and LSTMs [16]. Word2Vec was applied to vectorize text input and build word representations in the vector space (See Fig. 2). Sequences of such vectors were processed using various neural net architectures.

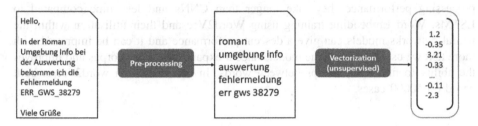

Fig. 2. Text Vectorization

Word2Vec was built using 300,000 historical workflow cases in an unsupervised training mode. All networks were built with one hidden layer, and utilized the a custom trained Word2Vec model. To train the three different neural net models, we have also used 300,000 old tickets with known priorities in a supervised learning process. An additional 10,000 tickets were used to evaluate the models in prioritizing the test tickets automatically. Table 1 summarizes the prioritizing stage results.

Table 1. Prioritization Results

Neural Network Model	Accuracy	Precision	Recall	F1
Convolutional Neural Net (CNN)	82.67%	82.52%	82.64%	82.58%
Recurrent Neural Net (**RNN**)	89.28%	89.19%	89.27%	89.23%
Long Short-Term Memory Net (**LSTM**)	92.35%	92.13%	92.23%	92.16%

Further to the initial results, a second form evaluation was conducted using the best performing algorithm on cases. The evaluation was conducted among the company experts and it was based on DeepTMS's performance on a qualitative level. DeepTMS suggested 10 solutions to any new workflow case. Experts were called to decide whether the most relevant solution was included in the retrieved corpus of cases. 4 slots were created among 10000 workflow cases and the following results were obtained:

Was it between retrieved wokflows one and three: 7764 cases − 77.64%
Was it between retrieved wokflows four and seven: 1468 cases − 14.68%
Was it between retrieved wokflows eight and ten: 692 cases − 6.92%
Was not listed: 76 cases − 0.76%

DeepTMS is using neural networks in case pre-processing to eliminate the redundant text and pass the most relevant text to deep neural networks for prioritization purposes. For our evaluation LSTM seems to out- performed all the other neural network models, however it is prone to computational overheads both during its training phase, and its text processing afterwards. CNNs seem appropriate to areas where changes occur in the network architecture and can give promising results in text processing as well [17]. CNNs are faster in training and processing phases than RNNs and LSTMs. Since an LSTM is a special RNN case they seemed to per- form well on text tasks, better t standard CNNs and worse than LSTMs. In terms of training and processing performance they take longer than CNNs and less time compared to LSTMs. Word Embedding training using Word2Vec and their utilisation within the neural networks models can give a descent performance and it can be improved with more text we use in building the model, since it expands the word corpus and improves the ability to find relationships between words. In our evaluation word2vec is built based on 50000 cases.

5   Conclusions

This paper presents a novel approach to Workflow management systems using textual CBR and Deep neural networks. Automatic feature extraction can be possible using such a hybrid technique and the results are promising as it has been seen in a real application. DeepTMS seems a solid framework to begin our work in this area and we aim to expand it towards real time case processing as well as experimenting with more advanced deep learning algorithms such as adversarial generative networks or Siamese networks. This work has shown that it is possible to have a solid, hybrid, text handling architecture using CBR however more work is required to demonstrate its general applicability.

References

1. Brynjolfsson, E., McElheran, K.: Data in action: data-driven decision making in U.S. manufacturing. Center for Economic Studies (CES) (2016)
2. Aamodt, A., Plaza, E.: Case-based reasoning: foundational issues, methodological variations, and system approaches. AI Commun. 1(7), 39–59 (1994)
3. Chen, X.-W., Lin, X.: Big data deep learning: challenges and perspectives. IEEE Access 2, 514–525 (2014)
4. Bengio, Y.: Deep learning of representations: looking forward. In: Dediu, A.-H., Martín-Vide, C., Mitkov, R., Truthe, B. (eds.) SLSP 2013. LNCS (LNAI), vol. 7978, pp. 1–37. Springer, Heidelberg (2013). https://doi.org/10.1007/978-3-642-39593-2_1

5. Bengio, Y., LeCun, Y.: Scaling learning algorithms towards, AI. In: Bottou, L., Chapelle, O., DeCoste, D., Weston, J. (eds.) Large Scale Kernel Machines, vol. 34, p. 321360. MIT Press, Cambridge (2007)
6. Bengio, Y., Courville, A., Vincent, P.: Representation learning: a review and new perspectives. IEEE Trans. Pattern Anal. Mach. Intell. **35**(8), 17981828 (2013). https://doi.org/10.1109/TPAMI.2013.50
7. Lenz, M., Burkhard, H.-D., Bartsch-Spörl, B., Wess, S. (eds.): Case-Based Reasoning Technology. LNCS (LNAI), vol. 1400. Springer, Heidelberg (1998). https://doi.org/10.1007/3-540-69351-3
8. Richter, M.M., Weber, R.: Case-Based Reasoning: A Textbook. Springer-Verlag GmbH, Berlin (2016). https://doi.org/10.1007/978-3-642-40167-1
9. Ashley, K.: Modeling Legal Argument, Reasoning with Cases and Hypotheticals. MIT-Press, Cambridge (1990)
10. Aleven, V.: Teaching case-based argumentation through a model and examples. Ph.D. dissertation, University of Pittsburgh, Intelligent Systems Program (1997)
11. Brninghaus, S., Ashley, K.D.: How machine learning can be beneficial for textual case-based reasoning. In: Proceedings of the AAAI-98/ICML-98 Workshop on Learning for Text Categorization (AAAI Technical Report WS-98-05), Madison, WI, pp. 71–74 (1998)
12. Mikolov, T., Chen, K., Corrado, G., Dean, J.: Efficient estimation of word representations in vector space. In: NIPS 2013 Proceedings of the 26th International Conference on Neural Information Processing Systems, vol. 2 (2013)
13. Altszyler, E., Sigman, M., Slezak, D.F.: Comparative study of LSA vs Word2vec embeddings in small corpora: a case study in dreams database (2016). arXiv preprint arXiv:1610.01520
14. Maddern, M., Maull, R., Smart, A.: Customer satisfaction and service quality in UK financial services. Int. J. Prod. Oper. Manag. **27**, 998–1019 (2007)
15. Bach, K., Althoff, K.-D., Newo, R., Stahl, A.: A case-based reasoning approach for providing machine diagnosis from service reports. In: Ram, A., Wiratunga, N. (eds.) ICCBR 2011. LNCS (LNAI), vol. 6880, pp. 363–377. Springer, Heidelberg (2011). https://doi.org/10.1007/978-3-642-23291-6_27
16. Hochreiter, S., Schmidhuber, J.: Long short-term memory. Neural Comput. **9**, 1735 (1997)
17. Kim, Y.: Convolutional neural networks for sentence classification. In: Conference on Empirical Methods in Natural Language Processing (2014)
18. Stram, R., Reuss, P., Althoff, K.-D.: Weighted one mode projection of a bipartite graph as a local similarity measure. In: Aha, D.W., Lieber, J. (eds.) ICCBR 2017. LNCS (LNAI), vol. 10339, pp. 375–389. Springer, Cham (2017). https://doi.org/10.1007/978-3-319-61030-6_26
19. Reuss, P., Witzke, C., Althoff, K.-D.: Dependency modeling for knowledge maintenance in distributed CBR systems. In: Aha, D.W., Lieber, J. (eds.) ICCBR 2017. LNCS (LNAI), vol. 10339, pp. 302–314. Springer, Cham (2017). https://doi.org/10.1007/978-3-319-61030-6_21
20. Reuss, P., et al.: FEATURE-TAK - Framework for extraction, analysis, and transformation of unstructured textual aircraft knowledge. In: Goel, A., Díaz-Agudo, M.B., Roth-Berghofer, T. (eds.) ICCBR 2016. LNCS (LNAI), vol. 9969, pp. 327–341. Springer, Cham (2016). https://doi.org/10.1007/978-3-319-47096-2_22
21. Roth-Berghofer, T.R.: Learning from HOMER, a case-based help desk support system. In: Melnik, G., Holz, H. (eds.) LSO 2004. LNCS, vol. 3096, pp. 88–97. Springer, Heidelberg (2004). https://doi.org/10.1007/978-3-540-25983-1_9
22. Göker, M., et al.: The development of HOMER a case-based CAD/CAM help-desk support tool. In: Smyth, B., Cunningham, P. (eds.) EWCBR 1998. LNCS, vol. 1488, pp. 346–357. Springer, Heidelberg (1998). https://doi.org/10.1007/BFb0056346

23. Öztürk, P., Prasath, R.R., Moen, H.: Distributed representations to detect higher order term correlations in textual content. In: Szczuka, M., Kryszkiewicz, M., Ramanna, S., Jensen, R., Hu, Q. (eds.) RSCTC 2010. LNCS (LNAI), vol. 6086, pp. 740–750. Springer, Heidelberg (2010). https://doi.org/10.1007/978-3-642-13529-3_78

24. Sizov, G., Öztürk, P., Štyrák, J.: Acquisition and reuse of reasoning knowledge from textual cases for automated analysis. In: Lamontagne, L., Plaza, E. (eds.) ICCBR 2014. LNCS (LNAI), vol. 8765, pp. 465–479. Springer, Cham (2014). https://doi.org/10.1007/978-3-319-11209-1_33

25. Khoo, C.S.G.: Automatic identification of causal relations in text and their use for improving precision in information retrieval. Ph.D. thesis, The University of Arizona (1995)

26. Minor, M., Tartakovski, A., Bergmann, R.: Representation and structure-based similarity assessment for agile workflows. In: Weber, R.O., Richter, M.M. (eds.) ICCBR 2007. LNCS (LNAI), vol. 4626, pp. 224–238. Springer, Heidelberg (2007). https://doi.org/10.1007/978-3-540-74141-1_16

27. Business Process Management Initiative (BPMI): BPMN 1.1: OMG Specification, February 2008. http://www.bpmn.org/. Accessed Oct 2010

28. OASIS: BPEL, The Web Services Business Process Execution Language Version 2.0, May 2006. http://www.oasis-open.org/apps/org/workgroup/wsbpel

29. Workflow Management Coalition (WfMC): XPDL 2.1 Complete Specification, Updated 10 October 2008. http://www.wfmc.org/xpdl.html. Accessed Oct 2010

30. Kapetanakis, S., Petridis, Ma, J., Bacon, L.: Providing explanations for the intelligent monitoring of business workflows using case-based reasoning. In: Roth-Berghofer, T., Tintarev, N., Leake, D.B., Bahls, D. (eds.) Proceedings of the 5th International Workshop on Explanation- Aware Computing Exact (ECAI 2010), Lisbon, Portugal (2010)

31. Kapetanakis, S., Petridis, M., Knight, B., Ma, J., Bacon, L.: A case based reasoning approach for the monitoring of business workflows. In: Bichindaritz, I., Montani, S. (eds.) ICCBR 2010. LNCS (LNAI), vol. 6176, pp. 390–405. Springer, Heidelberg (2010). https://doi.org/10.1007/978-3-642-14274-1_29

32. Kapetanakis, S., Petridis, M.: Evaluating a case-based reasoning architecture for the intelligent monitoring of business workflows. In: Montani, S., Jain, L.C. (eds.) Successful Case-based Reasoning Applications-2, pp. 43–54. Springer, Berlin (2014). https://doi.org/10.1007/978-3-642-38736-4_4

33. Bandis, L., Kapetanakis, S., Petridis, M., Fish, A.: An architecture for process mining using CBR on rail transport industry. In: Petridis, M. (ed.) Proceedings of the 22nd UK CBR workshop, Peterhouse, December 2017, pp. 11–18. Brighton Press (2017)

The Dreaming Variational Autoencoder for Reinforcement Learning Environments

Per-Arne Andersen[✉], Morten Goodwin, and Ole-Christoffer Granmo

Department of ICT, University of Agder, Grimstad, Norway
{per.andersen,morten.goodwin,ole.granmo}@uia.no

Abstract. Reinforcement learning has shown great potential in generalizing over raw sensory data using only a single neural network for value optimization. There are several challenges in the current state-of-the-art reinforcement learning algorithms that prevent them from converging towards the global optima. It is likely that the solution to these problems lies in short- and long-term planning, exploration and memory management for reinforcement learning algorithms. Games are often used to benchmark reinforcement learning algorithms as they provide a flexible, reproducible, and easy to control environment. Regardless, few games feature a state-space where results in exploration, memory, and planning are easily perceived. This paper presents *The Dreaming Variational Autoencoder* (DVAE), a neural network based generative modeling architecture for exploration in environments with sparse feedback. We further present Deep Maze, a novel and flexible maze engine that challenges DVAE in partial and fully-observable state-spaces, long-horizon tasks, and deterministic and stochastic problems. We show initial findings and encourage further work in reinforcement learning driven by generative exploration.

Keywords: Deep reinforcement learning · Environment modeling
Neural networks · Variational autoencoder
Markov decision processes · Exploration · Artificial experience-replay

1 Introduction

Reinforcement learning (RL) is a field of research that has quickly become one of the most promising branches of machine learning algorithms to solve artificial general intelligence [2,10,12,16]. There have been several breakthroughs in reinforcement learning in recent years for relatively simple environments [6,14,15,21], but no algorithms are capable of human performance in situations where complex policies must be learned. Due to this, a number of open research questions remain in reinforcement learning. It is possible that many of the problems can be resolved with algorithms that adequately accounts for planning, exploration, and memory at different time-horizons.

In current state-of-the-art RL algorithms, long-horizon RL tasks are difficult to master because there is as of yet no optimal exploration algorithm that is

M. Bramer and M. Petridis (Eds.): SGAI-AI 2018, LNAI 11311, pp. 143–155, 2018.
https://doi.org/10.1007/978-3-030-04191-5_11

capable of proper state-space pruning. Exploration strategies such as ϵ-greedy is widely used in RL, but cannot find an adequate exploration/exploitation balance without significant hyperparameter-tuning. Environment modeling is a promising exploration technique where the goal is for the model to imitate the behavior of the target environment. This limits the required interaction with the target environment, enabling nearly unlimited access to exploration without the cost of exhausting the target environment. In addition to environment-modeling, a balance between exploration and exploitation must be accounted for, and it is, therefore, essential for the environment model to receive feedback from the RL agent.

By combining the ideas of variational autoencoders with deep RL agents, we find that it is possible for agents to learn optimal policies using only generated training data samples. The approach is presented as the dreaming variational autoencoder. We also show a new learning environment, Deep Maze, that aims to bring a vast set of challenges for reinforcement learning algorithms and is the environment used for testing the DVAE algorithm.

This paper is organized as follows. Section 3 briefly introduces the reader to preliminaries. Section 4 proposes *The Dreaming Variational Autoencoder* for environment modeling to improve exploration in RL. Section 5 introduces the Deep Maze learning environment for exploration, planning and memory management research for reinforcement learning. Section 6 shows results in the Deep Line Wars environment and that RL agents can be trained to navigate through the deep maze environment using only artificial training data.

2   Related Work

In machine learning, the goal is to create an algorithm that is capable of constructing a model of some environment accurately. There is, however, little research in *game* environment modeling in the scale we propose in this paper. The primary focus of recent RL research has been on the value and policy aspect of RL algorithm, while less attention has been put into perfecting environment modeling methods.

In 2016, the work in [3] proposed a method of deducing the Markov Decision Process (MDP) by introducing an adaptive exploration signal (pseudo-reward), which was obtained using deep generative model. Their method was to compute the Jacobian of each state and used it as the pseudo-reward when using deep neural networks to learn the state-generalization.

Xiao et al. proposed in [22] the use of generative adversarial networks (GAN) for model-based reinforcement learning. The goal was to utilize GAN for learning dynamics of the environment in a short-horizon timespan and combine this with the strength of far-horizon value iteration RL algorithms. The GAN architecture proposed illustrated near authentic generated images giving comparable results to [14].

In [9] Higgins et al. proposed DARLA, an architecture for modeling the environment using β-VAE [8]. The trained model was used to extract the optimal policy of the environment using algorithms such as DQN [15], A3C [13], and Episodic Control [4]. DARLA is to the best of our knowledge, the first algorithm to properly introduce learning without access to the target environment during training.

Buesing et al. recently compared several methods of environment modeling, showing that it is far better to model the state-space then to utilize Monte-Carlo rollouts (RAR). The proposed architecture, state-space models (SSM) was significantly faster and produced acceptable results compared to auto-regressive (AR) methods [5].

Ha and Schmidhuber proposed in [7] *World Models*, a novel architecture for training RL algorithms using variational autoencoders. This paper showed that agents could successfully learn the environment dynamics and use this as an exploration technique requiring no interaction with the target domain.

3   Background

We base our work on the well-established theory of reinforcement learning and formulate the problem as a MDP [20]. An MDP contains $(\mathcal{S}, \mathcal{A}, \mathcal{T}, r)$ pairs that define the environment as a model. The state-space, $\mathcal{S}$ represents all possible states while the action-space, $\mathcal{A}$ represents all available actions the agent can perform in the environment. $\mathcal{T}$ denotes the transition function $(\mathcal{T} : \mathcal{S} \times \mathcal{A} \to \mathcal{S})$, which is a mapping from state $s_t \in \mathcal{S}$ and action $a_t \in \mathcal{A}$ to the future state s_{t+1}. After each performed action, the environment dispatches a reward signal, $\mathcal{R} : \mathcal{S} \to r$.

We call a sequence of states and actions a *trajectory* denoted as $\tau = (s_0, a_0, \ldots, s_t, a_t)$ and the sequence is sampled through the use of a stochastic policy that predicts the optimal action in any state: $\pi_\theta(a_t|s_t)$, where π is the policy and θ are the parameters. The primary goal of the reinforcement learning is to *reinforce* good behavior. The algorithm should try to learn the policy that maximizes the total expected discounted reward given by, $\mathcal{J}(\pi) = \mathbb{E}_{(s_t,a_t) \sim p(\pi)} \left[\sum_{i=0}^{T} \gamma^i \mathcal{R}(s_i) \right]$ [15].

4   The Dreaming Variational Autoencoder

The Dreaming Variational Autoencoder (DVAE) is an end-to-end solution for generating probable future states $\hat{s}_{t+n}$ from an arbitrary state-space $\mathcal{S}$ using state-action pairs explored prior to s_{t+n} and a_{t+n}.

The DVAE algorithm, seen in Fig. 1 works as follows. First, the agent collects experiences for utilizing experience-replay in the *Run-Agent* function. At this stage, the agent explores the state-space guided by a Gaussian distributed policy. The agent acts, observes, and stores the observations into the experience-replay buffer $\mathcal{D}$. After the agent reaches terminal state, the DVAE algorithm encodes state-action pairs from the replay-buffer D into probable future states. This is stored in the replay-buffer for artificial future-states $\hat{D}$.

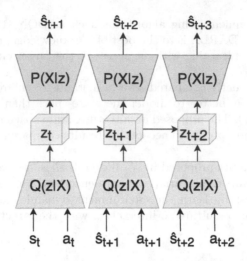

Fig. 1. Illustration of the DVAE model. The model consumes state and action pairs, yielding the input encoded in latent-space. Latent-space can then be decoded to a probable future state. $\mathcal{Q}(z|X)$ is the encoder, z_t is latent-space, and $\mathcal{P}(X|z)$ is the decoder. DVAE can also use LSTM to better learn longer sequences in continuous state-spaces.

Table 1 illustrates how the algorithm can generate sequences of artificial trajectories using $\mathcal{T}_\theta = \mathcal{P}(X|\mathcal{Q}(z|X))$, where $z = \mathcal{Q}(z|X)$ is the encoder, and $\mathcal{T}_\theta = \mathcal{P}(X|z)$ is the decoder. With state s_0 and action $\mathcal{A}_{right}$ as input, the algorithm generates state $\hat{s}_1$ which in the table can be observed is similar to the real state s_1. With the next input, $\mathcal{A}_{down}$, the DVAE algorithm generates the next state $\hat{s}_2$ which again can be observed to be equal to s_2. Note that this is without ever observing state s_1. Hence, the DVAE algorithm needs to be initiated with a state, e.g. s_0, and actions follows. It then generates (dreams) next states.

Table 1. DVAE algorithm for generating states using $\mathcal{T}_\theta$ versus the real transition function $\mathcal{T}$. First, a real state is collected from the replay-memory. DVAE can then produce new states from current the trajectory τ using the state-action pairs. θ represent the trainable model parameters.

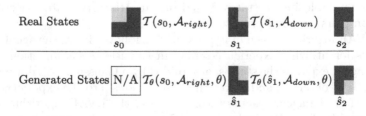

Algorithm 1. The Dreaming Variational Autoencoder

1: Initialize replay memory $\mathcal{D}$ and $\hat{\mathcal{D}}$ to capacity $\mathcal{N}$
2: Initialize policy π_θ
3: **function** RUN-AGENT($\mathcal{T}$, $\mathcal{D}$)
4:     **for** i = 0 to N_EPISODES **do**
5:         Observe starting state, $s_0 \sim \mathcal{N}(0, 1)$
6:         **while** s_t not TERMINAL **do**
7:             $a_t \leftarrow \pi_\theta(s_t = s)$
8:             $s_{t+1}, r_t, terminal_t \leftarrow \mathcal{T}(s_t, a_t)$
9:             Store experience into replay buffer $\mathcal{D}(s_t, a_t, r_t, s_{t+1}, terminal_t)$
10:            $s_t \leftarrow s_{t+1}$
11:        **end while**
12:    **end for**
13: **end function**
14: Initialize encoder $\mathcal{Q}(z|X)$
15: Initialize decoder $\mathcal{P}(X|z)$
16: Initialize DVAE model $\mathcal{T}_\theta = \mathcal{P}(X|\mathcal{Q}(z|X))$
17: **function** DVAE
18:    **for** d_i in D **do**
19:        $s_t, a_t, r_t, s_{t+1} \leftarrow d_i$ ▷ Expand replay buffer pair
20:        $X_t \leftarrow s_t, a_t$
21:        $z_t \leftarrow \mathcal{Q}(X_t)$ ▷ Encode X_t into latent-space
22:        $\hat{s}_{t+1} \leftarrow \mathcal{P}(z_t)$ ▷ Decode z_t into probable future state
23:        Store experience into artificial replay buffer $\hat{\mathcal{D}}(\hat{s}_t, a_t, r_t, \hat{s}_{t+1}, terminal_t)$
24:        $\hat{s}_t = \hat{s}_{t+1}$
25:    **end for**
26:    **return** $\hat{\mathcal{D}}$
27: **end function**

The requirement is that the environment must be partially discovered so that the algorithm can learn to behave similarly to the target environment. To predict a trajectory of three timesteps, the algorithm does nesting to generate the whole sequence: $\tau = \hat{s}_1, a_1, \hat{s}_2, a_2, \hat{s}_3, a_3 = \mathcal{T}_\theta(\mathcal{T}_\theta(\mathcal{T}_\theta(s_0, \mathcal{A}_{rnd}), \mathcal{A}_{rnd}), \mathcal{A}_{rnd})$. The algorithm does this well in early on, but have difficulties with long sequences beyond eight in continuous environments.

5   Environments

The DVAE algorithm was tested on two game environments. The first environment is Deep Line Wars [1], a simplified Real-Time Strategy game. We introduce Deep Maze, a flexible environment with a wide range of challenges suited for reinforcement learning research.

5.1   The Deep Maze Environment

The Deep Maze is a flexible learning environment for controlled research in exploration, planning, and memory for reinforcement learning algorithms.

Maze solving is a well-known problem, and is used heavily throughout the RL literature [20], but is often limited to small and fully-observable scenarios. The Deep Maze environment extends the maze problem to over 540 unique scenarios including Partially-Observable Markov Decision Processes (POMDP). Figure 2 illustrates a small subset of the available environments for Deep Maze, ranging from small-scale MDP's to large-scale POMDP's. The Deep Maze further features custom game mechanics such as relocated exits and dynamically changing mazes.

The game engine is modularized and has an API that enables a flexible tool set for third-party scenarios. This extends the capabilities of Deep Maze to support nearly all possible scenario combination in the realm of maze solving.[1]

State Representation. RL agents depend on sensory input to evaluate and predict the best action at current timestep. Preprocessing of data is essential so

(a) A Small, Fully Observable MDP   (b) A Large, Fully Observable MDP

(c) Partially Observable MDP having a vi-   (d) Partially Observable MDP having ray-
sion distance of 3 tiles   traced vision

Fig. 2. Overview of four distinct MDP scenarios using Deep Maze.

---

[1] The Deep Maze is open-source and publicly available at https://github.com/CAIR/deep-maze.

that agents can extract features from the input. For this reason, Deep Maze has built-in state representation for RGB Images, Grayscale Images, and raw state matrices.

Scenario Setup. The Deep Maze learning environment ships with four scenario modes: (1) Normal, (2) POMDP, (3) Limited POMDP, and (4) Timed Limited POMDP.

The first mode exposes a seed-based randomly generated maze where the state-space is modeled as an MDP. The second mode narrows the state-space observation to a configurable area around the player. In addition to radius based vision, the POMDP mode also features ray-tracing vision that better mimic the sight of a physical agent. The third and fourth mode is intended for memory research where the agent must find the goal in a limited number of time-steps. In addition to this, the agent is presented with the solution but fades after a few initial time steps. The objective is the for the agent to remember the solution to find the goal. All scenario setups have a variable map-size ranging between 2×2 and 56×56 tiles.

5.2   The Deep Line Wars Environment

The Deep Line Wars environment was first introduced in [1]. Deep Line Wars is a real-time strategy environment that makes an extensive state-space reduction to enable swift research in reinforcement learning for RTS games.

The game objective of Deep Line Wars is to invade the enemy player with mercenary units until all health points are depleted, see Fig. 3. For every friendly unit that enters the far edge of the enemy base, the enemy health pool is reduced

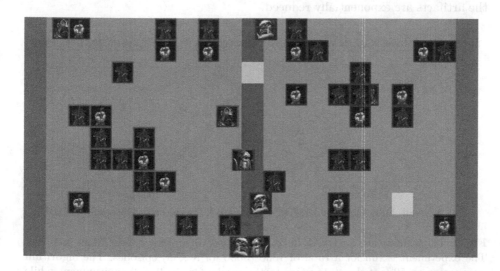

Fig. 3. The graphical user interface of the deep line wars environment.

by one. When a player purchases a mercenary unit, it spawns at a random location inside the edge area of the buyers base. Mercenary units automatically move towards the enemy base. To protect the base, players can construct towers that shoot projectiles at the opponents mercenaries. When a mercenary dies, a fair percentage of its gold value is awarded to the opponent. When a player sends a unit, the income is increased by a percentage of the units gold value. As a part of the income system, players gain gold at fixed intervals.

6   Experiments

6.1   Deep Maze Environment Modeling Using DVAE

The DVAE algorithm must be able to generalize over many similar states to model a vast state-space. DVAE aims to learn the transition function, bringing the state from s_t to $s_{t+1} = T(s_t, a_t)$. We use the deep maze environment because it provides simple rules, with a controllable state-space complexity. Also, we can omit the importance of reward for some scenarios.

We trained the DVAE model on two *No-Wall Deep Maze* scenarios of size 2×2 and 8×8. For the encoder and decoder, we used the same convolution architecture as proposed by [17] and trained for 5000 epochs for 8×8 and 1000 epochs for 2×2 respectively. For the encoding of actions and states, we concatenated the flattened state-space and action-space, having a fully-connected layer with ReLU activation before calculating the latent-space. We used the Adam optimizer [11] with a learning-rate of 1e-08 to update the parameters.

Figure 4 illustrates the loss of the DVAE algorithm in the No-Wall Deep Maze scenario. In the 2×2 scenario, DVAE is trained on only 50% of the state space, which results in noticeable graphic artifacts in the prediction of future states, see Fig. 5. Because the 8×8 environment is fully visible, we see in Fig. 6 that the artifacts are exponentially reduced.

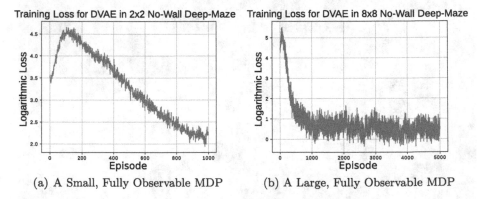

(a) A Small, Fully Observable MDP   (b) A Large, Fully Observable MDP

Fig. 4. The training loss for DVAE in the 2×2 No-Wall and 8×8 Deep Maze scenario. The experiment is run for a total of 1000 (5000 for 8×8) episodes. The algorithm only trains on 50% of the state-space to the model for the 2×2 environment while the whole state-space is trainable in the 8×8 environment.

$\hat{s}_{t+1}$ Right $\hat{s}_{t+2}$ Down $\hat{s}_{t+3}$ Left $\hat{s}_{t+4}$ Up $\hat{s}_{t+5}$ Down $\hat{s}_{t+6}$ Right $\hat{s}_{t+7}$ Up $\hat{s}_{t+8}$

Fig. 5. For the 2×2 scenario, only 50% of the environment is explored, leaving artifacts on states where the model is uncertain of the transition function. In more extensive examples, the player disappears, teleports or gets stuck in unexplored areas.

Table 2. Results of the deep maze 11×11 and 21×21 environment, comparing DQN [15], TRPO [18], and PPO [19]. The optimal path yields performance of 100% while no solution yields 0%. Each of the algorithms ran 10000 episodes for both map-sizes. The last number represents at which episode the algorithm converged.

Algorithm	Avg Performance 11×11	Avg Performance 21×21
DQN-$\hat{\mathcal{D}}$	94.56% @ 9314	64.36% @ N/A
TRPO-$\hat{\mathcal{D}}$	96.32% @ 5320	78.91% @ 7401
PPO-$\hat{\mathcal{D}}$	98.71% @ 3151	89.33% @ 7195
DQN-$\mathcal{D}$	98.26% @ 4314	84.63% @ 8241
TRPO-$\mathcal{D}$	99.32% @ 3320	92.11% @ 4120
PPO-$\mathcal{D}$	99.35% @ 2453	96.41% @ 2904

6.2 Using $\hat{\mathcal{D}}$ for RL Agents in Deep Maze

The goal of this experiment is to observe the performance of RL agents using the generated experience-replay $\hat{\mathcal{D}}$ from Fig. 1 in Deep Maze environments of size 11×11 and 21×21. In Table 2, we compare the performance of DQN [14], TRPO [18], and PPO [19] using the DVAE generated $\hat{\mathcal{D}}$ to tune the parameters.

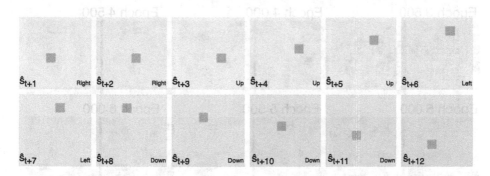

$\hat{s}_{t+1}$ Right $\hat{s}_{t+2}$ Right $\hat{s}_{t+3}$ Up $\hat{s}_{t+4}$ Up $\hat{s}_{t+5}$ Up $\hat{s}_{t+6}$ Left

$\hat{s}_{t+7}$ Left $\hat{s}_{t+8}$ Down $\hat{s}_{t+9}$ Down $\hat{s}_{t+10}$ Down $\hat{s}_{t+11}$ Down $\hat{s}_{t+12}$

Fig. 6. Results of 8×8 Deep Maze modeling using the DVAE algorithm. To simplify the environment, no reward signal is received per iteration. The left caption describes current state, s_t, while the right caption is the action performed to compute, $s_{t+1} = \mathcal{T}(s_t, a_t)$.

Figure 7 illustrates three maze variations of size 11 × 11, where the AI has learned the optimal path. We see that the best performing algorithm, PPO [19] beats DQN and TRPO using either $\hat{\mathcal{D}}$ or $\mathcal{D}$. The DQN-$\hat{\mathcal{D}}$ agent did not converge

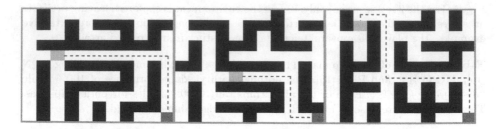

Fig. 7. A typical deep maze of size 11 × 11. The lower-right square indicates the goal state, the dotted-line indicates the optimal path, while the final square represents the player's current position in the state-space. The controller agent is DQN, TRPO, and PPO (from left to right).

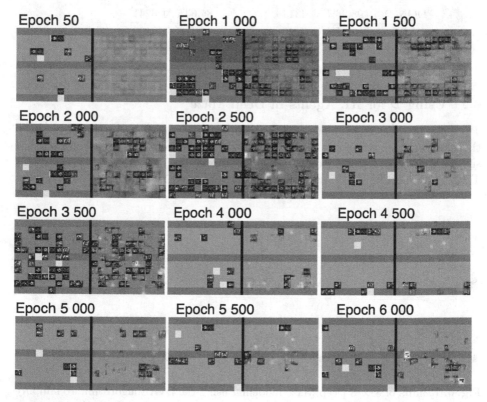

Fig. 8. The DVAE algorithm applied to the Deep Line Wars environment. Each epoch illustrates the quality of generated states in the game, where the left image is real state s and the right image is the generated state $\hat{s}$.

in the 21 × 21 environment, but it is likely that value-based algorithms could struggle with graphical artifacts generated from the DVAE algorithm. These artifacts significantly increase the state-space so that direct-policy algorithms could perform better.

6.3 Deep Line Wars Environment Modeling Using DVAE

The DVAE algorithm works well in more complex environments, such as the Deep Line Wars game environment [1]. Here, we expand the DVAE algorithm with LSTM to improve the interpretation of animations, illustrated Fig. 1.

Figure 8 illustrates the state quality during training of DVAE in a total of 6000 episodes (epochs). Both players draw actions from a Gaussian distributed policy. The algorithm understands that the player units can be located in any tiles after only 50 epochs, and at 1000 we observe the algorithm makes a more accurate statement of the probability of unit locations (i.e., some units have increased intensity). At the end of the training, the DVAE algorithm is to some degree capable of determining both towers, and unit locations at any given time-step during the game episode.

7   Conclusion and Future Work

This paper introduces the *Dreaming Variational Autoencoder* (DVAE) as a neural network based generative modeling architecture to enable exploration in environments with sparse feedback. The DVAE shows promising results in modeling simple non-continuous environments. For continuous environments, such as Deep Line Wars, DVAE performs better using a recurrent neural network architecture (LSTM) while it is sufficient to use only a sequential feed-forward architecture to model non-continuous environments such as Chess, Go, and Deep Maze.

There are, however, several fundamental issues that limit DVAE from fully modeling environments. In some situations, exploration may be a costly act that makes it impossible to explore all parts of the environment in its entirety. DVAE cannot accurately predict the outcome of unexplored areas of the state-space, making the prediction blurry or false.

Reinforcement learning has many unresolved problems, and the hope is that the Deep Maze learning environment can be a useful tool for future research. For future work, we plan to expand the model to model the reward function $\hat{\mathcal{R}}$ using inverse reinforcement learning. DVAE is an ongoing research question, and the goal is that reinforcement learning algorithms could utilize this form of *dreaming* to reduce the need for exploration in real environments.

References

1. Andersen, P.-A., Goodwin, M., Granmo, O.-C.: Towards a deep reinforcement learning approach for tower line wars. In: Bramer, M., Petridis, M. (eds.) SGAI 2017. LNCS (LNAI), vol. 10630, pp. 101–114. Springer, Cham (2017). https://doi.org/10.1007/978-3-319-71078-5_8
2. Arulkumaran, K., Deisenroth, M.P., Brundage, M., Bharath, A.A.: Deep reinforcement learning: a brief survey. IEEE Signal Process. Mag. **34**(6), 26–38 (2017)
3. Bangaru, S.P., Suhas, J., Ravindran, B.: Exploration for multi-task reinforcement learning with deep generative models. arxiv preprint arXiv:1611.09894, November 2016
4. Blundell, C., et al.: Model-free episodic control. arxiv preprint arXiv:1606.04460, June 2016
5. Buesing, L., et al.: Learning and querying fast generative models for reinforcement learning. arxiv preprint arXiv:1802.03006, February 2018
6. Chen, K.: Deep Reinforcement Learning for Flappy Bird. cs229.stanford.edu, p. 6 (2015)
7. Ha, D., Schmidhuber, J.: World Models. arxiv preprint arXiv:1803.10122, March 2018
8. Higgins, I., et al.: beta-VAE: learning basic visual concepts with a constrained variational framework. In: International Conference on Learning Representations, November 2016
9. Higgins, I., et al.: DARLA: improving zero-shot transfer in reinforcement learning. In: Precup, D., Teh, Y.W. (eds.) Proceedings of the 34th International Conference on Machine Learning. Proceedings of Machine Learning Research, vol. 70, pp. 1480–1490. PMLR, International Convention Centre, Sydney, Australia (2017)
10. Kaelbling, L.P., Littman, M.L., Moore, A.W.: Reinforcement learning: a survey. J. Artif. Intell. Res. (1996)
11. Kingma, D.P., Ba, J.L.: Adam: a method for stochastic optimization. In: Proceedings, International Conference on Learning Representations 2015 (2015)
12. Li, Y.: Deep reinforcement learning: an overview. arxiv preprint arXiv:1701.07274, January 2017
13. Mnih, V., et al.: Asynchronous methods for deep reinforcement learning. In: Balcan, M.F., Weinberger, K.Q. (eds.) Proceedings of The 33rd International Conference on Machine Learning. Proceedings of Machine Learning Research, vol. 48, pp. 1928–1937. PMLR, New York (2016)
14. Mnih, V., et al.: Playing atari with deep reinforcement learning. Neural Inf. Process. Syst. December 2013
15. Mnih, V., et al.: Human-level control through deep reinforcement learning. Nature **518**(7540), 529–533 (2015)
16. Mousavi, S.S., Schukat, M., Howley, E.: Deep reinforcement learning: an overview. In: Bi, Y., Kapoor, S., Bhatia, R. (eds.) IntelliSys 2016. LNNS, vol. 16, pp. 426–440. Springer, Cham (2018). https://doi.org/10.1007/978-3-319-56991-8_32
17. Pu, Y., et al.: Variational autoencoder for deep learning of images, labels and captions. In: Lee, D.D., Sugiyama, M., Luxburg, U.V., Guyon, I.R.G. (eds.) Advances in Neural Information Processing Systems, pp. 2352–2360. Curran Associates, Inc. (2016)
18. Schulman, J., Levine, S., Abbeel, P., Jordan, M., Moritz, P.: Trust region policy optimization. In: Bach, F., Blei, D. (eds.) Proceedings of the 32nd International Conference on Machine Learning. Proceedings of Machine Learning Research, vol. 37, pp. 1889–1897. PMLR, Lille (2015)

19. Schulman, J., Wolski, F., Dhariwal, P., Radford, A., Klimov, O.: Proximal Policy Optimization Algorithms. arxiv preprint arXiv:1707.06347 (jul 2017)
20. Sutton, R.S., Barto, A.G.: Reinforcement Learning: An Introduction, vol. 9. MIT Press, Cambridge (1998)
21. Van Seijen, H., Fatemi, M., Romoff, J., Laroche, R., Barnes, T., Tsang, J.: Hybrid reward architecture for reinforcement learning. In: Guyon, I., et al. (eds.) Advances in Neural Information Processing Systems, vol. 30, pp. 5392–5402. Curran Associates, Inc. (2017)
22. Xiao, T., Kesineni, G.: Generative adversarial networks for model based reinforcement learning with tree search. University of California, Berkeley, Technical report (2016)

Short Technical Papers

Abnormality Detection in the Cloud Using Correlated Performance Metrics

Sally McClean[1], Naveed Khan[1(✉)], Adam Currie[1], and Kashaf Khan[2]

[1] School of Computing, Ulster University, Newtownabbey, Co. Antrim BT37 0QB, Northern Ireland
{si.mcclean,n.khan,currie-a5}@ulster.ac.uk
[2] BT Innovate and Design, Martlesham, England
kashaf.khan@bt.com

Abstract. Virtualisation has revolutionised computing, enabling applications to be quickly provisioned and deployed compared to traditional systems and ensuring that client applications have an ongoing quality of service, with dynamic resourcing in response to demand. However, this requires the use of performance metrics, to recognise current or evolving resourcing situations and ensure timely reprovisioning or redeployment. Associated monitoring systems should thus be aware of not only individual metric behaviours but also of the relationship between related metrics so that system alarms can be triggered when the metrics fall outside normal operational parameters. We here consider multivariate approaches, namely analysis of correlation structure and multivariate exponentially weighted moving averages (MEWMA), for detecting abnormalities in cloud performance data with a view to timely intervention.

Keywords: Cloud computing
Multivariate Exponentially Weighted Moving Average (MEWMA)
Abnormality detection · Online monitoring

1 Introduction

Virtualisation in the Cloud has revolutionised the way that computing can be provided, allowing applications and services easy access to resources [5]. Cloud computing allows applications to be efficiently provisioned and deployed compared to traditional systems [2], ensuring that client applications have an ongoing quality of service, with resources that can be added or removed as demand increases or decreases. However, capacity planning teams currently have to manually, or semi-manually, detect abnormalities when KPIs (Key Performance Indicators) and SLAs (Service Level Agreements) have been breached. Once the source of this problem is identified, they must then determine the source of the problem before finding a suitable solution. As well as such short term interventions, it is also highly desirable to identify longer term trends in application

K. Khan—Principal Research Scientist

© Springer Nature Switzerland AG 2018
M. Bramer and M. Petridis (Eds.): SGAI-AI 2018, LNAI 11311, pp. 159–164, 2018.
https://doi.org/10.1007/978-3-030-04191-5_12

behavior and intervene, if necessary, before there are adverse effects on customer KPIs and SLAs. In the following sections, we discuss related work, a methodology to investigate to identify patterns and identify anomalies, the architecture of an experimental cloud environment, and some corresponding experiments. To this end we explore some multivariate approaches, namely analysis of correlation structure and multivariate exponentially weighted moving averages (MEWMA), for detecting abnormalities in cloud performance data with a view to timely intervention. A conclusion and discussion of future work are also included.

2 Methodology

2.1 Background

Cloud computing has emerged as a combination of virtualisation and grid/cluster computing, allowing resources to be offered as a service. For this provision to be efficient, monitoring techniques and related approaches need to be extended, including topics ranging from metric selection [2] to resource prediction [6]. Several authors have studied fundamental aspects of monitoring on the cloud, including those aimed at maintaining required and agreed cloud services [3]. Such topics resonate clearly with the developing cloud mobile market and deployment of the cloud to different sectors. A particular aspect of monitoring within the cloud environment, is the intensive and dynamic need for resources [10].

However, there is limited work progress to date with regard to exploring individual metric behaviour as well as the inter-dependence between related metrics, as a means of proactively detecting the emergence of resourcing situations and raising appropriate alarms. Monitoring in a dynamic and flexible cloud environment provides challenges in maintaining a high-quality user experience while maximising profit and server utilisation. Not only do the resources need to be monitored but so too do the relationship and behaviour profiles, in order to detect the source of a developing problem and identify its possible solution automatically.

2.2 Correlating Performance Metrics to Characterise Resource Patterns

Within the cloud, a large number of metrics are collected through time, to measure resources. These metrics provide information on how busy and overloaded each resource is. However, it is only by considering inter-relationships between the metrics that we can fully understand the real problems that are emerging and the causes of these problems. Thus, metric correlation can help provide a necessary understanding of application behaviour, based on performance metrics, application load and usage trends.

Correlation coefficients are used to measure the relationship between two time-series where values range from -1.0 to $+1.0$, and two time-series are completely in step if the correlation between them is 1.0, inversely related of the correlation is -1.0 and unrelated if it is zero. On the basis of the correlation matrix we can then start to learn motifs, illustrating which metrics, or group of metrics, represent contention or a bottleneck and where resources are aligned.

2.3 Proactive Resource Management Using MEWMA

The Multivariate Exponentially Weighted Moving Average (MEWMA) is a statistical control method to monitor simultaneously two or more correlated variables and also provide sensitive detection of small and moderate shifts in time series data. The MEWMA statistic incorporates information of all prior data including historical and current observation with a user-defined weighted factor [8]. MEWMA has achieved better performance in detecting small and moderate changes than other multivariate control charts like the T-Square and Shewhart control chart [1].

MEWMA can be defined using the following equation.

$$\mathbf{Z}_i = \wedge \mathbf{X}_i + (1 - \wedge)\mathbf{Z}_{i-1} \qquad i = 1, 2, 3, ..., n \tag{1}$$

where $\mathbf{Z}_i$ is the ith MEWMA vector, $\wedge$ is the diagonal matrix with elements λ_i which weight the current and historical data for $i = 1, ..., p$ where p is the number of dimensions and $0 < \lambda_i \leq 1$, and $\mathbf{X}_i$ is the ith input observation vector, $i = 1, 2, 3, ..., n$. The out-of-control statistics is defined in Eq. 2.

$$\mathbf{T}_i^2 = \mathbf{Z}_i' \boldsymbol{\Sigma}_i^{-1} \mathbf{Z}_i < h \tag{2}$$

where $\mathbf{Z}_i$ is the MEWMA vector and $\mathbf{Z}_i'$ is its transpose, $\boldsymbol{\Sigma}_i$ is the variance covariance matrix of $\mathbf{Z}_i$ and $h(> 0)$, chosen to achieve a specified in-control value. Multivariate analysis is used to measure more than one characteristic of a system and also evaluate the relationship among these characteristics. In general the λ value lies between 0 and 1, but, the standard value used in literature for MEWMA algorithm is $\lambda = 0.3$ [9].

In multivariate analysis, the data points $\mathbf{X}_1, \mathbf{X}_2, \mathbf{X}_3, ..., \mathbf{X}_n$ are subsequences of a data stream where n is the length of a data stream. Each data point $\mathbf{X}_i$ is a vector of n observations. The data points in the data stream may be from various distributions, for example, $\mathbf{X}_1, \mathbf{X}_2, \mathbf{X}_3, ..., \mathbf{X}_{i-1}$ and $\mathbf{X}_i, \mathbf{X}_{i+1}, ..., \mathbf{X}_n$ can be from distributions D_1 and D_2 respectively. The aim of the algorithm is to determine and classify the position of change points x_i in the data stream. In the first step, the MEWMA algorithm calculates the exponentially weighted moving average of the multivariate input observations to find the change points. Here, we consider window size of 25 s, which are used to analyse the data using a sliding window with an increment of 1 s to perform sequential analysis. These window size is chosen to combine some historical data with new data to balance the data and identify if a change has happened. In a window, the index variable, i slides subsequently to determine the global statistics for each index i, $1 < i \leq n$. Each input vector of multivariate data is used to find the MEWMA vector represented by $\mathbf{Z}_i$.

3   Experimental Design

For the benchmark experiment, we used a shared resource test bed previously described in more detail in [4]. In the experiment, we monitored each level of the architecture: the applications resource usage, the user resource container (URC) and the server resource usage. Metric readings were taken of several resources, including CPU, memory, disk I/O and network packets to understand how the cloud environment changes while reacting to requests and how the behavior of its metrics reflects these loads. Here, we focus on the resource usage to identify metric correlations without system or environmental effects. After allowing the application to run idle, we then started to load the VM by increasing the number of requests being sent to the application, where every ten minutes the load sent to the application increased in sets of five; these requests were sent equally between the client machines. We also recorded the response time of each request.

4   Results

4.1   Metric Correlation Results

These results have previously been described in detail in [4]; here we present a shortened version which has been refocused onto the use of the correlation matrix as a tool for abnormality detection. In our experiment, the highest significant correlation was shown between the CPU and network with a correlation of 0.92, suggesting that, as the number of requests increases so to do the workload (Table 1). Likewise, there was a significant correlation between the CPU and memory, as expected. However, the disk exhibited a significant negative correlation with the network traffic, suggesting that is has become a bottleneck and is queueing the requests rather than sending responses through the network in a timely manner. The correlation significance was tested using a t-test.

Table 1. Experimental results for metric correlation matrix

	CPU	Memory	Disk	Network
CPU	1.0			
Memory	0.69	1.0		
Disk	−0.30	0.42	1.0	
Network	0.92	0.38	−0.63	1.0

NB the significant correlations are bold in red

4.2   Proactive Abnormality Detection Results

The MEWMA model was fitted in an online manner and identified 4 specific change-points as illustrated in Fig. 1. The 4 specific change-points detected can be interpreted as follows:

1. At 11.28 min the network traffic started to ramp up, as can be seen in Fig. 1. This resulted in a corresponding increase in CPU and memory usage.
2. At 21.56 min there was a further increase in network traffic, with CPU reaching almost 100% utilization, and memory usage also increasing.
3. At 31.18 min, there is a further significant increase in memory utilisa-tion.
4. At 51.42 min, another change-point was identified. This flagged the point at which the disk started to become active, with a resulting drop in CPU utilization, as discussed earlier.

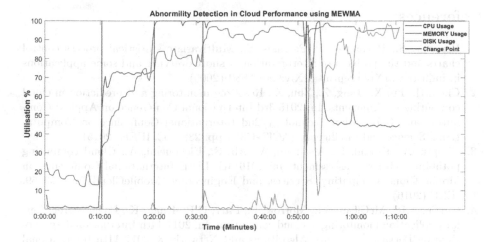

Fig. 1. Abnormality detection in cloud performance using MEWMA.

By interpreting these change-points alongside the network usage and other performance metrics, we can characterise the change-points in terms of flagging increased network load or jumps in component utilisation. Maxing out on these components is an extreme situation where reallocation of resources becomes imperative. By using a multivariate approach, we can identify joint changes in the different metrics and notify the appropriate stakeholders.

5   Summary

Through our benchmark example we were able to demonstrate that the correlation matrix can be used to identify abnormal patterns and furnish evidence as to the cause of the abnormality. In our example, the cause was an under-provisioned disk, which subsequently became very overloaded, and drastically reduced the response rate. In other experiments, by changing the resource allocations we have seen different correlation structures corresponding to different resources being under-provisioned. In particular, we have demonstrated that a multivariate change-point detection algorithm, in this case MEWMA, can be used to predict when an abnormality is about to occur. In further work we will extend the use of such techniques to different scenarios and contexts. Also, in order to extract change-points at an appropriate level of detail it is generally necessary to tune the MEWMA parameters such as window size, significance and forgetting factor vector λ. We have done some previous work on this topic [7] and will extend to the current context in further work.

Acknowledgement. This research is supported by the BTIIC (BT Ireland Innovation Centre) project, funded by BT and Invest Northern Ireland.

References

1. Bersimis, S., Panaretos, J., Psarakis, S.: Multivariate statistical process control charts and the problem of interpretation: a short overview and some applications in industry. arXiv preprint arXiv:0901.2880 (2009)
2. Chen, H., Fu, X., Tang, Z., Zhu, X.: Resource monitoring and prediction in cloud computing environments. In: 2015 3rd International Conference on Applied Computing and Information Technology/2nd International Conference on Computational Science and Intelligence (ACIT-CSI), pp. 288–292. IEEE (2015)
3. Chopra, A., Prasad, P., Alsadoon, A., Ali, S., Elchouemi, A.: Cloud computing potability with risk assessment. In: 2016 4th IEEE International Conference on Mobile Cloud Computing, Services, and Engineering (MobileCloud), pp. 53–59. IEEE (2016)
4. Currie, A.R., McClean, S.I., Morrow, P., Parr, G.P., Khan, K.: Using correlations for application monitoring in cloud computing. In: 2017 14th International Symposium on Pervasive Systems, Algorithms and Networks & 2017 11th International Conference on Frontier of Computer Science and Technology & 2017 Third International Symposium of Creative Computing (ISPAN-FCST-ISCC), pp. 211–217. IEEE (2017)
5. Garg, A., Bagga, S.: An autonomic approach for fault tolerance using scaling, replication and monitoring in cloud computing. In: 2015 IEEE 3rd International Conference on MOOCs, Innovation and Technology in Education (MITE), pp. 129–134. IEEE (2015)
6. Hu, Y., Deng, B., Peng, F., Wang, D.: Workload prediction for cloud computing elasticity mechanism. In: 2016 IEEE International Conference on Cloud Computing and Big Data Analysis (ICCCBDA), pp. 244–249. IEEE (2016)
7. Khan, N., McClean, S., Zhang, S., Nugent, C.: Optimal parameter exploration for online change-point detection in activity monitoring using genetic algorithms. Sensors **16**(11), 1784 (2016)
8. Khoo, M.B.: An extension for the univariate exponentially weighted moving average control chart. Matematika **20**(1), 43–48 (2004)
9. Lucas, J.M., Saccucci, M.S.: Exponentially weighted moving average control schemes: properties and enhancements. Technometrics **32**(1), 1–12 (1990)
10. Peng, J., Chen, J., Kong, S., Liu, D., Qiu, M.: Resource optimization strategy for CPU intensive applications in cloud computing environment. In: 2016 IEEE 3rd International Conference on Cyber Security and Cloud Computing (CSCloud), pp. 124–128. IEEE (2016)

Directed Recursion Search: A Directed DFS for Online Pathfinding in Random Grid-Based Environments

Paul M. Roberts[✉]

School of Computing and Digital Technologies,
Staffordshire University, Stoke-on-Trent ST4 2DE, UK
paul.roberts@staffs.ac.uk

Abstract. The most popular pathfinding approach used in video games is the A* algorithm. This paper looks at depth-first search to determine if, with modifications, it can be made into a viable alternative. Proposed is a method of directing a search, which utilises a scoring system. Tests conducted on randomly generated maps of varying sizes showed that Directed Recursion Search calculated near-optimal paths in less time, by expanding fewer nodes, and with less memory required to store the paths, than A* or depth-first search.

Keywords: Pathfinding · DRS · Depth-first search · A* · Grid-based Heuristic

1 Introduction

Pathfinding is a problem particularly prevalent in video games and is responsible for the calculation of a route between two points for an agent to follow, which avoids all obstacles enroute. This process can be extremely inefficient and consume a huge amount of the processing time available at each update. To compound this issue, the algorithm must also return a valid path quickly; if one is available [1]. A valid path is a route between the start and end nodes, however an optimal path is more desirable, which is a valid path with the mathematical shortest length. Ultimately, there is a trade-off between the speed of processing and the accuracy of the resultant path [2]. Given the impact upon other resources, near-optimal paths can be deemed as acceptable in video games if the calculated path is not obviously worse from a player perspective [3]. Near-optimal is classified as a path with a length in the range of 10% when compared to the optimal path calculated by the A* algorithm [4].

In this paper is presented a novel online algorithm, denoted as Directed Recursion Search (DRS), to calculate near-optimal paths within random grid-based environments. Tests will compare results from DRS against standard implementations of depth-first search (DFS) and the A* algorithm.

M. Bramer and M. Petridis (Eds.): SGAI-AI 2018, LNAI 11311, pp. 165–170, 2018.
https://doi.org/10.1007/978-3-030-04191-5_13

2 Related Work

The A* algorithm is a best-first search algorithm that uses lists to hold nodes encountered during a search [5]. With each iteration, the node with the least cost is expanded. Any connected nodes are then added to the list. A heuristic function is used to calculate the cost, which can be either admissible or inadmissible. If the heuristic function used is admissible, A* will always find the optimal path if one exists [6], however, in grid-based environments the path may actually be 8% longer than the true optimal path. This is because A* does not pass through cells at any angle [7]. It is a relatively fast algorithm [8], but is still a time-consuming process, which performs poorly in large scale environments [2]. Within the algorithm, A* makes use of two lists for storing nodes - an open list for the nodes generated in the search, but yet to be expanded, and a closed list containing the nodes that have been both generated and expanded to produce successor nodes. Manipulation of these lists is where a lot of the processing time for A* is consumed.

DFS can search any environment that can be described as a graph. Once a starting node is selected, DFS will follow an unexplored edge to a connected node, itself yet to be explored. This process continues until there are no further unexplored edges to follow, at which point the search will backtrack to a previous node which still has an unexplored edge. Navigating a graph in this manner will result in a full search of the graph, where each node is explored only once [9]. In practice, once the destination node has been discovered it is possible to generate a path. However, there is no guarantee that the first solution returned will be the optimal one [10]. By modifying the order in which the connected edges are searched, a DFS becomes a directed search, which can be very efficient [9] compared to its undirected predecessor.

3 The Proposed Directed Recursion Search (DRS)

DRS has been developed for use in static grid-based environments and consists of a three-stage process: Search, Enhancement and Refinement. All three stages take place online, with no precomputation required. Upon completion of all three stages the algorithm returns a valid, near-optimal path. There are two important elements of DRS that set it apart from a standard DFS. The first is how the search is directed; the second is how it builds a knowledge of the environment, and then uses this knowledge to determine which cells have more potential to be part of the optimal path. The full algorithm is supplied in Figs. 1, 2, 3, and are called in the order they are listed.

4 Experiment

Test environments were randomly generated grid-based maps of the following dimensions: 10×10, 25×25, 50×50 and 100×100. Each environment conducted 1000 searches for each of the following criteria: no blocked cells, 10%, 20%, 30% and 40% of cells blocked. Therefore, each environment size was tested 5,000 times, resulting in a total of 20,000 path calculations. Octile movement was allowed for all three approaches, enabling searches to progress in eight directions. However,

Search(*c* = current position, *t* = target position)
1. Check if *c* is equal to *t*.
2.   If so,
3.   Add this position to *Potential Nodes* list.
4.   Calculate *threshold* for a cell to be considered a potential node.
5.   Return true.
6. Check if c is a valid position.
7.   If cell at *c* is BLOCKED,
8.   return false.
9.   Else,
10.   If cell at c has already been visited.
11.   Increment cost of cell at this position by 0.5.
12.   Set cell at this position as visited.
13.   Else,
14.   Set the cost of cell at this position to 1.0.
15. Let *v* = vector from *c* to *t* scaled to Search Length.
16. Let *c'* = *c* + *v*.
17. Check if a move to *c'* is a valid move.
18.   If so, recursively call Search(*c'*, *t*)
19.   If function call to Search() returned true,
20.   If cost <= *threshold*, add this position to *Potential Nodes* list.
21.   Return true.
22. Let *rotation* = 0.
23. While *rotation* < 180,
24.   Increment *rotation* by desired angle.
25.   Let *negRot* = *c* + (*c'* rotated by -*rotation*), and *posRot* = *c* + (*c'* rotated by +*rotation*).
26.   Check if a move to *posRot* is a valid move.
27.   If so, recursively call Search(*posRot*, *t*)
28.   If function call to Search() returned true,
29.   If cost <= *threshold*, add this position to *Potential Nodes* list.
30.   Return true.
31.   Check if a move to *negRot* is a valid move.
32.   If so, recursively call Search(*negRot*, *t*)
33.   If function call to Search() returned true,
34.   If cost <= *threshold*, add this position to *Potential Nodes* list.
35.   Return true.
36. End while.
37. Return false.

Fig. 1. DRS search algorithm

Enhancement()
1. Let *index* = 0.
2. While *index* < the number of nodes in *Potential Nodes* list - 1.
3.   Let *a* = the element from the *Potential Nodes* list at *index*.
4.   Let *b* = the element from the *Potential Nodes* list at *index*+1.
5.   If the distance between *a* and *b* < Search Length,
6.   Add *a* to *Enhanced Nodes* list.
7.   Else,
8.   Call Search(*a*, *b*).
9.   Add nodes found in Search() function to *Enhanced Nodes* list.
10.   Increment *index* by 1.
11. End while.

Fig. 2. DRS enhancement algorithm

Refinement()
1. Let *endIndex* = the number of nodes in *Enhanced Nodes* list − 1, and startIndex = 0.
2. While *Enhanced Nodes* list is not empty,
3.   Let *collided* = false.
4.   Let *a* = the element from the *Enhanced Nodes* list at *endIndex*.
5.   Let *b* = the element from the *Enhanced Nodes* list at *startIndex*.
6.   Let *searchVector* = the vector between a and b.
7.   If length of *searchVector* > 0.
8.   Let *v* = *searchVector* scaled to Search Length.
9.   While length of *v* < *searchVector* length,
10.   If cell at position *a* + *v* is ACCESSIBLE,
11.   Let *v* = *v* + *searchVector* scaled to Search Length.
12.   Else,
13.   Let *collided* = true.
14.   Exit while.
15.   End while.
16.   If *collided* equals true,
17.   Let *endIndex* = *endIndex* − 1.
18.   Let *startIndex* = 0.
19.   Else,
20.   Add *b and a* to *Refined Nodes* list.
21.   Delete *a, b* and all nodes in between these nodes from *Enhanced Nodes* list.
22. End while.

Fig. 3. DRS refinement algorithm

diagonal moves were only allowed during the search if the neighbouring cardinal moves were allowed. The positions for the search were located at opposite sides of the environment to ensure that, at a minimum, the width of the environment was searched. The start node was always positioned at the bottom left cell and a random position selected for the end node from the right-hand border.

To compare the results of DRS, the A* algorithm and DFS were tested in the exact same environments, including the same start and end points. A* used an euclidean heuristic, and the order of connected cells in the DFS implementation started with the cell to the north and rotated counter-clockwise. The following metrics were recorded: path length, path optimality, number of nodes in the path, and the number of node expansions. As an additional metric, the time in milliseconds from the start of the search to the time a path is returned was also recorded.

All tests have been conducted on the same hardware to ensure a fair depiction of the performance of the algorithms within the same constraints.

5   Results

It is clear from the results in Table 1 that DRS outperforms DFS by all metrics recorded, across all environments. This is to be expected, as DRS directs the search, whereas DFS does not. The more interesting comparisons are between DRS and A*. Looking at the Time (m/s) column, it is shown that DRS outperforms A* in terms of search time in all environments. Furthermore, as time taken is closely related to the number of expansions, observations of this metric reveal similar improvements. Path Length shows mixed results. Those calculated by DRS in 10×10 maps were shorter

Table 1. Averages per search

	Algorithm	Time (m/s)	Cells expanded	Path length	Optimality %	Nodes in path
10 × 10	A*	5.79	20.22	11.98		11.89
	DFS	0.88	34.28	18.87	57.59	18.01
	DRS	**0.65**	**14.25**	**11.55**	−3.54	**3.77**
25 × 25	A*	54.00	104.65	**32.12**		29.88
	DFS	4.66	221.66	90.77	182.61	78.43
	DRS	**2.27**	**53.18**	32.41	0.92	**7.52**
50 × 50	A*	528.61	414.18	**67.23**		61.22
	DFS	17.17	861.28	299.32	345.25	251.68
	DRS	**9.32**	**150.89**	69.84	3.89	**14.92**
100 × 100	A*	6692.83	2044.67	**144.07**		128.39
	DFS	49.76	3626.99	1084.86	653.01	893.72
	DRS	**33.55**	**536.10**	155.45	7.90	**32.42**

than those found by A*, however, for all subsequent maps the A* algorithm finds the shorter paths. Paths calculated in 25 × 25 maps are fractionally longer for DRS with the average path being less than one percent longer. In 50 × 50 maps, the length of the DRS path increases to 3.89% longer, and in 100 × 100 maps the DRS path is 7.9% longer.

6 Discussion

Within the tests conducted for this paper, it has been demonstrated that DRS outperforms DFS in all categories and betters the A* algorithm on all but one metric identified as being critical to pathfinding in video games. The one metric not surpassed was path length, which can still be considered acceptable as the paths were within the 10% range to be considered as near-optimal. The number of nodes required by DRS to depict this path was consistently lower than the other approaches. This is a desirable feature for pathfinding in video games as storing fewer nodes allows the unused computer memory to be used on other processes. It is important to recognise that the tests conducted forced the searches to the extremes of the maps. It is very unlikely in a real-world game scenario that the AI agents will continually be pathfinding from one side of an environment to the other. Therefore, it can be assumed that most searches will be on smaller subsections of an environment, comparable to the smaller grids tested in this paper. In which case DRS should be extremely competitive in video games.

In video games, where agent response time is crucial to maintaining the illusion of intelligence, processing speed is extremely important. DRS outperformed the other approaches in all tests in terms of time. Another desirable trait is for an algorithm to require fewer expansions, indicating lower memory requirements and less processing. DRS was the clear winner in all tests when looking at cell expansions.

7 Conclusions and Future Work

The tests conducted have shown that DRS expands far fewer nodes than either A* or DFS. It can be concluded that this is indeed an effect of the directed nature of DRS, as similar results were not shown in the standard DFS approach. As there are no list searches carried out by DRS, as is done by the A* algorithm, there was an inevitable reduction in search time. However, a reduction in expansions will have also had an impact upon processing speed. Therefore, it is difficult to conclude that the speed improvements were solely down to the use of lists.

DRS can be viewed as a starting point of a new direction in pathfinding. It has been shown to be a valid alternative to A* in terms of path length, calculation time, the number of nodes stored in the resultant path, and the overall number of expansions. Testing the algorithm in real game world scenarios now needs to take place, as testing in random grid-based environments was just that, a test. For DRS to be considered by the games industry as an alternative to A*, similar results will need to be seen in more ecologically valid environments.

In conclusion, DRS has been shown to expand fewer nodes whilst still returning a near-optimal path - making it potentially a more efficient alternative for pathfinding in video games.

References

1. Algfoor, Z.A., Sunar, M.S., Abdullah, A.: A new weighted pathfinding algorithm to reduce the search time on grid maps. Expert Syst. Appl. **71**, 319–331 (2017)
2. Mathew, G.E., Malathy, G.: Direction based heuristic for pathfinding in video games. In: 2nd International Conference on Electronics and Communication Systems, ICECS 2015, pp. 1651–1657 (2015)
3. Cui, X., Shi, H.: An overview of pathfinding in navigation mesh. Int. J. Comput. Sci. Netw. Secur. **12**, 48–51 (2012)
4. Valenzano, R., Arfaee, S.J., Thayer, J., Stern, R., Sturtevant, N.R.: Using alternative suboptimality bounds in heuristic search. In: Association for the Advancement of Artificial Intelligence (2013)
5. Hart, P.E., Nilsson, N.J., Raphael, B.: A formal basis for the heuristic determination of minimum cost paths. Trans. Syst. Sci. Cybern. **SSC4**, 100–107 (1968)
6. Cui, X., Shi, H.: A*-based pathfinding in modern computer games. Int. J. Comput. Sci. Netw. Secur. **11**, 125–130 (2011)
7. Nash, A., Koenig, S.: Theta* for any-angle pathfinding. In: Game AI Pro 2. CRC Press (2015)
8. Graham, T., McCabe, H., Sheridan, S.: Pathfinding in computer games. ITB J. **4**, 57–81 (2003)
9. Tarjan, R.: Depth-first search and linear graph algorithms. In: IEEE Switching and Automata Theory, pp. 114–121. Stanford University, California (1971)
10. Korf, R.E.: Depth-first iterative-deepening: an optimal admissible tree search. In: Artificial Intelligence 27, pp. 97–109. Elsevier Science Publishers (1985)

Modelling Trust Between Users and AI

Simon Thompson[✉]

Orion Building, BT Adastral Park, Martlesham Heath, Suffolk, UK
simon.2.thompson@bt.com

Abstract. Individual and Societal Trust in AI will determine the scope of application and level of adoption of AI technology. A model of trust is proposed with its partial implementation as a numerical simulation. It is shown by simulation that the introduction of multi-agent dynamics of the sort observed in the case studies we describe has a significant impact on the behaviour of the system. The contributions of this paper are; a new model of trust in AI systems, the partial realisation of the model as a simulator and the results of the preliminary experiments over our simulation.

Keywords: AI ethics · Trust · AI winter

1 Introduction

The widespread application of AI will mean that a very wide community of people will be asked to accept the decisions that AI's are making. The evolution of the adoption of technologies such as genetically modified organisms and nuclear power has been significantly affected by public perception.

For AI to be exploited successfully it must be trusted. Trust is a positive outcome required for users to want to use and interact with AI systems. In the context of the three issues described above for AI to be widely used people need to feel that they won't be harmed, will retain their freedom and can understand what and who is in control at any given moment; in short they need to trust the systems that they are working with.

Therefore convenient and simple methods of creating trust in these systems that can be accessed by ordinary people are desired. Sometimes policy makers and the media discuss the need for "Explainable AI". Explanation can be seen as an act made by an agent or entity with the intent to establish trust in its decision making. Agents are motivated to do this because those who can be trusted are accountable and therefore can be given responsibility for decisions, and being allowed to make independent decisions has high utility.

But simplistic ideas of an explaining AI excludes the wider system in which it is embedded. People using AI's may not wish to reveal their intents by requesting or receiving explanations; they may want to audit and observe rather than inquire and solicit information. Individuals may want to come to a view on the drivers for a decision independently of the AI. And, as noted above, diffusion of control can mean that the notion of a single explaining agent doesn't make sense.

M. Bramer and M. Petridis (Eds.): SGAI-AI 2018, LNAI 11311, pp. 171–176, 2018.
https://doi.org/10.1007/978-3-030-04191-5_14

Trust is used as a construct in the reasoning of AI systems to determine the value of information received [for example: 2], this tradition is important to the discussion presented here in so far as it will allow the simulation and design of systems of AI's and people. A model of trust for AI systems which is then formalized and examined later in the paper.

Trust in human systems is created over time by accumulating evidence of behaviour that allows expectations to be established [1]. Humans will accumulate trust in artificial decision makers by being able to gather evidence over a number of episodes. The quality and amount of evidence will be proportional to the number of episodes required, the trust created will be conditional and qualified in nature [3].

Fundamental constraints on creating trusted AI are imposed by ethical considerations as well as limitations of the art. It may be hard to gather appropriate data, and algorithms can be unreliable. Individual experiences and perceptions may be colored by these constraints.

2   Simulation

We develop triangular model of trust in AI as a three way interaction between [a user and the AI], an [impassive third party and the AI] and [the user and the impassive third party]. This model simplifies the idea of a transactional system and a structural/cultural modifier (the third party) such as the media or a community perception of the AI. The perception of the individual is modeled as transformed by the individuals view of the limitations of the technology, and the perception of the individual is also modified by the way that the third party perceives the performance of the technology as well.

The user understands the AI at a step in the simulation by comparing the AI's decision to a random number simulating the possibility that the AI is correct or not, if the random number is lower than the quality of the AI then the user evaluates this as a mistake. An explanation process is then run to moderate this outcome – if the explanation offered by the AI is of high quality this is modelled as a high probability that the user's trust in the AI will be positively increased by the current interaction. If the explanation is low quality, and the AI's decision is poor then the user's trust will be changed negatively.

The third party is treated in a similar way, but we model the explanation to the third party as a different level of mistakes, simplifying the difference in the perception between users and community. The user incorporates the third-parties current trust in the AI into its calculation of the AI's trustworthiness, the users trust at any step is an average of its raw update described above and its current belief about the trust in the AI of the third-party biased by its belief in the third party.

In Fig. 1 we show this setting (LHS) and also LHS-2 showing disconnection between the User and the Third Party. And a more complete model (RHS) which would use a graph of user agents in an attempt to model the cultural dynamics of different communities more or less connected to the third party and the user, and each other. The RHS model is a topic for future work, and will contain a large number of free variables (size and density of community, number and structure of sub communities, behaviour of individual agents, degree of connectivity to user and third party entities and so on).

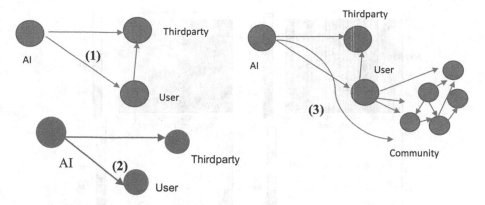

Fig. 1. LHS (1), (2) the simulations we constructed and tested; RHS (3) an idealised future simulation including a graph of similar agents interacting and independently spreading information about the AI based on independent thresholds and beliefs.

3 Experiments and Initial Results

A Julia program was implemented embodying the model described, Julia was chosen as an implementation system because it offers high speed matrixes processing and a powerful visualization system. This was run vs 100 episodes of consultation for 10000 trials. For each trial the random number representing the AI's performance was the same at each step – the parameters of quality of explanation (qAI), the user perception of the AI (αTP), the third-party perception of the AI (αU) and the users perception of the third-party (trustUTP) were varied between 0.0 and 1.0.

Figures 2 and 3 show results extracted from the simulator. Currently it is not possible to make strong claims about the meanings of these outputs, a substantial investigation is required to validate the simulator and to characterize the mass of data that is generated. However we can make some observations about the data obtained so far. Both the dynamics and final state of the evolution of the trust parameter are clearly affected by the flow of information between the third-party and the user.

Top LHS of Fig. 2 shows the variation of user trust evolution in the simulator where the user consults the third party. The dark bars represent journeys where user trust has collapsed early and in this implementation it cannot recover (the user agent ceases to interact below a certain threshold). The striation indicate journeys in which the users trust is fluctuating, The Top RHS shows that there are distinct transitions in the regions explored by the simulator which are not generated by the smooth distributions of starting parameters.

The bottom two charts in Fig. 2 show the evolution of third party trust in the absence of a noisy update from another party. An observation here is that the variation and collapse features observed in the user dynamics are absent. Figure 4 shows the charts in the model (2) scenario from Fig. 2. Here the user is evolving trust in the AI in the absence of a third party. As we would intuitively predict in this case the dynamics of trust evolution in the third party and the agent are similar over the range of

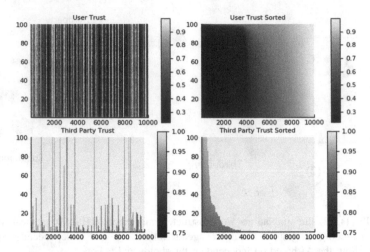

Fig. 2. Model where User interacts with Third-party (1) User trust evolving for 10k interactions using randomised parameters for quality of explanation, AI performance for user, AI performance for the third party and between the user and the third party.

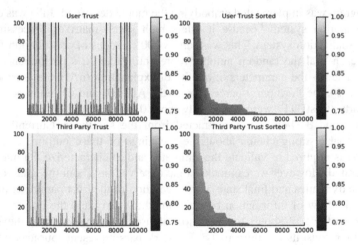

Fig. 3. Model where User does NOT interact with third-party (2), Top LHS shows 10k user journeys, top RHS shows trust sorted, bottom LHS shows third-party journeys and bottom RHS shows sorted trust values for the third party.

parameters chosen in the simulated journeys, with the caveat that in the top charts it can be observed that some journeys collapse because of the user trust threshold, leading to low final trust values for the user.

Figure 4 shows some statistics on the first 100 journeys, the comparison between model 1 (LHS) and model 2 (RHS) shows the variation that would be expected given the observations above. However another result of interest here is the variation in standard deviation and the lack of correlation (0.0826 vs −0.54) between standard

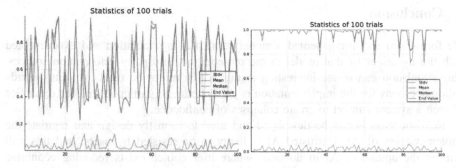

Fig. 4. Statistical behaviour over the first 100 journeys. LHS - model (1) consulting third party, RHS (2) no interaction.

deviation and outcome for the user agent consulting the third-party. As noted these observations require development and validation but they do demonstrate that interesting and varied behaviour in trust evolution can be simulated by models of the type that we propose.

4   Future Work

We have reported preliminary results from experiments using a simplified model described above. An extensive systematic investigation of the properties of our model is required, both to understand the behaviour of the current instantiation and to determine more realistic and robust realizations.

In our current model we instantiate both the cultural and structural components of the model as a single agent. We believe that the dynamics of communities and their behaviours are much richer and a model that uses a graph of interacting agents possibly in combination with a third-party "structural" meta agent would be likely to generate interesting insights.

The results obtained demonstrate that introducing multi-agent dynamics to a trust evolution system of the sort we have modelled creates a substantially different behaviour. Our longer term ambition is to modify and use our simulator to develop answers to questions like:

- What is the outcome for users that choose not to consult the AI for a period of time at the beginning of the game? What conditions lead users to trust an AI enough to try it out? What impact do irrational strategies have?
- Conversely if the user is an "early adopter" what are the trust strategies, outcome probabilities and trust update functions that potentially corrode users willingness to trust and use an AI?
- If the user loses trust in the AI and stops engaging or engages negatively what is the length of time that is required to re-establish trust?

5 Conclusion

We formalized and implemented a model of trust as a simulation and experimented with the dynamics of that model in the presence of third-party information sources. This simulation can create interesting results which might be used to point towards policy decisions for the implementation of AI systems, in particular that the dynamics of such a system can set to create collapses of confidence.

Realistic models can be developed and used to robustly design and regulate the implementation of AI. Untrusted AI is likely to be resisted by users, and this will hamper the uptake of AI in domains where user choice exists reducing economic benefit and limiting the scope of use for AI to solve the massive problems that face our society. In the past AI has undergone several crisis of trust resulting in AI-Winters, our model shows one way that this dynamic can operate. By ensuring that the information channels to third-party (media) and individuals don't become flooded with the failures of AI driven by overblown claims of its applicability we may still be able to avoid another crash.

References

1. Gambetta, D.: Can we trust, trust? Trust: making and breaking cooperative relations, vol. 13, pp. 213–237 (2000)
2. Teacy, W.L., Patel, J., Jennings, N.R., Luck, M.: Travos: trust and reputation in the context of inaccurate information sources. Auton. Agent. Multi-Agent Syst. **12**(2), 183–198 (2006)
3. Venanzi, M., Rogers, A., Jennings, N.R.: Trust-based fusion of untrustworthy information in crowdsourcing applications. In: Proceedings of the 2013 International Conference on Autonomous Agents and Multi-Agent Systems, pp. 829–836. International Foundation for Autonomous Agents and Multiagent System, May 2013

Multi-criteria Decision Making with Existential Rules Using Repair Techniques

Nikos Karanikolas[1](✉), Madalina Croitoru[2], Pierre Bisquert[3],
Christos Kaklamanis[1,4], Rallou Thomopoulos[3], and Bruno Yun[2]

[1] Department of Computer Engineering and Informatics, University of Patras,
Patras, Greece
{nkaranik,kakl}@ceid.upatras.gr
[2] University of Montpellier, Montpellier, France
{croitoru,yun}@lirmm.fr
[3] INRA Iate/INRIA GraphIK, Montpellier, France
{pierre.bisquert,rallou.thomopoulos}@inra.fr
[4] Computer Technology Institute and Press "Diophantus" (CTI), Patras, Greece

Abstract. In this paper, we explain how to benefit from the reasoning capabilities of existential rules for modelling an MCDM problem as an inconsistent knowledge base. The repairs of this knowledge base represent the maximally consistent point of views and inference strategies can be used for decision making.

Keywords: Multi-criteria decision-making · Existential rules
Knowledge representation

1 Introduction

The way to reach a group's decision is a very complex task and depends on the nature of the decision problem. This paper deals with the multi-criteria decision making (MCDM) problem, where a set of agents $\mathcal{I}$ (corresponds to the decision makers) have preferences over multiple criteria on a set of alternatives $\mathcal{C}_A$. MCDM has been an active research area where many different approaches have been proposed.

In this paper we take a different research avenue and see the MCDM problem from a knowledge representation and reasoning point of view. The advantage of doing so is two fold. First, it allows for the use of expressive languages for describing the decision problem (and their subsequent reuse in applications). Second, it paves the way for synergies between the two fields. MCDM could thus benefit from recent advances on explanation and user interaction developed within the techniques we employ in this paper.

Concretely, we propose to define the MCDM problem as an inconsistent knowledge base expressed using existential rules. The inconsistency will be

© Springer Nature Switzerland AG 2018
M. Bramer and M. Petridis (Eds.): SGAI-AI 2018, LNAI 11311, pp. 177–183, 2018.
https://doi.org/10.1007/978-3-030-04191-5_15

addressed using repair techniques [7], a state of the art method of reasoning in presence of inconsistency that outputs the consistent subsets of the knowledge base maximal with respect to set inclusion. The reasoning is then performed on these subsets (also called repairs of the knowledge base).

2   Background Notions

In this section we define the logical language employed in this paper. The notions below represent classical logical notions with some minor changes to reflect the MCDM setting. In "http://students.ceid.upatras.gr/ nkaranik/ sgai-appendix.pdf" the reader can find an example showing the logical language and some examples which clarify our modeling. We consider *the positive existential* fragment of first-order logic $\text{FOL}(\exists, \wedge)$ [5,9]. Its language $\mathcal{L}$ is composed of formulas built with the usual quantifiers $(\exists, \forall)$ and *only* two connectors: implication $(\rightarrow)$ and conjunction $(\wedge)$.

We consider usual first-order vocabularies with constants but no other function symbols. A vocabulary is a pair of two disjoint sets $\mathcal{V} = (\mathcal{P}, \mathcal{C})$, where $\mathcal{P}$ is a finite set of predicates and $\mathcal{C}$ is a set of constants. The following refining on the vocabulary definition is proper to the way we formalize the decision problem. The set of predicates $\mathcal{P}$ is partitioned in two disjoint sets $\mathcal{P} = \mathcal{P}_R \cup \mathcal{P}_C$ with $\mathcal{P}_R \cap \mathcal{P}_C = \emptyset$. $\mathcal{P}_C$ represents the criteria predicates we consider for decision making while $\mathcal{P}_R$ represents the other predicates (relations) which are used for describing the world in general (and thus not considered directly by the decision process). The set of constants $\mathcal{C}$ is partitioned into four pairwise disjoint sets $\mathcal{C} = \mathcal{C}_A \cup \mathcal{C}_\mathcal{I} \cup \mathcal{C}_V \cup \mathcal{C}_C$ and for all $x, y \in \{A, \mathcal{I}, V, C\}$ s.t. $x \neq y$, $\mathcal{C}_x \cap \mathcal{C}_y = \emptyset$. The set $\mathcal{C}_A$ is representing the constants that are naming the various alternatives involved in the decision process. The set $\mathcal{C}_\mathcal{I}$ represents the constants that are naming the agents/decision makers of $\mathcal{I}$ that are taking part in the MCDM problem. Let $\mathcal{C}_V = \bigcup_{c \in \mathcal{P}_C} \mathcal{C}_V^c$, where a set $\mathcal{C}_V^c$ represents the different values the criteria $c \in \mathcal{P}_C$ can have. Therefore the interpretation of a predicate c in $\mathcal{P}_C$ will only take values from $\mathcal{C}_A$ and their corresponding $\mathcal{C}_V^c$. Note that, the interpretation of an n-ary predicate symbol is a set of n-tuples of elements of the domain of discourse. The set $\mathcal{C}_C$ represents the other constants used eventually by $\mathcal{P}_R$. The domain of interpretation of $\mathcal{P}_R$ is $\mathcal{C}_A \cup \mathcal{C}_C$. Furthermore, for each predicate c in $\mathcal{P}_C$ we define on the values of its interpretation $\mathcal{C}_A \times \mathcal{C}_V^{c\,(n-1)}$, where n is the arity of the predicate, a total order $\gg_{\mathcal{C}_A \times \mathcal{C}_V^c}$. By abuse of notation, when the set of alternatives is given, we denote the preference $\gg_{\mathcal{C}_V^c}$.

An **atomic formula** (or atom) over $\mathcal{V}$ is of the form $p(t_1, ..., t_n)$ where $p \in \mathcal{P}$ is an n-ary predicate, and $t_1, ..., t_n$ are terms, with t over $\mathcal{V}$ a constant or a variable. A ground atom is an atom with no variables. A conjunction of atoms is called a *conjunct*. A conjunction of ground atoms is called a *ground conjunct*. A variable in an atom is free if it is not in the scope of any quantifier. A formula is *closed* if it has no free variables. A closed formula is called a *sentence*. Factual knowledge (a fact) about the world is represented by *ground atoms*. In the Existential Rules framework this concept has been extended so that a fact on $\mathcal{V}$

is the existential closure of a conjunction of atoms over $\mathcal{V}$ [5]. Let F be a fact, we denote by $terms(F)$ (resp. $vars(F)$) the set of terms (resp. variables) that occur in F.

A *profile* for alternative $A \in \mathcal{C}_A$ of decision maker $I \in \mathcal{C}_\mathcal{I}$, denoted $profile_I(A)$, is a conjunction of facts of the form $p_0(A) \wedge \bigwedge_{1 \le i \le n} p_i(A, \boldsymbol{t})$ with A representing an alternative (i.e., $A \in \mathcal{C}_A$), p_0 an unary predicate in $\mathcal{P}_R$ representing the type of the alternative, $\{p_i | 1 \le i \le n\}$ a set of criteria that apply for the alternative A and $\boldsymbol{t}$ a vector of the other terms except A of the respective criterion predicate. Note that, in a decision problem multiple types of alternatives can be proposed as the solution and hence, the need to define p_0. Each decision maker $I \in \mathcal{C}_\mathcal{I}$ will express her set of profiles over the set of alternatives $\mathcal{C}_{A,\mathcal{I}}$, i.e., $Profile_I(\mathcal{C}_{A,\mathcal{I}})$. Hence, $Profile_I(\mathcal{C}_{A,\mathcal{I}}) = \bigwedge_{A_k \in \mathcal{C}_{A,\mathcal{I}}} profile_I(A_k)$. When I is implicit we denote it simply by $Profile(\mathcal{C}_A) = \bigwedge_{A_k \in \mathcal{C}_{A,\mathcal{I}}} profile_I(A_k)$.

Given a set of variables $\mathcal{X}$ and a set of terms $\mathcal{T}$, a **substitution** σ of $\mathcal{X}$ by $\mathcal{T}$ (notation $\sigma : \mathcal{X} \rightarrow \mathcal{T}$) is a function from $\mathcal{X}$ to $\mathcal{T}$. Given a fact F, $\sigma(F)$ denotes the fact obtained from F by replacing each occurrence of $x \in X \cap vars(F)$ by $\sigma(x)$. A **homomorphism** from a fact F to a fact F' is a substitution σ of $vars(F)$ by (a subset of) $terms(F')$ such that $\sigma(F) \subseteq F'$.

A conjunctive query (CQ) has the following form: $\mathcal{Q} = \text{ans}(x_1, \ldots, x_k) \leftarrow B$, where B (the "body" of $\mathcal{Q}$) is an existential closed atom or a conjunction of existential closed atoms, and $x_1, \ldots, x_k$ are variables that occur in B and ans is a special k-ary predicate, whose elements are used to build an answer. Given a set of facts $\mathcal{F}$, an answer to $\mathcal{Q}$ in $\mathcal{F}$ is a tuple of constants $(D_1, \ldots, D_k)$ such that there is a homomorphism σ from B to $\mathcal{F}$, with $\sigma(\text{ans}(x_1, x_2, \ldots x_k)) = \sigma(\text{ans}(D_1, D_2, \ldots D_k))$. If $k = 0$, i.e., $\mathcal{Q} = \text{ans}() \leftarrow B$, $\mathcal{Q}$ is called a Boolean conjunctive query, the unique answer to $\mathcal{Q}$ is the empty tuple if there is a homomorphism from B to $\mathcal{F}$, otherwise there is no answer to $\mathcal{Q}$. Note that a query $\mathcal{Q}$ can be shortly referred to by its body B. For its simplicity, this notation will be used hereafter. In order to represent enriched knowledge about the facts, we use rules that encode domain-specific knowledge. Rules are regarded as an ontological layer that reinforces the expressiveness of the knowledge base. Rules are logical formulae that allow us to infer new facts (conclusion) from existing facts (hypothesis). **Existential rules** [5] introduce new variables in the conclusion having ability to represent unknown individuals. We denote by $\boldsymbol{x}$ in a bold font a vector of variables. An *existential rule* (or simply a rule) is a closed formula of the form $R = \forall \boldsymbol{x} \forall \boldsymbol{y}(B \rightarrow \exists \boldsymbol{z} H)$, where B and H are conjuncts, with $vars(B) = \boldsymbol{x} \cup \boldsymbol{y}$, and $vars(H) = \boldsymbol{x} \cup \boldsymbol{z}$. The variables in vector $\boldsymbol{z}$ are called the existential variables of the rule R. B and H are respectively called the *body* and the *head* of R. We denote them respectively $body(R)$ for B and $head(R)$ for H.

Existential rules are more expressive than Description Logics as they can represent complex relations between individuals and overcome the "cycle on variables" [9]. Another important aspect of the existential rules framework is the possibility of having *unbounded predicate arity*, i.e., predicates with an arbitrary number of parameters. Entailment is undecidable for general existential rules

[8]. However, we work with classes of existential rules that ensure decidability (while keeping expressiveness) [5].

We also account for a special kind of rules called *negative constraints*, i.e., knowledge that imposes constraints about the world. A negative constraint is a rule of the form $N = \forall \boldsymbol{x}(B \to \bot)$, where $vars(B) = \boldsymbol{x}$. Negative constraints in the existential rules framework fully capture *concept disjointness* of DLs. From now on we omit quantifiers in front of formulae as there is no ambiguity.

An individual decision maker's I **knowledge base** is a tuple $\mathcal{K} = (\mathcal{F}, \mathcal{R}, \mathcal{N})_I$ (denoted as $\mathcal{K} = (\mathcal{F}, \mathcal{R}, \mathcal{N})$ when there is no ambiguity) of finite sets of facts (thus including profiles), rules and negative constraints respectively. Reasoning with a knowledge base of facts, rules and negative constraints is done via a mechanism called saturation of facts by the rules.

A rule $R = \forall \boldsymbol{x} \forall \boldsymbol{y}(B \to \exists \boldsymbol{z} H)$ is **applicable** [5] to a fact F if there exists a homomorphism σ from B to F. The *application of R to F w.r.t.* σ produces a fact $\alpha(F, R, \sigma) = F \cup \sigma(safe(H))$, where $\mathtt{safe}(H)$ is obtained from H by replacing existential variables with fresh variables (not used variables). $\alpha(F, R, \sigma)$ is said to be an **immediate derivation** from F. Let F be a fact and $\mathcal{R}$ be a set of rules. A fact F' is called an $\mathcal{R}$-**derivation** of F if there is a finite sequence (called the **derivation sequence**) $\langle F_0 = F, ..., F_n = F' \rangle$ such that for all $0 \le i < n$ there is a rule $R \subseteq \mathcal{R}$ which is applicable to F_i and F_{i+1} is an immediate derivation from F_i. The saturation operator $(C\ell)$ can be seen as a *fixed-point operator* where we denote by $C\ell_{\mathcal{R}}^*(\mathcal{F})$ the saturation of $\mathcal{F}$ with respect to $\mathcal{R}$. Note that $C\ell_{\mathcal{R}}^*(\mathcal{F})$ is a finite set [6] for the classes of existential rules considered in this paper. In the next section we will see how to reason with facts in the presence of inconsistency using repair based methods.

3   Multi-criteria Decision Making as Repair Techniques

In what follows we recall the formal definition of *inconsistency* in the existential rules framework; then we introduce the subset-repairing techniques which is inspired by the work from the database community [10] and Description Logics [11].

Definition 1 (Inconsistency). *A set of facts $\mathcal{F}$ is inconsistent with respect to a set of rules $\mathcal{R}$ and negative constraints $\mathcal{N}$ (or inconsistent for short) if and only if there exists a constraint $N \in \mathcal{N}$ such that $C\ell_{\mathcal{R}}^*(\mathcal{F}) \models body(N)$.*

This means that the set of facts *violates* the negative constraint N or triggers it. Correspondingly, a knowledge base $\mathcal{K} = (\mathcal{F}, \mathcal{R}, \mathcal{N})$ is inconsistent (with respect to $\mathcal{R}$ and $\mathcal{N}$) if and only if there exists a set of facts $\mathcal{F}' \subseteq \mathcal{F}$ such that $\mathcal{F}'$ is inconsistent. An alternative writing is $C\ell_{\mathcal{R}}^*(\mathcal{F}) \models \bot$.

One way to cope with inconsistency is to construct *maximal consistent subsets* of the knowledge base [12]. This corresponds to "Data Repairs" [1]. A data repair of a knowledge base $\mathcal{K} = (\mathcal{F}, \mathcal{R}, \mathcal{N})$ is a set of facts $\mathcal{F}'$ such that $\mathcal{F}'$ is consistent and there exists no consistent subset of $\mathcal{F}$ that strictly contains $\mathcal{F}'$ [11]. Since repairs are computed exclusively on the set of facts and given that the factual part of the knowledge base is the only source of inconsistency we, from now on, abuse slightly the notation and refer to $\mathcal{K}'$ by its set of facts $\mathcal{F}'$. The set of all repairs of $\mathcal{K}$ is denoted by $\mathcal{R}epair(\mathcal{K})$.

For an individual decision maker $I \in \mathcal{C}_\mathcal{I}$ and the set of alternatives $\mathcal{C}_A$ we use repair techniques in order to obtain one single, maximal consistent subset of $Profile(\mathcal{C}_A)$. For a given set of alternatives $\mathcal{C}_A$ and for each of the individual decision makers $I \in \mathcal{C}_\mathcal{I}$, the $Profile_I(\mathcal{C}_A)$ is consistent wrt to the commonly agreed set of rules and negative constraints[1]. Note that we need to have a common structure for all the profiles and we do not consider that the preferences of an individual decision maker are inconsistent. The first step is to construct $Profile_I(\mathcal{C}_A)$ for every decision maker $I \in \mathcal{C}_\mathcal{I}$. It is very important to mention the fact that each decision maker also has a (strict) total preference ordering on the set of criteria they consider in their profiles.

At this step we consider a fresh set of constants that correspond to those criteria that decision maker I considers in her aggregation function. We also need to consider the set of constants naming the decision makers, i.e., for every $c \in \mathcal{P}(c)$ the new constant name is C^*. We introduce two meta predicates: *consider* (a ternary predicate taking a decision maker's identifier, an alternative and a constant corresponding to the criterium name) and *preferred* (a ternary predicate stating that I prefers criterion i to j). Inconsistencies that can arise at this step are due to the following factors.

Inconsistency Regarding the Consideration of Different Criteria. Each $I \in \mathcal{C}_\mathcal{I}$ gives a set of rules: $\mathcal{R}_I = \{\forall A \in \mathcal{C}_A\ type(A) \wedge \mathcal{J}_{I_i} \rightarrow consider(I, A, C^*)\}$, where C^* is the constant that corresponds to a criterion that I considers for alternative A. We have that *type* is a predicate and A is in its interpretation. By $\mathcal{J}_i$, we denote the justification made by the decision maker for her rule R_i. Negative constraints are of the form $\forall I, J \in \mathcal{C}_\mathcal{I} \forall A \in \mathcal{C}_A \forall C^* \in \mathcal{C}_C, consider(I, A, C^*) \wedge not\_consider(J, A, C^*) \wedge type(A) \wedge diff(I, J) \rightarrow \bot$, i.e., different decision makers do not consider the same criteria. The predicate $not\_consider(I, A, C^*)$ means that C^* is not considered by I for A and predicate $diff(I, J)$ stands for two different decision makers I and J.

Inconsistency Regarding the Consideration of Different Alternatives. $I \in \mathcal{C}_\mathcal{I}$ set of rules: $R_I = \{\forall A \in \mathcal{C}_A\ type(A) \wedge \mathcal{J}_{I_i} \rightarrow alternative(A, I)\}$ which corresponds to the alternatives considered by I. Negative constraints: $\forall I, J \in \mathcal{C}_\mathcal{I} \forall A \in \mathcal{C}_A\ alternative(A, I) \wedge not\_alternative(A, J) \wedge diff(I, J) \rightarrow \bot$. When A is not considered by I we denote it by $not\_alternative(A, I)$.

Inconsistency Regarding the Consideration of Different Preferences on Criteria. $I \in \mathcal{C}_\mathcal{I}$ set of rules: $\mathcal{R}_I = \{\forall A \in \mathcal{C}_A, \forall C_i^*, C_j^* \in \mathcal{C}_C\ consider(I, A, C_i^*) \wedge consider(I, A, C_j^*) \wedge \mathcal{J}_{I_i} \rightarrow preferred(I, C_i^*, C_j^*)\}$. Negative constraints: $\forall A \in \mathcal{C}_A \forall I, J \in \mathcal{C}_\mathcal{I} \forall C_i^*, C_j^* \in \mathcal{C}_C, preferred(I, A, C_i^*, C_j^*) \wedge not\_preferred(J, A, C_i^*, C_j^*) \wedge diff(I, J), preferred(I, A, C_i^*, C_j^*) \wedge equivalent(J, A, C_i^*, C_j^*) \wedge diff(I, J), equivalent(I, A, C_i^*, C_j^*) \wedge not\_preferred(J, A, C_i^*, C_j^*) \wedge$

---

[1] Please remember that we are in the OBDA case where the inconsistency can only come from facts thus we agree upon a common ontology (i.e., set of rules and negative constraints) a priori.

$diff(I, J) \rightarrow \perp$. Atom $not\_preferred(I, A, C_i^*, C_j^*)$ means that C_i^* is not pairwise preferred to C_j^* by I and predicate $equivalent(I, A, C_i^*, C_j^*)$ means that C_i^* and C_j^* are equally preferred by I.

Inconsistency on the Criteria Values (Evaluation Ratings resp.) of the Decision Makers over the Alternatives. $I \in \mathcal{C_I}$ set of rules: $\mathcal{R}_I = \{\forall A \in \mathcal{C}_A \; type(A) \wedge \mathcal{J}_{I_i} \rightarrow has\_value(I, A, C^*, V)\}$ that corresponds to the value (evaluation rating resp.) $V \in \mathcal{C}_V^c$ I gives for C^*. Inconsistencies occur when different decision makers have different valuation (evaluation rating resp.) for the same alternative on a specific criterion. The value corresponds to a metric that is related to real data. Although one could think that, since value is objective, it would be the same for all of them, this is not the case in real life simply because not all the decision makers have the same information. The evaluation rating corresponds to a metric that is related to their subjective preferences. Negative constraints are of the form $\forall I, J \in \mathcal{C_I} \forall A \in \mathcal{C}_A \forall C^* \in \mathcal{C}_C \forall V_1, V_2 \in \mathcal{C}_V^c, has\_value(I, A, C^*, V_1) \wedge has\_value(J, A, C^*, V_2) \wedge type(A) \wedge diff(I, J) \wedge diff(V_1, V_2) \rightarrow \perp$.

4 Discussion and Related Work

In this work, we modelled the MCDM problem as reasoning in presence of an inconsistency problem. We used existential rules for the modelling language of the knowledge base and employed repair techniques for reasoning. In knowledge representation and reasoning, argumentation is also a well known method for handling inconsistency. Using argumentation for reasoning was proven to yield semantically equivalent results as to repair techniques. Furthermore, argumentation has been studied for its principled human computer interaction advantages, e.g., [2–4]. However, in this context, argumentation is a computationally hard process.

Acknowledgements. The work of Nikos Karanikolas was supported with a scholarship from IKY funded by the action "Support of Postdoctoral Researchers" from the resources of the EP "Human Resources Development, Education and Lifelong Learning" with priority axes 6, 8, 9 and is and co-funded by the European Social Fund - ESF and the Greek state. Part of this work has been carried out while N. Karanikolas was employed by INRA. The authors acknowledge the support of the H2020 NoAW project.

References

1. Arenas, M., Bertossi, L., Chomicki, J.: Consistent query answers in inconsistent databases. In: Proceedings of the Eighteenth ACM SIGMOD-SIGACT-SIGART Symposium on Principles of Database Systems, pp. 68–79. ACM (1999)
2. Arioua, A., Croitoru, M.: DALEK: a tool for dialectical explanations in inconsistent knowledge bases. In: Proceedings of the 6th International Conference on Computational Models of Argument, COMMA 2016 (2016)
3. Arioua, A., Croitoru, M.: Dialectical characterization of consistent query explanation with existential rules. In: Proceedings of the 29th International Florida Artificial Intelligence Research Society Conference (FLAIRS 2016), pp. 14–19 (2016)

4. Arioua, A., Croitoru, M., Papaleo, L., Pernelle, N., Rocher, S.: On the explanation of SameAs statements using argumentation. In: Schockaert, S., Senellart, P. (eds.) SUM 2016. LNCS (LNAI), vol. 9858, pp. 51–66. Springer, Cham (2016). https://doi.org/10.1007/978-3-319-45856-4_4

5. Baget, J.F., Leclère, M., Mugnier, M.L., Salvat, E.: On rules with existential variables: walking the decidability line. Artif. Intell. **175**(9–10), 1620–1654 (2011)

6. Baget, J.F., Mugnier, M.L., Rudolph, S., Thomazo, M.: Walking the complexity lines for generalized guarded existential rules. In: Proceedings of the International Joint Conference on Artificial Intelligence (IJCAI 2011), pp. 712–717 (2011)

7. Baget, J.F., et al.: Inconsistency-tolerant query answering: rationality properties and computational complexity analysis. In: Michael, L., Kakas, A. (eds.) JELIA 2016. LNCS (LNAI), vol. 10021, pp. 64–80. Springer, Cham (2016). https://doi.org/10.1007/978-3-319-48758-8_5

8. Beeri, C., Vardi, M.Y.: The implication problem for data dependencies. In: Even, S., Kariv, O. (eds.) ICALP 1981. LNCS, vol. 115, pp. 73–85. Springer, Heidelberg (1981). https://doi.org/10.1007/3-540-10843-2_7

9. Chein, M., Mugnier, M.: Graph-based Knowledge Representation - Computational Foundations of Conceptual Graphs. In: Advanced Information and Knowledge Processing. Springer, London (2009). https://doi.org/10.1007/978-1-84800-286-9

10. Chomicki, J.: Consistent query answering: five easy pieces. In: Schwentick, T., Suciu, D. (eds.) ICDT 2007. LNCS, vol. 4353, pp. 1–17. Springer, Heidelberg (2006). https://doi.org/10.1007/11965893_1

11. Lembo, D., Lenzerini, M., Rosati, R., Ruzzi, M., Savo, D.F.: Inconsistency-tolerant semantics for description logics. In: Hitzler, P., Lukasiewicz, T. (eds.) RR 2010. LNCS, vol. 6333, pp. 103–117. Springer, Heidelberg (2010). https://doi.org/10.1007/978-3-642-15918-3_9

12. Rescher, N., Manor, R.: On inference from inconsistent premises. Theor. Decis. **1**(2), 179–217 (1970)

GramError: A Quality Metric
for Machine Generated Songs

Craig Davies(✉), Nirmalie Wiratunga©, and Kyle Martin©

Robert Gordon University, Aberdeen, Scotland
{c.davies,n.wiratsunga,k.martin}@rgu.ac.uk

Abstract. This paper explores whether a simple grammar-based metric
can accurately predict human opinion of machine-generated song lyrics
squality. The proposed metric considers the percentage of words written
in natural English and the number of grammatical errors to rate the
quality of machine-generated lyrics. We use a state-of-the-art Recurrent
Neural Network (RNN) model and adapt it to lyric generation by retraining on the lyrics of 5,000 songs. For our initial user trial, we use
a small sample of songs generated by the RNN to calibrate the metric.
Songs selected on the basis of this metric are further evaluated using
"Turing-like" tests to establish whether there is a correlation between
metric score and human judgment. Our results show that there is strong
correlation with human opinion, especially at lower levels of song quality.
They also show that 75% of the RNN-generated lyrics passed for human-
generated over 30% of the time.

Keywords: Natural language generation · Quality metric
Recurrent neural network

1 Introduction

Artificial Intelligence (AI) has in recent years proved to be effective in a variety of
Natural Language Processing (NLP) applications such as neural translation [2]
and caption generation [12]. Much of this has been driven by the success of
sequence-to-sequence learning algorithms [11]. Model learning and evaluation
commonly relies on metrics (such as BLEU and NIST) which were developed for
machine translation tasks [3,10]. These metrics compare the machine-written
output of a translation task to a human-written translation and rate the quality
based on the similarity of the two translations, with a more similar translation
said to be of higher standard. This makes it less suitable for creative Natural
Language Generation (NLG) tasks, as it is virtually impossible to get a human
and a machine to write creatively in a way that can be compared in any meaningful form on the basis of exact matching.

In our work, we explore the role of lyrical composition and consider semantics
such as sentence structure, language formation and punctuation to formulate
an alternative evaluation metric for song generation. With this in mind, we

M. Bramer and M. Petridis (Eds.): SGAI-AI 2018, LNAI 11311, pp. 184–190, 2018.
https://doi.org/10.1007/978-3-030-04191-5_16

introduce a simple metric, GRAMERROR, that analyses the lyrical composition of songs. We show that such a metric correlates well with human evaluation of song lyrics. The metric proposed in this paper is studied using songs generated by a sequence-to-sequence model trained on a corpus of songs from the classic rock genre. We created user tests to allow us to compare human judgments with metric scoring. Here judgments refer to the ability to identify whether a song was written by a machine. We found a strong correlation between increasing metric generated scores with decreasing human judgment accuracy. Our results also suggest that 75% of the lyrics generated by the Recurrent Neural Network (RNN) passed for human-generated over 30% of the time when compared adversarially to human-written song lyrics. These results demonstrate the utility of the lyrical composition metric proposed in our work.

In this paper, we explore work on lyric generation and discuss why existing automated metrics are unsuitable for rating the quality of work produced by NLG systems (Sect. 2). Our proposed metric appears in Sect. 3 followed by the song generation model in Sect. 4. The evaluation in Sect. 5 presents the utility of GRAMERROR following a user survey and two user evaluation trials. Conclusions appear in Sect. 6.

2   Related Work

There have been several attempts at using NLG systems for song lyric generation [8,9]. Templates [6] are commonly used to guide the NLG process where the focus is on using existing music and breaking the beat down into rhythm patterns (beats, rests). Thereafter random words are selected to fit the rhythm whilst the generative grammar strategy writes words that best fit pre-written grammar templates. Another approach is referred to as a Generate and Test strategy since sentences are generated on the basis of the grammar templates and tested on the basis of a best fit ranking. Here fit relates to rhythm, rhyme (with other lines) and number of syllables. Oliveira's PoeTryMe [7] is a typical example of this strategy.

Machine evaluation of song quality is often challenging due to the multi-faceted criteria. Work in NLG (although less complex than song analysis) has successfully adopted overlap metrics such as BLEU and NIST [1,10]. Although these metrics were not originally intended for use in creative NLG, BLEU has been used to rate generated poetry [5] and results suggest a good correlation with human judgment quality, but only for low BLEU scores (between 0.11 and 0.15). One problem with using such metrics is the reliance on reference texts (for the comparison). Even if such a resource existed, creative writing is not about matching previous content from the past.

3   A Grammar Based Quality Metric

In formulating a quality metric for lyric comparison, we take inspiration from findings reported in [8], where generative models with a focus on grammar were shown to outperform more complex models. The strong performance of a grammar-based model performed suggested that a metric which considered the quantity and severity of grammatical errors machine-written song lyrics would be effective. In our work we utilise the popular online grammar correction system "Grammarly"[1] to evaluate text and categorise errors into "major grammatical errors" and "minor grammatical errors". Thereafter a metric is used to aggregate these errors to form the quality score.

Major grammatical errors typically relate to punctuation errors or spelling mistakes, whilst minor grammatical errors are related to poor sentence structure. Accordingly we combine both these error counts using a weighted formula as follows:

$$\textsc{GramError} = \alpha pE - \beta MG - \gamma mG - C \tag{1}$$

Here pE is the percentage of words in the song written in natural English, MG is the number of Major grammatical errors, mG is the number of minor grammatical errors and C is a constant that manages the sensitivity of the score. Here α, β and γ are mixing weights used to help calibrate the metric. This is informed by our findings from an initial user survey discussed in Sect. 5. After learning the weights we assign a value to C such that the metric is capped at 100. This offers greater granularity when compared to a lower cap such as 10, which would lack the sensitivity to measure the calibre of songs that might be similar in quality. The metric has no lower limit.

4   Generating Song Lyrics with an RNN

A Recurrent Neural Net (RNN) was used to generate song lyrics. The recurrent nature of this model means that the output at each step is fed back into the network and provides important contextual information based on word locality, improving the semantic coherence of its output. As our aim was to test how well the proposed metric correlates with human opinion, we adapted a pre-trained RNN from an existing NLG system which generated plays in the style of William Shakespeare by retraining it on a Kaggle dataset scraped from the Lyrics Freak website[2]. This dataset contains the English lyrics for 57,650 songs and informed two aspects of our work. To retrain the RNN to suit the task of lyric generation, we extracted 5,000 classic rock songs to form the training set. Classic rock was selected because the RNN proved susceptible to repetition in the training set, meaning repetitive genres (i.e. pop music) demonstrated poorer performance.

Due to the size of this dataset, we used a mini-batchs to iteratively train the model. We also extended the network by adding a further hidden layer as we found it improved the quality of generated lyrics. Thus we constructed an RNN with 4 hidden layers, 3 of which used tanh activation functions while the final layer used a softmax classifier to feed into a cross-entropy loss function using

---

[1] www.grammarly.com/.
[2] https://www.kaggle.com/mousehead/songlyrics.

Adam optimiser. We then re-trained the model for 20 epochs on the training set of 5,000 classic rock songs. Note that we needed few epochs to retrain the system as we were adapting an already competent network to the task of lyric generation. The sequence length of the data was set at 50. This parameter identifies the max length of a sequence that can be generated by the RNN. The batch size was set to 256. These parameters were selected following extensive empirical evaluation.

5 Evaluation

The aims of our evaluation were two-fold. Firstly, we wished to identify appropriate weights for our proposed metric. Secondly, we aimed to measure the correlation between the metric and human judgment of lyric quality. Accordingly we defined a two stage evaluation. In the first stage we used a survey to measure the influence of major and minor grammatical errors on human judgment of song quality. This allowed us to calibrate the mixing weights of GRAMERROR and improve its scoring. In the second stage we performed 'Turing-like' tests to investigate whether our metric was indicative of when machine-generated lyrics would be confused for human-written songs.

Test Survey. To determine how well GRAMERROR correlates with human opinion, users were recruited to complete a survey on song quality. Users were presented with 5 bot-written songs and asked to answer four questions using one of six possible answers. The questions were evenly weighted with the most positive answer worth 25 points. The highest achievable score was therefore 100 (designed to match the maximum score GRAMERROR could give), enabling us to measure the discrepancy between GRAMERROR scoring and human ratings to improve calibration of weights in our equation.

The Turing-Like Tests. We adopted a two-stage 'Turing-like' evaluation to investigate whether lyrics scored highly by our metric would be more likely to be mistaken for human-written. In the first stage, users were presented with 13 songs (4 human-written, 9 machine-generated) in isolation and asked to identify whether the song was written by a bot or a human. We used 8 songs generated by our RNN and a song presented in [4]. We observed that it received the highest possible score by GRAMERROR, thus giving it the best chance of passing the Turing test and forming an upper bound for our tests.

The second stage only used machine-generated songs which passed for human a threshold percentage of times (30%) in the first stage. Users were presented with a bot-written song alongside human-written lyrics and were asked to identify which was which. We could then measure the correlation between GRAMERROR and human opinion when lyrics were in isolation and when presented alongside human-written songs.

5.1   Results

The Test Survey. In total, 13 users responded to the first survey. When compared to an uncalibrated (i.e. all mixing weights set to zero) version of GRAMERROR, the total discrepancy between the proposed metric and human ratings was 154 points. We observed that GRAMERROR more accurately reflected human opinion at the lower end of the rating scale, showing deviation of just 3 points on the lowest ranked song, but differing by 28 points on the highest rated song.

These results indicated that GRAMERROR should rate songs more strictly. Iteratively testing weights for each variable in the metric, we found the optimal formula:

$$\text{GRAMERROR} = 4pE - 2MG - 2mG - 300 \tag{2}$$

suggesting that human evaluators assign equal weight to major and minor grammatical errors. The constant C was set to 300, capping the metric's score at 100. After this recalibration the total discrepancy between GRAMERROR scores and user ratings was reduced to 114. Figure 1 shows the comparison between the recalibrated GRAMERROR scores and the human rating for five of the songs.

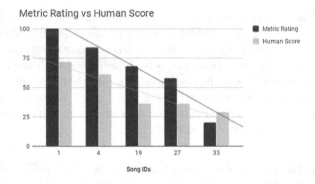

Fig. 1. Rating from metric scoring vs human ratings

The Turing-Like Tests. In the first stage, 14 users completed the survey. Their responses are summarised in Fig. 2. We observe that a song's GRAMERROR score correlated well with how often it was thought to be human-written when presented in isolation. Four of the machine-generated songs were labeled as human-written by 30% or more users, including the three songs highest rated by GRAMERROR. The three songs which received the lowest score from our metric were labeled as human by less than 20% of users. Dropout was low, with only 3 users failing to complete the survey after starting.

The second Turing test demonstrated similar results. Using the four machine-generated songs which had been mislabeled as human most often in the last test,

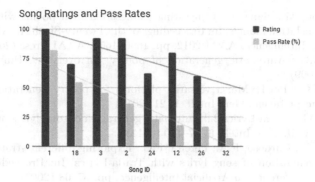

Fig. 2. Comparing automated ratings and test 1 pass rates

we observed that three of the four machine-written songs were passed for human by over 30% of tested users once more. This suggests that GRAMERROR's scoring is robust to whether songs are viewed in isolation or alongside human-written lyrics. The response rate for this test was high - 62 people started the test and only 4 failed to finish.

6 Conclusions

In this paper we introduced a new grammar focused metric, GRAMERROR, for measuring NLG. When this metric is used to rate song lyrics, it matches human judgment reasonably well, with a difference of 9% between the metric and user opinion at lower levels of quality and a difference of 28% at higher levels of quality. The metric also correlates well with how likely a set of song lyrics is to pass for a set of human-written song lyrics, both when in isolation and when alongside a human-written counterpart.

References

1. Adeyanju, I., Wiratunga, N., Lothian, R., Sripada, S., Lamontagne, L.: Case Retrieval Reuse Net (CR2N): an architecture for reuse of textual solutions. In: McGinty, L., Wilson, D.C. (eds.) ICCBR 2009. LNCS (LNAI), vol. 5650, pp. 14–28. Springer, Heidelberg (2009). https://doi.org/10.1007/978-3-642-02998-1_3
2. Cho, K., et al.: Learning phrase representations using rnn encoder-decoder for statistical machine translation. In: Proceedings of the 2014 Conference on Empirical Methods in Natural Language Processing, pp. 1724–1734. ACL (2014)
3. Doddington, G.: Automatic evaluation of machine translation quality using n-gram co-occurrence statistics. In: Proceedings of the Second International Conference on Human Language Technology Research, pp. 138–145. Morgan Kaufmann Publishers Inc. (2002)
4. Ghazvininejad, M., Shi, X., Choi, Y., Knight, K.: Generating topical poetry. In: Proceedings of the 2016 Conference on Empirical Methods in Natural Language Processing, pp. 1183–1191. ACL (2016)

5. He, J., Zhou, M., Jiang, L.: Generating Chinese classical poems with statistical machine translation models. In: Proceedings of the Twenty-Sixth AAAI Conference on Artificial Intelligence, AAAI 2012, pp. 1650–1656. AAAI Press (2012)

6. Oliveira, H.G.: Automatic generation of poetry: an overview. Universidade de Coimbra (2009)

7. Oliveira, H.G.: PoeTryMe: a versatile platform for poetry generation. Comput. Creat., Concept Inven., Gen. Intell. 1, 21 (2012)

8. Oliveira, H.G.: Tra-la-Lyrics 2.0: automatic generation of song lyrics on a semantic domain. J. Artif. Gen. Intell. 6, 87–110 (2015)

9. Oliveira, H.G., Cardoso, F.A., Pereira, F.C.: Exploring different strategies for the automatic generation of song lyrics with Tra-la-Lyrics. In: Proceedings of 13th Portuguese Conference on Artificial Intelligence, pp. 57–68 (2007)

10. Papineni, K., Roukos, S., Ward, T., Zhu, W.J.: BLEU: a method for automatic evaluation of machine translation. In: Proceedings of the 40th Annual Meeting on Association for Computational Linguistics, ACL 2002, ACL, Stroudsburg, PA, USA, pp. 311–318 (2002)

11. Sutskever, I., Vinyals, O., Le, Q.V.: Sequence to sequence learning with neural networks. In: Proceedings of the 27th International Conference on Neural Information Processing Systems - Volume 2, NIPS 2014, pp. 3104–3112. MIT Press, Cambridge (2014)

12. Vinyals, O., Toshev, A., Bengio, S., Erhan, D.: Show and tell: a neural image caption generator. In: Proceedings of the IEEE Conference on Computer Vision and Pattern Recognition, pp. 3156–3164 (2015)

Computational Complexity Analysis of Decision Tree Algorithms

Habiba Muhammad Sani[✉], Ci Lei, and Daniel Neagu

University of Bradford, Bradford, UK
{hmsani,clei1,dneagu}@bradford.ac.uk

Abstract. Decision tree is a simple but powerful learning technique that is considered as one of the famous learning algorithms that have been successfully used in practice for various classification tasks. They have the advantage of producing a comprehensible classification model with satisfactory accuracy levels in several application domains. In recent years, the volume of data available for learning is dramatically increasing. As a result, many application domains are faced with a large amount of data thereby posing a major bottleneck on the computability of learning techniques. There are different implementations of the decision tree using different techniques. In this paper, we theoretically and experimentally study and compare the computational power of the most common classical top-down decision tree algorithms (C4.5 and CART). This work can serve as part of review work to analyse the computational complexity of the existing decision tree classifier algorithm to gain understanding of the operational steps with the aim of optimizing the learning algorithm for large datasets.

Keywords: Classification · Decision trees · Complexity

1 Introduction

Today, the world is overwhelmed with the continuous growth in the amount of data available for learning. Useful information is hidden within this large amount of data. With machine learning techniques, we can analyse these data and extract meaningful information that can aid in decision making [6,19]. As large data are becoming a common norm in many application domains, trying to discover useful pattern and information from these real-world data pose several challenges such as memory and time complexities. Managing and analysing such amount of data requires special and very expensive hardware and software, which often causes various companies and organizations to exploit only a small part of the stored data. According to [3], one of the major challenges for the data mining research community is to develop methods that facilitate the use of learning algorithms for real-world databases. Machine learning is a sub-field of computer science with the goal of training and programming machines to learn

© Springer Nature Switzerland AG 2018
M. Bramer and M. Petridis (Eds.): SGAI-AI 2018, LNAI 11311, pp. 191–197, 2018.
https://doi.org/10.1007/978-3-030-04191-5_17

from experiences to become expert in applying their experiences in new situation [14,17]. There are many classification algorithms available. Decision tree algorithms are among the successful and widely used technique for classification tasks. Decision tree techniques have been around over three decades now and are still actively used in many real-world applications. Given the long history and interest in decision tree algorithms, it is surprising that there has been few work done on the computational complexity of the decision tree algorithm in the literature [11,20]. The goal of this paper is to theoretically and experimentally analyse and compare the complexity of decision tree algorithm for classification task. The decision tree classifiers chosen are the ones with high number of citation and implemented in Scikit-learn python packages for machine learning. The rest of the paper has the following organization: Sect. 2 provides some background of basic concepts in relation to the paper. Theoretical analysis is presented in Sect. 3. Experimental and result analysis were provided in Sect. 4. Finally, Sect. 5 presents the conclusion about this paper as well as a highlight on the future work.

2 Background

2.1 Classification

Classification is a type of supervised learning task in which a training set of labelled examples is given, and the goal is to form a description that can be used to predict previously unseen examples. Formally, the training set is denoted as $S\langle X, y \rangle$. Where X is the set of input attributes $X = \{x_1, x_2, ..., x_n\}$ and y represents the target or class attribute such that $y = \{c_1, c_2, ..., c_n\}$.

2.2 Decision Tree Algorithm

Decision tree inducers are algorithms that automatically construct a decision tree from a given dataset [13]. Typically, the goal is to find the optimal decision tree by minimizing the generalization error. There are various top-down decision tree algorithms such as IDE [12], C4.5 [16], and CART [8]. Some implementation consists of both the tree growing and tree pruning phase such as (C4.5 and CART) and other algorithms are designed to perform only the tree growing phase [1,10].

2.3 Computational Complexity

Computational resources are crucial in any practical application of learning algorithm. These computational resources are of two basic types: Sample complexity and computational complexity [2,4,7,15]. Algorithm analysis is an important part of a broader computational complexity theory which provides theoretical estimates for resources needed for any given algorithm which solves a given computational problem.

3   Theoretical Analysis

Generally, the actual runtime analysis of an algorithm depends on the specific machine on which the algorithm is being implemented upon. To avoid machine dependence analysis, it is a common approach in literature to analyse the runtime of an algorithm using asymptotic sense which is a standard approach in computational complexity theory [5, 18]. In these kind of analysis, it is required that the input size n of any instance to which the algorithm is expected to be applied be clearly defined. However, in the context of machine learning algorithms, there is no clear notion of the input size since learning algorithms are expected to detect some pattern from a dataset and can only access random sample of that data [17]. Therefore, the computational analysis is usually performed to determine the worst-case scenario.

3.1   Analysis of C4.5 Algorithm

Given that in general the decision tree algorithm follows the divide and conquer scheme which is similar to quick sort algorithm. When an algorithm contains a recursive call to itself, its running time can often be described by a recurrence equation which describes the overall running time on a problem of size n in terms of the running time on smaller inputs. In decision tree basically, the computational complexity of building decision tree is mainly concentrated on the criterion function consisting of two basic primary operations the entropy gain calculation of the class attribute and the entropy of the input variables in the training set with respect to the class. The estimated complexity of computing the probability for each class labelled is bounded by the size of the sample. So, the cost is $O(n)$. The computation performed on one input attribute requires $O(n\ log_2\ n)$ and since all attributes are considered then the total cost for this operation will be $O(mn\ log_2\ n)$. Similarly, to analyse the recursive call of the algorithm on the subset of the training set, the estimated complexity for such operation is $O(n\ log_2\ n)$ since at each partition, the algorithm considers the instances and their respective target values. Hence, the total running time complexity for C4.5 algorithm can be estimated by combining the cost for each of the basic operations in decision tree building as:

$$T(S, X, y) = O(n) + O(mnlog_2n) + O(nlog_2n) \tag{1}$$

where S is the training set, X is the input attributes and y represents the target. This running time can be simply expressed asymptotically as $O(mn\ log_2\ n)$ which is the dominant factor and it is thus a logarithmic function of n. However, with some approach in which the algorithm repeatedly re-evaluate the dataset each time the procedure is called, the running time can exponentially scale up to $O(m^k n^q)$ where k and q can be any constant c≥2.

3.2   Analysis of CART Algorithm

The complexity of CART can also be estimated using the same notion as in C4.5 since in theory the key operational steps of constructing decision tree generally follows the same structure. One major difference between the two algorithms lies in the splitting criterion used for the selection of attribute. CART uses gini index splitting criteria. Hence, the process of constructing decision tree using CART algorithm can also be estimated as $O(mn \ log_2 \ n)$ where m is the attributes and n is the observations.

4   Experimental Analysis

This section experimentally study the running time of decision tree algorithms. We are basically interested in the behaviour of the algorithms as the number of instances increases.

4.1   Datasets Used

To compare the performance of the classifiers, some frequently used datasets obtained from UCI machine learning repository are used. The characteristics of the datasets is given in Table 1.

Table 1. Characteristics of datasets

Datasets	Sample size (n)	Features	Classes (c)
Breast cancer	699	9	2
Pima diabetes	768	9	2
Banknote	1372	5	2

4.2   Experimental Setup

The experiment was carried out on a 64- bit computer with windows 10 operating system, dual-core Intel i7-6700 (3.4 GHz) desktop with 16 GB RAM running windows 10 operating system. The algorithms used for the experiment were implemented in the popular scikit-learn python library for data analysis and Anaconda-Jupyter Notebook editor 3.6 was used to obtain our results. Even though, our concern is basically on complexity analysis, but the accuracy was also considers since there is usually a trade-off between the two [9].

4.3   Results and Discussion

The goal of the experimental work is to analyse the behaviour of the decision tree algorithms as the size of the input dataset increases. Table 2 shows accuracy score over 10 cross validation runs as well as the running time measured in milliseconds for cancer, diabetes and banknote datasets respectively. Similarly, Figs. 1, 2 and 3 shows the graphical plot of only the running time results presented in Table 2 respectively. Overall, the results show that the running time of both algorithms grows nearly linearly as the size of the input increases as expected. However, CART algorithm outperforms the C4.5 across all the datasets in terms of the running time; but the differences is not significantly pronounced.

Table 2. Accuracy(*Acc.*) and time (*t*) result for cancer, diabetes and banknote datasets respectively.

Sample size n	Cancer dataset				Diabetes dataset				Banknote dataset			
	C4.5		CART		C4.5		CART		C4.5		CART	
	Acc.	*t*	*Acc.*	*t*	*Acc.*	*t*	*Acc.*	*t*	*Acc.*	*t*	*Acc.*	*t*
50	88.8	16.3	85.0	16.2	42.5	18.5	54.6	17.4	1.0	15.1	1.0	15.0
100	90.0	19.3	84.0	18.9	57.6	23.2	52.6	19.5	1.0	15.6	1.0	15.2
200	93.8	22.8	88.8	22.6	69.8	32.3	65.3	26.9	1.0	15.9	1.0	15.8
300	90.6	26.9	90.8	25.8	60.8	42.3	57.8	32.5	1.0	16.4	1.0	15.9
400	91.7	29.9	89.7	29.0	67.6	54.2	64.8	39.7	1.0	16.5	1.0	16.1
500	92.3	33.7	93.1	32.7	67.5	63.7	67.7	48.5	1.0	16.6	1.0	16.3
600	93.3	36.5	94.3	35.6	69.1	69.8	68.2	54.8	1.0	16.8	1.0	17.0
700	-	-	-	-	68.6	79.2	68.3	60.4	1.0	17.1	1.0	15.9
800	-	-	-	-	-	-	-	-	1.0	44.4	1.0	42.8
900	-	-	-	-	-	-	-	-	1.0	45.5	1.0	45.2
1000	-	-	-	-	-	-	-	-	1.0	62.1	1.0	49.1

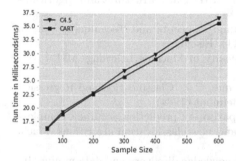

Fig. 1. Run time vs sample size for cancer dataset

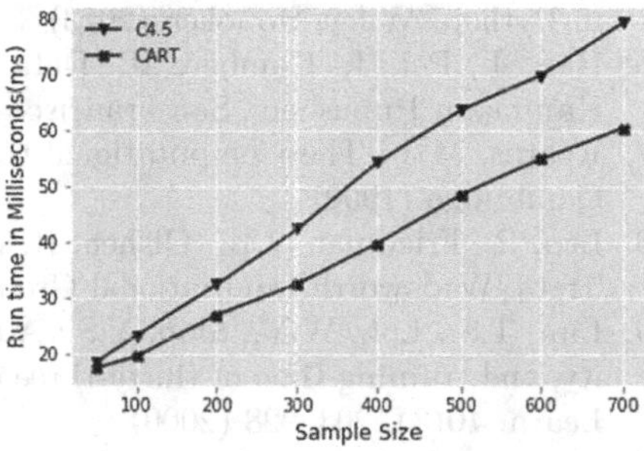

Fig. 2. Run time vs sample size for diabetes dataset

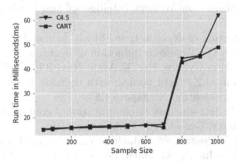

Fig. 3. Run time vs sample size for banknote dataset

5   Conclusion and Future Work

This paper theoretically and experimentally analysed and compared the execution time of the two basic decision tree algorithms implementation in scikit-learn python machine learning library (C4.5 and CART). The deeper investigation into the algorithm behaviour with different problem settings and techniques for possible improvement over the complexity of the algorithm remains the future work to further consider.

References

1. Barros, R.C., De Carvalho, A.C., Freitas, A.A., et al.: Automatic Design of Decision-Tree Induction Algorithms. Springer, Heidelberg (2015). https://doi.org/10.1007/978-3-319-14231-9
2. Bovet, D.P., Crescenzi, P., Bovet, D.: Introduction to the Theory of Complexity. Citeseer (1994)
3. Fayyad, U., Piatetsky-Shapiro, G., Smyth, P.: From data mining to knowledge discovery in databases. AI Mag. **17**(3), 37 (1996)
4. Gács, P., Lovász, L.: Complexity of Algorithms, Lecture Notes. Yale University (1999)
5. Goodrich, M.T., Tamassia, R., Goldwasser, M.H.: Data Structures and Algorithms in Python. Wiley, Hoboken (2013)
6. Han, J., Pei, J., Kamber, M.: Data Mining: Concepts and Techniques. Morgan Kaufmann Publishers, San Francisco (2011). Elsevier
7. Kearns, M.J.: The Computational Complexity of Machine Learning. MIT Press, Cambridge (1990)
8. Leo, B., Friedman, J.H., Olshen, R.A., Stone, C.J.: Classification and Regression Trees. Wadsworth International Group, Belmont (1984)
9. Lim, T.S., Loh, W.Y., Shih, Y.S.: A comparison of prediction accuracy, complexity, and training time of thirty-three old and new classification algorithms. Mach. Learn. **40**(3), 203–228 (2000)
10. Maimon, O., Rokach, L.: Introduction to knowledge discovery and data mining. In: Maimon, O., Rokach, L. (eds.) Data Mining and Knowledge Discovery Handbook, pp. 1–15. Springer, Boston (2009). https://doi.org/10.1007/978-0-387-09823-4_1
11. Martin, J.K., Hirschberg, D.: On the complexity of learning decision trees. In: International Symposium on Artificial Intelligence and Mathematics, pp. 112–115. Citeseer (1996)
12. Quinlan, J.R.: Induction of decision trees. Mach. Learn. **1**(1), 81–106 (1986)
13. Rokach, L., Maimon, O.: Top-down induction of decision trees classifiers-a survey. IEEE Trans. Syst. Man Cybern. Part C Appl. Rev. **35**(4), 476–487 (2005)
14. Rokach, L., Maimon, O.Z.: Data mining with decision trees: theory and applications, vol. 69. World Scientific, Singapore (2008)
15. Roos, M., Rothe, J.: Introduction to computational complexity. Technical report, Institut fur Informatik, Dusseldorf, Germany (2010)
16. Salzberg, S.L.: C4. 5: Programs for Machine Learning by J. Ross Quinlan Morgan Kaufmann Publishers Inc., 1993. Mach. Learn. **16**(3), 235–240 (1994)
17. Shalev-Shwartz, S., Ben-David, S.: Understanding Machine Learning: From Theory to Algorithms. Cambridge University Press, Cambridge (2014)

18. Sipser, M.: Introduction to the Theory of Computation, vol. 2. Thomson Course Technology, Boston (2006)
19. Witten, I.H., Frank, E., Hall, M.A., Pal, C.J.: Data Mining: Practical Machine Learning Tools and Techniques. Morgan Kaufmann, San Francisco (2016)
20. Zaki, M.J., Meira Jr., W., Meira, W.: Data Mining and Analysis: Fundamental Concepts and Algorithms. Cambridge University Press, Cambridge (2014)

Forecasting Student's Preference in E-learning Systems

Paulo Novais[1](✉)(iD), Filipe Gonçalves[1](✉)(iD), and Dalila Durães[2,3](✉)(iD)

[1] Algoritmi Research Centre/Department of Informatics,
University of Minho, Braga, Portugal
pjon@di.uminho.pt, fgoncalves@algoritmi.uminho.pt
[2] Department of Artificial Intelligence,
Technical University of Madrid, Madrid, Spain
d.alves@alumnos.upm.es
[3] CIICESI, ESTG, Polytechnic Institute of Porto, Felgueiras, Portugal

Abstract. The need for qualified people is growing exponentially, requiring limited resources allocated to education/training to be used most efficiently. However some problems can occur: (1) relying on learning theories, it is crucial to improve the learning process and mitigate the issues that may arise from technologically enhanced learning environments; (2) each student presents a particular way of assimilating knowledge, i.e. his/her learning procedure. It's essential that these systems adapt to the learning preferences of the students. In the present study, we propose an intelligent learning system able to monitor the patterns of students' behaviour during e-assessments, to support the teaching procedure within school environments. Results show that there are still mechanisms that can be explored to understand better the complex relationship between human behaviour, attention, and assessment which could be used for the implementation of better learning strategies. These results may be crucial for improving learning systems in an e-learning environment and for predicting students' behaviour in an exam, based on their interaction with technological devices.

Keywords: Learning · Intelligent mentoring systems
Biometric behaviour

1 Introduction

Technology emerges as a way of improving teaching/learning process, offering new ways to achieve better results and overcoming some known constraints, such as the availability of qualified teachers, time constraints, and individual monitoring. In this sense, the use of technological tools for teaching, with the consequent separation of teacher-student and student-student, can represent a risk as a significant amount of context information is lost [6].

In this paper, we propose an approach of an intelligent e-learning system able to monitor the patterns of students' behaviour during e-assessments, to support the teaching procedure within school environments. Especially behaviour

© Springer Nature Switzerland AG 2018
M. Bramer and M. Petridis (Eds.): SGAI-AI 2018, LNAI 11311, pp. 198–203, 2018.
https://doi.org/10.1007/978-3-030-04191-5_18

patterns are calculated based on mouse dynamics, keystrokes, student attention, and electronic assessment activity [4]. This approach used a non-intrusive method to assess the preferences of students while interacting with the computer. The hypothesis is that each student may be affected differently by each type of assess activity style and that this approach is a valid one for measuring such differences.

2   How Preferences Affects Attention

Previous research suggests that, in the context of learning and e-learning activities, different learning styles can influence learning performance [5]. Besides, each student has its own particular way of assimilating knowledge, that is, his learning preference. When the given instruction style matches the student's learning preference, the process is maximised which guarantees that the student learns more and more easily.

To accomplish this task, different fields were studied, such as Behavioural Biometrics [8], Ambient Intelligence [1] and Behaviourism [2], to develop a state classification of students with their interaction with computers and more specifically with e-Learning platforms. In [8], the authors propose a system based on a classification of the state-of-the-art in behavioural biometrics which is based on skills, style, preference, knowledge, motor-skills or strategy used by people while accomplishing different everyday tasks such as driving an automobile, talking on the phone or using a computer. In [1] the authors propose an Ambient Intelligence (AmI) that is about sensitive, adaptive electronic environments that respond to the actions of persons and objects and cater for their needs.

Mouse and keyboard tracking are techniques also used to measure and classify attention. The mouse and keyboard tracking technique is a non-invasive approach because the data captured is compiled by a background software and the user does not have the perception that he/she is being monitored. In previous work, we were focused on the analysis of student's attention based on tasks defined by the teacher [3] and found that people tend to interact differently with different applications and in different contexts. For example, although both tasks involve typing, people tend to type differently if they are in a messaging application and in a word processing application [7].

3   Materials and Methods

In the case of this work, one of the fundamental requirements is that the routines of the students while doing the computer-based assess activity are not disturbed by the data collection process as, any disturbance may have negative consequences on the outcome. The approach followed in this paper thus relies on Mouse and keystrokes Dynamics, in an attempt to put forward a completely non-intrusive method for assessing stress in Human-Computer Interaction. These results may be crucial for improving learning systems in an e-learning environment and for predicting students' behaviour in an assess activity, based on their interaction with technological devices. This specific population (vocational students) was selected to participate in this study, given these characteristics, since they are students who easily give up activities and, consequently, the learning and evaluation processes can give up easily.

3.1 Population

The study took place at the Caldas das Taipas High School, where assess activities take place on the computer. Each computer has a keyboard, a mouse, and a screen. The assess activity begins at the same time for all students and they log in the pre-defined software using their personal credentials and the activity begins. The experiment took place in four different multimedia lessons, with a maximum of 100 min to complete the assessment. In each assessment, different activity styles for the same subject were applied, where the first lesson was based on exercises related to video editing; the second lesson, the proposed tasks was related to image editing; in the third lesson, the proposed tasks was related to text editing; and in the fourth lesson, the proposed tasks was related to audio editing. For this purpose, a group of 14 (all girls) students was selected to participate in this experience.

Table 1. Summary of the characteristics of each assess activity.

Class	Date	Duration (minutes)		
		$\bar{x}$	$\tilde{x}$	S
Video	21-05-2018	7.31612E+15	8.4653E+15	3.00389E+15
Image	24-05-2018	9.99167E+15	1.21798E+16	4.7135E+15
Text	25-05-2018	6.19021E+15	7.29301E+15	2.64201E+15
Audio	29-05-2018	7.0459E+15	8.95808E+15	3.55391E+15

Their average age is 15.9 years old (SD = 1.5 years). Information regarding each assessment's duration is presented in Table 1. The data collection is completely transparent from the point of view of the student, i.e. their participation in the study has no effect whatsoever on their routine as all the relevant information is collected in a transparent manner.

3.2 Features Extraction

The construction of the logs presents the necessary conditions for (1) reconstruct the actions of each student, providing information for when interactions occur (2) information can be used to extract information/knowledge necessary to quantify the interaction performance of each student. Regarding mouse dynamics features, the process focuses on the individual's interaction with the mouse device, more specifically the system events triggered by the movement, clicks, and scroll. A similar process is verified in the retrieval of information related to keystroke and student's activity events. In other words, the proposed system presents the necessary requirements to generate high-level information on the user's behaviour patterns.

3.3 Dataset

After applying a survey to the students, they indicated that their preferred style was: for 70% image and for 30% was video. Based on this results and in the results obtained in the four assess lessons, presented in Table 2 and Fig. 1 we can conclude that: (1) the time spent in the application defined by the teacher has the higher level for lesson assess in the video, which is the preferred style only for 30% of the students. In the preferred style of the most of the students, image, they have a level of attention of 91,36, lowest average. (2) In case of mouse velocity, the higher level was for the assessment level of video and image.

Table 2. Summary of the biometric features variation for each exam.

Class	CD	DBC	DDC	DPLBC	KDT	MA	MV	APP%	TBK
Units	ms	px	px	ms	px	px/s^2	px/ms	%	ms
Video	188.31	206.1	214.24	2819.12	1002.8	0.6811	0.5931	94.14	1865
Image	150.73	150.73	161.88	3725.35	2669.1	0.6659	0.5413	91.36	1738
Text	146.43	227.4	152.52	2838.14	1223.0	0.6056	0.5312	89.23	1073.1
Audio	281.0	189.2	119.10	2408.52	714.1	0.5828	0.4986	93.7	1758
$\bar{x}$	187.66	227.0	165.70	2946.41	1384.2	0.6367	0.5447	92.08	1599.3

4 Analysis and Results

Based on the preparation process mentioned, we now focus on the relevance of the features analysed for the prediction of the student's learning method preference. With this work's step, it is intended: on the one hand, to identify and remove unnecessary, irrelevant and redundant features of the dataset that do not contribute to the prediction of the student's learning method preference; on the other hand, to verify, within the relevant features, those that present greater relevance, making it possible to order them by degree of importance.

As such, for the selection of most relevant features, the Boruta technique (a wrapper method built around the random forest classification algorithm) was applied along with the 10-fold cross-validation process. The Boruta follows a completely relevant feature selection method, which captures all the attributes that are relevant to the outcome variable. Its results are shown in Fig. 2, where

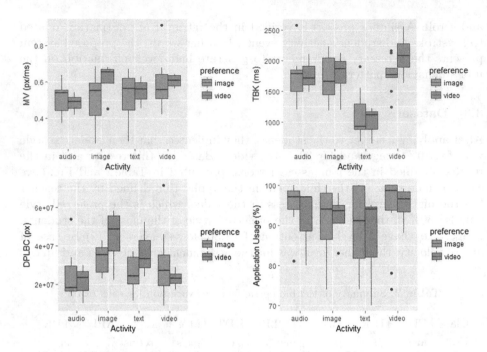

Fig. 1. Activity for the four lessons.

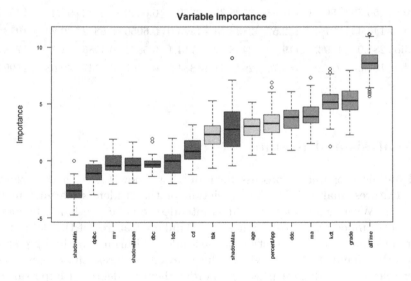

Fig. 2. Feature selection - Boruta method.

the Exam Duration feature is presented as the most relevant for predicting the student's learning preference, followed by the Assessment Grade, the Key Down Time, the Mouse Acceleration, and the Duration Distance Clicks.

5 Discussion and Conclusions

Results show that there are still mechanisms that can be explored to understand better the complex relationship between human behaviour, attention, and assessment, which could be used for the implementation of better learning strategies. These results may be crucial for improving learning systems in an e-learning environment and for predicting students' behaviour in an exam, based on their interaction with technological devices. The proposed paper focuses in this field, through a first analysis regarding the possibility of predicting students' learning preferences by monitoring student-computer interaction during an online exam. Briefly, we have verified that the main features to be analysed for this prediction focuses on the variation of exam duration, followed by Assessment Grade, Key Down Time, Mouse Acceleration, and the Duration Distance Clicks. However, since students' learning preferences varied only between "video" and "image" activities, there is a need to acquire new case studies to complement the remaining activities (i.e. "audio" and "text") and as a way to increase the number of cases to be applied in the process of learning and validation of the future prediction model. In addition, as future work, we intend to apply this knowledge to the development of a classification model capable of predicting, in an effective and non-intrusive way, students' learning preferences in real-time.

Acknowledgement. This work has been supported by COMPETE: POCI-01-0145-FEDER-007043 and FCT- Fundação para a Ciência e Tecnologia within the Project Scope: UID/CEC/00319/2013.

References

1. Aarts, E., Wichert, R.: Ambient intelligence. In: Bullinger, H.J. (ed.) Technology Guide, pp. 244–249. Springer, Heidelberg (2009). https://doi.org/10.1007/978-3-540-88546-7_47
2. Bouton, M.E.: Behaviourism, thoughts, and actions. Br. J. Psychol. **100**(S1), 181–183 (2009)
3. Durães, D., Cardoso, C., Bajo, J., Novais, P.: Learning frequent behaviors patterns in intelligent environments for attentiveness level. In: De la Prieta, F., et al. (eds.) PAAMS 2017. AISC, vol. 619, pp. 139–147. Springer, Cham (2018). https://doi.org/10.1007/978-3-319-61578-3_13
4. Duraes, D., Carneiro, D., Jimenez, A., Novais, P.: Characterizing attentive behavior in intelligent environments. Neurocomputing **272**, 46–54 (2018)
5. Ford, N., Chen, S.Y.: Individual differences, hypermedia navigation, and learning: an empirical study. J. Educ. Multimed. Hypermedia **9**(4), 281–311 (2000)
6. Novais, P., Carneiro, D.: Interdisciplinary Perspectives on Contemporary Conflict Resolution. Advances in Linguistics and Communication Studies. IGI Global (2016). https://books.google.pt/books?id=irFjjwEACAAJ
7. Pimenta, A., Carneiro, D., Neves, J., Novais, P.: A neural network to classify fatigue from human-computer interaction. Neurocomputing **172**, 413–426 (2016)
8. Yampolskiy, R.V., Govindaraju, V.: Behavioural biometrics: a survey and classification. Int. J. Biom. **1**(1), 81–113 (2008)

Human Motion Recognition Using 3D-Skeleton-Data and Neural Networks

Jan P. Vox[✉] and Frank Wallhoff

Institute for Assistive Technologies, Jade University of Applied Sciences,
Oldenburg, Germany
{jan.vox,frank.wallhoff}@jade-hs.de

Abstract. This work addresses the recognition of human motion exercises using 3D-skeleton-data and Neural Networks (NN). The examined dataset contains 16 gymnastic motion exercises (e.g. squats, lunges) executed from 21 subjects and captured with the second version of the Microsoft™ Kinect sensor (Kinect v2). The NN was trained with eight datasets from eight subjects and tested with 13 unknown datasets. The investigation in this work focuses on the configuration of NNs for human motion recognition. The authors will conclude that a backpropagation NN consisting of 100 neurons, three hidden layers, and a learning rate of 0.001 reaches the best accuracy with 93.8% correct.

Keywords: Neural networks · Human motion recognition
3D-skeleton-data

1 Introduction

Human motion recognition is widely researched and offers many possible applications. Common areas include sport sciences, ergonomics analysis, virtual activity games, and the in-depth analysis of motions. The investigated recognition framework in this work refers to a training system for therapeutic purposes. In general the recognition should work regardless of the user respectively of the individual body size. In order to adapt to individual movement executions of its respective user and to improve the overall recognition accuracy iteratively, the recognition model should be capable of optimizing its exercise models after the initial training by adapting to new training material (learning). In previous work, the authors investigated the recognition of human motion exercises using multiclass Support Vector Machines (SVM). In this work it was generally concluded, that SVMs are well suited for the recognition of 19 human motions [7]. However, the extension of the training material with new gymnastic exercises and the individualization of certain motions to the respective user led to a decrease of the recognition accuracy was occasionally observed with SVMs.

This work was supported by EU grants in the INTERREG project *Vitale Regionen* and by the Jade University of Applied Sciences with the graduate track Jade2Pro.

M. Bramer and M. Petridis (Eds.): SGAI-AI 2018, LNAI 11311, pp. 204–209, 2018.
https://doi.org/10.1007/978-3-030-04191-5_19

This work investigates whether NN are an alternative and better suitable for adapting to personal variances in human motions. In particular for the recognition with optical motion capturing systems i.e. the Kinect v2 and the processing of 3D-skeleton-data (cartesian positions from body joints) is focused. The best topology, respectively the configuration (hidden layers, neurons and learning rate) of NN for the purpose of human motion recognition using 3D-skeleton-data is investigated in this work.

2 State of the Art

NNs are used in many applications for prediction and recognition [6]. Nevertheless, for the recognition of human motions other machine learning methods such as Decision Trees, Hidden Markov Models (HMM), Dynamic Time Warping (DTW) and SVM are often used, e.g. in [3] or [1]. Gaglio et al. combined K-Means, SVMs and HMMs and evaluated this method with the Kinect Activity Recognition Dataset (KARD). The KARD contains 18 activities e.g. arm waves, sit down, side kick, etc. With their method they achieved an accuracy above 84% [2]. The KARD differs from the dataset examined in this work and thus the classification problem also differs. The reason is that the motions in the KARD are mainly carried out by the upper or lower limbs (e.g. arm wave, side kick). In contrast, the gymnastic motions studied in this work are carried out by the whole body. Furthermore, some movements have lateral synchronisms (left arm as well as right arm). In a previous work, the authors achieved an accuracy of up to 81% for the recognition of 19 motion exercises using SVMs [7]. Patsadu et al. used backpropagation NN with 60 neurons and one hidden layer and 3D-skeleton-data for the recognition of stand, sit down and lie down. They achieved an accuracy of 100% for the recognition of three human motions [4]. To conclude, there is no general method which optimizes all recognition problems. Thus the focus in this work refers to the recognition of 16 gymnastic exercises using NNs.

3 Dataset

The examined dataset in this work contains 16 motion exercises from 21 subjects (9 male, 12 female) aged from 19 to 81. The data was examined within a study about a training assistant in a previous work [7]. Physical motion exercises were automatically captured in the form of 25 body joint positions (3D-skeleton-data) as time series with a sampling rate of 50 Hz. The subject was placed 2.5 m in front of the Kinect v2 and was asked to perform dedicated motion exercises. The dataset includes ten repetitions per subject from each motion exercise. The description of all examined motions exercises are listed in Table 1. The character L_-R in the shortcut means that the motion exercises were performed left and right respectively.

Table 1. Description of the motion exercises in the dataset

No.	Shortcut	Description
1, 2	abdArmElbow90L_R	abduction elbow left and right
3	abdLegL	sideward abduction with left leg
4	armsFrontLBackR	right arm forward and left arm to the rear
5	diagoArmLLegR	left arm up and right leg sideward abduction
6, 7	flexElbowL_R	flexion elbow right and left arm
8	fullSquat	squat with arms
9	jumpingJack	jumping jack
10, 11	kneeUpL_R	flexion left and right knee
12, 13	sideLungeLegL_R	sideward lunge left and right
14	lungeLegL	lunge with left leg in front
15	swingArmBackwardL	left arm swing backward
16	swingArmForwardR	right arm swing forward

4 Preprocessing and Testing of NN Configurations

Preprocessing: As in all machine learning applications, in addition to the particular configuration of a NN, the preprocessing step has an important impact for the overall performance. The obeyed feature vector includes normalized position data and calculated joint angles. In order to normalize the position data, the origin of the coordinate system was normalized with regard to the right ankle. Subsequently, the lengths of the limbs were re-calculated to a reference skeleton. The dimension of the reference skeleton is re-calculated from the mean body dimensions in the training data for the latter presentation to the NN. In order to calculate the joint angles (e.g. knee, elbow, hip), three positions are required. For example, the angle in the elbow is calculated with the Cartesian positions from hand, elbow and shoulder. The joint angles ranging from 0°–180° were normalized to a range of 0–1. In total 14 joint angles from elbow, shoulder, armpit, knee, leg (left and right), pelvis, hip, torso, and head were used in conjunction with the position data to form a feature vector.

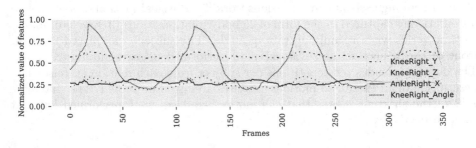

Fig. 1. Normalized data from four features per frame when performing four full squats.

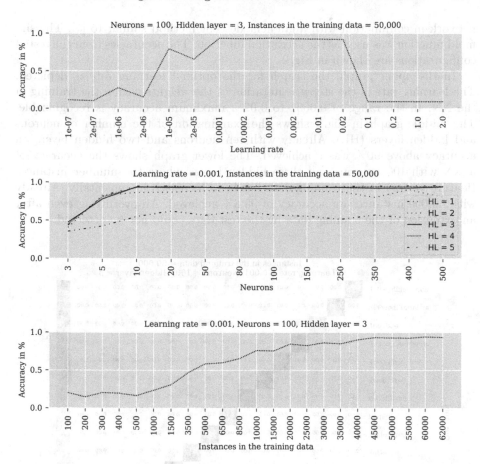

Fig. 2. Accuracies of the tested configurations incrementally increasing the learning rate, number of neurons and the hidden layer as well as the number of instances in the training data.

The feature selection was achieved using variance analysis. All features with low information were rejected based on thresholds. The entire feature vector includes 52 features out of 89 possible features (25 x, y, z-positions and 14 joint angles). The x, y, z-positions and the calculated joint angles from the right knee when performing four squats are shown in Fig. 1.

Testing Configurations: Finally, to determine which configuration and topology of a NN is best suitable for the recognition, the learning rate, the number of neurons, and hidden layers as well as the number of instances or rather frames in the training data are incrementally increased until a saturation of the accuracy rate was observed. The neural network was trained in a supervised manner with eight subjects and tested with datasets of 13 unknown subjects. The architecture and training context of the NN were implemented as a backpropagation network in conjunction with a gradient descent method similar to [5]. The sigmoid function was used as the activation function. The accuracies from the tested configurations are shown in Fig. 2.

In the upper graph, the search for the optimal learning rate is depicted. The learning rate is the stepwise iteration of the weights within the training of the NN. In the range of 0.0001 to 0.02 a maximum accuracy is recognizable. The middle graph in Fig. 2 shows the examination of the number of neurons and hidden layers (HL). Already with ten neurons and two hidden layers an accuracy above 90% was e achieved. The lower graph shows the accuracy of a NN with 100 neurons and three hidden layers where the number instances (feature vector) in the training data has been increased incrementally. Already with 50,000 instances an accuracy of 93.8% achieved. An overfitting even after an extension of the training data by the test data could not be detected.

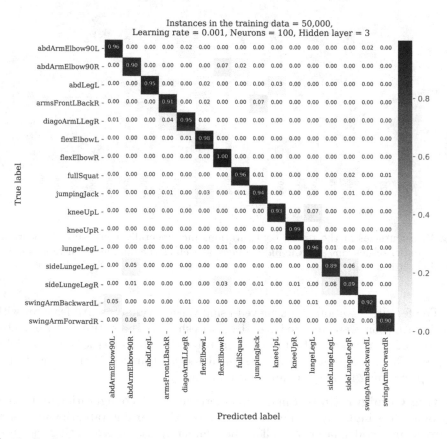

Fig. 3. Confusion matrix of the classification accuracies from 16 motion exercises with eight subjects in the training set and tested with 13 unknown datasets. The total accuracy of all tested exercises is 93.8%.

5   Results and Conclusion

The study in this work aims at determining the configuration and topology of a NN for human motion recognition. The results of the tested configurations are summarized in Fig. 2. The study shows that a learning rate around 0.001 is meaningful. It was also shown that already with a number of ten neurons and three hidden layers, an accuracy of 91.1% may be achieved. With a number of 100 neurons, the accuracy increases to 93.8%. Finally it is concluded that a training data set with at least 50,000 instances (eight subjects) is recommended. As an early adoption it has to be ensured that different body sizes are among the training subjects. Considering the accuracy of each individual exercise in the confusion matrix, it can finally be shown that almost any motion exercise can be recognized with over 90% accuracy. The full confusion matrix from the 16 tested motion exercise is shown in Fig. 3.

The experiments show that backpropagation NNs with a learning rate of 0.001, 100 neurons, three hidden layers, and the sigmoid function as activation function reach an accuracy up to 93.8%, tested with 13 unknown datasets (117,679 instances). In the ongoing research, the behaviour of NNs using new motion exercises are added to the training set is investigated. Another investigation will address the performance of NNs based on only one training dataset from one subject and artificial increased data.

Acknowledgements. The authors gratefully acknowledge the contribution of Jannik Flessner, Johannes Hurka, Tobias Theuerkauff, Jana Tessmer and Yves Wagner.

References

1. Cippitelli, E., Gasparrini, S., Gambi, E., Spinsante, S.: A human activity recognition system using skeleton data from rgbd sensors. Comput. Intell. Neurosci. **2016**, 21 (2016)
2. Gaglio, S., Re, G.L., Morana, M.: Human activity recognition process using 3-d posture data. IEEE Trans. Hum. Mach. Syst. **45**(5), 586–597 (2015)
3. Kale, G.V., Patil, V.H.: A study of vision based human motion recognition and analysis. arXiv preprint arXiv:1608.06761 (2016)
4. Patsadu, O., Nukoolkit, C., Watanapa, B.: Human gesture recognition using kinect camera. In: 2012 International Joint Conference on Computer Science and Software Engineering (JCSSE), pp. 28–32. IEEE (2012)
5. Rashid, T.: Make Your Own Neural Network. CreateSpace Independent Publishing Platform, London (2016)
6. Schmidhuber, J.: Deep learning in neural networks: an overview. Neural Netw. **61**, 85–117 (2015). https://doi.org/10.1016/j.neunet.2014.09.003
7. Vox, J.P., Wallhoff, F.: Recognition of human motion exercises using skeleton data and SVM for rehabilitative purposes. In: 2017 IEEE Life Sciences Conference (LSC), pp. 266–269, December 2017. https://doi.org/10.1109/LSC.2017.8268194

Autonomous Swarm Agents
Using Case-Based Reasoning

Daniel O'Connor[1], Stelios Kapetanakis[2(✉)], Georgios Samakovitis[3],
Michael Floyd[4], Santiago Ontañon[5], and Miltos Petridis[6]

[1] Keble College, Oxford University, Oxford, UK
`daniel.oconnor@keble.ox.ac.uk`
[2] School of Computing, Engineering and Mathematics, University of Brighton,
Brighton, UK
`s.kapetanakis@brighton.ac.uk`
[3] School of Computing and Mathematical Sciences, University of Greenwich,
London, UK
`g.samakovitis@gre.ac.uk`
[4] Knexus Research Corporation, Springfield, VA, USA
`michael.floyd@knexusresearch.com`
[5] Department of Computer Science, Drexel University, Philadelphia, USA
`santi@cs.drexel.edu`
[6] Department of Computing, Middlesex University, London, UK
`m.petridis@mdx.ac.uk`

Abstract. Dynamic planning is a hot topic in autonomous computing. This
work presents a novel approach of simulating swarm computing behaviour in a
sandbox environment where swarms of robots are challenged to fight against
each other with a goal of "conquering" any environment bases. Swarm strategies
are being used which are decided, modified and applied at run time. Autonomous swarm agents seem surprisingly applicable to several problems where
combined artificial intelligence agents are challenged to generate innovative
solutions and evaluate them prior to proposing or adopting the best possible one.
This work is applicable in areas where AI agents should make selections close to
real time within a range of available options under a multi-constraint, multi-
objective mission environment. Relevance to Business Process workflows is
also presented and documented.

Keywords: Case-based reasoning · Swarm Intelligence · Swarm robotics
Multi-agent systems · Real-time strategy · Goal-driven agent
Autonomous computing

1 Introduction

Swarm Intelligence (SI) is the discipline of a collective behaviour of natural or artificial
decentralized systems comprising many individuals that can govern themselves in a
self-organized way. An SI system or colony has a population of simple units, referred
as agents, that can interact among each other and with/within their environment.
Several examples of SI systems can be found in Natural Sciences, such as Biology,

© Springer Nature Switzerland AG 2018
M. Bramer and M. Petridis (Eds.): SGAI-AI 2018, LNAI 11311, pp. 210–216, 2018.
https://doi.org/10.1007/978-3-030-04191-5_20

where decentralised species with no leadership or master control can demonstrate complex behaviours and intelligent global performance that is usually unknown or not possible to perform by any single individual. Several natural examples exist including bird flocking, ant colonisation, bacterial growth, animal herding, etc. Artificial Intelligence (AI) is mimicking such behaviours and several algorithms appear under SI or "SI applications in robotics" that can be applied on multi-sensory input from various sources e.g. drone swarms or Unmanned Ground Vehicles (UGVs).

This work presents a SI robot application, named RoboWars [6] which can be configured based on real world requirements adhering to drone cases, UGVs or any other autonomous mechanical application scenario provided by the user. This paper presents a Case-based Reasoning (CBR) [1] application and evaluation as it was applied on a variation of the Capture the Flag (CtF) game, demonstrating its applicability in versatile environments and algorithmic scenarios.

RoboWars has been used for educational purposes and at limited scale, however its applicability can be expanded on open field scenarios. This paper investigates a simple mission using CBR and is structured as follows: Sect. 2 presents the relevant work in CBR, SI and Business Workflow Scenarios; Sect. 3 illustrates our environment configuration; Sect. 4 shows the system evaluation and results; and finally, Sect. 5 discusses the future steps of this work and possible improvements.

2   Related Work

CBR works as a continuous problem-oriented, solution-embedded process where experience supports learning [2]. CBR uses extensively any knowledge within its application domain and is based on a solid case representation and rigid similarity mechanics that allow its continuous 5-R step of retrieve, reuse, revise, review, retain.

CBR has been applied in a variety of domains with substantial success including recommender systems, business process workflows, medical domain, etc. CBR has a few examples in Swarm Intelligence applications with the most notable of Lorenzi et al. [3] in task allocation, Nouaouria and Boukadoum [4] in CBR retrieval optimisation, Ben Yahia et al. [5] in fuzzy CBR and particle swarm optimisation for decision making support and Teodorovic et al. [24] in ensemble CBR and Bee colony optimisation for dose planning in cancer treatment. A lot of work on CBR relevant to swarm computing and complementary to our work can be seen in the fields of agent-based computing and games.

On the agent-based computing we can see the work of Floyd and Esfandiari on learning by observation [17], Sebestyénová on agent-based Decision Support systems [7], agent-based CBR for computation resource allocation within a cloud environment [8], multi-based collaborative reasoning using CBR [9], ensemble CBR and multi-agents for collaborative management in supply chain [10] and distributed agent-based CBR for large scale operations [11].

CBR and games literature shows an extensive range of applications from Real-time strategical decisions [12–14], hybrid approaches combining CBR and Reinforcement Learning [15], CBR and real-time pathfinding [16] to automatic feature selection for robocup agents [18] and automatic CBR-game case generation(s) [19].

Close to our work is also the work on CBR and business process workflow monitoring, remedy finding and reasoning having several examples on temporal-spatial workflows [20–22] and advanced path finding scenarios [23].

3 Environment Configuration

RoboWars allows several usages to simulate different scenario requirements and maps. For this work we used randomly generated maps simulating a capture "as many bases as possible" game. A simple description of the environment is the following: When a simulation is initiated, a random map is generated as shown in Fig. 1, having an odd number of "bases".

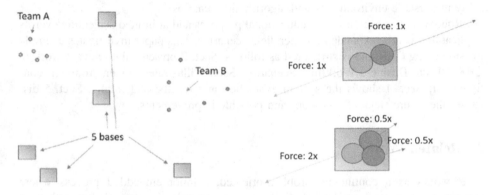

Fig. 1. Graphical representation of two adversarial teams and random "bases"

Fig. 2. Agent collisions scenarios

Upon the successful generation of a map, two teams of 3 to 5 agents each are deployed on the map starting from opposite directions e.g. Team A on the East of the map whereas Team B on the West, North vs. South, etc. Each team's mission is to capture as many bases as possible. Upon a successful capture each team is rewarded with a score bonus [6]. The agents do not destroy each other when they collide but instead push each other with a standard amount of force (Fig. 2).

The case representation is detailed in [6], where each case $C = \langle d, c, s, r \rangle$, where:

- d is a set of continuous agent positions as captured per second over time. If pos_n^t is the position of agent n at time t, $d = \{pos_1^1, \ldots, pos_n^1, \ldots, pos_1^t, \ldots, pos_n^t\}$ and contains $n \times t$ items.
- c is a set of actions performed by the agents over time. If ac_n^t is the action performed by agent n at time t, $c = \{ac_1^1, \ldots, ac_n^1, \ldots, ac_1^t, \ldots, ac_n^t\}$ and contains $n \times t$ items.
- s is the chosen strategy of the team
- r is the actual result of using the case's strategy is a simulation

4   Evaluation

For the CBR evaluation 3 case bases were created: for Team A, Team B, and a Global case base which contained any "new" combination of strategies used by either of the teams. We ran between 40–50 h of simulations to tackle the CBR cold start problem (i.e., the generation of initial cases) where each team was randomly assigned a strategy and learned how its chosen actions affected the outcome (i.e., perform exploration). We used the trained case bases as the initial experiment where each team competed against each other. The outcomes of these simulations were converging to something like: "conquer a base" by accident or to a "defend one base all together" strategy until the end of the round. This strategy seemed to provide the best results for any swarm.

To eliminate the case base bias, we allowed for an evolved model of choosing strategies where: teams could opt for different strategies over time based on their score (e.g., if a swarm was noticing that its score was lower than its opponents it would attempt to change its strategy mode to acquire a higher score over time). Additionally, if a team was ahead of score it would attempt to maintain it by opting for a more risk-averse strategy. For this experiment the initial case bases seemed not sufficient, and the cold start training had to be repeated to have an appropriate set of cases for the swarms to choose from. We conducted 200 h of simulations with longer simulation rounds (5–10 min each) to allow for a more comprehensive case base formulation. All the experiments contained 3-min rounds with the swarms able to choose from any combination of strategies that would maximise their score, regardless of the time taken in the training period. This second experiment contained more than 60 h of simulations allowing for a more comprehensive view of how swarms could behave over time while attempting to maximise their score. A few interesting observations that came into light from this experiment were the following:

(a) Swarms tended to reuse often their "best" tactics. For example, a rapid succession between "attack any base" scenario and "defend our bases equally" seemed to work very well for a specific swarm and such sequences of strategies were heavily utilised across time.

(b) Swarms were strongly biased upon their original training and were slow to adjust their strategy sequences. This was expected to some extent due to the nature of CBR. However, interestingly once a better strategy sequence was achieved, it was rapidly evolving into the "most keen to use" one from the swarms.

(c) There were rounds were a swarm could end up being "confused". This phenomenon was prevalent when the case base exceeded a few thousand sequences and the equal "ranking" of cases made difficult to swarms to take the right decision.

Our final experiment was among the trained swarms and a new swarm, called the Golden Swarm (GS), which was trained with the Global case base (i.e., the hybrid case base containing the novel cases from each case base). We ran additional simulations and observed several interesting outcomes. After several rounds of equal wins and losses two phenomena were observed as the most prevalent:

(1) GS tended to "exploit" the limitations of its opponent by resorting to cases that its opponent has never seen before and extreme scenarios that have probably come from a past swarm's initial training

(2) GS managed to "confuse" its opponent several times, by adopting series of strategies its opponent has regarded as mediocre due to its past performance.

5   Conclusions and Challenges

This work has investigated an interesting concept in CBR and swarm optimisation. A new simulator was developed to allow the simulation of UGVs and drones, and at the same time being able to apply different AI techniques and measure their outcomes and impact. For this work we have demonstrated several CBR vs. CBR evaluations, illustrating how a CBR system can evolve and be able to achieve superior performance based on its original training and after having several rounds of iterations with a worthy opponent. However, this was just a brief demonstration of what can be really achieved with the proposed tool and AI methodology.

Our future work will focus on overcoming the challenges we encountered, from both CBR and the Swarm design limitations. Our focus will be on redesigning and revaluating any early steps and allow for a more advanced workflow representation and similarity finding e.g. consider each case's log of agent actions per second. We have observed cases where CBR seemed to restrict each swarm. In such cases and to allow for future evolution we are planning to investigate more appropriate techniques to allow for deviation in behaviour. Finally, more advanced robot formations and strategies and advanced teams and skill within the robots can provide a more realistic experience and adherence to real life scenarios.

Acknowledgements. We would like to thank UK Nuffield Research and the European Defence Agency (EDA) for providing support to the initial stages of this work.

References

1. Leake, D.B.: Case-based reasoning. In: Ralston, A., Reilly, E.D., Hemmendinger, D. (eds.) Encyclopedia of computer science, 4th edn, pp. 196–197. Wiley, Chichester (2003)
2. Aamodt, A., Plaza, E.: Case-based reasoning: foundational issues, methodological variations, and system approaches. AI Commun. 7(1), 39–59 (1994)
3. Lorenzi, F., Santos, D.S., de Oliveira, D., Bazzan, A.L.C.: Task allocation in case-based recommender systems: a swarm intelligence approach. Information Science Reference, pp. 268–279 (2007)
4. Nouaouria, N., Boukadoum, M.: A particle swarm optimization approach for the case retrieval stage in CBR. In: Bramer, M., Petridis, M., Hopgood, A. (eds.) Research and Development in Intelligent Systems XXVII: Incorporating Applications and Innovations in Intelligent Systems XVIII Proceedings of AI-2010, pp. 209–222. Springer, London (2011). https://doi.org/10.1007/978-0-85729-130-1_15

5. Ben Yahia, N., Bellamine, N., Ben Ghezala, H.: Integrating fuzzy case-based reasoning and particle swarm optimization to support decision making. Int. J. Comput. Sci. Issues **9**(3), 117–124 (2012)
6. O' Connor, D., Kapetanakis, S., Floyd, M., Ontanon, S., Petridis, M.: RoboWars: autonomous swarm robotics using case-based reasoning. In: Petridis, M. (ed.) Proceedings of the 22nd UK CBR Workshop, Peterhouse, December 2017, pp. 5–10. Brighton Press (2017)
7. Sebestyénová, J.: CBR in agent-based decision support system. In: Acta Polytechnica Hungarica, vol. 4, no. 1, pp. 127–138. Andras Bako, Budapest Tech (2007)
8. De la Prieta, F., Bajo, J., Corchado, J.M.: A CBR approach to allocate computational resources within a cloud platform. In: Novais, P., Camacho, D., Analide, C., El Fallah Seghrouchni, A., Badica, C. (eds.) Intelligent Distributed Computing IX. SCI, vol. 616, pp. 75–84. Springer, Cham (2016). https://doi.org/10.1007/978-3-319-25017-5_7
9. Manousakis-Kokorakis, V., Petridis, M., Kapetanakis, S.: Collaborative reasoning in workflow monitoring using a multi-agent architecture. J. Expert Update **15**(1), 37–47 (2015)
10. Fu, J., Fu, Y.: Case-based reasoning and multi-agents for cost collaborative management in supply chain. Int. Workshop Inf. Electron. Procedia Eng. **29**, 1088–1098 (2012)
11. Agorgianitis, I., Petridis, M., Kapetanakis, S., Fish, A.: Evaluating distributed methods for CBR systems for monitoring business process workflows. In: Proceeding of ICCBR 2016, Workshop on Reasoning About Time in CBR, Atlanta, GA, October 28–November 2, 2016, pp. 122–131 (2016)
12. Ontañón, S., Mishra, K., Sugandh, N., Ram, A.: Case-based planning and execution for real-time strategy games. In: Weber, R.O., Richter, M.M. (eds.) ICCBR 2007. LNCS (LNAI), vol. 4626, pp. 164–178. Springer, Heidelberg (2007). https://doi.org/10.1007/978-3-540-74141-1_12
13. Ontañón, S: Case acquisition strategies for case-based reasoning in real-time strategy games. In: FLAIRS 2012. AAAI Press (2012)
14. Mishra, K., Ontañón, S., Ram, A.: Situation assessment for plan retrieval in real-time strategy games. In: Althoff, K.-D., Bergmann, R., Minor, M., Hanft, A. (eds.) ECCBR 2008. LNCS (LNAI), vol. 5239, pp. 355–369. Springer, Heidelberg (2008). https://doi.org/10.1007/978-3-540-85502-6_24
15. Wender, S., Watson, I.: Combining case-based reasoning and reinforcement learning for unit navigation in real-time strategy game AI. In: Lamontagne, L., Plaza, E. (eds.) ICCBR 2014. LNCS (LNAI), vol. 8765, pp. 511–525. Springer, Cham (2014). https://doi.org/10.1007/978-3-319-11209-1_36
16. Bulitko, V., Bjornsson, Y., Lawrence, R.: Case-based subgoaling in real-time heuristic search for video game pathfinding. J. Artif. Intell. Res. **39**, 269–300 (2010)
17. Floyd, M.W., Esfandiari, B.: Building learning by observation agents using jLOAF. In: Proceedings of Workshop on Case-Based Reasoning for Computer, ICCBR 2011, pp. 37–41, 12–15 September 2011
18. Acosta, E., Esfandiari, B., Floyd, M.W.: Feature selection for CBR in imitation of RoboCup agents: a comparative study. In: Proceedings of the Workshop on Case-Based Reasoning for Computer Games (Held at the 18th International Conference on Case-Based Reasoning), Alessandria, Italy, July 19–22, pp. 25–34 (2010)
19. Floyd, M.W., Esfandiari, B.: An active approach to automatic case generation. In: McGinty, L., Wilson, D.C. (eds.) ICCBR 2009. LNCS (LNAI), vol. 5650, pp. 150–164. Springer, Heidelberg (2009). https://doi.org/10.1007/978-3-642-02998-1_12
20. Kapetanakis, S., Petridis, M., Knight, B., Ma, J., Bacon, L.: A case based reasoning approach for the monitoring of business workflows. In: Bichindaritz, I., Montani, S. (eds.) ICCBR 2010. LNCS (LNAI), vol. 6176, pp. 390–405. Springer, Heidelberg (2010). https://doi.org/10.1007/978-3-642-14274-1_29

21. Kapetanakis, S., Petridis, M., Knight, B., Ma, J., Bacon, L.: Providing explanations for the intelligent monitoring of business workflows using case-based reasoning. In: Workshop Proceedings of ExACT-10 at ECAI 2010, Lisbon, Portugal (2010)
22. Kapetanakis, S., Petridis, M.: Evaluating a case-based reasoning architecture for the intelligent monitoring of business workflows. In: Montani, S., Jain, L.C. (eds.) Successful Case-based Reasoning Applications-2, pp. 43–54. Springer, Berlin (2014). https://doi.org/10.1007/978-3-642-38736-4_4
23. Niu, L., Zhuo, G.: An improved real algorithm for difficult path finding situation. In: Proceeding of the International Archives of the Photogrammetry, Remote Sensing and Spatial Information Sciences 2008, Beijing, China, vol. 37 (2008)
24. Teodorovic, D., Šelmic, M., Mijatovic-Teodorovic, L.: Combining case-based reasoning with bee colony optimisation for dose planning in well differentiated thyroid cancer treatment. Expert Syst. Appl. 40(5), 2147–2155 (2013)

Application Papers

Papers Included in the Application Stream
of AI-2018

The following six sections comprise refereed papers accepted for the application stream of AI-2018, divided into the following categories:

- Industrial Applications of Artificial Intelligence
- Planning and Scheduling in Action
- Machine Learning in Action
- Applications of Machine Learning
- Applications of Agent Systems and Genetic Algorithms
- Short Application Papers

The Rob Milne Memorial Award for the best refereed application paper in the conference was won by a paper entitled "Beat the Bookmaker – Winning Football Bets with Machine Learning" by Johannes Stübinger (Friedrich-Alexander-Universität Erlangen-Nürnberg, Germany) and Julian Knoll (Technische Hochschule Nürnberg, Germany).

The final section comprises the text of short application papers which were presented as posters at the conference.

Beat the Bookmaker – Winning Football Bets with Machine Learning (Best Application Paper)

Johannes Stübinger[1](✉) and Julian Knoll[2](✉)

[1] Friedrich-Alexander-Universität Erlangen-Nürnberg,
Lange Gasse 20, 90403 Nuremberg, Germany
johannes.stuebinger@fau.de

[2] Technische Hochschule Nürnberg Georg Simon Ohm,
Keßlerplatz 12, 90489 Nuremberg, Germany
julian.knoll@th-nuernberg.de

Abstract. Over the past decades, football (soccer) has continued to draw more and more attention from people all over the world. Meanwhile, the appearance of the internet led to a rapidly growing market for online bookmakers, companies which offer sport bets for specific odds. With numerous matches every week in dozens of countries, football league matches hold enormous potential for developing betting strategies. In this context, a betting strategy beats the bookmaker if it generates positive average profits over time. In this paper, we developed a data-driven framework for predicting the outcome of football league matches and generating meaningful profits by betting accordingly. Conducting a simulation study based on the matches of the five top European football leagues from season 2013/14 to 2017/18 showed that economically and statistically significant returns can be achieved by exploiting large data sets with modern machine learning algorithms. Furthermore, it turned out that these results cannot be reached with a linear regression model or simple betting strategies, such as always betting on the home team.

Keywords: Football · Betting strategy · Machine learning
Statistical arbitrage · Sports forecasting

1 Introduction

The anticipated outcome of a favorite football team's upcoming match is often a topic of discussion for a large part of the population. In some offices, the skill to accurately predict these outcomes results in admiration and is often even rewarded. Aside from these more superficial implications, guessing the correct football match results may have a far larger impact on a sector which, within the last decade, has grown to become a huge industry: online bookmakers. If one is able to estimate the outcome of football matches in a more accurate way

© Springer Nature Switzerland AG 2018
M. Bramer and M. Petridis (Eds.): SGAI-AI 2018, LNAI 11311, pp. 219–233, 2018.
https://doi.org/10.1007/978-3-030-04191-5_21

than these online bookmakers, the reward would not only be admiration but also significantly high returns on the betting amount.

This paper describes a way to estimate the outcome of football matches based on large data sources and common machine learning algorithms. For this purpose, different approaches were compared to discover whether more complex approaches like machine learning algorithms result in better outcomes. Furthermore, the possibility of beating the prediction accuracy of one of the world's leading online gambling bookmakers was examined as well as the capability to use our strategy to generate positive returns on average. In that context, methods of the field of statistical arbitrage stock market trading were incorporated. Throughout the whole article, the term "football" refers to the popular sport association football (soccer) rather than to other sports like American football or rugby.

We make the following main contributions to the literature. First, we constructed a betting strategy for football league matches based on machine learning algorithms and findings from the field of statistical arbitrage trading. Second, we benchmarked our strategies with trading variants which rest upon betting odds of the online bookmaker. Third, we performed a large-scale simulation study based on a data set including in total 39 variables for 8,082 football matches of the big five football leagues. Fourth, we showed favorable risk-return characteristics for the betting strategies based on machine learning algorithms and demonstrated that risk-averse strategies perform better than risk-taking ones.

The remainder of this work is structured as follows. In Sect. 2, we give an overview of the related work. After describing the data and the simulation study conducted in Sect. 3, we discuss its results in Sect. 4. Concluding remarks and an outlook on our future work are contained in Sect. 5.

2   Related Work

2.1   Literature on Sports Bets

Betting and Financial Markets. Several publications exist regarding the efficient market hypothesis in the betting exchange market. For example, Gil et al. [13] analyzed the market during the 2002 FIFA World Cup and found that the patterns observed provide only mixed support for the efficient market hypothesis. In contrast, Croxson and Reade [7] did a similar study and found that prices adjust swiftly and fully. Although prices vigorously increased immediately after a goal, these prices still remained higher 10 to 15 min afterwards. Forrest and Simmons [9] aimed to research the betting market of the top tier of Spanish football. They found that the relative number of fans of each club in a match appears to have an impact on betting odds, with supporters of more popular teams offered more favorable conditions. Franck et al. published an inter-market comparison of the forecasting accuracy of bookmakers and a major betting exchange [10] and researched the inter-market arbitrage in betting [11].

They claimed that the combination of knowledge from bookmakers and information from the bet exchange market yields a guaranteed positive return. In addition, empirical studies and meta-studies about the accuracy of sports experts and the bet exchange market [26,29] regarding the outcome of a sporting event were published. Choi and Hui [6] analyzed the over- and under-reaction to unanticipated events using the in-play football betting market. They found that, in general, market participants under-react to new events but over-react to events that are highly surprising.

Furthermore, some articles present research about the influence of the match results of publicly traded sports teams on the corresponding stock price. Palomino et al. [23] examined how football team stocks react regarding the outcome of a match. They found evidence that abnormal returns for winning teams do not reflect rational expectations, but are high due to overreactions induced by investor sentiment. Levitt [19] analyzed the differences between sports betting markets and financial markets for NFL football teams and found that, due to bookmakers being able to set prices, they yield greater profits than could be obtained if they acted like traditional brokers and attempted to balance out supply and demand. Bernile and Lyandres [4] examined whether investors' biased ex-ante beliefs regarding outcomes of a future event can explain the stock market inefficiencies. They investigated publicly traded European football clubs around important matches and found that an investor sentiment is attributable in part to a systematic bias in the investors' ex-ante expectations.

Prediction of the Outcomes of Sporting Events. Some publications about betting on football matches refer specifically to the major sporting events FIFA World Cup and UEFA Euro Cup. In 1980 Stefani [27] had already introduced a least squares betting approach and applied it to the FIFA World Cup 1976. Archontakis and Osborne [2] formulated a Fibonacci betting strategy, which relies on the Fibonacci sequence to generate bets. Using this approach on the FIFA World Cup finals data, they claimed it is possible to earn economic profits through this method with fairly large risk. Luckner et al. [22] published the results of an empirical study that compares the forecast accuracy of a prediction market of the FIFA World Cup 2006 to predictions derived from the FIFA world ranking. They found that prediction markets for the FIFA World Cup outperform predictions based on the FIFA world ranking in terms of forecast accuracy. Zeileis et al. [35] introduced a probabilistic forecast for the 2018 FIFA World Cup based on the bookmaker consensus model to predict the winner of the FIFA World Cup. They predicted the winner of the UEFA Euro Cup with a similar strategy two years before [34].

In addition to predicting outcomes of the FIFA World Cup, Stefani [27] applied the least squares betting approach to other sports such as American football and basketball as well. Likewise, Lisi and Zanella [20] published an article which investigated a betting strategy based on 501 tennis matches resulting in a cumulative return of 16.3%.

Prediction of Football League Match Results. This paper aims to predict the outcome of football league matches based on characteristics of former matches. In this context, we only found a few publications in the periphery of this topic:

- Rue and Salvesen [25] applied a Bayesian dynamic generalized linear model to estimate the time dependent skills of the teams of the English Premier League and the Spanish Primera Division. Based on only the data about the match results of former matches, they used an MCMC algorithm to find the parameters of their model and then predicted the next football matches. For a total of 3,892 football matches between 1993 and 1997, they calculated a final cumulative return of 40% for the English Premier League and 54% for the Spanish Primera Division.
- Godin et al. [14] described another approach for predicting Premier League football matches. They analyzed how to incorporate Twitter Microposts in which users made a guess how a football match would end up. Therefore, they had to extract this information from unstructured text which required a parsing algorithm to be defined. They predicted the outcome of about 200 match results in 2013/14 and claimed to be able to realize a theoretical profit of 30%.
- Tax and Joustra [33] predicted match results of the Dutch Eredivisie between 2000 and 2013. Their data were mainly based on the results of the former matches. In addition, they incorporated data about whether the team played in a lower league the season before, whether a new coach was hired, or whether the top scorer was injured. Based on these data, they analyzed different machine learning algorithms (e.g., Naive Bayes, Neural Networks, or Decision trees) regarding their accuracy.

In conclusion, no published article exists which examines the topic this paper focuses on. Much literature can be found regarding the relation between betting and financial markets as well as some articles about the forecast of sporting events. In the area of predicting the outcome of football league matches, two studies for a maximum of two leagues based on data about the former match outcomes [25,33] and one study including data from social media [14] were identified. To date, there is neither a study about incorporating match characteristics (e.g., shots at the goal, pass quota, or number of fouls), nor one which predicts football matches for the big five football leagues (England, France, Germany, Italy, Spain). This article fills these and other gaps.

2.2 Literature on Statistical Arbitrage

Statistical arbitrage is a trading strategy developed by a group of mathematicians and physicists at Morgan Stanley in the mid-eighties. According to Hogan [16] and Avellaneda and Lee [3], the self-financing strategy describes a long-term trading opportunity that exploits persistent capital market anomalies to generate economically and statistically significant positive profits over time. The corresponding data-driven trading recommendations are identified using inter-disciplinary methods - the spectrum ranges from plain vanilla approaches to state-of-the-art models from the fields of mathematics, physics, computer science and operations research.

In recent years, interest in statistical arbitrage trading has risen sharply in the academic community. The research work focuses either on theoretical foundations or empirical fields of application. Key representatives are Alexander and Dimitriu [1], Gatev et al. [12], Pole [24], and Liu et al. [21]. It is surprising that so far there is no academic study presenting a statistical arbitrage strategy in the field of sports betting.

3 Simulation Study

3.1 Data Sources

For our empirical application, we collected football match data from the five top European leagues, i.e., the Premier League, Ligue 1, Bundesliga, Serie A, and Primera Division from season 2013/14 to 2017/18. This data set serves as a true acid test for any back-testing study because analyst coverage and investor scrutiny is especially high for these large capitalized leagues. If a match result was subsequently changed by an arbitrating body for other reasons, the original result was still used. In the following, the data set used within our simulation study is described in more detail.

Match Characteristics. Table 1 presents a summary (minimum, median, maximum, and mean) of the match characteristics of all 8,082 football matches analyzed. The data set contains information about the general game, pass behavior, defense and disciplinary measures, and attack capacities for both the home and the away team. The table provides a good illustration of the well-known home advantage. The average values of most characteristics show higher values for the home team. Only attributes characterizing defensive behavior tend to be greater for the away teams, e.g., "number of intercepted balls", "number of clarifying actions", "number of fouls", or "number of sending-offs".

Match Results. The goal statistics for the analyzed football matches are presented in Fig. 1 in more detail. As mentioned above, the main focus of this research paper is to predict which team would win a specific football league match. Therefore, the difference between the number of goals of the home team and the number of goals of the away team plays a decisive role.

In total, 3,723 home team wins (46%), 1,967 draws (24%), and 2,392 away team wins (30%) were observed. This illustrates the home advantage also found in the match characteristics. This fact is well in line with the finding that the distribution of the goal difference (home team goals minus away team goals) is asymmetric, which means that there are more matches with a positive goal difference (home teams wins) than with a negative goal difference (away team

Table 1. Summary of the match characteristics data from season 2013/14 to 2017/18.

	Home team				Away team			
	Min	Median	Max	Mean	Min	Median	Max	Mean
General game								
Ball possession	15.5%	51.6%	83.4%	51.3%	16.6%	48.4%	84.5%	48.7%
Duel quota[1]	28.4%	50.4%	66.7%	50.3%	33.0%	49.5%	70.5%	49.5%
Air duel quota	11.5%	50.0%	100%	50.7%	0.0%	50.0%	88.5%	49.3%
Intercepted balls	0	15	47	15.47	0	15	43	15.78
Number of offsides	0	2	14	2.38	0	2	14	2.15
Number of corners	0	5	20	5.63	0	4	18	4.43
Pass								
Number of passes	135	433	1015	447.79	161	412	1078	426.25
Long passes proportion	2.3%	14.7%	40.7%	15.2%	2.9%	15.4%	42.7%	16.0%
Pass quota[2]	41.9%	78.7%	94.1%	78.0%	41.0%	77.5%	93.1%	76.7%
Pass quota (opposing half)	31.7%	70.5%	92.8%	70.2%	32.8%	68.8%	92.4%	68.5%
Number of crosses	1	20	81	21.36	1	16	55	16.83
Cross quota[3]	0.0%	23.1%	75.0%	23.6%	0.0%	22.2%	100%	22.7%
Defense and discipline								
Number of tackles	3	18	48	18.80	3	19	45	19.07
Tackle quota[4]	22.2%	75.0%	100%	74.3%	0.0%	74.1%	100%	73.6%
Clarifying actions[5]	1	20	68	21.52	2	24	89	25.55
Number of fouls	2	13	33	13.41	0	14	32	13.80
Number of sending-offs	0	0	2	0.10	0	0	3	0.13
Attack								
Goals	0	1	10	1.55	0	1	9	1.17
Shots	1	13	43	13.94	0	11	35	11.22
Shots at the goal	0	5	16	4.85	0	4	15	3.89
Shots inside the box	0	8	26	8.20	0	6	23	6.38
Shots outside the box	0	5	23	5.74	0	5	19	4.84
Shooting accuracy	0.0%	45.5%	100%	45.3%	0.0%	44.4%	100%	44.9%

[1]Number of successful duels divided by the total number of duels.
[2]Number of successful passes divided by the total number of passes.
[3]Number of successful crosses divided by the total number of crosses.
[4]Number of successful tackles divided by the total number of tackles.
[5]Number of successful defense actions 2017/18.

wins). Though, the most frequent outcome of the football match was no difference between home and away team (draw).

Betting Odds. To obtain a financial performance evaluation of our approach, we also collected the betting odds corresponding to the analyzed football matches from the online bookmaker Bet365[1], one of the leading betting suppliers with

[1] We thank http://www.football-data.co.uk/data.php for providing the data.

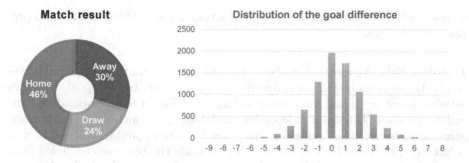

Fig. 1. Properties of the match results from season 2013/14 to 2017/18.

about 23 million customers globally. The analysis is based on the very common decimal odds, which work as follows: A bet amount b is placed on a specific event and a given betting odd o. If the event occurs, the bet amount multiplied by the betting odd $b \cdot o$ is paid out. If the event does not occur, nothing is paid out. Thus, the relative return on b is always either $o - 1$ (for a successful bet) or -1 (for an unsuccessful bet), which means a complete loss of b.

Table 2 shows a short summary of the collected betting odds. It is remarkable that a win for one of the teams leads to far more extreme betting odds than for a draw. Apart from this, it is hardly surprising that the bookmaker is aware of the aforementioned home advantage which can be seen by comparing the average odds of a home win with the average away win odds.

Table 2. Summary of the betting odds from season 2013/14 to 2017/18.

	Min	Median	Max	Mean
Home team wins	1.02	2.15	26	2.793
Draw	2.5	3.5	17	4.077
Away team wins	1.08	3.5	51	4.957

3.2 Simulation Setup

The simulation study aimed (1) to predict football matches with the aid of data-driven methods and (2) to exploit the obtained information using a statistical arbitrage strategy. Specifically, different machine learning approaches were applied to forecast the goal difference between home team and away team (dependent variable y) based on the football match data observed up to that point (independent variables x). According to Jegadeesh and Titman [17], Gatev et al. [12], and Tax and Joustra [33], the data set was divided into overlapping study periods, each shifted by one match day. Each study period included a test set, which represents the considered match day, and a training set, which contains all previous match days.

Training Set. As mentioned above, the training set contains all information about the previous match days. Specifically, y_{train} describes the goal difference between home team and away team and x_{train} defines the corresponding football match data. The set of independent variables x_{train} includes the characteristics from the sections "general game", "pass", "defense and discipline" as well as "attack" (see Table 1). The variable "shots inside the box" was excluded from x_{train}, since it can be calculated by "shots" and "shots outside the box". Based on a similar thought three other variables were removed: The knowledge of "ball possession", "duel quota", and "air duel quota" of the home team makes the respective variable for the away team redundant. To model the relation of the dependent variable y_{train} as a function of the 39 independent variables x_{train}, different common machine learning approaches were employed:

- Random forest (RFO): An important representative of machine learning is the random forest, which is an ensemble learning method that works by building a variety of decision trees to output the class, i.e. the mean prediction of each tree. The approach corrects the habit of decision trees to overfit to the training set. For further details about this approach, see Hastie et al. [15].
- Boosting (BOO): Boosting is a meta-algorithm for machine learning that merges several weak classifiers into a single strong classifier. This technology reduces bias and variance as well as memory requirements and runtime. Please refer to Zhou [36] for more information.
- Support vector machine (SVM): Support vector machine divides a set of objects into classes in such a way that as wide an area as possible remains free of objects around the class boundaries. The kernel trick is used in the case of non-linear separable data. Steinwart and Christmann [28] described this approach in more detail.

Test Set. For each study period, the aim was to predict the match results $\hat{y}_{test}$ of the considered match day. The corresponding match data were not used as independent variables x_{test}, since only information before the match starts was included to avoid any look-ahead bias. Therefore, x_{test} was determined based on the team characteristics of the last matches. For each home (away) team, the average characteristic value of each considered variable was calculated based on the past three home (away) matches – this procedure avoids any look-ahead bias and takes the home advantage into account[2]. Specifically, we determined the weighted median, a measure that is more robust against outliers than the weighted mean. It should be noted that home (away) teams had to possess at least team characteristics for three home (away) matches of the current season.

---

[2] Without loss of generality, our model can also be used for matches without home advantage, e.g., FIFA World Cup and UEFA Euro Cup. In this case both teams would be neutral teams.

Finally, the dependent variable was predicted based on the fitted models (RFO, BOO, SVM) and the team characteristics x_{test}.

This simulation study assumed that past team characteristics contain pieces of information that have a substantial effect on match results in the future. If our hypothesis holds and this relationship is reflected by the outlined models, we would be able to identify market inefficiencies in order to draw positive expected profits. The aim was to capture this circumstance with the following statistical arbitrage strategy:

- $\hat{y}_{train} > 2$ means the model predicted that the home team will win. Consequently, we bet 1 monetary unit on the home team, i.e. $b = 1$.
- $\hat{y}_{train} < -2$ means the model predicted that the away team will win. Consequently, we bet 1 monetary unit on the away team, i.e. $b = 1$.
- $-2 \leq \hat{y}_{train} \leq 2$ means the model does not provide a clear sign for "home team wins" or "away team wins". Consequently, we do not execute any bets, i.e. $b = 0$.

The trading thresholds of ± 2 was introduced because increasing deviations of the estimation from 0 depict higher chances of success. Since we are a conservative investor, the thresholds to ± 2 result from the objective of only betting on clear predictions. This parameter setting is consistent with the literature – the large-scale analyses of Bollinger [5] and Stübinger and Endres [31] show that trading thresholds of ± 2 are optimal in the context of financial bets.

To assess the value-add of the trading strategies based on several machine learning approaches, they were benchmarked with a variant based on linear regression (LIR). This well-known method is a linear approach to model the relationship between dependent variables and one or more independent variables. The statistical properties of the resulting estimators can easily be determined.

Furthermore, three strategies based on the betting odds served as a benchmark: (1) Strategy BET bets 1 monetary unit per match on the outcome of the match result with the lowest odd. If two odds are identical, no action is taken. In this context, the lowest betting odd means always either "home team wins" or "away team wins". (2) Strategy HOM bets 1 monetary unit per match on the outcome "home team wins". Other circumstances are not taken into account. (3) Strategy RAN randomly bets 1 monetary unit per match on the outcome "home team wins" or "away team wins".

4   Results

4.1   Statistical Analysis

The general results of the simulation study are shown in Table 3. While the rows are divided into different characteristics, the columns each reflect a different method or betting strategy. In terms of prediction quality, RFO achieves the best results, i.e. the highest accuracy, the lowest root mean squared error (RMSE), and the lowest mean absolute deviation (MAD). RFO is followed by the other two machine learning methods BOO and SVM. After this, we find the less complex LIR followed by the unsophisticated approaches BET and HOM. It is not surprising that the random bet RAN clearly leads to the poorest performance.

Another finding is that the accuracy of the different approaches is in line with the resulting average payoff. In addition, the machine learning approaches (RFO, BOO, SVM) reveal average payoffs greater than 1, in contrast to the other less complex methods. In this context it should be noted that an average payoff greater than 1 means that the betting party beats the bookmaker on a long term perspective. Like the prediction quality, the average payoffs follow the complexity of the corresponding methods.

Moreover, betting that the home team wins is clearly preferred by all approaches except RAN. This makes sense since RAN is supposed to bet on the home team in about half of the cases. All other methods identified the home advantage we described in Sect. 3. Furthermore, we find that a higher number of bets leads to lower average payoffs. It could be carefully concluded that the machine learning methods are better at selecting the more secure match outcomes out of the pool of all possible bets. Finally, we notice that the minimum and maximum of the predicted goal difference between home team and away team goals are in a reasonable range. The machine learning approaches in particular lead to values between 4.9 goals difference for the home team and 4.6 goals difference for the away team.

Table 3. Statistical characteristics for the strategies RFO, BOO, SVM, LIR, BET, HOM, and RAN from season 2013/14 to 2017/18.

	RFO	BOO	SVM	LIR	BET	HOM	RAN
Prediction quality							
Accuracy	75.62%	70.95%	66.12%	63.60%	54.49%	46.10%	37.82%
RMSE	1.9986	2.2441	2.2899	2.2740	9.3875	9.7927	10.1494
MAD	1.5909	1.7964	1.8610	1.8631	9.2288	9.6182	9.9739
Betting details							
Number of bets	324	482	614	566	6586	6664	6664
Bet on home team	89.51%	79.67%	81.43%	71.20%	71.24%	100%	51.19%
Bet on away team	10.49%	20.33%	18.57%	28.80%	28.76%	0.00%	48.81%
Average payoff	1.0542	1.0217	1.0054	0.9957	0.9705	0.9676	0.9370
Predicted values							
Maximum	4.1788	4.8992	4.5194	4.2173	-	-	-
Minimum	−3.4892	−4.6230	−4.1254	−5.7978	-	-	-

4.2 Financial Analysis

Table 4 depicts the risk-return characteristics per match of the seven considered strategies. First of all, we observe that the findings from the statistical analysis (see Subsect. 4.1) are also reflected in the finance context – strategies with a high prediction quality generate meaningful profits and vice versa. The approaches based on machine learning algorithms provide positive returns ranging between 0.5% per match for SVM and 5.42% per match for RFO. In contrast, the benchmark methods achieve negative returns between −0.43% (LIR) and −3.24% (HOM). As expected, the naive strategy RAN produces a clear loss of −6.30% per match. Applying RFO results in economically and statistically significant returns – the p-value of the non-parametric Wilcoxon-Test (WT) is 0.28%. It is not surprising that the minimum of all strategies is −1, as at least one predicted event does not occur. Analyzing quartile 1 confirms the outperformance of RFO – more than 75% of all returns are in the positive range. The maximum is vastly different between RFO, BOO, SVM, LIR, and BET on the one hand and HOM and RAN on the other hand. RFO achieves the highest hit ratio, i.e. the percentage of matches with positive returns, with 75.62% per match. In summary, the strategies based on machine learning methods outperform classic approaches in a multitude of return characteristics and risk metrics – this statement is particularly true for RFO.

Table 4. Risk-return characteristics per match for the strategies RFO, BOO, SVM, LIR, BET, HOM, and RAN from season 2013/14 to 2017/18. WT denotes the non-parametric Wilcoxon-Test.

	RFO	BOO	SVM	LIR	BET	HOM	RAN
Mean	0.0542	0.0217	0.0054	−0.0043	−0.0295	−0.0324	−0.0630
p-value of WT	0.0028	0.1108	0.8439	0.3235	0.0000	0.0000	0.0000
Minimum	−1.0000	−1.0000	−1.0000	−1.0000	−1.0000	−1.0000	−1.0000
Quartile 1	0.0375	−1.0000	−1.0000	−1.0000	−1.0000	−1.0000	−1.0000
Median	0.1650	0.1800	0.1700	0.1800	0.2000	−1.0000	−1.0000
Quartile 3	0.3525	0.4000	0.4400	0.5000	0.8000	0.7800	0.7200
Maximum	5.2500	6.0000	6.0000	5.2500	1.8500	13.5000	20.0000
Standard deviation	0.7545	0.7816	0.8844	0.8818	0.9433	1.2993	1.5510
Skewness	1.2106	0.9184	1.2001	0.7542	0.1608	2.1598	3.0134
Kurtosis	7.8638	6.4619	5.3599	2.3316	−1.5890	9.9730	18.4355
Share with return > 0	0.7562	0.7095	0.6612	0.6360	0.5449	0.4610	0.3782

Following Knoll et al. [18] and Stübinger [30], we analyze the performance of the strategies over time. Figure 2 shows the cumulative returns of RFO, BOO, SVM, LIR (upper graph) and BET, HOM, RAN (lower graph) from 2013/14 to 2017/18. The difference in the length of the seven time series is caused by the varying number of executed bets (see Table 3). As expected, RFO is the best in class with an end value of 17.55% – the smooth and steady growth is particularly pleasant for any potential investor. BOO displays medium drawdowns and a final cumulative return of 10.46%. For SVM and LIR, gains and losses offset each other over time. In contrast, the remaining strategies possess a steady race to the bottom. As a result, BET and HOM achieve a cumulative return of −194.60% and −216.11% at the end of season 2017/18. The naive strategy RAN performs even worse: the loss totals −420.11% within the considered time period. In summary, the findings obtained so far are not driven by outliers, but rather the result of permanent correct or incorrect predictions.

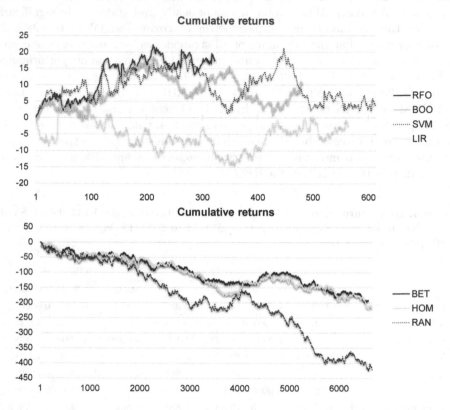

Fig. 2. Development of cumulative returns of the strategies RFO, BOO, SVM, and LIR (upper graph) as well as BET, HOM, and RAN (lower graph) from season 2013/14 to 2017/18.

Figure 3 examines the risk aversion of the individual strategies by showing the relative proportions of the executed bets. For each strategy, the betting odds are divided into the following five classes: low (1.00–1.50), low-medium (1.51–2.00), medium (2.01–3.00), medium-high (3.01–4.00), high (> 4.01). First of all, a clear asymmetry between strategies based on dependent variables (first row) and strategies based on betting odds (second row) can be identified. RFO selects low betting odds in approximately 69% of all executed bets – low-mid betting odds are used in 20%. One could conclude that this approach relies to a high degree on "safe" outputs and avoids risky bets. The strategies BOO, SVM, and LIR also tend to focus more on lower odds, but the willingness to take risks steadily increases. BET only applies low, low-medium, and medium betting odds because one of the odds for "home team wins" or "away team wins" is always less than 3.00. As expected, RAN chooses the trading rule independently of the available betting odds – matches with low or high betting odds are chosen similarly often. In conjunction with Table 4, it can be summarized that risk-averse strategies lead to the most profitable returns – this finding is well in line with the literature ([8], [32]).

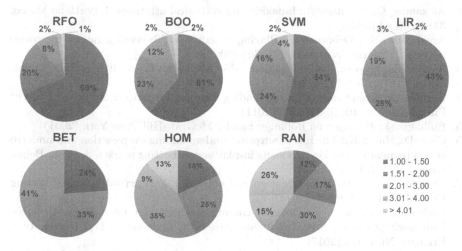

Fig. 3. Relative proportions of used betting odds of the strategies RFO, BOO, SVM, and LIR (first row) as well as BET, HOM, and RAN (second row) from season 2013/14 to 2017/18.

5   Conclusions and Future Work

In this paper, we have described a data-driven approach for predicting the outcome of football league matches and generating positive returns by betting accordingly. These positive returns could be achieved by analyzing large data sets with machine learning algorithms. In the empirical back-testing study, the random forest approach generated statistically and economically significant returns of 5.42% per match. In contrast, less complex approaches, such as linear regression, placing all bets on the home team, betting on the outcome with the lowest (and therefore most likely) betting odd, or choosing a random match result, were not able to yield positive returns. Finally, it turned out that risk-averse strategies lead to the most profitable returns.

This study may serve as a starting point for future work. In general, it could be used as a blueprint for research applying data-driven approaches to predict the outcome of future events. Furthermore, more data (e.g. performance in previous matches) could be incorporated as variables into the described data set in order to further increase the accuracy of the analyzed approaches. Finally, the presented approach could be applied to football leagues in other countries as well as second or lower leagues. In addition, other types of sports with corresponding leagues, such as rugby (RFL), American football (NFL), or basketball (NBA) could be targeted by our approach.

References

1. Alexander, C., Dimitriu, A.: Indexing and statistical arbitrage. J. Portfolio Manag. **31**(2), 50–63 (2005)
2. Archontakis, F., Osborne, E.: Playing it safe? A Fibonacci strategy for soccer betting. J. Sports Econ. **8**(3), 295–308 (2007)
3. Avellaneda, M., Lee, J.H.: Statistical arbitrage in the US equities market. Quant. Financ. **10**(7), 761–782 (2010)
4. Bernile, G., Lyandres, E.: Understanding investor sentiment: the case of soccer. Financ. Manag. **40**(2), 357–380 (2011)
5. Bollinger, J.: Bollinger on Bollinger bands. McGraw-Hill, New York (2001)
6. Choi, D., Hui, S.K.: The role of surprise: understanding overreaction and underreaction to unanticipated events using in-play soccer betting market. J. Econ. Behav. Organ. **107**, 614–629 (2014)
7. Croxson, K., Reade, J.: Information and efficiency: goal arrival in soccer betting. Econ. J. **124**(575), 62–91 (2014)
8. Endres, S., Stübinger, J.: Optimal trading strategies for Lévy-driven Ornstein-Uhlenbeck processes. FAU Discussion Papers in Economics (17). University of Erlangen-Nürnberg (2017)
9. Forrest, D., Simmons, R.: Sentiment in the betting market on Spanish football. Appl. Econ. **40**(1), 119–126 (2008)
10. Franck, E., Verbeek, E., Nüesch, S.: Prediction accuracy of different market structures–bookmakers versus a betting exchange. Int. J. Forecast. **26**(3), 448–459 (2010)
11. Franck, E., Verbeek, E., Nüesch, S.: Inter-market Arbitrage in Betting. Economica **80**(318), 300–325 (2013)
12. Gatev, E., Goetzmann, W.N., Rouwenhorst, K.G.: Pairs trading: performance of a relative-value arbitrage rule. Rev. Financ. Stud. **19**(3), 797–827 (2006)
13. Gil, R.G.R., Levitt, S.D.: Testing the efficiency of markets in the 2002 World Cup. J. Predict. Mark. **1**(3), 255–270 (2012)
14. Godin, F., Zuallaert, J., Vandersmissen, B., de Neve, W., van de Walle, R.: Beating the bookmakers: leveraging statistics and Twitter microposts for predicting soccer results. In: Workshop on Large-Scale Sports Analytics (2014)
15. Hastie, T., Tibshirani, R., Friedman, J.: The Elements of Statistical Learning: Data Mining, Inference, and Prediction. SSS. Springer, New York (2009). https://doi.org/10.1007/978-0-387-84858-7
16. Hogan, S., Jarrow, R., Teo, M., Warachka, M.: Testing market efficiency using statistical arbitrage with applications to momentum and value strategies. J. Financ. Econ. **73**(3), 525–565 (2004)
17. Jegadeesh, N., Titman, S.: Returns to buying winners and selling losers: implications for stock market efficiency. J. Financ. **48**(1), 65–91 (1993)
18. Knoll, J., Stübinger, J., Grottke, M.: Exploiting social media with higher-order factorization machines: statistical arbitrage on high-frequency data of the S&P 500. Quanitative Finance, Forthcoming (2018)

19. Levitt, S.D.: Why are gambling markets organised so differently from financial markets? Econ. J. **114**(495), 223–246 (2004)
20. Lisi, F., Zanella, G.: Tennis betting: can statistics beat bookmakers? Electron. J. Appl. Stat. Anal. **10**(3), 790–808 (2017)
21. Liu, B., Chang, L.B., Geman, H.: Intraday pairs trading strategies on high frequency data: the case of oil companies. Quant. Financ. **17**(1), 87–100 (2017)
22. Luckner, S., Schröder, J., Slamka, C.: On the forecast accuracy of sports prediction markets. In: Gimpel, H., Jennings, N.R., Kersten, G.E., Ockenfels, A., Weinhardt, C. (eds.) Negotiation, Auctions, and Market Engineering. LNBIP, vol. 2, pp. 227–234. Springer, Heidelberg (2008). https://doi.org/10.1007/978-3-540-77554-6_17
23. Palomino, F., Renneboog, L., Zhang, C.: Information salience, investor sentiment, and stock returns: the case of British soccer betting. J. Corp. Financ. **15**(3), 368–387 (2009)
24. Pole, A.: Statistical Arbitrage: Algorithmic Trading Insights and Techniques. Wiley, Hoboken (2011)
25. Rue, H., Salvesen, O.: Prediction and retrospective analysis of soccer matches in a league. J. Roy. Stat. Soc.: Ser. D (Stat.) **49**(3), 399–418 (2000)
26. Spann, M., Skiera, B.: Sports forecasting: a comparison of the forecast accuracy of prediction markets, betting odds and tipsters. J. Forecast. **28**(1), 55–72 (2009)
27. Stefani, R.T.: Improved least squares football, basketball, and soccer predictions. IEEE Trans. Syst. Man Cybern. **10**(2), 116–123 (1980)
28. Steinwart, I., Christmann, A.: Support Vector Machines. Springer, New York (2008). https://doi.org/10.1007/978-0-387-77242-4
29. Stekler, H.O., Sendor, D., Verlander, R.: Issues in sports forecasting. Int. J. Forecast. **26**(3), 606–621 (2010)
30. Stübinger, J.: Statistical arbitrage with optimal causal paths on high-frequency data of the S&P 500. Quant. Financ. (2018, forthcoming)
31. Stübinger, J., Endres, S.: Pairs trading with a mean-reverting jump-diffusion model on high-frequency data. Quant. Financ. **18**, 1735–1751 (2018)
32. Stübinger, J., Mangold, B., Krauss, C.: Statistical arbitrage with vine copulas. Quant. Financ. **18**, 1831–1849 (2018)
33. Tax, N., Joustra, Y.: Predicting the Dutch football competition using public data: a machine learning approach. Trans. Knowl. Data Eng. **10**(10), 1–13 (2015)
34. Zeileis, A., Leitner, C., Hornik, K.: Predictive Bookmaker Consensus Model for the UEFA Euro 2016 (2016)
35. Zeileis, A., Leitner, C., Hornik, K.: Probabilistic forecasts for the 2018 FIFA World Cup based on the bookmaker consensus model. Working Papers in Economics and Statistics - Universität Insbruck (2018)
36. Zhou, Z.H.: Ensemble Methods: Foundations and Algorithms. Chapman and Hall, Boca Raton (2012)

Industrial Applications of Artificial Intelligence

Rule-Mining and Clustering in Business Process Analysis

Paul N. Taylor$^{(\boxtimes)}$ (iD) and Stephanie Kiss

Applied Research, BT, Ipswich, UK
{paul.n.taylor,steph.kiss}@bt.com

Abstract. The analysis of complex business processes is a challenging topic. Machine learning provides many tools to help with the analysis/understanding of complex data. In this paper we present the application of two types of technique to this domain. First, rule mining techniques to discover relationships between process behaviour and outcomes. Second, a technique presented is one suitable for clustering arbitrary length directed acyclic graphs such as those that represent business process executions. Both cases are presented in the context of a real business process.

Keywords: Business process · Rule mining · Clustering
Sequence alignment

1 Introduction

Business processes are essential to the running of modern businesses. Complex businesses inherently have complex processes involving multiple actors both inside and outside the business to complete the tasks. The analysis of these processes is essential to keep the process system running smoothly. Inefficiencies in business processes can have a major impact, can slow down progress within a company, can be very costly and can have a negative impact on customer satisfaction.

The motivation for this paper is to discuss the application of two methods that we are investigating for use in a large multinational corporation. Using these techniques, we aim to speed up the analysis of these processes and to discover deeper insights that are difficult to do manually or through visualisation to enable domain experts to address the inefficiencies and streamline the processes. The processes used as examples within the paper are large-scale order fulfilment processes. There exist a variety of ways analysing orders eg. flow charts, which can be very useful to identify key paths and recurring events [5]. There are also workflow mining algorithms, which discover workflows from complex process data [1].

In this paper we will discuss the application of two machine-learning techniques for use in process analysis. The first of those, discussed in Sect. 2 is the use

© Springer Nature Switzerland AG 2018
M. Bramer and M. Petridis (Eds.): SGAI-AI 2018, LNAI 11311, pp. 237–249, 2018.
https://doi.org/10.1007/978-3-030-04191-5_22

of rule mining to look for previously unknown relationships between sequences in the data and between such sub-sequences and process failures. The second technique that will be discussed is that of clustering databases of process sequences in Sect. 3 which aims to discover meaningful differences in behaviour in a process database.

2   Rule Mining in Process Sequences

The problem we aim to solve by analysing these order sequences is that of orders being delayed. One of BT's measures for order success is whether the order completes on time. The target date for delivery is a pre-allocated upon order confirmation. If the order needs to pass to a supplier because it might be a new line and the cables have to be installed, the delivery date has to be updated for the customer, which already means delay. We can refer to these incomplete or delayed orders as failed. We first aim to discover frequent sets of tasks within orders to get an idea of the general structure of them and also to inform us of any jointly occurring and non-independent sets of tasks. By finding frequent sub-sequences, which take into account the temporal aspect of our dataset, we also aim identify discriminating features which may appear significantly more frequently in either successful or failed orders.

The business value this brings by identifying these features, is to inform they way we create order paths in the future and helps us make the customer experience more streamlined and to the point. This can have great effect on the number of complaints and can improve customer satisfaction.

This section we will present the application of well-known rule mining techniques to the large scale business process data available at BT.

2.1   Association Rule Mining

The development of association rule mining can be traced back to Agrawal, Imieliński and Swami [2], who developed the first algorithm to gain more insight into customer's shopping habits in supermarkets, based on their large transaction databases. They created the algorithm to find frequent items bought together by shoppers which could then inform the placement of these items in shops. This idea was applied at many physical and online retailers, including Amazon but mostly in marketing use cases.

Our aim was to apply the *Apriori* algorithm to our processes dataset to discover interesting and informative rules about our tasks and paths taken to fulfil customer orders. The reason we chose to use association rule mining is because it is a great way to find frequent tasks within processes and it can also inform us of tasks that frequently occur together. *Apriori* also gives us interestingness measures which we can utilise to make decisions based on our results. We also aimed to find tasks and groups of tasks which relate to each other by always or never occurring together. From these kinds of insights, we can develop a more informed way of creating processes and are able to identify integral tasks within certain types of processes and also help us interpret results from our clustering.

Our dataset contains more than 350,000 orders which have a unique process ID number and contain a path in the form of Fig. 1. These paths are made of tasks, all with unique task ID numbers. They all have start and end points, which can also been seen in Fig. 1.

```
PROTOTYPE_ID                                                    PATH
      119304 start -> 100332 -> 100404 -> 100404 -> end.
```

Fig. 1. Example path string

We took each unique task in our dataset as an element of the itemset I, in our case this was 1181 unique tasks. Our database table contains 356,358 orders, let this be our set T. Each of these orders has a unique ID number and is made up of tasks from I.

We defined a rule to be $A \Rightarrow B$ such that $A, B \subseteq I$. The associated measures we used to evaluate the interestingness of our rules were support and confidence.

Support gave us the frequency of A and B occurring together in our processes.
$Supp(A \Rightarrow B) = Supp(A \cup B)$

Whilst *confidence* was the frequency of B occurring given A occurs in our rules.
$Conf(A \Rightarrow B) = \frac{Supp(A \cup B)}{Supp(A)}$

We also used *lift* to ascertain whether the probability of the occurrence of the left hand side(*lhs*) and right hand side(*rhs*) are independent of each other. Lift is the ratio of the confidence of the rule over the expected confidence of a rule. If lift is equal to 1, we can say that the *lhs* and *rhs* are independent of each other, if lift > 1 we can observe a level of dependency between them.
$Lift(A \Rightarrow B) = \frac{Supp(A \cup B)}{Supp(A) \times Supp(B)}$

The thresholds by which we defined our rules as interesting were defined by us. The initial *support* chosen was 0.2 and *confidence* was 0.6. This gave us a large enough set of rules (410 rules).

The algorithm we used in this application was the *Apriori* algorithm [3], implemented in the R package *arules*. We required 3 steps in order to find our association rules:

1. Transform order from string of task IDs (Fig. 1) to vector containing tasks (Fig. 2).
2. Create transaction matrix from orders.
3. Run *apriori* function using transaction matrix to create association rules.

A subset of the resulting rules using *support* $= 0.2$, *confidence* $= 0.6$ can be found in Fig. 3. The names of the tasks in those rules are shown in Fig. 4.

The empty {} *lhs* in the first five rules indicates that the tasks in the itemset occur very frequently with every other task in our task set. We can also assert

```
$`119304`
[1] "  100332  " "  100404  " "  100404  "
```

Fig. 2. Example path vector

```
            lhs            rhs     support confidence    lift  count
[1]          {} =>     {100887} 0.6782580  0.6782580 1.000000 107198
[2]          {} =>     {100199} 0.6549361  0.6549361 1.000000 103512
[3]          {} =>     {101002} 0.7623205  0.7623205 1.000000 120484
[4]          {} =>     {100442} 0.9949320  0.9949320 1.000000 157248
[5]          {} =>     {100332} 1.0000000  1.0000000 1.000000 158049
[6]    {100403} =>     {100500} 0.2046644  0.9848379 1.673684  32347
[7]    {100403} =>     {100442} 0.2078153  1.0000000 1.005094  32845
[8]    {100403} =>     {100332} 0.2078153  1.0000000 1.000000  32845
[9]    {100959} =>     {100921} 0.2184576  0.8995623 1.607332  34527
[10]   {100959} =>     {100199} 0.2424058  0.9981762 1.524082  38312
[11]   {100959} =>     {101002} 0.2107195  0.8676984 1.138233  33304
[12]   {100959} =>     {100442} 0.2428487  1.0000000 1.005094  38382
[13]   {100959} =>     {100332} 0.2428487  1.0000000 1.000000  38382
[14] {26729917} => {14098816} 0.2160849  0.9861685 2.906860  34152
[15] {14098816} => {26729917} 0.2160849  0.6369384 2.906860  34152
[16] {26729917} =>    {100921} 0.2001215  0.9133147 1.631904  31629
[17] {26729917} =>    {100199} 0.2080494  0.9494961 1.449754  32882
[18] {26729917} =>    {100442} 0.2188435  0.9987583 1.003846  34588
```

Fig. 3. Results of the Apriori algorithm (first 18 rules)

```
                          NAME TASK_DEF_ID
                 Order Created      100332
               Order Submitted      100442
     OrderActivation/htmlEmail      100887
   OrderConfirmation/htmlEmail      101002
          Wholesale: 510\\n(KCI1)  100199
```

Fig. 4. Itemset of tasks present (in first 18)

that *Order Created* occurs in all of our orders, since the rule {} ⇒ {100332} has support 1 and confidence 1.

We can also see that the most frequent tasks that occur together are *Order Created* and *Order Submitted*, but that also *Order Submitted* very often goes together with *OrderConfirmation/htmlEmail*. The lift in the first five rules is obviously 1 as the *rhs* is independent of the *lhs*. This reinforces what we already know about our order processes, meaning in general orders are created, they are submitted and the customer is informed via email or sms.

Since we have more than 400 rules, we need to restrict this set to find the most interesting ones. We do this by sub-setting our set of rules to only include rules with *confidence* > 0.85 and *lift* > 2.3. These thresholds were arrived at through a consultancy process with the process owners. Higher lift indicates that our *lhs* and *rhs* occur more frequently together than expected. By restricting *confidence* to be greater than 0.85, we intend to choose rules with high frequency of the *rhs* occurring given *lhs*. Given these conditions, the subset contains 68 rules which is easier to further analyse.

2.2   Sequential Rule Mining

Sequential rule mining is a form of association rule mining, but it takes into account the temporal properties of transactions. Whilst association rules $A \Rightarrow B$ mean "if A takes place then also B takes place", sequential rules imply "if A takes places then it is followed by B". This makes it very appealing to use for us as it enables us to see in what order certain tasks appear. The order is important for us as we can learn about the way processes progress, which sub-sequences are more frequent in failed orders and also what prompts certain errors and what is their effect.

Our dataset is structured so that each of our tasks in our dataset are assigned a time stamp to mark when the task starts and ends. All of the tasks in this dataset are instantaneous, meaning their start time and end time are the same. Hence we can label each task instead with a rank as in Fig. 5, its position within the process. We have added an OTD column to show if the order has been delivered on time. This will be useful later, when finding discriminating sub-sequences.

PROCESS_INST_ID	TASK_INST_ID	OTD	RANK
45894415	45894542	0	1
45894415	45894496	0	2
45894415	45894512	0	3
45894415	45894518	0	4
45894415	45894469	0	5
45894415	45894510	0	6
45894415	45894489	0	7
45894415	45894514	0	8
45894415	45894504	0	9
45894415	45894488	0	10

Fig. 5. Example sequence

To find frequent sub-sequences in our data, we use R's *TraMineR* package. In this package, we utilise functions related to event sequence analysis. The *TraMineR* package uses a pattern-growth based PrefixSpan-like algorithm to compute frequent sub-sequences and also contains functions related to finding discriminating sub-sequences and sequential association rules [12]. To work with these functions, we need to convert each order in the data to an event sequence object which can then be fed into the sequence mining algorithm. Once the frequent sub-sequences are found, we also compute the sequential association rules. The interestingness measure we use here is support.

We followed these four steps to find the sequential association rules:

1. Convert from path in Fig. 1 to TSE format [6] in Fig. 5.
2. Create event sequence object from each order.
3. Run *seqefsub* function to find frequent sub-sequences with minimum support specified.
4. Using these frequent sub-sequences, run *seqerules* function to find sequential association rules.

Once complete, we end up with a set of frequent sub-sequences like the ones in Fig. 6

```
              Subsequence  Support   Count
                 (100332) 1.0000000 362745
                 (100442) 0.9614137 348748
       (100332)-(100442) 0.9589629 347859
                 (101002) 0.6172518 223905
       (100332)-(101002) 0.6172490 223904
       (100442)-(101002) 0.6140071 222728
(100332)-(100442)-(101002) 0.6138499 222671
                 (100887) 0.5882176 213373
       (100332)-(100887) 0.5882093 213370
       (100442)-(100887) 0.5872610 213026
```

Fig. 6. Subset of the most frequent sub-sequences

The most interesting use for finding frequent sub-sequences in our data is to look at discriminating sub-sequences. It has been previously mentioned that BT is measured against certain targets, one of which is on-time delivery. This relates to providing new services and is a date given to customers at order confirmation. There are a variety of reasons why this target is not reached and we want to discover if the data can give us more ideas as to why customer orders are late. We want to use this on-time delivery as a measure to discriminate groups by and to understand the differences between these groups.

The first step here is to subset the full set of orders to only contain processes related to the services being analysed. We can label each process with an on-time delivery (OTD) flag; if 1 the order has been processed on-time, if 0 it has failed to complete within date. This will be our discriminating variable, from which we can group the orders into two groups Success and Failure.

Once we have done this, we need to rerun the function to find the frequent sub-sequences on this subset and then we can apply these frequent sub-sequences to the *seqecmpgroup* function which will evaluate whether the sub-sequences are found more or less frequently in either OTD group based on a Chi-square test. Then we are able to identify discriminating sub-sequences by evaluating the Pearson residuals. If the residuals ≤ -2 the subsequence is significantly less frequent than expected under independence whilst if the residuals > 2, the subsequence is significantly more frequent than expected.

2.3   Results

The results of the association rule mining are 68 rules with strong lift, on average 2.83, which implies a high level of dependency. For reference, the top 10 rules with highest *confidence* and *lift* can be found in Fig. 7.

By running the discriminating subsequence search, we are also able to identify what sequence of tasks are more likely to cause failure or success. As we can see in Fig. 8, the tasks on the left hand chart are significantly less likely to be in

lhs		rhs	support	confidence	lift	count
{100403}	=>	{100500}	0.2022633	0.9910981	2.611869	73370
{100271}	=>	{100500}	0.2091965	0.9931292	2.617221	75885
{100198}	=>	{100921}	0.2083888	0.9224724	2.904757	75592
{100198}	=>	{100199}	0.2097810	0.9286351	2.576271	76097
{100921}	=>	{100199}	0.3171071	0.9985330	2.770186	115029
{100403,100442}	=>	{100500}	0.2022633	0.9910981	2.611869	73370
{100332,100403}	=>	{100500}	0.2022633	0.9910981	2.611869	73370
{100271,100442}	=>	{100500}	0.2091965	0.9931292	2.617221	75885
{100271,100332}	=>	{100500}	0.2091965	0.9931292	2.617221	75885
{100198,100921}	=>	{100199}	0.2080552	0.9983993	2.769815	75471

Fig. 7. Top 10 rules with measures

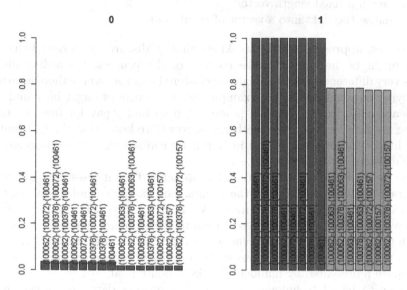

Fig. 8. Discriminating sub-sequences

a failed process, whilst the ones on the right hand chart are significantly more likely to occur in a successful order.

We presented these results to our domain experts where they were validated against domain knowledge. In this case many of the rules discovered are well known and understood. Several of the rules indicated behaviour that the process owners believed to be erroneous. As a result of this study we were able to provide them with the evidence needed to justify changes in the process to remove the issues. Specific outcome results are commercially sensitive.

3   Clustering

Another approach which could be utilised to discover information in databases of business processes is that of clustering. Clustering will allow the discovery of hidden sub-structures within the business process database. These might be known sub-structures (eg. different products with different provision processes) or might be unknown (eg. different processes being followed in different geographies when the process should be nationally standardised).

Most common clustering techniques such as k-Nearest Neighbour require data to be represented as a fixed size feature vector for each observation. These vectors are then processed algorithmically to produce the final set of clusters. In order to represent sequence data as a fixed length vector there are two common approaches:

1. Use a sliding window approach where only the most recent n tasks are included in a fixed length vector.
2. Summarise the data into a vector of event counts.

The first approach has the weakness that it discards historical behaviour which might be important in the context of the process. Discarding history means very different sequences might be clustered together where there is no solid underlying reason for that. For example, two car journeys might both end with the "leave motorway","visit fuel pump", "pump fuel","pay for fuel" sequence causing them to be clustered together, however if we know that the first journey starts in London and the second in Berlin we can see that these processes are highly different in the real world.

The major weakness of the second approach is that it loses data about the temporal relationships between the events. For example, and event sequence ABCDABCDE might be turned into a A = 2, B = 2, C = 2, D = 2, E = 1, F = 0, which would be an identical representation to the sequence AABBCCDDE even though they are completely different sequences. This can be offset by summarising the transitions explicitly however this rapidly becomes untenable when the state space represented by number of tasks is non-trivial.

Similarity based techniques to work with process data are known in the literature in the context of case-based reasoning approaches. CBR is typically examined in the literature with reference to the automated monitoring of a process executions [8], or as a vehicle for adaptation of the workflows at runtime [10]. The focus of this paper is rather to investigate the use of similarity based clustering to aid the human understanding of a complex business process system, and then to try and discover the underlying logic that determines the differences in behaviour.

3.1   Minimum Spanning Tree Based Clustering

An alternative clustering approach to k-means which can be used with only a distance function that is able to assign a value of difference between pairs of items utilises minimum spanning tree (MST) techniques [7]. The distance between each pair of process instances can be calculated using a metric such as edit distance. Using edit distance as a metric on sequence data can itself be problematic because we would need to ensure the lowest cost is calculated each time to get the highest quality clusters. In order to meet this requirement we can calculate the distance between two process samples using Sequence Alignment techniques popular in Bioinformatics. For this investigation of the MST clustering technique we have utilised the Needleman-Wunsch algorithm for global sequence alignment [11]. An implementation of Needleman-Wunch in python is available in the Python Alignment library [4].

Now that we have a technique that can produce the distances between observations we can use Kruskal's algorithm [9] to produce the minimum spanning tree. Applying Kruskal's algorithm will produce the minimum-spanning-tree for all of the paths in the dataset. An example of one of these is shown in Fig. 9. The relative frequency of each path is indicated by the size of the node representing that path.

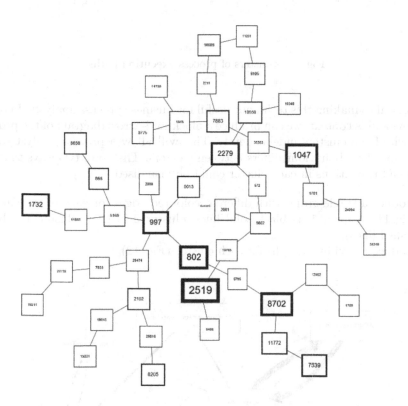

Fig. 9. An example minimum spanning tree of process execution paths

Once the minimum spanning tree is produced then we can remove the most expensive edges in turn until either the desired number of clusters is produced or the remaining edges have a distance below a given threshold. The example data being used here produces 3 clusters as shown in Fig. 10.

Whilst Fig. 9 illustrates the relationship between the process execution paths in our example dataset, and Fig. 10 shows 3 clusters discovered from that data, it does not show any business context to those clusters. Giving a business context

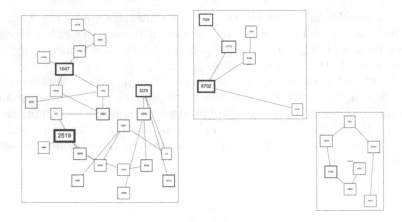

Fig. 10. Clusters of process execution paths

is essential to making this technique useful for business process analysts. In order to provide this context, we can produce a block-and-arrow diagram of the process for each of the clusters independently. This will allow a process analyst to see at a glance how behaviour differs between clusters. There are two ways that the tasks and transitions in each cluster could be visualised:

– Produce a single graph with different coloured edges for each of the clusters (Fig. 11 - cluster 1 as black solid lines, cluster 2 in grey, cluster 3 is black dashed lines).
– Produce individual graphs for each cluster (Fig. 12)

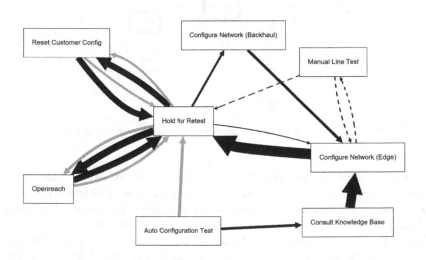

Fig. 11. Clusters of process execution paths

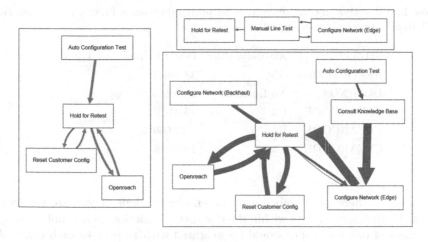

Fig. 12. Clusters of process execution paths - one per box.

Whilst it is difficult to get quantitative figures on how good or bad clusters are for analysis we were able to get some basic qualitative feedback by surveying business process analysts at BT. We showed the different possible representations to business analysts within BT and the second (Fig. 12) was judged to be significantly more useful by our audience.

3.2 Discovering Cluster Rationale

The diagrams of individual clusters are very useful for process analysis projects, however we do not have any data in the cluster diagrams themselves regarding the reasons for the clusters. Are they consistent with regards to some variable, or is the underlying reason for this partitioning unknown? In order to provide some context to the clusters we've attempted an additional layer of analysis to try to determine the cluster drivers.

For a selected cluster, the categorical labelling of the process traces are identified. The probability mass function (PMF) for each of the values of the categorical variables is calculated for the selected cluster and for the overall population of process traces. The two sets of PMF values can then be compared for differences. This will then provide some insight about how the population of process traces in the cluster differs from the global population. For example, we might see that Product A is four times more likely to be in Cluster 1 than the other clusters. Having clusters strongly associated with one attributes would be a strong indicator that attribute is driving the discovered sub-structure in the process. An example of such output is shown in Table 1.

3.3 Possible Extensions

In terms of the work on clustering with minimum spanning trees, one potential extension being investigated is the extension of the distance calculation to take

Table 1. Table showing the differences in probability mass function for categorical attributes for one cluster in Fig. 12

Attribute name	Attribute value	Percent change vs. Global
REPORTCODE	NSC	38.101%
DOMINOS	No Dominos	26.889%
CLEARCODE	C2	25.312%
CLEARCODE	R3	−22.069%
CLEARCODE	C3	19.959%

into account differences in labelling between observations. There are challenges with including labelled data within the distance calculation as it is not clear how differences of different types would be weighted with respect to each other. An external optimisation approach might be needed to tune the appropriate weights prior to clustering.

4   Conclusion

In this paper the application of two machine learning techniques to business process analysis have been presented and discussed. The nature of business process execution data as arbitrary length directed graphs makes the application of standard techniques difficult without using encoding schemes that lose significant amounts of data. By adapting the two techniques presented here we were able to overcome some of the data-loss issues normally required for the application of rule-mining or clustering of business processes.

References

1. Van der Aalst, W., Weijters, T., Maruster, L.: Workflow mining: discovering process models from event logs. IEEE Trans. Knowl. Data Eng. **16**(9), 1128–1142 (2004)
2. Agrawal, R., Imieliński, T., Swami, A.: Mining association rules between sets of items in large databases. In: ACM SIGMOD Record, vol. 22, pp. 207–216. ACM (1993)
3. Agrawal, R., Srikant, R., et al.: Fast algorithms for mining association rules. In: Proceedings of the 20th International Conference on Very Large Data Bases, VLDB, vol. 1215, pp. 487–499 (1994)
4. Aygün, E.: Python-Alignment, May 2017. https://github.com/eseraygun/python-alignment
5. Croxton, K.L.: The order fulfillment process. Int. J. Logist. Manag. **14**(1), 19–32 (2003)
6. Gabadinho, A., Ritschard, G., Studer, M., Müller, N.S.: Mining sequence data in R with the TraMineR package: a users guide for version 1.2. University of Geneva, Geneva (2009)

7. Grygorash, O., Zhou, Y., Jorgensen, Z.: Minimum spanning tree based clustering algorithms. In: 2006 18th IEEE International Conference on Tools with Artificial Intelligence (ICTAI 2006), pp. 73–81 (2006)
8. Kapetanakis, S., Petridis, M., Knight, B., Ma, J., Bacon, L.: A case based reasoning approach for the monitoring of business workflows. In: Bichindaritz, I., Montani, S. (eds.) ICCBR 2010. LNCS (LNAI), vol. 6176, pp. 390–405. Springer, Heidelberg (2010). https://doi.org/10.1007/978-3-642-14274-1_29
9. Kruskal, J.B.: On the shortest spanning subtree of a graph and the traveling salesman problem. Proc. Am. Math. Soc. **7**(1), 48–50 (1956)
10. Minor, M., Bergmann, R., Görg, S., Walter, K.: Towards case-based adaptation of workflows. In: Bichindaritz, I., Montani, S. (eds.) ICCBR 2010. LNCS (LNAI), vol. 6176, pp. 421–435. Springer, Heidelberg (2010). https://doi.org/10.1007/978-3-642-14274-1_31
11. Needleman, S.B., Wunsch, C.D.: A general method applicable to the search for similarities in the amino acid sequence of two proteins. J. Mol. Biol. **48**(3), 443–453 (1970)
12. Ritschard, G., Bürgin, R., Studer, M.: Exploratory mining of life event histories. In: Contemporary Issues in Exploratory Data Mining in the Behavioral Sciences, pp. 221–253 (2013)

Machine Learning in Control Systems: An Overview of the State of the Art

Signe Moe[(⊠)], Anne Marthine Rustad, and Kristian G. Hanssen

Department of Mathematics and Cybernetics, SINTEF Digital, Oslo, Norway
{Signe.Moe,AnneMarthine.Rustad,Kristian.Gaustad.Hanssen}@sintef.no

Abstract. Control systems are in general based on the same structure, building blocks and physics-based models of the dynamic system regardless of application, and can be mathematically analyzed w.r.t. stability, robustness and so on given certain assumptions. Machine learning methods (ML), on the other hand, are highly flexible and adaptable methods but are not subject to physic-based models and therefore lack mathematical analysis. This paper presents state of the art results using ML in the control system. Furthermore, a case study is presented where a neural network is trained to mimic a feedback linearizing speed controller for an autonomous ship. The neural network outperforms the traditional controller in case of modeling errors and measurement noise.

Keywords: Control systems · Machine learning · Hybrid analytics

1 Introduction

The use of Machine Learning (ML) is increasing rapidly within numerous applications. These highly flexible, adaptable methods are in several settings, such as natural language processing [13] and medical diagnosis [19], showing better performance, higher robustness and adaptability beyond that of traditional approaches. However, these methods are lacking in terms of stability proofs and mathematical analysis and explanation.

On the other hand, traditional control systems are mostly based on the same blocks, regardless of the application. These blocks are illustrated in Fig. 1 and are described in detail in Sect. 2. In general, such control loops are based on system and parameter identification, and are designed to give the controlled system desired properties such as stability and robustness given reasonable assumptions. However, identifying and modeling a system is challenging and in some cases infeasible due to unobservability and highly non-linear effects. This paper presents an overview of state of the art of machine learning in the control system, where one or more of the traditional control blocks have been replaced or combined with a machine learning-approach. This results in a *hybrid analytics control system*, which may benefit from the strengths of both approaches.

M. Bramer and M. Petridis (Eds.): SGAI-AI 2018, LNAI 11311, pp. 250–265, 2018.
https://doi.org/10.1007/978-3-030-04191-5_23

This paper is organized as follows. Section 2 presents the traditional control loop and the different system blocks, their main purpose and the most commonly used techniques and considerations. State of the art results of ML in the control system are described in Sect. 3. Furthermore, a case study is presented in Sect. 4, where a traditional, model-based speed controller for an autonomous surface vessel is replaced with a neural network controller. Finally, conclusions are given in Sect. 5.

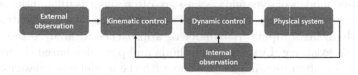

Fig. 1. The traditional control loop consists of multiple components for observation and control.

2   The Control Loop

This section briefly describes the overall function and interaction of the blocks in a traditional control loop (Fig. 1). Furthermore, the most commonly used approaches and considerations for the different control blocks are briefly described. Control loops are used to regulate a number of states such as motion, temperature and voltage, and can be applied to various physical systems, e.g. robotic manipulators, autonomous vehicles and process systems. The dynamics of the system is modeled using the laws of physics, and these models are commonly used for simulations and in the design of the different control components, which are described below.

In a control loop, the **internal observation** block provides information on the internal states of the system, either from direct sensor measurements or from estimations based on sensor data combined with the system model [10]. Furthermore, the control system may require information about its surroundings to properly be able to perform its tasks. This occurs in the **external observation** block. The relevant states of the system and the external observations are used by the **kinematic** and **dynamic controllers**. The kinematic controller calculates the desired behavior of the system, i.e. what the states of the system should be to achieve one or more tasks [3]. These reference states are given as input to the dynamic controller in addition to the actual states, and the objective of the dynamic controller is to use the control inputs to drive the difference between these to zero, i.e. to bring the system to the desired state [17].

An illustrative example is an adaptive cruise control of a car. In this case, the internal observation block estimates the velocity of the car by measuring the rotations per minute of the wheels and calculating the resulting velocity. The external observation block uses sensors such as radars or cameras to detect other vehicles or obstacles ahead. The original reference velocity is constant and manually set by the driver. However, based on the external observations, this velocity may be altered by the kinematic controller should it for instance be necessary to slow down to avoid collisions with slower-moving vehicles. Finally, the dynamic controller ensures that the engine speeds up if the car is moving slower than the reference velocity and vice versa.

2.1 Modeling of Physical Systems

Physics-based models of dynamic systems are often given as differential equations describing the relationship between the system states, their derivatives w.r.t. time and the control inputs. A number of approaches to analyze the behavior of the system exist, e.g. Lyapunov's methods and passivity-based theorems [17]. Hence, they are often used in combination with the model when designing of the control system to ensure that the estimated states converge to the actual states, or that the actual states converge to the reference states.

For a robotic manipulator, the state is given by the joint angles q. The position and orientation of the end effector is denoted η. The system model is then given as

$$\dot{\eta} = J(q)\dot{q}, \tag{1}$$

$$M(q)\ddot{q} + C(q, \dot{q})\dot{q} + g(q) = \tau, \tag{2}$$

where J is the configuration-dependent Jacobian matrix, M and C are the mass/inertial and Coriolis matrices, g is a vector describing the gravitational forces and τ are the forces produced by the joint actuators [31]. This model assumes frictionless joints.

Although such mathematical models are useful tools based on a solid foundation of physics and reasoning, there are also challenges related to achieving a sufficiently accurate model. They are often based on assumptions that may not always be satisfied, e.g. frictionless joints or negligible forces at low velocities [34]. Furthermore, accurate modeling of non-linear effects such as damping and friction and parameter estimation is highly challenging [7]. Finally, such models, often referred to as *process plants*, may be too complex to be utilized in the control system, and are often replaced by simplified models, called *control plants* describing only the most essential physical effects of the system [6,16].

2.2 Kinematic Control and Decision Making

A system may have one or multiple tasks in a prioritized order that may be in conflict, or several modes of operation. The kinematic controller considers the desired overall behavior of the system and calculates the desired states to achieve this based on the current states of system and external observations.

A common type of kinematic controller is based on **inverse kinematics**. For instance, a robot manipulator is controlled through actuators at the joints q. A given joint configuration corresponds to an exact end effector position and orientation η, but a given position/orientation may be achieved by multiple joint configurations. Based on specified tasks such as desired end effector configuration η_{des} and the current configuration q, the kinematic controller calculates the corresponding desired joint angles q_{des} [4]. However, the stability analysis is based on the assumption that the reference q_{des} is tracked perfectly [3]. Furthermore, it is unsuitable for tasks requiring force control, such as manipulation tasks [18].

Unlike the example above, many systems are **underactuated**, i.e. do not have a control input related to every state. One example of this is surface vessels, which typically only have two control inputs (a rudder and a thruster) in spite of having 6 states (described in Sect. 4). Thus, the kinematic controller must calculate the reference for the states that are controlled such that the desired behavior is achieved [11].

Furthermore, a system may have multiple modes of operations. For complex systems, it is highly challenging to make a rule-based **decision maker** to handle all eventualities. A common approach is to use fuzzy logic [2], which ensures a smooth transition between different modes of operation.

2.3 Dynamic Control

The dynamic controller receives the desired and actual states q_{des} and q. The necessary control forces τ to drive the states to their references, i.e. the error $e \triangleq q_{\text{des}} - q$ to zero, are then calculated.

A widely used dynamic controller is the proportional integral derivative **(PID)** controller (3). This is based on a linear combination of the error, its derivative and its integral, and gain matrices K_{p}, K_{i} used for controller tuning. Thus, it is not affected by modeling errors and is applicable to almost any system. However, optimal control or stability can not be guaranteed, and badly tuned PIDs may even result in unstable systems. Furthermore, it performs poorly on systems with strong non-linear effects, and it is susceptible to measurement noise in sensors [1].

$$\tau(t) = K_{\text{p}}e(t) + K_{\text{i}} \int_0^t e(s)ds + K_{\text{d}}\dot{e}(t). \tag{3}$$

The **feedback linearizing** controller is model-based and aims to cancel out non-linear effects of the system to overcome one of the weaknesses of the PID-controller. Thus, it is possible to guarantee stability using such controllers, but they are susceptible to modeling errors and measurement noise. For instance, for the dynamics of a manipulator given by (2), a feedback linearizing PD-controller is given in (4) (the argument t is omitted for readability). The resulting closed loop system has a uniformly globally exponentially stable equilibrium point at $e = 0$, i.e. the error will converge to zero in a finite amount of time [17]. Furthermore, it is clear that the effects related to gravity, centripetal and Coriolis forces have been compensated for by the control system.

$$\tau = M(q)(\ddot{q}_{\text{des}} + K_{\text{p}}e + K_{\text{d}}\dot{e}) + C(q,\dot{q})\dot{q} + g(q). \tag{4}$$

A model predictive controller (**MPC**) is implemented by solving an optimization problem at every control step. The system behavior is predicted by the use of a model, and a trajectory of the system states over the prediction horizon is obtained. This allows formulating constraints on both decision variables and the predicted states. Only the first control step is used; at the next control step new state estimates are obtained, and the optimization problem is solved over again. The success of MPC has been attributed to the ability to handle multivariable systems with both input and output constraints in a consistent manner [25]. However, the controller can be computationally heavy and its performance depends heavily on the accuracy of the process model [28].

2.4   Internal and External Observation

A variety of **sensors** are available to provide relevant information about internal states, such as encoders, Global Positioning System (GPS), Inertial Measurement Units (IMUs) and thermometers. However, physical sensors have several shortcomings. First, certain sensors are expensive and may constitute a large part of the total cost of a control system in addition to inducing errors such as stochastic noise and biases. Furthermore, certain states and signals are challenging to measure directly [10] and must be estimated using an observer. For instance, the **Kalman filter** is a widely used observer to estimate missing states from indirect and noisy measurements and the system model. Although the traditional Kalman filter is only applicable to linear systems, the **extended Kalman filter** is based on linear approximations of non-linear systems [14]. Note that this is computationally heavy for complex systems.

In certain situations, it is necessary to gather and process information about the environment to assist the kinematic or dynamic controller. Examples of such **external observations** are environmental disturbances such as wind and waves and obstacle detection. Commonly used sensors for the latter include radars, lasers and cameras, where the sensor data must be analyzed through computer vision algorithms to determine whether a given area is free of obstacles [29]. Traditionally, computer vision methods have been based on camera imaging geometry, feature detection, stereo vision, and so on [32]. However, the use of machine learning is highly increasing in the field of image analysis. The following section will provide several examples of this.

3   ML in Control Systems

This section will present examples of machine learning approaches being used in one or more blocks of the control loop in Fig. 1.

3.1 Modeling of Physical Systems

As mentioned in Sect. 2, several components in the control loop are often based on differential equations describing the behavior of the system, which are are highly challenging to solve explicitly. However, ML may provide additional tools for analyzing such equations. In [20–22], neural networks in various forms are used to approximate solutions of ordinary and partial differential equations (PDEs). In [30], an algorithm for approximating the solution of a PDE using a deep neural network is presented. The network is trained assuming no knowledge of the solution and a theorem is presented stating that the neural network will converge to the solution of the PDE as the size of the network increases.

ML may also be applied to learn a dynamic model on the same form as (2) without solving the equation. In [33], a neural network is used to identify parts of a model for an underwater vehicle as illustrated in Fig. 2. In most practical cases, all parameters apart from the hydro-dynamic damping parameters can be calculated with sufficient accuracy with ordinary methods. Hence, the term $\hat{\Phi}$ is estimated using a neural network, whereas the known parameters are represented by the known model Φ_M. After training, the neural network is used in a feedback linearizing controller to compensate for the damping.

In [8], a neural network is used to approximate the dynamics of the leader and follower, and this approximation is utilized in a feedback

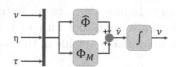

Fig. 2.   Illustration reproduced from [33]. The nonlinear dynamic equations with neural network $\hat{\Phi}$ to model unknown parameters in parallel with known parameters and model structure Φ_M is used to estimate the vehicle accelerations $\dot{\nu}$ given the position/orientation η, velocities ν and control inputs τ.

control law to achieve formation control. This control law also requires information about the internal states of the agents, and to achieve this another neural network is applied as an observer to estimate linear and angular velocities of the robots, which are assumed to have limited communication between them. Thus, machine learning techniques are applied both in the dynamic controller and internal observer of the control loop.

3.2 Kinematic Control/Decision Making

ML is often applied in the kinematic control component in situations requiring online analysis of the environment. In such cases, the input to the algorithms are often camera images or other sensor data from the external observation component. In [15], a quadrotor is trained to autonomously follow a forest trail to assist in search and rescue missions. To achieve this, the robot has a front view camera. The images are given as input to the kinematic controller, where a deep convolutional neural network (CNN) outputs a calculated probability of the trail being left, straight or right relative to the camera reference frame. These probabilities are then recalculated into desired orientation and forward velocity.[1]

---

[1] A narrated video summary is available at http://bit.ly/perceivingtrails.

Similarly, in [27] a deep convolutional neural network is used in the kinematic controller for an underwater snake robot to ensure proper docking. The snake head is equipped with a single camera which provides images as input to the kinematic controller. During training, the position (x, y) and orientation ψ of the robot are measured through a camera positioning system and used with a traditional kinematic controller to calculate the desired heading ψ_{des} required to follow a path to the docking station. The path is designed so that the docking station is visible from the camera on the path. The error $\tilde{\psi} = \psi_{\text{des}} - \psi$ is the input to the dynamic controller. However, in uncontrolled environments such as subsea, it is not straightforward to obtain the position and orientation of the robot. Therefore, a neural network is trained to estimate $\tilde{\psi}$ given only camera input. Hence, the network is trained to mimic the behavior of the traditional kinematic controller without being dependent on state measurements that may be unavailable outside of the controlled environment (see Fig. 3).

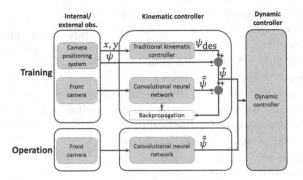

Fig. 3. Illustration reproduced from [27]. A CNN is trained to provide the same heading error as a traditional kinematic controller without depending on state measurements that are not available in uncontrolled environments.

3.3 Dynamic Control

Machine learning may also be applied as dynamic controllers. In fact, *Machine Learning Control* (MLC) is the concept of using machine learning algorithms to learn an effective control law $b = K(s)$ that maps the system input (sensors s) to the system output (actuators b) motivated by problems involving complex control tasks where it may be difficult or impossible to model the system and develop a useful control law. Instead, data is utilized to learn effective controllers [9].

A similar approach as in [27] is applied in [36] for the dynamic control component. Here, a deep neural network is trained to mimic the behavior of an MPC for a quadcoptor that should avoid columns in its path. The MPC requires estimation or measurements of position. The neural network, however, is not dependent on position but is based only on observations that are directly available from the vehicle's onboard sensors. Since the MPC is only used at training time, one can perform training in a controlled environment where the full state is known at training time (e.g. using motion capture), but unavailable at test time. During test time, the neural network performs very well both in the face of modeling errors and never before seen scenarios such as multiple obstacles[2].

In [35], a bipedal robot is considered. The dynamics are modeled similar to (2), but also include static and dynamic friction and other disturbance torques and faults that occur in robot manipulator. These are considered unknown, hence they cannot be directly included in a feedback linearizing controller. Therefore, the dynamic controller of the bipedal robot is

$$\tau_{\text{total}} = \tau + \tau_{\text{c}}(\hat{y}_{\text{rnn}}), \tag{5}$$

where τ is given by (4) and τ_{c} is a term to compensate for the error and disturbance terms, and in turn to improve system response speed and reduce the steady state error. This term is based on the output of a recurrent neural network (RNN) $\hat{y}_{\text{rnn}}$, and simulations confirm that the tracking error e is decreased significantly when the RNN is activated compared to only using the feedback linearizing controller.

3.4   Internal and External Observation

In [26], a Radial Basis Function neural network (RBF NN) is trained to predict air data for a small unmanned aerial vehicle (UAV). Traditional air databooms are sensor-based and are therefore physically impractical for small UAVs. The RBF NN has a 5-dimensional input consisting of pressure measurements from sensors on the leading edge of the wing and outputs estimates of the freestream static pressure, freestream airspeed and UAV angle of attack, which is important information for the remainder of the control system. Data is gathered in a wind tunnel where the network output variables are known and the network is then trained in a supervised manner.

4   Case Study: Speed Controller

This section presents a case study of ML-in-the-loop, where a neural network replaces the dynamic speed controller of an autonomous unmanned surface vessel (USV). The neural network is trained to mimic the behavior of a feedback linearizing controller. The entire control system including the original speed controller is presented below, followed by a description of the training and evaluation of the controller.

The states of the USV are given by $\boldsymbol{\eta} \triangleq [x, y, \psi]^T$ and $\boldsymbol{\nu} \triangleq [u, v, r]^T$ and are illustrated in Fig. 4(a). The control inputs T and δ are the thruster force and rudder angle, respectively. In this use case, we assume that measurements of the full state are available. Furthermore, we assume that there are no external elements and disturbances to consider.

---

[2] A video summary is available at http://rll.berkeley.edu/icra2016mpcgps/.

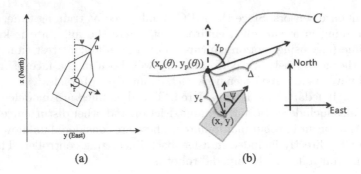

Fig. 4. (a) The states of the USV: position (x, y) and orientation ψ of the USV with respect to the North-East-Down (NED) frame and surge, sway and yaw rate u, v and r w.r.t. the body-fixed frame. (b) Desired path C, path-tangential reference frame with orientation $\gamma_p(\theta)$ and cross-track error y_e illustrated.

4.1   Model of Physical System

The simulation model in component form is given in [5,11] as

$$
\begin{aligned}
\dot{x} &= \cos(\psi)u - \sin(\psi)v, \\
\dot{y} &= \sin(\psi)u + \cos(\psi)v, \\
\dot{\psi} &= r, \\
\dot{u} &= F_u(v, r) - \frac{d_{11}}{m_{11}}u + \frac{b_{11}}{m_{11}}T, \\
\dot{v} &= X(u)r + Y(u)v, \\
\dot{r} &= F_r(u, v, r) + \frac{m_{22}b_{32} - m_{23}b_{22}}{m_{22}m_{33} - m_{23}^2}\delta.
\end{aligned}
\tag{6}
$$

This model assumes non-zero velocity. The expressions for $F_u(v, r)$, $X(u)$, $Y(u)$ and $F_r(u, v, r)$ are given in [23]. The control inputs consist of the thruster force T and rudder angle δ of the USV, and the model constants m_{ij}, d_{ij} and b_{ij} are mass/inertia, hydrodynamic damping and actuator configuration parameters that depend on the physical properties of the ship. The numeric values for these parameters are given in [12].

4.2   Kinematic Control

For this case study, the control system should make the vessel follow a given smooth path C and maintain a desired constant surge velocity u_{des}. The path variables are illustrated in Fig. 4(b). The path C is parametrized by $\theta \geq 0$ with respect to the NED-frame as $(x_p(\theta), y_p(\theta))$. The cross-track error y_e is computed as the orthogonal distance between the vessel position (x, y) and the path-tangential reference frame defined by the point (x_p, y_p). Note that the position of the path-tangential reference frame is always such that the along-track error $x_e \equiv 0$. The orientation of the path-tangential frame is defined as

$$\gamma_{\mathrm{p}}(\theta) = \mathrm{atan}\left(\frac{y_{\mathrm{p}}'(\theta)}{x_{\mathrm{p}}'(\theta)}\right) \tag{7}$$

It is clear from Fig. 4(b) that $y_e = 0$ implies that the vessel is on the desired path. Hence, we define the control objectives as

$$\lim_{t \to \infty} u(t) = u_{\mathrm{des}},$$
$$\lim_{t \to \infty} y_e(t) = 0. \tag{8}$$

The kinematic controller in this case should provide the desired states to ensure that the control objectives are satisfied. In case of the desired velocity, this is trivially equal to the constant, desired velocity u_{des}. It is proven in [24] that if the reference heading

$$\psi_{\mathrm{des}} = \gamma_{\mathrm{p}}(\theta) - \underbrace{\mathrm{atan}\left(\frac{v}{u_{\mathrm{des}}}\right) - \mathrm{atan}\left(\frac{y_e}{\Delta}\right)}_{\triangleq \beta_{\mathrm{des}}} \tag{9}$$

is tracked, the USV will converge to and follow the path. Here, the constant $\Delta > 0$ is the lookahead-distance, and the term β_{des} is a side-slip term to compensate for the sideways motion that occurs when a ship turns. In this case study, $\Delta = 75$ m.

4.3 Dynamic Control

Feedback linearizing controllers are highly suitable to ensure tracking of the desired surge velocity u_{des} and heading ψ_{des} for the system (6) due to the many non-linear components of the system. The controllers are given as

$$T = \frac{m_{11}}{b_{11}}\left(-F_u(v,r) + \frac{d_{11}}{m_{11}}u_{\mathrm{des}} + \dot{u}_{\mathrm{des}} - k_u(u - u_{\mathrm{des}})\right), \tag{10}$$

$$\delta = \frac{m_{22}m_{33} - m_{23}^2}{m_{22}b_{32} - m_{23}b_{22}}\left(-F_r(u,v,r) + \ddot{\psi}_{\mathrm{des}} - k_\psi(\psi - \psi_{\mathrm{des}}) - k_r(\dot{\psi} - \dot{\psi}_{\mathrm{des}})\right), \tag{11}$$

where the gains k_u, k_ψ and k_r are strictly positive constant controller gains. It is proven in [23] that the controllers (10) and (11) ensure that the references u_{des} and ψ_{des} are tracked. In this case study, the controller gains are chosen as $k_u = 0.1$ s^{-1}, $k_\psi = 0.04$ s^{-2} and $k_r = 0.9$ s^{-1}.

4.4   Training of the Neural Network Speed Controller

The model and control system presented in Sects. 4.1, 4.2 and 4.3 was implemented in Matlab. The neural network surge controller is trained using supervised learning to mimic the behavior of the feedback linearizing controller (10). Therefore, the network input $X \in \mathbb{R}^5$ is composed of the USV velocity u, v and r and the desired surge velocity and acceleration u_{des} and $\dot{u}_{\mathrm{des}}$, and the output is the estimated thruster force $\hat{T}$. Note that in this particular case study the reference velocity is always constant, and therefore $\dot{u}_{\mathrm{des}} = 0 \; m/s^2$ for all data points except the moment the velocity reference changes from one to another constant value. Future work includes training for time-varying surge velocity references.

Simulations with a perfectly known model and no measurement noise are run to collect training data. To ensure tracking of the reference surge velocity for all types of paths, simulations are performed on a large number of sine wave paths and a straight line path, given as

$$x_{\mathrm{p}}(\theta) = \theta, \quad y_{\mathrm{p}}(\theta) = A\sin\left(\frac{2\pi}{L}\theta\right), \qquad (12)$$

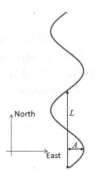

where A and L are the amplitude and period of the path in meters (Fig. 5). In the data gathering, simulations have been run for every combination of $A \in [0, \; 100]$ and $L \in [500, \; 1500]$ in 5 and 100 m intervals, respectively. Each path is simulated for 800 s and data is saved with a frequency of 20 Hz. The reference velocity u_{des} is chosen randomly from a predefined set of values every 200 s. This interval is given as $u_{\mathrm{des}} \in [0.5, \; 5.75]$ m/s, where u_{des} increases in 0.25 m/s increments. The simulation data is then used to train the neural network using TensorFlow. Several possible architectures were evaluated. The chosen network has three hidden layers of 100 nodes each with ReLu activation functions, which are suitable as they do not squeeze the input and they are less likely to have vanishing gradient problems than activation functions like sigmoid and hyperbolic tangent functions. The Adam optimizer was used to train the network to minimize the cost-function

Fig. 5. Sine wave path used to gather training data for multiple combinations of A and L.

$$\mathrm{Cost} = \frac{1}{m}\sum_{i=1}^{m}(\hat{T} - T)^2, \qquad (13)$$

where m is the number of data points, T is the thruster force calculated by the feedback linearizing controller (10), and $\hat{T}$ is the output of the neural network. Since training data is saved with high frequency it was not necessary to reuse any points in the training. We therefore use a batch size of $m = 1000$ data points and run training until all data from simulations have been used once.

4.5   Evaluation of the Neural Network Speed Controller

To evaluate the performance of the neural network speed controller, simulations are performed with a new path and reference velocities that the network has not been specifically trained for and compared to the performance of the feedback linearizing controller (10). This is described in Case I below. In addition, robustness is tested by introducing measurement noise (Case II) and modeling errors (Case III). In all test cases, simulations are run for 500 s where the reference velocity is increased from $u_{des} = 1.82$ m/s to $u_{des} = 3.64$ m/s after 250 s. The new path is illustrated in Fig. 6 and is defined as

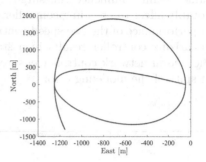

Fig. 6. Curved path used in simulations to evaluate the neural network.

$$x_p(\theta) = 1.2\theta \sin(0.005\theta), \quad y_p(\theta) = 600\cos(0.005\theta) - 650. \tag{14}$$

Case I - Perfect model and no measurement noise: In this case the feedback linearizing controller (10) perfectly cancels out the nonlinear terms, stabilizes the system and guarantees that the surge velocity converging to and tracking the reference velocity. This is confirmed by Fig. 7(a)–(b), where the thruster force calculated by the controller results in the surge velocity u converging to u_{des}. Similarly, the neural network controller has learned to mimic the behavior of the feedback linearizing controller and also results in tracking of the reference velocity u_{des} in spite of simulating a new path and setting u_{des} to values the network was not explicitly trained on. The main difference occurs early in the simulation, where the neural network controller imposes less thrust force than the feedback linearizing controller, resulting in a slightly slower convergence to the first reference value. This occurs in all test cases.

Case II - Perfect model and measurement noise: In this case, white noise with a zero mean and a standard deviation of 0.4 m/s, 0.04 m/s and 3.0 rad/s is added on the velocity measurements u, v and r, respectively. This corresponds to around 10% of the actual maximum value during simulations. In this case, the feedback linearizing controller is unable to ensure perfect tracking of the reference velocity. As seen in Fig. 7(c)–(d), the resulting surge velocity u converges to a near-stationary error of approximately 0.2 m/s. However, the neural network controller ensures nearly perfect tracking of u_{des} in spite of the measurement noise.

Case III - Modeling errors and no measurement noise: In this case, the numeric values in the feedback linearizing controller and neural network remain unchanged, but some of the numeric values in the simulation model are altered. In particular, the parameters m_{11}, d_{11} and b_{11} are set to 85%, 110% and 108% of their original value, respectively. Thus, we evaluate the effects of notable modeling errors of magnitudes over and under the actual value. These values mainly influence the surge dynamics, so these modeling errors do not notably affect the heading controller (11). This is desirable to test the difference in performance of the two speed controllers only. Similar to Case II, the feedback linearizing controller results in a stationary deviation (Fig. 7(e)–(f)), whereas the neural network controller ensures perfect tracking of the reference velocity in spite of the modeling errors.

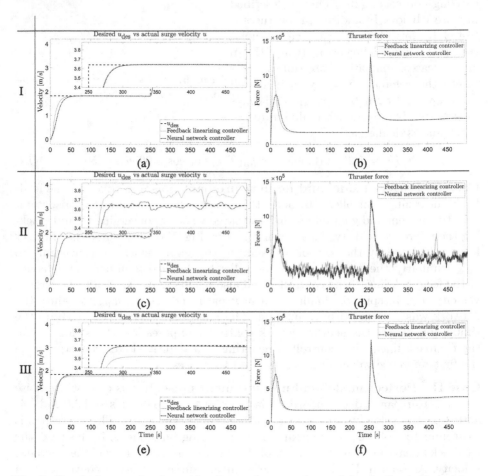

Fig. 7. Simulation results for evaluation and comparison of the feedback linearizing and neural network surge controller for three test cases. Confirming the theoretical results, the feedback linearizing controller performs very well in Case I, but results in a stationary deviation in case of measurement noise and modeling errors (Case II and III, respectively). The neural network is trained to mimic the behavior of the feedback linearizing controller on simulation data without modeling errors or measurement noise, but outperforms the original controller and achieves tracking also for Case II and III.

5 Conclusions

This paper presents the building blocks of a general control system along with some of the most used traditional methods. In general, traditional control methods are based on simple principles which are not sufficiently accurate for complex systems, or on a physics-based dynamic model of the system, which is time-consuming, challenging to derive and subject to assumptions and simplifications.

ML is in general highly adaptable and flexible, and may be introduced in a control system to a large degree (e.g. replacing and merging several blocks) or as a small addition to the existing system (e.g. accounting for unmodeled effects) to increase robustness, accuracy, and to remove simplifying assumptions. Finally, ML controllers may be trained to mimic the behavior of more complex, traditional controllers using fewer and/or cheaper sensors, thereby lowering the cost of the control system and increasing the applicability.

A use case is presented where a neural network is trained to mimic the behavior of a feedback linearizing controller to control the surge velocity of an autonomous ship. Training data is collected in simulations with a perfectly known model and no measurement noise. During the testing phase, the performance of the two controllers is compared also when measurement noise and modeling errors are present. In spite of being trained to mimic the feedback linearizing controller under ideal circumstances, the neural network controller performs better in the more challenging test cases and is thereby more robust and accurate than the original controller.

Acknowledgments. This project has been supported through the basic funding from the Norwegian Research Council.

References

1. Aastrøm, K.J., Murray, R.M.: Feedback Systems: An Introduction for Scientists and Engineers. Princeton University Press, Princeton (2008)
2. Abdullah, L.: Fuzzy multi criteria decision making and its applications: a brief review of category. Procedia Soc. Behav. Sci. **97**, 131–136 (2013)
3. Antonelli, G.: Stability analysis for prioritized closed-loop inverse kinematic algorithms for redundant robotic systems. IEEE Trans. Robot. **25**(5), 985–994 (2009)
4. Antonelli, G., Arrichiello, F., et al.: The null-space-based behavioral control for autonomous robotic systems. Intell. Serv. Robot. **1**(1), 27–39 (2008)
5. Caharija, W., Candeloro, M., et al.: Relative velocity control and integral LOS for path following of underactuated surface vessels. In: Proceedings of the 9th IFAC Conference on Manoeuvring and Control of Marine Craft, pp. 380–385 (2012)
6. Candeloro, M., Sørensen, A.J., et al.: Observers for dynamic positioning of ROVs with experimental results. IFAC Proc. Vol. **45**(27), 85–90 (2012)
7. Chin, C., Lau, M.: Modeling and testing of hydrodynamic damping model for a complex-shaped remotely-operated vehicle for control. J. Mar. Sci. Appl. **11**(2), 150–163 (2012)
8. Dierks, T., Jagannathan, S.: Neural network output feedback control of robot formations. IEEE Trans. Syst. Man Cybern. **40**(2), 383–399 (2010)

9. Duriez, T., Brunton, S.L., Noack, B.R.: Machine learning control (MLC). Machine Learning Control – Taming Nonlinear Dynamics and Turbulence. FMIA, vol. 116, pp. 11–48. Springer, Cham (2017). https://doi.org/10.1007/978-3-319-40624-4_2

10. Ellis, G.: Observers in Control Systems: A Practical Guide. Academic Press, Cambridge (2002)

11. Fossen, T.I.: Handbook of Marine Craft Hydrodynamics and Motion Control. Wiley, Hoboken (2011)

12. Fredriksen, E., Pettersen, K.Y.: Global kappa-exponential way-point manoeuvering of ships. In: Proceedings of the 43rd IEEE Conference on Decision and Control, pp. 5360–5367 (2004)

13. Goodfellow, I., Bengio, Y., et al.: Deep Learning. MIT Press, Cambridge (2016)

14. Grewal, M.S., Andrews, A.P.: Kalman Filtering : Theory and Practice. Wiley, Hoboken (2001)

15. Guisti, A., Guzzi, J., et al.: A machine learning approach to visual perception of forest trails for mobile robots. Robot. Autom. Lett. 1(2), 661–667 (2016)

16. Kelasidi, E., Pettersen, K.Y., et al.: A control-oriented model of underwater snake robots. In: Proceedings of the 2014 IEEE International Conference on Robotics and Biomimetics, pp. 753–760 (2014)

17. Khalil, H.K.: Nonlinear systems. Prentice Hall PTR, Upper Saddle River (2002)

18. Khatib, O.: A unified approach for motion and force control of robot manipulators: the operational space formulation. IEEE J. Robot. Autom. 3(1), 43–53 (1987)

19. Kononenko, I.: Machine learning for medical diagnosis: history, state of the art and perspective. Artif. Intell. Med. 23(1), 89–109 (2001)

20. Lagaris, I.E., Likas, A., et al.: Artificial neural networks for solving ordinary and partial differential equations. IEEE Trans. Neural Netw. 9(5), 987–1000 (1998)

21. Lagaris, I.E., Likas, A.C., et al.: Neural-network methods for boundary value problems with irregular boundaries. IEEE Trans. Neural Netw. 11(5), 1041–1049 (2000)

22. Malek, A., Shekari Beidokhti, R.: Numerical solution for high order differential equations using a hybrid neural network – optimization method. Appl. Math. Comput. 183(1), 260–271 (2006)

23. Moe, S., Pettersen, K.Y.: Set-based line-of-sight (LOS) path following with collision avoidance for underactuated unmanned surface vessel. In: Proceedings of the 1st Conference on Control Technology and Applications (2016)

24. Moe, S., Pettersen, K.Y., et al.: Line-of-sight curved path following for underactuated USVs and AUVs in the horizontal plane under the influence of ocean currents. In: Proceedings of the 1st IEEE Conference on Control Technology and Applications (2016)

25. Qin, J., Badgwell, T.: A survey of industrial model predictive control technology. Control Eng. Pract. 11, 733–764 (2003)

26. Samy, I., Postlethwaite, I., et al.: Neural-network-based flush air data sensing system demonstrated on a mini air vehicle. J. Aircr. 47(1), 18–31 (2010)

27. Sans-Muntadas, A., Pettersen, K.Y., et al.: Learning an AUV docking maneuver with a convolutional neural network. In: Proceedings of the IEEE Oceans (2017)

28. Seborg, D.E., Edgar, T.F., et al.: Process dynamics and control. AIChE J. 54(11), 3026–3026 (2008)

29. Singh, S., Keller, P.: Obstacle detection for high speed autonomous navigation. In: Proceedings of the 1991 IEEE International Conference on Robotics and Automation, pp. 2798–2805 (1991)

30. Sirignano, J., Spiliopoulos, K.: DGM: a deep learning algorithm for solving partial differential equations (2017). http://arxiv.org/abs/1708.07469

31. Spong, M.W., Hutchinson, S.: Robot Modeling and Control. Wiley, Hoboken (2005)
32. Szeliski, R.: Computer Vision: Algorithms and Applications. Springer, London (2011). https://doi.org/10.1007/978-1-84882-935-0
33. van de Ven, P.W.J., Johansen, T.A., et al.: Neural network augmented identification of underwater vehicle models. Control Eng. Pract. **15**(6), 715–725 (2007)
34. Vidoni, R., Carabin, G., Gasparetto, A., Mazzetto, F.: Stability analysis of an articulated agri-robot under different central joint conditions. Robot 2015: Second Iberian Robotics Conference. AISC, vol. 417, pp. 335–346. Springer, Cham (2016). https://doi.org/10.1007/978-3-319-27146-0_26
35. Wu, Y., Song, Q., et al.: Robust recurrent neural network control of biped robot. J. Intell. Robot. Syst. **49**(2), 151–169 (2007)
36. Zhang, T., Kahn, G., et al.: Learning deep control policies for autonomous aerial vehicles with MPC-guided policy search. In: Proceedings of the 2016 International Conference on Robotics and Automation, pp. 528–535 (2016)

Predicting Fluid Work Demand in Service Organizations Using AI Techniques

Sara AlShizawi[1(✉)], Siddhartha Shakya[1], Andrzej Stefan Sluzek[2], Russell Ainslie[3], and Gilbert Owusu[3]

[1] EBTIC, Khalifa University, Abu Dhabi, UAE
100036685@kustar.ac.ae
[2] Electrical and Computer Engineering, Khalifa University, Abu Dhabi, UAE
[3] BT, Adastral Park, Ipswich, UK

Abstract. Prediction is about making claims on future events based on past information and the current state. Predicting workforce demand for the future can help service organizations adjust their resources and reach their goals of cost saving and enhanced efficiency. In this paper, a use case for a telecom service organization is presented and a framework for predicting workforce demand using neural networks is provided. The experiments were performed with real-world data, and the results were compared against other popular techniques such as linear regression and also moving average which served as a simulation of the technique historically applied manually in the organization. The results show that the accuracy of prediction is improved with the use of neural networks. The technique is being built into a tool that is being tested by the partner telecom organization.

Keywords: Prediction · Moving average · Linear regression · Neural network

1 Introduction

Large service organizations such as telecoms, utility companies (including water and electricity), retailers, logistics providers and many other similar institutions have large workforces. These service organizations are mobilized in different locations to deliver different services for a different customer base. Based on the company's product portfolio, they can have diverse skills to do multiple sets of tasks. Successful service organizations are those who provide the right person, with the needed skill, at the right time, in the right place. Assuring this to the customer is the key to the successful delivery of services. Moreover, proactive planning of resources helps to reach a higher level of service by optimizing the deployment of the workforce, maximizing utilization, reducing leakage as much as possible and minimizing the cost of maintaining the service [1, 2].

Despite the fact that service organizations are concerned mostly about the importance of excellent customer service, they still need to manage their resources to achieve their goals. The first step to effectively manage the resources is to have full visibility of their future demand. In other words, having an idea of expected demand will give the company a great opportunity to change or make important decisions on how best to

© Springer Nature Switzerland AG 2018
M. Bramer and M. Petridis (Eds.): SGAI-AI 2018, LNAI 11311, pp. 266–276, 2018.
https://doi.org/10.1007/978-3-030-04191-5_24

utilize their limited capacity to meet the expected demand. Some demands can be estimated in advance, such as in the case where a contract is signed to provide a fixed service for a fixed period, e.g. delivering routine service to vehicles for an organization. However most of the demands in service industries, particularly in retail environments, are not fixed in advance, and therefore require a careful analysis of historical demand patterns together with associated parameters, to predict the future demand [3].

Big data, or historical data, provided by the service organizations are very important to predict future demand. Nowadays, with the advancement in IoT, Big Data and corresponding IT infrastructures, these data are easy to collect, store and process. Moreover, monitoring and record keeping systems also offer real time data. They also provide scene-relevant measurements such as the number of customers, their gender, service times and many other facts for a specific location. These scene data can be used to provide better services to the customers by using different analytical techniques to optimize services for specific customers.

In this paper, a real-world scenario from a telecom service organization is investigated. This project is part of an ongoing collaboration between EBTIC and its telecom's partner. The aim here is to predict how much work will be available for completion on a given day in the future. This differs from the total amount of work currently known about as it takes account of extra factors, such as when customers have selected appointments or when access to a location is available etc., to give the maximum number of tasks that could be completed that specific day. This value is used during the planning process to set the portion of the demand to target for completion on each day in order to maximize service levels. The accuracy of this value is important as it drives decisions on resourcing levels for the telecom partner's large workforce of field engineers and technicians. Predicting too high will result in over-resourcing resulting in waste but predict too low and under-resourcing will occur resulting in reduced service levels.

The paper is organized as follows. Several well-known prediction techniques and their applications are reviewed in Sect. 2. The problem formulation and the training algorithms used to solve the problem are described in Sect. 3. Empirical results using the real data set in three separate experiments are reported in Sect. 4 together with the discussion of the results. Section 5 contains the concluding remarks.

2 Background

Different resource demand prediction models have been built using different forecasting techniques, well-known in the literature. They include moving average [5], linear regression [4] including ARIMA [6, 7], and neural networks [8].

The moving average technique is used to get the general idea of the trends in a certain data set and it's basically the average of any subset of numbers. This technique is a good baseline to compare the other techniques to [5], particularly as it is analogous to current manual methods used by the organization. Linear regression is used to predict the unknown value of one variable from a known value of another variable. If x and y are two related variables, then the linear regression method will help to predict the value of y for a given value of x as described in Eqs. 1 and 2 [4].

$$m = \frac{xy - \bar{x}\bar{y}}{x^2 - (\bar{x})^2} \tag{1}$$

$$b = \bar{y} - m\bar{x} \tag{2}$$

where $\bar{x}$ and $\bar{y}$ indicate the means.

Autoregressive integrated moving average (ARIMA) is considered as one of the popular linear models in time series prediction [6]. The ARIMA model with AR (autoregressive) order of p and MA (moving average) order of q is denoted as ARMA (p, q) where the time series that fits the model is denoted as $x = \{x_t\}_{t=1}^n$ and it has the following form.

$$x_t = \Phi_0 + \sum_{j=1}^p \Phi_j x_{t-j} + \sum_{j=1}^q \theta_j e_{t-j} + e_t \quad t = 1, 2, \ldots, n \tag{3}$$

where $\Phi 0$ is a constant term, n denotes the length of the time series and et denotes the independent and identically distributed (IID) Gaussian white noise with zero mean and constant variance $\sigma 2$ [7]. From Eq. 3, the ARIMA model is considered to be a pure AR model if q = 0 and it is considered to be a pure MA if p = 0.

Finally, neural networks (NN), specifically feed forward NNs, are common models used for prediction in forecasting problems. Neural networks are made up of a number of nodes, divided into input layer, hidden layer and output layer. In general, historical data or the available data are divided into two sets, which are a training set and a testing set. The training set is used in the training phase of the neural network model where the weights of the connections between the nodes within the network are changed to attempt to achieve the required output. The testing set is then used to evaluate the accuracy of these trained models. The choice of algorithm used for training the neural network is very important. In this paper a resilient back propagation algorithm is used. Also, we make use of the early stopping strategy to avoid overfitting during the training process. The early stopping strategy further subdivides the training set into training and validation sets. The training set is used during the training process as before but now the validation set is used to evaluate the accuracy of the trained model during that process. Once the accuracy of the model on the validation set stops improving and instead starts to decrease this indicates that overfitting is starting to occur on the training set and thus the training process is then stopped [8].

Some of the recent work on forecasting in service industries using advanced techniques is discussed in [9], where an application related to transportation is presented where travel demand for short-term and long-term forecasting is investigated. The goal is to predict the passenger flow in train stations, buses and tram stops. For both short-term and long-term prediction, three techniques are used which are Random Forest (RF), Long-Short Term Memory (LSTM) and neural network. Another application related to maintenance is presented in [10], where the goal is to predict the condition of the components that need to be replaced or maintained before their end of life in performing their tasks. The prediction technique used for this is again LSTM. In the telecom sector, the ability to detect subscribers who intend to terminate their service in advance gives the company the opportunity to retain their customer by proposing special offers to them. In [11], a prediction model based on the logistic regression technique is built. This is done by assigning a value to subscribers based on the relationship between the historical data and their future behavioral pattern.

3 Problem Formulation

3.1 General Problem Definition

The main problem discussed in this paper is to predict how much work will be available for completion on a given day in the future. This prediction is important since the company has a large workforce of field engineers and technicians, based in different locations and with different skill sets, delivering services, such as installing new facilities or fixing faults to customers, on a daily basis. Thus, planning the technician's availability such as rostering, shifts, absences, etc., will help to make sure there are enough resources available to cover the required task completions. The main issue here is that having less resources will result in failing some of the work and having more resources than needed will result in unnecessary costs. The work itself is categorized into fluid work and non-fluid work, with the total amount of work available called the workstack for that skill. Fluid work are tasks that have passed through all stages of validation and inventory clearance and are available to be done on a specific day. Non-fluid work are the ones that are still in that process and can't yet be completed on that specific day. The requirement is to predict the fluid workstack for future based on the past workstack and other capacity, and demand related parameters. Predicting the fluid workstack can be more difficult than predicting the total workstack due to it being a percentage of the total workstack and that percentage can be different for different days, based on additional external and internal factors. Also, the prediction has to be done for each geographical area and for each skill's fluid workstack separately.

The data set provided from the telecom company consists of 543 data points, and each data point represents the total volume for all inputs and outputs per day. The data set includes 59 separate areas with 3 resource type's capacity levels. Since the data is anonymized, we represent capacity/resource types as (R_1, R_2 and R_3) and workstacks, intakes and fluid workstacks for 5 different skills as (W_1, W_2, W_3, W_4 and W_5), (N_1, N_2, N_3, N_4 and N_5) and (F_1, F_2, F_3, F_4 and F_5) respectively.

3.2 Mathematical Model of Built Neural Network

We propose to use a feedforward neural network model as it is the most commonly used model for forecasting and has been proven to work well. For the purpose of this work, a fixed topology network with three standard layers are used which are input layer, hidden layer and output layer [12]. We build a set of N neural networks, each of them is modeling the relationship between the outputs, $F = \{F_1, F_2, \dots F_5\}$, and the inputs ($R_1$, R_2 and R_3), (W_1, W_2, W_3, W_4 and W_5) and (N_1, N_2, N_3, N_4 and N_5). Figure 1 shows the structure of the neural network used.

It is noted in Fig. 1 that a fixed value of 1 is added as a bias node to the input layer and the hidden layer which helps in fitting the model to the data more accurately.

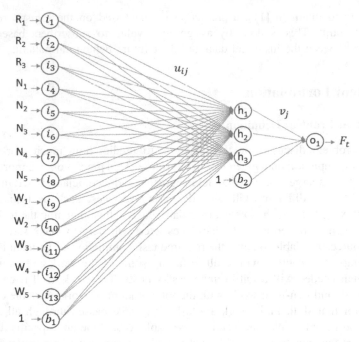

Fig. 1. The structure of neural network with 13 inputs, a single output and one hidden layer with 3 nodes.

Moreover, the relationship between the inputs and the output is described mathematically as shown in Eq. 4.

$$Ft = \alpha\left(\sum\nolimits_{j=1}^{M}\left(\alpha\left(\sum\nolimits_{i=1}^{N} P_i u_{ij} + u_{bj}\right)v_j\right) + v_b\right) \tag{4}$$

Where, P_i = {P1, P2, ..., P13} are the inputs (R1, R2 and R3), (W1, W2, W3, W4 and W5) and (N1, N2, N3, N4 and N5), u_{ij} represents the weight between input node (i) and hidden node (j), while u_{bj} represents the weights between the bias node in the input layer and the hidden node (j). Similarly, v_j represents the weight between hidden node (j) and the output node, while v_b represents the weight between the bias node in the hidden layer and the output node. Resilient back propagation, as described in Sect. 2, was used to estimate the parameters u_{ij} and v_j. Also, an activation function α (x) for the neural network nodes, which we choose to be of a sigmoid form for each layer, is shown in Eq. 5.

$$\alpha(x) = \frac{1}{1 + e^{-x}} \tag{5}$$

Furthermore, since a sigmoid form is chosen, the values of the inputs are mapped to 0 and 1, and the output value in Eq. 4 is between 0 and 1 [12].

Usually, a simple network structure with a small number of hidden nodes works well in out-of-sample predictions, and this is due to the overfitting effect. The over fitted model has a poor generalization ability for data out of the sample. However, it has a good fit to the sample used for model building. Hence, selection of the number of hidden nodes is a data dependent parameter and there is no specific rule in choosing this parameter [6].

4 Experiments and Results

We performed experiments with many different settings for the topology of the neural network in order to achieve a higher accuracy of prediction. We describe some of the key experiments in this section. The data set supplied by our partner telecom company included one year of historical data containing inputs and outputs, as described in Eq. 4, for 5 different types of tasks (skills) and for 59 different geographical locations. For the purpose of this paper we only detail the experiments performed for skill type 1 and area type 1 (referred to as skill1 and area1 here after).

We started by performing correlation analysis to check the relationship between different input variables and the output variables. This helps us to find the variables that have contributions to the output and also will help to decide the structure of the neural network. Figure 2 shows the correlation matrix for all inputs against skill 1 (shown as SKILL1_FLWK in the figure). Dark colored squares indicate that the relationship between the two variables are highly correlated while it is considered to be less correlated when the color of the squares get lighter. On the other hand, white squares mean that there is no correlation between the two variables.

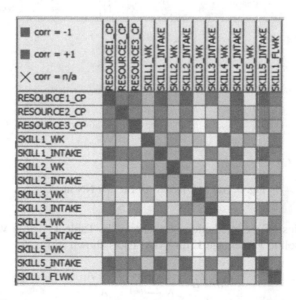

Fig. 2. Correlation matrix for all 13 inputs and one output (SKILL1_FLWK).

The network was implemented using the Encog [13] library in Java for all three experiments. Also, the data was divided into two sets, training set and testing set. 70% of the data was included in the training set, while the rest was included in the testing set. For each experiment, different topologies of neural networks, together with the additional inputs where required, were used. This was to check if there are any signals in the additional inputs and if they can help improve the accuracy. We first describe the experimental setups and the output of the experiments and then explain the results under each table.

4.1   Experiment 1

The aim of experiment 1 is to check how accurately we can predict on-the-day fluid workstacks by using on-the-day inputs of that day's resources, that day's workstacks and that day's intakes. For this, a neural network was built using the above mentioned inputs and compared against moving average and linear regression models. The inputs and output for experiment 1 for all three models are shown in Fig. 3. Figure 3a shows the moving average inputs where $(F_t)^{-1}$, $(F_t)^{-2}$ and $(F_t)^{-3}$ are the fluid workstack for the same day from previous 3 weeks. The linear regression and neural network have the same inputs sets as shown in Fig. 3b.

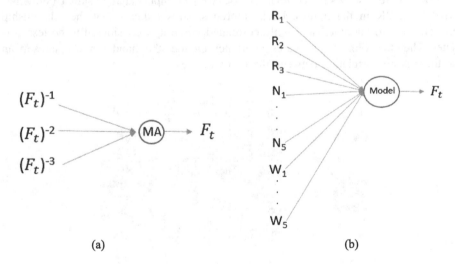

(a)   (b)

Fig. 3.   (a) MA model (b) LR and NN model.

The accuracies of the predictions are shown in Table 1. These were calculated using Mean Absolute Percentage Error (MAPE) as shown in Eq. 6.

$$MAPE = \frac{1}{N} \sum\nolimits_{t=1}^{n} \frac{|P_t - A_t|}{A_t} \qquad (6)$$

Table 1. Experiment 1 results - Accuracies of each technique and each day.

	Sat	Sun	Mon	Tue	Wed	Thu	Fri	Avg.
MA	73.6%	77.2%	51.8%	74.9%	57.0%	75.4%	78.7%	69.8%
LR	73.7%	95.2%	84.4%	80.1%	1.1%	85.9%	89.4%	72.8%
NN	44.8%	92.3%	87.6%	82.0%	89.9%	73.8%	87.9%	79.8%

Where P_t and A_t refers to the predicted and actual values respectively, and N is the sample size. The accuracy then will be 1 - *MAPE*. It is important to note that for each weekday we build and train separate models. This is to capture the trend that each weekday may have on the output.

It can be noted that MA had the worst average accuracy of 69.8% in comparison to the other two methods. The linear regression performed better at 72.8% and the NN has the best accuracy of 79.8%. Since the moving average had the lowest accuracy amongst the techniques, we did not use it for experiments 2 and 3.

4.2   Experiment 2

The motivation for experiment 2 is to see if there is any additional signal from the past values of the fluid workstacks on the current day's fluid workstack which can be used to further improve the accuracy. For this, we first calculate the moving average and add it as an extra parameter in our model. This additional input is shown in Fig. 4, as $A_3(F_t)$ and it models the aggregated information about the fluid workstack in past periods.

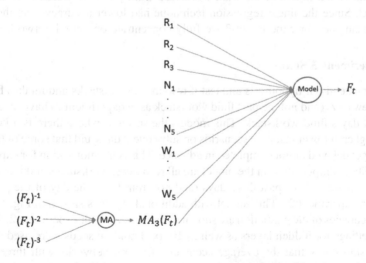

Fig. 4. NN model with additional moving average input.

For this experiment, we try three different settings for hidden layers with the number of layers ranging from 1 to 3. The number of nodes in each of the hidden layers was set to 12 as it performed best during our empirical experiments. Also, 10 different fixed random seeds were used to initialize the network for each type and for each day of the week. The trained network with the highest accuracy was selected for prediction and accuracy reporting. The motivation for using fixed random seeds was to help replicate the results. Also, having 10 of these seeds gives confidence that we have considered different possibilities of training the network. It was the requirement from our partner telecom that the results should not change each time they run the prediction model and having fixed random seeds would achieve this. The accuracies of the prediction are shown in Table 2 using linear regression and neural network techniques.

Table 2. Experiment 2 result - Accuracies of each technique and each day.

	Sat	Sun	Mon	Tue	Wed	Thu	Fri	Avg
LR	87.7%	90.6%	78.3%	81.7%	−5.2%	79.0%	87.6%	71.4%
NN (Hlayer = 1)	55.7%	91.3%	84.0%	73.6%	81.9%	69.7%	76.9%	76.2%
NN (Hlayer = 2)	41.5%	99.2%	85.6%	78.9%	73.9%	65.8%	90.2%	76.4%
NN (Hlayer = 3)	64.6%	95.9%	81.7%	76.3%	80.5%	72.1%	88.6%	80.0%

The results show that the neural network technique performed better than the linear regression technique. However, it did not significantly improve the results from experiment 1. The best accuracy results were for neural networks with 3 hidden layers with the average accuracy of 80.0% in comparison to the results in experiments 1 where the average accuracy was 79.8%. This shows that for the tested instance of the problem, additional inputs of the fluid workstack from previous weeks does not have much effect. Since the linear regression technique had lower accuracy than the neural network technique, for experiment 3 we fully concentrate on neural network models.

4.3   Experiment 3 Setup

We further extend our hypothesis and test if resources, workstacks and intakes from the previous few days (and not the past fluid workstack as in experiment 2) have an effect on the current day's fluid workstack. This models the scenario where there is a knock-on effect of higher or lower resource scenarios on subsequent days and that some of the work may have got delayed or got completed in advance. This is the motivation for experiment 3. The additional inputs used in the model are all resources, workstacks and intakes for a current day as well as for past three days (and not from the same day of the past three weeks as in experiment 2). This model with additional inputs is shown in Fig. 5.

The accuracies of the prediction are shown in Table 3. As with experiment 2, the three different settings for hidden layers as well as 10 fixed random seeds were used here.

The results show that the average accuracy of neural networks with three hidden layers was best with 83.1%. It also shows that using 3 hidden layers was better than using 1 or 2 hidden layers (which was also the case with experiment 2). This is a significant improvement from experiment 2 and shows that the previous days' resources, workstacks and intakes have an effect on the current days' fluid work which can help to improve the prediction accuracy by about ∼ 4%.

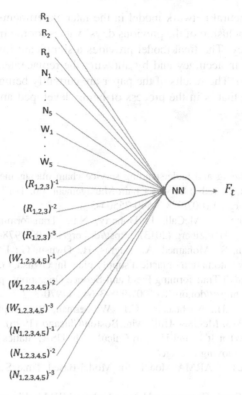

Fig. 5. NN model with additional inputs.

Table 3. Experiment 3 result - Accuracies of each technique and each day.

	Sat	Sun	Mon	Tue	Wed	Thu	Fri	Avg
NN (Hlayer = 1)	57.6%	93.7%	84.4%	77.5%	85.9%	77.1%	71.0%	78.2%
NN (Hlayer = 2)	69.1%	95.7%	85.6%	81.1%	85.2%	77.7%	81.8%	82.3%
NN (Hlayer = 3)	70.9%	92.7%	84.6%	83.6%	88.0%	75.6%	86.3%	83.1%

5 Conclusion

In this paper we investigated methods to solve a real-world forecasting scenario within a telecoms company, the goal was to predict the number of tasks available to complete on a given day in the future. For this purpose, we looked at several different forecasting methods, including linear regression, moving average and neural network, with the moving average being the closest to the current manual process used. We outlined the techniques and defined the problem together with the neural network model used to solve it. We then performed experiments on the real-world data and compared the accuracy of the models built with the moving average (the current process). We found that the neural network model produced better accuracy than the current process. We then focused on the neural network model in the later experiments to further refine it, discovering that the inclusion of the previous days' values for the inputs used increased the prediction accuracy. The final model provides a significant improvement over the current process, both in accuracy and by allowing the replacement of a manual technique with automation. The results of the paper are currently being incorporated into a new planning system that is in the process of being developed and tested.

References

1. Voudouris, C.: Defining and understanding service chain management. In: Voudouris, C., Lesaint, D., Owusu, G. (eds.) Service Chain Management, pp. 1–17. Springer, Heidelberg (2008). https://doi.org/10.1007/978-3-540-75504-3_1
2. Owusu, G., O'Brien, P., McCall, J., Doherty, N.F.: Transforming Field and Service Operations. Springer, Heidelberg (2013). https://doi.org/10.1007/978-3-642-44970-3
3. Shakya, S., Kassem, S., Mohamed, A., Hagras, H., Owusu, G.: Enhancing field service operations via fuzzy automation of tactical supply plan. In: Owusu, G., O'Brien, P., McCall, J., Doherty, N.F. (eds.) Transforming Field and Service Operations, pp. 101–114. Springer, Heidelberg (2013). https://doi.org/10.1007/978-3-642-44970-3_7
4. Neter, J., Kutner, M.H., Nachtsheim, C.J., Wasserman, W.: Applied Linear Statistical Models, vol. 4, p. 318. McGraw-Hill/Irwin, Boston/Chicago (1996)
5. Moving Average: What It Is and How to Calculate It, USA. Statics How To. http://www.statisticshowto.com/moving-average/
6. Xiong, Y.: Mixtures of ARMA Models for Model-Based Time Series Clustering, Hong Kong, p. 4 (2003)
7. Zhang, G.P.: Time Series Forecasting Using a Hybrid ARIMA. Elsevier, Amsterdam (2003)
8. Gardner, M.W., Dorling, S.R.: Artificial neural networks (the multilayer perceptron)—a review of applications in the atmospheric sciences. Atmos. Environ. 32(14–15), 2627–2636 (1998)
9. Meenakshi, R.S.: Efficient taxi dispatching system in distributed. In: International Conference on Information, Communication, Instrumentation and Control (ICICIC), Chennai, India, p. 6 (2017)
10. Aydin, O., Guldamlasioglu, S.: Using LSTM networks to predict engine condition on large scale data processing. In: 2017 4th International Conference on Electrical and Electronics Engineering, Ankara, Turkey, p. 5 (2017)
11. Toqu, F., Khouadjia, M.: Short & long-term forecasting of multimodal transport passenger. In: 2017 IEEE 20th International Conference on Intelligent Transportation Systems (ITSC), France, p. 7 (2017)
12. Shakya, S., Kern, M., Owusu, G., Chin, C.M.: Dynamic pricing with neural network demand models and evolutionary algorithms. In: Bramer, M., Petridis, M., Hopgood, A. (eds.) Research and Development in Intelligent Systems XXVII. SGAI 2010. Springer, London (2011). https://doi.org/10.1007/978-0-85729-130-1_16
13. Heaton, J.: Encog: library of interchangeable machine learning models for Java and C#. J. Mach. Learn. Res. 16, 1243–1247 (2015)

Workforce Rostering via Metaheuristics

Mary Dimitropoulaki[✉], Mathias Kern, Gilbert Owusu,
and Alistair McCormick

BT Research and Innovation, Ipswich, UK
{mary.dimitropoulaki,mathias.kern,gilbert.owusu,ali.mccormick}@bt.com

Abstract. Staff scheduling and planning in a cost effective manner has been a topic of scientific discussion for many years, driven by the need of many organisations to fully and effectively utilise their workforce to meet costumer demand and deliver service. Due to the varying nature of industry sectors, problems often require tailoring for particular business needs and types of work. This paper presents an overview of how a version of this problem was solved in a business with a large field workforce. The automation of this process has proved vital in ensuring that there is the right amount of resources rostered in on each day of the week, transforming a lengthy, manual procedure into an operation of a matter of seconds. The paper discusses how a Simulated Annealing approach was implemented, and provides a comparison of its performance versus a standard Hill Climber. We also include a detailed description of how rules and constraints were incorporated into the work, and what effect these had on rostered attendance.

Keywords: Rostering · Heuristic search · Industrial applications of AI

1 Introduction

An abundance of work has been undertaken in the area of automation and improvement of workforce rostering in areas such as call centres, health care systems, civic services & utilities and hospitality & tourism [8]. The diverse and complex dynamics of problems of this type mean that generalisation can prove difficult. Maximising operational effectiveness is known to lead to better customer experience and compliance to service level agreements. Prior to the automation of scheduling, one of the first steps to achieve this is to optimise resourcing and planning processes. Ensuring that there is a sufficient resource available on each day is key to successful field service management, and therefore the automation and optimisation of this process is essential. This work presents a solution to a rostering process problem of a large workforce of field resources via the use of metaheuristic methods.

The process of rostering resources is performed by a dedicated team and consists of the following manual steps, which can require days to complete:

- Create roster patterns

© Springer Nature Switzerland AG 2018
M. Bramer and M. Petridis (Eds.): SGAI-AI 2018, LNAI 11311, pp. 277–290, 2018.
https://doi.org/10.1007/978-3-030-04191-5_25

- Allocate resources to roster patterns
- Update allocation and implement roster assignments

These are building blocks of employee rostering, but the challenges occur with workload prediction, staffing requirements, shift design and allocation [15]. An important factor to note is that each business' operational requirements such as laws, planning periods and shift types can make this process very complex, and thus solutions ought to be tailored accordingly [15]. This paper will focus on assigning the ideal start week within their roster pattern for each resource. Rosters in this context are cyclical and we will be imposing a set of modifiable constraints (rules) with varying objectives. We are optimising the attendance across teams of approximately 100 to 300 field resources in a typical scenario. Roster patterns usually vary between 5 and 25 weeks in length, meaning each field resource could be on one of 5 to 25 positions within their pattern. This means there is a very large number of possible combinations of where the 100 to 300 resources are within their roster patterns. Over time attendance can become unbalanced, leaving some days with more field resources than needed and others with not enough. Shifting resources within their roster pattern will re-balance, but it is important to take as well into account the aim to minimise changes to individual resources and to ensure rules compliance.

The most studied and well-known rostering optimisation is the nurse rostering problem, which has been solved using many approaches and methods. Some of these are based on heuristics such as Tabu Search, Simulated Annealing and Genetic Algorithms [5]. A comparative study of solving the NRP performed by Kundu et al. [11] shows that constraints are best enforced through weightings, something which will be incorporated into our work and discussed in Sect. 1.1. They found that Simulated Annealing out-performed the Genetic Algorithm, with the most efficient roster being cyclic. In Hadwan and Ayob [10], we also see a similar approach in which shifts are created and then optimised via the use of Simulated Annealing with constraints introduced as weightings. A theoretical discussion can be found in Ernst et al. [8] who noted that the demands of different businesses result in different approaches when it comes to the automation of rostering. They discuss that the modules required to construct a roster vary from organisation to organisation, as some areas require demand modelling and others do not require task assignment. In our scenario task assignment cannot be done in advance, and thus after the roster design phase it is vital to assign the roster patterns to resources effectively. Once this stage has been completed, the best combination of start weeks for the field resources within their roster patterns is required for a balanced attendance. Scheduling and rostering in most cases are interrelated and a combined solution can be seen as more effective, with an example of this being achieved in [14] where this is applied to the driver rostering problem. When it comes to very large organisations, it is almost impossible to combine these two problems and thus these should be separated procedures. The sheer size of the workforce available in our scenario does not allow individual shift allocation, and further legal constrains and agreements limit the scope for regular changes of roster pattern. In our problem scenario, we consider the roster pattern of each resource as given and fixed but the actual position of each resource within their roster pattern can be changed, and our aim is to find the best current assignment of these positions to achieve the best overall attendance balance over a certain period into the future.

Airline crew rostering is another widely studied scheduling problem. This is an area in which we see most benefits in the automation of scheduling, with almost a \$50 million dollar cost saving per year for large airlines [1]. The most common methods rosters are assigned to crew is via bidline systems, personalised rostering or bidding systems. However many challenges remain unsolved such as crew pairing and fleet assignment [1]. Thiel [12] presents an interesting solution to crew pairing through team oriented rostering, a method which enhances team stability and team work quality, but the large amount of rosters and combinations were found to be major issues. In our case the same problems arise as human decision makers usually cannot deal with the amount of data available, and therefore a tool supporting such procedures is vital in more complex organisations [12]. Other public transport rostering has been studied in [4,7,9] in which we see applications in railway crew management, and in [14,16] where the driver rostering problem in public bus transportations is investigated.

1.1   Problem Overview

In this our problem scenario, we consider individual geographical areas which contain between 100 to 300 resources. Each of these geographical areas is divided into 4 to 10 sub-areas. The typical number of roster patterns used by the resources in each area can vary, but is typically below 15.

Roster patterns run over a given sequence of weeks. Upon the assignment of resources to a roster pattern, they will be given a start week number specifying their starting point within the roster pattern cycle. For example, a 13-week pattern means that if a resource starts working on week 9 of this pattern, they will continue working on week 10, 11, 12 and 13 followed by weeks 1 to 8. Afterwards they will repeat this cycle with weeks, 9, 10 and so on.

Roster patterns can also contain certain types of sub-cycles which determine the number of days worked in each week. For example, a resource could be on a 14 week roster pattern with 7 2-week sub-cycles, with the resource working 4 days in the first week and 5 days in the second week of each sub-cycle, i.e. working 9 days across each 2-week sub-cycle.

Over time, attendance across a longer time period can become unbalanced. For example over a 13-week period, one Saturday can see 40 working engineers while another Saturday can only have 25 rostered engineers. These different Saturday starting positions would pose a serious challenge for the operational teams, and a more stable figure of approximately 33 engineers each Saturday would be beneficial. Such imbalances are driven by resources leaving and joining, and by moving to different roster patterns. Proportionally, such imbalances can be even higher when looking at particular sub-areas or certain skilled cohorts of resources.

We have developed an approach, and tool, to aid the process of rostering in resources in order to balance attendance (a) at the overall area level and (b) also within certain sub-area and skill. The ultimate aim is to keep the variation of resource attendance seen across all Mondays over a certain future time period to a minimum, and Tuesdays, and Wednesdays, and so on.

As mentioned previously, we impose a set of constrains when searching for the optimal combination of roster start weeks:

(A) Hard Constraints
  - Optimise attendance at skill & sub-area level by grouping resources by this criteria.
  - Resources can only move to weeks that satisfy the completion of the sub-cycles. If a resource is currently on a 4-day week in their sub-cycle, we can only move them to another 4-day week of a different sub-cycle.
  - A specified gap between working Saturdays must be ensured.
  - Restrict percentage of resources allowed to change start weeks in order to minimise disruption and impact on their schedules.

(B) Soft Constraints[1]
  - We group engineers by skill & sub-area to ensure optimisation both for the overall area and across these lower level cohorts, and use weights to determine which groups to focus on.
  - Days like Saturdays are often more volatile due to the smaller number of resources working. We thus prefer to see Saturdays more optimised, which is ensured by a higher weighting of the Saturday resource balance compared to other weekdays.

(C) Cost function[2]
  The measure of attendance is given by the difference between the minimum and maximum number of employees attending on a single weekday over the span of all weeks in the roster pattern (e.g. all Mondays). From now on this will be referred to as the **range**, and so our main goal is to minimise the range for every day of the week.
  Assume we have an attendance matrix, A, of dimension $n \times 7$, where the rows, i, represent the week numbers and the columns, j, represent the days. This matrix is represented as

$$A = \begin{pmatrix} a_{11} & a_{12} & \cdots & a_{17} \\ a_{21} & a_{22} & \cdots & a_{27} \\ \vdots & \vdots & \ddots & \vdots \\ a_{n1} & a_{n2} & \cdots & a_{n7} \end{pmatrix}. \tag{1}$$

  We take the min A and max A for each column j, $1 \leq j \leq 7$, to calculate the relativity factor between these two values. This would be given by

$$\frac{\text{Range}_j}{\max_j A} = \frac{\max_j A - \min_j A}{\max_j A},$$

---

[1] Emphasis on specific areas to ensure targeted optimisation through the use of penalties/weights.

[2] The cost function is dependant on the different types of soft constraints.

and so for example on a weekday where we have 60 as the maximum number of resources and 50 as the minimum, the relativity would be 16%. The score for each group of employees is given by

$$cost = \sum_{1 \leq j \leq 7} w_j \left(\frac{\text{Range}_j}{\max_j \mathbf{A}} \right)^2, \tag{2}$$

in which the relativity has been squared, resulting in smoother range values when optimising. w_j are weekday-specific weights.

The overall cost function is then given by the sum of all the scores,

$$Overall \; group \; cost = \sum_{i=1}^{G} \left(cost_{group_i} \right), \tag{3}$$

where G is the number of resource groups, or cohorts.

As mentioned previously, we have to account for volatile weekdays such as Saturdays where the number of attending resources is significantly less than on other days of the week, resulting in a higher relativity factor. To prevent the score from being affected by the larger relativity, we multiply the cost function by a penalty/weight for each day of the week.[3] For example, we can use an attendance weight vector like $w = (1, 1, 1, 1, 1, 10, 10)$ to focus particularly on minimising Saturday and Sunday ranges.

The next step is to split this amongst the resource groups or cohorts. Recall, we have a single group corresponding to the attendance of all resources across the entire area and groups/cohorts consisting of resources sharing the same sub-area and/or skill level. In order to ensure well-balanced optimisation of ranges overall and within the smaller groups, we weigh the impacts of these two elements differently. We have achieved good results with a 40% weight for the optimisation across the overall areas and a 60% weight for optimising the smaller resource cohorts.

2   Methodology

The type of optimisation problem discussed in this paper is combinatorial as there is a finite set of solutions. Due to the size of the solution space it is not possible to search it exhaustively, and instead we are searching for good solutions close to the maximum fitness in the solution space. We have implement and tested two different techniques, Hill Climbing and Simulated Annealing. Heuristic approaches have been popular when it comes to crew rostering and planning, such as in [2,3,13]. As previously mentioned and commonly discussed in the literature, organisations have different requirements and hence a unique implementation is often necessary for the specific problem scenario.

---

[3] For example, a range of 10 on Saturday should not be considered the same as a range of 10 on any other day of the week due to the smaller number of attending resources.

2.1   Simulated Annealing

Simulated annealing is a widely used optimisation method derived from statistical thermodynamics. Annealing is the process of heating metals beyond melting point and then by cooling it slowly until solidified into a crystalline structure [6].

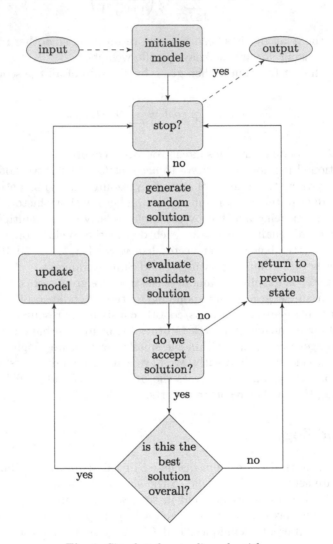

Fig. 1. Simulated annealing algorithm

An overview of the algorithm used in this tool is shown in Fig. 1. We start the process by initialising the model using attendance data, e.g. a 13-week attendance period for all resources starting from a specified date. We build this attendance picture both overall for all resources and for each individual group/cohort of resources. We evaluate the fitness of the current solution, f_c, and then choose a non-fixed[4] resource at random to set their start week to a random week[5]. Let f_n denote the value of the new fitness. Let s and s^* denote the current and neighbouring state/solution, respectively. The acceptance of states depends on the value of the new fitness given after evaluation, but also the *acceptance probability*, a function obtained through

$$P(f_n, f_c, T) = e^{\frac{f_c - f_n}{T}}, \tag{4}$$

where T denotes the temperature of the system, a global time-varying parameter used as a stopping condition. Stopping conditions in simulated annealing depend on the *cooling schedule* implemented.

In order to gain a deeper understanding as to how simulated annealing algorithms are formed, we will discuss the physical interpretation of this process. If $f_n(s^*)$ and $f_c(s)$ are the "internal energies" of each state, these are equivalent to the energies of a physical system. Ultimately, we wish to find the minimum $f_n(s^*)$ of the system. We see in Eq. 4 that the acceptance probability P depends on both energies and the temperature T. We require P to always be positive, hence the method does not get stuck in a local minimum that is worse than the global one. When $T \to 0$,

$$P(f_n, f_c, T) \begin{cases} \to 0, & \text{for } f_n(s^*) > f_c(s) \\ > 0, & \text{otherwise} \end{cases}$$

Hence, for sufficiently small T, the system increasingly favours moves that minimise the energy function and avoids moves that increase this. This is where the cooling schedule becomes important to the formulation of this method. A cooling schedule mainly depends on the cooling rate, which should be low enough for the probability distribution to always be near equilibrium. Simulated annealing is used to solve a wide range of problems and thus cooling schedules tend to be unique and tailored for each requirement.

The cooling schedule in our implementation starts with an initial temperature of $T_0 = 1$. After each iteration we decrease it by multiplying with a cooling rate, $c = 0.99995$ (i.e. $T = T \cdot c$) while $T > 0.01$. This results in approximately 92,101 iterations.

Note that, due to the fitness function described in Eq. 2, the highest fitness/internal energy we can obtain is 0. To account for this fact Eq. 4 is replaced with

$$P(f_n, f_c, T) = e^{\frac{f_n - f_c}{T}}. \tag{5}$$

This means that we are looking for the maximum energy f_n our system can achieve and so for P to be positive, $f_n(s^*) < f_c(s)$.

For each T we generate a random number $r \in [0, 1]$, and so solutions only get accepted if $P > r$ or $f_n > f_c$.

---

[4] A "fixed" resource simply means that they cannot change start week.

[5] Note, some resources are only allowed certain start weeks due to constraints related to factors such as sub-cycles and consecutive Saturdays.

Now let f_o be the best score found over all iterations. If $f_n > f_o$, we set $f_o = f_n$ and update the attendance by adding the new start week for the resource chosen at random. If solutions do not get accepted, i.e. $f_n \leq f_o$, we return to previous state and generate another random solution, until temperature reaches the minimum value set.

In Fig. 2 we see how the cooling rates affect the value of the fitness. As expected, for larger cooling rates we see the value of the maximum fitness converging to zero. This is due to the fact that for larger cooling rates, the temperature takes longer to converge to the value of 0.01 (i.e. the minimum temperature of the system chosen and thus the stopping condition) and so the number of iterations increases.

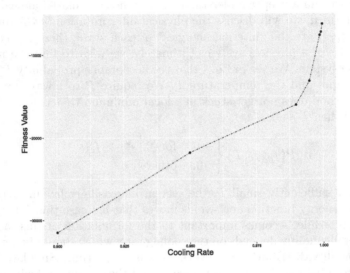

Fig. 2. Maximum fitness values against different cooling rates for $T_0 = 1$ and $T_{min} = 0.01$.

By looking at the best fitness achieved for each iteration we see that f_o starts converging to zero above 20,000 iterations which can be observed in Fig. 3. We also note that between ≈5,000 and ≈20,000 iterations, there is no significantly better solution found and thus the fitness value stops increasing. Note that the example used is on a specific set of test data, but we have observed the same general behaviour for a number of test scenarios.

3   Results

As mentioned previously, to solve this problem we initially implemented a Hill Climbing technique. In this section we discuss and compare the effectiveness of both the basic Hill Climber and the Simulated Annealing approach. We will also be observing how different constraints affect the results and discuss what

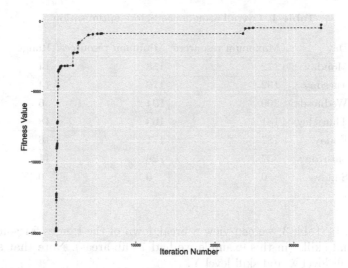

Fig. 3. Best overall fitness, f_o, against iteration numbers with $T_0 = 1$, $T_{min} = 0.01$ and $c = 0.99995$.

compromises, or choices, one can make when addressing a problem of such complexity.

3.1 Hill Climber vs Simulated Annealing

Hill Climbing is a basic local search optimisation technique: we look for the best solution in the neighbourhood of solutions similar to the current one, and do not accept any move that worsens the overall fitness (in contrast to Simulated Annealing). While the first run of the Hill Climber started from the original solution, we allowed for for a number of randomised restarts thereafter.

In general, we see that both methods significantly optimise, i.e. balance, resource attendance. For testing purposes, we will examine how these methods compare for a particular problem scenario, based on including the following constraints:

- Engineers are grouped by sub-area and skill, with appropriate weighting added (i.e. 60% of weight value split within groups and 40% for the overall area).
- Saturdays are weighted with a penalty ×10.
- Potential new start weeks obey sub-cycle rules.

By running the tool for the overall area, we get attendance results that look like the example shown in Table 1. We see the maximum & minimum number of resources attending on each day of the week over a certain time period, as well as their difference, the range. Note that, on Saturday we see a much lower attendance, and so a range of 11 cannot be considered the same as a range of 14

Table 1. Overall attendance before optimisation.

Day	Maximum resources	Minimum resources	Range
Monday	172	158	14
Tuesday	192	178	14
Wednesday	200	194	6
Thursday	181	163	18
Friday	187	171	16
Saturday	37	26	11
Sunday	0	0	0

on Monday. In Table 3, we can view a breakdown of the ranges for some of the sub-areas and skills (in this example we had 7 sub-areas). Note that skills are split into skill level X and skill level Y.

Table 2. Optimised ranges for the overall area produced by Simulated Annealing and the Hill Climber.

Day	Simulated Annealing	Hill Climber
Monday	3	4
Tuesday	5	6
Wednesday	3	4
Thursday	2	5
Friday	2	4
Saturday	1	1
Sunday	0	0

A good way to view the results after running the algorithm is to look at the new ranges across the weekdays. In Table 2, we see the improved ranges for the overall domain, and corresponding views exist for the smaller resource groups determined by sub-area and/or skill. Both the Hill Climber and Simulated Annealing produce good results in our example scenario in the overall domain, but especially so at individual skills and work areas (see Table 3). Simulated Annealing is generally more effective, as our experiments over a larger number of problem scenarios have shown, in particular when more constraints were added. It is well known that Hill Climbers can get more easily stuck in a local optimum, whereas the Simulated Annealing approach allows for escaping such local optima.

In Table 3, we see the optimised ranges in the example sub-areas and skill groups after both techniques, indicating that grouping by skill and sub-area optimises both sub-area and skills. Simulated Annealing with constraints will be discussed in more detail in the next section.

Table 3. Ranges pre-optimisation and after optimisation using Simulated Annealing and Hill Climbing in sub-areas and skills.

Day	Sub-area A			Sub-area B			Skill level X			Skill level Y		
	Pre	SA	HC	Pre	SA	HC	Pre	SA	HC	Pre	SA	HC
Monday	5	3	4	5	3	4	8	3	4	7	3	3
Tuesday	4	4	5	2	3	5	7	4	6	5	3	3
Wednesday	2	1	2	1	2	2	6	2	2	5	3	3
Thursday	5	4	6	3	5	3	10	2	5	8	2	3
Friday	5	5	5	4	3	4	11	3	3	8	2	4
Saturday	4	2	6	4	3	3	8	1	1	6	1	1
Sunday	0	0	0	0	0	0	0	0	0	0	0	0

By comparing the best fitness values of the two algorithms for 20 different geographical areas, i.e. problem instances, as shown in Fig. 4, we see that Simulated Annealing produces better scores in the majority of scenarios. The two cases in which this was not true, the randomised restarts of the HC allowed it to start from more promising initial solutions. Given more time, we expect the SA

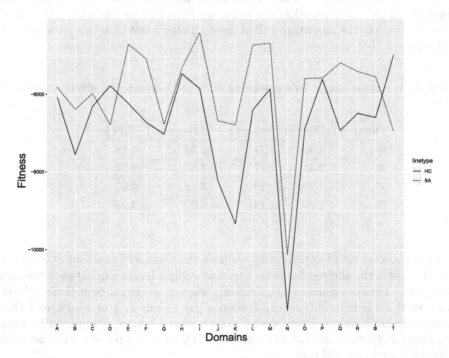

Fig. 4. Best overall fitness values produced for 20 domains by simulated annealing and hill climbing.

algorithm to match or better the HC solutions in these scenarios as well, however our SA solution was balanced for both speed and solution quality. Therefore we will be focusing on the SA approach going forward.

3.2   Optimising with Constraints

In this section we will discuss the results produced by the Simulated Annealing approach when applying the constraints discussed in Sect. 1.1. One of the hard constraints is that a break between working Saturdays must be enforced, ensuring a fair distribution of working Saturdays across all resources. In other words, roster week changes for an individual resource must not result in a resource working on a Saturday too soon after the previous working Saturday. We have also studied how to set the proportion of engineers for which the starting week can be changed, and how low this proportion can be before solution quality suffers significantly. For example, a 40% threshold means that no more than 40% of engineers can change start week.

In our first set of experiments, we have averaged results over 20 scenarios (geographical areas). We vary the aforementioned threshold values while maintaining a Saturday gap of 2 weeks (i.e. no work on two consecutive Saturdays). Table 4 shows that ranges improve - reduce - significantly from a threshold value of 10% to a value of 30%, but further reductions are rather more limited for larger thresholds. For practical purposes, we therefore recommend a threshold value of 30%, i.e. the algorithm will at most change 3 out of 10 resource's roster pattern week.

Table 4. Average of ranges for a number of skills and sub-areas for different threshold values.

Threshold	Domain	Sub-area A	Sub-area B	Skill level Y
10	4.00	3.71	4.57	5.58
30	2.43	2.17	4.57	4.57
50	2.29	2.14	3.42	3.85
70	2.29	2.14	3.7	4.28

In our second set of experiments, we keep the threshold constant at 30% but vary the size of the allowed Saturday gap. Enforcing a larger gap between working Saturdays - 3 weeks - leads to a significantly worse average range at domain level. However there is little difference between a gap of one or two weeks, and thus we recommend a value of two weeks, ensuring no resource is required to work two consecutive Saturdays at the point when the new improved overall solution is implemented (see Table 5).

Table 5. Average of ranges for a number of skills and work areas for different Saturday gap values.

Saturday gap	Domain
1 week	2.42
2 weeks	2.43
3 weeks	3.71

4 Discussion

In this paper, we introduced and described a rostering problem for a large workforce of field resources, discussed two solution techniques - a Hill Climber and a Simulated Annealing approach, and analysed and compared their performance. It is vital to understand and handle the specific business requirements in order to meaningfully address such real-life problem scenarios. Both algorithms consistently improved the initial roster setup in all test scenarios, and Simulated Annealing produced superior results over the more basic Hill Climber in the majority of cases. Furthermore, we showed how the amount of necessary (roster pattern week) changes can be limited without impacting the quality of the overall solution too much, thereby striking a balance between the need of the business to find better roster setups and the desire of individual field resources for minimal disruption.

The output of our approach has been used to improve the roster pattern setup across a large workforce of several thousand field resources. As a result, a more stable basic resource attendance has been achieved, meaning the fluctuations in attendance from one week to the next have been reduced. The greatest impact has been seen on Saturdays where we now see more similar numbers of available resources each week, rather than alternating weeks of too much or too little resource. This, in turn, has positively impacted - simplified - the resource planning process, and the need to cover supply shortages with overtime has diminished.

Going forward, we are planning to focus our research and development efforts on four key areas. Firstly, we want to fully automate the optimisation process so that it runs regularly and automatically flags if the quality of the current roster setup has declined too much. Secondly, we would like to strengthen the fairness aspect of our approach, ensuring that changes to roster pattern start weeks are shared equally among field resources over a longer period. Thirdly, we want to extend our approach from changing the start week within a fixed roster pattern per resource to an approach where we can also consider changing the roster pattern itself for a resource. And finally, we would like to further assess the performance of the chosen Simulating Annealing solution by comparing it to more alternatives such a Genetic Algorithm (GA) and Greedy Randomized Adaptive Search Procedure (GRASP) approaches. All four developments will enhance the applicability of our proposed solution in real-life scenarios.

References

1. Barnhart, C., Cohn, A.M., Johnson, E.L., Klabjan, D., Nemhauser, G.L., Vance, P.H.: Airline crew scheduling. In: Hall, R.W. (ed.) Handbook of Transportation Science. International Series in Operations Research & Management Science, vol. 56, pp. 517–560. Springer, US (2003). https://doi.org/10.1007/0-306-48058-1_14
2. Brusco, M.J., Jacobs, L.W.: A simulated annealing approach to the cyclic staff-scheduling problem. Nav. Res. Logist. (NRL) **40**(1), 69–84 (1993)
3. Burns, A., Hayes, N., Richardson, M.F.: Generating feasible cyclic schedules. Control Eng. Pract. **3**(2), 151–162 (1995)
4. Caprara, A., Fischetti, M., Toth, P., Vigo, D., Guida, P.L.: Algorithms for railway crew management. Math. Program. **79**, 125–141 (1997)
5. Cheang, B., Li, H., Lim, A., Rodrigues, B.: Nurse rostering problems - a bibliographic survey. Eur. J. Oper. Res. **151**(3), 447–460 (2003)
6. Du, K.L., Swamy, M.N.S.: Search and Optimization by Metaheuristics: Techniques and Algorithms Inspired by Nature. Birkhäuser, Basel (2016)
7. Ernst, A., Krishnamoorthy, M., Dowling, D.: Train crew rostering using simulated annealing. In: Caccetta, L., Teo, K.L., Sieq, P.F., Leung, Y.H., Jennings, L.S., Rehbock, V. (eds.) Proceedings of International Conference on Optimisation Techniques and Applications, pp. 859–866 (1998)
8. Ernst, A.T., Jiang, H., Krishnamoorthy, M., Sier, D.: Staff scheduling and rostering: a review of applications, methods and models. Eur. J. Oper. Res. **153**(1), 3–27 (2004)
9. Gonçalves, R., Gomide, F., Lagrimante, R.: Methodology and algorithms for railway crew management. IFAC Proc. Vol. **33**(9), 323–328 (2000)
10. Hadwan, M., Ayob, M.: A constructive shift patterns approach with simulated annealing for nurse rostering problem. Proceedings of 2010 International Symposium on Information Technology - Visual Informatics, ITSim 2010, p. 1 (2010)
11. Kundu, S., Mahato, M., Mahanty, B., Acharyya, S.: Comparative performance of simulated annealing and genetic algorithm in solving nurse scheduling problem. In: Proceedings of the International MultiConference of Engineers and Computer Scientists, p. 1 (2008)
12. Thiel, M.P.: Team-oriented airline crew scheduling and rostering: problem description, solution approaches, and decision support. Ph.D. thesis, Faculty of Business Administration and Economics at the University of Paderborn, Germany (2005)
13. Thompson, G.M.: A simulated annealing heuristic for shift scheduling using non-continuously available employees. Comput. Oper. Res. **23**(3), 275–288 (1996)
14. Valdes, V.A.V.: Integrating crew scheduling and rostering problems. Ph.D. thesis, Alma Mater Studiorum Universita di Bologna, Italy (2010)
15. Voudouris, C., Owusu, G., Dorne, R., Lesaint, D.: Service Chain Management: Technology Innovation for the Service Business. Springer, Heidelberg (2008). https://doi.org/10.1007/978-3-540-75504-3
16. Xie, L., Kliewer, N., Suhl, L.: Integrated driver rostering problem in public bus transit. Procedia Soc. Behav. Sci. **54**, 656–665 (2012)

Planning and Scheduling in Action

Incorporating Risk in Field Services Operational Planning Process

Chenlu Ji[1]([⊠]), Rupal Mandania[1], Jiyin Liu[1] ⓘ, Anne Liret[2] ⓘ,
and Mathias Kern[3]

[1] Loughborough University, Loughborough LE11 3TU, UK
c.ji2@lboro.ac.uk
[2] BT France, Paris, France
[3] British Telecommunications, London, UK

Abstract. This paper presents a model for the risk minimisation objective in the Stochastic Vehicle Routing Problem (SVRP). In the studied variant of SVRP, service times and travel times are subject to stochastic events, and a time window is constraining the start time for service task. Required skill levels and task priorities increase the complexity of this problem. Most previous research uses a chance-constrained approach to the problem and their objectives are related to traditional routing costs whilst a different approach was taken in this paper. The risk of missing a task is defined as the probability that the technician assigned to the task arrives at the customer site later than the time window. The problem studied in this paper is to generate a schedule that minimises the maximum of risks and sum of risks over all the tasks considering the effect of skill levels and task priorities. The stochastic duration of each task is supposed to follow a known normal distribution. However, the distribution of the start time of the service at a customer site will not be normally distributed due to time window constraints. A method is proposed and tested to approximate the start time distribution as normal. Moreover, a linear model can be obtained assuming identical variance of task durations. Additionally Simulated Annealing method was applied to solve the problem. Results of this work have been applied to an industrial case of SVRP where field engineering individuals drive to customer sites to provide time-constrained services. This original approach gives a robust schedule and allows organisations to pay more attention to increasing customer satisfaction and become more competitive in the market.

Keywords: Vehicle routing with time windows
Stochastic service time and travel time · Risk minimisation

1 Introduction

Increasing customer satisfaction is always an exciting topic for managers and re-searchers in order to build a more customer-oriented business. It is in particular true when planning geographically distributed services on customer sites. Therefore, the consideration of visit time windows, the stochastic service time and travel time in the workforce scheduling and vehicle routing problems (VRP) becomes crucial for service providing organisations [1]. Specifically, in the studied application domain, a start-of-day

© Springer Nature Switzerland AG 2018
M. Bramer and M. Petridis (Eds.): SGAI-AI 2018, LNAI 11311, pp. 293–307, 2018.
https://doi.org/10.1007/978-3-030-04191-5_26

planned tour of visits is created overnight, and then updated throughout the day as more and new information becomes available. The start-of-day schedule has to make certain assumptions such as technician availability, travel times, how long certain engineering tasks will take, whether technicians will be able to successfully complete work or whether they have to come back again, how much additional work will arrive during the day, and so on [2]. In terms of traffic networks, the travel time varies due to traffic congestion especially in big cities, which affects not only the service quality but also the air pollution [3].

The environment in which services need to be delivered is inherently dynamic and subject to disruption in the workstack estimates, in the execution of jobs by workforce as well as the travel conditions [4, 5]. Our research studies how elements of the risk can be incorporated into the scheduling approach, i.e., how the scheduling can manage and address the aforementioned sources of the risk to build both an optimal but also a robust schedule that minimises the risks and increases the likelihood of successful service delivery. A better schedule can help to improve the level of customer satisfaction as well as the work efficiency of technicians. Consequently, the company may get more customers and become more competitive in the market.

This research focuses on the Stochastic Vehicle Routing Problem (SVRP), in which technicians drive to customer sites to provide services. In the problem, we assume that service times and travel times are stochastic, and a time window is associated with the start time of the service.

Most previous relevant researches on VRP consider time windows and stochastic demands, [6–12] use a chance-constrained approach to the problem. Limited researches [1, 3, 5, 13] investigate the routing problem with time windows and stochastic travel time. We note that in these approaches, the objectives of the problem are related to traditional routing costs. In this paper, we introduce a new risk model that can be incorporated into the set of objectives to be minimised during the optimisation process.

In this paper, we present an application of the proposed model to a real scheduling problem in the field-engineering-service world. In that context, technicians offer services to customers, associating with a time window to each visit, and services are subject to disturbance in delivery causing the actual service time to be inherently stochastic, as well as the travel time to be uncertain. Section 2 gives a short description about the risk according to our previous research; while in Sect. 3, a complicated estimation of risks is proposed in order to prove that the normal distribution can be used in the risk calculation. In Sect. 4 a mathematical model is constructed by considering risks in the objective and can be solved by an exact method. Due to the complexity of the problem, heuristic methods show advantages while solving massive size problems. Thus Sect. 5 gives several a heuristic method – Simulated Annealing method – for this problem, followed by some results and discussions in Sect. 6.

2   Risk Definition

The risk in the problem is defined as the probability that the arrival time is after the upper limit of the time window [14]. More specifically, as it is shown in the Fig. 1, given a schedule, with a sequence of tasks $\{i_1, i_2, i_3, \cdots\}$ allocated to technician k,

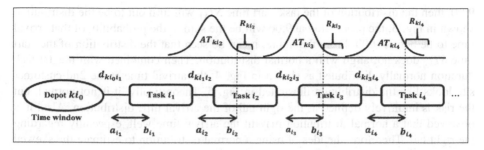

Fig. 1. Description of risks

$T_1, T_2, T_3\ldots$ are the task duration times, $d_{ki_0i_1}$ is the travel time from the depot of technician k to his first task, $d_{ki_1i_2}, d_{ki_2i_3}, d_{ki_3i_4}$ are the travel times between tasks $(e.g., d_{ki_1i_2}$ from 1st task to 2nd task). Suppose the arrival time follows a normal distribution, then we define the risk of missing the appointment for task i, R_{ki}, as the probability of the arrival time AT_{ki} being later than the upper limit of the time window b_i. The stochasticity of the arrival time arises from the uncertainty of the travel time and task duration. Moreover, an important property is that the risk increases simultaneously as it propagates for each technician, it is reasonable because the uncertainty aggregates as there is more uncertainty of the travel time and task time. In addition, from a previous study [14], the mathematical expression of risks can be derived as

$$R_{ki_n} = P(AT_{ki_n} > b_{i_n}) = 1 - \int \cdots \int_D \prod_{l=1}^{n-1} f_{ki_l}(X_l)dX_1dX_2\cdots dX_{n-1}, \quad (1)$$

where X_1 denotes the arrival time $AT_{ki_2}, X_l = \delta_{ki_l} + d_{ki_li_{l+1}}$ for $l \geq 2$, $f_{ki_l}(X_l)$ represents the probability density function of X_l, and $D = \{(X_1, \ldots, X_{n-1}) :$

$$\sum_{l=1}^{n-1} X_l \leq b_{i_n}, \sum_{l=2}^{n-1} X_l \leq b_{i_n} - a_{i_2}, \sum_{l=3}^{n-1} X_l \leq b_{i_n} - a_{i_3}, \ldots, X_{n-1} \leq b_{i_n} - a_{i_{n-1}}\}.$$

3 Estimate of Risks

To begin with, by analysing 72114 task data over a 12 month period [15], according to the task types that have a large number of samples, we found that the distributions of the actual time spent on the task, for each task type mostly are normally distributed or follow gamma distributions. Therefore, it is reasonable for us to use a normal distribution to calculate risks.

In the problem, due to the effect of time windows, technicians have to start work after the lower limit of the time window, so the distribution of the start time will be of the format in Fig. 3, which is not a normal distribution shape. More specifically, given a technician, suppose the arrival time at his/her 1st customer service spot AT_{k1} follows the normal distribution in Fig. 2 and the lower bound of the task time window a_1 is

9:00, then the distribution of the task start time ST_{k1} will turn out to be the distribution shown in Fig. 3, the probability at 9:00 will be the sum of the probability of that arrival time to be before 9:00. From the figure, it can be seen that the distribution of the start time ST_{k1} does not align with a normal distribution. Then combined with the 1st task duration normally distributed as shown in Fig. 4, the arrival time at the 2nd customer site looks like the distribution illustrated in Fig. 5. Theoretically, it is not normal, but the risk is intuitively defined as the right tail of the arrival time distribution. Also, it is observed that a normal distribution may fit the arrival time well, especially regarding the right tail. Therefore, the idea of using a normal distribution to estimate the skewed start time distribution comes naturally.

Furthermore, it is easy to conclude that the closer the average arrival time at the 1st customer site μ is to the lower limit of 1st task time window a_1, the more the start time distribution changes. From the Fig. 6, it is easy to observe that if the time window $a_1 = \mu - 2\sigma$, where σ is the standard deviation of the arrival time at the 1st customer site, the effect of the time window is small as shown in (b), compared to the original arrival time distribution shown in (a). In terms of the time window closer to the average arrival time, such as $a_1 = \mu - 0.5\sigma$, the effect of the time window is shown in Fig. 6(c), the shape of the start time is completely different from the arrival time. As for the scenario where the mean of the arrival time μ is much earlier than the lower limit of

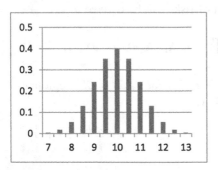

Fig. 2. Arrival time

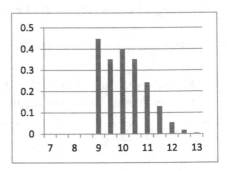

Fig. 3. Start time

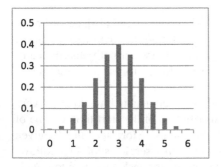

Fig. 4. Work time

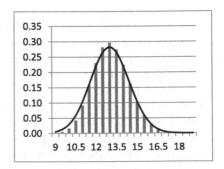

Fig. 5. Arrival time at the next task

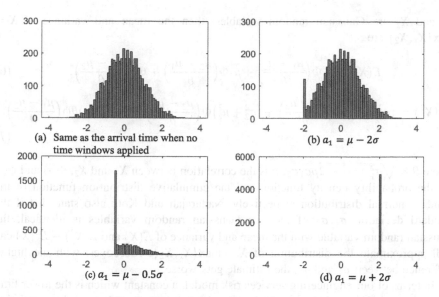

Fig. 6. Time window effect on the start time

time window a_1, i.e., $a_1 = \mu + 2\sigma$, the task is likely to start at time a_1 with a high probability so that the variance of the arrival time can be omitted.

Therefore, the estimation consists of three scenarios. To start with, if the mean μ of the arrival time AT_1 is much later than a_1, i.e., $a_1 \in [\mu - 3\sigma, \mu - \sigma)$, it is reasonable to use the normal distribution estimation model I below for the arrival time AT_2 that

$$\mu(AT_2) = \mu(ST_1) + \mu(TT_1) \tag{2}$$

$$\sigma^2(AT_2) = \sigma^2(ST_1) + \sigma^2(TT_1), \tag{3}$$

where TT_1 is the operation time of the 1st task plus the travel time from the 1st task to the 2nd task. In this scenario, the effect of the time window is so little that can be ignored. In contrast, if the mean μ of the arrival time is much earlier than a_1, i.e., $a_1 \in (\mu + \sigma, \mu + 3\sigma]$, which is shown in the example of the Fig. 6(d), the variance of the start time can be ignored because of the long waiting time till a_1. Then the estimation model II for the arrival time AT_2 is as below

$$\mu(AT_2) = a_1 + \mu(TT_1) \tag{4}$$

$$\sigma^2(AT_2) = \sigma^2(TT_1). \tag{5}$$

Then for the complicated scenario where $a_1 \in [\mu - \sigma, \mu + \sigma]$, the calculation may follow the approach from Madarajah and Kotz [15] who investigated the exact distribution of the maximum and minimum of two Gaussian random variables. Suppose

X_1 and X_2 are Gaussian random variables, then the mean and variance of $X = \max\{X_1, X_2\}$ are

$$E(X) = \mu_1 \Phi\left(\frac{\mu_1 - \mu_2}{\theta}\right) + \mu_2 \Phi\left(\frac{\mu_2 - \mu_1}{\theta}\right) + \theta\phi\left(\frac{\mu_1 - \mu_2}{\theta}\right), \tag{6}$$

$$E(X^2) = (\sigma_1^2 + \mu_1^2)\Phi\left(\frac{\mu_1 - \mu_2}{\theta}\right) + (\sigma_2^2 + \mu_2^2)\Phi\left(\frac{\mu_2 - \mu_1}{\theta}\right) + (\mu_1 + \mu_2)\theta\phi\left(\frac{\mu_1 - \mu_2}{\theta}\right), \tag{7}$$

where $\theta = \sqrt{\sigma_1^2 + \sigma_2^2 - 2\rho\sigma_1\sigma_2}$, ρ is the correlation between X_1 and X_2, $\Phi(\cdot)$ and $\phi(\cdot)$ are the probability density function and the cumulative distribution function of the standard normal distribution respectively. Nadarajah and Kotz also state that if the standard deviation σ_1, σ_2 of the two Gaussian random variables is identical, the Gaussian random variable with the mean and variance of $E(X)$ and $E(X^2) - E^2(X)$ can well approximate the distribution of $X = \max\{X_1, X_2\}$. Moreover, with the higher difference between σ_1 and σ_2, the estimate gets worse.

In terms of our engineering services risk model, a constant which is the lower limit of the time window replaces one of the Gaussian random variables and the correlation ρ is set to $0 (\rho = 0)$. Therefore the parameters of the normal distribution estimation for $ST_1 = \max\{AT_1, a_1\}$ are

$$E(ST_1) = \mu_1 \Phi\left(\frac{\mu_1 - a_1}{\sigma_1}\right) + a_1 \Phi\left(\frac{a_1 - \mu_1}{\sigma_1}\right) + \sigma_1\phi\left(\frac{\mu_1 - a_1}{\sigma_1}\right), \tag{8}$$

$$E(ST_1^2) = (\sigma_1^2 + \mu_1^2)\Phi\left(\frac{\mu_1 - a_1}{\sigma_1}\right) + a_1^2\Phi\left(\frac{a_1 - \mu_1}{\sigma_1}\right) + (\mu_1 + a_1)\sigma_1\phi\left(\frac{\mu_1 - a_1}{\sigma_1}\right), \tag{9}$$

where μ_1 and σ_1 are the mean and standard deviation of the arrival time AT_1. Then the estimated risk of the 2nd task is obtained via the ST_1 estimation and the normal distribution of the mixed time TT_1. Thus the normal distribution estimation model III for the arrival time AT_2 is as below

$$\mu(AT_2) = E(ST_1) + \mu(TT_1) \tag{10}$$

$$\sigma^2(AT_2) = E(ST_1^2) - E^2(ST_1) + \sigma^2(TT_1). \tag{11}$$

If we suppose that

$$error = real\ risk - estimate\ risk,$$

the estimation gives relative small error terms based on a 5000-sample test, which are shown in Fig. 7, in which the vertical axis represents the error value according to the number codes of 5000 samples shown in the horizontal axis (Fig. 7).

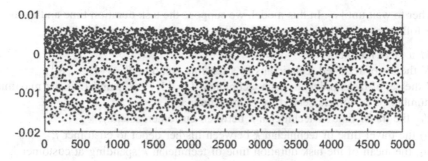

Fig. 7. Error of the estimation model

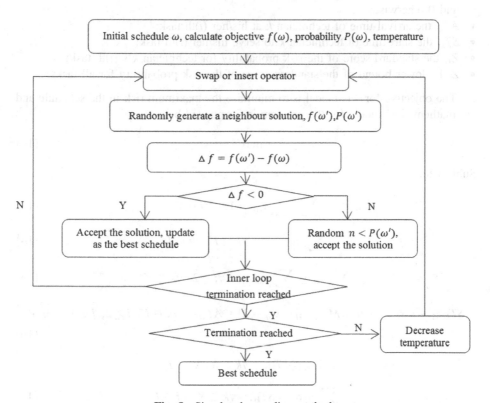

Fig. 8. Simulated annealing method

4 Mathematical Model

Let $G = (V, A)$ be a complete graph, where $V = V_0 \cup V_c$, and $V_c = \{1, \ldots, N\}$ is a set of vertices which denote customer locations and $A = \{(l, j) : l, j \in V_c, l \neq j\}$ is a set of arcs. While $V_0 = \{D_1, D_2, \ldots, D_k\}$ represents the depots. Each customer $j \in V_c$ has a time window $[a_j, b_j]$. If the technician arrives at customer j before a_j, it is necessary for him/her to wait until a_j. In this model, we suppose the task duration time and the travel time follow normal distributions. The following notations are defined:

- M a large number;
- K the set of required technicians in a feasible solution $K = \{1, \ldots, K\}$;
- I the set of tasks order for each technician, $I = \{1, \ldots, C\}$ and C is the maximum number of customers served by each technician;
- d_{klj} the travel time of technician k between customers l and j;
- t_{kj} the travel time of technician k between his/her depot to customer j;
- μ_{kj} the mean of the task duration time of technician k spending at customer j;
- σ^2 the variance of the task duration time, suppose it is identical for all tasks;
- x_{kij} a binary variable equal to 1 if technician k serves customer j as his/her (i)th task and 0 otherwise;
- AT_{ki} the arrival time of technician k at his/her (i)th task;
- ST_{ki} the start time of technician k to serve his/her (i)th task;
- Z_{ki} the standard score of the risk probability for technician k's (i)th task;
- Z the lower bound of the standard score of the risk probability for all tasks.

The objective for this model is to minimise the maximum risk in the schedule and the mathematical model for the problem is formulated below:

$$\max Z \tag{12}$$

Subject to:

$$\sum_k \sum_i x_{kij} = 1, \quad \forall j \in V \tag{13}$$

$$\sum_j x_{kij} \leq 1, \quad \forall k \in K, \, \forall i \in I \tag{14}$$

$$\sum_j x_{kij} \leq \sum_j x_{ki-1j}, \quad \forall i \geq 2, \, \forall k \in K \tag{15}$$

$$ST_{ki-1} + \mu_l x_{ki-1l} + t_{lj} + M\left(x_{ki-1l} + x_{kij} - 2\right) \leq AT_{ki}, \quad \forall k \in K, \, i \geq 2, \, j \in V, \, l \in V \tag{16}$$

$$AT_{ki} \leq ST_{ki}, \quad \forall k \in K, \, \forall i \in I \tag{17}$$

$$\sum_j a_j x_{kij} \leq ST_{ki}, \quad \forall k \in K, \, \forall i \in I \tag{18}$$

$$AT_{k1} \geq ST_{k0} + \sum_j t_{kj} x_{k1j}, \quad \forall k \in K \tag{19}$$

$$AT_{ki} \leq \sum_j b_j x_{kij}, \quad \forall k \in K, \, \forall i \in I \tag{20}$$

$$\sqrt{i-1} \cdot \sigma \cdot Z_{ki} \le \sum_j b_j x_{kij} - AT_{ki}, \quad \forall k \in K, \forall i \in I \qquad (21)$$

$$Z \le Z_{ki}, \quad \forall k \in K, i \in I \qquad (22)$$

Constraints (13) indicate that each customer is served by one technician. Constraints (14) and (15) make sure that the task list of each technician is consecutive. Constraints (16) show that for each technician the arrival time of the current task is the previous task start time combined with the previous task duration and the travel time to the current task. Constraints (17) and (18) endure that the start time is after both arrival time and the lower limit of the time window. Constraints (19) state that the arrival time of the first task for each technician is the travel time from his depot to the first task based on the technician start work time. Constraints (20) make sure the expected arrival time is before the latest time window. Constraints (21) calculate the z-score corresponding to the probability of the risk, the risk is defined as the probability of the value which is greater than Z_{ki} for the standard normal distribution, while Z denotes the lower bound of Z_{ki} as shown in constraints (22).

Note that in order to obtain a linear model, the variance of the duration for different tasks is supposed to be equal, and the z-score is introduced to present the same trend of the probability for risks, instead of calculating risks which are not linear.

5 Simulated Annealing Method

Due to the fact that the risk is defined as a probability and considered in the objective of the model, the exact method may solve a small size problem as shown in the previous section. However, there are some limitations such as the variance for the uncertainty needs to be identical for all tasks. Also, it cannot solve the problem if the objective is to minimise the average risk in the schedule, because the average z-score is not the same as the average value of risks. Therefore, one of the heuristic methods, Simulated Annealing (SA) is applied to solve problems of a larger size and with multiple objectives. Before the illustration of the SA method, two search operators that are used in the searching process are explained first.

Given a specific task, the swap operator swaps the task with another task, while the insert operator withdraws this task and inserts it to another technician's task list according to the order of the lower limits of these task time windows. To be more specific, given a task m of technician p and task n of technician q, the swap operator exchanges the task m of p and task n of q. The insert operator withdraws the task m from technician p and assigns it to technician q.

Simulated Annealing (SA) is a probabilistic method proposed for finding the global minimum of a cost function that may possess several local minima [16, 17]. While Burkard and Rendl [18] first applied SA method to solve quadratic assignment problems, computational results indicated that they could obtain the best-known solution with a relatively high probability.

The Simulated Annealing algorithm was originally inspired from the process of annealing in metal work, a technique involving heating and controlled cooling of a material to increase the size of its crystals and reduce their defects. Both are attributes of the material that depends on its thermodynamic free energy. While the same amount of cooling brings the same amount of decrease in temperature, it will bring a different decrease in the thermodynamic free energy depending on the rate that it occurs, with a slower rate producing a more prominent decrease.

In Simulated Annealing, a temperature variable is used to simulate this heating and cooling process. We initially set it high and then allow it to slowly 'cool' as the algorithm runs. While this temperature variable is high the algorithm will be allowed, with a higher probability, to accept solutions that are worse than our current solution. It gives the algorithm the ability to jump out of any local optima as it explores the solution space. The chance of accepting worse solutions is reduced due to the decline of the temperature, which allows the algorithm to gradually focus in an area of the search space close to the optimum solution.

6   Experimental Results and Discussions

6.1   Basic Experiments

In our experiments, the risk is a result of the uncertain task duration and the fluctuating travel time. Besides, several factors are considered during the scheduling process. On the one hand, tasks have different time windows, different means and variances of the estimated duration time, different necessary skill levels and different priorities. On the other hand, technicians have different depots and different skill ability. Moreover, the travel time is also treated as an uncertain factor and the variance of the travel time is distinct in the morning or the afternoon. In addition, the distributions of uncertain factors in the model are all supposed as normal distributions.

In the basic experiment, the testbed is based on 120 tasks and 20 technicians. In order to see the effect of considering risks in the scheduling, as well as the effect of considering task priorities, we suppose that the required skill level for tasks are all equal and the priorities are distinguished as two levels: high and low.

Hence there are three scheduling models: the travel time model is of a traditional scheduling problem that the objective is to minimise the total travel time; while the risk model and priority risk model aim at minimising the average risk of all tasks. Moreover, in the risk model, all tasks are treated as the same importance while for the priority risk model each task has one of the two different priorities. Figure 9 shows the average risks of high and low priority tasks for the three models. From the comparison of the travel time model and the risk model, the average risk for all tasks in the case of travel time model is much higher than that obtained when minimising task and travel risk; it is reasonable because we did not consider risk when minimising the total travel time during scheduling. Meanwhile, Fig. 9 shows that the average risk for the travel time model is not significantly high in value; this is because risks are limited by the time window threshold constraints in the travel time model.

Furthermore, in the real world, tasks appear to have different importance or priority according to the business objectives. If a technician fails to start a high priority task in time, then the penalty should be higher. Therefore, the priority risk is introduced in the scheduling where the priority risk of a particular task is defined as the risk of the task

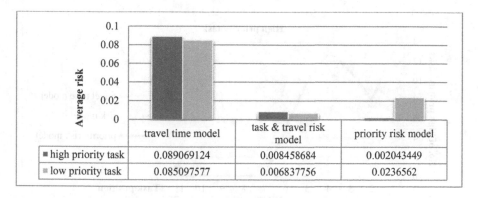

Fig. 9. Risks for different models

multiplied by an adjusted task importance score, in order to force high priority tasks to possess low risks. As we can see in Fig. 9, the average risk of high priority tasks is smaller at the cost of the increased average risk for low priority tasks.

Additionally, a comparison of the average travel time is shown in Table 1. The average travel time is the total travel time spent by all technicians divided by the total number of tasks. As expected, the travel time model results in the smallest travel time among the three models; but the risk model and priority risk model also show relatively short travel time. An explanation could be that by minimising the risks, there is a side effect of minimising the travel time simultaneously. Specifically, the risk is considered as the area of the distribution of the arrival time fell after the latest time of the time window, and the mean of the arrival time is associated with the estimated operation time of all previous tasks and the travel time between the depot to the 1st customer and between previous tasks for each technician. Therefore, during scheduling, when we try to minimise risks we also minimise the travel time simultaneously.

Table 1. Travel time for different models

Model	Travel time model	Risk model	Priority risk model
Travel time (mins)	19.56	31.65	21.46

6.2 Structures of the Task Priority

From the definition of risks, a conclusion can be drawn that the risk increases as it propagates because the variance of the arrival time increases along the task list for each technician. The position of the task in the planned tour of visits is the essential information for the robustness of the plan during the day against disturbances. From Fig. 9, we notice that the risk for high priority tasks becomes smaller in the priority risk model. By analysing the structure of the task priority at each position in the task list for every technician, we can find that high priority tasks are completed at the early position

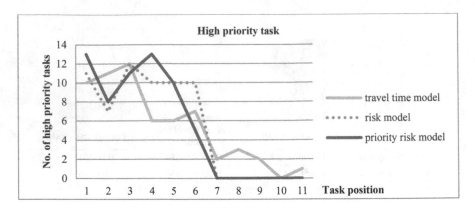

Fig. 10. High priority task position composition

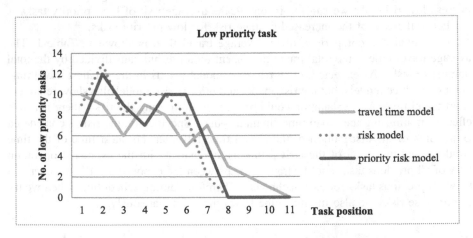

Fig. 11. Low priority task position composition

in the tour of visits. It models the real-world fact that technicians prefer to do the important task first to make sure its completion will be achievable.

In our application case, the average number of tasks for each technician is 6, which is derived from 120 tasks divided by 20 technicians. Figure 10 illustrates the number of high priority tasks as the vertical axis (figures on lines) according to each position number in task lists for all technicians on the horizontal axis. For instance, there are 13 high priority tasks assigned to technicians as their 1st task in the schedule obtained by priority risk model, whereas 11 tasks for the risk model and 10 tasks for the travel time model. In other words, there are 13 technicians scheduled by a high priority task as their 1st task in the priority risk model, and 11 technicians and 10 technicians processing a high priority task in their 1st task position for the risk model and the travel time model respectively. We can notice that the graph shows in the case of the travel time model, some technicians may have more than 8 tasks which are really tense for them and accordingly the risks for missing them may be much high. In both risk models, technicians may have at most 7 tasks.

Moreover, the high priority tasks at position 1 and 4 are more in the priority risk model than those in the risk model, which explains the high priority tasks are executed earlier both in the morning and in the afternoon. Also, there is a cost of focusing on high priority tasks: the low priority tasks are pushed to late positions as is shown in Fig. 11. In addition, we may observe that the number of tasks in the travel time model and risk model did not fluctuate as much as that in the priority risk model.

6.3   Structures of the Task Priority

In order to study the technicians' behaviour, the productivity for a technician is introduced, it can be defined as

$$\text{technician's productivity} = \frac{\text{number of tasks}}{\text{work hours}} \cdot \text{roster hours}. \tag{23}$$

First, we get the number of tasks done per hour (number of tasks/total work hours), then we get the maximum number of tasks achievable per day, by multiplying by the technician daily rostered hours.

From the definition, the productivity states a certain task number for a technician only considering the work time factor. Then Fig. 12 shows the number of technicians (vertical axis) according to the value of productivity (horizontal axis). For example, there are around 7 technicians whose productivity is around 12 tasks when building the start-of-day service visits plan with the priority risk model. Thus from the graph, we may conclude that by introducing risks in scheduling, technicians will have even workload among them, which also means a robust schedule can be obtained.

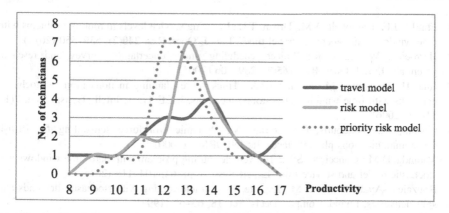

Fig. 12. Productivity distribution

7 Conclusion

This research aims at modelling the risks observed in field force services delivery operations and incorporate risks in the operational planning process from a new perspective. The risks, which interpret the possibility of missing appointments regarding time windows, arise from the stochastic service time and travel time. Moreover, the model also demonstrates the risk increases simultaneously as it propagates for each technician. In addition, this model has been applied to a real-world problem in the telecommunication sector. Results have shown that the schedule generated is more robust while minimising the risk of failure, pushing high-priority tasks earlier in the schedule to avoid failure of these tasks.

In a risk assessment tool or a risk-based scheduling engine under a dynamic environment, the calculation needs to be fast enough but also realistic. In the first step, we proposed an addition method to estimate risk distributions and test the accuracy. Then a linear model is built for this problem by limiting some factors and can be solved by exact methods. Concerning the application area, the Simulated Annealing method is utilised in the scheduling process to obtain a good solution in an acceptable time.

As for the future work, the task duration which follows a gamma distribution will be considered; even the combination of gamma and normal distributions will be taken into consideration. Furthermore, it is worthwhile to work on a simulation which mimics a real-time task process in one day to demonstrate the advantage of considering risk in the scheduler. Additionally, in the simulation we may study how to re-schedule at specified time points based on the information from completed tasks, in order to obtain the pros and cons that rescheduling or updating technician task lists several times in a day.

References

1. Ehmke, J.F., Campbell, A.M., Urban, T.L.: Ensuring service levels in routing problems with time windows and stochastic travel times. Eur. J. Oper. Res. **240**(2), 539–550 (2015)
2. Herroelen, W., Leus, R.: Project scheduling under uncertainty: survey and research potentials. Eur. J. Oper. Res. **165**(2), 289–306 (2005)
3. Jula, H., Dessouky, M., Ioannou, P.A.: Truck route planning in nonstationary stochastic networks with time windows at customer locations. IEEE Trans. Intell. Transp. Syst. **7**(1), 51–61 (2006)
4. Lesaint, D., Voudouris, C., Azarmi, N.: Dynamic workforce scheduling for British Telecommunications plc. Interfaces. In: INFORMS (2000)
5. Miranda, D.M., Conceição, S.V.: The vehicle routing problem with hard time windows and stochastic travel and service time. Expert Syst. Appl. **64**, 104–116 (2016)
6. Bouzaiene-Ayari, B., Dror, M., Laporte, G.: Vehicle routing with stochastic demands and split deliveries. Found. Comput. Decis. Sci. **18**, 63–69 (1993)
7. Bertsimas, D.J.: Probabilistic combinatorial optimization problems. Ph.D. Thesis, Report No. 193 (1988)
8. Bastian, C., Rinnooy-Kan, A.H.G.: The stochastic vehicle routing problem revisited. Eur. J. Oper. Res. **56**, 407–412 (1992)

9. Gendreau, M., Laporte, G., Seguin, R.: A tabu search algorithm for the vehicle routing problem with stochastic demands and customers. Oper. Res. **44**(3), 469–477 (1996)
10. Gendreau, M., Laporte, G., Potvin, J-Y.: Metaheuristics for the capacitated VRP. In: Toth, P., Vigo, D. (eds.), The Vehicle Routing Problem, pp. 129–154. Society for Industrial and Applied Mathematics, Philadelphia (2002)
11. Chang, M.: A vehicle routing problem with time windows and stochastic demands. J. Chin. Inst. Eng. **28**(5), 783–794 (2005)
12. Lei, H., Laporte, G., Guo, B.: The capacitated vehicle routing problem with stochastic demands and time windows. Comput. Oper. Res. **38**, 1775–1783 (2011)
13. Li, X., Tian, P., Leung, S.C.H.: Vehicle routing problems with time windows and stochastic travel and service times: models and algorithm. Int. J. Prod. Econ. **125**(1), 137–145 (2010)
14. Ji, C., Liu, J., Liret, A., Dorne, R., Owusu, G., Rana, R.: Service scheduling to minimise the risk of missing appointments. In: Conference Proceedings on Proceedings, Computing Conference (2017)
15. Nadarajah, S., Kotz, S.: Exact distribution of the max/min of two Gaussian random variables. IEEE Trans. Very Large Scale Integr. Syst. **16**(2), 210–212 (2008)
16. Kirkpatrick, S., Gelatt Jr., C.D., Vecchi, M.P.: Optimisation by simulated annealing. Science **220**(4598), 671–680 (1983)
17. Cerny, V.: Thermodynamical approach to the traveling salesman problem: an efficient simulation algorithm. J. Optim. Theory Appl. **45**(1), 41–51 (1985)
18. Burkard, R.E., Rendl, F.: A thermodynamically motivated simulation procedure for combinatorial optimization problems. Eur. J. Oper. Res. **17**, 169–174 (1984)

Machine Learning in Action

Risk Information Recommendation
for Engineering Workers

Kyle Martin[1]([✉]) [ID], Anne Liret[2] [ID], Nirmalie Wiratunga[1] [ID], Gilbert Owusu[3],
and Mathias Kern[3]

[1] Robert Gordon University, Aberdeen, Scotland
{k.martin,n.wiratunga}@rgu.ac.uk
[2] BT France, Paris, France
anne.liret@bt.com
[3] British Telecommunications, London, UK
{gilbert.owusu,mathias.kern}@bt.com

Abstract. Within any sufficiently expertise-reliant and work-driven domain there is a requirement to understand the similarities between specific work tasks. Though mechanisms to develop similarity models for these areas do exist, in practice they have been criticised within various domains by experts who feel that the output is not indicative of their viewpoint. In field service provision for telecommunication organisations, it can be particularly challenging to understand task similarity from the perspective of an expert engineer. With that in mind, this paper demonstrates a similarity model developed from text recorded by engineer's themselves to develop a metric directly indicative of expert opinion. We evaluate several methods of learning text representations on a classification task developed from engineers' notes. Furthermore, we introduce a means to make use of the complex and multi-faceted aspect of the notes to recommend additional information to support engineers in the field.

Keywords: Case-Based Reasoning · Information retrieval
Machine learning · Metric learning · Similarity modeling
Deep metric learning

1 Introduction

Within any expertise-reliant and work-driven domain there is a requirement to understand the similarities between specific work tasks. Sufficiently understanding the similarity between work elements in these sectors presents an opportunity to improve transfer of experiential content [5] and provide services such as work recommendation [12]. We notice this problem frequently within field provision of services for telecommunication organisations.

Though we had previously published our findings regarding a fuzzy logic-based recommender system [12], engineers have demonstrated a reluctance in uptake of the system. In particular, it was highlighted that the system was

© Springer Nature Switzerland AG 2018
M. Bramer and M. Petridis (Eds.): SGAI-AI 2018, LNAI 11311, pp. 311–325, 2018.
https://doi.org/10.1007/978-3-030-04191-5_27

opaque in terms of its decision-making process and that the similarity model it generated was not representative of engineer's own expert perspective. In answer to this, we have built a Case-Based Reasoning (CBR) system with greater explanatory capabilities and drawing on text documents recorded by the engineers' themselves to inform its similarity model. We have discussed the explanatory capabilities in other work [10] and thus in this paper will focus on how we utilised the complex information source of engineer notes to develop a similarity model which can act as a basis for additional information recommendation.

This work is motivated by the need to learn similarity from a user's perspective. We believe that using notes written by engineers themselves as the information source for a similarity metric will ensure that the cases retrieved through similarity-based return are more representative of this point of view. In essence, we wish to achieve a similarity model which is indicative of what a domain expert's own experiences have lead them to believe is the truth. We believe this can be achieved by basing it on experts' notations regarding the subject.

Beyond this however, the notes offer potential as a multi-faceted source which can inform a number of decision support systems. The notes are a large semi-structured source of information detailing specific experiences of human experts in the field. Thus, we view this as an opportunity to develop a corporate memory of human experience, improving the effectiveness of engineers in the field and enabling business robustness to the departure of experts from employment. Though in this work we focus on the development of the similarity model and the recommendation of information to counter explicit risks, we suggest this is an equally suitable method to achieve goals such as autonomous fault diagnosis and expert assistance recommendation.

We offer several contributions in this paper. We (1) evaluate methods of developing representations from expert-written documents for similarity-based return on the basis of their accuracy on a simple classification task. We (2) showcase a generalisable method to recommend additional information from complex and multi-faceted information sources that the notes represent. Lastly, we (3) present all of our findings with a specific use case in the telecommunications engineering domain. Though presented as a field services recommender, the concept could be adapted to fit other domains.

This paper is split into the following sections. Section 2 talks about related work. Section 3 highlights aspects of the notes which lend themselves towards developing a similarity model and additional information recommendation. Section 4 contains an evaluation of the text representation learning methods and analyses their impact learning a similarity model. In Sect. 5 we formalise our approach to additional information recommendation and demonstrate the completed system. Finally, in Sect. 6 we examine the system within the context of future work and in Sect. 7 we offer some conclusions.

2 Related Work

This work primarily considers the learning of similarity between telecommunication tasks. In previous work a fuzzy recommender system was used to recommend tasks to engineers [12]. However, it was found that engineers resented the lack of clarity behind its recommendations. This informed our drive to develop a similarity metric which is robust to scrutiny from an expert perspective and can be used to develop an explanation. We have previously identified the explainability aspects of this work [10], and so we focus upon learning experiential content from the expert perspective in this work.

Sharing and managing expertise is a necessary aspect of knowledge management [1]. However, knowledge transfer between expert-level users is a difficult task [4]. When seeking to automatise such an interaction, it often means that a user is directed towards another expert user, rather than presented with specific information itself [5]. This is because the information sources that store experience are necessarily complex, as experiential content is difficult to elicit and therefore difficult to query effectively [17].

Due to the above reasons, human experience composes one of the more difficult areas to manage in an organisational memory [16]. We feel that the notes recorded by engineers themselves offer a bridge between explicit corporate storage and the otherwise inaccessible content of human memory.

2.1 Learning Representations from Text

The notes detailing complex task information are recorded in text, and so in this paper we consider approaches to develop a similarity model for text documents. We compare a range of techniques to improve document representation, such as distributional and distributed methods, as well as a deep metric learner. Distributional approaches utilise statistical-based methods to measure co-occurence of words. An example of this is tf-idf [14], which calculates the term-frequency/inverse-document-frequency for each term in a document to produce a sparse representation. Distributed approaches, often associated with word embeddings such as those obtained through Word2Vec [11], produce dense representations which are representative of latent or syntactical features within individual words. These are obtained by examining the context in which words appear. For example, Word2Vec [11] uses a sliding window which considers the words both before and after the target term to provide input to a one-layer neural network. The network is exposed to multiple sliding windows containing the target term to build an understanding of its latent features based upon the context in which it appears. These latent features are represented by real numbers and can be used to build a vectorial representation of individual words. A document is then represented by an average of the word vectors (or embeddings) which it contains. This process is known as Doc2Vec [7].

Deep metric learners are a group of architectures (including the Siamese Neural Network [2,3] and Triplet Network [15]) that use neural network techniques to learn a metric. They receive multiple examples as input simultaneously to develop embeddings which are optimised based on an objective. This objective is defined by a 'matching criteria' - a principle which identifies whether two examples are similar or not. Importantly, this matching criteria is not necessarily reliant upon class knowledge [6]. Deep metric learners develop a space which is optimised for similarity-based return by minimising the distance between examples which adhere to the matching criteria and maximising the distance between examples that do not. Due to this they have demonstrated application in areas where fine-grained similarity knowledge is important, such as face verification [15] and similar text retrieval [13].

2.2   Provision of Additional Information

Finally, since our desire is to use the generated model as the basis for recommendation of additional information, we review methods of similarity-based recommendation. From the literature, we can observe a number of examples of similarity-based recommendation being used to take advantage of complex sources and provide decision support services for experts. One such field is interpersonal trust modeling [8,9].

In [8,9], the authors utilise similarity measures to develop a prediction of how effectively an expert will integrate with a team to complete group-work reliant tasks. This is based on understanding of interpersonal trust between group members gained from individual member feedback. A similarity model is then generated using the similarity between members' prior task preferences, as gained from ratings that each member of the group had given to tasks they themselves had previously completed. This is similar in nature to the approach we adopt in this paper for additional information recommendation. We are reliant on users to explicitly describe reasons for task failure to form the basis of our system to identify risk information. However, this information is captured by the business anyway, and so does not require additional data collection from the engineer as a rating would provide. Furthermore, the information we are able to extract from the text documentation is more complex than a single numerical rating value, and therefore more valuable.

3   Similarity from an Expert's Perspective

It is common within complex services provisioning that the personnel which fulfill the required technical work gradually become highly skilled in their domain. In this paper specifically, we highlight the telecommunications engineering force whom develop expertise in network equipment installation and repair. To ensure continuous service delivery, they traditionally are allocated tasks. A task, in this scenario, represents either a time-constrained action to perform on a piece of equipment or an investigation regarding a delayed step of a wider network process. Field engineers record information about the tasks they have completed in text documents called "notes". These notes form an heterogeneous base of mixed types of information, such as work order, identified problem, failure reason, task progression, task context, and sometimes informal recommendation. The notes are categorised based upon their contents. For example, Order notes contain information about the work requirements of a task. Details of task completion are stored in Closure notes, while records of task failure and the reason behind it are stored in Further notes. Lastly, an engineer can enter additional miscellaneous information about a task in its in User notes.

The notes are a semi-structured source of expert information describing a specific task. However, they are made complex by the fact that different only certain note types may be present in certain tasks. For example, a task which has never been attempted will only be associated with Order notes, while there may be both Further and Closure notes describing another task if it had been failed at least once before it was successfully completed. Furthermore, a task will often not only be associated with multiple different types of notes, but also multiples of the same note type (i.e. two Further notes if the task has been failed twice). However, certain note types (such as Order notes) will never be duplicated. Figure 1 displays the relationship between notes and tasks for two examples.

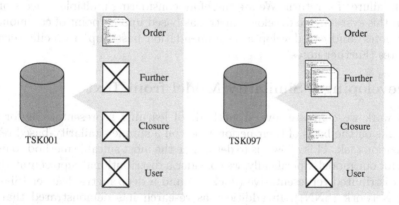

Fig. 1. The relationship between tasks and notes. Task TSK001 is an example of a newly created task, where only the Order notes have been generated. Meanwhile, TSK097 is an example of a task that has been attempted twice and failed (notice two Further notes) before being successfully completed (detailed in the Closure notes). In both instances the engineer has declined to add more information in the User notes.

In this paper, we demonstrate a similarity model generated based upon Order notes, which are representative of the original work order calling for the task to be completed. Since an Order note is created at the same time as the original task, this guarantees that a task can be used to query the model immediately upon creation. This is an important component of a timely system, as it would be less useful to query the model after a task has already been allocated, or even failed.

We also propose a method to use the notes for recommendation of additional information. For this purpose, we consider the specific use case of risk information recommendation and so we are primarily interested in the reasons that govern task failure. These are recorded in Further notes, while details of successful task completion are recorded in Closure notes. However, as aforementioned, neither Further nor Closure notes are available for every task, as these note types are only generated when a task is attempted and failed or succeeded respectively. This has two consequences: (1) that a task which is completed on first attempt (the most common scenario) does not become associated with any point of failure and so is not associated with a risk and (2) that newly generated tasks will not be associated with either of these note types.

Since it is necessary for the similarity model to be equally valid across the entire case-base, these note types would be ineffective to use as a basis for a similarity model. Hence we utilise a similarity model which is generated based upon a shared point of commonality across all of the case-base (Order notes). However, Order notes alone are not sufficient to develop a recommendation of additional information. To provide this, we need the information that is present within these specialised note types. The result is that we will only consider a specific subset of tasks in which these notes are present (i.e. Further notes detailing task failure) for return. We are therefore considering multiple aspects of the notes in this system - we develop a metric as based upon a point of commonality (Order notes) and can develop a recommendation based upon specific relevant task notes (Further notes).

4   Developing a Similarity Model from Text

In this work we compare several methods of learning representations for text documents on the basis of their performance on a simple similarity-based return classification task. This allows us to determine the most suitable method to use as a basis for our model. Specifically, we consider a distributional representative (tf-idf), a distributed representative (doc2vec) and a deep metric learner (Siamese Neural Network (SNN)). In addition, as research has demonstrated that the performance of a deep metric learner can be enhanced through the selection of a suitable training strategy [15], we also consider an SNN which uses DYNEE sample selection.

Term frequency-inverse document frequency (tf-idf) is a statistical measure that calculates a real value for each term in a document. The value for each term is calculated by dividing the frequency of its usage within a document over the number of documents which contain the term within the corpus [14]. Therefore, each feature of a document vector is a value which represents an individual word from the corpus vocabulary and so vectors can be very sparse. As a result, tf-idf becomes steadily less effective in large corpora with a varied vocabulary.

Document-2-Vector (Doc2Vec) [7] is an extension of the Word2Vec algorithm [11]. Word2Vec uses contextual knowledge from the measurement of word co-occurrence to capture latent or syntactical features and develop word embeddings. The result is a feature space where words that have similar contexts exist close together. To retrieve a representation for a document (Doc2Vec), the embeddings for terms within the document are simply averaged. Sparseness of representation is thereby avoided, as feature values are not reliant on specific words being present.

The Siamese Neural Network (SNN) is a deep metric learner. It has a unique neural architecture comprised of two matching sub-networks with identical weights and parameters. This allows the network to receive example input in pairs, thereby enabling the network to train based on the relationships that exist between examples. When input to the network, pairs of examples are labeled on the basis of a 'matching criteria'. The metric space which is learned by the SNN is optimised to fit the stated matching criteria, such that positive pairs (in which member examples adhere to the matching criteria) exist close together, while negative pairs (in which members do not) exist far apart.

Learning of representations in this manner is controlled by SNN's unique contrastive loss function, introduced in [3] and we summarise here. Contrastive loss is split into two elements; L_G for positive (genuine) pairs and L_I for negative (impostor) pairs. The use of both genuine and impostor error means that the similarity metric can be directly learned by the network through the comparison of the actual pair label Y_A (equal to 0 for genuine and 1 for impostor pairs) and the distance between pair members, D_W. This means that distance between constituents of genuine pairs are minimised over the course of training, whilst ensuring that impostor pairs maintain at least a set margin of M distance apart.

$$L_G = (1 - Y_A) \cdot D_W{}^2 \tag{1}$$
$$L_I = Y_A \cdot (max(0,\ M - D_W))^2 \tag{2}$$
$$L = L_G + L_I \tag{3}$$

The output of the identical sub-networks form feature embeddings for each member of the input pair. During training it is these embeddings that are used for any distance computations, thereby ensuring iterative model refinement. An example SNN architecture is presented in Fig. 2.

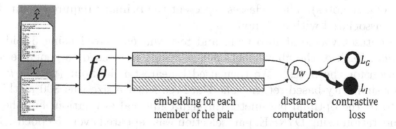

Fig. 2. The Siamese Neural Network (SNN) architecture

As SNNs receive pairs of examples as input, this presents an additional parameter that can be fine-tuned. In its basic form, the network will receive randomly generated pairs as input during training. However, research has demonstrated that a higher optima and quicker convergence can be achieved if an appropriate pairing strategy is adopted. With this in mind, we also considered an SNN supported by DYNEE sample selection. DYNEE is a pairing strategy which optimises pair creation through the use of a combined exploration and exploitation strategy. DYNEE exploits knowledge gained in previous stages of training by identifying pairs which had generated high loss values. It then uses them to augment a randomly generated pair set which provides exploratory coverage of the space. This is repeated over the course of training to ensure that the pair set is formed from contemporary information.

4.1 Evaluation

In this section we evaluate the vectorial representation of notes gained through each method - tf-idf, Doc2Vec, SNN and an SNN with DYNEE sample selection - to determine which develops the best representation in terms of accuracy on a classification task. Although a subject study would be desirable to understand whether the model develops a score which is representative in an expert's opinion, we will empirically evaluate the model using a simple classification task as a proxy. In future work we plan to complete such a subject study to accompany and strengthen this empirical evaluation.

4.2 Experimental Setup

For the purposes of comparison we have created a simple classification task where notes are classified according to one of four work types. The goodness of each of the learned representations are assessed by their performance on this classification task.

We extracted two months of Order notes written by telecommunication engineers between March and April 2018. We filtered out any note which contained less than 50 characters, as we judged them not to be adequately meaningful. This resulted in a dataset of 1,610 notes split into four classes - Cabling (CAB - 227 notes), Jointing (JRT - 789 notes), Overhead (OVH - 503 notes) and Power Testing (PTO - 91 notes). These classes represent the primary required competence which is associated with each note.

The dataset was split into train and test and evaluated using 5-fold cross evaluation. Each of the abovementioned methods were used to generate a representation for the notes[1]. We then used k-nearest neighbour (with a k value of 3) for similarity-based return. The Doc2Vec feature size was 300 as this was found to be the optimal parameter through empirical evaluation. For the SNN implementation using DYNEE, pair selection was repeated every 5 epochs. The α exploitation ratio used for DYNEE was $|P|/10$. This means that 10% of the training pairs at any one time were formed through exploitation, while the remainder were randomly generated to provide exploration.

---

[1] Both SNN sub-network architectures were comprised of 3-layer perceptrons which used an SGD optimizer, ReLU activations and were trained for 250 epochs.

4.3   Results

The results are presented in Table 1[2]. It is unsurprising that deep metric learners perform better than either tf-idf or Doc2Vec on the classification task, as they are designed to produce embeddings which are optimal for similarity-based return. We can observe that the SNN with the DYNEE training strategy achieved the highest accuracy, though this was only marginally greater than its vanilla counterpart. This is likely due to the small size of the dataset. Tf-idf performed the worst. This was as expected, because as a statistical measure tf-idf does not consider the context of terms.

Table 1. Results of representation learning methods on a classification task.

Architecture	Accuracy (%)
Tf-Idf	62.24
Doc2Vec	63.79
SNN	66.25
SNN DYNEE	66.83

Figure 3 presents a principle component analysis of the representation distribution gained from the Doc2Vec and SNN on a multi-dimension scaling scatter plot. We can observe that the representation distribution gained from SNN demonstrates significantly better similarity clusters. It confirms that concepts learned by SNNs form better clusters around class boundaries when compared to Doc2Vec. This also provides supporting evidence towards the performance gains observed with SNNs.

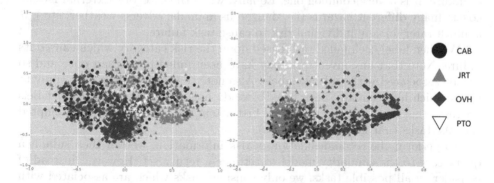

Fig. 3. Representation distribution gained from Doc2Vec (left) and SNN (right)

---

[2] The displayed results for SNNs used Doc2Vec embeddings as input, as they performed better. When using tf-idf representations as input, both SNNs still outperformed tf-idf and Doc2Vec.

5   Recommendation of Additional Information

Additional information can take many forms and assist an engineer in the field in different ways. We formally view additional information in this paper as the provision of extra knowledge which can contribute to the successful completion of a task. Of particular interest is additional information which may allow a user to pre-emptively identify possible task failure and potentially avoid it. In this manner, we hope to either prevent task failure or 'fail fast' such that minimum resources are wasted on a doomed task.

We propose a method to make further use of the engineering notes. We suggest that based upon the developed similarity model, we can recommend additional information to users with the purpose of supporting their work. Specifically, we will identify the likelihood of potential risk categories to an incoming task and make a recommendation based on knowledge from the notes to counter the risk where appropriate. Though we focus on recommendation of risk information in this work, the same principle can apply to other problems and domains with similarly recorded expertise.

5.1   Formalising Risk

Firstly, we extract a set of risk categories from the Further notes of previously failed tasks. These categories are an abstraction of specific risks that are collected into a single related concept (i.e. both "the customer was not ready" and "the customer was not present" would fall into the Customer risk category). This presented us with six risk categories - Contractor, Customer, Duct Blockage, External Event, Planning and Time. These categories were formed based upon feedback from telecommunication engineering experts and the most common sources of risk. For example, though Duct Blockage is a reasonably specific point of failure, it is a very common one. Equally, while the category External Events covers many different hazards (i.e. dangerous animals, adverse weather, etc.), it is much rarer for any individual risk to cause task failure.

We then label each failed task based upon the risk category which caused its failure. Note that any given task may have been failed more than once and so can be associated with multiple labels. Also note that these labels only apply to tasks which have already been failed - we do not generate risk category labels for tasks that were successful on their first attempt or have yet to be attempted (i.e. the tasks that lack Further notes).

To perform the recommendation of risk information, we can then submit a query case to the similarity model to retrieve a return set. However, instead of considering all possible tasks, we only consider tasks which are associated with Further notes (and therefore at least one risk label). We can then perform a vote weighted by similarity to gauge the likelihood of a given risk occurring in the query task (see Fig. 4). We perform this vote in the following manner.

Let us describe an individual risk category as r and a function to induce a score for the risk category of an unseen example $r()$. We will also describe a task as x and our full set of task examples as X. Similarly we will identify a

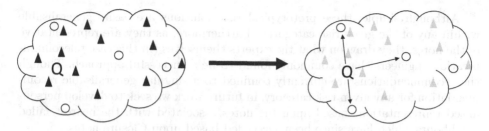

Fig. 4. Vote weighted by similarity. If the triangles represent successfully completed tasks, while the circles represent tasks that failed at least once, then we can observe only the latter feed into the weighted by similarity vote.

failed task as $\hat{x}$, such that $\hat{x} \in \hat{X}$ and $\hat{X} \subset X$. We can retrieve a label for a given failed task using the function $y(\hat{x})$. We compare a query, q, with its set of nearest failed neighbours, $\hat{x}^{NN}$. To develop a score, each risk category is calculated by the following formula:

$$r(q) = \frac{1}{k} \sum_{i}^{k} sim(x_i^{NN}, q) \cdot s_r \tag{4}$$

where k denotes the neighbourhood size parameter and s_i denotes a binary value 'switch' which is set to 1 if x_i^{NN} has previously failed due to the given risk (i.e. $r = y(\hat{x})$), or 0 otherwise. What this means is that a risk category's score is based upon a similarity weighted vote of its nearest failed neighbours. In this manner, we can develop a score of the likelihood for the occurrence of each risk in a given query.

5.2   Generating Recommendations

Though it is useful to demonstrate the likelihood of individual risks to an engineer, this is not necessarily helpful if they do not understand how to circumvent those risks. Therefore, we also generate a recommendation to answer any sufficiently likely risks. This is achieved by comparing each individual risk category score against a threshold. We have three possible classifications of risk - Low ($r(q) < 30\%$), Medium ($r(q) > 30\%$ and $r(q) < 60\%$) and High ($r(q) > 70\%$). The recommendations themselves are based upon the most common solution successful solution derived from the Closure notes of previously failed task. For example, most of the Closure notes suggest that many task failures relating to the Customer label can be avoided by phoning the customer ahead of time. It is worth noting that this will not necessarily prevent the task itself from failing. If the Customer has still not completed necessary pre-work, then the task will fail regardless. It does however offer an opportunity to 'fail fast' (i.e. prevent the engineer wasting time traveling to the customer's location). This in itself will improve productivity, as the engineer will then be free to complete another task.

Although simple, these prototypical risk solutions are easily generalisable within any of the given risk categories. Furthermore, as they are representative of the notes, they draw on what the experts themselves (in this case telecommunication engineers) have commonly found to be a successful approach. Though the recommendations are currently confined to a singular generalisable recommendation for any given risk category, in future work we seek to develop personalised representations based upon the notes associated with the nearest failed neighbours which have since been succeeded based upon Closure notes.

An example of the system is presented in Fig. 5. Note the text area on the left provides details of the original task, while the window on the right details the scoring across the list of risk categories. The bottom window is used to provide a recommendation - notice that the greatest risk being Contractor is highlighted and the system recommends that the user contact the Contractor in advance to ensure that the work is ready to begin.

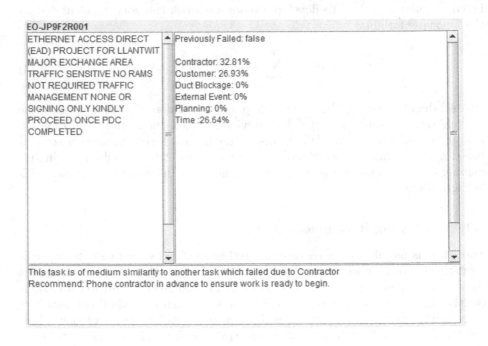

Fig. 5. Additional information recommendation for a medium risk task

5.3   Previously Failed Tasks and Progressed Tasks

Field service provisioning is a field where large scale jobs can frequently occur. These jobs are usually broken down into a series of related, often sequential, tasks which we describe as a work chain. Therefore, this environment must be considered when recommending additional risk information. Equally, there is potential for tasks to have been failed by one engineer before being attempted by another. Thus it is necessary for our system to consider at least some evidence of task history in order to make its recommendations.

We adopt a strict stance towards failure in task history for our additional information recommender; if a task, or any of the previous tasks in its work chain, has ever been failed previously, then we make a strong recommendation to counter this risk. The system will still display scoring for other risk categories, but will highly recommend that action be taken to answer this specific risk. Furthermore, it will highlight that this task (or a member of its work chain) has been failed in the past and provide the Further notes regarding the failure. These notes include contact information for the engineer that previously attempted the task, as well as specific information on the failure. This enables the engineer to form a response to the risk or contact the engineer for further information as required.

An example of the recommendation made regarding a previously failed task is shown in Fig. 6. We can observe that the right text area has been extended to include the Further notes of the previously failure. Note also that the bottom text area highlights which risk category caused this task to fail on its previous attempt. If more than one Further note was associated with this task, then all previously written Further notes would appear in the right text area. Similarly, if a previous task in the work chain had failed, the bottom window would identify this.

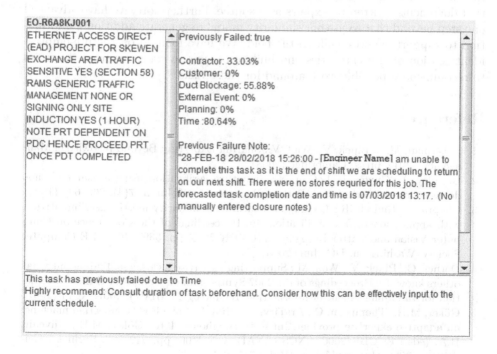

Fig. 6. Additional information recommendation for a previously failed task

6   Future Work

In future work we would like to evaluate the risk recommendation method demonstrated in this paper by performing a full subject study on engineers to retrieve qualitative feedback on the system. This would improve the robustness of the empirical evaluation to measure embedding goodness.

Ultimately, we would like to offer explanations of why a certain risk has been identified and offer recommendations on how best to circumvent the identified risk which are both personalised to the given task. We believe these personalisation can also be produced from the engineers' notes. In our current work, we are attempting to learn a generalisable breakdown of the notes, such that we can quickly identify the most appropriate passage to present to an engineer by way of an explanation. A similar method could also be applied to find the most likely solution to a risk. We believe this could be a very useful tool in the field to support engineering workers - a system which is able to pinpoint similar tasks as a method to provide additional information, support this information through an explanation and offer a recommendation on how to take advantage of that knowledge effectively.

7   Conclusion

In conclusion we have demonstrated a similarity model which is built upon textual documents written by experts as a source. Furthermore, we have advanced one step beyond that to use our similarity model to generate additional information to support experts while in the field. We have focused on the pre-emptive identification of risk categories and build on common solutions from the notes to recommend a possible work around for these risks.

References

1. Ackerman, M.S., Pipek, V., Wulf, V.: Sharing Expertise: Beyond Knowledge Management. MIT press, Cambridge (2003)
2. Bromley, J., Guyon, I., LeCun, Y.: Signature verification using a 'siamese' time delay neural network. Int. J. Pattern Recognit. Artif. Intell. **7**(4), 669–688 (1993)
3. Chopra, S., Hadsell, R., LeCun, Y.: Learning a similarity metric discriminatively, with application to face verification. In: Proceedings of the Conference on Computer Vision and Patter Recognition, CVPR 2005, pp. 539–546. IEEE Computer Society, Washington, DC, June 2005
4. Dörner, C., Pipek, V., Won, M.: Supporting expertise awareness: finding out what others know. In: Proceedings of the 2007 Symposium on Computer Human Interaction for the Management of Information Technology, CHIMIT 2007. ACM (2007)
5. Göker, M.H., Thompson, C., Arajärvi, S., Hua, K.: The PwC connection machine: an adaptive expertise provider. In: Roth-Berghofer, T.R., Göker, M.H., Güvenir, H.A. (eds.) ECCBR 2006. LNCS (LNAI), vol. 4106, pp. 549–563. Springer, Heidelberg (2006). https://doi.org/10.1007/11805816_40

6. Koch, G., Zemel, R., Salakhutdinov, R.: Siamese neural networks for one-shot image recognition. In: Deep Learning Workshop, ICML 2015, July 2015
7. Le, Q., Mikolov, T.: Distributed representations of sentences and documents. In: Proceedings of the 31st International Conference on International Conference on Machine Learning, ICML 2014, vol. 32, pp. II-1188–II-1196. JMLR.org (2014)
8. Malinowski, J., Keim, T., Weitzel, T., Wendt, O.: Decision support for team building: incorporating trust into a recommender-based approach. In: The Ninth Pacific Asia Conference on Information Systems, pp. 604–617 (2005)
9. Malinowski, J., Weitzel, T., Keim, T.: Decision support for team staffing: an automated relational recommendation approach. Decis. Support. Syst. 45(3), 429–447 (2008). special Issue Clusters
10. Martin, K., Liret, A., Wirtaunga, N., Owusu, G., Kern, M.: Explainability through transparency and user control: a case-based recommender for engineering workers. In: XCBR Workshop, ICCBR 2018, July 2018
11. Mikolov, T., Chen, K., Corrado, G., Dean, J.: Efficient estimation of word representations in vector space. CoRR abs/1301.3781 (2013)
12. Mohamed, A., Bilgin, A., Liret, A., Owusu, G.: Fuzzy logic based personalized task recommendation system for field services. In: Bramer, M., Petridis, M. (eds.) SGAI 2017. LNCS (LNAI), vol. 10630, pp. 300–312. Springer, Cham (2017). https://doi.org/10.1007/978-3-319-71078-5_26
13. Neculoiu, P., Versteegh, M., Rotaru, M.: Learning text similarity with siamese recurrent networks. In: Rep4NLP@ACL (2016)
14. Ramos, J.: Using TF-IDF to determine word relevance in document queries. In: Proceedings of the First Instructional Conference on Machine Learning, pp. 133–142 (2003)
15. Schroff, F., Kalenichenko, D., Philbin, J.: Facenet: a unified embedding for face recognition and clustering. In: Proceedings of the 2015 IEEE Conference on Computer Vision and Pattern Recognition, CVPR 2015, pp. 815–823. IEEE Computer Society, Washington, DC, June 2015. https://doi.org/10.1109/cvpr.2015.7298682
16. Walsh, J.P., Ungson, G.R.: Organizational memory. Acad. Manag. Rev. 16(1), 57–91 (1991)
17. Wright, G., Ayton, P.: Eliciting and modelling expert knowledge. Decis. Support. Syst. 3(1), 13–26 (1987)

Generalised Decision Level Ensemble Method for Classifying Multi-media Data

Saleh Alyahyan[1,2(✉)] and Wenjia Wang[1]

[1] University of East Anglia, Norwich, UK
{S.Alyahyan,Wenjia.Wang}@uea.ac.uk
[2] Shaqra University, Shaqra, Saudi Arabia

Abstract. In recent decades, multimedia data have been commonly generated and used in various domains, such as in healthcare and social media due to their ability of capturing rich information. But as they are unstructured and separated, how to fuse and integrate multimedia datasets and then learn from them effectively have been a main challenge to machine learning. We present a novel generalised decision level ensemble method (GDLEM) that combines the multimedia datasets at decision level. After extracting features from each of multimedia datasets separately, the method trains models independently on each media dataset and then employs a generalised selection function to choose the appropriate models to construct a heterogeneous ensemble. The selection function is defined as a weighted combination of two criteria: the accuracy of individual models and the diversity among the models. The framework is tested on multimedia data and compared with other heterogeneous ensembles. The results show that the GDLEM is more flexible and effective.

Keywords: Multimedia · Classification · Heterogeneous ensemble
Diversity · Model selection

1 Introduction

Multimedia data usually consist of multiple media types of data, such as text, images, graphics, audio and video etc. [1,2]. They can be generated in many fields and internet. For example, in healthcare, a patient with a potential complex disease may be examined through a series of tests to investigate their underlying problems with blood test, screening (X-rays, CT, MRI), Electroencephalography(EEG), or Electrocardiogram(ECG), Endoscopy(video), etc. These tests generate data represented in multimedia, as illustrated by Fig. 1, and they need to be considered together by doctors in order to make an accurate diagnosis and carry out appropriate treatments. Then, as more and more multimedia data have been rapidly generated and accumulated in various applications, analysing, discovering useful knowledge and learning from them have become a challenge in machine learning and data mining fields. Although many different algorithms

© Springer Nature Switzerland AG 2018
M. Bramer and M. Petridis (Eds.): SGAI-AI 2018, LNAI 11311, pp. 326–339, 2018.
https://doi.org/10.1007/978-3-030-04191-5_28

have been developed for dealing with multimedia data with different strategies, how best to combine many sets of different media data for effective machine learning is still a research issue [3,4]. It should be stressed that there seems a misrepresentation of multimedia data in some published researches which were presented as the work on multimedia whilst actually used only one media of data, mostly just imagery or video, instead of several media datasets together [5,6].

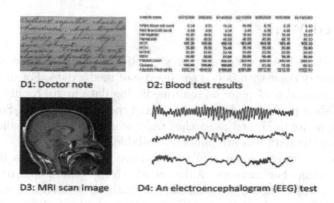

D1: Doctor note   D2: Blood test results

D3: MRI scan image   D4: An electroencephalogram (EEG) test

Fig. 1. An example of multimedia medical data.

So for clarity, we define Multi-Media Data (MMD) as a collection of several sub datasets that are represented by at least two or more different media formats: numbers, text, image, video, graphics, animation, audio, time series data, etc.

Multimedia data are usually unstructured so they need to be transformed into a structured representation through feature extraction. Then their features are aggregated to form a big flat single dataset for further analysis. This is arguably the most common approach for integrating multimedia data Then the analysis can be done just like any other data. In this way, one obvious possible problem is that the integrated dataset may have a very high dimensionality, i.e. too many features that can often overwhelm machine learning and data mining algorithms to produce good results [7].

In this research, we apply another strategy, contrary to above approach of integrating multimedia datasets into one big dataset. Firstly we use each dataset to generate some models, and then combine these models' decisions to produce the final solution. This is called the decision-level fusion. Moreover, with this approach, it provides us a natural platform to build heterogeneous ensembles for classifying multimedia data.

A heterogeneous ensemble for classification combines multiple classifiers that are created by using different algorithms on different or same datasets, with an aim of making the classifiers more diverse and hence possibly increasing accuracy [8–10].

Following our previous studies [11,12], this study presents a new generalised function for selecting classifiers to build a heterogeneous ensemble based on two criteria - accuracy and diversity, combined with variable weights.

The rest of the paper is organized as follows. Section 2 briefly reviews some related previous studies. Section 3 describes our proposed methods in detail, including the tools and programs used in the research. Section 4 provides details of the experiment conducted and our results. Section 5 gives conclusions and suggestions for the further work.

2   Related Work

As mentioned, although there are many publications on multimedia domains, they mostly only dealt with only a single type of media data. For instance, on a major international conference on multimedia big data in 2017, only about 15% of the published papers used more than one type of media data. So, there are actually not many published researches truly working on multimedia data, nor many multimedia data sets are publicly available.

There are, however, some studies that have used multimedia datasets for machine learning. For instance, Aalaa et al. [7,13] generated five small heterogeneous datasets containing a mixture of both structured and unstructured datasets and then applied clustering ensemble methods to them. Their experiments showed that the results using all available types of media outperform the results using the best individual types of media.

Yamanishi and Jenjia [14] conducted a study of the distributed learning system for Bayesian learning strategies. In their system each instance was observed by different classifiers which were called agents. They aggregated the outputs from the agents to give significantly better results. They demonstrated that distributed learning systems work approximately (or sometimes exactly) as well as the non-distributed Bayesian learning strategy. Thus, by employing their method, they were able to achieve a significant speeding-up of learning.

Onan [15] applied ensemble classification methods to text datasets. In his experiment the data sets ware represented by 5 different formats. Five types of classifiers were used: Naive Bayes, Support Vector Machine, K-Nearest Neighbour, Logistic Regression and Random forest. He compared individual classifiers and their homogeneous ensemble using Bagging and Boosting. The results showed that ensembles out-performed individuals.

Ballard and Wang [16] developed a dynamic ensemble selection methods for heterogeneous data mining. Although their datasets are not multimedia, their basic idea of combining multiple datasets at decision level inspired this work.

Some recent studies published in a major international conference on Multimedia Big Data (2017) used multimedia data. For instances, Amato et al. [17] used a multimedia dataset collected from the social media networks to develop a recommendation system. The data they used include text messages, tags, photos and possible interactions between the users. Their results show that using these multimedia data in their filtering and ranking based method helped to achieve a promising accuracy of recommendation, even though they did not use any machine learn methods. Liu et al. [18] used both image and audio data to detect drones. They used the feature level integration approach to generate a big dataset for training SVM models for classifying drones.

In summary, previous studies have used decision-level combination methods and different machine learning approaches to analyse so-called heterogeneous datasets, whilst in fact their datasets mostly come from different data sources of the same type. Thus, these studies were limited by their single medial of data and how their methods may perform on multimedia datasets is unknown. Also, much of this previous work is limited to applying some issues which affect the ensemble out comes, including diversity and accuracy for candidate models. In other words, model selection criteria have not been applied.

3 The Generalised Decision Level Ensemble Method(GDLEM)

3.1 The Generalised Decision Level Ensemble Method Framework

Our decision-level ensemble method(DLEM), as shown in Fig. 2, consists of four modules namely: (1) the multimedia data representation and feature extraction, (2) the modelling, (3) the model selection and, (4) the combination. In the first stage, the DLEM extracts features from each subset of media data to create D_i's $(1 < i < n)$ such that each D_i represents the unique type of media features, i, for each instance.

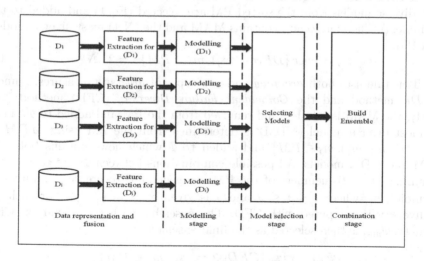

Fig. 2. The general framework for DLEM

In the second stage, the DLEM employs some heterogeneous machine learning algorithms to generate individual models for each dataset D_i. The total number of the generated individual models for the MMD, D, is determined by $m * n$. This modelling stage produces a pool of models, PM, with members PM_{ij} representing the individual model fitted using D_i with the base classifier method $B_j, 1 < j < m$.

The third stage selects models from the model pool PM using accuracy and diversity as selection criteria, either individually or jointly in some predefined rules. Using these criteria, three different rules: $R0$, $R1$, $R2$, were derived. After some intensive experiments in our earlier studies, we then devised a new rule that uses a function to combine accuracy and diversity in a more generalised manner to select the models.

Rules R0, R1 and R2 are described in our earlier work [11,12]. We give a brief summary of them here for convenience as they are the bases of the new rule.

R0: This rule only uses *accuracy* as the criterion for model selection. The DLEM firstly computes the accuracy, ($Acc(m_i)$), for each of the n models in the model pool PM and sort them in a descending order based their accuracy. Then the DLEM selects the N most accurate models from the PM, i.e., $m_i = max\{Acc(m_j), m_j \in PM\} i = 1...N$, and add them to the ensemble, ϕ.

R1: It uses both *accuracy* and *diversity* as criteria separately to select models at different stages. The DLEM first removes the most accurate model (MAM) from PM; using $m_1 = max\{Acc(m_j), m_j \in PM\}$ and add it to the ensemble, ϕ. Then the pairwise diversities between MAM and remaining models in PM, are calculated by the Double Fault (DF) method [19] and the models in the PM are sorted in a decreasing order based on the magnitude of the DF's. The (N-1) most diverse models from the sorted PM are selected (Eq. 1) and added to the ensemble, ϕ. Therefore ϕ now contains MAM and the (N-1) most diverse models from PM.

$$m_i = max\{DF(m_1, m_j), m_j \in PM\} i = 2...N \qquad (1)$$

R2: This rule uses both *accuracy* and two types of *diversity* measures, namely the *DF* method and the *Coincident Failure Diversity* (CFD) method [20]. Firstly, the MAM is selected and removed from the PM and added to Φ. Then the most diverse model (MDM) is determined from the PM using $MDM = max\{DF(m_1, m_j), m_j \in PM\}$ and added to Φ which now contains both the MAM and MDM models. All possible combinations between Φ and each of the remaining $(N - 2)$ members of the PM are generated to create J number of ensembles, ϕ_i, where $1 \leq i \leq J$ and J is given by $J = \binom{|PM|}{N-2}$. For each ϕ_i, its diversity is computed with CFD. The ensemble with the maximum CFD diversity, Φ_{md}, is then selected as the final ensemble.

$$\Phi_{md} = max\{CFD(\Phi \Leftarrow m_j), m_j \in PM\} \qquad (2)$$

The relevant literature shows that most studies, including some of our own rules. e.g. R0, only used one measure, either accuracy or diversity as the model selecting criterion, but our results as well as others demonstrated that the ensembles built in such ways are not really utilizing the balanced strengths of individual models but only focused on one aspect over others. Although our rules R1 and R2 use two measures but they use them separately in a sequential manner. So in this study, we proposed a new rule that combines both accuracy and diversity with a weighted function and the combined score is used for selecting candidate models.

R3: This new rule uses a combination of accuracy (Acc) and diversity(Div) as a generalised criterion for selecting models to build an ensemble. The combined measure is defined below.

$$\gamma_i = \alpha(Acc)_i + \beta(Div)_i . \tag{3}$$

Where α and β are the weights for accuracy, Acc, and diversity, Div, of model m_i ($1 \leq i \leq n - 1$) in the PM. The diversity measure Div in this rule is flexible can be a pairwise on non-pairwise diversity as long as it is considered as appropriate. In this study, we use the CFD.

After taking the best model out from the model pool PM, the combined score, γ_i, is calculated for the remaining $n - 2$ models in PM. The model with $max(\gamma_i)$ is selected from PM and added to Φ.

R3 is considered as a generalised rule because all other three rules R0, R1 and R2 are just its special cases with specific values for the weights and the diversity measure. When set $\alpha = 1$ and $\beta = 0$, R3 becomes R0. If we use the DF as the diversity measure and set $\alpha = 0$ and $\beta = 1$, then R3 becomes R1. if we use non-pairwise diversity measure such as the CFD and set $\alpha = 0$ and $\beta = 1$, R3 becomes R2.

Based on this new rule, a corresponding algorithm for building a decision level ensemble is derived and named as generalised Decision-level Ensemble Method (GDLEM) as it is flexible with R3 to apply various rules for selecting models by manipulating the weights or changing the measures used in the relationship γ in Eq. 3. The GDELM as follows. The first step is the same as that of the other three rules, i.e. choosing the MAM from PM as the first member of Φ. The key difference starts from the second step where the selection of candidate models uses the newly defined γ_i. This second step is repeated until N models with $max(\gamma_i)$ completely fills Φ.

3.2   Implementation of the GDLEM

The experiment was carried out on a normal PC, with an I7 processor and 16 GB RAM. As the GDLEM is flexible for selecting candidate classifiers, we have selected 10 efferent base classifiers that are provided in the WEKA library [21]. These base classifiers are: trees(*J48, RandomTree, REP-Tree*), bayes(*NaiveBayes, BayesNet*), function(*SMO*), rules(*JRip, PART*) and Lazy(*IBk, LWL*).

4   Experiment Design and Results

4.1   Dataset

We conducted a series of experiments using a benchmark dataset – 8 Scene Categories Dataset [22], which contains two subsets in different media: 2688 images and their annotations represented by XML files. The images are categorized into eight classes in according to their scenes and objects captured by the images. Each XML file contained a number of tags that describe an image. The annotations were dealt with as text and 782 textual features were extracted out from the texts to form a data subset D_t. For the imagery data, 567 features were extracted out from the images using Histograms of Oriented Gradients (HOG) [23] to form another data subset, i.e. imagery data D_g.

Ten base classifiers were used to learn from the textual and the imagery features subsets, which gave twenty heterogeneous models in total. This gave the GDLEM the opportunity to have more variety of models.

4.2   Experiment Design and Results

We carried out a series of experiments to investigate the performance of the GDLEM, using three selection rules separately, on the multimedia data. The investigated issues included (1) the performance measures and classifier selection criteria represented by the rules: R0, R1, R2 and R3, and (2) the ensemble size. A total of 135 experiments were conducted. This involved running all possible combination of these parameters. Each experiment was repeated five times with different samplings of the datasets.

In parallel, we conducted the experiments to investigate the influence of CFDs on the accuracy of all the ensembles built with the first three rules although the CFD is not used by R0 and R1.

With R3, through varying the values of the weights α and β from 0 to 1 with an increment of 0.1, such that $\alpha + \beta = 1$, and using the above experiment settings, 850 experiments were carried out in total.

Some summarised results are shown in Fig. 3. They clearly shows that the GDLEMs built with the three rules are generally superior to individual classifiers, because that the mean accuracies (shown in red lines on the figures) of the GDLEMs are approximately 10% higher than the mean accuracies (illustrated by blue lines) of the individual classifiers in the GDLEMs. In addition, it further demonstrated that our ensemble results have a higher level of accuracy overall than the best individual models, the MAMs. Hence, our GDLEM had the best reliability overall because the reliability of an MAM was not consistent over a succession of experiments. On the hand, the ensembles built with our method, the GDLEM, are more consistent and reliable as well as more accurate.

Figure 4 compares the results of GDLEMs built with the three rules and variable sizes from 3, 5, 7 to 19 on the test data. This shows the weakness of R1. Our previous studies indicated that there were accuracy issues with this rule. However, these became much more apparent in the current work when the

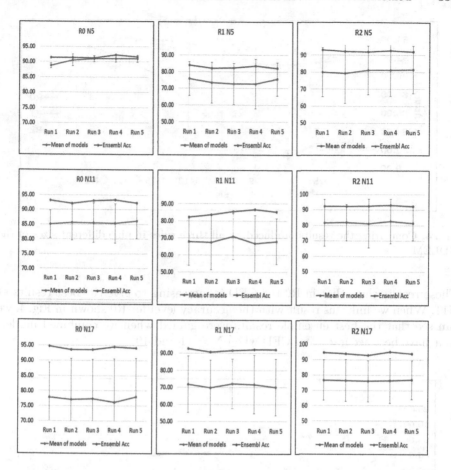

Fig. 3. Summaries of GDLEM results for rules R0, R1 and R2 and the size of ensemble 5, 11 and 17 are shown in each sub-graph. Tow lines (red and blue) are the accuracy of GDLEM and the mean accuracy for models that are chosen for the GDLEM respectively. The stranded deviation is shown by whiskers over 5 runs. (Color figure online)

high number of models were used. The increase in model numbers highlighted very clearly the disadvantages of R1. As can be seen, its accuracy levels varied inconsistently: started low and wend further lower; it only improved when N = 11. On all the way up to N = 19, it is still worse than two other rules.

R0 performed reasonably well because it combines all the models in the PM, which have the best accuracies. R2 is same as R0 when N = 3, but improved while R0 went down when the size increased, although they are similar after N = 11. But R2 is more favourable as it performed better when the size of ensembles is smaller, which means it is more efficient.

Figure 5 shows the average values of the CFD in the ensembles built with R0, R1 and R2, although the CFD is not used in R0 and R1. The purpose is to see if the CFD can be used to explain why some ensembles are better than others.

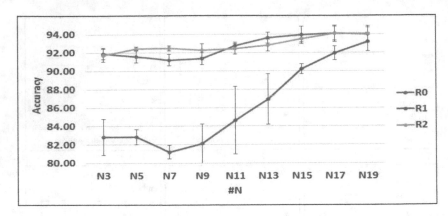

Fig. 4. Comparing the results produced by all three rules in nine different sizes of the GDLEM.

These results show that in R0 the CFD is increasing to give the best results at N11. When we link this result with the accuracy level for R0 shown in Fig. 4, we can see that the best ensemble results were gained when we combined models that have best accuracy and CFD when N = 11 and 19.

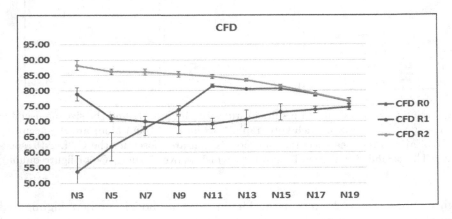

Fig. 5. Comparing the CFDs for all three rules in nine different sizes of the ensembles.

As R3 is a generalised and flexible rule, it gives the chance to do more investigation into the influences of the CFD in the ensemble. Figure 6 shows improvement in accuracy for model selection for some ensembles of size 3 to 9, given α is set between 0.5 and 0.6. For ensembles of size greater than 9, varying α and β does not have much impact on the accuracy level for the ensemble (See Fig. 7) and that is because the size of the model pool is too small. When the size of the ensemble reaches and succeeds the 50% of the model pool, there is not much space for selecting models and hence the ensembles could be more or less the same regardless of whatsoever models are chosen.

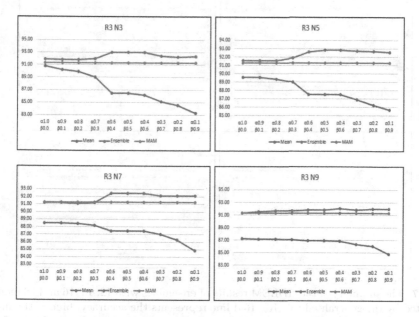

Fig. 6. Sample of GDLEM results for the generalised rule R3 with ensemble size 3, 5, 7 and 9 are shown in each sub-graph. Three lines: red for the accuracy of GDLEM, blue for the mean accuracy for models that are chosen for the GDLEM and grey for MAM. (Color figure online)

The best results are produced by R3 when the weight of the accuracy α is equal to 0.4 as it is shown in the critical difference digram in Fig. 8 and the weight for diversity is 0.6. And this means, when more weight, about 20%, is put on the diversity than on the accuracy, the ensembles with less accurate but more diverse modules achieved the best results. Moreover, the digram shows that the range between 0.4 and 0.6 for α performs better than others.

Thus, it can be seen that the generalised selection rule R3 is a combination of accuracy and CFD measures, gives chances to the GDLEM to select the models that can help improve the accuracy of heterogeneous ensembles. The systematic empirical investigations found the best ensembles are produced when the weights for accuracy and diversity are split at 0.4 to 0.6 respectively. That effect clearer when a large pool of models and we select number of models below the half. In summary, the ensembles built with model selection criteria that use a combination of CFD and DF and accuracy measures, gives good results. They are superior to those results obtained using either pair-wise diversity (R1) or just accuracy (R0).

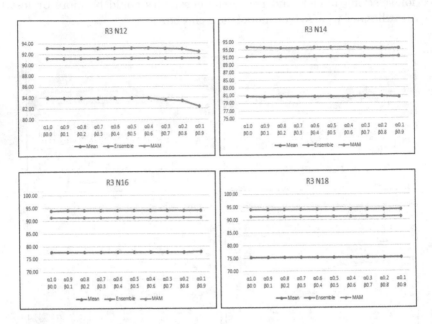

Fig. 7. The summary of the GDLEM results of ensembles with 12, 14, 16 and 18 models selected by the generalised rule R3. Red line represents the accuracy; blue = the mean accuracy of the models in the ensembles, and grey = MAM in the ensembles. (Color figure online)

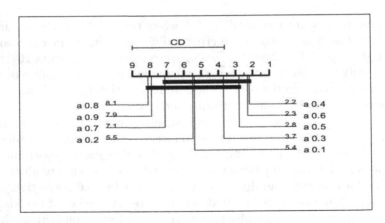

Fig. 8. A diagram shows critical differences of the average results of ensembles with different sizes from 3 to 19, when the accuracy weight α varied from 0.1 to 1.0 with a step size of 0.1.

4.3   Critical Comparison with Other Ensembles

The results of GDLEM were compared with the feature-level ensemble method(FLEM) and various heterogeneous ensembles based on the single media data, text (HEST) and image data (HESG). The full comparative results between the FLEM and the HESG were published in [12] and the full results for the HEST were published in [11]. Figure 9 shows the critical difference diagram for the GDLEM, DLEM, FLEM, HEST and HESG, with all rules R0, R1, R2 and R3. The GDLEM-R3 is the best on average and a credible explanation is this R3 with appropriate weights can produce the optimal combination between the accuracy and CFD to improve classification accuracy.

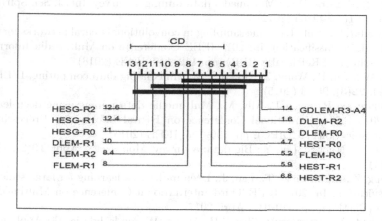

Fig. 9. Critical difference diagram for the ensembles built with GDELM, DLEM, Feature-Level Ensemble Method (FLEM), Hybrid Ensembles Built with Textual Data (HEST) and with Imagery Data (HESG) for all rules R0, R1, R2 and R3. It shows that the GDLEM with R3 is the best.

5   Conclusion and Future Work

In this study, we developed a generalised heterogeneous ensemble method to classify multi-media datasets at the decision level (GDLEM) aiming to achieve the best and most reliable accuracy results. Our GDLEM consists of four stages: extracting features from multi-media subsets, modelling the subsets datasets, selecting models with different rules based on various criteria, and building heterogeneous ensembles. The new model selection rule, R3, has been demonstrated to have a capability to select the individual models that are less accurate but more diverse. Hence, in some points, e.g. accuracy weight from 40% to 60%, it achieved the best level of ensemble accuracy beating those obtained by other ensembles, including DLEM, FLEM, HEST and HESG in the same dataset. Other obvious observation from this study is that heterogeneous ensemble gives better results when we combine accuracy and diversity measurements for model selection.

Suggestions for future work to improve our approach include (1) increasing model pool size so that there are more choices for model selection, (2) creating other complex selection rules by adding more measures in the relationship on the generalised R3, (3) of course, the approach should be tested on more multimedia datasets. Finally it should be extended to other different problems such as time serious classification.

References

1. More, S., Mishra, D.K.: Multimedia data mining: a survey. Int. J. Sci. Spirit. Bus. Technol. **1**(1), 49–55 (2012)
2. Pouyanfar, S., et al.: Dynamic sampling in convolutional neural networks for imbalanced data classification. In: 2018 IEEE Conference on Multimedia Information Processing and Retrieval (MIPR), pp. 112–117. IEEE (2018)
3. Zhu, W., Cui, P., Wang, Z., Hua, G.: Multimedia big data computing. IEEE Multimed. **22**(3), 96-c3 (2015)
4. Wlodarczak, P., Soar, J., Ally, M.: Multimedia data mining using deep learning. In: 2015 Fifth International Conference on Digital Information Processing and Communications (ICDIPC), pp. 190–196. IEEE (2015)
5. Chen, M., Mao, S., Liu, Y.: Big data: a survey. Mob. Netw. Appl. **19**(2), 171–209 (2014)
6. Kuang, Z., Li, Z., Zhao, T., Fan, J.: Deep multi-task learning for large-scale image classification. In: 2017 IEEE Third International Conference on Multimedia Big Data (BigMM), pp. 310–317, April 2017
7. Mojahed, A., Bettencourt-Silva, J.H., Wang, W., de la Iglesia, B.: Applying clustering analysis to heterogeneous data using similarity matrix fusion (SMF). In: Perner, P. (ed.) MLDM 2015. LNCS (LNAI), vol. 9166, pp. 251–265. Springer, Cham (2015). https://doi.org/10.1007/978-3-319-21024-7_17
8. Wang, W.: Some fundamental issues in ensemble methods. In: IEEE International Joint Conference on Neural Networks, IJCNN 2008. (IEEE World Congress on Computational Intelligence), pp. 2243–2250. IEEE (2008)
9. Krawczyk, B., Minku, L.L., Gama, J., Stefanowski, J., Woźniak, M.: Ensemble learning for data stream analysis: a survey. Inf. Fusion **37**, 132–156 (2017)
10. Woźniak, M., Graña, M., Corchado, E.: A survey of multiple classifier systems as hybrid systems. Inf. Fusion **16**, 3–17 (2014)
11. Alyahyan, S., Farrash, M., Wang, W.: Heterogeneous ensemble for imaginary scene classification. In: Proceedings of the 8th International Joint Conference on Knowledge Discovery, Knowledge Engineering and Knowledge Management (IC3K 2016), KDIR, Porto, Portugal, 9–11 November 2016, vol. 1, pp. 197–204 (2016)
12. Alyahyan, S., Wang, W.: Feature level ensemble method for classifying multi-media data. In: Bramer, M., Petridis, M. (eds.) SGAI 2017. LNCS (LNAI), vol. 10630, pp. 235–249. Springer, Cham (2017). https://doi.org/10.1007/978-3-319-71078-5_21
13. Mojahed, A., de la Iglesia, B.: An adaptive version of k-medoids to deal with the uncertainty in clustering heterogeneous data using an intermediary fusion approach. Knowl. Inf. Syst. **50**(1), 27–52 (2017)
14. Yamanishi, K.: Distributed cooperative Bayesian learning strategies. Inf. Comput. **150**(1), 22–56 (1999)

15. Onan, A.: An ensemble scheme based on language function analysis and feature engineering for text genre classification. J. Inf. Sci. **44**, 28–47 (2016). https://doi.org/10.1177/0165551516677911

16. Ballard, C., Wang, W.: Dynamic ensemble selection methods for heterogeneous data mining. In: 2016 12th World Congress on Intelligent Control and Automation (WCICA), pp. 1021–1026. IEEE (2016)

17. Amato, F., Moscato, V., Picariello, A., Sperlì, G.: Recommendation in social media networks. In: Third IEEE International Conference on Multimedia Big Data, Laguna Hills, CA, USA, 19–21 April 2017 (2017)

18. Liu, H., Wei, Z., Chen, Y., Pan, J., Lin, L., Ren, Y.: Drone detection based on an audio-assisted camera array. In: Third IEEE International Conference on Multimedia Big Data, Laguna Hills, CA, USA, 19–21 April 2017, pp. 402–406. IEEE Computer Society (2017)

19. Giacinto, G., Roli, F.: Design of effective neural network ensembles for image classification purposes. Image Vis. Comput. **19**(9), 699–707 (2001)

20. Partridge, D., Krzanowski, W.: Software diversity: practical statistics for its measurement and exploitation. Inf. Softw. Technol. **39**(10), 707–717 (1997)

21. Witten, I.H., Frank, E., Hall, M.A., Pal, C.J.: Data Mining: Practical Machine Learning Tools and Techniques. Morgan Kaufmann, Burlington (2016)

22. Oliva, A., Torralba, A.: Modeling the shape of the scene: a holistic representation of the spatial envelope. Int. J. Comput. Vis. **42**(3), 145–175 (2001)

23. Dalal, N., Triggs, B.: Histograms of oriented gradients for human detection. In: IEEE Computer Society Conference on Computer Vision and Pattern Recognition, CVPR 2005, vol. 1, pp. 886–893. IEEE (2005)

Applications of Machine Learning

Spotting Earnings Manipulation: Using Machine Learning for Financial Fraud Detection

Kumar Rahul, Nandini Seth[(⊠)], and U. Dinesh Kumar

Indian Institute of Management, Bangalore, India
kumar.rahulra@iimb.ac.in,
{nandini.seth15, dineshk}@iimb.ernet.in

Abstract. Earnings manipulation and accounting fraud leads to reduced firm valuation in the long run and a public distrust in the company and its management. Yet, manipulation of accruals to hide liabilities and inflate earnings has been a long-standing fraudulent conduct amongst many listed firms. As auditing is time consuming and restricted to a sample of entries, fraud is either not detected or detected belatedly. We believe that supervised machine learning models can be used to determine high risk firms early enough for auditing by the regulator. We also discuss the anomaly detection unsupervised learning methodology. Since the proportion of manipulators is much lower than the non-manipulators, the biggest challenge in predicting earnings manipulation is the imbalance in the data leading to biased results for conventional statistical models. In this paper, we build ensemble models to detect accrual manipulation by borrowing theory from the seminal work done by Beneish. We also showcase a novel simulation-based sampling technique to efficiently handle imbalanced dataset and illustrate our results on data from listed Indian firms. We compare existing ensemble models establishing the superiority of fairly simple boosting models whilst commenting on the shortfall of area under ROC curve as a performance metric for imbalanced datasets. The paper makes two major contributions: (i) a functional contribution of suggesting an easily deployable strategy to identify high risk companies; (ii) a methodological contribution of suggesting a simulation-based sampling approach that can be applied in other cases of highly imbalanced data for utilizing the entire dataset in modeling.

Keywords: Earnings manipulation · Accrual manipulation · Data analytics
Bagging · Boosting · Gaussian model · Supervised learning
Unsupervised learning · Ensemble methods · Sampling · Simulation

1 Introduction

1.1 Context

Advancements in technology, early stage funding, improved regulations and increased foreign investment has led to the emergence of many new businesses in the last decade in India. The two operational stock exchanges in India-National Stock Exchange of India and Bombay Stock Exchange are the 10th and 12th largest stock exchanges in the

© Springer Nature Switzerland AG 2018
M. Bramer and M. Petridis (Eds.): SGAI-AI 2018, LNAI 11311, pp. 343–356, 2018.
https://doi.org/10.1007/978-3-030-04191-5_29

world respectively. In 2017, the total number of listed companies in Indian stock exchange was approximately 5600 [1]. While these businesses have prudent revenue models, high competition and socio-economic factors act as deterrents in sustaining growth and facilitating expansion in the market. This shrinking market share directly impacts the financial health of these companies. Their publicly declared earnings are signals to the stakeholders about management performance as well as the future resources and prospects of the firm. It has been observed that to maintain a better public image, moderate share prices and manage shareholder pressure, firms usually want to publicly report positive turnarounds only. The phenomena of earnings manipulation is not new globally. In 2001, Enron filed for bankruptcy after an accounting fraud resulted in $ 74 billion loss to the shareholders [2]. The industry giant Lehman Brothers also met with similar fate in 2008 despite the $ 639 billion in assets [3]. Despite manipulations close to $ 1.7 billion, the promoters of Indian front runner Satyam Computers were not penalized due to a delayed investigation [4]. Since investigation of fraud is often tedious and time consuming, an early warning system about earnings manipulation will be useful both the regulatory authorities and the stakeholders. Earnings manipulation has been an area of academic interest for over 30 years now. The 1970s and early 1980s witnessed a number of studies investigating the elements of accounting choices. The period following mid-1980s was used up in studying accrual-based earnings manipulation while the turn of the century marked increased focus on researching real earnings manipulation. Despite all advancements, authorities still rely on insider input (whistle blowers) and sample-based auditing to identify defaulters.

1.2 Relevant Literature

In financial literature, earnings management and fraud are defined to be subparts of earnings manipulation. While they differ in intensity and technique, they are utilized to achieve a favorable level of firm earnings. Schipper [5] defines earnings management as:

> *"a purposeful intervention in the external financial reporting process, with the intent of obtaining some private gain [as opposed to, say, merely facilitating the neutral operation of the process]... Under this definition, earnings management could occur in any part of the external disclosure process, and could take a number of forms. A minor extension of this definition would encompass "real" earnings management, accomplished by timing investment or financing decisions to alter reported earnings or some subset of it"*

This is in line with the definition later provided by Healy and Wahlen [6] who define earnings management as the activity where

> *"managers use judgment in financial reporting and in structuring transactions to alter financial reports to either mislead some stakeholders about the underlying business of the company or to influence contractual outcomes that depend on reported accounting numbers..."*

Primarily, firms can manipulate earnings by utilizing their accounting choices known as accrual manipulations. This includes clever use of accounting moderations permissible under generally accepted accounting principles (GAAP) such as deferred tax expense, stock repurchase, restructuring charge reversals etc. Extensive research has been done in understanding the pervasiveness of accrual-based manipulation [7]. Alternatively, earnings can also be manipulated through altering operating cash flow known as real earnings manipulation. Real earnings management is the modification of the timing and scale of business activities to manipulate earnings. This includes activities such as research and development (R&D) expenditures, capital investments, and the production, sale and disposal of long-term assets etc. [8]. It has been observed that real manipulations used to meet earnings benchmarks impact future performance of the firm [9] There is empirical evidence to establish that managers typically use these two types of manipulation as substitutes but switch between the two depending on the auditing atmosphere [10, 11]. Managers' sequential decisions about both kinds of manipulation have been studied with evidence [12]. Alleged manipulator firms manipulate more than one income statement line item in their financial statements with the topmost choices being revenue, inventory and cost of goods sold [13]. Researchers have also tried to understand the behavioral aspects of earnings manipulation such as auditor's responses to high risk firms [14] and CEO's earnings manipulation behavior [15].

2 Conceptual Framework

Research on detecting earnings manipulation is long standing yet inadequate. Earlier models used discretionary components of reported income to detect manipulators. While these models (Healy model, DeAngelo Model, Jones Model, Industry Model) appeared to be well specified, they all generated tests of low power for earnings management of economically plausible magnitude [16]. Despite the performance, these models lay the ground work for aggregate accrual models. Beneish [17] combined three things (i) cash flow and accrual variables from Healy and Jones models; (ii) Concept of contract-based incentive for earnings manipulation [18] and (iii) signals on poor future prospects of a firm to build a model for detecting manipulation. Our paper builds on this foundational model to provide a functional machine learning approach to manipulation detection. Beneish showcased the use of an econometric model to analyze companies' financial data for prediction. He used the probit regression on eight derived financial ratios to build a score-based model to differentiate manipulators and non-manipulators. While this work was a beneficial attempt to solving this problem, regression (with logit or probit link functions) for classification builds on the fact that there is ample data to provide enough learning opportunities for both classes. In real life, the proportion of manipulators is likely to be disproportionately lesser compared to non-manipulators. A highly imbalanced data such as this one requires advanced algorithms to correctly demarcate the two existing classes. In this paper, we have used two modelling approaches – supervised and unsupervised learning to build upon Beneish's work.

3 Data Description

Using the SEBI (Security and Exchange Board of India) reports and the LexisNexis database, we collected information pertaining to earnings manipulation for the time period 2005–2015. A total of 39 manipulator firms which have been publicly declared to have committed fraud were identified through SEBI annual reports and LexisNexis database. We extracted the financial data for these 39 companies along with 1,200 high sales volume non-manipulator firms using the Prowess database. As expected, the dataset thus obtained was highly imbalanced containing 96.86% non-manipulators and 3.14% manipulators. The data has a final status column with labels "No" and "Yes" with "No" signaling companies that were not identified as manipulator and "Yes" signaling companies identified as manipulators by SEBI and LexisNexis. We used this data to calculate the financial ratios reported by these 1239 companies to SEBI in their quarterly filing.

In line with the common approach - the total observations were randomly split into training and test set. The 70% of the observations i.e. 868 data points were used for model training and the remaining 30% i.e. 371 observations were used for model testing. Figure 1 provides a descriptive summary for all the variables presented in Table 1 for the collected data set. The summary is provided separately for both the classification classes, also to check the distribution of the variables. We use these ratios as independent variables to build our models.

4 Sampling Strategy

Computation statistical algorithms use sampling as an approach to create varied experiences for the machine to learn on. While dealing with imbalanced datasets, we need to create a more stable distinction between the majority and minority class. As we observed, we have 1200 non-manipulators i.e. instances belonging to the majority class and 39 manipulators i.e. instances belonging to the minority class in the current dataset.

In this paper, we propose a sampling strategy based on monte-carlo simulation technique. The sampling technique uses the existing data to generate new experiences i.e. new observations to obtain a balance in the modelling dataset. This sampling technique performs better than the existing techniques such as up-sampling, bootstrap sampling and synthetic sampling of minority class (SMOTE). The key idea here is to use the distribution parameters of these variables to generate new data-points for the minority class. This way, we are not repeating the same observations to create a balanced dataset as in the case of bootstrap sampling and up-sampling. We are also using 100% data available in the test sample and therefore not losing any information as in the case of down-sampling. The down-sampling strategy would use only 6% of the observations for the new sample generation. Since we are following the method of monte-carlo simulation, we need to draw randomly from a normally distributed sample. We assume that the variables of interest here have a distribution which is a member of the Johnson family of distribution. This system covers a wide variety of distributions which can be transformed into normal distribution by optimally choosing one of the three families of distributions. The parameters are estimated using the sample quartile

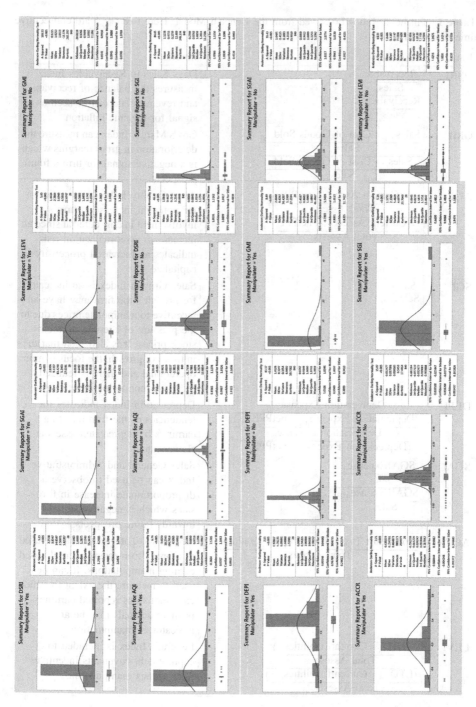

Fig. 1. Summary of the variables given in the Beneish model calculated for the available dataset

Table 1. Financial Ratios borrowed from the Beneish Model. Here t & t − 1 are consecutive time periods in Years

Ratio	Formula	Intuition
DSRI	$$\dfrac{\dfrac{Receivable_{(t)}}{Sales_{(t)}}}{\dfrac{Receivable_{(t-1)}}{Sales_{(t-1)}}}$$	Days Sales to Receivables Index measures the balance of receivables and revenues and can be seen as a signal for revenue inflation
GMI	$$\dfrac{\dfrac{Sales_{(t-1)} - Cost\ of\ Goods\ Sold_{(t-1)}}{Sales_{(t-1)}}}{\dfrac{Sales_{(t)} - Cost\ of\ Goods\ Sold_{(t)}}{Sales_{(t)}}}$$	Gross Margin Index can measure the deterioration in gross margins which is a negative signal for firm's future prospects
AQI	$$\dfrac{\dfrac{1-(Current\ Assest_{(t)} + netPPE_{(t)})}{Total\ Assests_{(t)}}}{\dfrac{1-(Current\ Assest_{(t-1)} + netPPE_{(t-1)})}{Total\ Assests_{(t-1)}}}$$	Asset Quality Index is an indicator for potential increase in firm's involvement in cost deferral since an increase in asset realization risk indicates an increased propensity to capitalize
SGI	$$\dfrac{Sales_{(t)}}{Sales_{(t-1)}}$$	Sales Growth Index is an indicator for growth - the firm may have an incentive to manipulate prices due to the pressure of keeping up their stock prices. It is also seen that the in times of growth, the focus is more operational and there is reduced focus on monitoring and reporting
DEPI	$$\dfrac{\dfrac{Depreciation\ Expense_{(t-1)}}{(Depreciation\ Expense_{(t-1)} + netPPE_{(t-1)})}}{\dfrac{Depreciation\ Expense_{(t)}}{(Depreciation\ Expense_{(t)} + netPPE_{(t)})}}$$	Depreciation Index indicates the tendencies of the firm boosting earnings by depreciated assets at a slower rate
SGAI	$$\dfrac{\dfrac{SGAIExpense_{(t)}}{Sales_{(t)}}}{\dfrac{SGAIExpense_{(t-1)}}{Sales_{(t-1)}}}$$	Sales General and Administrative Index can be used to observe a disproportionate increase in firm sales which is negative signal towards future prospects
ACCR	$$\dfrac{Profit\ after\ Tax_{(t)} - Cash\ from\ Operations_{(t)}}{Total\ Assests_{(t)}}$$	Accruals to Total Assets can be used as a proxy to measure accrual based earning manipulations. It can be used to measure the extent to which cash motivates reported earnings-positive accruals may be an indicator of manipulation
LEVI	$$\dfrac{\dfrac{(LTD_{(t)} + CurrentLiabilities_{(t)})}{Total\ Assests_{(t)}}}{\dfrac{(LTD_{(t-1)} + CurrentLiabilities_{(t-1)})}{Total\ Assests_{(t-1)}}}$$	Leverage Index is included to capture debt covenants incentives for earnings manipulation

ratio along with Shapiro–Wilk test of normality [19]. Readers are encouraged to read [19] for more details on transformation and estimation methodology.

As can be seen from the summary, none of the eight variables exhibited a normal distribution pattern directly, however Johnson transformation on the five variables (AQI, SGAI, ACCR, LEVI and DEPI) resulted in normal distributions. We use only these five variables to generate simulated samples from the data. We generated a total of 812 new observations so that the training set has 50% representation of each class (840 non manipulators, 28 + 812 = 840 manipulators). The distribution identification analysis for manipulators and non-manipulators was done for the transformed variables and is summarized in Fig. 2.

5 Ensemble Model Results

5.1 Supervised Learning Algorithm

In this section we show the superiority of using ensemble methods over statistical models to perform classification. For classification problems, ensemble refers to the process of aggregating the results of several models using a systematic approach of majority voting or weighted majority voting. Two of the most commonly used ensemble methods are bagging and boosting. Both of these ensemble methods in turn rely on the sampling strategy to give superior performance on an imbalanced dataset. Bagging is the process of iteratively taking bootstrap sample from the training dataset to determine outcome and aggregating the results. Each of these iterations is trained independently on a full-sized sample picked randomly but with replacement from the original dataset. These models can be trained in parallel since they train independently. We expect predictions from different models to be different since the samples have overlaps but are different with high probability.

We applied the bagging ensemble method to our given data using the Random Forest technique [20] on the simulated sample explained in the previous section (Table 2).

The performance of the random forest model on the test set is shown in Table 3.

The ensemble technique of Boosting creates a strong classifier using multiple weak classifiers. This leads to a model which is sequential in nature. The initial model assigns equal weights to all the observations and is based on a full-sized sample randomly selected with replacement. These weights decide the likelihood of the observation being picked in the next sample. The observations which have the highest error (for a regression model) have higher probability of being picked in the consecutive trials. This is achieved by adjusting the weight parameter. Therefore, with each step, the patterns which are most difficult get chosen by the algorithm. As expected, different models are better in different part of the observation space. Regressors are combined using weighted median. Models which are more confident about their predictions are weighted more heavily.

Ada boost is the simplest of boosting algorithm which can be used for solving classification problem. In its naïve form, ada boost makes one level decision tree. However, there are many variations to the ada boost model. We implemented two

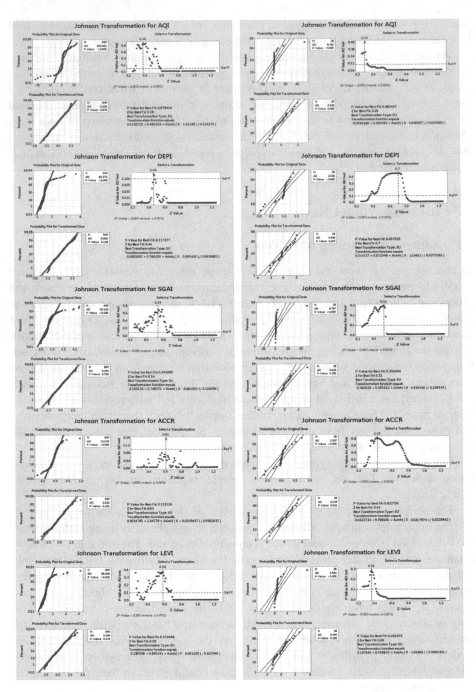

Fig. 2. Distribution pattern of the 5 financial ratios used for model building. (Column 1: Non-Manipulators, Column 2: Manipulators)

specific boosting algorithms on our dataset. Adaboost.M1 using Adaboost.M1() and eXGBoost Gradient Boosting using xgbTree() in R. We applied these two algorithms on the original training data as well as by resorting the simulation-based sampling suggested in the earlier section. With all the three fine tuning parameters, the search grid functionality of caret package reported the best model with mfinal = 100, max-depth = 4 and coeflearn = Breiman. The outcome of the ada boost with simulated sampling is shown in Table 4.

Table 2. Classification matrix on simulation sampling using random forest

Summary: 1680 (entries are percentual average cell counts across resamples)

		Reference	
		No	Yes
Prediction	No	28.6	21.9
	Yes	22.1	27.4
Accuracy (average): 0.5599			

Table 3. Classification matrix on test set with random forest using simulation sampling

Confusion matrix and statistics

		Reference	
		No	Yes
Prediction	No	217	4
	Yes	143	7
Accuracy (average): 0.604; Sensitivity: 0.6027; Specificity: 0.6363			

Table 4. Classification matrix on synthetic sampling using ada boost

Summary: 1680 (entries are percentual average cell counts across resamples)

		Reference	
		No	Yes
Prediction	No	29.8	22.8
	Yes	20.2	27.2
Accuracy (average): 0.5702			

The performance of the ada boost model on 371 observation reserved as test is shown in Table 5.

With all the fine-tuning parameters implemented using the search grid functionality of caret package the outcome of the XG boost with simulated sampling is shown in Table 6.

The performance of the random forest model on 371 observation reserved as test is shown in Table 7.

As can be seen by the confusion matrix, we are able to achieve a high level of specificity making the number of firms that need to be audited less. We can also see that

Table 5. Classification matrix on test set with ada boost using synthetic sampling

Confusion matrix and statistics		Reference	
		No	Yes
Prediction	No	216	2
	Yes	144	9
Accuracy (average): 0.605; Sensitivity: 0.6000; Specificity: 0.8181			

Table 6. Classification matrix on synthetic sampling using XGboost

Summary: 1680 (entries are percentual average cell counts across resamples)		Reference	
		No	Yes
Prediction	No	27.4	21.5
	Yes	22.6	28.5
Accuracy (average): 0.5595			

Table 7. Classification matrix on test set with XG boost using synthetic sampling

Confusion matrix and statistics		Reference	
		No	Yes
Prediction	No	192	2
	Yes	168	9
Accuracy (average): 0.542; Sensitivity: 0.5333; Specificity: 0.8181			

a high number of manipulators are being classified correctly which was not the case when conventional models like logistic, neural networks, random forest etc. were used without sampling. While down-sampling gave comparable results, the biggest disadvantage with it is the reduction of data significantly.

After seeing the results for the various models in the previous section, one is also compelled to question the ability of ROC to be a suitable metric to judge the performance of the model. Under circumstances such as this, standard measures such as sensitivity, specificity, precision, area under the ROC curve and the Youden's index may fail to identify the best model (Fig. 3).

5.2 Unsupervised Learning Algorithms

Unsupervised learning algorithms do not use the information available on the dependent variable and use only the distribution of the independent variables to build models. The models identify structures i.e. data patterns and groups within the data to determine the labels. The most popular approaches to unsupervised learning are clustering, independent component analysis and association rules. Unsupervised learning is

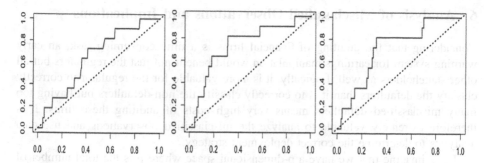

Fig. 3. ROC Curve with simulating sampling for (i) random forest: AUC 0.6460 (ii) ada boost: AUC 0.7442 (iii) XG boost: AUC 0.7199

believed to be much closer to artificial intelligence than supervised learning as we let the algorithm determine the complex processes within data without much external guidance.

Since our data is characterized by high skewness – our approach should accommodate that. The key idea we explore is that of anomaly detection. Anomalies are patterns in our data that do not conform to a well-defined notion of normal behavior. The drawback of using supervised learning is that while the usual training methods may detect fraudulent behavior similar to the one that it has been trained on effectively, it may fail to detect new anomalies in data.

It is relatively easier to make use of the Gaussian distribution when talking of anomaly detection. A data that is normally distributed will conform to a set of predefined probabilistic rules. Any new set of values will have to conform to those rules for the algorithm to recognize them as being "normal" or "usual". The values that do not conform would be labelled as unusual or anomalous. We used the well-known approach of Gaussian anomaly detection as an exploratory starting point to understand the label-less approach. We encourage readers to read [21] for a better understanding of anomaly detection. We obtained the confusion matrix shown in Table 8.

Table 8. Confusion matrix for Gaussian anomaly detection

Confusion matrix and statistics			
		Reference	
		No	Yes
Prediction	No	214	86
	Yes	10	29
Accuracy (average): 0.7168			

6 Analysis of Misclassified Observations and Implications

Considering that the auditing of financial firms is a time consuming task, an early warning system for earnings manipulation would benefit not just the regulators but all other stakeholders as well. Logically, it is more valuable for the regulator to correctly classify the defaulters than it is to correctly classify the non-defaulters but having too many misclassified defaulters means very high costs of auditing these firms. It is therefore extremely valuable to analyze the misclassified observations and use data analytics to determine the correct deployment strategy.

Let's imagine that we have a p-dimensional space where p is the total number of variables of interest. For instance, in the given data, p is 8. Each instance of our data will be a point in this space. If we are able to identify regions where probability of default is high, we can flag all firms belonging to that area as "high risk" and consider them eligible for regulatory audit. We can do this by simply observing the data points closer to firms that have committed fraud. This is the deployable approach we are suggesting in the paper. We consider all the correctly classified defaulter firms and calculate p-sphere around them to be the high risk region. We propose that these contain high risk firms which should be audited.

We analysed the most basic form of nearest neighbourhood for the correctly classified defaulter firms and concluded that on the basis of Euclidean distance, a p-sphere of radius 2.64 can accommodate all the misclassified values if bagging algorithm is used along with the simulated sampling approach that we suggested. Similarly for the boosting algorithms – Adaboost and XGboost, we would need spheres of radius 2.17 and 2.11 respectively if the same sampling strategy is followed. While these distances look imprecise on the onset, the key idea here is to construct a region within which instances can be treated as highly risky. These regions will get smaller (number of firms will reduce) as we keep identifying more defaulters. As expected, the regulator will always prefer to audit additional firms in order to capture all the defaulters. It is also interesting to note that while the set of defaulters used in the current dataset are declared by SEBI and LexisNexis, there is a possibility that there are firms which perform earnings manipulations but haven't been caught. When the manipulation is a result of a malicious and intended action, the adversaries will try to make the fraudulent observation appear like its normal, thereby making its detection difficult. Since the approach presented here suggests the audit of all the firms displaying behaviour similar to know defaulters, it highly likely that the regulators might discover other defaulters too. It is also worth noting that since the machine is learning on the basis of the given data, the more information we get on defaulters, the more our results are likely to improve.

Identifying anomalies in the data i.e. identifying which firms are behaving out of their usual character is highly valuable in detection of earnings manipulation. This deployment strategy holds an increased importance in the case of a new firms. If these new firms do not conform to the "normal" of the market – this might indicate that they are running a high risk of being a manipulator and should therefore be audited. Given the approach that we suggested in this paper, one can determine the p-dimensional Euclidean distance of the new instance from the existing defaulters to determine if it is close enough to be flagged as high risk. The accrual behaviour of these firms may resemble that of fraudulent firms as flagged by SEBI and LexisNexis. There is tremendous managerial value in deploying this strategy to identify defaulters in advance.

7 Limitations and Future Scope

This is the first paper by the authors in this ongoing stream of work. We have identified some limitations and possible future extensions of this foundational paper which are discussed in this section. We have used various sampling strategies in an attempt to remove the data bias, however random forest is the only technique used from the ensemble family of bagging models. For further improvements, we propose the use of other mature ensemble techniques such as model averaged neural network, randomGLM, random ferns, bagged logicFS, bagged discrimination analysis and understand the efficiency of these techniques. The authors are also working on developing a simulated sampling strategy which does not require normality in variable data. While we have relied on the financial ratios used in the Beneish model to carry out our analysis, it may be useful to investigate the other financial ratios which may help in improving the classification of companies based on earnings manipulation. As for the deployment strategy, one may also want to explore other distance metrices other than the Euclidean distance to identify manipulator-like cases as well as other unsupervised learning methodologies.

We see that sampling plays a critical role in machine learning algorithms. The usefulness of sampling intensifies when the dataset is imbalanced. Though traditional methods of data analysis have long been used to detect fraud, they require complex and time-consuming investigations and an inherent knowledge of finance, economics, business practices and corporate law. However, modern day machine learning techniques and technological capabilities can help with fraud detection well before the damage is done. In this paper we have attempted to provide an easily applicable pre-auditing methodology for shortlisting which firms need to be scrutinized by the regulators.

References

1. NSE: https://en.wikipedia.org/wiki/National_Stock_Exchange_of_India
2. Enron Scam: https://www.history.com/this-day-in-history/enron-files-for-bankruptcy
3. Lehman Scam: https://en.wikipedia.org/wiki/Bankruptcy_of_Lehman_Brothers
4. Satyam Scam: https://en.wikipedia.org/wiki/Satyam_scandal
5. Schipper, K.: Earnings management. Account. Horiz. 3(4), 91 (1989)
6. Healy, P.M., Wahlen, J.M.: A review of the earnings management literature and its implications for standard setting. Account. Horiz. 13(4), 365–383 (1999)
7. Beneish, M.D.: Earnings management: a perspective. Manag. Finan. 27(12), 3–17 (2001)
8. Xu, R.Z., Taylor, G.K., Dugan, M.T.: Review of real earnings management literature. J. Account. Lit. 26, 195 (2007)

9. Gunny, K.A.: The relation between earnings management using real activities manipulation and future performance: evidence from meeting earnings benchmarks. Contemp. Account. Res. **27**(3), 855–888 (2010)

10. Zang, A.: Evidence on the tradeoff between real manipulation and accrual manipulation. Account. Rev. **84**, 675–703 (2007)

11. Chi, W., Lisic, L.L., Pevzner, M.: Is enhanced audit quality associated with greater real earnings management? Account. Horiz. **25**(2), 315–335 (2011)

12. Zang, A.Y.: Evidence on the trade-off between real activities manipulation and accrual-based earnings management. Account. Rev. **87**(2), 675–703 (2011)

13. Dechow, P.M., Sloan, R.G., Sweeney, A.P.: Causes and consequences of earnings manipulation: an analysis of firms subject to enforcement actions by the SEC. Contemp. Account. Res. **13**(1), 1–36 (1996)

14. Bedard, J.C., Johnstone, K.M.: Earnings manipulation risk, corporate governance risk, and auditors' planning and pricing decisions. Account. Rev. **79**(2), 277–304 (2004)

15. Zhang, X., Bartol, K.M., Smith, K.G., Pfarrer, M.D., Khanin, D.M.: CEOs on the edge: earnings manipulation and stock-based incentive misalignment. Acad. Manag. J. **51**(2), 241–258 (2008)

16. Dechow, P.M., Sloan, R.G., Sweeney, A.P.: Detecting earnings management. Account. Rev. **70**, 193–225 (1995)

17. Beneish, M.D.: The detection of earnings manipulation. Financ. Anal. J. **55**(5), 24–36 (1999)

18. Watts, R., Zimmerman, J.: Positive Accounting Theory. Prentice-Hall Inc., Upper Saddle River (1996)

19. Chou, Y.M., Polansky, A.M., Mason, R.L.: Transforming non-normal data to normality in statistical process control. J. Qual. Technol. **30**(2), 133–141 (1998)

20. Breiman, L.: Random forests. Mach. Learn. **45**(1), 5–32 (2001)

21. Chandola, V., Banerjee, A., Kumar, V.: Anomaly detection: a survey. ACM Comput. Surv. (CSUR) **41**(3), 15 (2009)

Context Extraction for Aspect-Based Sentiment Analytics: Combining Syntactic, Lexical and Sentiment Knowledge

Anil Bandhakavi[1], Nirmalie Wiratunga[1(✉)], Stewart Massie[1], and Rushi Luhar[2]

[1] School of Computing, Robert Gordon University, Aberdeen, UK
{a.s.bandhakavi,n.wiratunga,s.massie}@rgu.ac.uk
[2] SentiSum, London, UK
rushi@sentisum.com

Abstract. Aspect-level sentiment analysis of customer feedback data when done accurately can be leveraged to understand strong and weak performance points of businesses and services and also formulate critical action steps to improve their performance. In this work we focus on aspect-level sentiment classification studying the role of opinion context extraction for a given aspect and the extent to which traditional and neural sentiment classifiers benefit when trained using the opinion context text. We introduce a novel method that combines lexical, syntactical and sentiment knowledge effectively to extract opinion context for aspects. Thereafter we validate the quality of the opinion contexts extracted with human judgments using the BLEU score. Further we evaluate the usefulness of the opinion contexts for aspect-sentiment analysis. Our experiments on benchmark data sets from SemEval and a real-world dataset from the insurance domain suggests that extracting the right opinion context combining syntactical with sentiment co-occurrence knowledge leads to the best aspect-sentiment classification performance. From a commercial point of view, accurate aspect extraction, provides an elegant means to identify "pain-points" in a business. Integrating our work into a commercial CX platform (https://www.sentisum.com/) is enabling the company's clients to better understand their customer opinions.

Keywords: Aspect extraction · Sentiment analysis
Natural language processing · Machine learning

1 Introduction

Sentiment analysis (SA) is the computational study of opinionated text with increasing relevance to on-line commercial applications. Sentence level analysis of opinionated content is common but these ignore sentence structure and semantic

M. Bramer and M. Petridis (Eds.): SGAI-AI 2018, LNAI 11311, pp. 357–371, 2018.
https://doi.org/10.1007/978-3-030-04191-5_30

constructs [10,14]. Basically they attempt to detect the overall polarity of a sentence, paragraph, or text span, irrespective of the entities mentioned (e.g. restaurant) and their aspects (e.g. price). Increasingly, more granular analysis is needed to better understand the target of the opinion, referred to as the aspect, as well as the context within which that sentiment is being expressed [13]. Indeed the ability to analyze opinionated content beyond just the surface level is crucial to discover meaningful business insights for companies. For instance given *the food was amazing but the service could have been better*, we can observe that although the overall sentence polarity can be viewed as being positive, there is to some degree a level of negative polarity also being expressed towards aspect, *service*, when sentence context, *the service could have been better*, is inspected more closely.

Context-aware analysis calls for methods that not only extract aspects, but also extract relevant context about each aspect from within the sentence in order to infer the polarity of sentiment (positive, negative or neutral) and its strength expressed numerically on a positive to negative scale [12]. For example, in the sentence *food is good at the restaurant but the price is too high*, there are two aspects (food, price) discussed with differing sentiment. In this example, traditional SA would identify the sentiment to be either positive or negative which is less useful for understanding the specific opinion of the user about food and price at the restaurant.

Typically feedback content has multiple aspects with differing sentiment towards them. Context can allow us to map the relevant sentiment to its associated aspect. Therefore context extraction is important to support the disambiguation of this mapping and therefore improve aspect level sentiment analysis. Accordingly our contributions are:

- a comparative study of context extraction approaches on benchmark and real-world data sets;
- a novel hybrid approach for aspect context extraction which combines syntactic analysis and sentiment co-occurrence knowledge; and
- integration of the approach as a scalable extension into a commercial system that analyses high volume real-world customer feedback data for insight discovery.

In the rest of the paper we review related literature in Sect. 2. In Sects. 3 and 4 we formulate the different methods of opinion context extraction and also describe the sentiment classifiers used. Section 5 describes our evaluation with insights on the experimental datasets and analysis of the results. In Sect. 6 we consider the role of context extraction in a real world analytics system before presenting our conclusions in Sect. 7.

2   Related Work

Aspect-Based Sentiment Analysis identifies both the sentiment present in the text as well as the specific target on which the sentiment is expressed. Context plays a key role in mapping sentiment to its target aspect. Aspect-Based

Sentiment Analysis can be considered as three staged pipeline: aspect extraction, opinion context extraction and aspect-level sentiment analysis.

Various methods have been used for identifying and extracting aspect terms, for example Conditional Random Fields (CRF), Support Vector Machines (SVM), Random Trees and Random Forest. One approach is to extract all the different nouns and noun phrases from the text and consider them as candidate aspect terms [9]. Schouten develop a co-occurrence based method for category discovery using a dictionary-based sentiment classification algorithm through which aspects can be identified by an annotation process [20]. Alternatively, aspect extraction can be modeled as a sequential labeling task with features extracted for CRF training [22]. In addition to the common features used in Named Entity Recognition (NER) systems, it also uses available external resources for building different name lists and word clusters.

Supervised machine learning can also be used to extract the aspect term [22]. An aspect can be expressed by a noun, adjective, verb or adverb. In [17] the aspect term is extracted by casting it as a sequence tagging task, in which each token in a candidate sentence is denoted as either *beginning, inside* or *outside* (BIO). CRFs are used for extracting aspect terms along with the BIO model for representation [3]. The CRFs together with a linear chain CRF are used for determining conditional probability. The authors employ a graph co-ranking approach, to model aspect terms and opinion words as graph nodes, and then they generate three different sub-graphs defining their bond between the nodes [6]. To obtain a list of dependable aspect terms, the candidate nodes are ranked using a combined random walk on the three sub graphs. In this work we extract aspects manually and focus on evaluating different approaches for extracting the context associated with each aspect and also the impact of such contexts on different sentiment classifiers to predict aspect level sentiment.

In order to analyze opinion with reference to a specific aspect (feature) requires, firstly the extraction of phrases or context, followed by the specific aspects related to sentiment or opinion analysis. Context extraction methods tend to utilize frequency related metrics such as relevance and interestingness metrics [24]; as well as the use of dependency parser based extraction patterns [4,23]. Common to both is the use of noun and verb phrases (NPs, VPs) as indicators of product features and the surrounding dictionary opinion words as opinions. Features are constructed using the phrase dependency tree to extract relations among all product features and opinions that were later used in aspect and opinion expression extraction. Although, these approaches fail to discover aspect specific opinion phrases, the use of NPs in extracting candidate opinion phrases has that effect, and is similar to [5]. In other relevant work on extracting opinion contexts related to aspects include the use of specific rules to refine the dependency tree parse by only accepting it when it fits the specific patterns [18]. Analyzing information regarding predecessors, successors and siblings in a given predecessor tree are common strategies used in these syntax-based methods [8]. Our work also takes advantage of dependency parsers, but additionally we combine analysis of the tree with sentiment co-occurrence statistics to extract candidate opinion phrases for aspect-sentiment analysis. Specifically this allows us to effectively prune the parse tree and home-in on the relevant context content.

The state-of-the-art in sentiment analysis shows a diverse landscape in terms of approaches - from rule-bases and sentiment lexicons [15] to the more supervised classification models generated by shallow and deep learning methods [19]. Rule-based systems and general-purpose lexicons are normally manually created, whilst domain-specific lexicons tends to be generative by leveraging labeled or weakly-labeled text with sentiment classes (e.g. positive, negative) [7]. On the other hand machine/deep learning systems for sentiment analysis apply supervised learning to learn sentiment classifiers to predict the polarity of a given text. A common approach is to learn features from text related to vocabulary (e.g. n-grams), part-of-speech (POS) information, polarity, negation [1,14,16]. Recent success in neural architectures include both shallow (e.g. fastText) [10] and deep networks (e.g. convolutional neural networks, recursive/recurrent neural networks) [11,21]. Typically these have been found to be effective at learning features when there is large amounts of training data. In this paper we do not propose a new sentiment classifier, however we evaluate the effectiveness of different state-of-the-art sentiment analyzers trained using the text generated from the proposed opinion context extraction methods for predicting aspect-level sentiment.

3   Opinion Context Extraction Approaches

The main question we address in this paper is how best to choose the words that constitute the context of a given aspect. Possible approaches are to select words from the full sentence, from a lexical window, or from a syntactic window. The context of the aspect can then be taken as the bag-of-words contained in the associated sentence or window. The sentiment associated with the aspect can then be determined by passing the extracted context to one of several supervised state-of-the-art sentiment classifiers.

3.1   Sentence Level Context

The baseline strategy for context extraction is to simply use the entire sentence as containing the relevant context for any given aspect, a, in that sentence. Sentiment classification is applied to the entire sentence bearing a and the corresponding prediction assigned to a:

$$sentiment\_classifier(a, \text{sentence}(a)) \tag{1}$$

Where $sentiment\_classifier()$ is a function that predicts the sentiment expressed, in relation to the aspect as positive, negative or neutral. This context extraction approach is reasonable if the sentence contains only a single aspect and the sentiment words in the sentence are used to express opinion towards that aspect. However in real life data, e.g. customer feedback data, sentences often contain multiple aspects and the sentiment towards each can be either positive, negative or neutral. Therefore using the entire sentence as a context is not ideal to accurately determine the opinion towards aspects. In the following sections we propose three alternative approaches that extract part of a sentence with an aim to identify the opinion targeted towards specific aspects.

3.2 Lexical Window of Context

In this approach we identify a window of k words around an aspect as the context window from which to extract text for sentiment analysis. The size of the window is chosen empirically to be 3. More formally, let a sentence be denoted as $S = \{w_1, \ldots, w_n\}$. Assuming $w_x \in S$ as the aspect a, the lexical window of context for w_x is extracted as follows:

$$Context_{lex}(w_x) = \begin{cases} [w_{x-k} : w_{x+k}] \ if \ x < n - k \ and \ x > k \\ [w_1 : w_{x+k}] \quad if \ x < k \\ [w_{x-k} : w_n] \quad if \ x + k > n \end{cases} \quad (2)$$

This approach assumes that the opinion words targeting an aspect occur close by, in the window of k words from the aspect, and that extracting the words within that window gives a useful bag-of-words for analyzing the sentiment of the aspect. For instance with $k = 3$ we would extract just, *The*, to the left-side and, *was amazing but*, to the right-side as our context given the underlined aspect in the following sentence:

| The *food was amazing but* | the service could have been better.

Sentiment classification is applied using the lexical context associated with the aspect a and the corresponding prediction is assigned to a as follows:

$$sentiment\_classifier(a, Context_{lex}(a)) \quad (3)$$

3.3 Syntactical Window of Context

With complex sentences involving multiple aspects one cannot rely solely on adjacency of text as a cue to context identification. For instance in the following examples, *We use that restaurant for Italian food on week days and have always found they serve promptly and the sauces are great*, sentiment about the food itself appears towards the end of the sentence, whilst the mention of the aspect (*food*) is at the beginning of the sentence. Accordingly to link opinion to aspects we need to study syntactical relationships between these components.

In the syntactically-informed windowing approach, we study the dependency relationships within a sentence to extract the window of k words to form the context for aspect, w_x. Unlike the lexical window which ignores the syntactic relationships between words, this approach starts from the aspect node and incrementally traverses the dependency parse tree in either direction to arrive at the context text for sentiment analysis. The standard tool used in natural

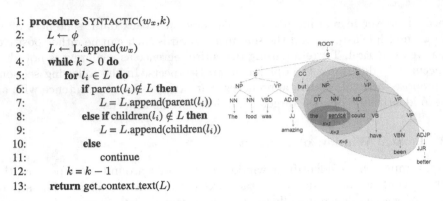

```
1:  procedure SYNTACTIC(w_x,k)
2:      L ← φ
3:      L ← L.append(w_x)
4:      while k > 0 do
5:          for l_i ∈ L do
6:              if parent(l_i) ∉ L then
7:                  L = L.append(parent(l_i))
8:              else if children(l_i) ∉ L then
9:                  L = L.append(children(l_i))
10:             else
11:                 continue
12:         k = k − 1
13:     return get_context_text(L)
```

Fig. 1. Algorithm1 - Syntactical window of context algorithm (left) and parse tree analysis for k up to 3 (right).

language processing for learning the syntactic structure of sentences is a dependency parser. In this work we use trees constructed through Spacy[1] to extract the relevant text window.

More formally given a sentence, $S = \{w_1, \ldots, w_n\}$, we make use of its dependency tree, $T = \{t_1, \ldots, t_n\}$, where each $t_i \in T$ is a triplet $(w_i, parent(w_i), children(w_i))$ where $parent(w_i) \in S$ and $children(w_i) \in S$. Assuming $w_x \in S$ as the aspect a, the syntactical window of context for w_x is extracted using the algorithm detailed in Fig. 1. Essentially the approach as described in algorithm 1 traverses the dependency tree to increasing levels guided by the parameter k to collect tree nodes and their corresponding words in order to generate the context for a given aspect.

The example tree (see Fig. 1) illustrates how for different values of k we are able to traverse the tree from a given aspect node (such as *service*) to form the neighborhood and therein extract the relevant text appearing within that neighborhood. Clearly the higher the value of k the greater the neighborhood reach. In our experiments we explore the impact of neighborhood size on the different datasets for context extraction.

Once the context text is extracted sentiment classification is applied using the discovered syntactic context associated with the aspect a and the corresponding prediction is assigned to a as follows:

$$sentiment\_classifier(a, Context_{synt}(a)) \tag{4}$$

3.4   Syntactical Sentiment Weighted Co-occurrence Window of Context

A sentiment-rich corpus of text can be used to learn how often a list of sentiment words and aspects co-occur. Furthermore, this knowledge can be used to guide the traversal of the dependency tree to collect the words that influence the aspect

---

[1] https://spacy.io/.

unlike the previous approach which uses distance between words within the tree. Essentially the co-occurrence statistics provides a gauge of how relevant a specific node is likely to be for a given aspect. Aggregating these scores for any candidate sub-tree associated with the aspect provides a heuristic with which we can select the most relevant sub-tree for our context extraction. Unlike 3.3, here we are able to commit to the most promising sub-tree thereby disregarding neighboring sub-trees that are less promising in terms of aspect sentiment relatedness.

In our example tree in Fig. 2 we can see two candidate sub-trees associated with the aspect *service*. However the correct context relates to the sub-tree containing the opinionated words *but, could* and *better*, whilst that containing *tasty* should actually be relevant only to aspect *food*. To disambiguate this context we aggregate co-occurrence statistics within each candidate sub-tree, and associate the sub-tree to the aspect having the higher score. Accordingly the higher co-occurrence score with the sentiment-rich word, *better*, suggests that *service* is more likely to be assigned to the right sub-tree over the left, because *food* is likely to have a stronger co-occurrence with *tasty* (this score is not shown in figure). In this way we combine the syntactic dependencies between words with co-occurrence statistics between aspects and sentiment bearing words to extract context for aspect-sentiment analysis from a sentence.

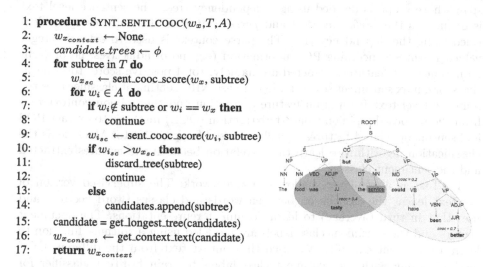

1: **procedure** SYNT_SENTI_COOC(w_x,T,A)
2:     $w_{x_{context}} \leftarrow$ None
3:     $candidate\_trees \leftarrow \phi$
4:     **for** subtree in T **do**
5:         $w_{x_{sc}} \leftarrow$ sent_cooc_score(w_x, subtree)
6:         **for** $w_i \in A$ **do**
7:             **if** $w_i \notin$ subtree or $w_i == w_x$ **then**
8:                 continue
9:             $w_{i_{sc}} \leftarrow$ sent_cooc_score(w_i, subtree)
10:            **if** $w_{i_{sc}} > w_{x_{sc}}$ **then**
11:                discard_tree(subtree)
12:                continue
13:            **else**
14:                candidates.append(subtree)
15:     candidate = get_longest_tree(candidates)
16:     $w_{x_{context}} \leftarrow$ get_context_text(candidate)
17:     **return** $w_{x_{context}}$

Fig. 2. Algorithm2 - Syntactical sentiment weighted co-occurrence window of context (left) and parse tree illustration (right) for arbitrary subtree.

More formally, let a sentence be denoted as $S = \{w_1, \ldots, w_n\}$. Let T be the dependency tree corresponding to S and T^* be a subtree of T. Let A be the set of aspects identified for a corpus of reviews. Assuming $w_x \in S$ as the aspect a, the algorithm for co-occurrence informed window of context for w_x is extracted as shown in the algorithm in Fig. 2. The aggregated sentiment weighted co-occurrence statistics for any given tree is obtained using *get_senti_cooc_score*.

Note that although the illustration (in Fig. 2) shows two arbitrary subtrees, essentially the approach described in algorithm 2 for a given aspect a, extracts all the subtrees that contains it and selects the sub-tree from them such that there is no other aspect in the subtree with a sentiment weighted co-occurrence score higher than that of a. Sentiment classification is applied using the discovered context associated with the aspect a and the corresponding prediction is assigned to a as follows:

$$sentiment\_classifier(a, Context_{synt\_senti\_coocc}(a)) \qquad (5)$$

4 Sentiment Classifier

A diverse set of sentiment classifiers ranging from feature engineering-based (e.g. NRC sentiment) [12] to shallow neural networks (e.g. fastText) [10] to deep neural networks (e.g. convolutional neural network (CNN)) [11] is used to evaluate context extraction quality.

NRC sentiment applies feature engineering to extract different features based on n-grams, part-of-speech (POS) information and sentiment information. n-grams are extracted from text at the sentence level and also within a sentence span whose scope is decided using a dependency tree. The sentence level text is defined as the *surface context* and *parse context* is the sentence span identified using the dependency tree. The parse context is used to extract integer valued features concerning POS information (e.g. no of adjectives, no of verbs etc). Sentiment features extracted are namely: total positive score, total negative score, max sentiment score etc. In our case NRC sentiment classifier uses the sentence level text for n-gram feature extraction and the opinion context text from the proposed Opinion Context Extraction (OCE) methods to extract POS and sentiment related features. Finally we used Support Vector Machine as the classification algorithm to learn the co-relation between the features extracted and the sentiment classes.

fastText is a one-layer shallow neural network. The supervised version of fastText learns the association between words and classes (word vectors) and uses that in turn (average) to learn document representations. The document vectors and the sentiment class labels are modeled using a softmax function to learn a sentiment classifier. We used the context text from the different OCE methods along with the sentiment class labels to train fastText classifier for aspect sentiment prediction.

The CNN used in this work applies one layer of convolution and one layer of pooling on top of word embeddings. The word embeddings are generated for each of the domains (restaurants and insurance) using the unsupervised version of fastText. We used fastText embeddings as it is known to enrich the word embeddings with sub-word information thereby better capturing syntactic variations in the vocabulary [2]. Similar to supervised fastText we feed the context text from the different OCE methods as input for CNN to learn a neural sentiment classifier for aspect sentiment prediction.

5   Evaluation

The aim of the evaluation is to measure the quality of the opinion contexts extracted against human judgments and also to validate the usefulness of the proposed opinion context extraction methods for effective aspect-sentiment analysis. Our evaluation is a comparative study of the performance of the different opinion context extraction methods using evaluation tasks such as text overlap and sentiment analysis.

5.1   Datasets

We used three different data sets (customer reviews) from the domains of restaurants and insurance for our evaluation. The restaurant data sets are official benchmark data sets from the SemEval competition for 2015[2] and 2016[3]. The data set for the insurance domain is a commercial data set. The SemEval data sets are provided with marked aspects and aspect level sentiment labels. We have manually identified a list of about 700 aspects from the insurance domain reviews and have created a sample data set containing these aspects and passed them to Amazon Mechanical Turk to get the aspect level sentiment annotations. Further we have used a sample of sentences from the SemEval and the insurance data sets to manually annotate the opinion contexts for the aspects. Table 1 captures the volume of data (sentences) for SemEval and insurance data sets.

Table 1. Sentiment datasets

Class	SemEval-2015		SemEval-2016		Insurance	
	Train	Test	Train	Test	Train	Test
Positive	941	193	1008	568	3615	1811
Negative	274	123	430	196	2077	1042
Neutral	36	22	52	36	757	381

5.2   Methods

The following different methods are part of our comparative study:

1. Opinion context extraction method using sentence as a context (refer Sect. 3.1)
2. Opinion context extraction method using lexical window of words as a context (refer Sect. 3.2)
3. Opinion context extraction method using syntactic window of k words as a context (refer Sect. 3.3)
4. Opinion context extraction method using syntactic features and sentiment co-occurrence statistics (refer Sect. 3.4)
5. Each of the above methods are used to generate a context text for aspects which in turn is used to train the 3 sentiment classifiers from Sect. 4.

---

[2] http://alt.qcri.org/semeval2015/task12/.
[3] http://alt.qcri.org/semeval2016/task5/.

5.3   Results and Analysis

In this section we present the results obtained for different opinion context extraction approaches in text overlap and aspect-sentiment classification tasks.

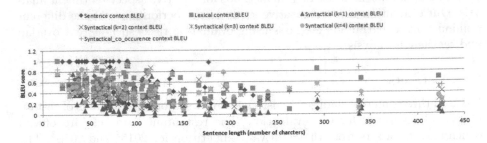

Fig. 3. BLEU score for opinion context extraction methods on insurance data

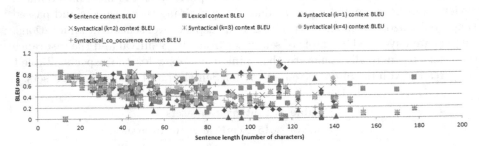

Fig. 4. BLEU score for opinion context extraction methods on SemEval data

Text Overlap Analysis. Figures 3 and 4 show the text overlap between the dataset's human annotated opinion phrases and the extracted opinion phrases from sentences using the proposed methods. We used BLEU score as a metric to quantify the quality of the extracted opinion phrases. The figures capture sentences sorted by length (ascending order) on the x-axis and BLEU score on the y-axis. It was observed that for shorter sentences the best BLEU score was from sentence based opinion context extraction approach. On the other hand for longer sentences approaches that extract a span of text within the sentence were found to have better BLEU score. This suggests that it is useful to have a context that accurately captures the opinion about an aspect instead of using the entire sentence.

Further we also investigated the aspect composition in the sample sentences selected for text overlap analysis. We have segregated the data into two categories namely: sentences with *single aspect* and sentences with *multiple aspects* and observed the BLEU scores within each category. Figure 5 shows the BLEU scores for insurance and SemEval datasets organized by the aspect composition in the sentences.

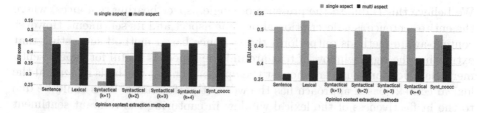

Fig. 5. BLEU score by aspect composition for Insurance (left) and SemEval (right) data

As before we found that for single aspect sentences, considering the complete sentence as a context has higher BLEU score compared to using part of a sentence as a context. On the other hand, for multi-aspect sentences (specially with the insurance data) context extraction was found to have higher BLEU scores than using the entire sentence. This suggests that it is important to identify the right spans of text within a sentence and associate each with the aspects contained in the sentence.

Aspect Sentiment Classification. Here we use sentiment classification as a means to find out how effective each extraction method is for aspect-level sentiment prediction. Table 2 shows the aspect level sentiment prediction results (best overall accuracy highlighted in bold) for SemEval and the insurance data sets. It was observed that using sentence text as the context for aspect sentiment analysis is a strong competition for the other methods which use only a span of text within the sentence as context text for aspect sentiment prediction.

Table 2. Aspect sentiment classification results

Classifier	Sentence	Lexical	Syntactic (k = 1)	Syntactic (k = 2)	Syntactic (k = 3)	Syntactic (k = 4)	Syntactic Senti_co_occur
SemEval-2015 data							
FastText	65.28	58.45	60.83	66.76	66.17	68.24	69.45
NRC	69.76	72.81	70.13	70.67	69.12	69.37	**75.24***
CNN	67.14	60.45	62.23	67.35	68.12	70.42	72.26
SemEval-2016 data							
FastText	73.29	62.72	67.75	71.66	76.19	76.44	77.15
NRC	74.68	77.83	77.14	78.33	78.46	**79.72***	78.67
CNN	72.86	63.24	68.12	70.83	74.12	75.89	76.68
Insurance data							
FastText	75.72	62.85	64.78	68.37	70.93	70.09	77.45
NRC	78.74	80.05	81.69	82.65	82.77	82.73	**82.87***
CNN	76.12	64.12	66.23	70.23	72.89	74.57	78.67

We believe this is due to the presence of single aspect bearing sentences, where the entire sentence is a description about one aspect and its sentiment. However context-aware methods outperform the sentence based method suggesting that extracting the right window of text around the aspect is useful for aspect sentiment classification. Further amongst the opinion context methods in general the lexical context based approach has the weakest performance. This could be due to the ineffectiveness of the lexical window in capturing the relevant sentiment words that target the aspects.

For the syntactic context approach the performance of sentiment analysis improves consistently as the value of k increases from 1 to 4. This suggests that having longer context which include immediate as well as distant syntactic dependents for the aspect is more effective to capture the relevant opinion words that target the aspects thereby boosting the sentiment classifier performance. Further the approach which combines the syntactic dependency information with the sentiment co-occurrence information to extract the opinion context surrounding an aspect either records the best performance (SemEval-2015, insurance) or is comparable with the performance of the approach which uses only the syntactic context (SemEval-2016). Overall these results suggests that the sentiment co-occurrence guided sub-tree selection heuristic for disambiguating aspect contexts, is specifically beneficial for multi-aspect sentence analysis.

Amongst the different sentiment learners used, NRC sentiment classifier performs best consistently outperforming its neural counterparts. Amongst the neural methods CNN performs better than fastText. This suggests that with more depth in the neural network there is scope for learning better predictive models. We believe that NRC sentiment classifier learns features that are complementary and are collectively effective in predicting the sentiment at the aspect level. Further in the case of NRC since it uses both the sentence level text and opinion context within the sentence for feature extraction we found it to be having an advantage over the neural classifiers which consider only the opinion context text as input.

Finally we observed that overall performance scores tend to be higher on the real-world insurance data set compared to the SemEval data sets. This could be due to the fact that the insurance data set has more training examples than the SemEval data sets. Nevertheless it is extremely promising to find that the context-aware methods outperform the sentence based method in aspect sentiment predictions confirming our assumption that identifying sentiment at the level of entities and aspects present in the sentence is more important than overall sentiment analysis for extracting value from customer feedback data.

6   Real World Analytics System

The technology described in this paper is used by SentiSum to help their clients better understand feedback in the form of on-line reviews and customer satisfaction surveys. The aspect extraction method discussed here helps identify key aspects (referred to as topics) in the feedback text. Topics are grouped into

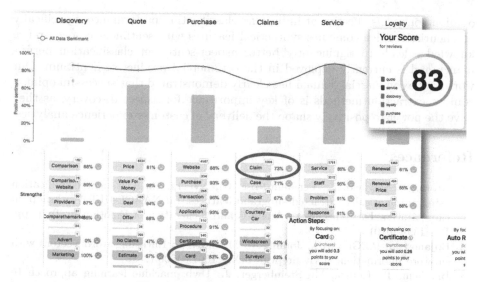

Fig. 6. SentiSum dashboard analytics

higher level categories which correspond to stages in a customer's interaction with the company. This is known as a customer journey (see Fig. 6). Here, we have highlighted the topic "claim" which is part of the "claims" customer journey stage for a UK insurer. The system further extracts sentence fragments that describe the sentiment towards the identified topics. This fragment is then fed into domain specific sentiment classifiers generating a positive/negative/neutral label. The distribution of classes over topics and over time forms the info graphic which is used to generate trend insights on customer feedback.

We also compute a customer satisfaction score which is a weighted average of sentiment over selected topics (83% Fig. 6). Notice how aspect extraction directly contributes to the discovery of action steps - by unearthing topics that have attracted negative opinion which if fixed can further boost the overall score. These are the customer "pain points" and drawing attention to these are a valuable feature of the SentiSum offering.

7 Conclusion

In this paper we investigated the role of opinion context extraction for aspect-level sentiment classification with the aim of evaluating the extent to which traditional and neural sentiment classifiers benefit when trained using the opinion context text. We proposed four methods to extract opinion contexts surrounding aspects using lexical, syntactic and sentiment co-occurrence knowledge. Further we validated the quality of the opinion contexts extracted with human judgments using the BLEU score and also through standard aspect-sentiment classification tasks. Our experiments on benchmark data sets from SemEval and a real-world dataset from the insurance domain suggests that extracting the right opinion context is effective at improving classification performance. Specifically our heuristic which combines syntactical features with sentiment co-occurrence knowledge leads to significantly better aspect-sentiment classification performance and is currently deployed in the commercial product of SentiSum. Our work in the commercial domain has clearly demonstrated that successful opinion context extraction methods is of key importance for aspect discovery, as they have the power to positively shape the delivery of customer experience analytics.

References

1. Arora, S., Mayfield, E., Penstein-Rosé, C., Nyberg, E.: Sentiment classification using automatically extracted subgraph features. In: NAACL-HLT Workshop on Computational Approaches to Analysis and Generation of Emotion in Text, pp. 131–139 (2010)
2. Bojanowski, P., Grave, E., Joulin, A., Mikolov, T.: Enriching word vectors with subword information. arXiv preprint arXiv:1607.04606 (2016)
3. Brychcın, T., Konkol, M., Steinberger, J.: Uwb: machine learning approach to aspect-based sentiment analysis. In: SemEval 2014, p. 817 (2014)
4. Chen, Y.Y., Wiratunga, N., Lothian, R.: Effective dependency rule-based aspect extraction for social recommender systems. In: 21st Pacific Asia Conference on Information Systems (2017)
5. Fei, G., Chen, Z., Liu, B.: Review topic discovery with phrases using the polya urn model. In: COLING, pp. 667–676 (2014)
6. Garcıa-Pablos, A., Cuadros, M., Rigau, G.: V3: unsupervised aspect based sentiment analysis for semeval-2015 task 12. In: SemEval-2015 (2015)
7. Go, A., Bhayani, R., Huang, L.: Twitter sentiment classification using distant supervision. Processing (2009)
8. Hazem, A., Morin, E.: Improving bilingual lexicon extraction from comparable corpora using window-based and syntax-based models. In: Gelbukh, A. (ed.) CICLing 2014. LNCS, vol. 8404, pp. 310–323. Springer, Heidelberg (2014). https://doi.org/10.1007/978-3-642-54903-8_26
9. Hu, M., Liu, B.: Mining opinion features in customer reviews. In: Proceedings of the 19th National Conference on AI 2004 (2004)
10. Joulin, A., Grave, E., Bojanowski, P., Mikolov, T.: Bag of tricks for efficient text classification. arXiv preprint arXiv:1607.01759 (2016)
11. Kim, Y.: Convolutional neural networks for sentence classification. In: Proceedings of the Conference on Empirical Methods in NLP (EMNLP), pp. 1746–1751 (2014)
12. Kiritchenko, S., Zhu, X.D., Cherry, C., Mohammad, S.: NRC-Canada-2014: detecting aspects and sentiment in customer reviews. In: SemEval@COLING (2014)
13. Laddha, A., Mukherjee, A.: Extracting aspect specific opinion expressions. In: Proceedings of the Conference on Empirical Methods in NLP, pp. 6270–637 (2016)
14. Mohammad, S.M., Kiritchenko, S., Zhu, X.: NRC-Canada: building the state-of-the-art in sentiment analysis of tweets. In: Proceedings of the 7th International Workshop on Semantic Evaluation, pp. 321–327 (2013)
15. Muhammad, A., Wiratunga, N., Lothian, R.: Contextual sentiment analysis for social media genres. Knowl.-Based Syst. 108, 92–101 (2016)
16. Nakagawa, T., Inui, K., Kurohashi, S.: Dependency tree-based sentiment classification using CRFs with hidden variables. In: Human Language Technologies: Conference of the North American Chapter of the ACL, pp. 786–794 (2010)

17. Nandan, N., Dahlmeier, D., Vij, A., Malhotra, N.: SAP-RI: a constrained and supervised approach for aspect-based sentiment analysis. In: SemEval 2014, p. 517 (2014)
18. Gamallo Otero, P.: Comparing window and syntax based strategies for semantic extraction. In: Teixeira, A., de Lima, V.L.S., de Oliveira, L.C., Quaresma, P. (eds.) PROPOR 2008. LNCS (LNAI), vol. 5190, pp. 41–50. Springer, Heidelberg (2008). https://doi.org/10.1007/978-3-540-85980-2_5
19. Ribeiro, F.N., Araujo, M., Goncalves, P., Goncalves, M.A., Benevenuto, F.: Sentibench- a benchmark comparision of state-of-the-paractice sentiment analysis methods. EPJ Data Sci. 5, 23 (2016)
20. Schouten, K., Frasincar, F., de Jong, F.: COMMIT-P1WP3: a co-occurrence based approach to aspect-level sentiment analysis. In: Proceedings of the 8th International Workshop on Semantic Evaluation (SemEval 2014) (2014)
21. Socher, R., Perelygin, A., Wu, J., Chuang, J., Manning, C., Ng, A., Potts, C.: Recursive deep models for semantic compositionality over a seniment treebank. In: Proceedings of the EMNLP (2013)
22. Toh, Z., Wang, W.: DLIREC: aspect term extraction and term polarity classification system. In: Proceedings of the 8th International Workshop on Semantic Evaluation (SemEval 2014), pp. 235–240 (2014)
23. Wu, Y., Zhang, Q., Huang, X., Wu, L.: Phrase dependency parsing for opinion mining. In: Proceedings of the Conference on Empirical Methods in NLP, vol. 3, pp. 1533–1541 (2009)
24. Zhao, W.X., et al.: Topical keyphrase extraction from twitter. In: Proceedings of the 49th Annual Meeting of the ACL: Human Language Technologies-Volume 1, pp. 379–388 (2011)

Confidence in Random Forest
for Performance Optimization

Kennedy Senagi[1,2(✉)] and Nicolas Jouandeau[2]

[1] Department of Information Technology, Dedan Kimathi University
of Technology, Nyeri, Kenya
kennedy.senagi@dkut.ac.ke
[2] LIASD, University of Paris8, Paris, France
n@ai.univ-paris8.fr

Abstract. In this paper, we present a non-deterministic strategy for searching for optimal number of trees ($NoTs$) hyperparameter in Random Forest (RF). Hyperparameter tuning in Machine Learning (ML) algorithms optimizes predictability of an ML algorithm and/or improves computer resources utilization. However, hyperparameter tuning is a complex optimization task and time consuming. We set up experiments with the goal of maximizing predictability, minimizing $NoTs$ and minimizing time of execution (ToE). Compared to the deterministic algorithm, e-greedy and default configured RF, this research's non-deterministic algorithm recorded an average percentage accuracy (acc) of approximately 98%, $NoTs$ percentage average improvement of 29.39%, average ToE improvement ratio of 415.92 and an average improvement of 95% iterations. Moreover, evaluations using Jackknife Estimation showed stable and reliable results from several experiment runs of the non-deterministic strategy. The non-deterministic approach in selecting hyperparameter showed a significant acc and better computer resources (i.e. cpu and memory time) utilization. This approach can be adopted widely in hyperparameter tuning, and in conserving utilization of computer resources i.e. green computing.

Keywords: Machine Learning · Random Forest
Hyperparameter tuning · Number of trees

1 Introduction

RF was first introduced by Breiman [2]. It is an ensemble classifier that builds many decision trees from the same dataset using bootstrapping and randomly sampled variables. Predictions at the leaves are combined to form a single prediction; for each tree. When performing classifications, the input query instances traverse each tree, which casts its vote for a class. RF considers the class with the most votes as the answer to a classification query [2]. The inception of RF has led to development of many RF libraries and diverse usage of RF on a variety

© Springer Nature Switzerland AG 2018
M. Bramer and M. Petridis (Eds.): SGAI-AI 2018, LNAI 11311, pp. 372–386, 2018.
https://doi.org/10.1007/978-3-030-04191-5_31

of datasets. RF has been implemented in several software libraries: scikit-learn, SPRINT and Random Jungle. It has been studies and applied in diverse domain [11,12,15].

RF is a supervised ML algorithm that requires tuning to improve predictability, speed and utilization of computer resources. Tuning RF involves adjusting hyperprameters. Hyperparameters can be set by default or configured manually. In default settings, the ML algorithm sets hyperprameter values while manually setting requires users to set specific values. Hyperparameters specify interoperability of the underlying model. When adopting ML algorithm to specific datasets, hyperparameter tuning can be cumbersome and time consuming [6,14].

Default hyperprameter values do not give better results compared to tuned RF. Many theories have been put forward to optimize hyperparameter RF including grid search and Bayesian optimization [14]. Some researchers focus on optimizing specific hyperprameters [1,10,11]. For instance, Bernard et al. [1] discusses ways of selecting the number of features to consider in node splitting and Liu et al. [10] derived a nonparametric algorithm to estimate the categorical distributions of the internal nodes. $NoTs$ has been studied too [11].

This research focused on maximizing acc while minimizing $NoTs$ and ToE in RF. We did experiments on different datasets and saw that most datasets had maximum acc and minimum ToE between 2 to 512 $NoTs$, the *fertile region*. We formulated a non-deterministic algorithm that maximized acc while minimizing $NoTs$ and ToE in the fertile region. Moreover, we did further experiments using grid search, e-greedy algorithms, and compared results.

In this paper, Sect. 2 covers related works, Sect. 3 discusses experiments, results and analysis and Sect. 4 concludes the paper.

2   Related Works

Tuning ML systems can be time consuming and at times inaccurate and difficult. To solve this, a hyperparameter optimization strategy is proposed inspired by analysis of boolean function focusing on high-dimension datasets. The algorithm recorded at least an order of magnitude of speedup than Hyperband and Bayesian Optimization and outperform Random Search 8x [7].

Sensitive was more on $NoTs$ but less sensitive to the number of features in node split. MapReduce could made parameter optimization feasible on a massive scale [6]. RF grows trees rapidly and setting up a large $NoTs$ (e.g. 1000) is okay. If there are many variables, trees can grow more (up-to 5000) [3]. acc increased when $NoTs$ in RF was doubled. However, there was a threshold beyond which there was no significance gain in acc [11].

A full Bayesian treatment expected improvement parameter tuning, and algorithms (e.g. ANN) for dealing with variable time regimes and running experiments in parallel. Results of this experiment surpassed a human expert at selecting hyper-parameters on the competitive CIFAR-10 dataset; beating the state of the art by over 3%. SVM was used as a case study algorithm [14].

XGBoost algorithm proposed candidate splitting points according to percentiles of feature distribution, then maps the continuous features into buckets split, aggregates the statistics and finds the best solution among proposals based on the aggregated statistics [4].

Optimizing parameters of evolutionary algorithm values is a challenging activity. CMA-ES tuning algorithms gave better results in terms of utility. Tuning parameters of evolutionary algorithms does pay off in terms of performance, better other intuitions and usual parameter setting conventions [13].

A selection of supplemental training datasets was used in fine-tuning a high-performing ANN model. Natural Language Processing system ability is improved after being evaluated by Item Response [9].

3　Experiments, Results and Analysis

In this research, we considered 20 standardized datasets collected from UCI Machine Learning [5] and Kaggle [8] website, namely: Balance Scale (1), Breast Cancer Wisconsin - Original (2), Car Evaluation (3), Habermans Survival (4), Pen-Based Recognition of Handwritten Digits (5), Website Phishing (6), Yeast (7), Banknote Authentication (8), Contraceptive Method Choice (9), Diabetic Retinopathy Debrecen (10), EEG Eye State (11), Pima Indians Diabetes (12), Wine Quality - White (13), Wine Quality (14), Breast Cancer Wisconsin (Original) (15), Dota (16) Handwriting Verification Test (17), Ionosphere (18), Plant Leaf Classification (19) and Seeds (20). All experiments were run 20 times and results averaged. $NoTs$ (θ) was varied, as we measured accuracy (acc) and time of execution (t). Computer was: Intel(R) Xeon(R) CPU E5-4610 0 @ 2.40 GHz.

3.1　Considering 2 to 4096 Number of Trees

The parameter space was composed of a finite set of sorted even $NoTs$; 2 to 4096. RF predictability was evaluated by acc defined in Eq. 1; where n are samples, $\hat{y}_i$ is the predicted label and y_i is the original label. The results of acc and t are tabulated in Tables 1 and 2 respectively.

$$acc(y, \hat{y}) = \frac{1}{n} \sum_{i=0}^{n-1} 1(\hat{y}_i = y_i) \tag{1}$$

Table 1 shows acc increasing steadily with an increase in $NoTs$, then flattens. RF classification employs bagging principles, where a committee of trees, cast a vote for the predicted class. However, RF classifier introduces modifications in bagging where it builds a large collection of de-correlated trees, and then averages them. When the $NoTs$ become huge, we see RF acc varying insignificantly meaning the average acc of de-correlated trees vary insignificantly. Therefore, increasing the $NoTs$ increases acc, but there is a threshold where, increasing $NoTs$ does not contribute to a significantly positive acc. Maximum acc values are bolden in Table 1. Besides the 6th dataset having its average maximum acc at 2048 $NoTs$, the other datasets had their average accuracies between 2 and

Table 1. Accuracy (percentage) of RF with θ trees for 20 datasets (DS)

DS	Number of trees											
	2	4	8	16	32	64	128	256	512	1024	2048	4096
1	80.3	81.9	83.0	82.4	84.6	**85.6**	84.6	84.0	84.0	84.0	84.6	84.6
2	91.7	93.7	97.1	**98.0**	97.6	97.6	97.6	97.1	97.1	97.1	97.1	97.1
3	86.3	85.5	83.6	83.8	**84.8**	84.4	84.6	84.4	84.8	84.8	84.6	84.6
4	76.1	79.3	75.0	76.1	**79.3**	79.3	78.3	78.3	78.3	79.3	78.3	79.3
5	92.5	96.8	98.3	98.6	98.4	98.9	99.0	**99.1**	99.0	99.1	99.1	99.1
6	81.5	86.9	86.2	87.4	85.7	87.4	87.9	88.4	87.7	87.9	**88.7**	88.2
7	48.6	47.8	52.9	57.3	56.5	59.5	**59.8**	58.8	58.8	58.5	58.5	58.8
8	96.6	**97.8**	97.6	97.6	97.3	97.6	97.8	97.8	98.1	97.8	97.8	97.8
9	46.4	48.4	49.1	**51.6**	49.5	49.8	51.1	49.5	50.7	51.4	50.9	51.1
10	61.3	64.7	65.3	65.0	**69.9**	66.5	67.6	67.9	68.2	67.1	67.9	67.3
11	77.9	84.2	87.9	89.3	91.3	**92.7**	92.0	92.2	92.2	92.1	92.3	92.2
12	66.7	71.0	74.9	74.5	76.6	76.6	76.6	75.8	**77.5**	76.6	77.1	77.1
13	54.9	59.4	64.7	64.6	65.7	65.9	67.1	**67.3**	67.1	66.6	67.3	67.4
14	54.4	69.7	63.3	67.3	69.2	69.2	69.6	**70.2**	69.8	69.2	69.8	69.8
15	96.5	96.6	97.0	**97.2**	97.2	97.2	97.2	97.2	97.2	97.2	97.2	97.2
16	73.6	77.1	79.9	83.8	84.9	**86.0**	86.6	86.8	86.2	87.1	87.5	87.1
17	84.9	88.7	91.5	89.6	91.5	**92.5**	92.5	91.5	92.5	92.5	92.5	92.5
18	74.9	70.1	75.8	77.5	76.2	76.2	75.8	**76.6**	77.5	77.5	77.5	76.6
19	92.5	93.2	93.2	93.8	93.8	93.7	93.6	**94.1**	93.8	94.1	94.1	94.1
20	82.5	**90.5**	87.3	84.1	87.3	85.7	87.3	87.3	87.3	87.3	87.3	87.3

512 trees. These variations could have been caused by the randomness of RF. This research identified the range of 2 to 512 $NoTs$ to be the *fertile region*.

Table 2 shows ToE increasing steadily with an increase in $NoTs$. This tells us that building more $NoTs$ in RF demand more computing resources. We also observed a relative significant change in ToE; the threshold values are in bold.

Furthermore, this research notes that, different datasets gave different values of acc and ToE with the different $NoTs$. This is could be as a result of different dataset having different complexities (i.e. features, number of records and classes) and the random nature of RF. Therefore, it is important we maximize acc and minimize ToE (i.e. minimize computer resources utilized) in the fertile region.

3.2 Considering 2 to 512 Number of Trees

In Sect. 3.1, we defined the fertile region where we observed a lower ToE and maximum accuracies. In this region, we can avoid searching in regions (>512)

Table 2. Time of execution (sec) of RF with θ trees for 20 datasets (DS)

DS	Number of trees											
	2	4	8	16	32	64	128	256	512	1024	2048	4096
1	0.21	0.21	0.22	0.23	0.25	**0.30**	0.51	0.90	1.60	3.29	6.49	12.45
2	0.21	0.21	0.22	0.23	0.25	**0.30**	0.50	0.90	1.59	3.09	5.98	12.35
3	0.21	0.21	0.22	0.23	0.25	**0.30**	0.50	1.00	1.80	3.39	6.79	13.57
4	0.21	0.21	0.22	0.23	0.25	**0.30**	0.50	0.80	1.60	3.30	5.99	12.06
5	0.21	0.21	0.22	0.23	**0.26**	0.41	0.60	1.10	2.20	4.01	8.23	15.87
6	0.21	0.21	0.22	0.23	0.25	**0.30**	0.50	0.89	1.89	3.46	6.42	13.14
7	0.21	0.21	0.22	0.23	0.26	**0.30**	0.50	1.00	1.88	3.71	7.13	14.06
8	0.21	0.21	0.22	0.23	0.25	**0.30**	0.50	0.90	1.69	3.17	6.64	12.76
9	0.21	0.21	0.22	0.23	0.25	**0.30**	0.50	1.00	1.89	3.47	6.95	13.70
10	0.21	0.21	0.22	0.23	0.25	**0.30**	0.50	0.90	1.79	3.47	6.93	14.41
11	0.21	0.21	0.22	0.33	**0.46**	0.71	1.20	2.40	4.70	9.18	18.27	36.62
12	0.21	0.21	0.22	0.24	0.25	**0.30**	0.50	0.79	1.68	3.46	6.43	12.64
13	0.21	0.21	0.22	0.23	**0.25**	0.51	0.70	1.40	2.69	5.28	10.45	21.20
14	0.21	0.21	0.22	0.23	0.25	0.40	**0.60**	1.10	2.09	3.76	7.33	14.96
15	0.26	0.32	0.26	0.31	0.50	**0.62**	1.19	1.93	3.73	6.74	14.13	27.27
16	0.26	0.28	0.29	0.31	**0.47**	0.77	1.03	1.94	3.11	6.54	12.95	26.09
17	0.26	0.29	0.29	0.31	**0.37**	0.57	0.95	1.71	2.94	5.07	10.21	19.48
18	0.24	0.26	0.29	0.34	**0.35**	0.62	0.90	1.60	2.60	5.31	10.51	19.33
19	0.25	0.26	0.29	0.33	**0.31**	0.71	0.89	1.50	3.00	5.49	10.43	20.885
20	0.26	0.26	0.29	0.37	**0.37**	0.55	1.13	1.78	3.033	5.59	11.128	20.389

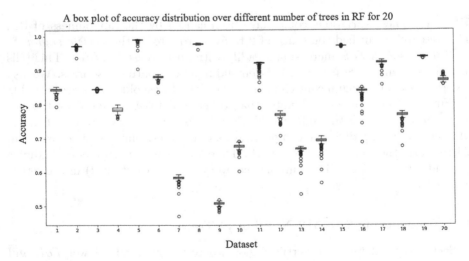

Fig. 1. Number of trees against datasets of accuracy in RF for 20 datasets

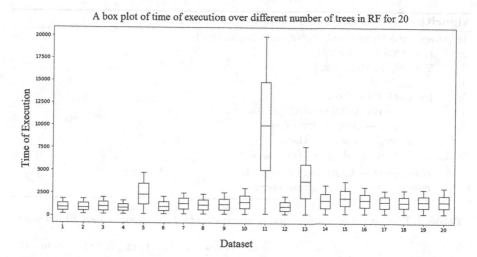

Fig. 2. Number of trees against datasets of time of execution in RF for 20 datasets

that showed higher ToE and significant flattening of acc. Within the fertile region parameter space, we defined a finite set of sorted even $NoTs$, θ. We configured, trained and tested RF with the respective θ and recorded acc and t; results are shown in Figs. 1 and 2.

Figure 1 shows a box plot of accuracy distribution for $NoTs$ against datasets across 20 datasets in the fertile region. Some datasets had a low inter-quartile range, low difference between the low and maximum points and more outliers below the lower whiskers. Some box plots also recorded some outliers above the upper whisker. A low difference in quartile ranges means there was a low variation in acc from the median. However, the outliers inform us that, some accuracies values were very far away from the median. Nonetheless, we see different acc distribution on different datasets. We therefore need to have a strategy that will dynamically search the best acc.

Figure 2 is a box plot of $ToEs$ distribution for $NoTs$ against datasets across 20 datasets in the fertile region. We observed the lower whisker having almost the same ToE; there could be some $NoTs$ that give almost the same minimum ToE. In most datasets, the lower whiskers being shorter than the upper whiskers. A shorter lower whisker means lower ToE were closer to the median.

From the above, we formulated: deterministic, non-deterministic, e-greedy and default configured RF (having 8 $NoTs$) algorithmic approaches to search an minimum $NoTs$ hyperparameter that maximized acc.

(a) Deterministic Hyperparameter Search

The deterministic search algorithm is outlined in Algorithm 1. This algorithm's goal was to maximize acc. Note that, $\exists acc_{max} \in acc$. The deterministic algorithm is greedy and exhaustive (linear search) and returns acc_{max}, with its corresponding NoT (θ_{best}) and ToE (t). Results are in Tables 4, 5 and 6.

Algorithm 1. The Deterministic Hyperparameter Search

1: **procedure** DETERMINISTICSEARCH($train, test$)
2:     $t_i \leftarrow$ CURRENTTIME()
3:     $\mathcal{T} \leftarrow [\theta_1, \theta_2, \theta_3, \ldots, \theta_n]$
4:     $acc_{max} \leftarrow 0$
5:     **for each** θ **in** $\mathcal{T}$ **do**
6:         $rf \leftarrow$ RANDOMFOREST($\theta, train$)
7:         $acc_{new} \leftarrow$ ACCURACY($rf, test$)
8:         **if** $acc_{new} > acc_{max}$ **then**
9:             $(acc_{max}, \theta_{best}) \leftarrow (acc_{new}, \theta)$
10:     $time\_spent \leftarrow$ CURRENTTIME() $- t_i$
11:     **return** $(acc_{max}, \theta_{best}, time\_spent)$

Table 3. Percentage of samples and average standard deviation across 20 datasets

DS	1	2	3	4	5	6	7	8	9	10	11	12	13	14	15	16	17
Percentage	90	80	30	10	20	30	40	20	50	50	10	10	20	20	10	30	30
Average STD $\times 10^{-4}$	1.1	0	1.1	3.9	0.5	1.1	1.4	0.5	0	1	1	3.9	2.6	1.2	0.5	2.4	1.1
Modal percentage	10																

(b) The Non-deterministic Hyperparameter Search Algorithm

This research was interested in maximizing acc and minimizing $NoTs$. Tables 1 and 2 shows different acc with different $ToEs$. Table 2 shows more $NoTs$ require more ToE (i.e. memory and cpu time). With this observation, we ought to maximize acc and minimize $NoTs$ to conserve computing resources i.e. green computing. This research therefore formulated a non-deterministic approach to converge close/to maximum acc and minimum $NoTs$. The algorithm is outlined in Algorithm 2, where $\theta_i = random(\in \mathcal{T}), \psi_1 = 1 + \frac{lim}{100},$ and $\psi_2 = 1 - \frac{lim}{100}$.

Experiment results of the non-deterministic algorithm are in Table 3. We see a significantly low average standard deviation across the percentage samples. This means there was a small variation in acc across the percentage samples. We considered 10% sample because it requires lesser CPU resources in generating random $NoTs$, using the function, GENERATE( ). Fewer $NoTs$ means lower ToE.

The goal of the non-deterministic algorithm was to maximize acc and minimize t through randomization. In this algorithm we assumption that, $\exists acc_{best} \in acc$ has θ_{best}. Note that the function GENERATE( ) returns 10% of elements in the parameter space and elements are sampled without replacement. We iterate through the random selected $NoTs$ as we configure RF. We considered percentage upper bound and lower bound of the acc_{best}. If acc_{rand} falls in the upper boundary, then $acc_{best} \leftarrow acc_{rand}, \theta_{best} \leftarrow \theta_{rand}$ and we $break$, with the assumption that we do not anticipate further percentage Δacc_{best}. If acc_{rand} falls in the lower boundary and θ_{rand} is less than θ_{best}, then $acc_{best} \leftarrow acc_{rand}, \theta_{best} \leftarrow \theta_{rand}$ and we also $break$, with the assumption that we have an insignificant Δacc_{best} and we have a better t_{best}. Moreover, if acc_{rand} falls above the upper boundary, then $acc_{best} \leftarrow acc_{rand}, \theta_{best} \leftarrow \theta_{rand}$, and we continue looping with the

---

Algorithm 2. The Non Deterministic Hyperparameter Search

```
1:  vals = []
2:  procedure GENERATE()
3:      while LEN(vals) ≤ 26 do
4:          val = 2 + rand()%512
5:          if val is not in vals then
6:              add val in vals
7:      return val
8:  procedure NONDETERMINISTICSEARCH(train, test)
9:      t_i ← CURRENTTIME()
10:     acc_rand, θ_rand, acc_best, θ_best, count ← 0
11:     T ← GENERATE()
12:     for each θ_rand in T do
13:         rf ← RANDOMFOREST(θ_rand, train)
14:         acc_rand ← ACCURACY(rf, test)
15:         if count == 0 then
16:             (acc_best, θ_best) ← (acc_rand, θ_rand)
17:         if ψ_1.acc_best > acc_rand > ψ_2.acc_best then
18:             if acc_rand < acc_best then
19:                 if θ_rand < θ_best then
20:                     (acc_best, θ_best) ← (acc_rand, θ_rand)
21:                     break
22:             else
23:                 (acc_best, θ_best) ← (acc_rand, θ_rand)
24:                 break
25:         else if acc_rand > ψ_1.acc_best then
26:             (acc_best, θ_best, count) ← (acc_rand, θ_rand, 0)
27:         count ← count + 1
28:         if count >= 10 then break
29:     time_spent ← CURRENTTIME() - t_i
30:     return (acc_best, θ_best, time_spent)
```

---

assumption that we anticipate further percentage Δ acc_{best}. Lastly, we *break* when iteration counts are 10% of the parameter space. Finally, we set the percentage boundary as 1% to increase the algorithm's *acc*. A larger percentage boundary will reduce the algorithm's *acc*. Results are in Tables 4, 5 and 6.

(c) RF configured with Default Parameters

RF took 8 number of trees by default as the NoT.

(d) The e-greedy Algorithm

A multi-bandit strategy is a mathematical model used to reason about how to make a decision when we have many actions to take and imperfect information about the rewards you would receive after taking these actions. Multi-armed bandit problem use the analogy of considering arms (options) to select in order to maximize a reward. e-greedy is an example of a multi-bandit algorithm. e-greedy uses the concept of exploiting and exploring. This algorithm is greedy in the sense that it exploits the best action at that time. However, the exploiting is regulated by the epsilon value that allows it to explore (trying out other options). We calculate the probability that an event will occur and match it with the epsilon value ϵ, set to 0.1, this guides us on when to exploit or explore. Exploiting considers the rewards for each arm/option and picks the arm with the highest reward, while exploring randomly chooses any arm. The arm/option that was either exploited or explored accumulates an reward [16]. This research looked at the problem of minimizing NoT using multi-armed bandit problem, whereby a user anticipates to chose an NoT that maximizes acc (exploiting) and can also considering other possible $NoTs$ could maximize acc (exploring). We initialize a counter and rewards arrays with lengths equivalent to $NoTs$ length. The chosen NoT increase it's count value, in it's index in the counter array c. Cumulative occurrences is got by summing up the counter array, C. These values are used in calculating the probability of an event will occur p, where $p = c/C$. If p is less than ϵ we choose to exploit, otherwise we explore. In exploring, we choose a random NoT from the other $NoTs$. After either exploiting or exploring, each NoT reward (in this case acc) is averaged in it's element index in the rewards array. This rewards array was used in considering future arms to exploit. We set-up experiments with 500 iterations.

3.3 Performance Comparisons: Number of Trees, Accuracy and Time of Execution

Table 4 contains results and analysis of minimum $NoTs$, selected by deterministic and non-deterministic hyperparameter search algorithms. The table also has average probabilities for e-greedy predicting θ_{best}. We observe a considerably good percentage improvement of $NoTs$ in the non-deterministic algorithm. At some instances, for example, in datasets 8 and 13, the non-deterministic algorithm was able to perfectly converged to the minimum $NoTs$ with 26 and 2 iterations respectively. Moreover, as observed in Table 4, about 65% of the datasets used less than 50% (i.e. less than 5% of random values in the search space) of random values while iterating, to converge close/to maximum acc and minimum $NoTs$. Generally, the percentage $NoTs$ improvement was 29.39% and the average number of iterations used were 11.8. We have average probabilities of e-greedy selecting the correct θ_{best} for each dataset. We were not able to get a good visualization of e-greedy learning performance (in terms of probabilities) across 500 iterations for the 20 datasets. However, we averaged the probabilities and we see e-greedy had an average 0.83 i.e. e-greedy can select θ_{best} quite well.

Table 5 shows accuracy recorded from running deterministic, non-deterministic and default configured RF. The default configured RF had a mean percentage difference of -4.9 while the non-deterministic and e-greedy algorithms had the same and considerably better percentage change of -1.81. In non-deterministic algorithm, datasets 2, 8 and 13 recorded a zero percentage change in acc.

Table 4. Recorded minimum number of trees (θ_{best}) and iterations for deterministic and non-deterministic algorithms, and e-greedy average probability of predicting θ_{best}

DS	Deterministic	Non-deterministic			e-greedy
	θ_{best}	θ_{best}	θ % improvement	Iteration	Avg probability of selecting θ_{best}
1	26	32	−23.08	5	0.821
2	46	48	−4.35	26	0.703
3	116	46	60.34	26	0.958
4	70	18	74.29	26	0.949
5	48	16	66.67	26	0.821
6	216	26	87.96	26	0.774
7	118	34	71.19	3	0.819
8	44	44	0	26	0.778
9	48	42	12.5	2	0.825
10	18	10	44.44	4	0.821
11	196	50	74.49	26	0.723
12	164	10	93.9	2	0.822
13	46	46	0	2	0.82
14	150	50	66.67	3	0.813
15	32	32	−1.133	11	0.808
16	500	46	−30.250	2	0.785
17	138	20	−7.118	3	0.761
18	26	26	−0.444	3	0.78
19	2	2	0.895	11	0.913
20	4	10	0.800	2	0.787
μ	100	30.40	29.39	11.8	0.814

Table 6 has results and analysis of time of execution of deterministic, non-deterministic, e-greedy algorithms and default configured RF. The ratio of deterministic: non-deterministic algorithms, deterministic:e-greedy, deterministic: default configured RF are calculated. Their averages are also calculated. Default-configured RF records a very high average ratio of 6223. Non-deterministic and e-greedy algorithms record relatively high ratios of 415 and 110 respectively. As discussed in this section, the deterministic algorithm is exhaustive and selects the minimum $NoTs$ that had the maximum acc. With these results, we benchmark the non-deterministic algorithm, e-greedy and default configured RF. The non-deterministic algorithm uses the principle of randomization, heuristics and terminating policies as outlined in Algorithm 2. With this strategy, the non-deterministic algorithm recorded $\approx 97\%$ average acc, and could run at an average of 415.92 faster, on an average of 11.8 iterations. Using the strategy formulated in Algorithm 2, the non-deterministic algorithm recorded 100% acc at three instances, and recorded zero $NoTs$ percentage improvement on two instances. Moreover, in the non-deterministic algorithm, we recorded $NoTs$ that are below the $NoTs$ threshold (64 trees), that showed a significant

Table 5. Maximum accuracy (acc_{best}) for deterministic, default configured RF and non-deterministic, and average acc for e-greedy recorded across 20 datasets (DS)

DS	Deterministic	Default configured RF		Non-deterministic		e-greedy	
	acc_{max}	acc_{best}	% Δ	acc_{best}	% Δ	Avg acc	% Δ
1	0.862	0.819	−4.99	0.856	−0.70	0.847	−1.74
2	0.976	0.971	−0.51	0.976	0.00	0.971	−0.51
3	0.85	0.846	−0.47	0.846	−0.47	0.849	−0.12
4	0.815	0.761	−6.63	0.804	−1.35	0.8	−1.84
5	0.993	0.973	−2.01	0.99	−0.30	0.988	−0.50
6	0.897	0.855	−4.68	0.887	−1.11	0.883	−1.56
7	0.601	0.552	−8.15	0.593	−1.33	0.588	−2.16
8	0.985	0.976	−0.91	0.985	0.00	0.98	−0.51
9	0.538	0.48	−10.78	0.505	−6.13	0.514	−4.46
10	0.711	0.627	−11.81	0.682	−4.08	0.685	−3.66
11	0.925	0.89	−3.78	0.919	−0.65	0.91	−1.62
12	0.797	0.74	−7.15	0.736	−7.65	0.775	−2.76
13	0.681	0.636	−6.61	0.681	0.00	0.669	−1.76
14	0.71	0.654	−7.89	0.679	−4.37	0.692	−2.54
15	0.973	0.97	−0.31	0.973	0.00	0.972	−0.10
16	0.88	0.826	−6.14	0.863	−1.93	0.863	−1.93
17	0.942	0.909	−3.50	0.933	−0.96	0.925	−1.80
18	0.797	0.735	−7.78	0.771	−3.26	0.773	−3.01
19	0.942	0.936	−0.64	0.94	−0.21	0.94	−0.21
20	0.919	0.883	−3.92	0.903	−1.74	0.887	−3.48
μ	0.840	0.802	−4.933	0.826	−1.812	0.826	−1.814

change in $ToEs$, as discussed in Sect. 3.1. This means the formulated strategy worked quite well. Considering dataset 2, we note that 0% percentage acc change, was got with more $NoTs$ (48 trees instead of 46 trees) but at 34.76 times faster. These shows 100% accuracies got, at more number trees but takes a shorter searching time. This makes the strategy formulated in this research relevant. Despite the 1% boundary policy and breaking policies strategies, 65% of the datasets recorded less than 1% change in percentage acc. The other 35% scored fairly good results too. Generally, a shorter ToE means the process will take a shorter time in memory and shorter cpu time, when tuning RF. We also observed the non-deterministic algorithm run an average of 4.6% iterations (i.e. 11.8 of 256 iterations in the parameter space). This is an improvement in iterations by 95.3%. Therefore, the non-deterministic algorithm can improve utilization of computing resources while maintaining a significant acc.

Table 6. Average time of execution (sec) recorded across 20 datasets (DS)

DS	Deterministic	Default configured RF		Non-deterministic		e-greedy	
	i (sec)	t (sec)	Ratio	t (sec)	Ratio	t (sec)	Ratio
1	224.11	0.03	7470	1.22	183.7	2.16	103.75
2	217.97	0.02	10899	6.27	34.76	7.16	100.91
3	239.22	0.03	7974	6.45	37.09	7.28	104.92
4	216.26	0.02	10813	6.43	33.63	7.16	100.12
5	282.42	0.07	4035	6.38	44.27	7.59	118.17
6	235.94	0.03	7865	6.25	37.75	7.96	104.4
7	249.68	0.04	6242	0.78	320.1	1.33	107.16
8	230.44	0.03	7681	6.34	36.35	7.9	104.75
9	246.37	0.03	8212	0.51	483.08	2.32	106.19
10	246.37	0.04	6159	0.94	262.1	2.26	109.01
11	622.88	0.29	2148	1.02	610.67	2.76	225.68
12	227.91	0.03	7597	0.46	495.46	2.25	101.29
13	360.73	0.11	3279	0.59	611.41	2.46	146.64
14	260.52	0.05	5210	0.77	338.34	2.31	112.78
15	230.42	0.15	1536	0.26	886.23	2.37	97.22
16	218.4	0.13	1680	0.29	753.1	2.26	96.64
17	195.28	0.03	6509	0.25	781.12	2.16	90.41
18	213.35	0.03	7112	0.28	761.96	2.25	94.82
19	227.81	0.04	5695	0.28	813.61	2.3	99.05
20	190.49	0.03	6350	0.24	793.71	2.16	88.19
μ	256.83	0.06	6223.3	2.30	415.92	3.82	110.61

As explained in this section, e-greedy algorithm heavily relies on the idea that, the probability of the chosen NoT should be less than the ϵ value, for it to exploit that (selected) arm. Otherwise, the algorithm explores (randomly selects other arms). Across the 20 datasets, on average, the probability that e-greedy will select the optimal arm is 0.814, as shown in Table 4. At some point, because of the exploring and exploiting ideas, e-greedy misses to select the best arms, that's why Table 5 shows e-greedy having a average acc score of 0.826. Nevertheless, in the same table, considering the deterministic algorithm selected the best acc value, e-greedy falls short of an averagely of −1.8% from the best score, and runs 110.61 faster than the deterministic algorithm. Comparing e-greedy and the non-deterministic, coincidentally, we see both of them having the same accuracy across the 20 datasets. However, the non-deterministic algorithm runs 415 times faster compared to the deterministic approach while e-greedy that run at 110 times faster than the deterministic approach. Generally we see the non-deterministic algorithm performing better than the e-greedy algorithm.

The RF algorithm configured by default $NoTs$ (8 trees) showed good results too. It recorded ≈94.5% average accuracy change and very good ToE ratio of 6223. Table 2 told us that fewer $NoTs$ give lesser times of execution. Comparing these results with the non-deterministic algorithm, Table 6 has a higher $ToEs$ because of the higher number of iterations (average of 30.40 across the 20 datasets). If we benchmark our results with the deterministic algorithm, RF algorithm configured by default $NoTs$ runs 6223 faster and give 94.5% chances to get the average best acc, on average. While the non-deterministic approach runs 415 faster and give 98.19% chances to get the average best acc, on average.

3.4 Evaluation Using Jackknife Estimation

Jackknife is used to evaluate the quality of the prediction of computational models. It uses resampling to calculate standard deviation error and estimate bias of a sample statistic, as shown in Eqs. 2 and 3 [15]. Table 7 shows Jackknife results across the 20 datasets. Different datasets record different values of Bias-Corrected Jackknifed Estimates. Standard error is used for null hypothesis testing and for computing confidence intervals. This is why confidence intervals deviating insignificantly. We also see the bias-corrected Jackknifed estimate

Table 7. Jackknife estimates for deterministic and non-deterministic algorithms

DS	Bias-corrected jackknifed estimate			Confidence interval					
				Deterministic		Non-deterministic		e-greedy	
	Deterministic	Non-deterministic	e-greedy	Lower	Upper	Lower	Upper	Lower	Upper
1	0.86	0.85	0.84	0.86	0.87	0.85	0.85	0.84	0.85
2	0.98	0.98	0.97	0.98	0.98	0.98	0.98	0.97	0.97
3	0.85	0.85	0.85	0.85	0.85	0.85	0.85	0.85	0.85
4	0.82	0.79	0.8	0.82	0.82	0.79	0.80	0.79	0.8
5	0.99	0.99	0.99	0.99	0.99	0.99	0.99	0.99	0.99
6	0.89	0.88	0.88	0.89	0.89	0.88	0.89	0.88	0.88
7	0.61	0.59	0.59	0.60	0.61	0.59	0.59	0.59	0.59
8	0.99	0.99	0.98	0.99	0.99	0.98	0.99	0.98	0.98
9	0.53	0.52	0.51	0.53	0.53	0.51	0.52	0.51	0.51
10	0.71	0.69	0.68	0.71	0.71	0.69	0.69	0.68	0.69
11	0.93	0.91	0.91	0.93	0.93	0.91	0.92	0.9	0.92
12	0.80	0.77	0.77	0.79	0.80	0.77	0.78	0.77	0.78
13	0.68	0.67	0.66	0.68	0.68	0.66	0.67	0.66	0.67
14	0.71	0.69	0.69	0.71	0.71	0.68	0.69	0.68	0.69
15	0.97	0.97	0.97	0.97	0.97	0.97	0.97	0.97	0.97
16	0.86	0.88	0.86	0.86	0.87	0.88	0.88	0.85	0.87
17	0.93	0.94	0.92	0.93	0.94	0.94	0.95	0.92	0.93
18	0.77	0.80	0.77	0.76	0.78	0.79	0.80	0.77	0.78
19	0.94	0.94	0.94	0.94	0.94	0.94	0.94	0.94	0.94
20	0.90	0.92	0.88	0.89	0.91	0.91	0.93	0.88	0.89
μ	0.84	0.83	0.82	0.83	0.84	0.83	0.83	0.82	0.83

deviating minimally because the standard error were zero across all the records. In the bias-corrected jackknifed estimate column, the non-deterministic algorithm records 0.83 compared to the e-greedy that recorded 0.82. Generally, the non-deterministic algorithm predictions are stable and reliable.

$$Var(\theta) = \frac{n-1}{n} \sum_{i=1}^{n} (\bar{\theta}_i - \bar{\theta}_{jack})^2, \quad \bar{\theta}_{jack} = \frac{1}{n} \sum_{i=1}^{n} (\bar{\theta}_i) \tag{2}$$

$$\bar{\theta}_{BiasCorrected} = N\bar{\theta} - (N-1)\bar{\theta}_{jack} \tag{3}$$

4 Conclusion

Hyperparameter tuning is a complex optimization task and time consuming. In this research, we formulated a non-deterministic strategy in searching an optimal $NoTs$ hyperparameter in RF algorithm. The goal of this strategy was to maximize predictability, minimizing $NoTs$ and minimizing $ToEs$. We compared experiment results with the deterministic algorithm, e-greedy and default configured RF. The non-deterministic strategy recorded significantly good results in maximizing acc, minimizing $NoTs$ and minimizing searching time. Moreover, evaluations using Jackknife Estimation show that its predictions are stable. The non-deterministic strategy had a significant acc levels and better utilization of cpu processing and time in memory. This research can be adopted in algorithms hyperparameter search and in green computing to preserve computing resources.

References

1. Bernard, S., Heutte, L., Adam, S.: Influence of hyperparameters on random forest accuracy. In: Benediktsson, J.A., Kittler, J., Roli, F. (eds.) MCS 2009. LNCS, vol. 5519, pp. 171–180. Springer, Heidelberg (2009). https://doi.org/10.1007/978-3-642-02326-2_18
2. Breiman, L.: Random forests. J. Mach. Learn. **45**(1), 5–32 (2001). https://doi.org/10.1023/A:1010933404324
3. Breiman, L., Cutler, A.: Random forests manual v4.0 (2017). https://www.stat.berkeley.edu/~breiman/Using_random_forests_v4.0.pdf
4. Chen, T., Guestrin, C.: XGBoost: a scalable tree boosting system. In: 22nd ACM SIGKDD International Conference on Knowledge Discovery and Data Mining, pp. 785–794. ACM (2016). https://doi.org/10.1145/2939672.2939785
5. Dheeru, D., Karra Taniskidou, E.: UCI machine learning repository (2017). http://archive.ics.uci.edu/ml
6. Ganjisaffar, Y., Debeauvais, T., Javanmardi, S., Caruana, R., Lopes, C.V.: Distributed tuning of machine learning algorithms using MapReduce clusters. In: 3rd Workshop on Large Scale Data Mining: Theory and Applications. ACM (2011). https://doi.org/10.1145/2002945.2002947
7. Hazan, E., Klivans, A., Yuan, Y.: Hyperparameter optimization: a spectral approach. arXiv preprint arXiv:1706.00764 (2017)
8. Kaggle: Kaggle datasets. https://www.kaggle.com/datasets

9. Lalor, J., Wu, H., Yu, H.: Improving machine learning ability with fine-tuning (2017)
10. Liu, X., et al.: Semi-supervised node splitting for random forest construction. In: IEEE Conference on Computer Vision and Pattern Recognition, pp. 492–499 (2013). https://doi.org/10.1109/CVPR.2013.70
11. Oshiro, T.M., Perez, P.S., Baranauskas, J.A.: How many trees in a random forest? In: Perner, P. (ed.) MLDM 2012. LNCS (LNAI), vol. 7376, pp. 154–168. Springer, Heidelberg (2012). https://doi.org/10.1007/978-3-642-31537-4_13
12. Senagi, K., Jouandeau, N., Kamoni, P.: Using parallel random forest classifier in predicting land suitability for crop production. J. Agric. Inform. 8(3), 23–32 (2017). https://doi.org/10.17700/jai.2017.8.3.390
13. Smit, S.K., Eiben, A.E.: Comparing parameter tuning methods for evolutionary algorithms. In: IEEE Congress on Evolutionary Computation, pp. 399–406. IEEE (2009). https://doi.org/10.1109/CEC.2009.4982974
14. Snoek, J., Larochelle, H., Adams, R.P.: Practical Bayesian optimization of machine learning algorithms. In: Advances in Neural Information Processing Systems, pp. 2951–2959 (2012)
15. Wager, S., Hastie, T., Efron, B.: Confidence intervals for random forests: the jackknife and the infinitesimal jackknife. J. Mach. Learn. Res. 15(1), 1625–1651 (2014)
16. White, J.: Bandit Algorithms for Website Optimization. O'Reilly Media, Inc., Farnham (2013)

Applications of Agent Systems and Genetic Algorithms

Designing a Website Using
a Genetic Algorithm

Lukas Günthermann[1] and John Kingston[2(✉)]

[1] School of Engineering and Informatics, University of Sussex, Brighton, UK
[2] Centre for Secure, Intelligent and Usable Systems, University of Brighton,
Brighton, UK
j.k.kingston@brighton.ac.uk

Abstract. This paper describes the use of a genetic algorithm to design a
website, according to principles of clarity, symmetry, golden ratio and image
size. The website's logo is used to calculate a matching colour scheme. Results
indicate that local maxima can be a problem but that with the right weighting of
the fitness function, a pleasing design can be achieved.

Such a program could be used when designing large numbers of websites;
when a website has to be re-designed regularly to match changing content; or to
provide a starting point for human website designers or users of interactive
genetic algorithms to improve.

Keywords: Genetic algorithms · Aesthetics · Design · Websites
Configuration

1 Introduction

Aesthetics is the subsection of philosophy examining the nature of beauty and taste.
Lavie and Tractinsky [1] divides it into classical aesthetics and expressive aesthetics.
Classical aesthetics describes characteristics such as clarity, orderliness, and symmetry;
the traits of expressive aesthetics are being original, fascinating, refined, or creative.

The perception of aesthetics in the design of a website influences how likely
visitors are to trust it and even how good they perceive the usability of the website to be
[2]. Since the majority of online users give a website only a few moments of attention
[3] and do not browse deeply to subpages [4] it is necessary to gain the viewer's
attention and trust within this short time span.

The goal of the work described in this paper is to produce a website design using
genetic algorithms that fits the principles of classical aesthetics and whose colours
blend with the logo provided. The focus is placed on the logo because of research that
suggests that companies can embed traits of credibility in the design of a logo and that
these logos can trigger positive credibility assessments of the sponsor of the website
[5]. If this is correct then a good logo fulfils both the need to gain attention and the need
to gain trust. However, attention can produce positive or negative results; for logos to
be visually appealing, they have to blend in with the design of the website.

This approach could be applied in situations, in which it is necessary to create or
maintain many pages with similar requirements. It could be used in web services which

© Springer Nature Switzerland AG 2018
M. Bramer and M. Petridis (Eds.): SGAI-AI 2018, LNAI 11311, pp. 389–402, 2018.
https://doi.org/10.1007/978-3-030-04191-5_32

offer a modular construction system for customers without experience in web design. They would select the content and the settings, so that the algorithm can create a basic solution, which could then be improved by human designers if required.

Other researchers have applied genetic algorithms to the optimisation of website design (e.g. [6–8]). However, all these approaches rely on user feedback to select preferred designs while the genetic algorithm, is running. The work described in this paper uses pre-programmed design principles instead which allows the algorithm to run through many more iterations in a reasonable time.

2 Genetic Algorithms

The theory of evolution posits that reproduction within a species occasionally produces an individual with one or more mutations; that some of these mutations are beneficial to survival, causing the mutation to spread throughout the population according to the principle of survival of the fittest; and that an accumulation of such mutations eventually produces a new species. Genetic algorithms mimic the first two of these three steps within a computer system in an attempt to produce optimised or near-optimal results. Genetic algorithms are usually applied to optimisation problems which are too complex to be solved arithmetically in a reasonable amount of time due the high number of possible combinations (e.g. the well-known Travelling Salesman problem).

The core of a genetic algorithm is the population of chromosomes: units of information which usually consists of a bit string. Each locus in the chromosome has two possible alleles (0 and 1); this allows every chromosome in the population to represent one possible set of parameters. The goal is to develop a genotype (set of parameters) which transforms the source code into the fittest phenotype (in this case, the most appealing website).

According to Mitchell [9], there are three operators in the most basic version of a GA used to evolve the population and create stronger solutions:

Selection: The higher the estimated value of a chromosome is, the more likely it is that the chromosome is selected for reproduction. However, if there is a dominating chromosome in the population, the entire population will slowly segue into similar characteristics, reducing diversity and adaptability; so it is important not to focus only on the most successful members of the population, but to keep variety high and eliminate members which are similar to the dominating member.

Crossover: This operator takes two selected chromosomes as parents and combines their genes into offspring with the same genotypic structure. There are several methods to recombine the two parent chromosomes. The most frequently used one is **single point crossover** [10] which selects a random locus within a chromosome and then takes the subsequence before the locus of the first chromosome and merges it with the subsequence after the locus of the second chromosome to form a new chromosome for the population. The same happens with the two remaining subsequences. Other alternatives are **N-point crossover** (using multiple randomly selected break points to recombine the two strings; this may impair the performance by splitting up interdependent gene blocks, but it does allow the head and tail section of a chromosome to stay together; and **uniform crossover** where the source parent for each gene of the offspring is chosen by chance, which covers a larger part of the search space [11].

Mutation: To increase the diversity in the population, each bit has a small chance of being flipped. The probability should not be too high, otherwise the algorithm will turn into a random search [12].

Once the reproduction process has finished, the value of chromosomes is estimated by a fitness function, and the process is repeated based on the new generation. The new generation is usually of a similar size to the previous one, but sometimes only the best members of the previous generation are carried forward – this is known as elitist selection [13]. This prevents the performance of the best solution in the population from decreasing [14] but may also prevent the algorithm from overcoming a local maximum.

3 Fitness of a Design

There is no objective way to describe beauty or good design in general, but we can evaluate a design according to classical aesthetic principles (clarity, orderliness and symmetry). Deciding how those features should be weighted requires drawing on fields such as psychology, cognitive science and neuroscience.

3.1 Gestaltung

According to [15] the first impression of a design influences all of the following perceptions. A user first views the whole Gestalt (German for "essence or shape of an entity's complete form") of the design and then starts noticing details.

The following Gestalt principles were suggested in [16]:

- Objects which are similar to each other in shape, size, colour, or texture will be perceived as part of a pattern.
- Lines or curves will lead the eye as a path and point attention towards breaking point like the end of the path or a crossing with another one.
- Viewers will subconsciously fill blanks and perceive structures as a whole, even if they are not closed.
- Simple and minimalistic designs reduce distraction.
- Similar elements can create the perception of combined objects, if they are close enough to each other. The eye tends to separate objects into background and foreground and shaping both in contrast to each other.
- A composition should provide order and balance, otherwise the viewer will feel unease and will not be able to decipher the content.

A fitness function could provide positive scores to simple and minimalist design; to order and balance; to paths that point attention to key elements (e.g. the logo); and perhaps to similarity of objects.

3.2 Page Layout

Three aspects of page layout are considered here: symmetry; the golden ratio; and images.

Symmetry. In [17] it is suggested that male users consider vertical symmetrical designed web pages more beautiful and appealing than asymmetrical ones. Surprisingly, the assessments by female participants seem not to be influenced by the factor whether a web page is symmetrical designed or not. Altaboli and Yin [18] confirm that the more similar the numbers and sizes of objects in two neighbouring areas are, the more appealing the visual aesthetics are perceived.

Golden Ratio. An asymmetrical design can be appealing as well, especially if it conforms to the *golden ratio*. The golden ratio is achieved when the ratio between two quantities is the same as the ratio between the bigger quantity and the sum of both quantities. The ratio is commonly believed to make a design more appealing to the human eye. Therefore, it is used, inter alia, in architecture, art, and music; the ancient Greek sculptor Phidias may have known of this ratio in 447 BC, when he created the sculptures for the Parthenon [19]. The golden ratio can also be found in nature, which might indicate that it offers some advantage in natural selection.

Images. Images are a critical part of a website as they help visitors to connect and feel comfortable [20]. They are also much more important than text because few visitors read all the text on any website.

Millennials favour websites with a large main picture; the users observed in [21] rated the visual appealing of such pages "significantly higher" compared to websites without such a main picture. Tullis and Tullis [22] showed that visual appeal ratings of e-commerce websites improved as the size of the largest image increased.

So a fitness function for page layout could evaluate symmetry; use of the golden ratio; and the size of the largest image.

3.3 Colour

When designing a website, it is important that the colour scheme matches the content, because it will determine in which way this content is perceived. The interpretation of colour depends on the social and cultural background of the viewer, some colours also create specific emotions: "Within the psychology of colors, warm colors show excitement, optimism, and creativity; cool colors symbolize peace, calmness, and harmony" [23].

The foundation of colour theory is the colour wheel as shown in Fig. 1. Complementary colours are colours which are on opposite sides of the wheel (e.g. yellow – violet). They create a high contrast when used in design. Analogous colours create a harmonious design by combining a colour and its neighbouring colours (e.g. red - red orange and red - red violet).

However, since this project aims to create a universal solution, it is not supposed to be optimised for a certain style or scheme. The nature of the colour theme is determined by the colour of the logo, which is given as an input variable. The fitness function will therefore evaluate the use of complementary colours to create a contrast between the main element and the background, and of analogous colours that harmonise with the logo.

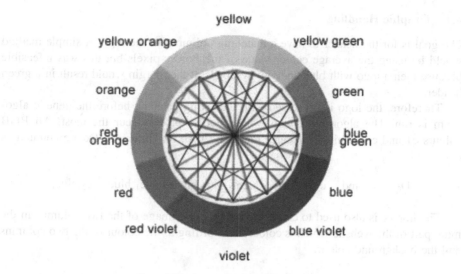

Fig. 1. The colour wheel

4 Implementation

A solution was developed using Microsoft Visual Design Studio 2017 and compiled in C++14. The genetic algorithm was drawn from the GALGO 2.0 template library for constrained optimisation.

The objective function has a vector of parameters as input. This vector represents the decoded chromosome. The return value of this function is the calculated fitness of the individual. The GALGO algorithm uses this function to determine which chromosomes should be selected for crossover.

The algorithm's settings were:

- The first generation is created with random chromosome values based on lower and upper bounds of colours (0 to 256), column widths (0 to 800), logo and images sizes, and padding.
- Stochastic universal sampling selection was used as a selection method and uniform crossover as a crossover method, following [24]:
- It was decided that flipping bits in a space of 256 options was not useful, so uniform mutation was used.
- A mutation rate of 0.03 turned out to convey the best results.
- The elite population size to 1, so that only the best member of each generation is carried on to the next one, thus preventing the performance of the solution from decreasing.
- Experimentation with different population sizes and number of generations determined that a good set-up involved 200 chromosomes mutating over 100,000 generations.
- Different coloured versions of the logo were introduced to enable multiple test runs.

4.1   Graphic Handling

The goal is for the header to have a matching colour with the logo. A simple method would be using the average colour value of the border pixels but this was infeasible because then a logo with blue and yellow pixels at the margin would result in a green header.

Therefore, the logo is processed with the CImg package before the genetic algorithm is run. The algorithm counts which border pixels occur the most. All RGB colours c1 and c2 within a tolerance range of 20 in the difference Dc are counted as one.

$$D_C = |c_1.\text{red} - c_2.\text{red}| + |c_1.\text{green} - c_2.\text{green}| + |c_1.\text{blue} - c_2.\text{blue}|$$

The library is also used to create the background image of the two columns in the main part of the website which is coloured according to the colour of the two columns and the background colour.

4.2   Web Design

The program converts the values of the three RGB channels to single colours and calculates the size of website elements based on the corresponding genes and the general width of the page, which is set in the input variables (1024px was used).

The output is in the form of CSS code (Fig. 2) and HTML code (Fig. 3). The head and body of the HTML document are represented by a vector of nodes (Fig. 4). Each node contains a name which represents the start tag and a Boolean value which determines whether the result string includes a closing tag or not. Optional components are attributes which will be included in the start tag; content which will be added between the start and end tag; and other nodes which enable the creation of a nested structure.

```
css += "#header {\n";
css += " text-align: center;\n";
css += " width: " + std::to_string(this->pageWidth - 2u * this->_padding) + "px;\n";
css += " padding: " + std::to_string(this->_padding) + "px;\n";
css += " height: "+ std::to_string(this->_heightLogo) + "px;\n";
css += " margin: " + std::to_string(this->_padding) + "px 0px " + std::to_string((int)(0.5 * this->_padding)) + "px 0px;\n";
css += " background: rgb(" + this->_colourTitle.toString() + ");\n";
css += "}\n";
css += "#header img {\n";
css += " float: left;\n";
css += " width: " + std::to_string(this->_widthLogo) + "px;\n";
css += " height: " + std::to_string(this->_heightLogo) + "px;\n";
css += "}\n";
css += "#header h1 {\n";
css += " position: absolute;\n";
css += " text-align: center;\n";
css += " line-height: " + std::to_string(this->_heightLogo) + "px;\n";
css += " left: 0;\n";
css += " right: 0;\n";
css += "}\n";
```

Fig. 2. CSS settings of the 'header' element

```
// ------------------------------------------------ //
// The class Node represents one line of html code //
// ------------------------------------------------ //
class Node
{
private:
    std::string _name;          // name
    bool _close;                // true = add a closing tag
    std::vector<Attribute> _att;// attributes
    std::vector<Node> _nodes;   // containing nodes
    std::string _content;       // the content between the tags
public:
    Node() {}
    Node(std::string v_name, bool v_close);
    Node& setContent(std::string v_content);
    Node& addAttribute(Attribute v_att);
    Node& addAttribute(std::string v_name, std::string v_value);
    Node& Node::addNode(Node v_node);
    std::string getString(unsigned int tab);
};
```

Fig. 3. HTML settings of the 'header'

```
doc.add2body(Node("div", true)
    .addAttribute("id", "wrapper")
    /* add header */
    .addNode((Node("div", true))
        .addAttribute("id", "header")
        .addNode(Node("img", false)
            .addAttribute("src", "\"logo.bmp\"")
            .addAttribute("alt", "\"logo\"")
        )

        .addNode((Node("h1", true))
            .setContent("Genetic Algorithms")
        )
    )
)
```

Fig. 4. Class 'node'

The fitness function mostly gives out penalties for aspects which deviate from design norms. The only exceptions are the differences in shade between the colour of the text and the background colours of header, footer, and the two columns. The darker the text is compared to the background, the higher the reward.

The colour of the left column is used as a point of reference and from now on referred to as main colour. Penalty points are applied for the difference between the colour of the background and the complementary colour of the main colour, for the difference between the colour of the header and the calculated colour of the border of the logo, and for the differences between the colours of header/footer and the colour of the right column and the analogous colours of the main colour.

4.3 Fitness Function

The difference Dc between two colours c1 and c2 is calculated using the following formula

$$D_c = (c_1.red - c_2.red)^2 + (c_1.green - c_2.green)^2 + (c_1.blue - c_2.blue)^2$$

The complementary colour ccomp is calculated by converting the original RGB colour into the HSL colour c0, adding 180° to the hue value, and converting it back into the complementary RGB colour. The analogous colours can1 and can2 are calculated in a similar way, but instead of adding 180°, in this case 30° are added to create the first, and 30° are subtracted to create the second analogous RGB colour. Since both of header/footer colour and the colour of the right column could be either one of the analogous colours, as long as they are not the same, both cases are calculated and the lesser penalty is applied.

$$c_{comp}.hue = c_0.hue + \frac{180°}{360°}$$

$$c_{an1}.hue = c_0.hue + \frac{30°}{360°}$$

$$c_{an2}.hue = c_0.hue - \frac{30°}{360°}$$

The following aspects are punished as well: height of the header too small/big compared to the height of the main body, main picture too small/big compared to the left column, additional picture too small/big compared to the right column, right column too small/big compared to the left column, and padding/margins too small/big compared to the mass of the content.

Furthermore, a penalty for lacking symmetry is applied by adding the mass of pictures (width * height) to the mass of the text (with a lower weighting) and comparing to the mass of the other side (left -> right) of the website. The result is the difference D_m. The masses m_1 and m_2 are not supposed to be equal, instead the golden ratio φ is applied.

$$D_m = (m_1 - \varphi * m_2)^2$$

5 Results

The algorithm was tested with different input logos and a varying number of generations. The layout was fixed to include two panes and a header that included the logo, but the sizes of the panes, header and logo could be adjusted by the algorithm, The population had a constant size of 200 members throughout the test runs of the program.

As shown in Table 1, the runtime increases almost linearly with the amount of generations

Table 1. Duration of the process depending on the number of generations

N generations (1000 s)	0.1	1	5	20	50	100
Runtime (mins:sec)		0:12	2:0	12:41	51:30	127:29	250:36

The results of the first generations in each run are very poorly designed solutions without an appropriate structure or colour harmony (see e.g. Figure 5). However, after only one hundred generations the first results can be seen (Fig. 6). Soon, a reasonable ratio between the different segments of the page evolves.

Then improvements usually stagnate, as it takes a very long time for all the different colour values to arrange in a pleasing way. Figure 7 shows the solutions after 1,000 (top left), 2,000 (top right), 6,000 (bottom left), and 20,000 generations (bottom right). Apparently, the reward for adjusting the colour of the header depending on the colour of the logo is barely enough to compensate the loss for shifting away from the analogous colour setting.

After configuring the weightings to reward the similarity between logo and header colour even more, the algorithm came up with an acceptable solution after just 2,000 generations (Fig. 8). However, this version was still likely to get stuck in local maxima; a different run of the same program produced a very small logo (about 5 mm wide). Because increasing the logo size would harm the achieved symmetry, this problem was still not solved after 100,000 generations.

In the final version (Fig. 9), the analogous colours are calculated correctly and the proportions are set appropriately, leading to a more harmonic design. This website took 60,000 generations although an identical layout with a slightly greener main colour was achieved in only 20,000 generations.

Fig. 5. First generation

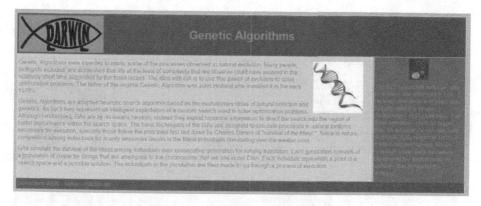

Fig. 6. 100 generations

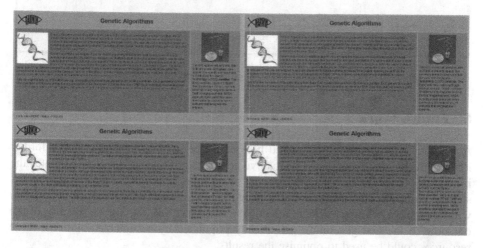

Fig. 7. 100–20 000 generations

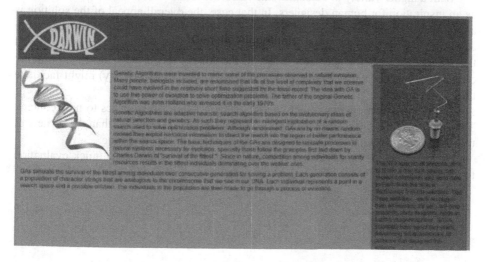

Fig. 8. Reconfigured algorithm, 2 000 generations

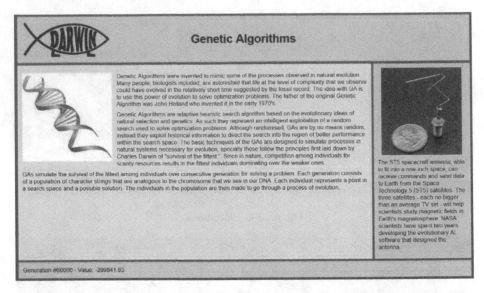

Fig. 9. Reconfigured algorithm, 60 000 generations

6 Future Work

A solution such as the one described here could be used as groundwork for further improvements. For example, an interactive genetic algorithm [25] which evaluates the individuals based on user feedback instead of set rules could take a created solution as starting point. Usually, interactive GAs need a lot of time and user feedback to come up with acceptable solutions, which fatigues the test users and impairs the quality of the outcome. If the first generation was already populated by acceptable solutions, these resources could be used to optimise the results.

With a higher variety in outcomes due to milder restraints, the results could be used as an inspiration for human designers. In that case, the overall appeal of the solution is arguably less important than single interesting aspects about the design which can serve as a source for a new design idea. A further experiment in which designers evaluated the system's results for attributes tested in the fitness function (symmetry, harmony etc.) and also aspects that are not included (e.g. boldness and novelty) might facilitate this.

Another application area might be dynamically adjusting websites to new content. This can be used if the content is uploaded or created by users rather than the owners of the page. It would enable the page to be adjusted in almost real-time.

Furthermore, the fitness function of this project can be used as a quick evaluation tool for existing websites. This might be a useful source of data for web crawlers.

Different fitness functions for other website types besides informational ones could be developed. Layout options that could be introduced would be:

- determining an appropriate font and size for the text;
- automatically dividing tabs;
- dynamic content placement.

However, adding more parameters greatly increases the time and generations needed for a satisfying solution so there may be practical limitations on the features that can be taken into account.

Technical changes that could be introduced include:

- mutation via bit flipping;
- dynamic mutation rates: If progress stagnates, a higher mutation rate might help to overcome local maxima, while the elite population prevents the solution from losing achievements by an extensive amount of random search.

Acknowledgements. The colour wheel image (Fig. 1) is from https://www.sessions.edu/color-calculator/. The GALGO algorithm was obtained from https://github.com/olmallet81/GALGO-2.0. CImg was obtained from http://cimg.eu/.

References

1. Lavie, T., Tractinsky, N.: Assessing dimensions of perceived visual aesthetics of websites. Int. J. Hum. Comput. Stud. **60**(3), 269–298 (2004)
2. Oyibo, K., Vassileva, J.: What drives perceived usability in mobile web design: classical or expressive aesthetics? In: Marcus, A., Wang, W. (eds.) DUXU 2017. LNCS, vol. 10288, pp. 445–462. Springer, Cham (2017). https://doi.org/10.1007/978-3-319-58634-2_33
3. Peracchio, L.A., Luna, D.: The role of thin-slice judgments in consumer psychology. J. Consum. Psychol. **16**, 25–32 (2006)
4. Thompson, C.: Search engines invite new problems. Market. Manag. **13**, 52–53 (2004)
5. Lowry, P.B., Wilson, D.W., Haig, W.L.: A picture is worth a thousand words: source credibility theory applied to logo and website design for heightened credibility and consumer trust. Int. J. Hum. Comput. Interact. **30**(1), 63–93 (2014)
6. Park, S.: Webpage design optimuization using genetic algorithm driven CSS. Retrospective Theses and Dissertations, 14548, Iowa State University (2007). https://lib.dr.iastate.edu/14548
7. Mensch, E.P.: Optimizing Website Design Through the Application of an Interactive Genetic Algorithm. Senior Projects Spring (2016). http://digitalcommons.bard.edu/senproj_s2016/313
8. Olliver, A., Monmarché, N., Venturini, G.: Interactiove design of web sites with a genetic algorithm. In: Proceedings of tne IADIS Internatiinal Conference WWW/Internet, pp. 355–362 (2002)
9. Mitchell, M.: An Introduction to Genetic Algorithms. MIT Press, London (1996)
10. Kora, P., Yadlapalli, P.: Crossover operators in genetic algorithms: a review. Int. J. Comput. Appl. **162**(10), 34–36 (2017)
11. Chawdhry, P.K., Roy, R., Pant, R.K. (eds.): Soft Computing in Engineering Design and Manufacturing. Springer, London (1998). https://doi.org/10.1007/978-1-4471-0427-8

12. Bäck, T.: Evolutionary Algorithms in Theory and Practice: Evolution strategies, Evolutionary programming, Genetic Algorithms. Oxford University Press, Oxford (1996)
13. Baluja, S., Caruana, R.: Removing the genetics from the standard genetic algorithm. In: Proceedings of the Twelfth International Conference on Machine Learning, Lake Tahoe, CA (1995)
14. Ahn, C.W., Ramakrishna, R.S.: Elitism-based compact genetic algorithms. IEEE Trans. Evol. Comput. **7**(4), 367–385 (2003)
15. Hussam, A.: The gestalt principle: design theory for web designers. Web Design Theory Blog, 12 January 2011. https://webdesign.tutsplus.com/articles/the-gestalt-principle-design-theory-for-web-designers–webdesign-1756
16. Arnheim, R.: Kunst und Sehen: Eine Psychologie des schöpferischen Auges, 3rd edn. De Gruyter, Berlin (2000)
17. Tuch, A.N., Bargas-Avila, J.A., Opwis, K.: Symmetry and aesthetics in website design: it's a man's business. Comput. Hum. Behav. **26**(6), 1831–1837 (2010)
18. Altaboli, A., Lin, Y.: Effects of unity of form and symmetry on visual aesthetics of website interface design. Proc. Hum. Factors Ergon. Soc. Annu. Meet. **56**(1), 728–732 (2012)
19. Hemenway, P., Ray, A.: Divine Proportion: Phi in Art, Nature, and Science. Sterling, New York (2005)
20. Lieberman, M.: How important are images in your website design? Inbound – the Blog, 22 March 2012. https://www.square2marketing.com/blog/bid/121405/how-important-are-images-in-your-website-design
21. Djamasbi, S., Siegel, M., Tullis, T., Generation, Y.: Web design, and eye tracking. Int. J. Hum. Comput. Stud. **68**(5), 307–323 (2010)
22. Tullis, T.S., Tullis, C.M.: Statistical analyses of E-commerce websites: can a site be usable and beautiful? In: 12th International Conference on Human-Computer Interaction, Beijing, China (2007)
23. Jones, B.: Color theory: the importance of color in Web design. Design and Promote Blog, 27 June 2014. https://www.designandpromote.com/color-theory-the-importance-of-color-in-web-design/
24. Alabsi, F., Naoum, R.: Comparison of selection methods and crossover operations using steady state genetic based intrusion detection system. J. Emerg. Trends Comput. Inf. Sci. **3** (7), 1053–1058 (2012)
25. Takagi, H.: Interactive evolutionary computation: fusion of the capacities of EC optimization and human evaluation. Proc. IEEE **89**(9), 1275–1296 (2000)

Regulated Information Sharing and Pattern Recognition for Smart Cities

John K. C. Kingston[✉]

Centre for Secure, Intelligent and Usable Systems, University of Brighton,
Brighton, UK
j.k.kingston@brighton.ac.uk

Abstract. This paper describes applications of BOBBIN, a multi-agent system based on a blackboard architecture, to supporting smart cities through regulated information sharing and pattern recognition. The first application uses the knowledge-based processing provided by a blackboard system to ensure that personal information is made available to all and only those who are entitled to see it, thus overcoming the objections raised by the UK Supreme Court to a recently proposed information sharing scheme. The second application extends the first to enable pattern recognition over appropriately regulated information about individuals, with the goal of identifying criminal offences and other patterns of behavior. The final application extends the second to deal with heterogeneous agents, public and private. Each application is illustrated with a scenario.

These three approaches can provide benefits in supporting the growth of intelligent public services and appropriate information sharing within a smart city.

Keywords: Regulated information · Smart cities · Pattern recognition · Blackboard systems

1 Introduction

This paper describes the use of BOBBIN (the Brighton Blackboard Information System) to support three different information sharing and pattern recognition applications that help to enable "smart cities". The applications are implemented in proof-of-concept demonstration systems.

The first application is called 'Named Person Lite'. It is based on the proposed 'Named Person' scheme that the Scottish Government planned to set up to allow a single individual with social care responsibilities to collect all relevant information about a child and to act on it if necessary. The scheme was declared illegal by the UK Supreme Court, partly because of concerns that the 'named person' was permitted to be selective in the information they shared and the institutions with whom they shared it. This paper proposes that BOBBIN is capable of enabling many of the planned benefits of the scheme whilst avoiding the Supreme Court's concerns by automating and regulating the sharing of information.

The second application extends the first with a higher 'blackboard' layer which draws appropriate information from each individual 'Named Person Lite' blackboard

M. Bramer and M. Petridis (Eds.): SGAI-AI 2018, LNAI 11311, pp. 403–415, 2018.
https://doi.org/10.1007/978-3-030-04191-5_33

agent. The goal is to recognise patterns that are known to recur across different cases in order to detect possible criminal offences or other undesirable behavior. The patterns are based on knowledge of typical precursors or indicators of common offences.

The last application extends the architecture again to draw information from various public and private sources including social media. The goal is to enable the public services to respond in a timely fashion based on near real-time information.

2   Intelligent Sharing of Regulated Information

There has been a long-running public debate between the need for privacy of personal data and information, and the value that can be obtained by sharing information and data. The debate covers sharing of health data for use in medical research (see e.g. [1]); allowing law enforcement access to private data [2]; and online gossip about celebrities (e.g. [3]) among other issues. As the law stands in the UK, most information about individuals can only be shared with the written consent of that individual; there are also restrictions on how that data can be processed [4].

The motivation for the work described in this paper arose from a recent conflict between information sharing and privacy in the context of the Scottish Government's proposed Named Person scheme. The proposal was that each child would have an assigned Named Person who would be available to listen, advise and help a child or young person and their parent(s), directly or by helping them to access other services. The Named Person would also be a clear point of contact if a child, young person or their parents wanted information or advice or to talk about any worries; and a point of contact for other services if they had any concerns about a child's or young person's wellbeing.

The scheme was controversial because it was perceived that the State wanted to appoint a guardian for every child who would replace some of the roles and responsibilities of parents. In the summer of 2016 before the scheme was implemented, the UK Supreme Court declared it to be partially illegal on the grounds of information sharing; the Named Person would have too much information to maintain privacy, and (crucially) there was no way to control how much of that information the Named Person chose to share with other responsible parties.

The Supreme Court did not rule that information sharing was a bad thing; it did, however, rule that unmonitored, unregulated, potentially selective information sharing was a bad thing. What if there was a way of sharing information automatically where the information flow is regulated both in terms of what cannot be shared (due to privacy or confidentiality) and what must be shared?

3   Information Sharing Architecture in BOBBIN

BOBBIN is designed as a 'blackboard' system [5] in which multiple agents communicate with each other via a central 'supervisor agent'. BOBBIN is implemented in JESS, the Java Expert System Shell [6]. This means that APIs with other packages can be programmed using Java.

The information sharing architecture designed within BOBBIN uses a three-tier model in which individual agents occupy the lowest level of the hierarchy; the middle level consists of 'departmental' agents that represent the department or group to which the individual agents belong; and there is a single 'supervisor' agent at the higher level whose role is to mediate information sharing. A diagram of the architecture can be seen in Fig. 1.

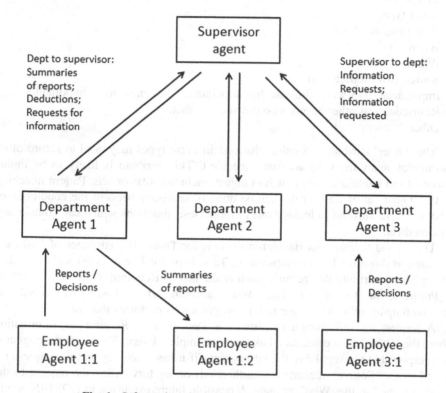

Fig. 1. Information sharing architecture within BOBBIN.

In a regulated information sharing scenario, an agent (e.g. a social worker) would gather information and send it to its departmental agent in the form of a report. The departmental agent would use knowledge to decide how much of that information could or should be shared with other agents in its department. It might also send the information or a summary of it to the supervisor agent. These decisions would be based on regulatory knowledge; existing information; and any requests for information sent by other departmental agents.

The supervisor agent may then communicate information to other departmental agents. Crucially, the supervisor agent will keep a record of all information that it receives, and that information will be made available to any other departmental agent that has appropriate authority.

Agents never communicate horizontally across the hierarchy; all communication is mediated by the departmental agents and the supervisor agent. This means an agent that sends an output up the hierarchy cannot control which other agents can see its outputs; that decision is made by the department and supervisor agents.

BOBBIN uses only two templates to represent information. The first template is for Event facts, which describe events that have occurred. The attributes of an Event are:

- Unique ID
- Event type
- Who (was involved)
- When
- Where
- Source (who reported it)
- Importance (0–5 scale; 0 means 'no importance', 5 means 'most important')
- Restriction (on other agents who can see this fact)
- Other

The 'Other' attribute recognises that certain event types may need to record other information apart from the attributes specified. This attribute is likely to be multi-valued; it can contain any type of Java object, including lists or sets. Pattern matching on the 'Other' attribute by rules can be done if necessary because the conditions of JESS rules are allowed to include one or more 'test' functions which can contain any Java predicate.

The second template for data/information is for Tasks. The attributes of Tasks are the same as those for Events (substituting Task Type for Event Type) with one addition: a Status attribute that records whether the task is Required; Optional; Assigned; In_Progress; or Completed. The 'Who' attribute of a Task will record the person/group/agent to whom the task is assigned/who performs the task.

A request for information consists of a Task of type Request_for_Information where the 'Other' field contains a link to an incomplete Event. The supervisor agent is then responsible for supplying the information (if it has it already and the requester – named in the 'Source' attribute – is authorised) or for forwarding the request to the agent(s) named in the 'Who' attribute. A possible future extension to BOBBIN would be to permit requests for information where 'Who' is unspecified; in such cases, the supervisor agent would monitor incoming information until it found a pattern that matched the request and/or use its knowledge to decide to which department the request should be sent.

4   Regulated Information Sharing: Named Person Lite

A demonstration system has been developed in BOBBIN's information sharing architecture to illustrate how a version of the Named Person scheme might operate within it. This application is called 'Named Person Lite'.

A walkthrough of how the system operates in a scenario is given below. The scenario used was published by the Scottish Government's Get It Right For Every

Child initiative to describe how the Named Person scheme would have worked [7]. An edited summary of the scenario is:

A health visitor on a home visit to assess the development of Emma a 2 year old girl notes that the home is very cold and appears unheated. Emma's mum, Ashley says the heating has been broken in the house for over a week and the private landlord has said that he would come and fix it but has not done so. Emma and her older sister, for whom the health visitor is also the Named Person, are dressed in layers of clothing and are sitting on the couch watching TV under a blanket reluctant to play. Both children have "runny noses" and mum is concerned that they both suffer from night-time coughing.

The health visitor asks mum if she would like her to try to contact the GP for a quick appointment for the children and also get advice and help to address the heating problem. Ashley is enthusiastic to get any help she can as she does not have any local support and was unclear of her rights in relation to the private landlord. The health visitor called the GP surgery and got an urgent appointment for the children the next day. She also called the local authority Crisis Grants Team and informed them of the family's situation and obtained an appointment with them for later in the day where Ashley is given an emergency grant for a small electric heater. In addition the health visitor gave Ashley the number of her local Citizen's Advice service to help her get information and advice about how to get the private landlord to accelerate repairs.

In the original scenario, the health visitor was expected to be Emma's 'named person'. How could BOBBIN support the same health visitor to achieve the same outcome using a 'Named Person Lite' approach?

In the demonstration system, BOBBIN contains a 'health visitor' agent for use by an individual health visitor. When the health visitor comes to write a report on her visit, the report is made through BOBBIN. In this scenario, the report includes two Events; it states that that there are two children suffering from minor ill-health; there is also a problem with the environment to which greater significance is attached.

BOBBIN asks who is responsible for fixing the environmental problem; a menu of common options is provided. In this case, 'Private landlord' is selected. This is added to the Event.

The health visitor agent in BOBBIN includes some rules, one of which is triggered whenever illness and environmental problem(s) are found in the same place. The rule asks the user whether the illness might be caused or triggered by the environmental problem. In this case, this answer is Yes, and that triggers further actions.

Firstly, the health visitor agent offers advice to be passed on to the client. In this case, it prompts the health visitor to suggest to Ashley that she might want to visit her GP and that the local Citizen's Advice Bureau may be able to help her negotiate with her landlord.

Secondly, it automates the request for a crisis grant by sending a task to a (notional or actual) Crisis Grants agent via the supervisor agent and the Crisis Grants departmental agent. The request provides the Events and asks for a decision on whether an emergency grant can be made available. The Crisis Grants agent is likely to send back a request for information such as how long the problem has persisted for, and how much money is required; this request should appear as a message to the health visitor who can supply the requested information. The Crisis Grants agent can then make a decision in principle based on the information supplied, and the Crisis Grants departmental agent can confirm or reject that decision based on knowledge of the budget and spending priorities. The health visitor does not need to know whether the decision has been made by a human or by an automated agent, or why it was made.

At this stage, the supervisor agent takes action. It has a record of an ongoing request from the Housing department for information on private landlords who are not fulfilling their obligations. While some actions by a landlord might be sufficiently private that the supervisor agent will not disclose them, in this case the supervisor agent determines (using rules) that the Housing department is entitled to see the information that the health visitor has gathered. A possible future enhancement to 'Named Person Lite' might be for the supervisor agent to 'push' certain information out to agents who might have an interest in it rather than waiting for requests.

In short, the supervisory agent is acting in the place of the Named Person in the role of sharing information between departments. However, it operates strictly according to its rules which are assumed to be regulation-based; any information that is not restricted by regulation is available to all those entitled to see it and only those entitled to see it. It therefore provides a way of sharing information between agents without falling foul of the Supreme Court's criticisms of the proposed Named Person scheme.

5   Pattern Recognition and Smart Cities

The architecture of BOBBIN is capable of more than just the regulated sharing of information. A second application extends the concept from information sharing to knowledge-based recognition of patterns in information. The goal of this application, as of all the applications described in this paper, is to support a 'smart city'.

There is no universally accepted definition of what a 'smart city' is. Albino et al. [8] review no fewer than twenty-one definitions. The definitions have a similar central conception, but differ in the degree to which the use of information and communication technologies is assumed and in the definitions of what a 'good' city is. For current purposes, smart cities will be defined as cities "that use all available technology and resources in an intelligent and co-ordinated manner to develop urban centers that are at once integrated, habitable and sustainable." [9]

The application proposed here focusses on the concepts of "intelligent" and "co-ordinated". One of the motivations for the Scottish Government's proposed Named Person scheme was to protect children who are suffering or at risk of suffering by allowing a single person to co-ordinate all information about that child, rather than having different indicators available to different departments. However, there are (fortunately rare) occasions in towns and cities where numerous children are suffering or at risk from the same source, as happened with the "grooming gangs" in Rochdale [10]. In such cases, a Named Person is needed initially to co-ordinate information about an individual child and then an agent that can co-ordinate information from different Named Persons and intelligently recognize patterns in that information is also required.

The knowledge that drives this pattern matching could be drawn from two sources: similarities observed amongst the experiences of the (actual or potential) victims, or knowledge of typical activities of perpetrators. The former can be handled using data mining techniques – either unsupervised learning to identify any patterns that might exist, or supervised learning to see if any minors or their known contacts fall into the profile of victims or perpetrators. The latter could draw on representations such as the "fraud plans" approach [11] to recognize generic plans and then variations on those plans applied locally.

5.1 Artificial Intelligence and Criminal Profiling

Criminal profiling is a technique for identifying likely suspects in a crime based on similarities in behavior to previous crimes, and (more controversially) to predict likely future crimes and victims. Attempts to apply artificial intelligence to support criminal profiling date back to the 1980s with the FBI's VICAP program for analyzing homicide-related violent crimes [12] which used case based reasoning to compare over 100 features of the modus operandi of a new crime with those already in the database and displays the 10 closest matches. Another program performed a similar function for crimes of arson; in one case, it was used to construct a criminal personality profile describing an individual who could have been responsible for a series of fires at religious homes and houses of worship that summer in a posh New England community, and it not only accurately described the suspect (who later confessed) but also pinpointed his residence.

AI systems that perform crime prediction use two approaches to profiling. The less controversial one is based on actions that are typical precursors to specific crimes: for example, a system is being trialed by the Chinese government that tracks the movements and behavior of individuals (using facial recognition from surveillance cameras) and highlights suspicious behavior [13]. A spokesman for the developers said, "Of course, if someone buys a kitchen knife that's OK, but if the person also buys a sack and a hammer later, that person is becoming suspicious".

The other approach is to use known factors about a person to predict their likelihood of committing crime. Controversy arises because any such system based on data mining inevitably includes demographic information about age, race and residence. An investigation into one such system – COMPAS (Correctional Offender Management Profiling for Alternative Sanctions), which is used in several state jurisdictions in the USA – found the system claiming that black people were almost twice as likely as white people to reoffend [14].

5.2 Approach Taken in BOBBIN

The approach taken in BOBBIN is to use knowledge about typical precursors to crimes. The precursors are identified by the 'department agents' and reasoned about by the supervisor's agent. If the department agent identifies a sufficient number of precursors, it passes that information to the supervisor which recommends further action and/or carries out appropriate information sharing with other departments. Table 1 lists some of the typical indicators/precursors of online purchase fraud.

Table 1. Indicators/precursors of purchase fraud [15]

Indicators / precursors of purchase fraud
Not mentioning the exact product that is for sale or other indications they haven't read the advert properly (e.g. requesting a 'best asking price' when the price is listed in the advert).
Being ready to pay 'without delay'.
Offering more than the asking price.
Item to be collected by a shipping company rather than the purchaser.
Paying through a third party
Bad grammar.

BOBBIN's supervisor agent links the knowledge about typical precursors to "fraud plans" [11]. This approach represents generic types of fraud and shows how the different generic steps are specialized to create different types of fraud. Figure 2 shows a generic plan for purchase fraud.

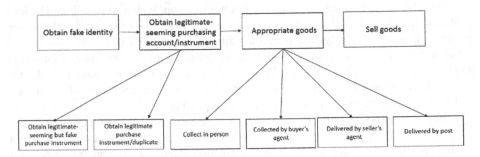

Fig. 2. Generic plan for purchase fraud (from [12]).

For example, assume that a motorcycle has been offered for sale online at a price of $5000. A potential purchaser who claims to live in a different US state replies as follows:

"I really want this as gift for my brother Can you give best asking price I will pay from Paypal account without delay and my shipping agent will collect."

If the purchaser feeds this message into BOBBIN, it will be sent to the Sales Department agent where the list of fraud precursors is stored. BOBBIN does not yet support identification of these precursors from natural language; instead it is able to present the request to a member of staff in the sales department along with a list of precursors and then to ask if any of the precursors appear to be present. Given that five of the six precursors listed in Table 1 are present, this information is sent to the supervisor agent which recommends sending a message to the buyer stating that the price has been increased (i.e. to test if the final, most damning precursor is also present). It could also notify other supervisor agents in other instances of BOBBIN (if suitable secure connections were available) to scan for messages from the same person/domain.

Precursors can be linked to specific steps in a crime plan. The use of a shipping company and bad grammar (from someone who claims to be a US resident) are linked to "Obtain fake identity"; paying through a third party (Paypal) is linked to "Obtain legitimate seeming purchase instrument". Others are linked to general characteristics of crime: failing to mention the exact product may be due to a fraudster re-using the same message in many attempts at fraud rather than tailoring them to individual targets, while "without delay" is typical of almost all frauds – for a fraudster, time is always vital because they want to complete their plan before the fraud is discovered. Using such a structured approach helps to explain why precursors are linked to offence types; to recognize unknown actions as being variants on previous precursors; to prompt human experts for further precursors; or to classify patterns of precursors found through machine learning.

6   Real Time Response in the Smart City

The architecture can be adapted to take input not only from Named Person agents but from other sources. These sources might include information websites about subjects such as transport, shopping, public events or weather, and social media sources.

Much of this information will be publicly available, but some may be regulated or otherwise restricted. For example, it is possible that a 'smart city' might include a social media network amongst shopkeepers. If a known shoplifter appears in one of their shops, they have agreed to share this information amongst themselves. Since publicising a claim that certain person is a known criminal could easily lead to a suit for defamation, they are careful to restrict that information from public availability; however, they may agree to share it, or a summary of it, with the police via an appropriately restricted channel. The BOBBIN architecture provides a suitable channel.

The primary benefit obtained from these sources is information that is updated in near real time. There are also secondary benefits in localization; some sources will address specific localities within a city.

An illustrative scenario assumes that a city contains

- A neighbourhood watch group that has its own page on social media where they share their observations of anything they deem anti-social, from rude teenagers to properties with overgrown gardens. They are only too happy to give the police access to their page.
- The local rail operator runs an opt-in alert service over social media through which travellers can be told of delays or cancellations to trains.

The scenario is:

It is early Saturday afternoon in Smarton. Most city council officials are off duty for the weekend, although their social media monitoring team has one person on duty. The police, in contrast, are out in force in the main shopping centre and at the football stadium where a big match is taking place in a couple of hours. The first supporters are already arriving at the ground.

The rail operator announces through its web service that a train from London will be arriving late. The train will be carrying many supporters of the away team. The police chief's tablet computer sends him a message reminding him that he is entitled to delay the kick-off of the football match if necessary but recommending that he does not do so based on current information about the train's arrival.

A message appears on the local neighbourhood watch group complaining about a group of young men walking purposefully along the middle of a suburban road (and temporarily blocking it) while singing rowdy songs. The police's social media monitoring team enter this into their intelligent software system. The software system recommends that since the group is moving rather than congregating and is not committing or attempting any criminal activity no immediate police presence is necessary.

The software assesses why such a group might have appeared. It is programmed to consider various possibilities including political rallies; organised fights; 'steaming' (mass theft/robbery); rioters; flashmobs; charity collectors; and missionaries/carol singers. Given the time of day, the time of year and the reported membership and behaviour of the group, it decides that the highest likelihood is that they are football supporters heading for the match. It calculates their likely routes.

An alert flashes on the police chief's tablet device. The information about the rowdy group has been combined with information about the late-arriving train. The police chief reads that the rowdy group is likely to pass the railway station at almost exactly the time that the train full of away fans will arrive.

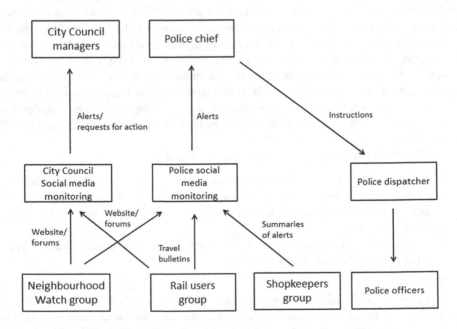

Fig. 3. Real Time Response Architecture for a Smart City.

He quickly deploys two officers to re-route the rowdy group down a different route that keeps them away from the station.

The architecture of such a system can be seen in Fig. 3. The current demonstrator version of BOBBIN lacks the capability to calculate routes or to access train timetables but is able to accept input from humans monitoring other information sources; to reason about why a large group of young men might have appeared; and to pass relevant information between agents. It uses a rule-based architecture for its reasoning; common groups are represented as objects with attributes such as gender, age, clothing, time of day and time of year and the rule-based system asks questions to distinguish groups based on those attributes.

7 Future Work

Possible enhancements to the systems described above could include.

7.1 Natural Language Understanding

One possible enhancement to this system would be to implement text mining on the web pages/messages of the various information groups, so that instead of a human being having to monitor the groups all the time, automated alerts could be sent when something important is posted by one of these groups.

7.2 Conflict Identification and Resolution

With many different information sources contributing to it, it is inevitable that BOBBIN will eventually be supplied with contradictory information about the same event, or contradictory cases that address the same 'problem'.

BOBBIN is well placed to identify such conflicts, since all information that is shared passes through the supervisor agent; all that is needed is a few rules to detect occasions where an event of the same type has been reported at the same time and/or location but with other details being different, or where two or more cases offer contradicting solutions to a 'problem'.

As for conflict resolution, the quickest method is to ask the system's user to resolve it. The next quickest is to establish a priority of sources; it may come down to trust (e.g. believing the rail operator over a local resident), although this should be treated as a heuristic rather than a firm rule.

A third method would be to send a message back to the agents who have supplied the contradicting/contradicted information reporting the contradiction, asking them to either change or explain the information that they have supplied. Experience suggests that often both information providers may well have been well-meaning but made different assumptions about the context surrounding the event.

A fourth approach is to treat both information items as provisionally true, and to mark any deductions made on the basis of these items as assumption-based. Assumption-based truth maintenance systems (ATMS) [16] are a recognised technology in Artificial Intelligence and can be used to reason with hypothetical or unproven information, with all such reasoning being retracted if the initial information is proven to be untrue.

7.3   Custom-Built Workflow

A further knowledge management application that could be built within BOBBIN would be to use the blackboard architecture to develop customised workflows. In this scenario, the 'agents' would be different individuals or departments who could offer specialised workflows that solved particular problems. A problem would be posted on the blackboard (a set of events and a request to analyse or transform those events to achieve a particular goal) and these would be matched against the various specialised workflows. If one of those specialised workflows applied, it would either simulate processing of the events or would actually be carried out and its results would be posted on the blackboard, which might achieve the goal or which might be used to trigger another specialised workflow that advances towards the goal. Finally, the set of workflows used to achieve the goal is assembled into a sequence that can be applied to achieve, or has already been used to achieve the real goal.

For example, imagine that a company had become aware that one of its employees might be mis-using company computers. If the company's various departments were running BOBBIN's custom workflow application, the company could post a description of the events (employee details) and goal (determine if any breach of company policy has occurred) to BOBBIN's supervisory agent. They might expect the Human Resources agent to be first to respond, but it would not do so because the HR agent only has workflows to deal with an employee who is known to be misbehaving. In fact it would be IT Services who would offer two workflows: one to run an automated keyword analysis of the employee's email traffic which is held on the central server; the other to create a disk image of the employee's computer that might be used by a later workflow that conducts forensic analysis of disk images.

The company is informed of IT's response via BOBBIN and authorises them to do the email analysis. The results will be posted onto BOBBIN. If it is found that the employee has emailed confidential documents to his personal email account, then one or more of HR's workflows would apply, and there might also be good reason to carry out the time-consuming forensic analysis; which was done first would depend on other priorities.

References

1. Abbas, A., Khan, S.U.: A review on the state-of-the-art privacy-preserving approaches in the e-health clouds. IEEE J. Biomed. Health Inform. **4**, 1431–1441 (2014)
2. Barrett, B.: The Apple-FBI Battle is over, but the new Crypto Wars have just begun. Wired, March 30th (2016). https://www.wired.com/2016/03/apple-fbi-battle-crypto-wars-just-begun/. Accessed 19 Aug 2016
3. Naomi Campbell v Mirror Group Newspapers (2002–2004). [2002] EWHC 499 (Q.B.); [2002] IP&T 944 (CA); [2004] IP&T 764 (HL), [2004] UKHL 22
4. Data Protection Act 1998. http://www.legislation.gov.uk/ukpga/1998/29/contents

5. Hayes-Roth, B.: A blackboard architecture for control. Artif. Intell. **26**(3), 251–321 (1985)
6. Friedman-Hill, E.J.: Jess, the Java Expert System Shell. Sandia National Laboratories Report SAND98-8206.UC-405. http://prod.sandia.gov/techlib/access-control.cgi/1998/988206.pdf. Accessed 19 Aug 2016 (1997)
7. Get It Right For Every Child initiative: Scenario 4: Emma's story. Scottish Government. ISBN 978-1-78652-292-4 (2016). http://www.gov.scot/Resource/0050/00502049.pdf. Accessed 19 Aug 2016
8. Albino, V., Berardi, U., D'Angelico, R.M.: Smart cities: definitions, dimensions, performance and initiatives. J. Urban Technol. **22**(1), 3–21 (2015)
9. Barrionuevo, J.M., Berrone, P., Ricart, J.E.: Smart cities: sustainable progress. IESE Insight **14**, 50–57 (2012)
10. Bunyan, N.: Rochdale grooming trial: gang convicted for sex trafficking. In: Daily Telegraph, London (2012). Accessed 8 May 2012
11. Kingston, J.: Representing, reasoning and predicting fraud using fraud plans. In: Proceedings of Research Challenges in Information Science (RCIS-2017), University of Brighton, 10–12 May 2017
12. Icove, D.J.: Automated crime profiling. FBI National Centre for the Analysis of Violent Crime, December 1986. http://www.icove.com/images/crimeprofiling.pdf
13. Yang, Y., Yang, Y., Ju, S.F.: China seeks glimpse of citizens' future with crime-predicting AI. Financial Times, 23 July 2017. https://www.ft.com/content/5ec7093c-6e06-11e7-b9c7-15af748b60d0
14. Angwin, J., Larson, J., Mattu, S., Kirchner, L.: Machine bias. ProPublica, 23 May 2016. https://www.propublica.org/article/machine-bias-risk-assessments-in-criminal-sentencing/
15. Provo, N.: Craigslist scams Revisited – 5 Main Scam Indicators, 30 May 2010. https://mollermarketing.com/2010/05/craigslist-scams-revisited-5-main-scam-indicators/
16. Reiter, R., de Kleer, J.: Foundations of assumption-based truth maintenance systems: preliminary report. In: Proceedings of the Sixth National Conference on Artificial Intelligence (AAAI 1987), Seattle, Washington, vol. 1, pp. 183–188. AAAI Press

A Middleware to Link Lego Mindstorms Robots with 4th Generation Language Software NetLogo

Syed K. Aslam[✉][ID], William J. Faithful, and William J. Teahan

Bangor University, Bangor, Wales, UK
{eep613,eep831,w.j.teahan}@bangor.ac.uk

Abstract. Lego Mindstorms has delivered low-cost amateur robotics to the public, where anyone can easily modify and develop new systems and extensions to extend its capabilities. However, no one has previously attempted to link a 4th generation agent-oriented language such as NetLogo with Mindstorms robots in order to provide an agent-oriented development environment along with simulation and modelling capabilities. This paper describes the development of middleware which can be used to control a Mindstorms robot via a NetLogo model which provides body-syntonic capabilities for real-time sensor feeds and robot commands to make and enact decisions. A couple of example NetLogo models to demonstrate the capabilities of this system (line-following ability and subsumption architecture roaming) have been developed and are described in this paper.

Keywords: Robotics · Middleware · Lego Mindstorms · Subsumption

1 Introduction

Robotics research has been conducted since the 1950s. The first industrial robot was introduced in 1961 which was used by GM for welding die casts onto car bodies [2]. Further research led to the development of many new and modern robots with more functionalities and features such as the computer controlled Stanford arm [11], first mobile robot Shakey [6], Genghis was capable of following a person based on the readings of an infrared sensor [7], Myrmex [1] was created with three principle layered behaviours: collect, avoid and safe-forward, and the winner of the 2005 DARPA Grand Challenge, Stanley [12] which was able to autonomously navigate a 175 miles off road course in under 10 h.

The release of LEGO Mindstorms robots in 1998 increased amateur interests in the development of intelligent mobile robots. Nowadays, LEGO kit is an essential part of educational institutions and extensions creating by community provide additional functionalities. However, these extensions/libraries require the users to have internal knowledge of the system and of 3rd generation languages such as Java. This paper describes the development of middleware

© Springer Nature Switzerland AG 2018
M. Bramer and M. Petridis (Eds.): SGAI-AI 2018, LNAI 11311, pp. 416–430, 2018.
https://doi.org/10.1007/978-3-030-04191-5_34

named NXTLogo for using an agent-oriented 4th generation language to control NXT 2.0 robots which can provide additional functionalities along with the functionalities of 3rd generation middleware extensions/libraries. In addition, the developer has access to simulation and modelling facilities provided by Net-Logo, and an ability to design using what Papert[1] called a 'body-syntonic' or first-person perspective—the developer designs the agent (imagined as a robotic 'turtle') to move using a perspective similar to their own perspective.

The next section introduces the background to this project, section three covers the design and implementation of the middleware in details. Section four describes two sample NetLogo models which have been written using the middleware to illustrate use of its capabilities and section five presents the results of these models. Finally, section six draws conclusions and provides some future work.

2   Background

Robots have long been predicted to become mainstream public agents which will require (at-least) basic intelligence (an ability to navigate, communicate and interact in the real world environment). Generally, robotics hardware is advanced enough to fulfil these objectives; however, complexity of design and implementation of thoughtful intelligence are holding back this prediction.

Rodney Brooks outlined the idea of subsumption [4] in which architecture breaks down complicated behaviour to be the sum of several behaviour layers and each layer is subsumed in priority by the one above it. Sensor based robots are characterised by four key phases, according to Brooks [9]: situatedness; embodiment; intelligence; and emergence.

To understand the Brooks approach, we need to understand cognitive and reactive behaviours. Cognitive behaviour for navigation maintains an internal model of an environment and comprehends relative position within it. In contrast, reactive behaviour does not maintain this relative position or internal model, it simply responds to stimuli. Wang [14] describes cognitive agents as being driven by intention and having a representation of their environment from which they can predict the future. For example, a robot vacuum cleaner can respond to simple stimuli to accomplish its tasks such as "Is this patch of floor dirty?", "Is there a wall in front of me?", or "Am I moving?" can be paired with appropriate instinctive responses.

The approach to designing autonomous systems has evolved over the years from being exclusively cognitive before the late 1980's to agents with more reactive elements and behaviour. Reactive approaches to robotics provide a simple and effective means of realising complicated behaviours.

In the context of this paper, a robot is capable of displaying aspects of Brook's behavioural approach if it can act immediately upon real world events by utilizing sensors and actuators and does not need an internal model to operate. Complex

---

[1] Papert was the original designer of NetLogo's parent language, Logo.

reaction, interaction and forward planning is all within scope. However, for our work, these capabilities are available if the robot is treated as a NetLogo turtle (NetLogo and Logo provides programming constructs using agents in the form of turtles, patches, links and the observer).

2.1   Related Work

NetLogo's API for Java extensions provides a wide range of possibilities especially for linking two independent systems such as NetLogo and MATLAB [10]. The approach for writing a NetLogo extension is seamless, with data passed from NetLogo, where it is acted upon in the secondary system and then passing back as a result. This is done in a way that the developer essentially has access to further NetLogo-like language commands without the need to be aware of the underlying implementation.

Many other middleware extensions/libraries for Mindstorms NXT have been developed such as RWTH, cliRobust, and JCSPre. RWTH Mindstorms NXT toolbox for MATLAB is the only other 4th generation language extension for Lego Mindstorms. RWTH is similar to having an application in which LeJOS commands can be written and run without compilation, whereas this project uses the capabilities of LeJOS to provide an abstraction of a robot in NetLogo instead of recycling LeJOS commands into another language.

cljRobust Clojure Programming API for Lego Mindstorms NXT [15] has been designed around clojure, which is a modern, concurrent dialect of LISP. The purpose of this extension is to allow control applications to be written in clojure. Extensions/libraries such as these have been designed to allow parallel programming elements to be used to control Mindstorms robots.

JCSPre [8] bears more resemblance to this project as it is also based on LeJOS firmware for NXT robots, but it links the robot and its LeJOS abstraction to a reduced version of the parallel programming environment JCSP (Communicating Sequential Processes for Java). Similar to cljRobust, this has been designed to provide a port for LeJOS functionality directly into the JCSP language.

2.2   Lego Mindstorms Robotics

The first version of the Lego Mindstorms kit was released in 1998, with subsequent versions released in 2006, 2009 and 2013. Lego Mindstorms comes with preinstalled firmware. However, a custom firmware can be installed to achieve required functionalities. Because of its availability to the public and its relatively cheap price for a robotics kit, several interesting robots have been developed by the community. Two well-known ones are a Rubik's cube solver and a Sudoko solver. These puzzle solvers demonstrate an application of the cognitive approach to AI and also demonstrate the flexibility of the Lego Mindstorms kit, and the capabilities of the sensors included with it. The fact that a robot with a light sensor on a sweeping arm can accurately scan and read numbers on a piece of paper opens up many possibilities for completely autonomous input, even if it is a relatively slow process.

2.3 NetLogo

NetLogo is a programmable multi-agent modelling and simulation language with a wide range of practical uses. It is free to download and provides a large number of example models which demonstrate the level of processes and behaviours that can be simulated. Its drag and drop interface makes it easy to use, create and monitor programs (called 'models') in real-time. Being an agent-oriented programming language makes it a uniquely interesting port destination for a robotics kit.

2.4 LeJOS

LeJOS is the custom firmware and API used in this project to program the control file on the robot and the communication in the extension. LeJOS is a lightweight Java replacement firmware for Lego Mindstorms NXT and RCX robots. LeJOS has its own JVM (Java Virtual Machine) which allows robots to be programmed in Java. The advantages of using Java are twofold:

- Java provides cross-platform system portability and NetLogo is also free and portable.
- NetLogo is written in Java, meaning that NetLogo and LeJOS can be linked with relative simplicity.

LeJOS flexibility and scope has already been used widely. For example, a team from Portugal [3] successfully used LeJOS to implement subsumption based roaming and environment mapping on a Lego Mindstorms robot. They linked the control file (Robot) and Java program (Laptop) via Bluetooth.

The next section describes the design and implementation of the system and the files and commands which make up the extension.

3 NXTLogo: Design and Implementation

The purpose of this middleware is to make the system heterogeneous, so that it works on all platforms and with all robot configurations, and to make the front end intuitive and easy to develop with, without the user needing internal knowledge of the system or the processes involved. In order to achieve that, a great number of challenges needs to be tackled through system design. The system needs to be efficient, configurable, dynamic and reliable while at the same time maintaining a simple, user friendly front end. There needs to be an emphasis on the usability of LEGO Mindstorms extensions to enthusiasts without specific 3rd generation programming skills. Doing away with the complicated programming, installations, and compiling should open-up development to people and parties less directly connected to the field.

The design of the Middleware (see Fig. 1) is divided into two parts: the Java extension to NetLogo; and the LeJOS Java control file which runs on the NXT. The extension handles the channelling and conversion of data both to the NXT

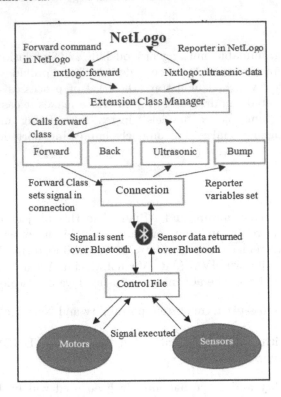

Fig. 1. The design for the middleware based on some sample classes in the extension.

over Bluetooth and to the extension via NetLogo reporters, and does no explicit processing of the data itself. The control file is the other end of the Bluetooth connection created in the extension, and runs on the LeJOS firmware on the NXT. It listens for incoming commands, actuates them and returns data from all sensors.

The Control File. There are many challenges in designing an efficient control file such as returning sensor data frequently, non-blocking, and data transfer. LeJOS is used to run on a robot (control file). However, several steps are required in order to compile a program to run on the NXT.

Firstly, the written program needs to be compiled into a .class file by the LeJOS NXJ compiler, nxjc, and then needs to be converted into a binary .nxj program to run on the robot. To achieve this, the program needs to be independent of its references and the wholly independent unit needs to be compiled into a .nxj binary instruction file using the nxjlink utility. Afterwards, the file is uploaded to the robot via Bluetooth or USB and executed as instructed.

The control file implements the LeJOS abstractions of robot peripherals and sits between the extension and the peripherals. For example, a pilot is used to control two motors, and colour, ultrasonic, and touch sensors. The sensors return their abstractions (boolean for the bump sensor, distance from 0–255 for the ultrasonic sensor, and 3 integer RGB for the colour sensor) and the pilot sends back a boolean indicating if the robot is moving, and associated tacho count, and approximate real turn angle after any given manoeuvre, and resets itself. The provided information is enough to allow simulation corrections in NetLogo which means we can move a turtle representation of the robot in the NetLogo simulation in a similar manner as the robot has moved itself.

The main polling loop of the control file is shown in Algorithm 1. In order to send back the sensor data, it requires every polling loop to ensure a constant stream besides making sure that sending and receiving is synchronised at both ends which is a difficult task. Synchronisation is one of the biggest issues that needs to be overcome in order for the robot to be able to generate a relative map of its environment upon which it can later rely. A switch statement is used to process the signal in case it is anything other than NO-ACTION is received, but everything else is designed using LeJOS's instant return arguments in motor calls which avoids using while loops or hanging the program. This allows the sending of sensor data even while the robot is moving forward.

This architecture allows the sending of data at the end of every iteration of the main while loop without blocking, hanging, or pausing the robot. This fast and regular return of the data is necessary for visualizing the sensors as event streams, otherwise, events can be reacted too slowly or missed completely.

Algorithm 1. Main Loop of Control File

```
1  while signal != terminate do
2  |   switch signal
3  |   |   case stop
4  |   |   |   stop robot;
5  |   |   |__ setsignal = NO-ACTION;
6  |   |   case foward-constant
7  |   |   |   robot keep going forward;
8  |   |___|__ setsignal = NO-ACTION;
9  |__ send sensor data;
```

In an ideal world, sensor data would be placed in an array; however, available I/O streams (OutputStream and DataOutputStream) in LeJOS only support primitives which means output has to be sequential for each sensor. The former is able to send bytes of data (integers) one at a time which is not particularly useful because tachometer and motor turn-angle estimations are floating point numbers. Although the later supports all the primitives (boolean, integer, float, double), it does not support an array. This leave us with two choices: (1) send back the numbers from each sensor individually and deal with them sequentially at the extension; or (2) write a serialising method to run on the robot which has limited power and memory. Our current solution is sequential. However, this may complicate things if we want to extend the project to involve multiple robots, but separate output and input for each robot is necessary if we wish to differentiate between messages.

The NetLogo Extension File, NXTLogo. The variables in the extension called NXTLogo are in the connection class and in the reporters. In the connection class, two methods are used to set the signal, buffered and checked. In buffered, if two different signals are sent at the same time, the second to arrive is placed in the buffer to be executed next. The buffer size is variable but two seems to operate best where the second signal is discarded if identical to the first one. In order to update the sensor streams frequently, the NetLogo simulation needs to keep executing which generates unwanted repeat instructions. Without discarding, the buffer would fill up quickly and the robot would not move as expected. Once the instruction is executed and removed from the buffer, a new one can take its place. In this way, repeat instructions can still work if required. However, they will not stack up into a backlog (see Fig. 2). The checked method can accept integers from 1 to 359, and sets a variable as such which tells the robot how far it is expected to turn when given a turning command.

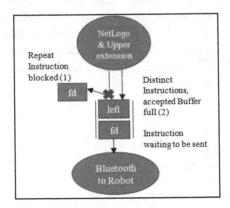

Fig. 2. The control file instruction buffer.

Instructions are each defined by a class and linked to an appropriate command in NetLogo. When an instruction is given in NetLogo, its defined class in the extension passes a representative integer to the signal setting method which checks the instruction duly and places it in the queue to be executed if accepted. Whenever the main program loop is repeated, the signal buffer is peeked (first element is investigated but not removed). If peek is null, the NO-ACTION signal is sent, otherwise, if peek is not null, the head of the queue is removed and sent to the robot along with the current turning angle.

These systems are synchronized by blocking each other. For example, the extension sends a signal and waits to hear a response from the robot to make sure the signal has been executed and the loop has been passed and the robot sends a response after executing and waits for the next signal. The steps between a command being sent and executed are shown in Fig. 1.

Implementation and Class Breakdown. The extension consists of 15 Java classes with most of them using standard practice when writing a NetLogo extension where every extension command to be called in NetLogo needs its own class. All of these command classes are referenced by the extension class manager file, which tells NetLogo which command is linked with which class. Commands and Reporters are two types of classes called by NetLogo. Commands do not return any information and are only capable of executing codes whereas reporters return data when called. The currently available commands in NXTLogo are listed and briefly summarized in Table 1.

Table 1. Commands currently available in NXTLogo.

nxtlogo:connect \<String robot-name\>	Connects to the specified NXT
nxtlogo:forward	Moves forward an arbitrary unit of distance
nxtlogo:forward-until-bump	Moves forward until told to stop or bump sensor hit
nxtlogo:backward	Move backward an arbitrary unit of distance
nxtlogo:turn-left \<int angle\>	Turns left the specified angle
nxtlogo:turn-right \<int angle\>	Turns right the specified angle
nxtlogo:stop	Stops the NXT's current action
nxtlogo:bump-data	Reporter for the touch sensor
nxtlogo:colour-data	Reporter for the colour sensor
nxtlogo:ultrasonic-data	Reporter for the ultrasonic sensor
nxtlogo:angle-data	Reporter for the approx. angle turned last manoeuvre
nxtlogo:tacho-data	Reporter for the wheel turns last manoeuvre
nxtlogo:moving	Reporter for whether the NXT is moving
nxtlogo:get-errors	Reporter pops the top error off the stack trace, if any
nxtlogo:terminate	Terminates the connection to the NXT

Each of the commands available in NetLogo in Table 1 has a respective class in the NXTLogo extension. The majority of the commands just pass data to or from the robot whereas the `get-errors` command and its associated java class make debugging much easier. Errors are stored in a buffer upon detection and can be accessed one-by-one from NetLogo with the `get-errors` command.

This extension architecture is sufficient for delivering the basic functionality required of the system. The control file and extension as described can perform connection and two-way Bluetooth communication between the external systems: NetLogo and Lego Mindstorms Robots. The robot can be completely controlled by NetLogo and it streams back real-time information not only from the sensors, but feedback from the actuators as well.

4   Sample NetLogo Models

In this section, sample NetLogo models will be designed and implemented using the new NXTLogo extension. The sample models are NetLogo simulations using a single robot in order to show some of the scope of the system.

4.1   Line Following

Line following is a complicated problem because it requires analysis of the colour sensor data to detect the change from the background colour. Line following with one colour sensor is not an optimal solution and it is best implemented with two sensors, one on each side of the line [13]. It is assumed that we are following a looped path which means we can turn in one direction. The sample program can also be used to keep the robot in a specific colour area.

It is assumed that the robot is set up with a downward facing colour sensor to measure in RGB 0–255 integers the colour of the floor and the line. The model is setup by running a control file on the robot and connecting to it in NetLogo. The robot should be placed with the colour sensor exactly over the line before the robot can follow the line and a button on the interface is pressed to learn the colour of the line. After deciding the line to be followed, the turn-angle (according to directions) and tolerance to the colour change (according to light settings) settings are adjusted before pressing the **go** button in the interface to run the NetLogo program.

This model contains just 50 lines of code which is reasonable for its accomplishments: line following and staying within a specific colour area. In order to iillustrate the simplicity of the final NetLogo code used to control the robot, an extract of this code (containing mostly NetLogo code but some pseudo-code) is shown below.

```
to go
    ask turtles [
        set color using nxtlogo:colour−data
        if color within tolerances [
          if (algorithm = 'left turn ']
```

```
            [ left−turn ]
            [ right−turn ]
        ]
        [ nxtlogo:forward−until−bump ]  ;  go forward
    ]
end
to left−turn
    nxtlogo:stop
    nxtlogo:turn−left turn−angle
end
to right−turn
    nxtlogo:stop
    nxtlogo:turn−right turn−angle
end
```

The code for this model has just six procedures (some of these are used above) which are summarised in Table 2 below.

Table 2. Six procedures of the line following model.

connect	Connects to the specified NXT robot
Set-line-colour	Saves the current colour under the sensor as the colour to follow
Check-colour	Displays the current colour under the sensor without moving the robot
Go	Follows the line: moves forward if the current colour matches the colour that is saved, and if not it turns in the specified direction. Displays the current colour in the environment
Left-turn	Turns the robot left the specified number of degrees
Right-turn	Turns the robot right the specified number of degrees

4.2   Subsumption Architecture Roaming

The purpose of this model is to show that the system is well suited to different AI paradigms, in this case the subsumption architecture [4]. As described in Sect. 2, to control a robot subsumption architecture employs a layered approach, with behaviours of different priorities subsuming one another. In other control systems for Lego Mindstorms Robots, this might be difficult to envision and implement, but in NXTLogo and NetLogo it is very straightforward. The main loop of the program as defined in the go procedure is as follows:

```
to go
    avoid−obstacles
    if not obstacle−detected? [
```

```
stay-on-this-colour
if not colour-change? [
    explore
]
]
end
```

This code is inspired by the Myrmix pseudocode for a basic subsumption architecture robot [5]. The subsumption roaming model contains five procedures. These are summarised in Table 3 below.

Table 3. Five procedures of the subsumption roaming model.

Connect	Connects to the specified NXT. Uses possible future convention for multi-robot simulations by keeping a record of the connected NXT in a hidden turtle. Allows the simulation to keep track of connected robots
Go	Executes layers of behaviours in order of subsumption. Reflexive behaviour has priority
Avoid-obstacles	Highest priority behaviour. Turns away from an obstacle if the ultrasonic sensor value is below a certain threshold
Stay-on-this-colour	Second priority behaviour. Turns if the colour sensor value is too far outside the tolerance
Explore	Lowest priority behaviour. Moves the robot forward unless the bump sensor is being pressed or another manoeuvre is attempted

By defining procedures for each behaviour, the main loop of the model becomes very easy to understand and can be implemented in close to natural language. In this case, the robot will prioritise the avoidance of physical obstacles, then try to remain on the same floor colour before it can move forward. This simple layered approach to behaviour means that we can see that apparently complex environment-aware roaming behaviour is the sum of three very simple behaviours, a hallmark of the subsumption architecture.

5 Results

In this section, we will analyse how well the programs perform and highlight any shortcomings in operation. The programs cover two quite different tasks which helps to highlight the potential for ease of behaviour development in many areas using different approaches.

5.1 Line Following

The line following program meets with mixed success based on a number of factors including but not limited to:

- Lighting conditions
- Remaining battery power
- Colour tolerance
- Excessive turn angle

The turn angle was set to 11 and the tolerance to 20. Based on the low light conditions, these settings were inadequate for line following in the environment the robot was situated in. A lower turn angle of five degrees was set to avoid overturning and a higher tolerance of 42 set to make the robot turn earlier when it is not completely over the line. The adjustment of these settings allowed for the success as shown in Fig. 3.

A set of ten runs was conducted with the same settings as described above and criteria of success for robot was to make a complete run without any assistance. The model was successful in six out of ten runs.

Because of the factors which can affect the program's success, it is difficult to draw solid conclusions from these results, but certain trends are noticeable.

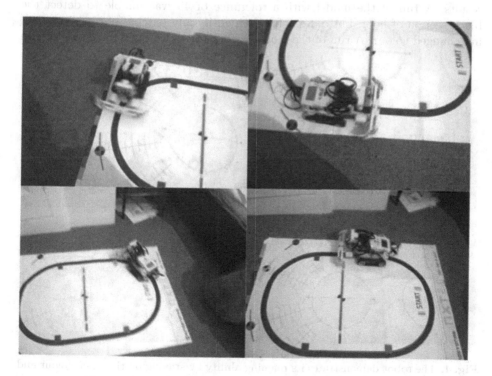

Fig. 3. Successful execution of the line following behaviour.

For one, this model relies upon one-way turning, so overturning is the most common reason for a failed run. The problem can be overcome by setting a lower turn angle which may slow down the robot in corners but will increase accuracy. Introduction of turning while moving would benefit this model; currently the system can only process one instruction at a time but future versions may include this capability easily by varying motor speed on the robot.

5.2   Subsumption Architecture Roaming

In the first attempt at running this simulation, the settings described in the previous section were found to be inadequate for the conditions and needed to be changed. The robot turned before reaching the black section of floor in the test environment (see Fig. 4) when there was no ultrasonic obstacle any detectable distance in front of it, suggesting that the chosen colour tolerance value was set too low. A colour tolerance of ±20 means that if any of the 3 values, R, G and B change by 20, the robot is told to turn and correct itself. After increasing the colour-tolerance value to 30, the robot could explore, turning when it detected the black section of floor and the far wall as shown in Fig. 4. This exploration is an emergent property of the combination of the three very simple behaviours implemented by the model.

Subsequent attempts with higher and lower tolerances provided mixed results. A run of the model with a tolerance of 45 was unable to detect the black section of floor, but did not falsely identify any patches of carpet as having changed colour. A run of the model with a tolerance of 25 yielded less false

Fig. 4. The robot demonstrates its roaming ability by staying on the same colour and avoiding solid obstacles.

positives than the initial run and could identify and steer away from the black section of floor, but did not match the faultless run at tolerance of 30.

It is worth noting that these runs were conducted on carpet, which can yield varying results for a colour sensor based on wear and light. If the runs were conducted again on a smooth matte floor, better results would be expected.

6 Conclusions

This paper has described the design and implementation of a middleware for Lego Mindstorms NXT robots where the robot can be controlled and linked directly to simulators in the agent-oriented programming language, NetLogo. The technologies that the middleware relies on are heterogeneous since it's built in Java which runs on the JVM on all platforms as does NetLogo, being free to download and able to run on any platform. Also the front end of the system is written in NetLogo, which is known for its simplicity of code. With regards to the Lego Mindstorms NXT hardware, sensor streams are implemented for all three native NXT sensors (touch, ultrasonic, colour). The middleware does not require any third generation programming from the end user in order to implement behaviours on the robot. Significant results can be achieved through minimal code and drag-and-drop interface creation for the controlling of simulations.

This paper has explored the feasibility and advantages of linking Lego Mindstorms robots with an agent-oriented multi-agent simulation language. Its significant contributions include the following:

- It has introduced a new and user friendly way of implementing cognitive and reactive behaviour on a mobile robot built from the Lego Mindstorms NXT 2.0 kit.
- It has demonstrated that the capabilities of other Mindstorms middleware extensions/libraries can be recreated in the system using relatively modest amounts of code.
- And it has provided the means for some of the extensive NetLogo capabilities to be adapted to feature real-world agents and therefore laid the foundations for further research and development using NetLogo and Lego Mindstorms robots.

While the basic functionality of the extension expected in the design brief has been met, there are areas in which the work could be extended, for example, extension of the system to involve multiple robots, and system heterogeneity. A series of control files based on multithreading can be implemented for the integrity and efficiency of the system. However, its effect on Mindstorms NXT and efficiency needs to be investigated before making further conclusions.

References

1. Bachega, R.P., Pires, R., Campo, A.B.: Force sensing to control a bio-inspired walking robot. IFAC Proc. Vol. **46**(7), 105–109 (2013)
2. Ballard, L.A., Sabanovic, S., Kaur, J., Milojevic, S.: George charles devol, jr. [history]. IEEE Robot. Autom. Mag. **19**(3), 114–119 (2012)
3. Björkelund, A., Bruyninckx, H., Malec, J., Nilsson, K., Nugues, P.: Knowledge for intelligent industrial robots. In: AAAI Spring Symposium: Designing Intelligent Robots, vol. 12, p. 02. CEUR-WS.org (2012)
4. Brooks, R.: A robust layered control system for a mobile robot. IEEE J. Robot. Autom. **2**(1), 14–23 (1986)
5. Burattini, E., de Francesco, A., De Gregorio, M.: Nsl: a neuro-symbolic language for a neuro-symbolic processor (NSP). Int. J. Neural syst. **13**(02), 93–101 (2003)
6. International, S.: Shakey. http://www.ai.sri.com/shakey/. Accessed: 21 Apr 2018
7. Karakurt, T., Durdu, A., Yılmaz, N.: Design of six legged spider robot and evolving walking algorithms. Int. J. Mach. Learn. Comput. **5**(2), 96–100 (2015). https://doi.org/10.7763/IJMLC.2015.V5.490
8. Kerridge, J.M., Panayotopoulos, A., Lismore, P.: JCSPRE: the robot edition to control LEGO NXT robots. In: CPA, pp. 255–270 (2008)
9. Müller, V.: Is there a future for AI without representation? Minds Mach. **17**(1), 101–115 (2007)
10. Robertson, S.H.: Multiscale computational analysis of xenopus laevis morphogenesis reveals key insights of systems-level behavior. BMC Syst. Biol. **1**(1), 46 (2007)
11. Scheinman, V.: The standford arm. http://infolab.stanford.edu/pub/voy/museum/pictures/display/1-Robot.htm. Accessed 21 Apr 2018
12. Sebastian, T.: Stanley: the robot that won the darpa grand challenge. J. Field Robot. **23**(9), 661–692 (2006)
13. Vannoy, R.: Building a line following robot. http://www.richardvannoy.info/building-a-line-following-robot.pdf. Accessed 21 Apr 2018
14. Wang, Y.: Cognitive robots. IEEE Robot. Autom. Mag. **17**(4), 54–62 (2010)
15. Wąs, J., Kułakowski, K.: Agent-based approach in evacuation modeling. In: Jędrzejowicz, P., Nguyen, N.T., Howlet, R.J., Jain, L.C. (eds.) KES-AMSTA 2010, Part I. LNCS (LNAI), vol. 6070, pp. 325–330. Springer, Heidelberg (2010). https://doi.org/10.1007/978-3-642-13480-7_34

Short Application Papers

A Holistic Metric Approach to Solving the Dynamic Location-Allocation Problem

Reginald Ankrah[1]([✉])[ID], Benjamin Lacroix[1][ID], John McCall[1][ID], Andrew Hardwick[2], and Anthony Conway[2]

[1] School of Computing and Digital Media, Robert Gordon University, Aberdeen, Scotland
r.b.ankrah@rgu.ac.uk
[2] Research and Innovation Department, British Telecommunications Plc, Adastral Park, Ipswich, UK

Abstract. In this paper, we introduce a dynamic variant of the Location-Allocation problem: Dynamic Location-Allocation Problem (DULAP). DULAP involves the location of facilities to service a set of customer demands over a defined horizon. To evaluate a solution to DULAP, we propose two holistic metric approaches: Static and Dynamic Approach. In the static approach, a solution is evaluated with the assumption that customer locations and demand remain constant over a defined horizon. In the dynamic approach, the assumption is made that customer demand, and demographic pattern may change over the defined horizon. We introduce a stochastic model to simulate customer population and distribution over time. We use a Genetic Algorithm and Population-Based Incremental Learning algorithm used in previous work to find robust and satisfactory solutions to DULAP. Results show the dynamic approach of evaluating a solution finds good and robust solutions.

Keywords: Dynamic Uncapacitated Location-Allocation Problem
GA · PBIL · Holistic metric · Stochastic model

1 Introduction

Location-Allocation Problem involves the location of a set of facilities to service a set of customers demands in such a way as to optimise a cost function, subject to a set of constraints [4]. LAP has been well-researched, and there are many formulations. LAP is, in general, a combinatorial problem and so the number of solutions increases exponentially with problem size, defined by the number of facilities and customers. Many metaheuristic methods have been proposed for LAP, including tabu search (TS) [2], simulated annealing (SA) [7], Variable

Supported by British Telecommunications plc.

neighborhood search [3], Genetic algorithms (GA) [5,11], Bees algorithm [9], Clustering search (CS) method using Simulated annealing (SA) [8], hybrid Particle swarm optimisation algorithm [10], hybrid intelligent algorithms [6]. LAP can be classified into capacitated problems (CLAP), where the capacity constraint of a facility applies, and uncapacitated problems (ULAP) where each facility is unconstrained in its service delivery. Our interest lies in ULAP, and in particular, a dynamic non-linear ULAP variant motivated by a real-world problem from the telecommunications industry.

ULAP is typically formulated with consideration to current parameters values. However, considering that customer distribution and growth will change over time, it becomes essential to plan the location of facilities with consideration to the time varying aspect of the problem. It is for this reason that we formulate the problem: Dynamic Uncapacitated Location-Allocation Problem (DULAP). DULAP involves the location of facilities to service a set of customer demands over a defined horizon, with the aim of reducing the overall total cost.

It is important to distinguish our approach in this paper from the dynamic optimisation literature. Classically, a dynamic optimisation is one where the value of solutions changes dynamically while a search algorithm is seeking an optimal solution. Here we explore the problem where the evaluation of a fixed solution incorporates dynamic or time-varying aspects of the problem.

To evaluate a solution to DULAP, we present two holistic metric approaches namely the Static and Dynamic approach. In the static approach, customers are assumed to remain the same over the defined period. In the Dynamic approach, customers are assumed to change over time. The change in customer movement is simulated using a stochastic model. To assess the benefits of simulating the movement of customers for decision making, we use a GA and a PBIL presented in [1]. Our objective is to study how a solution to DULAP can be assessed concerning robustness to forecast changes.

The paper is organised as follows: In Sect. 2 we present the problem formulation. In Sect. 3 we describe the experimental setup and results. Section 4 concludes the paper and highlights future work.

2   Problem Formulation

In this section, we discuss how the objective function is computed and how the movement of the customer population is simulated over time.

2.1   Objective Function

DULAP aims to minimise the overall total costs with regards to facilities and service costs over a defined horizon t expressed in years. Solutions to DULAP are evaluated using facilities and service costs. A solution x to the problem is defined by whether or not a facility is closed (0) or opened (1). We, therefore, select a binary representation, denoted by $x \in \{0,1\}^m$ where m is the number of possible facilities that can be opened. The objective function is expressed as:

$$f_{static}(x) = C_0(x) + \sum_{t=1}^{t_{max}} C_t(x)(1+r)^{-t} \tag{1}$$

where $r \in [0,1]$, $t_{max} = 25$.

The cost function C_0 involves the costs of opening and shutting down facilities, service costs of customers subject to main and backup connections, reassignment of customers and running costs of facilities at t_0. The cost function C_t calculates the discounted total costs for years $\{t_1, t_2, ..., t_{max}\}$. C_t involves service costs subject to main and backup connections and facility running costs. The discount rate r is set at 0.05. The two proposed ways of evaluating a solution both utilities the objective function but in two distinct ways. In the static and dynamic approach, the cost of C_0 remains constant.

For the static approach, we assume that customers will not change over the defined period. Hence, this makes the problem deterministic. This means that for time $\{t_1, t_2, ..., t_{max}\}$. The cost of C_t is the same for each year which is then discounted at a discount rate r.

For the dynamic approach, we assume that customers will change over time. This means that the problem is subject to changes in customer growth and distribution which are driven by a stochastic model. Hence, the problem becomes stochastic. Due to the stochastic nature of the problem, it becomes difficult to predict customer distribution in the future. The dynamic approach therefore proposes to simulate possible population movement for $\{t_1, t_2, ..., t_{max}\}$. The simulated customer movement gives varying costs for each year of the simulation. The cost for each year is then computed using C_t which are discounted at a discount rate r. While C_0, remains a deterministic function, future costs C_t are obtained from the expected costs over n simulations of customer growth. The dynamic approach then take the following form:

$$f_{dynamic}(x) = C_0(x) + E\left[\sum_{t=1}^{t_{max}} C_t(x)(1+r)^{-t}\right] \tag{2}$$

2.2 Simulation Model

Each facility is assumed to be located within a city. Parameters used in the model includes a growth rate, die-off rate, and a radius. For every year starting from time t_1, based on the growth rate of customers, new customers are generated randomly with a uniform probability of appearing anywhere within the defined radius of the city. Based on the die of rate, a percentage of customers are randomly removed from the city. Growth in customer sites within different regions varies in level of intensity depending on the demographics. The growth and die-off rates are based on the 2013 population statistics of the united states.

3 Experiments

In this section, we compare the two ways of evaluating a solution using the approaches described in Sect. 2.1.

3.1 Algorithms

To compare the two approaches for evaluating a solution, we use two algorithms: GA and PBIL. The two algorithms were used in our previous work [1] to solve the static variant of DULAP. The parameters used in this paper for the algorithms were the best parameters found in [1]. For both GA and PBIL, population size is set to 50. The total number of evaluations is set to 10000 for both algorithms. For GA, we employ tournament selection with a selected size of 2 and a tournament size of 3, uniform crossover with a crossover rate of 0.9, bit-Flip mutation with a mutation rate of 0.2 and an elitism rate of 20% of the population. For PBIL a learning rate of 0.1 is used with a truncation size of 20% of the population.

3.2 Problem Instances

For our experiments, 30 different instances of the problem are generated with an initial set of 10000 customers. For all 30 problems, we used $m = 100$ facilities which remain the same for all problems. $n = 100$.

The two algorithms (GA and $PBIL$) when combined with the two ways of evaluating a solution gives us four configurations: GA-f_{static}, GA-$f_{dynamic}$, PBIL-f_{static} and PBIL-$f_{dynamic}$. Each configuration is executed 20 times for each problem. At the end of each run, the best solution obtained by an algorithm is evaluated over 5000 simulations using $f_{dynamic}$ to allow for comparison of results.

3.3 Experimental Results

Table 1 shows the results obtained by each configuration on the 30 instances of the problem averaged over 20 runs. For each problem, the best algorithm is highlighted in bold. Table 2 shows the average ranking of the four configurations for all 30 instances of the problem. The best-ranked configuration is highlighted in bold.

We apply the Friedman statistical test to the results presented in Table 1 to find out if there is a statistical difference in the results obtained by each configuration. The p-value obtained by the Friedman test is 4.86E-11 which shows that there is a significant difference in results. We, therefore, apply the Holm's procedure to check the difference between the best ranking configuration and the other configurations in Table 3.

Table 3 shows PBIL-$f_{dynamic}$ to be the best configuration. Although the dynamic approach finds better results, the time complexity is much higher on the average when compared with the static approach. The average time for a run of a configuration is 1800 s for the dynamic and 70 s for the static.

Table 1. Results of GA and PBIL configurations over 20 runs

Problem	GA-f_{static}	PBIL-f_{static}	GA-$f_{dynamic}$	PBIL-$f_{dynamic}$
P1	5.64E+07	5.50E+07	5.62E+07	**5.49E+07**
P2	5.59E+07	5.50E+07	5.63E+07	**5.50E+07**
P3	5.59E+07	5.51E+07	5.60E+07	**5.49E+07**
P4	5.56E+07	5.49E+07	5.62E+07	**5.48E+07**
P5	5.64E+07	5.50E+07	5.63E+07	**5.48E+07**
P6	5.59E+07	5.51E+07	5.65E+07	**5.49E+07**
P7	5.59E+07	5.51E+07	5.60E+07	**5.49E+07**
P8	5.63E+07	5.51E+07	5.66E+07	**5.49E+07**
P9	5.62E+07	5.50E+07	5.60E+07	**5.48E+07**
P10	5.58E+07	5.51E+07	5.73E+07	**5.50E+07**
P11	5.57E+07	5.50E+07	5.62E+07	**5.48E+07**
P12	5.62E+07	5.51E+07	5.58E+07	**5.49E+07**
P13	5.62E+07	5.50E+07	5.58E+07	**5.48E+07**
P14	5.64E+07	5.50E+07	5.62E+07	**5.48E+07**
P15	5.59E+07	5.50E+07	5.57E+07	**5.49E+07**
P16	5.65E+07	5.50E+07	5.67E+07	**5.48E+07**
P17	5.56E+07	5.51E+07	5.59E+07	**5.49E+07**
P18	5.63E+07	5.50E+07	5.62E+07	**5.48E+07**
P19	5.67E+07	5.50E+07	5.60E+07	**5.48E+07**
P20	5.58E+07	5.50E+07	5.69E+07	**5.48E+07**
P21	5.67E+07	5.50E+07	5.65E+07	**5.48E+07**
P22	5.60E+07	5.51E+07	5.64E+07	**5.49E+07**
P23	5.65E+07	5.51E+07	5.61E+07	**5.48E+07**
P24	5.73E+07	5.49E+07	5.58E+07	**5.48E+07**
P25	5.68E+07	5.50E+07	5.56E+07	**5.48E+07**
P26	5.62E+07	5.50E+07	5.67E+07	**5.48E+07**
P27	5.72E+07	5.51E+07	5.64E+07	**5.49E+07**
P28	5.63E+07	5.50E+07	5.64E+07	**5.48E+07**
P29	5.67E+07	5.51E+07	5.70E+07	**5.49E+07**
P30	5.66E+07	5.50E+07	5.64E+07	**5.48E+07**

Table 2. Average rankings of the algorithms

Algorithm	Ranking
GA-f_{static}	3.50
PBIL-f_{static}	2.00
GA-$f_{dynamic}$	3.50
PBIL-$f_{dynamic}$	**1.00**

Table 3. Holm table for $\alpha = 0.05$

i	Algorithm	p	Holm
3	GA-$f_{dynamic}$	6.38E-14	0.016
2	GA-f_{static}	6.38E-14	0.025
1	PBIL-f_{static}	2.70E-03	0.050

4   Conclusion

In this paper, we introduced a dynamic variant of ULAP. We proposed two ways of evaluating a solution to DULAP. We used two algorithms from previous paper to find satisfactory and robust solutions to the new problem. The results show that PBIL-$f_{dynamic}$ produced the best results in all problem instances.

A comparison of the two approaches shows that when making important decision to establish facilities which are expected to service demand over a defined period. It becomes essential to consider how users demand and distribution might evolve. By simulating possible alternatives of how users might change, one can generate a solution that is robust enough to ensure that facilities can perform optimally for a defined time.

This approach of evaluating a solution can be extended to other fields of operational research where user demand and demographic patterns over time are often stochastic. Although the dynamic approach explored in this paper produces satisfactory solutions, the number of simulations needed to reflect real-world scenarios can be difficult to determine. Too many simulations may be computationally expensive in the time it takes to evaluate a solution. Too little simulations might not be reflective enough of the problem. Future work will, therefore, focus on finding a measure of balance between the number of simulations required and the time complexity of evaluating a solution to the problem.

References

1. Ankrah, R., Regnier-Coudert, O., McCall, J., Conway, A., Hardwick, A.: Performance analysis of GA and PBIL variants for real-world location-allocation problems (2018)
2. Brimberg, J., Mladenovic, N.: Solving the continuous location-allocation problem with tabu search. Stud. Locat. Anal. **8**(23–32), 41 (1996)
3. Brimberg, J., Hansen, P., Mladenović, N., Taillard, E.D.: Improvements and comparison of heuristics for solving the uncapacitated multisource weber problem. Oper. Res. **48**(3), 444–460 (2000)
4. Farahani, R.Z., Hekmatfar, M.: Facility Location: Concepts, Models, Algorithms and Case Studies. Springer, Heidelberg (2009). https://doi.org/10.1007/978-3-7908-2151-2
5. Mavani, K., Shah, M.: Synthesis of silver nanoparticles by using sodium borohydride as a reducing agent. Int. J. Eng. Res. Technol. **2**(3) (2013)

6. Mousavi, S.M., Niaki, S.T.A., Mehdizadeh, E., Tavarroth, M.R.: The capacitated multi-facility location-allocation problem with probabilistic customer location and demand: two hybrid meta-heuristic algorithms. Int. J. Syst. Sci. **44**(10), 1897–1912 (2013)
7. Murray, A.T., Church, R.L.: Applying simulated annealing to location-planning models. J. Heuristics **2**(1), 31–53 (1996)
8. de Oliveira, R.M., Mauri, G.R., Lorena, L.A.N.: Clustering search for the berth allocation problem. Expert Syst. Appl. **39**(5), 5499–5505 (2012)
9. Saeidian, B., Mesgari, M.S., Ghodousi, M.: Evaluation and comparison of genetic algorithm and bees algorithm for location-allocation of earthquake relief centers. Int. J. Disaster Risk Reduct. **15**, 94–107 (2016)
10. Shankar, B.L., Basavarajappa, S., Chen, J.C., Kadadevaramath, R.S.: Location and allocation decisions for multi-echelon supply chain network-a multi-objective evolutionary approach. Expert Syst. Appl. **40**(2), 551–562 (2013)
11. Tohyama, H., Ida, K., Matsueda, J.: A genetic algorithm for the uncapacitated facility location problem. Electron. Commun. Jpn. **94**(5), 47–54 (2011)

Identifying Variables to Define Innovator Group in the Healthy Food Industry: A Fuzzy Approach

Pooja Mohanty[✉], Nuria Agell Jane, and Monica Casabayo Bonas

ESADE Business School, Barcelona, Spain
{pooja.mohanty,nuria.agell,monica.casabayo}@esade.edu

Abstract. Customer adoption of innovation is a multi-disciplinary research area which has been extensively researched. However, identifying the most important variables that affect the adoption process remains unattended. In this paper, we propose Fuzzy TOPSIS method to rank variables that affect the Innovator Group customers. With an illustrative example we explain the method's applicability and we conclude by discussing implications for marketing research and healthy food industry.

Keywords: Fuzzy-TOPSIS · Innovator-Group · Variable-selection

1 Introduction

Any organization that wishes to be successful has to gain a profound understanding of its customers. Over the past decades, management research has emphasized acquiring and keeping good customers to garner superior value for the organizations [8,9,23]. Focus has shifted to customer-oriented strategies which are primarily built upon searching, acquiring and retaining specific customers [18,24]. Furthermore, to achieve this goal, organizations focusing on new product innovation face urgency to find and target the customers who adopt first. Hence, Innovator Group customers (henceforth IG) [16] are critical for success of innovations. Precise identification of this group leads to deeper understanding of customer adoption behaviour and helps streamlining organizational strategy, product development, and R&D in a fruitful direction.

Over the years, a multitude of research has been conducted in order to find key influencing factors of adoption for IG customers. However, there has been no integrated framework or model that combined all the information regarding the IG customers. By evaluating the existing research, an organizing framework was developed with 110 variables to identify the IG customers. This paper uses fuzzy-TOPSIS to obtain the most relevant variables among the identified ones. This paper has three sections: first, an introduction to the IG customer identification problem, second, a proposal with fuzzy-TOPSIS method to solve the problem, and third, an illustrative example to rank the variables according to their importance. To conclude, implications of the method for future researchers and managers are discussed.

© Springer Nature Switzerland AG 2018
M. Bramer and M. Petridis (Eds.): SGAI-AI 2018, LNAI 11311, pp. 440–445, 2018.
https://doi.org/10.1007/978-3-030-04191-5_36

2   Innovator Group Customers

Identification of customer groups based on the time of adoption of innovation was defined by Rogers and Bass [2,19] and much of marketing literature has been devoted to the identification of these customers and their individual characteristics. The customers who adopt innovations first are called innovators (they aren't involved in real innovation) and the group that follows them are called early adopters. Together these two groups are known as 'Innovator Group' [16]. Following IG customers in temporal order are early majority, late majority and laggards, segregated by their time of adoption. IG customers are key in assessing success or failure of innovations. In addition, early adoption time, heavy usage and influence on late adopters [3] make this group central in social contagion [14].

Unlike technology sector where most innovations are radical, food-industry innovations are incremental. Nonetheless, knowledge about adoption of innovation (AOI) is equally important in this sector because it caters to medical and baby food, water and healthy food in general to the households. Health is an important issue for both individuals and society. Efforts made to improve food quality in order to enhance health is a societal challenge [1]. IG customers can contribute by helping identify new healthy products.

Midgley and Dowling [17] defined an important characteristic of IG as 'innate innovativeness', which is an individual trait operating at a higher abstract-level. It influences a number of domain-specific behaviors including early purchasing of new products. However, translation from innate innovativeness to actual adoption behavior involves several other factors i.e. product innovativeness, customer perception on product/brand, external influences, social norms etc. Similar to findings of Midgley and Dowling's, Hirschman [10] proposed 'inherent novelty seeking attitude' construct. Foxall combined Innate innovativeness and inherent novelty seeking to develop a new construct: cognitive style [6], which is inspired from Kirton's [15] work and refers to mental information processing for decision-making or problem-solving, irrespective of one's intellectual ability.

The research presented here is based on a systematic literature review (SLR) of a previous study by the authors, where the SLR (1987–2017) of 30 years was conducted with a purpose to include both current and past research findings. 110 variables affecting AOI decision of the IG customers were collected, and an organizing framework was developed to capture the adoption process of these customers. This paper takes the framework further by reducing and obtaining the most important variables.

3   Methodology

Ranking multiple variables is a challenge and employing human experts for the task is even more complicated. To solve this problem, we looked into the decision-making literature especially into group decision making (GDM) research for our variable selection problem.

Nowadays multi-criteria decision making (MCDM) and GDM are important research domains in operations research and have wider applicability for organization, individual, and society. In marketing and social sciences, Delphi is one of the most applied techniques for decision making studies. However, Delphi requires repetitive surveys for convergence of a forecasting value [13]. Evaluating various MCDM methods (i.e. AHP, MAUT, ELECTRE, PROMETHEE, TOPSIS, VIKOR), we considered TOPSIS (Technique for Order Preference by Similarity to the Ideal Solution) [12] for its following advantages [4,20],

1. Simple, rational and easy to use
2. Increase in criteria or attribute has no effect on number of steps for execution
3. Considers linguistic data from decision makers without accounting for their prior similar experiences
4. Requires less cognitive effort from the decision makers
5. Easy to compute with good computational efficiency
6. Possibility of visualization

In most decision making situations, lack of information or impreciseness makes it difficult to consider only crisp (quantitative) values. Real life problems involve judgments and evaluations which are subjective in nature. To overcome these problems, natural languages employ fuzzy linguistic terms to convey the subjectiveness. These linguistics variables (using other magnitude values) can be expressed clearly with fuzzy set theory which captures the subjectiveness [7].

Hence, the ranking process proposed in this paper is based on the fuzzy version of a well-known distance-based approaches to rank variables in multi-criteria decision-making: FTOPSIS. The method uses fuzzy assessment of the variables, and constructs a decision matrix allowing comparison among the variables possible. Then it considers the distance between certain target points, named *ideal positive solution* and *ideal negative solution* that models the best and the worst alternatives respectively. The values of the distances are used to define closeness co-efficients (CC) for each variable and ranking of variables will be based on CC.

Assessment is provided by a group of experts in terms of linguistic judgments represented by fuzzy triangular numbers. Following the existing research [11,21], we propose a symmetric 5-point triangular fuzzy scale between 0 and 10 to represent the uncertainty inherent in experts' opinion (See Table 1).

Table 1. Left: Linguistic scale for rating variables. Right: Example matrix

Linguistic variable importance	Corresponding triangular fuzzy number
Very low	(0, 1, 3)
Low	(1, 3, 5)
Medium	(3, 5, 7)
High	(5, 7, 9)
Very high	(7, 9, 10)

$$
\begin{bmatrix}
L_{11} & L_{12} & \ldots \ldots & L_{1j} & \ldots \ldots & L_{1n} \\
L_{21} & L_{22} & \ldots \ldots & L_{2j} & \ldots \ldots & L_{2n} \\
\vdots & \vdots & \vdots \ \vdots & \vdots & \vdots \ \vdots \\
L_{i1} & L_{i2} & \ldots \ldots & L_{ij} & \ldots \ldots & L_{in} \\
\vdots & \vdots & \vdots \ \vdots & \vdots & \vdots \ \vdots \\
L_{m1} & L_{m2} & \ldots \ldots & L_{mj} & \ldots \ldots & L_{mn}
\end{bmatrix}
$$

Similar to the process explained by Chen and Tsao [5], we followed a 5-step process to conduct FTOPSIS ranking for the variables (See Fig. 1).

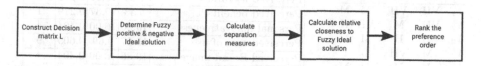

Fig. 1. Visual representation of the procedural steps in a Fuzzy-TOPSIS technique

Let L_{ij} be the $m \times n$ decision matrix where L_{ij} is the assessment of an expert j over the variable i, influencing the IG customers (See Table 1). Without any previous aggregation or normalization, we define the *ideal positive solution* and the *ideal negative solution* by considering the maximum and minimum respectively of each expert: $L_j^+ = (L_{1j}, L_{2j}, \dots L_{mj})$, where $I_j^+ = \max L_{ij}$, and $L_j^- = (L_{1j}, L_{2j}, \dots L_{mj})$, where $I_j^- = \min L_{ij}$. Then for each variable V_i we aggregate the fuzzy distances to ideal positive and ideal negative solution obtained from each experts, D_i^+ and D_i^- i.e.

$$D_i^+ = \sum_{j=1}^n d_j^+, \quad and \quad D_i^- = \sum_{j=1}^n d_j^- \tag{1}$$

where d is the euclidean distance between fuzzy numbers.

Finally, to rank the variables, the relative proximity to the ideal solution is computed for each V_i i.e. the closeness co-efficient as follows:

$$CC_i = \frac{D_i^+}{D_i^+ + D_i^-} \tag{2}$$

Note that all values of the relative proximity will be between 0 and 1. The best variable will be the variable with a relative proximity closest to zero.

4   An Illustrative Example

In this section, we present an illustrative example which is based on the top 15 cited variables from the framework and it demonstrates the applicability of FTOPSIS. We conducted an online survey with these 15 variables and collected information from 4 marketing experts. For contextualization, detailed explanation on AOI in healthy food industry and linguistic scale (Table 1) were provided at the beginning of the survey. After the experts provided values based on the importance to the adoption process, we completed the 5 steps (Fig. 1) and calculated closeness co-efficients and ranked the variables accordingly (Table 2).

Table 2. Left: Decision matrix from marketing experts. Right: Table of ranking

Var	Experts				Variable	D_i^+	D_i^-	CC_i	Rank
	E_1	E_2	E_3	E_4	Perceived usefulness	7.39	19.37	0.276	2
V_1	VH	VH	M	M	Perceived benefits	5.43	19.37	0.219	1
V_2	VH	M	VH	H	Personal innovativeness	10.86	16.00	0.404	4
V_3	H	H	M	M	Perceived ease of use	15.07	9.69	0.609	9
V_4	M	VH	L	L	Perceived Brand image	10.86	16.00	0.404	4
V_5	H	H	M	M	Perceived risk	6.93	16.00	0.302	3
V_6	H	H	H	H	Proce sensitivity	12.85	12.00	0.517	6
V_7	H	H	M	L	Hedonistic attitude	14.81	12.00	0.552	7
V_8	M	M	H	L	Availability of choice	14.81	12.00	0.552	7
V_9	L	M	H	M	Income	16.78	12.00	0.583	8
V_{10}	M	M	L	M	Information seeking attitude	5.43	19.37	0.219	1
V_{11}	M	VH	H	VH	Network externality	15.07	9.69	0.609	9
V_{12}	M	L	VH	L	Perceived compatibility	13.08	13.69	0.489	5
V_{13}	VH	M	M	L	Previous experience	6.93	16.00	0.302	3
V_{14}	H	H	H	H	Mass media influence	16.78	12.00	0.583	8
V_{15}	M	L	M	M					

5   Conclusions and Further Research

Our contribution to the fields of multi-criteria decision making and artificial intelligence (AI) will be primarily extending FTOPSIS technique to the marketing research domain. To best of our knowledge, the technique was never applied in this particular domain before. The study also aims to narrow the gap between AI and decision making domains by collaborating human experts with MCDM techniques. Moreover proposing a real application based on the illustrative example for European healthy food industry is expected. An extended study is planned with a Spanish FMCG firm, and learnings from the real-case will be applied to other industry. Hence, identifying IG customers from a parsimonious model will help managers promote improved quality of food and impact the society.

This study has some limitations. First, TOPSIS ignores any possibility of correlation among variables. Despite this disadvantage, solutions provided by TOPSIS confirms with correct solutions found by other MCDM methods [22]. Second, the study didn't consider weights for each variable from the experts while calculating for distances. Third, it didn't include a comparative analysis between FTOPSIS and MCDM or AI techniques for the variable selection and we will include comparison of techniques in our future studies.

References

1. Atkins, P., Bowler, I.: Food in Society: Economy Culture and Geography, 1st edn. Routledge, London (2001)
2. Bass, F.: A new product growth model for consumer durables. Manag. Sci. **15**(1), 215–227 (1969)

3. Catalini, C., Tucker, C.: When early adopters don't adopt. Science **357**(6347), 135–136 (2017)
4. Chen, C.T.: Extensions of the TOPSIS for group decision-making under fuzzy environment. Fuzzy Sets Syst. **114**(1), 1–9 (2000)
5. Chen, T.Y., Tsao, C.Y.: The interval-valued fuzzy TOPSIS method and experimental analysis. Fuzzy Sets Syst. **159**(11), 1410–1428 (2008)
6. Foxall, G.R.: Cognitive styles of consumer initiators. Technovation **15**(5), 269–288 (1995)
7. Gupta, R., Sachdeva, A., Bhardwaj, A.: Selection of 3PL Service Provider using Integrated Fuzzy Delphi and Fuzzy TOPSIS. In: Proceedings of the World Congress on Engineering and Computer Science, vol. 2 (2010)
8. Gupta, S.: Customer-based valuation. J. Interact. Mark. **23**, 169–178 (2009)
9. Gupta, S., Lehmann, D.R., Stuart, J.A.: Valuing customers. J. Mark. Res. (JMR) **41**(1), 7–18 (2004)
10. Hirschman, E.C.: Innovativeness, novelty seeking, and consumer creativity. J. Consum. Res. **7**, 283–295 (1980)
11. Hsieh, T.Y., Lu, S.T., Tzeng, G.H.: Fuzzy MCDM approach for planning and design tenders selection in public office buildings. Int. J. Proj. Manag. **22**(7), 573–584 (2004)
12. Hwang, C.L., Yoon, K.: Methods for multiple attribute decision making. In: Hwang, C.L., et al. (eds.) Multiple Attribute Decision Making, pp. 58–191. Springer, Heidelberg (1981). https://doi.org/10.1007/978-3-642-48318-9_3
13. Ishikawa, A., Amagasa, M., Shiga, T., Tomizawa, G., Tatsuta, R., Mieno, H.: The max-min Delphi method and fuzzy Delphi method via fuzzy integration. Fuzzy Sets Syst. **55**(3), 241–253 (1993)
14. Iyengar, R., Van den Bulte, C., Valente, T.W.: Opinion leadership and social contagion in new product diffusion. Mark. Sci. **30**(2), 195–212 (2011)
15. Kirton, M.: Adaptors and innovators: a description and measure. J. Appl. Psychol. **61**(5), 622–629 (1976)
16. Mahajan, V., Muller, E.: When is it worthwhile targeting the majority instead of the innovators in a new product launch? J. Mark. Res. (JMR) **35**, 488–495 (1998)
17. Midgley, D.F., Dowling, G.R.: Innovativeness: the concept and its measurement. J. Consum. Res. **4**, 229–241 (1978)
18. Min, S., Zhang, X., Kim, N., Srivastava, R.K.: Customer acquisition and retention spending: an analytical model and empirical investigation in wireless telecommunications markets. J. Mark. Res. **53**(5), 728–744 (2016)
19. Rogers, E.M.: Diffusion of Innovations, 1st edn. The Free Press - A division of Simon & Schuster Inc., USA (1962)
20. Roszkowska, E.: Multi-criteria decision making models by applying the TOPSIS method to crisp and interval data. In: Multi criteria decision making 10–11, pp. 200–230. The University of Economics, Katowice (2011)
21. Sun, C.C.: A performance evaluation model by integrating fuzzy AHP and fuzzy TOPSIS methods. Expert Syst. Appl. **37**(12), 7745–7754 (2010)
22. Velasquez, M., Hester, P.T.: An analysis of multi-criteria decision making methods. Int. J. Oper. Res. **10**(2), 56–66 (2013)
23. Weinstein, A.: Market Segmentation, revised edn. Probus Publishing Company, Chicago (1994). Revised edition
24. Woo, J.Y., Bae, S.M., Park, S.C.: Visualization method for customer targeting using customer map. Expert Syst. Appl. **28**, 763–772 (2005)

Business Process Workflow Mining Using Machine Learning Techniques for the Rail Transport Industry

Eleftherios Bandis[1], Miltos Petridis[1], and Stelios Kapetanakis[2(✉)]

[1] Department of Computer Science, Middlesex University, London, UK
{E.Bandis,M.Petridis}@mdx.ac.uk
[2] School of Computing, Engineering and Mathematics, University of Brighton, Brighton, UK
S.Kapetanakis@brighton.ac.uk

Abstract. Rail transportation is an important part of the transport infrastructure that supports modern advanced economies. Both public and private companies are highly concerned on how travel patterns, vehicle-passenger behaviours and other relevant phenomena such as weather affect their performance. Usually any travel network can be remarkably expensive to build and swiftly gets saturated after its construction and any subsequent upgrades. We propose suitable workflow monitoring methods for developing efficient performance measures for the rail industry using business process workflow pattern analysis based on Case-based Reasoning (CBR) combined with standard Data Mining methods. The approach focuses on both data preparation and cleaning and integration of data applied to a real industrial case study. Preliminary results of this work are promising against the complexity of the data and can scale on demand while showing they can predict to an efficient accuracy. Several modelling experiments are presented, that show that the proposed approach can provide a sound basis for effective and useful analysis of operational sensor data from train Journeys.

Keywords: Data mining · Case based reasoning · Process mining
Business process workflows · Workflow monitoring · Temporal reasoning

1 Introduction

The modernisation of the Rail industry has led to increasing usage of computer systems for logistics, tactical, planning, performance and maintenance reasons. Substantial growth in terms of operational method advancement (wayside detectors, wheel profile monitors, extended sensor network), processes, software and hardware equipment resulted to significant amounts of data being accumulated continuously. Such data is monitored and, at later stage, analysed with the aim to improve the performance of the industry and increase customer satisfaction.

Most rail operations, such as scheduled train services represent business workflows, mapped as event trails of spatio-temporal data. Techniques that have been developed for monitoring workflow operations [1, 20–22] can be used in the context of train

© Springer Nature Switzerland AG 2018
M. Bramer and M. Petridis (Eds.): SGAI-AI 2018, LNAI 11311, pp. 446–451, 2018.
https://doi.org/10.1007/978-3-030-04191-5_37

journeys. The rail industry can experience severe reduction in performance when it comes to unexpected disruptions in service that lead to experienced delays. To be able to identify the reasons behind delays, we propose process mining [5] techniques based on workflows to assist in deviation measurements from scheduled processes (i.e. timetable routes) against the workflows logged by the information system. To achieve that, workflow executions should be associated with the expected business process instances (i.e. timetable). However, this has proven to be a complicated task as several bottlenecks exist within the Railway system [6].

We introduce a multi-level Case-based Reasoning (CBR) approach to achieve workflow alignment between monitoring data and business processes by considering the railway domain unique characteristics and challenges as described above. This work follows on from earlier studies [5, 6] and provides further evaluation based on several experiments using predictive machine learning techniques.

The rest of this paper is organised as follows: Sect. 2 presents the relevant literature in terms of CBR, Workflows, Process mining and hybrid models, Sect. 3 formulates our proposed methodology for effective process mining of rail route workflows, Sect. 4 presents our experiments and results and finally, we discuss our overall findings and our future research steps.

2 Related Work

Modern organisations use business process workflows to coordinate their processes, tasks, roles and synchronise their resources with the aim to improve efficiency, efficacy and profitability. Workflows can automate processes, make them agile and can increase visibility of obscure, erroneous or complex events to company managers to increase productivity [4]. Business process workflow management differs across organisations. The size, sector and strategic orientation of an organization play a key role on how they adopt, analyse and practice Business workflows [8]. A common taxonomy includes the phases of: Design, Implementation, Enactment, Monitoring and Evaluation as the workflow life cycle in Business process management [8–10]. Among those the Monitoring phase enables the supervising of business processes in terms of management (e.g. performance, accuracy) and organization (e.g. utilization of resources, length of activities etc.) [10].

Cases are usually stored in a Case base along with their associated solutions. Based on this knowledge, CBR can produce a solution for a new problem by following the CBR process cycle defined in [12]. In the case of monitoring business process CBR has been shown to be able to be used to monitor process workflows using temporal similarity measures [21]. Process Mining (PM) is the technique used to extract knowledge and insights by discovering and analysing processes from event logs [13, 14].

In the literature, several algorithmic techniques have been introduced to solve the process mining problem, like Alpha miner and alpha+. Other heuristics, genetic and fuzzy algorithms have also been applied [7, 11]. Each algorithm has its limitations on a different aspect of the process discovery such as fitness, simplicity and precision, and they may be unfit to areas where uncertainty, inconsistency and fuzziness is present, therefore a CBR approach may be more appropriate. Workflows and process mining have received substantial focus from the literature [16–19] as well as graph-based systems in spatio-temporal workflows [20, 21]. The fundamental assumption in the latter is that a workflow structure is not met during execution. Therefore, the workflow instances are identical but not same. Consequently, workflow instances marked as problematic, that seem to be similar with other instances, they probably share the same problems and require similar solutions.

3   A CBR Approach for Aligning Workflow Executions

CBR has been shown effective in monitoring workflow instances under uncertainty [21, 22]. Delay patterns are often related to location and time e.g. rail platforms during peak hours can be overcrowded and this may lead to delays. Another common example are busy junctions during certain hours causing overheads to any related services. Therefore, it is presumed that same or similar routes share similar bottlenecks (delays).

To represent effectively workflows and their sequence and relationships in a formal way we use the General Time Theory (GTT) [3, 6]. In our graph representation each node represents a station whereas any edge represents the duration from station A to station B. A GTT workflow representation allows for a unified log interpretation which in conjunction with the multi-level similarity representation [6] presents a foundation for adequate CBR workflow cases. A workflow process consists of multiple activities. Activities involve tasks such as "start of a journey", "departure from a station", "arrive on a station" or "end of a journey". Each task contains: Time-related information, Location and task Relationships. A workflow respectively holds: The total duration of all activities, hardware identifies, temporal information and the workflow *start* and *end* time.

4   Experiments and Results

The proposed case representation and similarity measures allow for a rigid problem definition. A key challenge presented from the application domain is the lack of "solutions" due to the following reasons:

1. Constant changes at business process level. e.g. Rail timetable change every 6 months (seasonal). Variations occur in any normal operation per day.
2. Incomplete data.
3. Variant datasets with technical compatibility challenges and inconsistencies.

To overcome the above challenges the CBR cycle and case representation was defined as in [5, 6]. Following the work and experiments done we were able to produce reliable route data for just over one-year operation for the fleet of data of a Rail Operator based in the London Metropolitan area. This data covers the years 2015–2016. First a statistical data analysis and visualisation was conducted that allowed railway engineers and planners to get useful insights into the operation. Statistical data were provided for routes at different times of day, different days of the week focusing on specific known "trouble spots".

In the first instance, the experiments concentrate on supervised learning techniques concentrating on numerical prediction and classification. A specific known problematic route was selected. One year's worth of journeys was selected from the dataset. The dataset for the route had 6562 cases (all one-way travel). A series of experiments were conducted aiming at numerical prediction after binning of values on standard deviation multiples classification. The experiments were conducted using the IBM SPSS Modeler 18.0 tool [15]. Specific information on routes and stations have been anonymised to protect commercial sensitivities.

A first set of experiments was presented in [5]. The experiments presented here have been created based on the feedback at the workshop and by engineers who asked to use extra attributes such as the day of the week, peak/off peak and unit numbers. The current experiments contain better balanced data for classification and full 5-fold cross-validation.

A first set of experiments has been set to estimate how early data in a journey can be used to predict the arrival time of a service. As such, we used specific known problem spots early in the selected route (3 segments that intersect other lines and 3 dwell times in the corresponding starting stations) to predict the overall duration of the journey. The day of the week is also used as a predictor and an attribute showing morning/afternoon peak our and off-peak hour was also used for prediction. The results of this can be seen in Table 1 below.

Table 1. Numerical experiment results (journey time in sec)

	Generalised linear model	Regression	ANN (MLP)
Minimum error	−923.745	−925.043	−355.275
Maximum error	2010.244	2004.901	1996.996
Mean error	0	0	1.788
Mean absolute error	67.788	68.054	65.398
Standard deviation	98.345	98.599	94.674
Linear correlation	0.832	0.831	0.845
Occurrences	6,562	6,562	6,562

Table 1 shows that the neural network approach (Multi-layer perceptron - MLP) slightly improves on the other models. It must be stated that the regression algorithm does not consider the day of the week attribute or peak/off peak hour. An error in 70–80 s is a good level of accuracy, since a serious delay is defined as 3 min or more.

In addition to the numerical prediction above, classification algorithms were used after binning was applied to the predicted attribute (total Journey travel), the width of bins aligned to fit 2 bins of under and over the median value for journey times respectively. We used an averaged 5-way folding 80%–20% cross validation to evaluate the model accuracy. The results of this are presented in Table 2. It can be seen there that Logistic regression performs best. However, simple observation on the results shows that KNN picks up more late trains, but also suffers by more "false positives".

Table 2. Classification experiment results

	Log. regression	C5.1	ANN (MLP)	C&R tree	kNN
True	78.60%	74.08%	77.73%	74.30%	71.18%
False	21.40%	25.92%	22.27%	25.70%	28.82%
Total	1325	1325	1325	1325	1325

5   Conclusions

This work presents a transport friendly approach to break down the complexity of temporal spatial data and attempt to identify workflow patterns and trends over time. We propose a new multi-level similarity approach that can elicit meta-heuristic features and can assist in capturing relevant-granular features. We presented some preliminary results from our work on real industry case study, although our results were affected from the investigated dataset(s) bias, limited ranking and very large volume and variety. In our future work we plan to improve substantially our model towards automatic detection of workflow differences, mine patterns efficiently and work on ways to tackle large data volumes and dataset discrepancies and ill-balanced data. We will also work on establishing the right benchmark tools to enhance the accuracy, precision and recall of our proposed methodology while also combining the current analysis with more supervised and unsupervised machine learning algorithms to produce a more rounded view of the knowledge encapsulated in the data. This will be done by analysing the interaction between more than one routes and concentrating on known "trouble spots" in the network. Finally, the dataset to be analysed, will integrate more sources of information, including operations data, weather data, Twitter feeds etc. The purpose is to increase the accuracy of the models while retaining the transparency, auditability of data and explainability of the reasoning process.

References

1. Reijers, H.A., Weijters, A.J.M.M., Dongen, B.F.V., Medeiros, A.K.A.D., Song, M., Verbeek, H.: Business process mining: an industrial application. Inf. Syst. **32**, 713–732 (2007)
2. Network Rail. https://www.networkrail.co.uk/. Accessed 28 Oct 2017
3. Ma, J., Knight, B.: A general temporal theory. Comput. J. **37**(2), 114–123 (1994)
4. Accountants, Institute of Management Accountants: Implementing Automated Workflow Management. USA, Institute of Management Accountants 10 Paragon Drive Montvale, NJ 07645 (2000)
5. Bandis, E., Petridis, M., Kapetanakis, S.: Predictive process mining using a hybrid CBR approach for the rail transport industry. In: Proceedings of the 26th International Conference in Case Based Reasoning, RATIC 2018, Stockholm, Sweden, 9–12 July 2018
6. Bandis, E., Kapetanakis, S., Petridis, M., Fish, A.: Effective similarity measures for process mining using CBR on rail transport industry. In: Proceedings of the 22nd UKCBR Workshop, Cambridge UK, December 2017 (2017)

7. van der Aalst, W.M.P., de Medeiros, A.K.Alves, Weijters, A.J.M.M.: Genetic process mining. In: Ciardo, G., Darondeau, P. (eds.) ICATPN 2005. LNCS, vol. 3536, pp. 48–69. Springer, Heidelberg (2005). https://doi.org/10.1007/11494744_5

8. van der Aalst, W.M.P., ter Hofstede, A.H.M., Weske, M.: Business process management: a survey. In: van der Aalst, Wil M.P., Weske, M. (eds.) BPM 2003. LNCS, vol. 2678, pp. 1–12. Springer, Heidelberg (2003). https://doi.org/10.1007/3-540-44895-0_1

9. Zur Muehlen, M.: Workflow-Based Process Controlling: Foundation, Design and Application of Workflow-driven Process Information Systems. Logos (2004)

10. Reijers, H.A.: Design and Control of Workflow Processes: Business Process Management for the Service Industry. Springer, Heidelberg (2003). https://doi.org/10.1007/3-540-36615-6

11. Tiwari, A., Turner, C.J., Majeed, B.: A review of business process mining: state-of-the-art and future trends. Bus. Process Manag. J. 14(1), 5–22 (2008)

12. Aamodt, A., Plaza, E.: Case-based reasoning: foundational issues, methodological variations, and system approaches. AI Commun. 7(1), 39–59 (1994)

13. Van der Aalst, W.M.P.: Process Mining: Discovery, Conformance and Enhancement of Business Processes. Springer, Heidelberg (2011). https://doi.org/10.1007/978-3-642-19345-3

14. Van der Aalst, W.M.P., van Dongen, B.F., Herbst, J., Maruster, L., Schimm, G., Weijters, A.J.M.M.: Workflow mining: a survey of issues and approaches. Data Knowl. Eng. 47, 237–267 (2003)

15. IBM SPSS Modeller. https://www.ibm.com/products/spss-modeler

16. van der Aalst, W.M.P., de Medeiros, A.K.A., Weijters, A.J.M.M.: Process equivalence: comparing two process models based on observed behavior. In: Dustdar, S., Fiadeiro, J.L., Sheth, A.P. (eds.) BPM 2006. LNCS, vol. 4102, pp. 129–144. Springer, Heidelberg (2006). https://doi.org/10.1007/11841760_10

17. Dijkman, R., Dumas, M., García-Bañuelos, L.: Graph matching algorithms for business process model similarity search. In: Dayal, U., Eder, J., Koehler, J., Reijers, H.A. (eds.) BPM 2009. LNCS, vol. 5701, pp. 48–63. Springer, Heidelberg (2009). https://doi.org/10.1007/978-3-642-03848-8_5

18. Weber, B., Wild, W., Breu, R.: CBRFlow: enabling adaptive workflow management through conversational case-based reasoning. In: Funk, P., González Calero, P.A. (eds.) ECCBR 2004. LNCS (LNAI), vol. 3155, pp. 434–448. Springer, Heidelberg (2004). https://doi.org/10.1007/978-3-540-28631-8_32

19. Minor, M., Tartakovski, A., Bergmann, R.: Representation and structure-based similarity assessment for agile workflows. In: Weber, R.O., Richter, M.M. (eds.) ICCBR 2007. LNCS (LNAI), vol. 4626, pp. 224–238. Springer, Heidelberg (2007). https://doi.org/10.1007/978-3-540-74141-1_16

20. Kapetanakis, S., Petridis, M.J., Bacon, L.: Providing explanations for the intelligent monitoring of business workflows using case-based reasoning. In: Roth-Berghofer, T., Tintarev, N., Leake, D.B., Bahls, D. (eds.) Proceedings of the 5th International Workshop on Explanation—Aware Computing Exact (ECAI 2010), Lisbon, Portugal (2010)

21. Kapetanakis, S., Petridis, M., Knight, B., Ma, J., Bacon, L.: A case based reasoning approach for the monitoring of business workflows. In: Bichindaritz, I., Montani, S. (eds.) ICCBR 2010. LNCS (LNAI), vol. 6176, pp. 390–405. Springer, Heidelberg (2010). https://doi.org/10.1007/978-3-642-14274-1_29

22. Kapetanakis, S., Petridis, M.: Evaluating a case-based reasoning architecture for the intelligent monitoring of business workflows. In: Montani, S., Jain, L.C. (eds.) Successful Case-based Reasoning Applications-2, vol. 494, pp. 43–54. Springer, Berlin (2014). https://doi.org/10.1007/978-3-642-38736-4_4

Author Index

Printed in the United States
By Bookmasters